German

Stock Corporation

Act

German

STOCK CORPORATION ACT

Translation by

Friedrich K. Juenger
Associate Professor of Law, Wayne State University
and
Lajos Schmidt
Partner, Baker & McKenzie, Chicago

COMMERCE CLEARING HOUSE, INC.
PUBLISHERS *of* TOPICAL LAW REPORTS

NEW YORK   CHICAGO   WASHINGTON
BOSTON   PHILADELPHIA   LOS ANGELES   SAN FRANCISCO

PREFACE

According to its principal architect, Dr. Ernst Gessler, the new German *Aktiengesetz* "will for a long time to come be the basic law for our stock corporations." But the significance of the new Stock Corporation Act extends beyond the boundaries of the Federal Republic. The consequences of a revision of the corporate law of a major industrial and commercial nation for businessmen, investors, and their counsel are not limited to national confines. Several of the provisions of the Act claim "extraterritorial" application. Conversely, conflicts situations may arise where regulatory enactments of other countries, such as the American securities legislation, are applied to German corporations. In Europe, this Act and the recent codification of French company law are bound to influence the efforts towards Common Market corporate legislation. And in the United States, some of the solutions found in the present *Aktiengesetz* to fundamental corporate problems have already attracted comparative analysis of their potential usefulness despite a marked divergence of legal thinking and corporate practice.

We have attempted to facilitate access to this law by drafting a readable translation. The *Aktiengesetz* may be the longest corporate statute ever enacted. Its predecessor has been said to contain sections written in an "ungraceful and bombastic style" and some of the language added by the recent revision may be open to the same reproach. Moreover, the Act uses a great number of novel terms not contained in earlier German corporate legislation. Since a legal text is involved, accuracy was not to be sacrificed for style. Frequently, American legal terms were selected even though they are not exact counterparts of the German legal concepts. We were mindful of the danger that erroneous inferences can be drawn from the use of words with a technical meaning. However, this peril is somewhat counterbalanced by the numerous definitions contained in the Act. Where we could not resort to a reasonable approximation because German and Anglo-American thinking proved to be too far apart, an implicit acknowledgment of non-translatability will be apparent from such artificial terms as "post-formation acquisition," "control agreement," "company surrender agreement," and other terms that would be meaningless outside their particular context. In all of these instances, the temptation to footnote was strong. However, each explanation would merely call for others, and nothing short of an annotated code could satisfy the desire for perfection.

We are grateful to Frau Uda Klee, a German lawyer who assisted us in preparing the first draft of this translation, to Robert Gareis, who helped us find terms approximating those used in American securities practice, and to Charles Rimkus, C.P.A., who advised us on American accounting equivalents to the German terminology. We are also greatly indebted to the active cooperation and valuable suggestions of our publishers.

November, 1967

CONTENTS

Page

Introduction 1
Stock Corporation Act 25
Law Introducing the Stock
    Corporation Act 274
Glossary 287
Index 289

INTRODUCTION

I. Genesis of the Act

The present German Stock Corporation Act[1] is the successor of the *Gesetz über Aktiengesellschaften und Kommanditgesellschaften c 'f Aktien (Aktiengesetz)* of 1937.[2] This earlier statute was a comprehensive and thorough piece of modern corporate legislation. Although it had been enacted during the Hitler regime, it was not a product of the then prevailing ideology. Rather, it represented the culmination of earlier efforts to modernize the law, in part inspired by American practice. Much of its substance had already been anticipated in an emergency decree of 1931.[3] The 1937 Act permitted the issuance of non-voting preferred shares and, to a limited extent, provided for authorized capital. It broadened the powers of the managing board, strengthened minority safeguards, proclaimed responsibility of the corporation to the public, and provided for more effective disclosure of financial and business information. The earlier Act was also designed to restrain oppressive practices and self-perpetuation of management which resulted from practices such as the issuance of shares with multiple voting rights and the voting of treasury stock.

The present Act does not discard the gains of this earlier legislation. Despite the novelty of some of its features, the structure of German corporate law remains essentially unchanged. Nevertheless, the changes introduced are significant. Primarily, they are intended to strengthen the position of the shareholder by more meaningful disclosure requirements and by rules designed to protect his right to be consulted. Entirely new is the codification of the law governing related enterprises.

Proposals for a revision of the 1937 *Aktiengesetz* with a view to increased investor protection had been made at an early stage of Germany's economic revival following World War II. During that time several statutes were passed which affected the corporate law. These included statutes granting labor representation on corporate boards (the so-called co-determination laws),[4] and a 1959 statute which authorized the capitalization of surplus to permit,

---

[1] Law of September 6, 1965, [1965] 1 *Bundesgesetzblatt* 1089, effective as of January 1, 1966. The *Einführungsgesetz zum Aktiengesetz* (hereinafter cited as Introductory Law) of the same date and effective date was published in [1965] 1 *Bundesgesetzblatt* 1185.

[2] Law of January 30, 1937, [1937] 1 *Reichsgesetzblatt* 107.

[3] Decree of September 1, 1931, [1931] 1 *Reichsgesetzblatt* 493.

[4] Regarding this legislation see generally Vagts, "Reforming the 'Modern' Corporation: Perspectives from the German," 80 Harv. L. Rev. 23, 64-75 (1966). The present Act does not incorporate the co-determination laws but refers to them as they affect the composition of the managing board and the supervisory board, and establishes procedures for settling disputes concerning the applicability of their provisions. See, in particular, Sections 76, paragraph 2, and 95-99.

1

in effect, the issuance of tax-free stock dividends, and amended the 1937 Act to tighten financial disclosure requirements.[5]

The preparatory work on the present Act began in 1953 and led to a 1958 draft statute, the so-called *Referentenentwurf*, which was followed by a Government Draft *(Regierungsentwurf)* in 1960. These drafts were widely studied, discussed and debated before the present version was enacted on May 25, 1965.[6]

II. Some Features of German Corporate Law

A great deal of useful information on German stock corporations was published in English[7] before the passage of the present *Aktiengesetz*, and two major law review articles have appeared since.[8] It may suffice, therefore, briefly to refer to some of the principal aspects in which German corporate law and practice differ from our own.

Corporate Forms

The stock corporation is but one of several types of legal entities known to German law. Other corporate forms serve a variety of functions. Thus, the Civil Code, under the heading "juridical persons," deals with the so-called registered associations *(eingetragene Vereine)*, which are equivalent to membership corporations.[9] Specific statutes govern cooperatives *(eingetragene Genossenschaften)*,[10] mutual insurance companies *(Versicherungsvereine auf Gegenseitigkeit)*, and mining companies *(bergrechtliche Gewerkschaften)*.

---

[5] *Gesetz über die Kapitalerhöhung aus Gesellschaftsmitteln und über die Gewinn- und Verlustrechnung*, Law of December 23, 1959, [1959] 1 *Bundesgesetzblatt* 89 (the so-called "limited corporate law reform"). This statute, insofar as it relates to stock corporations and partnerships limited by shares, has been superseded by almost identical provisions contained in the present Act. To this extent it was expressly repealed by Section 33 of the Introductory Law. However, the provisions on capital increases remain applicable to limited liability companies.

[6] The various aspects of the reform of the Stock Corporation Act were the topic of numerous publications. Some of the more important contributions are listed in Rasch, *Richtige und falsche Wege der Aktienrechtsreform* 66-72 (1960).

[7] See, generally, Conard, "Organizing for Business," in II American Enterprise in the European Common Market 1, 43-151 (Stein & Nicholson ed. 1960); 1 Foreign Office, Manual of German Law 237-246 (Cohn & Wolff 1950); Spethmann, "West Germany," in Friedmann & Pugh, *Legal Aspects of Foreign Investment* 670 (1959); WTS: Germany, 1/4.6 (1963); Hay, "Four Lectures on the Common Market: Trade Provisions – German and French Company

Law – Establishment," 24 U. Pitt. L. Rev. 685, 719-734 (1963); Eckert, "Shareholder and Management: A Comparative View on Some Corporate Problems in the United States and Germany," 46 Iowa L. Rev. 12 (1960): Falkenhausen & Steefel, "Shareholders' Rights in German Corporations (AG and GmbH)," 10 Am. J. Comp. L. 407 (1961); Kessler, "The American Securities Act and Its Foreign Counterparts: A Comparative Study," 44 Yale L. J. 1133 (1935); Mann, "The New German Company Law and Its Background," 19 J. Comp. Leg. & Int'l L. (3d ser.) 220 (1937).

[8] Steefel & Falkenhausen, "The New German Stock Corporation Law," 52 Cornell L. Q. 518; Vagts, supra, note 4. For a summary of the Act, see CCH COMMON MARKET REPORTS ¶ 6622.25 – 6638.

[9] Treatment of the *Verein* in the General Part of the Civil Code has, as a matter of German statutory technique, the effect of making it the prototype of legal person. Accordingly, the rules of the Civil Code may be applicable to stock corporations.

[10] See generally Weisser & Fassnacht, "Cooperatives as an Aid to Small Business in Germany," 24 Law & Contemp. Prob. 209 (1959).

The usefulness of these entities is limited to the purposes for which they may be created. Three forms are available for incorporating a general business concern. In addition to stock corporations, the *Aktiengesetz* permits the formation of partnerships limited by shares *(Kommanditgesellschaften auf Aktien)*. The *"KGaA"* is considered to be a legal entity[11] despite the unlimited liability of the general partners and the applicability of partnership rules to a number of important incidents.[12] It is rarely found in practice.[13]

The real rival of the stock corporation is the limited liability company *(Gesellschaft mit beschränkter Haftung)*. This entity is the creature of a statute[14] enacted in response to the demands made by representatives of small business for a simplified corporate form. In effect, it is a statutory close corporation. This form is widely used in practice. Indeed, the large majority of businesses incorporated in Germany, including some very substantial ones, are limited liability companies.[15]

A number of reasons account for the popularity of the "GmbH." In contrast to the rigidity of the law governing stock corporations, the formal and substantive requirements to be observed in organizing and running a limited liability company are minimal; and the law affords great latitude in shaping its constitution to accommodate management and quotaholders by appropriate charter provisions.[16] Also, at present there is virtually no compulsion for a GmbH to disclose financial and other information,[17] and it has been surmised that the tightened disclosure provisions of the present Stock Corporation Act may induce a number of existing stock corporations to change their form and become limited liability companies.[18] Furthermore, quotaholders can, by entering into an appropriately drafted limited partnership arrangement with their company, avoid a double tax burden and enjoy the advantages of partnership taxation without losing the benefits of perpetuity and limited liability.[19]

---

[11] Stock Corporation Act, Section 278, paragraph 1. Sections hereinafter cited without further designation are those of the Stock Corporation Act.

[12] Section 278, paragraph 2.

[13] As of December 31, 1966, only 25 partnerships limited by shares existed in West Germany and West Berlin. Information furnished by *Statistisches Bundesamt*, Wiesbaden. This form developed as an alternative to the stock corporation at a time when corporations required the grant of a charter. Probably the strongest incentive for selecting this form is the strong position the general partners enjoy under the provisions of the Act.

[14] *Gesetz betreffend die Gesellschaften mit beschränkter Haftung*, Law of April 20, 1892, [1892] *Reichsgesetzblatt* 447

[15] In 1966, there were 2,420 stock corporations with a total stated capital of approximately 48 billion German marks, and 58,000 limited liability companies with a total stated capital of approximately 30 billion German marks. [1967] *Bundesanzeiger* No. 66, April 7, 1967, at 3.

[16] See generally DeVries & Juenger, "Limited Liability Contract: The GmbH," 64 Colum. L. Rev. 866 (1964).

[17] However, limited liability companies which are parent companies of an affiliated group are required to publish consolidated financial statements. See Introductory Law, Section 28.

[18] Möhring, "Das neue Aktiengesetz," 19 *Neue Juristische Wochenschrift* 1, 4 (1966) (commenting on the publication requirements concerning holdings of equity interests in related companies). This observation is confirmed by the statistics noted in the *Bundesanzeiger*, supra, note 15, which states that the total number of stock corporations decreased by 88, while that of limited liability companies increased by almost 4,000.

[19] Regarding the "GmbH & Co. KG" see DeVries & Juenger, supra, note 16 at 868 n. 11. This "Subchapter S" effect results from the fact that distributions are made to the quotaholders in their capacity as limited partners of, rather than as holders of an equity interest in, the limited liability company.

The possibility of doing business in the form of a limited liability company does, however, have a major drawback: the substantial advantages it offers are conditioned on forbearance from issuing shares. The limited liability statute bars free negotiability of quotas in such companies to assure continued closeness. It achieves this effect by restraining the embodiment of such interests in share certificates and conditioning their transfer on a notarial act.[20] The lack of negotiability inherent in the formalities and cost of a notarial transfer precludes public offerings. Thus, in order to be able to sell shares to the public, an enterprise. must adopt the form of a stock corporation or partnership limited by shares. Accordingly, stock corporations, though fewer in number, represent by far the greater concentration of economic power.

The co-existence of diverse corporate forms is reflected in the provisions of the Act on "transformation."[21] These provisions permit a limited liability company (or mining company) to change its corporate form so as to become a stock corporation or partnership limited by shares. In this manner, a close corporation can "go public." Conversely, a stock corporation or a partnership limited by shares may choose to adopt the form of a limited liability company.[22] Stock corporations may become partnerships limited by shares and vice versa. Specific provision for the transformation of various types of entities is also made in connection with the rules concerning merger and consolidation.[23]

Formation of a Stock Corporation

With the exception of the mining companies (bergrechtliche Gewerkschaften), which derive their corporate existence from state (Länder) legislation,[24] German corporation law has been federal in nature since 1870. Therefore, the necessity to treat the issuance of securities as a separate matter of national concern against the backdrop of divergent state laws did not arise. The absence of charter-mongering practices[25] may be the reason that Germany has no regulatory enactments comparable to our federal securities laws. Pro-

---

[20] The role and position of the notary in civil-law countries and the significance of the notarial act are explained in Schlesinger, "The Notary and the Formal Contract in Civil Law," [1941] N.Y. Law Revision Comm'n Rep. 403.

[21] See Sections 362-393. Concerning transformation of corporations into partnerships or sole proprietorships, transformation of mining companies into limited liability companies, and simplified mergers, see Umwandlungsgesetz (Statute Concerning Transformation), Law of November 12, 1956, [1956] 1 Bundesgesetzblatt 844, as amended by Section 39 of the Introductory Law.

[22] To prevent a squeeze-out of minority shareholders, who may be disadvantaged if they are given non-negotiable quota interests in lieu of shares, the present Act bars such a transformation if a minority of ten percent objects and provides for appraisal rights. See Section 369.

[23] See Sections 354-358.

[24] See Law Introducing the German Civil Code, [1896] Reichsgesetzblatt 604, Section 67, which exempted the mining laws of the German states, including state laws referring to mining companies, from the repealer provision of Section 55 of the same statute. The present Act deals only with companies which, pursuant to state law, have separate legal personality.

[25] But see 88 Entscheidungen des Reichsgerichts in Zivilsachen (hereinafter cited as R.G.Z.) 53 (1916). This decision would indicate that, because of the greater ease of incorporation, Gotha was preferred over Prussia as the place of incorporation for mining companies. The opinion also demonstrates how the concept of corporate domicile (Sitz) can be used to combat what a court may consider an improper incorporation in a "haven" jurisdiction.

visions deemed necessary to protect the investing public, including civil and penal sanctions, became part of a nation-wide corporate code. Existing institutions, such as the Commercial Register, notaries, the accounting profession,[26] the courts, and Chambers of Industry and Commerce, could be used to implement disclosure and other protective requirements.

Articles of Incorporation

It is for these reasons that incorporation of an *Aktiengesellschaft* is not a mere formality, but is conceived as an important transaction hedged with substantial safeguards. The articles of incorporation are an integral part of the organizational process which is designed to impart information and to assure adequate capitalization. The Act prescribes the necessary minimum content: the articles must set forth the name, purpose, domicile,[27] and stated capital of the company, the par value, number and classes of shares, any special advantages granted as a reward to promoters, and organizational expenses borne by the company and the members of its initial managing board.[28] They also must list any assets contributed upon formation, together with the names of the parties contributing them, and the number of shares or other consideration granted by the company in return for such contributions.[29]

The rules concerning the content of the articles of incorporation are mandatory.[30] The new Act provides that although the articles may contain collateral matter, their content may not vary from that prescribed by the statutory provisions unless the Act specifically authorizes a deviation.[31] The articles are the sole and exclusive organizational instrument; by-laws, in the sense of rules concerning the regulation and management of the affairs of the company, can

---

[26] The Act provides for audits in a great number of cases: e.g., upon formation of the company, Sections 33, 34; of annual reports, Section 162; in connection with capital increases, Sections 188, 194; and of dealings with related enterprises, Section 313.

[27]. Section 5, paragraph 1, provides that the domicile *(Sitz)* of a stock corporation is the place designated in the articles of incorporation. Paragraph 2 of the same section requires designation, "as a rule," of either a place of business or the place of administration or management. Thus, the Act permits selection of a domicile among various places with which the company has a connection. According to the language of this provision, the designation in the articles is decisive, even if there is no real connection with the place selected. In this respect, the concept of corporate domicile as used in the Act would seem to have a meaning different from that of "domicile" or "seat" as used in the context of German conflict of laws, where *"Sitz"* connotes the place of central management and control. See 25 *Entscheidungen des Bundesgerichtshofs in Zivilsachen* (hereinafter cited as B.G.H.Z.) 134, 144 (1957);

88 R.G.Z. 53, 54 (1916); 83 R.G.Z. 367 (1913); 2 Rabel, *Conflict of Laws* 41 (1960).

[28] Sections 23, 26. Contracts concerning the acquisition of assets by the company, compensation for services rendered in connection with the formation, or special advantages granted to promoters are not binding on the company unless they are referred to in the articles. Section 41, paragraph 3.

[29] Section 27. To prevent evasion of this provision through contribution of assets after formation, Section 52 requires for any sale of assets to the company within two years after its formation, at a price exceeding one-tenth of the stated capital, approval by a qualified majority of shareholders, as well as a special audit and appraisal. Such sales must also be recorded in the Commercial Register.

[30] In contrast to this rule, the quotaholders of a limited liability company enjoy almost unlimited freedom in shaping the charter to suit their purposes. See DeVries & Juenger, supra, note 16, at 868, 869.

[31] Section 23, paragraph 4.

be adopted neither by the shareholders nor by management.[32] Since this
instrument must be in the form of a notarial act,[33] it is assured that it meets
the statutory requirements.[34] The dissemination of the information it contains
is effected by filing with the Commercial Register,[35] which is open to every-
one, and by publication.[36]

Financing

The rules on incorporation are designed to guarantee an adequate initial
capitalization and to prevent stock watering. The minimum stated capital is
100,000 German marks.[37] In contrast to American practice, irrevocable subscriptions for all of the company's shares must be obtained[38] before the company can obtain recognition as a legal entity.[39] A minimum of twenty-five
percent of the par value (plus the full amount of any premium) of all shares
issued for cash must be paid in.[40] Issuance below par is not permitted.[41] As
discussed below, the value of assets contributed and the compensation of
promoters are subject to a fairly strict scrutiny.

Since in the case of public issues the incorporators and subscribers will
be syndicates of banks acting as underwriters,[42] their judgment, integrity and
solvency afford an additional measure of protection to investors.

Reports and Audits

The incorporators are required to make a written report concerning the
formation of the company, setting forth facts showing the reasonableness of

---

[32] The *Geschäftsordnung* of the managing
board referred to in Section 77, paragraph 2,
constitutes internal rules of procedure.

[33] Section 23, paragraph 1.

[34] Section 21, paragraph 1. The German
notary, who is a fully trained legal professional,
is required to advise the parties concerning
the legal significance of the documentation he
prepares for them. In effect, he is a guarantor
of the validity and legality of instruments
which are in the form of a notarial act. See
Schlesinger, supra, note 20, at 67, 68.

[35] Concerning the role and function of the
Commercial Register, see Schlesinger, *Comparative Law*, 285, 286, 341-343 (2d ed. 1959).

[36] Numerous provisions of the Stock Corporation Act require publication of corporate
transactions and notices in the "*Gesellschaftsblätter*." According to Section 25, this term refers to the Official Federal Gazette (*Bundesanzeiger*) and any additional newspapers that may
be designated in the articles of incorporation.

[37] "Authorized capital" is limited to an
amount equal to that of the stated capital, and
the authority of the management to issue new
shares is hedged with safeguards identical to
those applicable to capital increases. See
Sections 202-206.

[38] Section 7.

[39] See Section 29. Provision is made for
forfeiture of shares whose holders fail to pay
assessments and for liability of the transferors.
See Sections 64 and 65. Shareholders have no
cause of action against the company for rescis-
sion or damages on grounds of mistake, fraud or
duress. See 127 R.G.Z. 191 (1930); 88 R.G.Z.
187 (1916); Kessler, supra, note 7, at 1156-1158,
1161.

[40] Section 36, paragraph 2.

[41] Section 9, paragraph 1.

[42] A possibility of direct public offerings
(*Simultangründung*) existed under earlier
stock corporation acts, but it was rarely used
and has been discarded by the present Act.

shares or other consideration granted for assets contributed, the shares sub-scribed by members of the managing and supervisory boards, as well as special advantages granted to promoters and the compensation they were granted or promised for services in connection with the formation.[43] The process of for-mation and the incorporators' report are examined by the members of the initial managing and supervisory boards, who in turn must comment upon it in writing. If members of either board participated in the formation or acquired any interest or benefit in connection with the incorporation, the Act requires an additional examination by independent auditors appointed by the local Chamber of Industry and Commerce.[44] The same applies if assets are contrib-uted, in which event the auditors must appraise the assets and certify to the adequacy of their stated value. The audit reports are filed with the Chamber of Industry and Commerce.[45]

Registration

Before registration of the company in the Commercial Register, it does not exist as a legal entity and cannot issue shares.[46] The Act assures compliance with the rules concerning the organizational process by requiring that the application to record the corporation be accompanied by the articles of incor-poration and all pertinent documentation.[47] The promoters are liable for mis-statements and unfair transactions.[48]

The court of registry examines the documentation filed and may refuse to record the company if the reports do not comply with the statutory provisions or contain false or misleading statements, or if assets are overstated.[49] Details of the application to record are published.[50]

Investor Protection after Formation

The protection afforded to shareholders and creditors by the rules on "publicity," i.e., the disclosure of information through public registers and publication, and the guaranty of a "trust fund" of stated capital, is continued after formation. To bar evasion of the provisions concerning formation by subsequent offerings, they are complemented by essentially similar rules applicable to capital increases.[51] These rules also apply where an enterprise changes its corporate form to that of a stock corporation.[52] Contracts made

---

[43] Section 32.

[44] Sections 33, 34.

[45] Section 34.

[46] Section 41.

[47] See Section 37. The documentation re-quired to be filed includes the various reports, evidence of full subscription, of payments made on the shares, and of the organization expenses; contracts concerning the acquisition of assets by the company; documents showing the appointment of board members, as well as any governmental authorization that may be required for incorporation of the enterprise.

[48] See Section 46. Provision is also made for liability of undisclosed principals (Section 46, paragraph 5), of members of the managing and supervisory boards (Section 48), and of third parties who knowingly or recklessly caused damage to the company (Section 47). Regard-ing penal sanctions for false statements, see Section 399.

[49] Section 38.

[50] Section 40.

[51] Sections 182-191.

[52] Sections 370-383, 384, 385, 393.

by the company to acquire substantial assets within two years after registration ("post-formation acquisitions") are hedged with safeguards.[53] Continued
publicity is assured by periodic filing and the publication of audited financial
statements and business reports. The minimum content and the form of these
reports are prescribed in detail.[54] To protect the company's capital, the Act
prohibits repayment of capital[55] and the waiver of contributions.[56]

Less stringent in some respects than American securities legislation, the
German rules on disclosure and the preservation of stated capital (buttressed,
in the case of securities traded on a stock exchange, by the pertinent listing
and prospectus requirements[57]) offer a fairly effective protection to investors
and creditors. The improved disclosure provisions of the new Act further
increase this protection. Whether the creation of an agency similar to the
Securities and Exchange Commission entrusted with the specific task of
protecting the investing public might nonetheless be desirable is another
question.[58]

Capital Structure

In addition to common and (cumulative or non-cumulative) preferred stock,
German law permits the issuance of bonds,[59] as well as of hybrid and convertible securities.[60] Shares with disproportionate voting rights are looked upon
with disfavor.[61] Only cumulative preferred stock may be non-voting, and the
total par value of such stock may not exceed that of the outstanding voting
stock.[62] Shares with multiple voting rights may henceforth be created only

---

[53] Sections 52 and 53.

[54] See generally Sections 148-178, 329-338.

[55] Sections 57 and 62.

[56] Section 66.

[57] See generally Maurer & Spray, "The
Stock Exchanges of Germany," in *The Principal
Stock Exchanges of the World* (1964). For a
comparative discussion see Nussbaum, "American and Foreign Stock Exchange Legislation,"
21 Va. L. Rev. 839 (1935).

[58] See 1 Loss, *Securities Regulation*, n. 94
at 451 (1961); Jackson, "Public Offerings: A
Comparative Study of Disclosure in Western
Europe and the United States," 16 W. Res. L.
Rev. 44, 73-74; Kessler, supra, note 7 at 1164-
1165 (1935). Conceivably, a "federal" agency
paralleling the Securities and Exchange Commission may be established within the frame-
work of the European Common Market. See
CCH Common Market Reports ¶ 9149.

[59] The issuance of negotiable obligations
(including convertible bonds) requires the
approval of federal and state ministries. See
Civil Code, Sections 795, 808a; Statute Concerning Governmental Authorization for Bearer
Bonds, [1954] 1 *Bundesgesetzblatt* 147.

[60] See Section 221. A peculiar species are
the so-called *"Genussrechte"* (translated herein, for want of an appropriate English term, as
"debentures" or "other types of debentures"),
which the Act mentions in Sections 160 and
221. They are rights against the company,
rather than equity interests. Examples are
rights to participate in profits and liquidation
dividends, and rights to use the facilities of
the company (e.g., free tickets). They may be
granted to shareholders or to third parties.
They may, but need not, be embodied in an
instrument. They may be issued to raise capital,
but in practice are generally used to reward
promoters, management or employees, or as
consideration for services or rights granted to
the company.

[61] See Hueck, *Gesellschaftsrecht* 108-109,
149 (11th ed. 1963). It is for this reason that the
Act contains a number of provisions requiring
capital majorities (in addition to a majority of
the votes cast) and that minorities are determined by reference to percentages of capital,
rather than by votes.

[62] Sections 12, 139. The 1937 Act was even
more restrictive and provided for a ratio of only
1 to 2. In the event that the company is in
default with respect to dividends payable to
holders of preferred stock, the stock becomes
voting. See Section 140, paragraph 2.

in the rare case where a state economic ministry authorizes their issuance to protect "preponderant interests of the national economy."[63] However, the articles of incorporation may limit the number of shares that any one shareholder may vote.[64]

Proposals to introduce no-par value shares as part of the 1965 legislation were not successful. All shares must have a par value stated at fifty,[65] one hundred, or a multiple of one hundred German marks. If shares are issued above par, the premium becomes part of the statutory reserve, which is not available for dividend distribution.[66]

Bearer Shares[67] and Registered Shares

In recognition of the prevailing practice, the new Act specifies that unless the articles of incorporation provide for registered shares, certificates[68] for fully paid-up stock[69] shall be issued in bearer form.[70]

The fact that in Germany, as in many other civil-law countries, share certificates are customarily in bearer form has important consequences. The possibility of loss inherent in the ready negotiability of such an instrument, and the impossibility for the stock corporation to communicate directly with its anonymous owner, make it advisable to deposit the certificates with banks for safekeeping and the collection of dividends. The banks, realizing the potential offered by the possession of such shares, soon obtained blanket authorization for the exercise of voting rights from their depositors. Thus, rather than being mere depositaries, they in effect became intermediaries between shareholders and management. As holders of bearer paper, they did not even need proxies to vote in shareholders' meetings.

---

[63] Section 12, paragraph 2. Under the 1937 Act, a finding by the state economics ministry that issuance of such shares would be in the company's interest sufficed. The argument advanced in favor of permitting shares with multiple voting rights is the retention of control as against corporate take-overs by foreign interests (*"Überfremdung"*). See Hueck, supra, note 61. However, Section 101, paragraph 3, permits provisions in the articles giving shareholders the right to appoint up to one-third of the members on the supervisory board. Such a right is frequently exacted by governmental bodies which have an equity investment in a corporation.

[64] See Section 134, paragraph 1. This would seem to permit per capita voting provisions. Whether cumulative voting is permissible is doubtful. See Steefel & Falkenhausen, supra, note 8 at 534.

[65] Section 8, paragraph 1. The Act introduced the par value of fifty German marks to encourage purchases by small investors.

[66] Section 150, paragraph 2.

[67] Regarding bearer shares, see, generally, Schlesinger, supra, note 35, at 425-443; Vagts, supra, note 4, at 53-54.

[68] The term *"Aktie,"* in the terminology of the Stock Corporation Act, expresses either the share certificate or the right it embodies. This translation uses the term "share certificate" whenever appropriate.

[69] Shares may not be issued in bearer form before full payment of the subscription price. Section 10, paragraph 2.

[70] See Sections 10 and 24, paragraph 1. Conversely, the 1937 Act required a specific authorization in the articles for the issuance of bearer certificates.

The bankers' vote, combined with their own large holdings and those controlled by them through investment funds, is a major factor in the dominant
role played by German financial institutions.[71] The propriety of this practice
has been the subject of perennial discussion, those in favor viewing the banks
as the trustees of apathetic shareholders; those opposed, as self-seeking mo-
nopolists oblivious of conflict-of-interest problems. Prior legislation designed
to narrow the conditions for the exercise of the banker's vote had little practical effect, and it seems unlikely that the further restrictions contained in the
present Act will deprive the banks of the power concentrated in their hands.

If shares are in registered form, their transfer can be conditioned on the consent of the company.[72] Shares subject to this consent restriction may impose
on the holders the duty to render recurrent services or contributions (other
than money) to the company, if the articles of incorporation so provide.[73]

Management

In contrast to the dual role of directors and officers of an American corporation, the boards of an *Aktiengesellschaft* do not represent two echelons of authority but are placed in contraposition: the managing board (*Vorstand*) is the
executive arm of the company; the supervisory board (*Aufsichtsrat*) is its
overseer.

The Managing Board

The managing board is in charge of the day-to-day operations of the company, but it also performs the policy-making of the American board of directors.
The functions of the managing board are exercised by one or more members [74]
appointed by the supervisory board rather than elected by the shareholders.[75]
Its broad powers to bind the company[76] are limited neither by an ultra vires
doctrine nor by the requirement of the shareholders' consent to any transaction other than organic changes and enterprise agreements.[77] Limitations

---

[71] See Schlesinger, supra, note 35, at 438-
443; Vagts, supra, note 4, at 53-58, 62-63.

[72] Section 68, paragraph 2.

[73] Section 55. This provision was introduced
in 1900 to sanction the practice of growers of
sugar beets to operate jointly-owned sugar
factories in the form of stock corporations,
whose articles required the shareholders to
deliver their crops to the company. Such obligations are also found in the articles of other
enterprises run on a cooperative basis, such as
dairies and distilleries.

[74] Section 76, paragraph 2.

[75] Sections 84, 30, paragraph 4. In certain

instances, the court may fill a vacancy on the
managing board (Section 85). In enterprises of
the coal and steel industry having more than
1,000 employees, at least one of the members
of the managing board, the so-called labor
director (see Section 76, paragraph 2, third
sentence), must be approved by labor.

[76] Section 78, paragraph 1. Only in the event
that the conduct of the other party amounted to
collusion can a transaction involving an abuse
of the power to bind the company be set aside.
See 145 R.G.Z. 311 (1943).

[77] Concerning enterprise agreements, see
page 14, infra.

imposed by the articles of incorporation, by a resolution or the rules of procedure of either board or by a shareholders' resolution are ineffective as against third parties,[78] although board members may become liable to the company if they do not observe the restrictions limiting their managerial powers to the extent permitted by law.[79] Some measure of protection against the unfettered exercise of the power to bind the company is afforded by the rule that the managing board, in managing and representing the company, must act jointly.[80] However, the articles of incorporation or rules of procedure may make provision for some other form of representation, including individual action.[81]

Delegation of managerial tasks by the managing board to other executive personnel, comparable to corporate officers in American companies, is permissible and customary. The Act refers to the *Prokuristen*.[82] These are agents whose appointment is recorded in the Commercial Register and who are invested with fairly broad powers, specified in the Commercial Code,[83] to bind the company. The powers of unregistered agents *(Handlungsbevollmächtigte)*, who are also mentioned in the Act,[84] depend on the scope of the delegation and the provisions of civil and commercial law on apparent authority.

The Supervisory Board

The supervisory board's primary task is implicit in its name: it oversees the activities of management.[85] To preserve their independence, its members are prohibited from serving on the managing board or in any other managerial capacity.[86] They may not become active in the management of the company, although the articles may provide that specified categories of transactions require their approval.[87]

The supervisory board has a minimum of three members. Only in the case of family-owned companies having less than 500 employees are all of them elected by the shareholders[88]; this is an exception to the provisions of the co-determination legislation, which reserves a specified number of seats to representatives elected by labor.[89]

---

[78] Section 82, paragraph 1. However, the shareholders cannot effectively deprive the managing board of its functions or impair its managerial discretion.

[79] See Section 82, paragraph 2.

[80] Sections 77, paragraph 1, 78, paragraph 2. Section 77, paragraph 1, second sentence, expressly abolishes the curious rule of the 1937 Act whereby the chairman of the managing board, absent a provision in the articles to the contrary, had the autocratic power to outvote all other members.

[81] See Section 78, paragraphs 2-4. Regarding the requirement of joint action as far as acts of internal management are concerned, see Section 77.

[82] See, e.g., Sections 78, paragraphs 3 and 4, 89, 42, paragraph 2.

[83] See Commercial Code, Sections 48-53.

[84] See, e.g., Sections 89, 95, 117, paragraph 1.

[85] Section 111, paragraph 1. For a discussion of the role of this body as an intermediary between shareholders and management see Vagts, supra, note 4, at 50-53, 58-62, 64.

[86] Section 105.

[87] Section 111, paragraph 4. Transactions entered into by the managing board without such approval are nevertheless binding on the company. See Section 82, paragraph 1.

[88] Concerning the right of shareholders to appoint members of the supervisory board, see note 63, supra.

[89] The details of labor representation in management are described by Steefel & Falkenhausen, supra, note 8, at 537-539. For an evaluation of this feature of German law, see Vagts, supra, note 4, at 64, 78.

The new Act further curtails the proliferation of supervisory board memberships, engendered by the desire to attract prestigious and influential members,
by limiting the total number of board seats held by one person to fifteen[90]
and by specifying a maximum size for supervisory boards, with gradations
based on the stated capital of a company.[91] The Act also attacks interlocking
arrangements by barring the appointment to a supervisory board position of
managers of a company a member of whose supervisory board is a manager
of the appointing corporation,[92] and of any legal representative of a controlled
company.[93]

The managing board is required to keep the supervisory board informed
about prospective company policies, about the economic and financial condition of the company, and about major business transactions.[94] The supervisory board can request additional information and reports from the managing
board.[95] It can call a special shareholders' meeting,[96] may inspect the corporate books and records,[97] must examine the annual statements, and reports on
them at the annual shareholders' meeting.[98] The supervisory board, rather
than the shareholders, appoints the members of the managing board and may
dismiss them "for compelling reasons."[99] It also functions as the representative of the company in legal transactions and in litigation with members of
the managing board.[100]

III. Major Innovations Introduced
by the New Act

Related Enterprises and "Enterprise Agreements"[101]

The provisions of the present Act on related enterprises represent a new
departure. Prior German corporation statutes did not contain a comprehensive

---

[90] See Section 100, paragraph 2. This includes seats on boards of companies which are
not stock corporations but are required by law
to have a supervisory board. If none of the
companies are related as specified in Section
100, paragraph 2, last sentence, the maximum
number of permissible seats is ten.

[91] Section 95.

[92] Section 100, paragraph 2, No. 3.

[93] Section 100, paragraph 2, No. 2.

[94] Section 90, paragraphs 1 and 2. This provision is somewhat more extensive than the
corresponding one of Section 81 of the 1937 Act.

[95] See Section 90, paragraphs 3-5. Each of
its members can request that such information
and reports be made to the supervisory board
as a whole.

[96] Section 111, paragraph 3.

[97] Section 111, paragraph 2.

[98] Sections 170 and 171.

[99] Section 84, paragraph 3. The term "compelling reasons" (wichtiger Grund) does not
presuppose fault or incompetence on the part
of the member removed. Section 84, paragraph
3, specifically mentions a shareholders' vote
of no-confidence as a sufficient ground for
dismissal. Another ground would be continued
disagreement of the supervisory board with
the managing board member. Dismissal is
without prejudice to the rights under an employment contract. Section 84, paragraph 3.

[100] Section 112.

[101] See, generally, Rasch, Deutsches Kon-
zernrecht (3d ed. 1966).

set of rules governing this subject.[102] In fact, these provisions appear to be without precedent in corporate legislation. The phenomenon of legal separateness but factual dependency of juridical persons is, of course, not limited to Germany. However, its prevalence in that country is remarkable: approximately seventy percent of all German stock corporations are "related companies."[103]

The new provisions are not an effort to untangle this webwork. Nor are they antitrust legislation.[104] The increasing trend toward further concentration, even though it gave rise to enough concern to prompt investigations by the German Government[105] and the Commission of the European Economic Community,[106] has not met with legislative disapproval, and is in fact espoused by many who feel that concentration is necessary for effective competition with large American concerns.[107] However, the reporting requirements contained in the Act should serve to convey a clearer picture of the maze of interrelationships existing between German enterprises.

In the language of the Act, the generic term "related enterprises" includes entities linked together either by stock ownership or by other ties. The definitions in Sections 15 to 19 mention "enterprise agreements" together with majority-owned and majority-owning, controlled and controlling, interlocking, and affiliated enterprises. Before discussing the significance of these relationships, the reporting requirements established by the new Act will be mentioned.

---

[102] However, the 1937 Act contained a definition of "affiliated companies" and provided for some degree of reporting on relationships with such companies in the annual statements. It also limited the acquisition of shares in a controlling company, and the exercise of voting rights with respect to such shares, by a controlled company. See Sections 15, 131, paragraph 1, A II No. 6, A III Nos. 5, 9, 10, B V No. 7, and Section 134, No. 2, of the 1937 Act. Agreements to transfer profit and to lease the enterprise were mentioned in Section 256 of the 1937 Act.

[103] Gessler, "Das neue Aktienrecht," 20 *Der Betriebsberater* 677, 681 (1965). Many of the existing arrangements amount to de facto mergers. The reasons for shying away from taking this final step of legal oneness may be adverse transfer tax consequences or such reasons as the desire to bestow or to retain titles indicating a rank in the corporate and social hierarchy (*Herr Direktor*). See Rasch, supra, note 101, at 5.

[104] See Möhring, supra, note 18, at 2-3 (1966).

[105] Bericht über das Ergebnis einer Untersuchung der Konzentration in der Wirtschaft [Report on Results of the Inquiry into the Concentration of Industry], Parliamentary Document No. IV/2320, 1964. Report based on the *Gesetz über eine Untersuchung der Konzentration in der Wirtschaft*, December 31, 1960, BGBl 1961 I, 9.

[106] "Concentration of Enterprises in the Common Market," Memorandum of the EEC Commission to the Governments of the Member States on the Need for Larger Enterprises in the Common Market and the Problems Involved in Bringing This About, CCH COMMON MARKET REPORTS, Part I of Report No. 26 (March 17, 1966); see also CCH COMMON MARKET REPORTS ¶ 9081.

[107] Survey by the Union des Industries de la Communauté Européenne (U.N.I.C.E.), Brussels, February 1965; see CCH COMMON MARKET REPORTS ¶ 9029; Hans von der Groeben, member of the EEC Commission, in address to the European Parliament, Strasbourg, June 16, 1965; CCH COMMON MARKET REPORTS ¶ 9036.

Reporting of Holdings

Section 20 requires any "enterprise" (a term encompassing incorporated and unincorporated businesses, domestic and foreign)[108] whose holdings[109] in a German stock corporation amount to twenty-five percent or more[110] to notify the latter in writing. Further notification is required when the enterprise acquires a majority of shares or votes.[111] A report is also due if such interests subsequently fall below these marks.[112] A stock corporation receiving such notification is required to publish its content[113] and to refer to it in its annual business report.[114] Failure to comply with these reporting requirements suspends the shareholders' rights of the delinquent enterprise.[115] If a stock corporation acquires or relinquishes interest in the reportable amounts in a German entity incorporated in some form other than that of a stock corporation, it is required to notify the latter.[116] The acquisition and loss of a majority interest in unincorporated enterprises is also reportable.[117] However, that enterprise need not publish the information conveyed to it. There are no reporting or publication requirements if neither enterprise is a stock corporation.

The purpose of these provisions, according to the Government Draft, is to inform creditors and the public about existing holdings and future acquisitions of substantial interests, and to assure the enforceability of other rules concerning related enterprises.

Enterprise Agreements

These agreements fall into two categories:

(a) The first category[118] includes contracts in which a corporation, i.e., a stock corporation or partnership limited by shares, agrees to be managed by another enterprise ("control agreements"), and contracts in which a corporation agrees to transfer all of its profit to another enterprise, or to conduct its business for the account of the latter ("agreements to transfer profit").[119]

---

[108] It will be noted that the reporting and other consequences of existing relationships frequently depend on the form of the enterprise. This somewhat lopsided treatment of the law of related enterprises is a consequence of its treatment in the Stock Corporation Act, rather than in a separate statute. See Möhring, supra, note 18, at 5.

[109] Reportable holdings in existence at the time the Act went into effect had to be reported within one month from the effective date of the Act. Section 7 of the Introductory Law.

[110] Concerning attribution rules, see Section 20, paragraph 2, Section 16, paragraphs 2 and 4. A further duty to report applies to corporations and mining companies whose direct holdings in a stock corporation reach the 25 percent limit. Section 20, paragraph 3.

[111] Section 20, paragraph 4, Section 16, paragraph 1.

[112] Section 20, paragraph 5.

[113] Section 20, paragraph 6.

[114] Section 160, paragraph 3, No. 11.

[115] Section 20, paragraph 7, Section 21, paragraph 4.

[116] Section 21, paragraphs 1 and 3.

[117] Section 21, paragraphs 2 and 3.

[118] Section 291.

[119] The two types of contract of this category are usually combined. This combination is the so-called *"Organschaftsvertrag,"* a contractual device used to obtain favorable tax consequences for inter-company transactions.

(b) Agreements of the second category[120] involve a somewhat lesser degree of dependency. They include undertakings of a corporation to pool all or some of its profit with another enterprise ("profit-pooling agreements"), or to transfer part of its profit to it ("agreements to transfer a portion of profit"), or to lease or surrender its business to such other enterprise ("agreements to lease or surrender a business").

Since such contracts substantially affect the independence of a corporation, the Act subjects them to formal requirements resembling those provided for organic changes. They must be in writing, require a favorable shareholders' resolution adopted by a three-fourths majority of the obligor corporations, and must be recorded in the Commercial Register.[121] Control agreements and agreements to transfer profits must also be approved by the same majority of shareholders of the obligee company, if the latter is a corporation.[122] Provision is made for full explanation of the significance of pending enterprise agreements to the shareholders.[123]

These contracts are not an invention of the legislature. They evolved in practice as a result of corporate inbreeding and of peculiarities of German turnover and corporate income taxation.[124] To accord them statutory recognition appeared desirable in view of their widespread use and the reliance on tax rulings and decisions.[125] At the same time, their legal effect could be clarified. Finally, they could be used in connection with the delineation of permissible limits for the exertion of influence over a controlled company, and to establish safeguards for creditors and "outside shareholders" (i.e., minority investors not connected with the controlling group).

Consequences of a Given Relationship

In addition to the reporting requirements already discussed, several other provisions of the Act attach specific consequences to existing relationships, e.g., with regard to the right to hold or subscribe to shares,[126] the effect of interlocking holdings,[127] membership on corporate boards,[128] and the reporting of transactions in the annual statements.[129] Apart from the rules concerning con-

---

[120] Section 292 (entitled "Other Enterprise Agreements").

[121] Sections 293, 294. Concerning the amendment and termination of such agreements, see Sections 295-298.

[122] Section 293, paragraph 2.

[123] Section 293, paragraphs 3 and 4.

[124] See WTS: Germany, 2/4.5, 7/7, 16/2.3, 16/2.4 (1963); Karplus, "The German Integration Agreement as Corporate Guarantee," 19 Bus. Lawyer 295 (1963).

[125] The enforceability and effect of such contracts had been in doubt. See Rasch, supra, note 101, at 75, Karplus, supra, note 124, at 299. In particular, it was agreed that since they violated the rules on distribution of profit (Sec-

tions 52 and 54 of the 1937 Act), they might be illegal and void.

[126] Section 56, paragraph 2.

[127] Concerning restrictions on the exercise of shareholders' rights in the case of interlocking holdings, see Sections 328, 16; Section 6 of the Introductory Law. The idea underlying the highly complex interaction of Sections 56, paragraph 2, 328, and 19 is to bar acquisition of equity interests by two or more companies in each other and to neutralize existing interlocking holdings because of the undesirable effect of such holdings (misleading capital figures and self-perpetuating management).

[128] See Section 100, paragraph 2.

[129] See, e.g., Section 151, paragraph 1, III B No. 9; Section 157, paragraph 1, No. 7; Section 160, paragraph 3, Nos. 1, 2, 3, 10, 11.

solidated reports for affiliated enterprises,[130] the attempt to regulate the exercise of control by a dominant company seems to be the most significant aspect of this new legislation. Its objective is the adjustment of the conflicting interests of the controlling enterprise on the one hand and of outside shareholders and creditors of the controlled corporation on the other, on a somewhat more "scientific" basis than the American case law concerning the fiduciary duties and liabilities of majority shareholders. The statutory scheme is as follows:

The controlling enterprise must forbear from using its power to compel the management of the controlled corporation to perform or forego any act, unless it specifically compensates the controlled corporation, within the same fiscal year, for any detriment the latter may incur,[131] or unless both enterprises are parties to a control agreement. If such an agreement exists, the management of the controlled corporation must carry out any and all directives, however detrimental to the company, as long as they serve the purposes of the controlling enterprise or an enterprise affiliated with it.[132] Thus, absolute control is conditioned on a formal agreement sanctioning its exercise. Absent such an agreement, the failure to grant specific compensation renders the controlling enterprise liable in tort.[133] To ensure compliance with these provisions, the managing board of any controlled corporation which is not a party to a control agreement is required to report annually on its dealings with the controlling enterprise. This report must list all transactions and measures induced by or serving the interests of the controlling enterprise.[134]

The unfettered discretion which a controlling enterprise enjoys in the event that it has a control agreement with another enterprise is compensated by provisions protecting the creditors and shareholders of the controlled corporation. As the price for such an agreement, the law exacts the following safeguards: the controlling enterprise must underwrite the losses and maintain the statutory reserves of the controlled corporation, secure its creditors in the event of termination of the agreement,[135] guarantee appropriate dividend payments to outside shareholders, and grant them appraisal rights.[136]

If the corporation is the obligor under an agreement to transfer profit, its creditors and outside shareholders enjoy essentially the same protection.[137] Enterprise agreements of the second category,[138] however, need not provide for guaranteed dividends and appraisal rights to outside shareholders.[139]

---

[130] Sections 329-338; see page 18, infra.

[131] Section 311, paragraph 1.

[132] Section 308, paragraphs 1 and 2.

[133] Section 317, paragraphs 1 and 2. The executives of the controlling enterprise and the controlled corporation are jointly liable. See Section 317, paragraph 3, and Section 318.

[134.] Section 312. Regarding the audit of such reports, see Sections 313-315.

[135] Such creditors would otherwise lose the protection of Section 302: i.e., the guaranty effect of the underwriting of losses by the controlling enterprise.

[136] See Sections 300-305.

[137] Id.

[138] See note 120, supra.

[139] Sections 304 and 305 are inapplicable to such agreements. For the varying consequences of the several types of agreements of this second category, see Sections 300-303.

Integration

The provisions on integration[140] are entirely new. They permit the treatment of a parent and a subsidiary stock corporation as one economic entity without the requirement of a merger.

Integration is permissible whenever one stock corporation owns ninety-five percent or more of the shares of another. It is effected by shareholders' resolutions of the parent and the subsidiary and recording in the Commercial Register. The parent company's resolution requires a three-fourths majority.

After integration has been effected, the subsidiary maintains its separate legal identity. However, functionally and for accounting purposes it is treated as a mere division of the stock corporation. The parent becomes jointly liable for the obligations of the subsidiary – a statutory piercing of the corporate veil.

Accounting Rules

While the rules on related companies are interesting because of their novelty, the accounting provisions of the new Act[141] are of greater practical significance. Inspired by American practice, they are a substantial improvement over the statutory rules on financial statements contained in the 1937 Act. Most importantly, these provisions, through more stringent valuation rules,[142] eliminated the much debated practice of management's arbitrarily understating assets and overstating liabilities to create undisclosed reserves.[143] Allegedly an element of creditor protection, undisclosed reserves in effect permitted management to manipulate profits, thereby rendering illusory the statutory right of the shareholders to determine the amount of profit to be distributed as dividends.[144] Under present law, undisclosed reserves can result only from the application of scheduled depreciation and valuation methods conforming to proper accounting principles.[145] These methods must be set forth in the annual business report, and deviations from methods previously used must be explained. If such deviation generates an amount of ten percent or more of the annual profit or loss of the company, this amount must be listed separately.[146] In this manner the Act substituted truth in accounting and adequate information to the investors for the doubtful benefit of creditor protection through misstatement.

At the same time, the Act introduced remedies enabling shareholders to compel appropriate dividend distributions. Unless the company's articles provide otherwise, management is now required to put no less than one-half of the annual profit at the disposal of the shareholders[147] to assure that the amount

---

[140] Sections 319-327.

[141] Concerning accounting and audits, see Sections 148-178, 256-261, 329-338.

[142] See Sections 153 to 156.

[143] See Gessler, supra, note 103, at 679; Möhring, supra, note 18, at 89; Vagts, Book Review, 75 Harv. L. Rev. 1046, 1049-51 (1962).

[144] Section 174, paragraph 1. Compare Section 126 of the 1937 Act.

[145] See Sections 153, 154.

[146] Section 160, paragraph 2.

[147] See Sections 174, 58.

of such profit is not reduced by fictitious understatements. Shareholders representing five percent or more of the stated capital or shares having a combined par value of no less than one million German marks can appoint special auditors to examine wrongful understating of assets, and they can compel judicial review of the auditors' findings.[148] The same minority can contest oppressive and unwarranted allocation of profit to disclosed reserves by majority resolution to compel distribution of a dividend up to an amount of four percent of the stated capital.[149]

The rules on the minimum content of annual statements were further refined and the present provisions require substantially more detailed disclosure than those of the 1937 Act.[150]

In contrast to the prior Act, the new law requires consolidated statements for affiliated enterprises.[151] The pertinent provisions, inspired by foreign, in particular American, models[152] attempt to depict the true condition of the group as an economic entity and to prevent shuffling of profit among subsidiaries. They apply to German stock corporations and partnerships limited by shares which head a group of affiliates. The annual statements must include all group members domiciled in Germany more than 50 percent of whose equity is held by other group members.[153] If the enterprise heading the group is not a stock corporation or partnership limited by shares, but controls other group members through companies organized in either of these forms, the latter are required to file "partial consolidated statements" for the portion of the group controlled through them.[154] Similar provision is made for German corporations closest to the apex of a group controlled by a foreign entity.[155] The rules on partial consolidated statements are intended to encourage consolidated reports from companies which, because of their corporate form or a foreign domicile, are not compelled to do so, and to bar evasion by the simple expedient of changing the corporate form of the parent company.

An escape clause of the 1937 *Aktiengesetz* permitted suppression, in the business report, of facts if warranted by "preponderant interests of the company, a related company or the common weal."[156] Now such omissions can be justified only if full disclosure would be detrimental to the "welfare of the Federal Republic of Germany or one of its States."[157] Particulars concerning contingent liabilities and dealings with related companies may still be omitted

---

[148] See Sections 258-261.

[149] Section 254.

[150] Compare Sections 151-160 of the present Act with Sections 131-133 of the 1937 *Aktiengesetz*. Concerning exemptions for small and family-owned enterprises, see Section 157, paragraph 4.

[151] Sections 329-338. The principal criterion of an "affiliated group" is the common management of the group. Compare Section 18, paragraph 1, with Section 18, paragraph 2.

[152] The Official Explanation (*Begründung zum Regierungsentwurf*) refers to the Secu-

rities Act as well as to English, Canadian and Swedish legislation.

[153] Section 329.

[154] See Section 330, paragraph 1. Concerning consolidated reports in the event that a German limited liability company or mining company heads a group (or partial group) which also includes a corporation, see Introductory Law, Section 28.

[155] Section 330, paragraph 2.

[156] 1937 *Aktiengesetz*, Section 128, paragraph 3.

[157] Section 160, paragraph 4.

if their disclosure could reasonably be expected to cause substantial harm to the company. However, in this event the report must indicate that the escape clause was used and the item to which it was applied.

The significance of the new accounting rules is probably not limited to their mandatory applicability under the Stock Corporation Act. The German accounting profession is likely to consider them as the norm for "proper rules of accounting," to be applied to other enterprises as well. As a result, the information value of German financial statements will be vastly improved and approximate that required in international practice.

Shareholders

The Government Draft, in advocating a revision of the 1937 Act, emphasized the proprietary role of the shareholders and the desirability of encouraging the public to invest in stock corporations. In accordance with this policy, the new provisions attempt to strengthen the position of the shareholders.

Reacting to the perennial criticism of the banker's vote, changes designed to give shareholders a voice in corporate decision-making were introduced. The new provisions were inspired by and bear resemblance to the S.E.C. rules. They operate as follows:[158]

Together with the notice and a detailed agenda of each shareholders' meeting, management must send its proposals with respect to each item on the agenda and any nominations for office, to banks and shareholders' protective associations which in the preceding meeting voted as proxyholders, and to known shareholders. Shareholders are given an opportunity to make their views known by the requirement that management transmit shareholders' proposals and nominations for office in the same manner, unless such proposals are based on false or slanderous grounds, or if they are spurious, or would expose management to penal sanctions, or lead to an illegal resolution.[159] The recipient banks and shareholders' protective associations must forward the proposals and counterproposals to the owners of shares deposited with them.[160] If a bank intends to exercise voting rights for a shareholder, it must submit its own proposals (which are to take into account the shareholder's interest) to him, and request his instructions, indicating that it will vote as stated in the proposal unless instructions to the contrary are received. Shareholders' instructions bind the bank.[161] If none are received, the bank is bound by its own proposals.[162] If the bank does not vote in accordance with the

---

[158] See Sections 124-128.

[159] See Section 126, paragraph 2. The resemblance of this provision to the S.E.C. proposal rules goes so far as to duplicate the proviso that a statement containing more than 100 words need not be communicated. See S.E.C. Rule X-14A-8(b).

[160] Section 128.

[161] See Section 135, paragraphs 5, 8, 10, 11. Paragraphs 5 and 8 of this provision, which permit deviations from instructions and the bank's own proposals, are in line with the more general provision on the powers of agents contained in the Civil Code (Section 665).

[162] See Section 135, paragraphs 5, 8, 11.

shareholder's instructions or its own proposals, it must notify the shareholder and state the reasons for its action.[163] A waiver in advance of the bank's liability for failure to comply with these provisions is ineffective.[164]

A bank may not exercise voting rights of shareholders unless it holds their proxy.[165] However, such proxies need not relate to any specific meeting and can be issued in advance for a period of up to fifteen months.[166]

The present provisions represent a definite improvement over those of the 1937 *Aktiengesetz*. The new "proxy rules"[167] provide for more adequate information and establish a channel of communication between management and the unknown holders of bearer shares through the banks as intermediaries. In addition to existing minority rights concerning the calling of special meetings and proposals,[168] the rules permit dissemination of opposition nominations as well as proposals the cost of which is borne by the banks and the company.[169]

Considering that the Act permits blanket proxies which remain in effect over a substantial period of time and will, in practice, be automatically renewed, the practical effect of the new rules may well be limited.[170] Nor will these rules resolve any of the conflicts of interest inherent in the banks' variegated roles as advisers to both shareholders and management, holders of supervisory board seats, creditors, brokers, and investment bankers.

In addition to the improved accounting provisions and the "proxy rules," various other changes made by the new Act attempt to improve and strengthen the position of shareholders of German *Aktiengesellschaften*. These include extensive rights to corporate information,[171] the right of a qualified minority to contest understatement of assets,[172] and the reduction of fees and court

---

[163] Section 135, paragraph 8.

[164] See Section 128, paragraph 2, Section 135, paragraph 11.

[165] See Section 135, paragraph 1, first sentence. By calling the authorization to vote a proxy (*Vollmacht*), rather than a power (*Ermächtigung*), the new Act emphasizes that the bank acts as an agent rather than as a principal. Though it may not vote shares of another in its own name, the principal need not be disclosed. See Section 129, paragraphs 2 and 3, Section 135, paragraphs 1, 4 and 9.

[166] The Government Draft had originally provided that a proxy could be issued only for a specific meeting and after the call. The Legal and Economic Committees of the German Bundestag suggested that small shareholders would find this procedure tiresome and that it would infringe their right to appoint an agent. Their opinion prevailed.

[167] Vagts, supra, note 4, at 56-57, points out the similarity of the new German system to the practice under S.E.C. proxy rules and the rules of the New York Stock Exchange regarding securities held by nominee brokers in their own names ("street name").

[168] Section 122.

[169] See Section 128, paragraph 6, No. 2.

[170] *Cf.* Gessler, supra, note 103, at 679; Möhring, supra, note 18, at 88.

[171] See Sections 131, 132. These rights are still fairly limited when contrasted with those of shareholders in this country. In particular, shareholders of a German stock corporation have no access to corporate books and records.

[172] See Section 254.

costs for shareholders' actions to set aside corporate resolutions.[173] Though it may be doubtful whether the new Act has fully realized the ambitious aim of its supporters as a "magna charta" for shareholders, these changes are an important legislative recognition of the right of the investor to information and protection, as well as to active participation in the process of corporate decision-making.

IV. Translator's Note

Full understanding of a statute presupposes knowledge of the legal system from which it derives its existence. A cursory review of the text of the Stock Corporation Act will reveal numerous references to other enactments, such as the Civil Code, the Code of Civil Procedure, banking laws, and the co-determination statutes. Less obvious perhaps is the integrating function of terms of art. Innocuous to read, they are packed with meaning. To mention but a few: Section 3, by stating that a stock corporation is a "commercial company," subjects this entity to the rules of the Commercial Code. The recurring phrase *"unterliegt der sofortigen Beschwerde"* invokes the rules governing the special remedy against certain interlocutory decisions provided for in Sections 567-577 of the Code of Civil Procedure. Since no equivalent set of rules can be found in American procedural statutes, the translation cannot duplicate this incorporation by reference; it can only indicate that such decisions are appealable. The term *"Hauptversammlung"* (sometimes translated as "shareholders," sometimes as "shareholders' meeting") implies the notion of shareholders acting as the "supreme organ of the will" of the company, an idea not easily conveyed in terms of a legal system less preoccupied with theories of corporate existence. A similar difficulty is posed by the fact that German law takes a more legalistic approach to corporate life, conceiving, e.g., of shareholders' resolutions and financial statements as "acts" which change legal relationships and must be adopted, pronounced, and recorded in proper form. Such concepts as "transaction," "condition," "representation," and "performance" express complex legal ideas whose full import becomes apparent only after some immersion into German law.

---

[173] See Section 247 (reducing the maximum value of subject matter in issue, by which court costs and attorney's fees assessed against the losing party are measured; reduction of such value in case of economic hardship). The existing minority protection has been strengthened by defining minorities in various provisions by reference to fixed total par values in addition to percentages; by burdening the company with the expense of a special meeting called by a minority (see Section 122, paragraph 4); by extending the statute of limitations for special audits to five years (see Section 142) and im- posing the expenses thereof on the company (Section 146); by eliminating the requirement of a deposit of shares and the liability for gross negligence in the event of an action against promoters or management (Section 123 of the 1937 Act). Furthermore, appraisal rights were introduced for dissenting shareholders in the case of integration (Section 320, paragraph 5), control agreements and agreements to transfer profit (Section 305, paragraphs 1 and 2), and transformation of a corporation into a limited liability company (Section 375).

Many of the judicial and quasi-judicial agencies on which the Act relies to implement and police its provisions, such as the Commercial Register and the *Notar*, have no counterpart in American law. The absence of precise equivalents in terminology also proved to be troublesome in the translation of the accounting terminology employed by the Act.

These examples may suffice to indicate the serious obstacles to any attempt accurately to express the rules of the Act in the English language. An additional source of confusion is the fact that many of the rules governing stock corporations are not found in the Act. Thus, the tort liability of a stock corporation for acts of its management is based on Section 31 of the Civil Code, one of the provisions of the law of registered associations. Section 35 of that Code is pertinent to the question of whether the "vested rights" *(Sonderrechte)* of a shareholder can be cut off. The principle of good faith, mentioned in Sections 138, 157, and 242 of the Civil Code and interpreted in a vast body of case law and doctrinal writing, has been seized upon by German courts to modify corporate rights or to bar their exercise. Unexpressed are the canons of construction, methods of interpretation, and the tacit assumptions of German law, such as those concerning the value of precedent and doctrinal authorities.

Any translation of legal sources must of necessity be imperfect, for a statute cannot be severed from its natural surroundings and pressed into verbal patterns of a different culture without distortion. Nor do words used in legal texts lose their shades, nuances and emotional content. It is only fair to warn of these pitfalls. To what extent they can prove troublesome will depend on the nature of a given inquiry. Like other research material, a translation is merely a tool to be used with circumspection. In many instances it will give reliable guidance. Indeed, American counsel may more readily grasp the statute's purport than a German layman reading the *Aktiengesetz* in his native language. And the obscurity of a word or passage in the translation may point to a problem unresolved in the original text or whose solution lies outside the scope of the Stock Corporation Act.

Friedrich K. Juenger

German
Stock Corporation Act

Aktiengesetz

Vom 6. September 1965

Sammlung des Bundesrechts, Bundesgesetzbl. III 4121-1

Inhaltsübersicht

Erstes Buch

Aktiengesellschaft (§§ 1—277) §§

Erster Teil	Allgemeine Vorschriften	1— 22
Zweiter Teil	Gründung der Gesellschaft	23— 53
Dritter Teil	Rechtsverhältnisse der Gesellschaft und der Gesellschafter	54— 75
Vierter Teil	Verfassung der Aktiengesellschaft	76—147
1. Abschnitt	Vorstand	76— 94
2. Abschnitt	Aufsichtsrat	95—116
3. Abschnitt	Benutzung des Einflusses auf die Gesellschaft	117
4. Abschnitt	Hauptversammlung	118—147
1. Unterabschnitt	Rechte der Hauptversammlung	118—120
2. Unterabschnitt	Einberufung der Hauptversammlung	121—128
3. Unterabschnitt	Verhandlungsniederschrift. Auskunftsrecht	129—132
4. Unterabschnitt	Stimmrecht	133—137
5. Unterabschnitt	Sonderbeschluß	138
6. Unterabschnitt	Vorzugsaktien ohne Stimmrecht	139—141
7. Unterabschnitt	Sonderprüfung. Geltendmachung von Ersatzansprüchen	142—147
Fünfter Teil	Rechnungslegung. Gewinnverwendung	148—178
1. Abschnitt	Aufstellung des Jahresabschlusses und des Geschäftsberichts	148—161
2. Abschnitt	Prüfung des Jahresabschlusses	162—171
1. Unterabschnitt	Prüfung durch Abschlußprüfer	162—169
2. Unterabschnitt	Prüfung durch den Aufsichtsrat	170—171

STOCK CORPORATION ACT

of September 6, 1965
TABLE OF CONTENTS

Book One

Stock Corporation (§§ 1-277)

		Page
Part One	General Provisions (§§ 1-22)	35
Part Two	Formation of the Company (§§ 23-53) . . .	41
Part Three	Legal Relationships of the Company and of the Shareholders (§§ 54-75)	60
Part Four	Constitution of the Stock Corporation (§§ 76-147)	72
First Division	Managing Board (§§ 76-94)	72
Second Division	Supervisory Board (§§ 95-116)	83
Third Division	Abuse of Influence on the Company (§ 117)	99
Fourth Division	Shareholders' Meeting (§§ 118-147)	100
First Subdivision	Rights of Shareholders (§§ 118-120)	100
Second Subdivision	Calling of Shareholders' Meeting (§§ 121-128)	102
Third Subdivision	Minutes of Meeting. Right to Information (§§ 129-132)	108
Fourth Subdivision	Voting Rights (§§ 133-137)	111
Fifth Subdivision	Separate Resolutions (§ 138)	116
Sixth Subdivision	Non-voting Preferred Shares (§§ 139-141)	116
Seventh Subdivision	Special Audits. Assertion of Claims for Damages (§§ 142-147)	118
Part Five	Annual Statements. Disposition of Retained Earnings (§§ 148-178)	122
First Division	Preparation of Annual Financial Statements and Business Report (§§ 148-161)	122
Second Division	Examination of Annual Financial Statements (§§ 162-171)	138
First Subdivision	Audit by Annual Auditors (§§ 162-169) . . .	138
Second Subdivision	Examination by Supervisory Board (§§ 170-171)	143

§§

3. Abschnitt	Feststellung des Jahresabschlusses. Gewinnverwendung	172—176
1. Unterabschnitt	Feststellung des Jahresabschlusses	172—173
2. Unterabschnitt	Gewinnverwendung	174
3. Unterabschnitt	Ordentliche Hauptversammlung	175—176
4. Abschnitt	Bekanntmachung des Jahresabschlusses	177—178
Sechster Teil	Satzungsänderung. Maßnahmen der Kapitalbeschaffung und Kapitalherabsetzung	179—240
1. Abschnitt	Satzungsänderung	179—181
2. Abschnitt	Maßnahmen der Kapitalbeschaffung	182—221
1. Unterabschnitt	Kapitalerhöhung gegen Einlagen	182—191
2. Unterabschnitt	Bedingte Kapitalerhöhung	192—201
3. Unterabschnitt	Genehmigtes Kapital	202—206
4. Unterabschnitt	Kapitalerhöhung aus Gesellschaftsmitteln	207—220
5. Unterabschnitt	Wandelschuldverschreibungen. Gewinnschuldverschreibungen	221
3. Abschnitt	Maßnahmen der Kapitalherabsetzung	222—240
1. Unterabschnitt	Ordentliche Kapitalherabsetzung	222—228
2. Unterabschnitt	Vereinfachte Kapitalherabsetzung	229—236
3. Unterabschnitt	Kapitalherabsetzung durch Einziehung von Aktien	237—239
4. Unterabschnitt	Ausweis der Kapitalherabsetzung	240
Siebenter Teil	Nichtigkeit von Hauptversammlungsbeschlüssen und des festgestellten Jahresabschlusses. Sonderprüfung wegen unzulässiger Unterbewertung	241—261
1. Abschnitt	Nichtigkeit von Hauptversammlungsbeschlüssen	241—255
1. Unterabschnitt	Allgemeines	241—249
2. Unterabschnitt	Nichtigkeit bestimmter Hauptversammlungsbeschlüsse	250—255

Page

Third Division — Establishing Annual Financial Statements. Disposition of Retained Earnings (§§ 172-176) 144

First Subdivision — Establishing Annual Financial Statements (§§ 172-173) 144

Second Subdivision — Disposition of Retained Earnings (§ 174) 145

Third Subdivision — Ordinary Shareholders' Meeting (§§ 175-176) 146

Fourth Division — Publication of Annual Financial Statements (§§ 177-178) 147

Part Six — **Amendment of Articles of Incorporation. Measures to Acquire and Reduce Capital (§§ 179-240)** 149

First Division — Amendment of Articles of Incorporation (§§ 179-181) 149

Second Division — Measures to Acquire Capital (§§ 182-221) . 150

First Subdivision — Capital Increase Against Contributions (§§ 182-191) 150

Second Subdivision — Conditional Capital Increase (§§ 192-201) 155

Third Subdivision — Authorized Capital (§§ 202-206) 159

Fourth Subdivision — Capital Increase Out of Retained Earnings (§§ 207-220) 162

Fifth Subdivision — Convertible Bonds. Profit Participation Bonds (§ 221) 168

Third Division — Measures to Reduce Capital (§§ 222-240) 169

First Subdivision — Ordinary Capital Reduction (§§ 222-228) 169

Second Subdivision — Simplified Capital Reduction (§§ 229-236) 171

Third Subdivision — Capital Reduction by Cancellation of Shares (§§ 237-239) 175

Fourth Subdivision — Accounting Treatment of Capital Reduction (§ 240) 176

Part Seven — **Nullity of Shareholders' Resolutions and of Established Annual Financial Statements. Special Audit for Improper Understatement (§§ 241-261)** .. 177

First Division — Nullity of Shareholders' Resolutions (§§ 241-255) 177

First Subdivision — General Provisions (§§ 241-249) 177

Second Subdivision — Nullity of Specific Shareholders' Resolutions (§§ 250-255) 181

§§

2. Abschnitt	Nichtigkeit des festgestellten Jahresabschlusses	256—257
3. Abschnitt	Sonderprüfung wegen unzulässiger Unterbewertung	258—261
Achter Teil	Auflösung und Nichtigerklärung der Gesellschaft	262—277
1. Abschnitt	Auflösung	262—274
1. Unterabschnitt	Auflösungsgründe und Anmeldung	262—263
2. Unterabschnitt	Abwicklung	264—274
2. Abschnitt	Nichtigerklärung der Gesellschaft	275—277

Zweites Buch

Kommanditgesellschaft auf Aktien (§§ 278—290)

Drittes Buch

Verbundene Unternehmen (§§ 291—338)

Erster Teil	Unternehmensverträge	291—307
1. Abschnitt	Arten von Unternehmensverträgen	291—292
2. Abschnitt	Abschluß, Änderung und Beendigung von Unternehmensverträgen	293—299
3. Abschnitt	Sicherung der Gesellschaft und der Gläubiger	300—303
4. Abschnitt	Sicherung der außenstehenden Aktionäre bei Beherrschungs- und Gewinnabführungsverträgen	304—307
Zweiter Teil	Leitungsmacht und Verantwortlichkeit bei Abhängigkeit von Unternehmen	308—318
1. Abschnitt	Leitungsmacht und Verantwortlichkeit bei Bestehen eines Beherrschungsvertrags	308—310
2. Abschnitt	Verantwortlichkeit bei Fehlen eines Beherrschungsvertrags	311—318
Dritter Teil	Eingegliederte Gesellschaften	319—327
Vierter Teil	Wechselseitig beteiligte Unternehmen	328
Fünfter Teil	Rechnungslegung im Konzern	329—338

Page

Second Division	Nullity of Established Annual Financial Statements (§§ 256-257)	184
Third Division	Special Audit for Improper Understating (§§ 258-261)	186
Part Eight	**Dissolution and Declaration of Nullity of the Company (§§ 262-277)**	192
First Division	Dissolution (§§ 262-274)	192
First Subdivision	Grounds for Dissolution and Application to Record (§§ 262-263)	192
Second Subdivision	Liquidation (§§ 264-274)	192
Second Division	Declaration of Nullity of the Company (§§ 275-277)	197

Book Two

Partnership Limited by Shares (§§ 278-290)

Book Three

Related Enterprises (§§ 291-338)

Part One	**Enterprise Agreements (§§ 291-307)**	205
First Division	Types of Enterprise Agreements (§§ 291-292)	205
Second Division	Execution, Amendment and Termination of Enterprise Agreements (§§ 293-299)	206
Third Division	Protection of the Company and Its Creditors (§§ 300-303)	209
Fourth Division	Protection of Outside Shareholders in Case of Control Agreements and Agreements to Transfer Profit (§§ 304-307)	211
Part Two	**Power of Direction and Liability in Case of Controlled Enterprises (§§ 308-318)**	215
First Division	Power of Direction and Liability in Case of Control Agreement (§§ 308-310)	215
Second Division	Liability in Absence of Control Agreement (§§ 311-318)	217
Part Three	**Integrated Companies (§§ 319-327)**	222
Part Four	**Interlocking Enterprises (§ 328)**	228
Part Five	**Accounting Treatment of Affiliated Group of Companies (§§ 329-338)**	229

Viertes Buch   §§

Verschmelzung. Vermögensübertragung. Umwandlung (§§ 339—393)

Erster Teil	V e r s c h m e l z u n g	339—358
1. Abschnitt	Verschmelzung von Aktiengesellschaften	339—353
1. Unterabschnitt	Verschmelzung durch Aufnahme	340—352
2. Unterabschnitt	Verschmelzung durch Neubildung	353
2. Abschnitt	Verschmelzung von Kommanditgesellschaften auf Aktien sowie von Kommanditgesellschaften auf Aktien und Aktiengesellschaften	354
3. Abschnitt	Verschmelzung einer Gesellschaft mit beschränkter Haftung mit einer Aktiengesellschaft oder einer Kommanditgesellschaft auf Aktien	355—356
4. Abschnitt	Verschmelzung einer bergrechtlichen Gewerkschaft mit einer Aktiengesellschaft oder einer Kommanditgesellschaft auf Aktien	357—358
Zweiter Teil	V e r m ö g e n s ü b e r t r a g u n g	359—361
Dritter Teil	U m w a n d l u n g	362—393
1. Abschnitt	Umwandlung einer Aktiengesellschaft in eine Kommanditgesellschaft auf Aktien	362—365
2. Abschnitt	Umwandlung einer Kommanditgesellschaft auf Aktien in eine Aktiengesellschaft	366—368
3. Abschnitt	Umwandlung einer Aktiengesellschaft in eine Gesellschaft mit beschränkter Haftung	369—375
4. Abschnitt	Umwandlung einer Gesellschaft mit beschränkter Haftung in eine Aktiengesellschaft	376—383
5. Abschnitt	Umwandlung einer bergrechtlichen Gewerkschaft in eine Aktiengesellschaft	384—385
6. Abschnitt	Umwandlung einer Kommanditgesellschaft auf Aktien in eine Gesellschaft mit beschränkter Haftung	386—388
7. Abschnitt	Umwandlung einer Gesellschaft mit beschränkter Haftung in eine Kommanditgesellschaft auf Aktien	389—392
8. Abschnitt	Umwandlung einer bergrechtlichen Gewerkschaft in eine Kommanditgesellschaft auf Aktien	393

Page

Book Four

Business Combination. Transfer of Assets. Transformation (§§ 339-393)

Part One	**Business Combination (§§ 339-358)**	240
First Division	Combination of Stock Corporations (§§ 339-353)	240
First Subdivision	Merger (§§ 340-352)	240
Second Subdivision	Consolidation (§ 353)	246
Second Division	Combination of Partnerships Limited by Shares and of Partnerships Limited by Shares with Stock Corporations (§ 354)	248
Third Division	Merger of Limited Liability Company with Stock Corporation or Partnership Limited by Shares (§§ 355-356)	248
Fourth Division	Merger of Mining Company with Stock Corporation or Partnership Limited by Shares (§§ 357-358)	249
Part Two	**Transfer of Assets (§§ 359-361)**	250
Part Three	**Transformation (§§ 362-393)**	252
First Division	Transformation of Stock Corporation into Partnership Limited by Shares (§§ 362-365)	252
Second Division	Transformation of Partnership Limited by Shares into Stock Corporation (§§ 366-368)	254
Third Division	Transformation of Stock Corporation into Limited Liability Company (§§ 369-375)	255
Fourth Division	Transformation of Limited Liability Company into Stock Corporation (§§ 376-383)	259
Fifth Division	Transformation of Mining Company into Stock Corporation (§§ 384-385)	262
Sixth Division	Transformation of Partnership Limited by Shares into Limited Liability Company (§§ 386-388)	263
Seventh Division	Transformation of Limited Liability Company into Partnership Limited by Shares (§§ 389-392)	264
Eighth Division	Transformation of Mining Company into Partnership Limited by Shares (§ 393)	266

§§

Fünftes Buch
Sonder-, Straf- und Schlußvorschriften (§§ 394—410)

Erster Teil   Sondervorschriften bei Beteiligung von Gebietskörper-
                     schaften .... 394—395

Zweiter Teil   Gerichtliche Auflösung .... 396—398

Dritter Teil   Straf- und Bußgeldvorschriften, Schlußvorschriften .... 399—410

Page

Book Five

Special, Penal and Final Provisions (§§ 394-410)

Part One   **Special Provisions on Participation of**
                  Political Entities (§§ 394-395) 266

Part Two   **Judicial Dissolution (§§ 396-398)** 267

Part Three   **Provisions Concerning Penalties and**
  .   **Fines. Final Provisions (§§ 399-410)** . . . 268

Erstes Buch

Aktiengesellschaft

Erster Teil

Allgemeine Vorschriften

§ 1

Wesen der Aktiengesellschaft

(1) Die Aktiengesellschaft ist eine Gesellschaft mit eigener Rechtspersönlichkeit. Für die Verbindlichkeiten der Gesellschaft haftet den Gläubigern nur das Gesellschaftsvermögen.

(2) Die Aktiengesellschaft hat ein in Aktien zerlegtes Grundkapital.

§ 2

Gründerzahl

An der Feststellung des Gesellschaftsvertrags (der Satzung) müssen sich mindestens fünf Personen beteiligen, welche die Aktien gegen Einlagen übernehmen.

§ 3

Die Aktiengesellschaft als Handelsgesellschaft

Die Aktiengesellschaft gilt als Handelsgesellschaft, auch wenn der Gegenstand des Unternehmens nicht im Betrieb eines Handelsgewerbes besteht.

§ 4

Firma

(1) Die Firma der Aktiengesellschaft ist in der Regel dem Gegenstand des Unternehmens zu entnehmen. Sie muß die Bezeichnung „Aktiengesellschaft" enthalten.

(2) Führt die Aktiengesellschaft die Firma eines auf sie übergegangenen Handelsgeschäfts fort (§ 22 des Handelsgesetzbuchs), so muß sie die Bezeichnung „Aktiengesellschaft" in die Firma aufnehmen.

§ 5

Sitz

(1) Sitz der Gesellschaft ist der Ort, den die Satzung bestimmt.

(2) Die Satzung hat als Sitz in der Regel den Ort, wo die Gesellschaft einen Betrieb hat, oder den Ort

Book One
Stock Corporation

Part One
General Provisions

§ 1
Nature of the Stock Corporation

(1) The stock corporation is a company having separate legal personality. The recourse of creditors for obligations of the company is limited to the company's assets.

(2) The stock corporation has a stated capital represented by shares.

§ 2
Number of Incorporators

A minimum of five persons, who must subscribe to the shares for a consideration, shall execute the contract of association [articles of incorporation].

§ 3
The Stock Corporation as Business Organization

The stock corporation shall be deemed to be a business organization, even if it is not the purpose of the enterprise to engage in a commercial activity.

§ 4
Name

(1) As a rule, the name of the stock corporation shall be derived from the purpose of the enterprise. It must contain the designation "*Aktiengesellschaft.*"

(2) In the event that the stock corporation retains the name of a business taken over by it (§ 22 of the Commercial Code), it must add the designation "*Aktiengesellschaft*" to the name.

§ 5
Domicile

(1) The domicile of the company shall be the place specified in the articles of incorporation.

(2) As a rule, the articles of incorporation shall designate as the domicile the place where the

company is engaged in business, or the place from which the company is managed or administered.

zu bestimmen, wo sich die Geschäftsleitung befindet oder die Verwaltung geführt wird.

§ 6
Stated Capital

The stated capital as well as the shares must have a nominal value expressed in German marks.

§ 6
Grundkapital

Das Grundkapital und die Aktien müssen auf einen Nennbetrag in Deutscher Mark lauten.

§ 7
Minimum Nominal Amount of Stated Capital

The minimum nominal amount of the stated capital shall be one hundred thousand German marks.

§ 7
Mindestnennbetrag des Grundkapitals

Der Mindestnennbetrag des Grundkapitals ist einhunderttausend Deutsche Mark.

§ 8
Minimum Par Value of Shares

(1) The minimum par value of each share shall be fifty German marks. Shares specifying a lower par value shall be void. The parties issuing such shares shall be jointly and severally liable to the holders thereof for damage resulting from their issuance.

(2) Higher par values must be specified in multiples of one hundred German marks.

(3) The shares shall not be divisible.

(4) The above provisions also apply to the interim certificates issued to the shareholders prior to the issuance of the share certificates.

§ 8
Mindestnennbetrag der Aktien

(1) Der Mindestnennbetrag der Aktien ist fünfzig Deutsche Mark. Aktien über einen geringeren Nennbetrag sind nichtig Für den Schaden aus der Ausgabe sind die Ausgeber den Inhabern als Gesamtschuldner verantwortlich.

(2) Höhere Aktiennennbeträge müssen auf volle hundert Deutsche Mark lauten.

(3) Die Aktien sind unteilbar.

(4) Diese Vorschriften gelten auch für Anteilscheine, die den Aktionären vor der Ausgabe der Aktien erteilt werden (Zwischenscheine).

§ 9
Consideration for Shares

(1) Shares may not be issued for an amount below that of the par value.

(2) Issuance for an amount in excess of the par value is permissible.

§ 9
Ausgabebetrag der Aktien

(1) Für einen geringeren Betrag als den Nennbetrag dürfen Aktien nicht ausgegeben werden.

(2) Für einen höheren Betrag ist die Ausgabe zulässig.

§ 10
Shares and Interim Certificates

(1) Shares may be issued either in bearer or in registered form.

(2) They must be in registered form if issued prior to the full payment of the amount of the par value plus any premium. The amount of any installments paid shall be indicated on the share certificate.

(3) Interim certificates must be in registered form.

§ 10
Aktien und Zwischenscheine

(1) Die Aktien können auf den Inhaber oder auf Namen lauten.

(2) Sie müssen auf Namen lauten, wenn sie vor der vollen Leistung des Nennbetrags oder des höheren Ausgabebetrags ausgegeben werden. Der Betrag der Teilleistungen ist in der Aktie anzugeben.

(3) Zwischenscheine müssen auf Namen lauten.

(4) Zwischenscheine auf den Inhaber sind nichtig. Für den Schaden aus der Ausgabe sind die Ausgeber den Inhabern als Gesamtschuldner verantwortlich.

§ 11
Aktien besonderer Gattung

Die Aktien können verschiedene Rechte gewähren, namentlich bei der Verteilung des Gewinns und des Gesellschaftsvermögens. Aktien mit gleichen Rechten bilden eine Gattung.

§ 12
Stimmrecht. Keine Mehrstimmrechte

(1) Jede Aktie gewährt das Stimmrecht. Vorzugsaktien können nach den Vorschriften dieses Gesetzes als Aktien ohne Stimmrecht ausgegeben werden.

(2) Mehrstimmrechte sind unzulässig. Die für Wirtschaft zuständige oberste Behörde des Landes, in dem die Gesellschaft ihren Sitz hat, kann Ausnahmen zulassen, soweit es zur Wahrung überwiegender gesamtwirtschaftlicher Belange erforderlich ist.

§ 13
Unterzeichnung der Aktien

Zur Unterzeichnung von Aktien und Zwischenscheinen genügt eine vervielfältigte Unterschrift. Die Gültigkeit der Unterzeichnung kann von der Beachtung einer besonderen Form abhängig gemacht werden. Die Formvorschrift muß in der Urkunde enthalten sein.

§ 14
Zuständigkeit

Gericht im Sinne dieses Gesetzes ist, wenn nichts anderes bestimmt ist, das Gericht des Sitzes der Gesellschaft.

§ 15
Verbundene Unternehmen

Verbundene Unternehmen sind rechtlich selbständige Unternehmen, die im Verhältnis zueinander in Mehrheitsbesitz stehende Unternehmen und mit Mehrheit beteiligte Unternehmen (§ 16), abhängige und herrschende Unternehmen (§ 17), Konzernunternehmen (§ 18), wechselseitig beteiligte Unternehmen (§ 19) oder Vertragsteile eines Unternehmensvertrags (§§ 291, 292) sind.

(4) Interim certificates issued to bearer shall be void. The parties issuing them shall be jointly and severally liable to the holders thereof for damage arising out of such issuance.

§ 11
Different Classes of Shares

The rights imparted by different shares, in particular with respect to the distribution of profits and of corporate assets, may differ. Shares granting identical rights shall be considered as belonging to one class.

§ 12
Voting Rights. No Multiple Votes

(1) Each share shall carry the right to vote. Preferred shares may be issued, as permitted by the provisions of this Act, as non-voting stock.

(2) Multiple voting rights are prohibited. The highest authority having jurisdiction in economic affairs of the German state (Land) in which the company has its domicile may grant an exemption from this provision, if such should be necessary to safeguard overriding interests of the national economy.

§ 13
Signature on Share Certificates

With regard to the signature on share certificates and interim certificates, a facsimile shall be sufficient. The validity of a signature may be made dependent on compliance with a particular form requirement. Such form requirement must be specified on the certificate.

§ 14
Jurisdiction

Absent a provision to the contrary, "court" within the meaning of this Act shall be the court at the company's domicile.

§ 15
Related Enterprises

Related enterprises are legally independent enterprises which, in relation to each other, are majority-owned and majority-owning enterprises (§ 16), controlled and controlling enterprises (§ 17), members of an affiliated group of companies (§ 18), interlocking enterprises (§ 19), or parties to an enterprise agreement (§§ 291, 292).

§ 15

§ 16
Majority-Owned and Majority-Owning Enterprises

(1) An enterprise holding a majority of the shares of another legally independent enterprise, or having the majority of the votes (majority interest), shall be considered a majority-owning enterprise, and the other a majority-owned enterprise.

(2) The portion of the shares held by an enterprise shall be determined, in the case of a corporation, by reference to the proportion of the total par value of shares held by it to the stated capital; in the case of a mining company, by reference to the shares in the mining company. Shares of its own stock held by a corporation shall be deducted from the stated capital or, in the case of a mining company, from the number of the shares in the mining company. Shares held by another for the account of the enterprise shall be deemed to be shares of the enterprise's own stock.

(3) The portion of the votes to which an enterprise is entitled shall be determined by reference to the proportion of the number of votes it may cast for the shares held by it to the total number of votes. From the total number of votes are to be deducted the voting rights attributable to the enterprise's own shares as well as the shares which, pursuant to paragraph 2, third sentence, hereof, are deemed to be the enterprise's own shares.

(4) Shares owned by a controlled enterprise or owned by another for the account of the enterprise or of an enterprise controlled by it, and, in the event that the enterprise is a sole proprietorship, the shares held by the proprietor in his private capacity, shall be deemed to belong to the enterprise.

§ 17
Controlled and Controlling Enterprises

(1) Controlled enterprises are legally independent enterprises in which another enterprise (the controlling enterprise) can exert, directly or indirectly, a controlling influence.

(2) A majority-owned enterprise is presumed to be controlled by the majority-owning enterprise.

§ 16

§ 16
In Mehrheitsbesitz stehende Unternehmen und mit Mehrheit beteiligte Unternehmen

(1) Gehört die Mehrheit der Anteile eines rechtlich selbständigen Unternehmens einem anderen Unternehmen oder steht einem anderen Unternehmen die Mehrheit der Stimmrechte zu (Mehrheitsbeteiligung), so ist das Unternehmen ein in Mehrheitsbesitz stehendes Unternehmen, das andere Unternehmen ein an ihm mit Mehrheit beteiligtes Unternehmen.

(2) Welcher Teil der Anteile einem Unternehmen gehört, bestimmt sich bei Kapitalgesellschaften nach dem Verhältnis des Gesamtnennbetrags der ihm gehörenden Anteile zum Nennkapital, bei bergrechtlichen Gewerkschaften nach der Zahl der Kuxe. Eigene Anteile sind bei Kapitalgesellschaften vom Nennkapital, bei bergrechtlichen Gewerkschaften von der Zahl der Kuxe abzusetzen. Eigenen Anteilen des Unternehmens stehen Anteile gleich, die einem anderen für Rechnung des Unternehmens gehören.

(3) Welcher Teil der Stimmrechte einem Unternehmen zusteht, bestimmt sich nach dem Verhältnis der Zahl der Stimmrechte, die es aus den ihm gehörenden Anteilen ausüben kann, zur Gesamtzahl aller Stimmrechte. Von der Gesamtzahl aller Stimmrechte sind die Stimmrechte aus eigenen Anteilen sowie aus Anteilen, die nach Absatz 2 Satz 3 eigenen Anteilen gleichstehen, abzusetzen.

(4) Als Anteile, die einem Unternehmen gehören, gelten auch die Anteile, die einem von ihm abhängigen Unternehmen oder einem anderen für Rechnung des Unternehmens oder eines von diesem abhängigen Unternehmens gehören und, wenn der Inhaber des Unternehmens ein Einzelkaufmann ist, auch die Anteile, die sonstiges Vermögen des Inhabers sind.

§ 17
Abhängige und herrschende Unternehmen

(1) Abhängige Unternehmen sind rechtlich selbständige Unternehmen, auf die ein anderes Unternehmen (herrschendes Unternehmen) unmittelbar oder mittelbar einen beherrschenden Einfluß ausüben kann.

(2) Von einem in Mehrheitsbesitz stehenden Unternehmen wird vermutet, daß es von dem an ihm mit Mehrheit beteiligten Unternehmen abhängig ist.

§ 18
Konzern und Konzernunternehmen

(1) Sind ein herrschendes und ein oder mehrere abhängige Unternehmen unter der einheitlichen Leitung des herrschenden Unternehmens zusammengefaßt, so bilden sie éinen Konzern; die einzelnen Unternehmen sind Konzernunternehmen. Unternehmen, zwischen denen ein Beherrschungsvertrag (§ 291) besteht oder von denen das eine in das andere eingegliedert ist (§ 319), sind als unter einheitlicher Leitung zusammengefaßt anzusehen. Von einem abhängigen Unternehmen wird vermutet, daß es mit dem herrschenden Unternehmen einen Konzern bildet.

(2) Sind rechtlich selbständige Unternehmen, ohne daß das eine Unternehmen von dem anderen abhängig ist, unter einheitlicher Leitung zusammengefaßt, so bilden sie auch einen Konzern; die einzelnen Unternehmen sind Konzernunternehmen.

§ 19
Wechselseitig beteiligte Unternehmen

(1) Wechselseitig beteiligte Unternehmen sind Unternehmen mit Sitz im Inland in der Rechtsform einer Kapitalgesellschaft oder bergrechtlichen Gewerkschaft, die dadurch verbunden sind, daß jedem Unternehmen mehr als der vierte Teil der Anteile des anderen Unternehmens gehört. Für die Feststellung, ob einem Unternehmen mehr als der vierte Teil der Anteile des anderen Unternehmens gehört, gilt § 16 Abs. 2 Satz 1, Abs. 4.

(2) Gehört einem wechselseitig beteiligten Unternehmen an dem anderen Unternehmen eine Mehrheitsbeteiligung oder kann das eine auf das andere Unternehmen unmittelbar oder mittelbar einen beherrschenden Einfluß ausüben, so ist das eine als herrschendes, das andere als abhängiges Unternehmen anzusehen.

(3) Gehört jedem der wechselseitig beteiligten Unternehmen an dem anderen Unternehmen eine Mehrheitsbeteiligung oder kann jedes auf das andere unmittelbar oder mittelbar einen beherrschenden Einfluß ausüben, so gelten beide Unternehmen als herrschend und als abhängig.

(4) § 328 ist auf Unternehmen, die nach Absatz 2 oder 3 herrschende oder abhängige Unternehmen sind, nicht anzuwenden.

§ 18
Affiliated Groups and Members of Groups

(1) If a controlling and one or more controlled enterprises are subject to the centralized management of the controlling enterprise, they constitute an affiliated group of companies, and the individual enterprises are considered members of such group. If enterprises are parties to a control agreement (§ 291), or if one enterprise has been integrated into the other (§ 319), they shall be deemed to be subject to centralized management. A controlled enterprise shall be presumed to form an affiliated group with the controlling enterprise.

(2) Where legally independent enterprises are subject to centralized management but one does not control the other, they shall also constitute an affiliated group of companies, and the individual enterprises are considered members of such group.

§ 19
Interlocking Enterprises

(1) Interlocking enterprises are enterprises domiciled in Germany which have the legal form of a corporation or mining company and which are related in such a way that each of the enterprises holds more than one-fourth of the shares of any of the other enterprises. Whether an enterprise is the holder of more than one-fourth of the shares of another enterprise shall be determined by reference to § 16, paragraph 2, first sentence, and paragraph 4.

(2) If one of the interlocking enterprises holds a majority interest in the other enterprise, or if one of the enterprises can exert, directly or indirectly, a controlling influence over the other, one shall be deemed the controlling, and the other the controlled, enterprise.

(3) If each of the interlocking enterprises holds a majority interest in the other enterprise, or if each can exert, directly or indirectly, a controlling influence over the other, each shall be deemed to be a controlling and a controlled enterprise.

(4) § 328 shall not apply to enterprises that are deemed to be controlling or controlled enterprises pursuant to paragraph 2 or paragraph 3 hereof.

§ 20
Disclosure Requirements

(1) As soon as an enterprise acquires more than one-fourth of all of the shares of a stock corporation domiciled in Germany, it shall promptly inform such company of this fact in writing. Whether an enterprise holds more than one-fourth of the shares of another enterprise shall be determined by reference to § 16, paragraph 2, first sentence, and paragraph 4.

(2) For purposes of the disclosure requirement of paragraph 1 hereof, shares held by the enterprise shall include the following:

1. shares whose transfer can be demanded by the enterprise, by an enterprise controlled by it, or by another for the account of the enterprise or of an enterprise controlled by it;
2. shares which the enterprise, an enterprise controlled by it or another for the account of the enterprise or of an enterprise controlled by it, is obligated to acquire.

(3) If the enterprise is a corporation or a mining company, it shall also, as soon as it acquires more than one-fourth of the shares, not including the shares attributed to it pursuant to paragraph 2 hereof, promptly inform the company of that fact in writing.

(4) As soon as an enterprise acquires a majority interest (§ 16, paragraph 1), it shall likewise promptly inform the company of such fact in writing.

(5) If the interest held falls below the amount reportable under paragraph 1, 3, or 4 hereof, the company shall promptly be informed of this fact in writing.

(6) The company shall promptly publish, in the publications designated in the company's articles of incorporation, the existence of an interest of which it has been notified pursuant to paragraph 1 or 4 hereof, specifying the enterprise that holds such interest. If the company has been informed of the fact that the interest fell below the amount reportable under paragraph 1 or 4 hereof, this shall also be published promptly in such publications.

(7) Rights attributable to shares belonging to an enterprise that is subject to the disclosure requirement of paragraph 1 or 4 hereof may not, so long as the enterprise has not made the disclosure, be exercised by the enterprise, by an

§ 20
Mitteilungspflichten

(1) Sobald einem Unternehmen mehr als der vierte Teil der Aktien einer Aktiengesellschaft mit Sitz im Inland gehört, hat es dies der Gesellschaft unverzüglich schriftlich mitzuteilen. Für die Feststellung, ob dem Unternehmen mehr als der vierte Teil der Aktien gehört, gilt § 16 Abs. 2 Satz 1, Abs. 4.

(2) Für die Mitteilungspflicht nach Absatz 1 rechnen zu den Aktien, die dem Unternehmen gehören, auch Aktien,

1. deren Übereignung das Unternehmen, ein von ihm abhängiges Unternehmen oder ein anderer für Rechnung des Unternehmens oder eines von diesem abhängigen Unternehmens verlangen kann;
2. zu deren Abnahme das Unternehmen, ein von ihm abhängiges Unternehmen oder ein anderer für Rechnung des Unternehmens oder eines von diesem abhängigen Unternehmens verpflichtet ist.

(3) Ist das Unternehmen eine Kapitalgesellschaft oder bergrechtliche Gewerkschaft, so hat es, sobald ihm ohne Hinzurechnung der Aktien nach Absatz 2 mehr als der vierte Teil der Aktien gehört, auch dies der Gesellschaft unverzüglich schriftlich mitzuteilen.

(4) Sobald dem Unternehmen eine Mehrheitsbeteiligung (§ 16 Abs. 1) gehört, hat es auch dies der Gesellschaft unverzüglich schriftlich mitzuteilen.

(5) Besteht die Beteiligung in der nach Absatz 1, 3 oder 4 mitteilungspflichtigen Höhe nicht mehr, so ist dies der Gesellschaft unverzüglich schriftlich mitzuteilen.

(6) Die Gesellschaft hat das Bestehen einer Beteiligung, die ihr nach Absatz 1 oder 4 mitgeteilt worden ist, unverzüglich in den Gesellschaftsblättern bekanntzumachen; dabei ist das Unternehmen anzugeben, dem die Beteiligung gehört. Wird der Gesellschaft mitgeteilt, daß die Beteiligung in der nach Absatz 1 oder 4 mitteilungspflichtigen Höhe nicht mehr besteht, so ist auch dies unverzüglich in den Gesellschaftsblättern bekanntzumachen.

(7) Rechte aus Aktien, die einem nach Absatz 1 oder 4 mitteilungspflichtigen Unternehmen gehören, können für die Zeit, für die das Unternehmen die Mitteilung nicht gemacht hat, durch das Unternehmen, ein von ihm abhängiges Unternehmen oder

einen anderen für Rechnung des Unternehmens oder eines von diesem abhängigen Unternehmens nicht ausgeübt werden.

§ 21
Mitteilungspflichten der Gesellschaft

(1) Sobald der Gesellschaft mehr als der vierte Teil der Anteile einer anderen Kapitalgesellschaft oder bergrechtlichen Gewerkschaft mit Sitz im Inland gehört, hat sie dies dem Unternehmen, an dem die Beteiligung besteht, unverzüglich schriftlich mitzuteilen. Für die Feststellung, ob der Gesellschaft mehr als der vierte Teil der Anteile gehört, gilt § 16 Abs. 2 Satz 1, Abs. 4 sinngemäß.

(2) Sobald der Gesellschaft eine Mehrheitsbeteiligung (§ 16 Abs. 1) an einem anderen Unternehmen gehört, hat sie dies dem Unternehmen, an dem die Mehrheitsbeteiligung besteht, unverzüglich schriftlich mitzuteilen.

(3) Besteht die Beteiligung in der nach Absatz 1 oder 2 mitteilungspflichtigen Höhe nicht mehr, hat die Gesellschaft dies dem anderen Unternehmen unverzüglich schriftlich mitzuteilen.

(4) Rechte aus Anteilen, die einer nach Absatz 1 oder 2 mitteilungspflichtigen Gesellschaft gehören, können für die Zeit, für die sie die Mitteilung nicht gemacht hat, nicht ausgeübt werden.

§ 22
Nachweis mitgeteilter Beteiligungen

Ein Unternehmen, dem eine Mitteilung nach § 20 Abs. 1, 3 oder 4, § 21 Abs. 1 oder 2 gemacht worden ist, kann jederzeit verlangen, daß ihm das Bestehen der Beteiligung nachgewiesen wird.

Zweiter Teil
Gründung der Gesellschaft

§ 23
Feststellung der Satzung

(1) Die Satzung muß durch gerichtliche oder notarielle Beurkundung festgestellt werden. Bevollmächtigte bedürfen einer gerichtlich oder notariell beglaubigten Vollmacht.

(2) In der Urkunde sind der Nennbetrag, der Ausgabebetrag und, wenn mehrere Gattungen bestehen, die Gattung der Aktien anzugeben, die jeder Gründer übernimmt.

enterprise controlled by it, or by another for the account of the enterprise or of an enterprise controlled by it.

§ 21
Company's Disclosure Obligations

(1) As soon as the company acquires more than one-fourth of the shares of another corporation or mining company domiciled in Germany, it shall, promptly and in writing, inform the enterprise in which it holds such interest. Whether the company holds more than one-fourth of the shares of another shall be determined, *mutatis mutandis*, by reference to § 16, paragraph 2, first sentence, and paragraph 4.

(2) As soon as the company acquires a majority interest in another enterprise (§ 16, paragraph 1), it shall, promptly and in writing, inform the enterprise in which it holds such majority interest.

(3) If the interest held falls below the amount reportable under paragraph 1 or 2 hereof, the company shall promptly inform the other enterprise of this fact in writing.

(4) Rights attributable to shares belonging to a company which is subject to the disclosure requirement of paragraph 1 or 2 may not, so long as the company has not made the disclosure, be exercised.

§ 22
Proof of Interests Disclosed

An enterprise to which a disclosure has been made pursuant to § 20, paragraph 1, 3, or 4, or § 21, paragraph 1 or 2, can at any time request proof of the existence of the interest.

Part Two
Formation of the Company

§ 23
Execution of the Articles of Incorporation

(1) The articles of incorporation shall be executed in the form of a judicial or notarial record. Attorneys in fact shall require a power of attorney certified by a judge or notary.

(2) The instrument shall specify the par value of the shares, the amount for which they are issued and, if there are several classes of shares, the class of shares subscribed to by each incorporator.

§ 23

(3) The articles of incorporation shall set forth:

1. the name and the domicile of the company;
2. the purpose of the enterprise; in particular, in the case of industrial and commercial enterprises, the type of products and goods to be produced and traded shall be specifically indicated;
3. the amount of the stated capital;
4. the par value of each share and the number of shares of a given par value and, if there are different classes of shares, such classes;
5. the composition of the managing board;
6. the form in which the announcements of the company are published.

(4) The articles of incorporation may deviate from the provisions of this Act only if such deviation is expressly authorized. The articles of incorporation may set forth additional provisions not inconsistent with this Act.

§ 24
Bearer Shares and Registered Shares

(1) The shares shall be issued in bearer form, unless the articles of incorporation provide otherwise. § 10, paragraph 2, shall remain unaffected.

(2) The articles of incorporation may provide that a shareholder may request conversion of his bearer shares into registered shares or of his registered shares into bearer shares.

§ 25
Publication of Company Announcements

Whenever this Act or the articles of incorporation provide that an announcement of the company shall appear in the publications designated in the company's articles of incorporation, such announcement shall be published in the *Bundesanzeiger*. In addition, the articles of incorporation may designate other publications in which announcements of the company may appear.

§ 26
Preferences. Expenses of Formation

(1) Any preferences granted to a particular shareholder shall be stipulated in the articles of incorporation, designating the party entitled thereto.

§ 24

(3) Die Satzung muß bestimmen

1. die Firma und den Sitz der Gesellschaft;
2. den Gegenstand des Unternehmens; namentlich ist bei Industrie- und Handelsunternehmen die Art der Erzeugnisse und Waren, die hergestellt und gehandelt werden sollen, näher anzugeben;
3. die Höhe des Grundkapitals;
4. die Nennbeträge der einzelnen Aktien und die Zahl der Aktien jeden Nennbetrags sowie, wenn mehrere Gattungen bestehen, die Gattung der einzelnen Aktien;
5. die Zusammensetzung des Vorstands;
6. die Form der Bekanntmachungen der Gesellschaft.

(4) Die Satzung kann von den Vorschriften dieses Gesetzes nur abweichen, wenn es ausdrücklich zugelassen ist. Ergänzende Bestimmungen der Satzung sind zulässig, es sei denn, daß dieses Gesetz eine abschließende Regelung enthält.

§ 24
Inhaber- und Namensaktien

(1) Die Aktien sind als Inhaberaktien auszustellen, wenn die Satzung nichts anderes bestimmt. § 10 Abs. 2 bleibt unberührt.

(2) Die Satzung kann bestimmen, daß auf Verlangen eines Aktionärs seine Inhaberaktie in eine Namensaktie oder seine Namensaktie in eine Inhaberaktie umzuwandeln ist.

§ 25
Bekanntmachungen der Gesellschaft

Bestimmt das Gesetz oder die Satzung, daß eine Bekanntmachung der Gesellschaft durch die Gesellschaftsblätter erfolgen soll, so ist sie in den Bundesanzeiger einzurücken. Daneben kann die Satzung andere Blätter als Gesellschaftsblätter bezeichnen.

§ 26
Sondervorteile. Gründungsaufwand

(1) Jeder einem einzelnen Aktionär eingeräumte besondere Vorteil muß in der Satzung unter Bezeichnung des Berechtigten festgesetzt werden.

Formation of the Company

(2) Der Gesamtaufwand, der zu Lasten der Gesellschaft an Aktionäre oder an andere Personen als Entschädigung oder als Belohnung für die Gründung oder ihre Vorbereitung gewährt wird, ist in der Satzung gesondert festzusetzen.

(3) Ohne diese Festsetzung sind die Verträge und die Rechtshandlungen zu ihrer Ausführung der Gesellschaft gegenüber unwirksam. Nach der Eintragung der Gesellschaft in das Handelsregister kann die Unwirksamkeit nicht durch Satzungsänderung geheilt werden.

(4) Die Festsetzungen können erst geändert werden, wenn die Gesellschaft fünf Jahre im Handelsregister eingetragen ist.

(5) Die Satzungsbestimmungen über die Festsetzungen können durch Satzungsänderung erst beseitigt werden, wenn die Gesellschaft dreißig Jahre im Handelsregister eingetragen ist und wenn die Rechtsverhältnisse, die den Festsetzungen zugrunde liegen, seit mindestens fünf Jahren abgewickelt sind.

§ 27
Sacheinlagen. Sachübernahmen

(1) Sollen Aktionäre Einlagen machen, die nicht durch Einzahlung des Nennbetrags oder des höheren Ausgabebetrags der Aktien zu leisten sind (Sacheinlagen), oder soll die Gesellschaft vorhandene oder herzustellende Anlagen oder andere Vermögensgegenstände übernehmen (Sachübernahmen), so müssen in der Satzung festgesetzt werden der Gegenstand der Sacheinlage oder der Sachübernahme, die Person, von der die Gesellschaft den Gegenstand erwirbt, und der Nennbetrag der bei der Sacheinlage zu gewährenden Aktien oder die bei der Sachübernahme zu gewährende Vergütung.

(2) Ohne diese Festsetzung sind Verträge über Sacheinlagen und Sachübernahmen und die Rechtshandlungen zu ihrer Ausführung der Gesellschaft gegenüber unwirksam. Ist die Gesellschaft eingetragen, so wird die Gültigkeit der Satzung durch diese Unwirksamkeit nicht berührt. Ist die Vereinbarung einer Sacheinlage unwirksam, so ist der Aktionär verpflichtet, den Nennbetrag oder den höheren Ausgabebetrag der Aktie einzuzahlen.

(2) The full amount of any consideration paid by the company to shareholders or other persons as compensation or remuneration for the formation or the preparation thereof shall be stipulated separately in the articles of incorporation.

(3) Absent such stipulation, any agreements and transactions purporting to implement them shall be invalid as against the company. Once the company has been recorded in the Commercial Register, such invalidity cannot be cured by amending the articles of incorporation.

(4) Such stipulations may be amended no sooner than five years from the date of recording of the company in the Commercial Register.

(5) The provisions of the articles of incorporation containing such stipulations may be deleted by amendment no sooner than thirty years from the date of recording of the company in the Commercial Register, and after at least five years have elapsed since the liquidation of all legal relationships which constituted the basis for such stipulations.

§ 27
Contribution of Assets. Acquisition of Assets upon Formation

(1) If shareholders are to make contributions other than by cash payments (contribution of assets), in the amount of the par value plus any premium, or if the company is to acquire existing or future facilities or other assets (acquisition of assets upon formation), the articles of incorporation shall stipulate the object of such contribution or acquisition, as well as the person from whom the company is to acquire such asset, and the par value of the shares to be issued for the contribution of assets or the consideration for the assets to be acquired upon formation.

(2) Absent such stipulation, any agreements concerning contributions of assets or acquisitions of assets upon formation as well as the transactions purporting to implement them shall be invalid as against the company. The validity of the articles of incorporation shall not be affected by such invalidity once the company has been recorded. In the event that the agreement to make a contribution of assets is invalid, the shareholder shall be required to effect payment of the par value of the shares plus any premium.

(3) Once the company has been recorded in the Commercial Register, such invalidity cannot be cured by amending the articles of incorporation.

(4) § 26, paragraph 4, shall apply with respect to amendment of any such stipulations lawfully made. § 26, paragraph 5, shall apply to the deletion of the pertinent provisions of the articles of incorporation.

§ 28
Incorporators

Incorporators of the company are those shareholders who have executed the articles of incorporation.

§ 29
Establishment of the Company

The company is established upon the subscription of all the shares by the incorporators.

§ 30
Appointment of Supervisory Board, Managing Board, and Annual Auditors

(1) The incorporators shall appoint the initial supervisory board of the company as well as the annual auditors for the first full or partial fiscal year. Such appointment shall be in the form of a judicial or notarial record.

(2) The provisions for the appointment of employees' representatives to the supervisory board shall not apply to the composition and the appointment of the initial supervisory board.

(3) The members of the initial supervisory board may not be appointed to serve for a period beyond the adjournment of the shareholders' meeting which ratifies the acts of management for the initial full or partial fiscal year. Prior to the expiration of the term of office of the initial supervisory board, the managing board shall, in due time, announce the statutory provisions according to which, in its opinion, the subsequent supervisory board is to be composed; §§ 96 to 99 shall be applicable.

(4) The supervisory board shall appoint the initial managing board.

§ 28

(3) Nach Eintragung der Gesellschaft in das Handelsregister kann die Unwirksamkeit nicht durch Satzungsänderung geheilt werden.

(4) Für die Änderung rechtswirksam getroffener Festsetzungen gilt § 26 Abs. 4, für die Beseitigung der Satzungsbestimmungen § 26 Abs. 5.

§ 28
Gründer

Die Aktionäre, die die Satzung festgestellt haben, sind die Gründer der Gesellschaft.

§ 29
Errichtung der Gesellschaft

Mit der Übernahme aller Aktien durch die Gründer ist die Gesellschaft errichtet.

§ 30
Bestellung des Aufsichtsrats, des Vorstands und der Abschlußprüfer

(1) Die Gründer haben den ersten Aufsichtsrat der Gesellschaft und die Abschlußprüfer für das erste Voll- oder Rumpfgeschäftsjahr zu bestellen. Die Bestellung bedarf gerichtlicher oder notarieller Beurkundung.

(2) Auf die Zusammensetzung und die Bestellung des ersten Aufsichtsrats sind die Vorschriften über die Bestellung von Aufsichtsratsmitgliedern der Arbeitnehmer nicht anzuwenden.

(3) Die Mitglieder des ersten Aufsichtsrats können nicht für längere Zeit als bis zur Beendigung der Hauptversammlung bestellt werden, die über die Entlastung für das erste Voll- oder Rumpfgeschäftsjahr beschließt. Der Vorstand hat rechtzeitig vor Ablauf der Amtszeit des ersten Aufsichtsrats bekanntzumachen, nach welchen gesetzlichen Vorschriften der nächste Aufsichtsrat nach seiner Ansicht zusammenzusetzen ist; §§ 96 bis 99 sind anzuwenden.

(4) Der Aufsichtsrat bestellt den ersten Vorstand.

§ 31
Bestellung des Aufsichtsrats bei Sachgründung

(1) Ist in der Satzung als Gegenstand einer Sacheinlage oder Sachübernahme die Einbringung oder Übernahme eines Unternehmens oder eines Teils eines Unternehmens festgesetzt worden, so haben die Gründer nur so viele Aufsichtsratmitglieder zu bestellen, wie nach den gesetzlichen Vorschriften, die nach ihrer Ansicht nach der Einbringung oder Übernahme für die Zusammensetzung des Aufsichtsrats maßgebend sind, von der Hauptversammlung ohne Bindung an Wahlvorschläge zu wählen sind. Sie haben jedoch, wenn dies nur zwei Aufsichtsratmitglieder sind, drei Aufsichtsratmitglieder zu bestellen.

(2) Der nach Absatz 1 Satz 1 bestellte Aufsichtsrat ist, soweit die Satzung nichts anderes bestimmt, beschlußfähig, wenn die Hälfte, mindestens jedoch drei seiner Mitglieder an der Beschlußfassung teilnehmen.

(3) Unverzüglich nach der Einbringung oder Übernahme des Unternehmens oder des Unternehmensteils hat der Vorstand bekanntzumachen, nach welchen gesetzlichen Vorschriften nach seiner Ansicht der Aufsichtsrat zusammengesetzt sein muß. §§ 97 bis 99 gelten sinngemäß. Das Amt der bisherigen Aufsichtsratmitglieder erlischt nur, wenn der Aufsichtsrat nach anderen als den von den Gründern für maßgebend gehaltenen Vorschriften zusammenzusetzen ist oder wenn die Gründer drei Aufsichtsratmitglieder bestellt haben, der Aufsichtsrat aber auch aus Aufsichtsratmitgliedern der Arbeitnehmer zu bestehen hat.

(4) Absatz 3 gilt nicht, wenn das Unternehmen oder der Unternehmensteil erst nach der Bekanntmachung des Vorstands nach § 30 Abs. 3 Satz 2 eingebracht oder übernommen wird.

(5) § 30 Abs. 3 Satz 1 gilt auch für die nach Absatz 3 bestellten Aufsichtsratmitglieder.

§ 31
Appointment of Supervisory Board in Case of Incorporation of Existing Enterprise

(1) If the articles of incorporation specify as the object of a contribution of assets or of an acquisition of assets upon formation the contribution or the acquisition of an enterprise or part of an enterprise, the incorporators shall appoint to the supervisory board only as many members as are to be elected by the shareholders freely and not subject to binding nominations in accordance with the statutory provisions which, in their opinion, apply to the composition of the supervisory board after such contribution or acquisition of assets has been effected. However, should this result in only two members being designated, the incorporators shall appoint three members to the supervisory board.

(2) Unless the articles of incorporation provide otherwise, a quorum of the supervisory board appointed pursuant to paragraph 1, first sentence, hereof, shall exist if one-half of its members, but in no event less than three, take part in the adoption of a resolution.

(3) After the contribution or the acquisition of the enterprise or part of the enterprise has been effected, the managing board shall promptly announce the statutory provisions which, in its opinion, shall govern the composition of the supervisory board. §§ 97 to 99 shall apply *mutatis mutandis*. The office of the previous members of the supervisory board shall terminate only if the supervisory board should have been composed pursuant to provisions other than those the incorporators deemed to be applicable, or if the incorporators appointed three members to the supervisory board despite the fact that the supervisory board should also include employees' representatives.

(4) Paragraph 3 hereof shall not apply if the enterprise or part of the enterprise is contributed or acquired after the announcement of the managing board pursuant to § 30, paragraph 3, second sentence.

(5) § 30, paragraph 3, first sentence, shall also apply with respect to the members of the supervisory board appointed pursuant to paragraph 3 hereof.

§ 31

§ 32
Formation Report

(1) The incorporators shall make a written report concerning the process of the formation (formation report).

(2) The formation report shall contain the essential facts supporting the reasonableness of the consideration for the contributions of assets or the acquisitions of assets upon formation. The following shall be specified:

1. preceding transactions leading up to the acquisition by the company;
2. the costs of acquisition and production during the preceding two years;
3. in the event that an enterprise is transferred to the company, the earnings of the preceding two fiscal years.

(3) The formation report shall further specify whether and to what extent in connection with the formation shares have been subscribed to for the account of any member of the managing board or of the supervisory board, and whether and in what form any member of the managing board or of the supervisory board has requested for himself any special privilege or has requested any compensation or remuneration for the formation or its preparation.

§ 33
Examination of the Formation.
General Provisions

(1) The members of the managing board and of the supervisory board shall examine all the facts concerning the formation.

(2) In addition, an examination shall be made by one or more auditors (auditors of the formation) if

1. a member of the managing board or of the supervisory board is one of the incorporators, or
2. upon formation, shares have been subscribed to for the account of a member of the managing board or of the supervisory board, or
3. a member of the managing board or of the supervisory board has requested any special privilege for himself, or has requested any compensation or remuneration for the formation or its preparation, or
4. the formation involves a contribution or acquisition of assets.

§ 32

§ 32
Gründungsbericht

(1) Die Gründer haben einen schriftlichen Bericht über den Hergang der Gründung zu erstatten (Gründungsbericht).

(2) Im Gründungsbericht sind die wesentlichen Umstände darzulegen, von denen die Angemessenheit der Leistungen für Sacheinlagen oder Sachübernahmen abhängt. Dabei sind anzugeben

1. die vorausgegangenen Rechtsgeschäfte, die auf den Erwerb durch die Gesellschaft hingezielt haben;
2. die Anschaffungs- und Herstellungskosten aus den letzten beiden Jahren;
3. beim Übergang eines Unternehmens auf die Gesellschaft die Betriebserträge aus den letzten beiden Geschäftsjahren.

(3) Im Gründungsbericht ist ferner anzugeben, ob und in welchem Umfang ein Mitglied des Vorstands oder des Aufsichtsrats Aktien übernommen worden sind und ob und in welcher Weise ein Mitglied des Vorstands oder des Aufsichtsrats sich einen besonderen Vorteil oder für die Gründung oder ihre Vorbereitung eine Entschädigung oder Belohnung ausbedungen hat.

§ 33
Gründungsprüfung. Allgemeines

(1) Die Mitglieder des Vorstands und des Aufsichtsrats haben den Hergang der Gründung zu prüfen.

(2) Außerdem hat eine Prüfung durch einen oder mehrere Prüfer (Gründungsprüfer) stattzufinden, wenn

1. ein Mitglied des Vorstands oder des Aufsichtsrats zu den Gründern gehört oder
2. bei der Gründung für Rechnung eines Mitglieds des Vorstands oder des Aufsichtsrats Aktien übernommen worden sind oder
3. ein Mitglied des Vorstands oder des Aufsichtsrats sich einen besonderen Vorteil oder für die Gründung oder ihre Vorbereitung eine Entschädigung oder Belohnung ausbedungen hat oder
4. eine Gründung mit Sacheinlagen oder Sachübernahmen vorliegt.

(3) Die Gründungsprüfer bestellt das Gericht nach Anhörung der Industrie- und Handelskammer. Gegen die Entscheidung ist die sofortige Beschwerde zulässig.

(4) Als Gründungsprüfer sollen, wenn die Prüfung keine anderen Kenntnisse fordert, nur bestellt werden

1. Personen, die in der Buchführung ausreichend vorgebildet und erfahren sind;

2. Prüfungsgesellschaften, von deren gesetzlichen Vertretern mindestens einer in der Buchführung ausreichend vorgebildet und erfahren ist.

(5) Als Gründungsprüfer darf nicht bestellt werden, wer nach § 143 Abs. 2 und 3 nicht Sonderprüfer sein kann. Gleiches gilt für Personen und Prüfungsgesellschaften, auf deren Geschäftsführung die Gründer oder Personen, für deren Rechnung die Gründer Aktien übernommen haben, maßgebenden Einfluß haben.

§ 34
Umfang der Gründungsprüfung

(1) Die Prüfung durch die Mitglieder des Vorstands und des Aufsichtsrats sowie die Prüfung durch die Gründungsprüfer haben sich namentlich darauf zu erstrecken,

1. ob die Angaben der Gründer über die Übernahme der Aktien, über die Einlagen auf das Grundkapital und über die Festsetzungen nach §§ 26 und 27 richtig und vollständig sind;

2. ob der Wert der Sacheinlagen oder Sachübernahmen den Nennbetrag der dafür zu gewährenden Aktien oder den Wert der dafür zu gewährenden Leistungen erreicht.

(2) Über jede Prüfung ist unter Darlegung dieser Umstände schriftlich zu berichten.

(3) Je ein Stück des Berichts der Gründungsprüfer ist dem Gericht, dem Vorstand und der Industrie- und Handelskammer einzureichen. Jedermann kann den Bericht bei dem Gericht und bei der Industrie- und Handelskammer einsehen.

(3) The auditors of the formation shall be appointed by the court after hearing the Chamber of Industry and Commerce. Its decision can be appealed.

(4) Provided that the examination does not require additional expertise, the auditors of the formation shall be appointed only from among the following:

1. persons who are sufficiently trained and experienced in accounting;

2. auditing firms at least one of whose legal representatives is sufficiently trained and experienced in accounting.

(5) A person who is disqualified from acting as special auditor pursuant to § 143, paragraphs 2 and 3, may not be appointed as auditor of the formation. The same shall apply with respect to persons and auditing firms on whose management the incorporators or persons for whose account the incorporators have subscribed to shares exert a substantial influence.

§ 34
Scope of Examination of the Formation

(1) The examination by the members of the managing board and of the supervisory board, as well as the audit by the auditors of the formation, shall, in particular, cover:

1. whether the statements of the incorporators concerning the subscription of the shares, the contributions to the stated capital, and the stipulations made pursuant to §§ 26 and 27 are accurate and complete;

2. whether the value of the assets to be contributed or acquired is equal to the par value of the shares to be issued or to the value of the consideration to be rendered.

(2) A written report setting forth such facts shall be required with respect to each examination.

(3) The court, the managing board, and the Chamber of Industry and Commerce shall each be furnished a copy of the report of the auditors of the formation. The report shall be available for inspection by anyone at the court and at the Chamber of Industry and Commerce.

§ 35
Disputes between Incorporators and Auditors of the Formation. Remuneration and Expenses of Auditors of the Formation

(1) Disputes between the incorporators and the auditors of the formation concerning the extent of the information and the evidence to be furnished by the incorporators shall be decided by the court. The decision of the court is final. So long as the incorporators refuse to comply with such decision, the auditors of the formation shall not issue their report.

(2) The auditors of the formation shall be entitled to reimbursement for their reasonable cash expenditures and to remuneration for their services. The expenditures and the remuneration shall be determined by the court. The decision of the court can be appealed. It shall not be subject to further appeal. The final decision shall be enforceable in accordance with the provisions of the Code of Civil Procedure.

§ 36
Application to Record the Company

(1) The application to record the company in the Commercial Register shall be filed with the court by all of the incorporators and all of the members of the managing board and of the supervisory board.

(2) Except where a contribution of assets is stipulated, the application may not be filed before the amount assessed on each share has been duly paid (§ 54, paragraph 3) and, to the extent that it has not been used for the payment of taxes and fees due upon formation, is at the free disposal of the managing board. The amount assessed shall be at least one-fourth of the par value and, where shares are issued at a premium, also include one-fourth of such premium.

§ 37
Content of Application to Record the Company

(1) The application to record the company shall contain a statement to the effect that the requirements of § 36, paragraph 2, have been met; it shall specify the amount at which the shares are issued and the amount paid in. Proof shall be furnished

§ 35
Meinungsverschiedenheiten zwischen Gründern und Gründungsprüfern. Vergütung und Auslagen der Gründungsprüfer

(1) Bei Meinungsverschiedenheiten zwischen den Gründern und den Gründungsprüfern über den Umfang der Aufklärungen und Nachweise, die von den Gründern zu gewähren sind, entscheidet das Gericht. Die Entscheidung ist unanfechtbar. Solange sich die Gründer weigern, der Entscheidung nachzukommen, wird der Prüfungsbericht nicht erstattet.

(2) Die Gründungsprüfer haben Anspruch auf Ersatz angemessener barer Auslagen und auf Vergütung für ihre Tätigkeit. Die Auslagen und die Vergütung setzt das Gericht fest. Gegen die Entscheidung ist die sofortige Beschwerde zulässig. Die weitere Beschwerde ist ausgeschlossen. Aus der rechtskräftigen Entscheidung findet die Zwangsvollstreckung nach der Zivilprozeßordnung statt.

§ 36
Anmeldung der Gesellschaft

(1) Die Gesellschaft ist bei dem Gericht von allen Gründern und Mitgliedern des Vorstands und des Aufsichtsrats zur Eintragung in das Handelsregister anzumelden.

(2) Die Anmeldung darf erst erfolgen, wenn auf jede Aktie, soweit nicht Sacheinlagen vereinbart sind, der eingeforderte Betrag ordnungsgemäß eingezahlt worden ist (§ 54 Abs. 3) und, soweit er nicht bereits zur Bezahlung der bei der Gründung angefallenen Steuern und Gebühren verwandt wurde, endgültig zur freien Verfügung des Vorstands steht. Der eingeforderte Betrag muß mindestens ein Viertel des Nennbetrags und bei Ausgabe der Aktien für einen höheren als den Nennbetrag auch den Mehrbetrag umfassen.

§ 37
Inhalt der Anmeldung

(1) In der Anmeldung ist zu erklären, daß die Voraussetzungen des § 36 Abs. 2 erfüllt sind; dabei sind der Betrag, zu dem die Aktien ausgegeben werden, und der darauf eingezahlte Betrag anzugeben. Es ist nachzuweisen, daß der eingezahlte Be-

§ 35

trag endgültig zur freien Verfügung des Vorstands steht. Ist der Betrag durch Gutschrift auf ein Konto der Gesellschaft oder des Vorstands bei der Deutschen Bundesbank oder einem Kreditinstitut (§ 54 Abs. 3) eingezahlt worden, so ist der Nachweis durch eine schriftliche Bestätigung des Instituts zu führen. Für die Richtigkeit der Bestätigung ist das Institut der Gesellschaft verantwortlich. Sind von dem eingezahlten Betrag Steuern und Gebühren bezahlt worden, so ist dies nach Art und Höhe der Beträge nachzuweisen.

(2) Der Anmeldung sind beizufügen

1. die Satzung und die Urkunden, in denen die Satzung festgestellt worden ist und die Aktien von den Gründern übernommen worden sind;

2. im Fall der §§ 26 und 27 die Verträge, die den Festsetzungen zugrunde liegen oder zu ihrer Ausführung geschlossen worden sind, und eine Berechnung des der Gesellschaft zur Last fallenden Gründungsaufwands; in der Berechnung sind die Vergütungen nach Art und Höhe und die Empfänger einzeln anzuführen;

3. die Urkunden über die Bestellung des Vorstands und des Aufsichtsrats;

4. der Gründungsbericht und die Prüfungsberichte der Mitglieder des Vorstands und des Aufsichtsrats sowie der Gründungsprüfer nebst ihren urkundlichen Unterlagen; ferner die Bescheinigung, daß der Bericht der Gründungsprüfer der Industrie- und Handelskammer eingereicht worden ist;

5. wenn der Gegenstand des Unternehmens oder eine andere Satzungsbestimmung der staatlichen Genehmigung bedarf, die Genehmigungsurkunde.

(3) Die Vorstandsmitglieder haben ihre Namensunterschrift zur Aufbewahrung beim Gericht zu zeichnen.

(4) Die eingereichten Schriftstücke werden beim Gericht in Urschrift, Ausfertigung oder öffentlich beglaubigter Abschrift aufbewahrt.

that the amount paid in has been put at the free disposal of the managing board. In the event that the amount was paid by means of a transfer to a bank account of the company or of the managing board maintained with the Deutsche Bundesbank or another bank (§ 54, paragraph 3), such proof shall be furnished by means of a written confirmation issued by such bank. The bank shall be responsible to the company for the accuracy of this confirmation. If out of the amount paid in any portion was used for the payment of taxes and fees, evidence regarding the nature and amount of such payments shall be furnished.

(2) The application to record the company shall be accompanied by the following:

1. the articles of incorporation and the instruments containing the execution of such articles and the subscriptions to the shares by the incorporators;

2. in the event that § 26 or 27 applies, the agreements furnishing the bases for the relevant stipulations, or agreements entered into to carry them out, as well as an account of the expenses of formation assumed by the company; such account shall list the type and amount of any compensation and the various recipients thereof;

3. the documents concerning the appointment of the managing board and of the supervisory board;

4. the formation report and the examination reports of the members of the managing board and of the supervisory board as well as the report of the auditors of the formation, together with any documents pertaining thereto; in addition, a confirmation to the effect that the report of the auditors of the formation has been filed with the Chamber of Industry and Commerce;

5. in the event that the purpose of the enterprise or any other provision of the articles of incorporation requires governmental authorization, the instrument evidencing such authorization.

(3) The members of the managing board shall deposit their signatures with the court.

(4) An original, duplicate original, or certified copy of the documents filed shall be kept in the court records.

§ 37

§ 38
Examination by the Court

(1) The court shall examine whether the company has been duly constituted and whether registration has been duly applied for. Unless such is the case, the court shall not record the company.

(2) The court may also refuse registration if the auditors of the formation state, or if it is apparent, that the formation report or the report on the examination by the members of the managing board and of the supervisory board is either inaccurate or incomplete or does not comply with the statutory provisions. The same shall apply if the auditors of the formation state, or if it is the opinion of the court, that the value of the assets to be contributed or acquired is substantially less than the par value of the shares issued therefor or the value of the consideration to be rendered.

§ 39
Content of Registration

(1) The registration of the company shall set forth the name and the domicile of the company, the purpose of the enterprise, the amount of the stated capital, the date of execution of the articles of incorporation, and the members of the managing board.

(2) If the articles of incorporation contain any provisions regarding the duration of the company or the power of the members of the managing board or the liquidators to represent the company, or regarding the authorized capital, such provisions shall also be recorded.

§ 40
Publication of the Registration

(1) In addition to the content of the registration, the publication of the registration shall contain the following:

1. the information required in § 23, paragraph 3, §§ 24, 25, second sentence, §§ 26 and 27;

2. the amount for which the shares are issued;

3. the name, occupation, and residence of each of the incorporators;

4. the name, occupation, and residence of each of the members of the initial supervisory board.

§ 38
Prüfung durch das Gericht

(1) Das Gericht hat zu prüfen, ob die Gesellschaft ordnungsgemäß errichtet und angemeldet ist. Ist dies nicht der Fall, so hat es die Eintragung abzulehnen.

(2) Das Gericht kann die Eintragung auch ablehnen, wenn die Gründungsprüfer erklären oder es offensichtlich ist, daß der Gründungsbericht oder der Prüfungsbericht der Mitglieder des Vorstands und des Aufsichtsrats unrichtig oder unvollständig ist oder den gesetzlichen Vorschriften nicht entspricht. Gleiches gilt, wenn die Gründungsprüfer erklären oder das Gericht der Auffassung ist, daß der Wert der Sacheinlagen oder Sachübernahmen nicht unwesentlich hinter dem Nennbetrag der dafür zu gewährenden Aktien oder dem Wert der dafür zu gewährenden Leistungen zurückbleibt.

§ 39
Inhalt der Eintragung

(1) Bei der Eintragung der Gesellschaft sind die Firma und der Sitz der Gesellschaft, der Gegenstand des Unternehmens, die Höhe des Grundkapitals, der Tag der Feststellung der Satzung und die Vorstandsmitglieder anzugeben.

(2) Enthält die Satzung Bestimmungen über die Dauer der Gesellschaft oder über die Befugnis der Vorstandsmitglieder oder der Abwickler zur Vertretung der Gesellschaft oder über das genehmigte Kapital, so sind auch diese Bestimmungen einzutragen.

§ 40
Bekanntmachung der Eintragung

(1) In die Bekanntmachung der Eintragung sind außer deren Inhalt aufzunehmen
1. die Festsetzungen nach § 23 Abs. 3, §§ 24, 25 Satz 2, §§ 26 und 27;
2. der Ausgabebetrag der Aktien;
3. Name, Beruf und Wohnort der Gründer;
4. Name, Beruf und Wohnort der Mitglieder des ersten Aufsichtsrats.

(2) Zugleich ist bekanntzumachen, daß die mit der Anmeldung eingereichten Schriftstücke, namentlich die Prüfungsberichte der Mitglieder des Vorstands und des Aufsichtsrats sowie der Gründungsprüfer, bei dem Gericht, der Prüfungsbericht der Gründungsprüfer auch bei der Industrie- und Handelskammer eingesehen werden können.

(2) At the same time, it shall be announced that the documents filed with the application for registration, in particular, the examination reports of the members of the managing board and of the supervisory board as well as the auditors of the formation, may be examined at the court, and that the audit report of the auditors of the formation may also be examined at the Chamber of Industry and Commerce.

§ 41
Handeln im Namen der Gesellschaft vor der Eintragung. Verbotene Aktienausgabe

(1) Vor der Eintragung in das Handelsregister besteht die Aktiengesellschaft als solche nicht. Wer vor der Eintragung der Gesellschaft in ihrem Namen handelt, haftet persönlich; handeln mehrere, so haften sie als Gesamtschuldner.

(2) Übernimmt die Gesellschaft eine vor ihrer Eintragung in ihrem Namen eingegangene Verpflichtung durch Vertrag mit dem Schuldner in der Weise, daß sie an die Stelle des bisherigen Schuldners tritt, so bedarf es zur Wirksamkeit der Schuldübernahme der Zustimmung des Gläubigers nicht, wenn die Schuldübernahme binnen drei Monaten nach der Eintragung der Gesellschaft vereinbart und dem Gläubiger von der Gesellschaft oder dem Schuldner mitgeteilt wird.

(3) Verpflichtungen aus nicht in der Satzung festgesetzten Verträgen über Sondervorteile, Gründungsaufwand, Sacheinlagen oder Sachübernahmen kann die Gesellschaft nicht übernehmen.

(4) Vor der Eintragung der Gesellschaft können Anteilsrechte nicht übertragen, Aktien oder Zwischenscheine nicht ausgegeben werden. Die vorher ausgegebenen Aktien oder Zwischenscheine sind nichtig. Für den Schaden aus der Ausgabe sind die Ausgeber den Inhabern als Gesamtschuldner verantwortlich.

§ 41
Acting in the Name of the Company Prior to Registration. Prohibited Issuance of Shares

(1) Before registration in the Commercial Register, the stock corporation as such does not exist. A person acting in the name of the company before registration shall be liable personally; several persons so acting shall be liable jointly and severally.

(2) If the company agrees with a debtor to assume an obligation contracted in its name before registration, by substituting itself as debtor, the creditor's consent shall not be required to render the assumption of such obligation valid, provided that the agreement to assume the obligation is entered into, and the creditor is notified thereof, by the company or the debtor within three months from the date of registration of the company.

(3) Obligations resulting from agreements not stipulated in the articles of incorporation which concern special privileges, expenses of the formation, or contributions or acquisitions of assets, may not be assumed by the company.

(4) Before registration of the company, equity interests may not be transferred and share certificates or interim certificates may not be issued. Share certificates or interim certificates issued prior to such time shall be void. The issuers shall be jointly and severally liable to the holders for any damage arising out of such issuance.

§ 42
Errichtung einer Zweigniederlassung

(1) Die Errichtung einer Zweigniederlassung hat der Vorstand beim Gericht des Sitzes der Gesellschaft zur Eintragung in das Handelsregister des Gerichts der Zweigniederlassung anzumelden; der

§ 42
Establishment of a Branch

(1) Establishment of a branch requires the managing board to file an application with the court at the company's domicile to record it in the Commercial Register of the court where the

§ 42

branch is established; the application for registration shall be accompanied by a certified copy of the articles of incorporation. The court at the company's domicile shall promptly forward the application for registration to the court having jurisdiction over the branch, together with a certified copy of its entries concerning the company, to the extent that they are not concerned exclusively with other branches.

(2) The members of the managing board, as well as such of the *Prokuristen* whose powers of representation are not limited exclusively to the business of another branch, shall deposit their signatures and, in the case of the *Prokuristen,* the authorized signature for the company as well, with the court at the domicile of the branch.

(3) The court at the domicile of the branch shall examine whether the branch has been established and whether § 30 of the Commercial Code has been complied with. If this is the case, it shall record the branch without examining the facts reported to it if such facts have been recorded in the Commercial Register at the company's domicile. The registration shall contain the details specified in § 39 and the place of business of the branch; if the branch name contains an addition to the corporate name, such addition shall also be recorded.

(4) In addition to the content of the registration, the publication of the registration shall contain the information required in § 23, paragraph 3, §§ 24 and 25, second sentence. If the establishment of a branch is recorded in the Commercial Register of the court at the domicile of the branch within two years from the date on which the company was recorded in the Commercial Register of the court of its domicile, all information required by § 40 shall be published; in this event, the court at the company's domicile shall, upon transmittal of the application for registration, enclose a copy of the court's announcement made at the company's domicile.

(5) The registration of the branch shall be reported ex officio to the court at the company's domicile and shall be noted in the Commercial Register of that court; if the name of the branch contains an addition to the corporate name, this fact shall also be noted. The notation shall not be published.

Anmeldung ist eine öffentlich beglaubigte Abschrift der Satzung beizufügen. Das Gericht des Sitzes hat die Anmeldung unverzüglich mit einer beglaubigten Abschrift seiner Eintragungen, soweit sie nicht ausschließlich die Verhältnisse anderer Zweigniederlassungen betreffen, an das Gericht der Zweigniederlassung weiterzugeben.

(2) Die Vorstandsmitglieder sowie die Prokuristen, deren Prokura nicht ausschließlich auf den Betrieb einer anderen Niederlassung beschränkt ist, haben ihre Namensunterschrift, die Prokuristen auch die Firma, zur Aufbewahrung beim Gericht der Zweigniederlassung zu zeichnen.

(3) Das Gericht der Zweigniederlassung hat zu prüfen, ob die Zweigniederlassung errichtet und § 30 des Handelsgesetzbuchs beachtet ist. Ist dies der Fall, so hat es die Zweigniederlassung einzutragen und dabei die ihm mitgeteilten Tatsachen nicht zu prüfen, soweit sie im Handelsregister des Sitzes eingetragen sind. Die Eintragung hat die Angaben nach § 39 und den Ort der Zweigniederlassung zu enthalten; ist der Firma für die Zweigniederlassung ein Zusatz beigefügt, so ist auch dieser einzutragen.

(4) In die Bekanntmachung der Eintragung sind außer deren Inhalt die in § 23 Abs. 3, §§ 24, 25 Satz 2 vorgesehenen Bestimmungen aufzunehmen. Wird die Errichtung einer Zweigniederlassung in das Handelsregister des Gerichts der Zweigniederlassung in den ersten zwei Jahren eingetragen, nach dem die Gesellschaft in das Handelsregister ihres Sitzes eingetragen worden ist, so sind in der Bekanntmachung der Eintragung alle Angaben nach § 40 zu veröffentlichen; in diesem Fall hat das Gericht des Sitzes bei der Weitergabe der Anmeldung ein Stück der für den Sitz der Gesellschaft ergangenen gerichtlichen Bekanntmachung beizufügen.

(5) Die Eintragung der Zweigniederlassung ist von Amts wegen dem Gericht des Sitzes mitzuteilen und in dessen Register zu vermerken; ist der Firma für die Zweigniederlassung ein Zusatz beigefügt, so ist auch dieser zu vermerken. Der Vermerk wird nicht veröffentlicht.

§ 42

(6) Die vorstehenden Vorschriften gelten sinngemäß für die Aufhebung einer Zweigniederlassung.

(6) The foregoing provisions shall apply, *mutatis mutandis,* to the discontinuance of a branch.

§ 43
Behandlung bestehender Zweigniederlassungen

(1) Ist eine Zweigniederlassung in das Handelsregister eingetragen, so sind alle Anmeldungen, welche die Niederlassung am Sitz der Gesellschaft oder eine eingetragene Zweigniederlassung betreffen, beim Gericht des Sitzes zu bewirken; es sind so viel Stücke einzureichen, wie Niederlassungen bestehen.

(2) Das Gericht des Sitzes hat in der Bekanntmachung seiner Eintragung im Bundesanzeiger anzugeben, daß die gleiche Eintragung für die Zweigniederlassungen bei den namentlich zu bezeichnenden Gerichten der Zweigniederlassungen erfolgen wird; ist der Firma für eine Zweigniederlassung ein Zusatz beigefügt, so ist auch dieser anzugeben.

(3) Das Gericht des Sitzes hat sodann seine Eintragung unter Angabe der Nummer des Bundesanzeigers, in der sie bekanntgemacht ist, von Amts wegen den Gerichten der Zweigniederlassungen mitzuteilen; der Mitteilung ist ein Stück der Anmeldung beizufügen. Die Gerichte der Zweigniederlassungen haben die Eintragung ohne Nachprüfung in ihr Handelsregister zu übernehmen. In der Bekanntmachung der Eintragung im Register der Zweigniederlassung ist anzugeben, daß die Eintragung im Handelsregister des Gerichts des Sitzes erfolgt und in welcher Nummer des Bundesanzeigers sie bekanntgemacht ist. Im Bundesanzeiger wird die Eintragung im Handelsregister der Zweigniederlassung nicht bekanntgemacht.

(4) Betrifft die Anmeldung ausschließlich die Verhältnisse einzelner Zweigniederlassungen, so sind außer dem für das Gericht des Sitzes bestimmten Stück nur so viel Stücke einzureichen, wie Zweigniederlassungen betroffen sind. Das Gericht des Sitzes teilt seine Eintragung nur den Gerichten der Zweigniederlassungen mit, deren Verhältnisse sie betrifft. Die Eintragung im Register des Sitzes wird in diesem Fall nur im Bundesanzeiger bekanntgemacht.

§ 43
Treatment of Existing Branches

(1) If a branch has been recorded in the Commercial Register, all further applications for registration concerning the operation at the company's domicile or any registered branch shall be filed with the court at the company's domicile; the number of copies filed shall equal the number of places of operation.

(2) The court at the company's domicile shall, in its publication of the registration in the *Bundesanzeiger,* state that an identical registration will be made for the branches by the designated courts having jurisdiction over these branches; if the name of the branch contains any addition to the corporate name, such addition shall also be stated.

(3) The court at the company's domicile shall then ex officio give notice of the registration to the courts having jurisdiction over the branches, designating the issue of the *Bundesanzeiger* in which such registration was published; this notice shall be accompanied by a copy of the application for registration. The courts of the branches shall enter the registration in their Commercial Registers without further examination. The publication of the registration of the branch in Commercial Register shall state that the branch was registered in the Commercial Register of the court at the company's domicile and indicate the issue of the *Bundesanzeiger* in which this registration was published. The registration of the branch in the Commercial Register of the court having jurisdiction over the branch shall not be published in the *Bundesanzeiger.*

(4) If the registration concerns exclusively the status of particular branches, only as many copies shall be filed as the number of branches affected, together with one copy for the court at the company's domicile. The court at the company's domicile shall give notice of the registration only to the courts having jurisdiction over such branches as are affected thereby. In this event, the registration in the Commercial Register at the company's domicile shall be published only in the *Bundesanzeiger.*

§ 43

(5) Paragraphs 1, 3 and 4 hereof shall apply, *mutatis mutandis,* to the filing of documents and signatures.

(5) Die Absätze 1, 3 und 4 gelten sinngemäß für die Einreichung von Schriftstücken und die Zeichnung von Namensunterschriften.

§ 44
Branches of Companies Domiciled Abroad

§ 44
Zweigniederlassungen von Gesellschaften mit ausländischem Sitz

(1) If the company is domiciled abroad, the application to record the company shall be filed by all of the members of the managing board with the Commercial Register of the court of the district in which the company has a branch. The application for registration shall be accompanied by a certified copy of the articles of incorporation. § 37, paragraphs 1 and 2, shall not be applicable.

(1) Befindet sich der Sitz der Gesellschaft im Ausland, so ist die Gesellschaft zur Eintragung in das Handelsregister des Gerichts, in dessen Bezirk sie eine Zweigniederlassung besitzt, durch alle Vorstandsmitglieder anzumelden. Der Anmeldung ist die Satzung in öffentlich beglaubigter Abschrift beizufügen. § 37 Abs. 1 und 2 ist nicht anzuwenden.

(2) Upon filing the application, evidence of the existence of the corporation shall be submitted, and, if the purpose of the company or the permission to transact business in Germany requires governmental authorization, evidence of such authorization shall be furnished. Unless the foreign law requires a deviation from such provisions, the application for registration shall contain the details specified in § 23, paragraph 3, §§ 24 and 25, second sentence, and, if the application for registration is filed during the first two years after the company was recorded in the Commercial Register at its domicile, the additional details specified in § 40, paragraph 1. The application for registration shall be accompanied by the court's publication issued at the company's domicile.

(2) Bei der Anmeldung ist das Bestehen der Aktiengesellschaft als solcher und, wenn der Gegenstand des Unternehmens oder die Zulassung zum Gewerbebetrieb im Inland der staatlichen Genehmigung bedarf, auch diese nachzuweisen. Soweit nicht das ausländische Recht eine Abweichung nötig macht, sind in die Anmeldung die in § 23 Abs. 3, §§ 24, 25 Satz 2 vorgesehenen Bestimmungen und, wenn die Anmeldung in den ersten zwei Jahren nach der Eintragung der Gesellschaft in das Handelsregister ihres Sitzes erfolgt, auch die weiteren Angaben nach § 40 Abs. 1 aufzunehmen. Der Anmeldung ist die für den Sitz der Gesellschaft ergangene gerichtliche Bekanntmachung beizufügen.

(3) The registration shall contain the details specified in § 39 and shall indicate where the branch is located; if the name of the branch contains an addition to the corporate name, such addition shall also be recorded.

(3) Die Eintragung hat die Angaben nach § 39 und den Ort der Zweigniederlassung zu enthalten; ist der Firma für die Zweigniederlassung ein Zusatz beigefügt, so ist auch dieser einzutragen.

(4) The publication of the registration shall, in addition to the content of such registration, also contain the details specified in § 40, paragraph 1, to the extent that they are required to be set forth in the application for registration by the foregoing provisions.

(4) In die Bekanntmachung der Eintragung sind außer deren Inhalt auch die Angaben nach § 40 Abs. 1 aufzunehmen, soweit sie nach den vorstehenden Vorschriften in die Anmeldung aufzunehmen sind.

(5) In all other respects, the provisions concerning the establishment of a branch at the company's domicile shall apply, *mutatis mutandis,* to the applications to record, the deposit of signatures, and the registrations, unless the foreign law requires deviations therefrom.

(5) Im übrigen gelten für die Anmeldungen, Zeichnungen und Eintragungen, soweit nicht das ausländische Recht Abweichungen nötig macht, sinngemäß die Vorschriften für Niederlassungen am Sitz der Gesellschaft.

§ 44

§ 45
Sitzverlegung

(1) Wird der Sitz der Gesellschaft im Inland verlegt, so ist die Verlegung beim Gericht des bisherigen Sitzes anzumelden.

(2) Wird der Sitz aus dem Bezirk des Gerichts des bisherigen Sitzes verlegt, so hat dieses unverzüglich von Amts wegen die Verlegung dem Gericht des neuen Sitzes mitzuteilen. Der Mitteilung sind die Eintragungen für den bisherigen Sitz sowie die bei dem bisher zuständigen Gericht aufbewahrten Urkunden beizufügen. Das Gericht des neuen Sitzes hat zu prüfen, ob die Verlegung ordnungsgemäß beschlossen und § 30 des Handelsgesetzbuchs beachtet ist. Ist dies der Fall, so hat es die Sitzverlegung einzutragen und hierbei die ihm mitgeteilten Eintragungen ohne weitere Nachprüfung in sein Handelsregister zu übernehmen. Mit der Eintragung wird die Sitzverlegung wirksam. Die Eintragung ist dem Gericht des bisherigen Sitzes mitzuteilen. Dieses hat die erforderlichen Löschungen von Amts wegen vorzunehmen.

(3) Wird in den ersten zwei Jahren nach der Eintragung der Gesellschaft in das Handelsregister des ursprünglichen Sitzes eine Sitzverlegung aus dem Bezirk des Gerichts des bisherigen Sitzes eingetragen, so sind in der Bekanntmachung der Eintragung alle Angaben nach § 40 Abs. 1 zu veröffentlichen.

(4) Wird der Sitz an einen anderen Ort innerhalb des Bezirks des Gerichts des bisherigen Sitzes verlegt, so hat das Gericht zu prüfen, ob die Sitzverlegung ordnungsgemäß beschlossen und § 30 des Handelsgesetzbuchs beachtet ist. Ist dies der Fall, so hat es die Sitzverlegung einzutragen. Mit der Eintragung wird die Sitzverlegung wirksam.

§ 46
Verantwortlichkeit der Gründer

(1) Die Gründer sind der Gesellschaft als Gesamtschuldner verantwortlich für die Richtigkeit und Vollständigkeit der Angaben, die zum Zwecke der Gründung der Gesellschaft über Übernahme der Aktien, Einzahlung auf die Aktien, Verwendung eingezahlter Beträge, Sondervorteile, Gründungs-

§ 45
Transfer of Domicile

(1) In the event of a transfer of the company's domicile within Germany, such transfer shall be reported to the court at the former domicile.

(2) If the company's domicile is transferred from the jurisdiction of the court at the former domicile, this court shall promptly give notice ex officio of such transfer to the court at the new domicile. Such notice shall be accompanied by the entries concerning the former domicile as well as the documents kept by the court which theretofore had jurisdiction. The court at the new domicile shall examine whether the resolution concerning the transfer was duly adopted, and whether there was compliance with § 30 of the Commercial Code. If this is the case, it shall record the transfer of domicile and enter in its Commercial Register the entries reported to it, without further examination. The transfer of domicile shall become effective upon registration. The registration shall be reported to the court of the former domicile. This court shall, ex officio, effect the necessary cancellations.

(3) If a transfer of domicile from the jurisdiction of the court where it was originally domiciled is recorded within the first two years after registration of the company in the Commercial Register at the original domicile, the publication of the registration shall contain all of the details specified in § 40, paragraph 1.

(4) In the event that the domicile is transferred to another location within the jurisdiction of the court at the former domicile, the court shall examine whether the resolution concerning the transfer of domicile was duly adopted and whether there was compliance with § 30 of the Commercial Code. If this is the case, it shall record the transfer of domicile. The transfer of domicile shall become effective upon registration.

§ 46
Liability of Incorporators

(1) The incorporators shall be jointly and severally liable to the company for the accuracy and completeness of any information furnished for purposes of the formation of the company as to subscriptions to shares, payment on the shares, the use made of any amounts paid in, preferences,

§ 46

expenses of formation, contributions of assets, and acquisitions of assets upon formation. They shall also be responsible for ascertaining that the financial institution designated to receive payments on the capital stock is qualified for such purpose (§ 54, paragraph 3), and that any amounts paid in were put at the free disposal of the managing board. Without prejudice to their obligation to effect compensation for any other damage, they shall be required to make up deficiencies in the contributions and to pay any amounts that were not included in the expenses of the formation.

(2) In the event the company is damaged by the incorporators through contributions or acquisitions of assets or expenses of formation, either intentionally or through gross negligence, all of the incorporators shall be jointly and severally liable to the company.

(3) An incorporator shall not be liable if he did not have knowledge of the facts giving rise to such liability, and if he could not have obtained such knowledge even if he exercised the care of a reasonable businessman.

(4) If the company sustains a loss because a shareholder is insolvent or unable to contribute assets, the incorporators who accepted the subscription of such shareholder with knowledge of his insolvency or inability to perform shall be jointly and severally liable to the company for such loss.

(5) In addition to the incorporators, persons for whose account the incorporators subscribed to shares shall be liable in the same manner. They shall not be excused by a lack of personal knowledge as to circumstances which an incorporator acting for their account knew or should have known.

aufwand, Sacheinlagen und Sachübernahmen gemacht worden sind. Sie sind ferner dafür verantwortlich, daß eine zur Annahme von Einzahlungen auf das Grundkapital bestimmte Stelle (§ 54 Abs. 3) hierzu geeignet ist und daß die eingezahlten Beträge zur freien Verfügung des Vorstands stehen. Sie haben, unbeschadet der Verpflichtung zum Ersatz des sonst entstehenden Schadens, fehlende Einzahlungen zu leisten und eine Vergütung, die nicht unter den Gründungsaufwand aufgenommen ist, zu ersetzen.

(2) Wird die Gesellschaft von Gründern durch Einlagen, Sachübernahmen oder Gründungsaufwand vorsätzlich oder aus grober Fahrlässigkeit geschädigt, so sind ihr alle Gründer als Gesamtschuldner zum Ersatz verpflichtet.

(3) Von diesen Verpflichtungen ist ein Gründer befreit, wenn er die die Ersatzpflicht begründenden Tatsachen weder kannte noch bei Anwendung der Sorgfalt eines ordentlichen Geschäftsmannes kennen mußte.

(4) Entsteht der Gesellschaft ein Ausfall, weil ein Aktionär zahlungsunfähig oder unfähig ist, eine Sacheinlage zu leisten, so sind ihr zum Ersatz als Gesamtschuldner die Gründer verpflichtet, welche die Beteiligung des Aktionärs in Kenntnis seiner Zahlungsunfähigkeit oder Leistungsunfähigkeit angenommen haben.

(5) Neben den Gründern sind in gleicher Weise Personen verantwortlich, für deren Rechnung die Gründer Aktien übernommen haben. Sie können sich auf ihre eigene Unkenntnis nicht wegen solcher Umstände berufen, die ein für ihre Rechnung handelnder Gründer kannte oder kennen mußte.

§ 47
Liability of Persons Other Than Incorporators

In addition to the incorporators and the persons for whose account the incorporators subscribed to shares, the following shall be jointly and severally liable to the company:

1. a person receiving any compensation which, contrary to the applicable provisions, has not been listed as an item of expense of the formation, if such person knew, or under the

§ 47
Verantwortlichkeit anderer Personen neben den Gründern

Neben den Gründern und den Personen, für deren Rechnung die Gründer Aktien übernommen haben, ist als Gesamtschuldner der Gesellschaft zum Schadenersatz verpflichtet,

1. wer bei Empfang einer Vergütung, die entgegen den Vorschriften nicht in den Gründungsaufwand aufgenommen ist, wußte oder nach den Umständen annehmen mußte, daß die Verheimlichung

§ 47

beabsichtigt oder erfolgt war, oder wer zur Verheimlichung wissentlich mitgewirkt hat;

2. wer im Fall einer vorsätzlichen oder grobfahrlässigen Schädigung der Gesellschaft durch Einlagen oder Sachübernahmen an der Schädigung wissentlich mitgewirkt hat;

3. wer vor Eintragung der Gesellschaft in das Handelsregister oder in den ersten zwei Jahren nach der Eintragung die Aktien öffentlich ankündigt, um sie in den Verkehr einzuführen, wenn er die Unrichtigkeit oder Unvollständigkeit der Angaben, die zum Zwecke der Gründung der Gesellschaft gemacht worden sind (§ 46 Abs. 1), oder die Schädigung der Gesellschaft durch Einlagen oder Sachübernahmen kannte oder bei Anwendung der Sorgfalt eines ordentlichen Geschäftsmannes kennen mußte.

§ 48
Verantwortlichkeit des Vorstands und des Aufsichtsrats

Mitglieder des Vorstands und des Aufsichtsrats, die bei der Gründung ihre Pflichten verletzen, sind der Gesellschaft zum Ersatz des daraus entstehenden Schadens als Gesamtschuldner verpflichtet; sie sind namentlich dafür verantwortlich, daß eine zur Annahme von Einzahlungen auf die Aktien bestimmte Stelle (§ 54 Abs. 3) hierzu geeignet ist, und daß die eingezahlten Beträge zur freien Verfügung des Vorstands stehen. Für die Sorgfaltspflicht und Verantwortlichkeit der Mitglieder des Vorstands und des Aufsichtsrats bei der Gründung gelten im übrigen §§ 93 und 116 mit Ausnahme von § 93 Abs. 4 Satz 3 und 4 und Abs. 6.

§ 49
Verantwortlichkeit der Gründungsprüfer

§ 168 Abs. 1 bis 4 über die Verantwortlichkeit der Abschlußprüfer gilt sinngemäß.

§ 50
Verzicht und Vergleich

Die Gesellschaft kann auf Ersatzansprüche gegen die Gründer, die neben diesen haftenden Personen

---

circumstances should have known, that such concealment was intended or had occurred, or if he knowingly participated in the concealment;

2. a person who knowingly participated in an intentional or grossly negligent act causing damage to the company through the contribution or acquisition of assets;

3. a person who, prior to the registration of the company in the Commercial Register or during the first two years after registration, publicly advertises shares for the purpose of marketing them, if such person knew or by exercising the care of a reasonable businessman should have known of the inaccuracy or incompleteness of the statements made for purposes of the company's formation (§ 46, paragraph 1), or of the injury caused to the company through the contribution or acquisition of assets.

§ 48
Liability of Managing Board and of Supervisory Board

Members of the managing board and of the supervisory board who breach their duties in connection with the formation shall be jointly and severally liable to the company for any damage arising therefrom; they shall, in particular, have the duty to ascertain that a financial institution designated to receive payment for the shares (§ 54, paragraph 3) qualifies, and that any amounts paid in are put at the free disposal of the managing board. As to the care to be exercised by and the liability of the members of the managing board and of the supervisory board in the course of the company's formation, §§ 93 and 116, with the exception of § 93, paragraph 4, third and fourth sentences, and paragraph 6, shall likewise be applicable.

§ 49
Liability of Auditors of the Formation

§ 168, paragraphs 1 to 4, concerning the liability of the annual auditors, shall be applicable, *mutatis mutandis.*

§ 50
Waiver and Compromise

The company may waive or compromise a claim for damages against the incorporators, against any other persons who are also liable, or against the members of the managing board and of the supervisory board (§§ 46 to 48) only after the expiration of three years from the date of registration of the company in the Commercial Register, provided that the shareholders approve and a minority whose combined holdings amount to no less than one-tenth of the stated capital does not record its objection in the minutes. The time limit shall not apply if the party liable is unable to pay his debts as they mature and enters into a composition with his creditors to avert or terminate bankruptcy proceedings.

und gegen die Mitglieder des Vorstands und des Aufsichtsrats (§§ 46 bis 48) erst drei Jahre nach der Eintragung der Gesellschaft in das Handelsregister und nur dann verzichten oder sich über sie vergleichen, wenn die Hauptversammlung zustimmt und nicht eine Minderheit, deren Anteile zusammen den zehnten Teil des Grundkapitals erreichen, zur Niederschrift Widerspruch erhebt. Die zeitliche Beschränkung gilt nicht, wenn der Ersatzpflichtige zahlungsunfähig ist und sich zur Abwendung oder Beseitigung des Konkursverfahrens mit seinen Gläubigern vergleicht.

§ 51
Limitation on Damage Claims

Damage claims of the company pursuant to §§ 46 to 49 shall be barred after the expiration of five years. The period of limitations shall begin to run upon registration of the company in the Commercial Register or, if the act giving rise to the damage claim was committed subsequent thereto, upon the commission of the act.

§ 51
Verjährung der Ersatzansprüche

Ersatzansprüche der Gesellschaft nach den §§ 46 bis 49 verjähren in fünf Jahren. Die Verjährung beginnt mit der Eintragung der Gesellschaft in das Handelsregister oder, wenn die zum Ersatz verpflichtende Handlung später begangen worden ist, mit der Vornahme der Handlung.

§ 52
Post-Formation Acquisitions

(1) Agreements entered into by the company for acquisition of existing or future facilities or other assets for a consideration exceeding one-tenth of the stated capital, and executed within two years from the date of registration of the company in the Commercial Register, shall become valid only upon the approval of the shareholders and after registration in the Commercial Register. Absent such approval by the shareholders or registration in the Commercial Register, any transactions designed to implement such agreements shall also be invalid.

(2) An agreement pursuant to paragraph 1 hereof shall be in writing unless some other form is prescribed. It shall, from the time of the calling of the shareholders' meeting which is to adopt a resolution on the approval of the agreement, be exhibited at the company's premises for examination by the shareholders. Upon request, any shareholder shall promptly be furnished a copy. The agreement shall be exhibited at the shareholders' meeting. The managing board

§ 52
Nachgründung

(1) Verträge der Gesellschaft, nach denen sie vorhandene oder herzustellende Anlagen oder andere Vermögensgegenstände für eine den zehnten Teil des Grundkapitals übersteigende Vergütung erwerben soll, und die in den ersten zwei Jahren seit der Eintragung der Gesellschaft in das Handelsregister geschlossen werden, werden nur mit Zustimmung der Hauptversammlung und durch Eintragung in das Handelsregister wirksam. Ohne die Zustimmung der Hauptversammlung oder die Eintragung im Handelsregister sind auch die Rechtshandlungen zu ihrer Ausführung unwirksam.

(2) Ein Vertrag nach Absatz 1 bedarf der schriftlichen Form, soweit nicht eine andere Form vorgeschrieben ist. Er ist von der Einberufung der Hauptversammlung an, die über die Zustimmung beschließen soll, in dem Geschäftsraum der Gesellschaft zur Einsicht der Aktionäre auszulegen. Auf Verlangen ist jedem Aktionär unverzüglich eine Abschrift zu erteilen. In der Hauptversammlung ist der Vertrag auszulegen. Der Vorstand hat ihn zu

Beginn der Verhandlung zu erläutern. Der Niederschrift ist er als Anlage beizufügen.

(3) Vor der Beschlußfassung der Hauptversammlung hat der Aufsichtsrat den Vertrag zu prüfen und einen schriftlichen Bericht zu erstatten (Nachgründungsbericht). Für den Nachgründungsbericht gilt sinngemäß § 32 Abs. 2 und 3 über den Gründungsbericht.

(4) Außerdem hat vor der Beschlußfassung eine Prüfung durch einen oder mehrere Gründungsprüfer stattzufinden. § 33 Abs. 3 bis 5, §§ 34, 35 über die Gründungsprüfung gelten sinngemäß.

(5) Der Beschluß der Hauptversammlung bedarf einer Mehrheit, die mindestens drei Viertel des bei der Beschlußfassung vertretenen Grundkapitals umfaßt. Wird der Vertrag im ersten Jahre nach der Eintragung der Gesellschaft in das Handelsregister geschlossen, so müssen außerdem die Anteile der zustimmenden Mehrheit mindestens ein Viertel des gesamten Grundkapitals erreichen. Die Satzung kann an Stelle dieser Mehrheiten größere Kapitalmehrheiten und weitere Erfordernisse bestimmen.

(6) Nach Zustimmung der Hauptversammlung hat der Vorstand den Vertrag zur Eintragung in das Handelsregister anzumelden. Der Anmeldung ist der Vertrag in Urschrift, Ausfertigung oder öffentlich beglaubigter Abschrift mit dem Nachgründungsbericht und dem Bericht der Gründungsprüfer mit den urkundlichen Unterlagen beizufügen.

(7) Bestehen gegen die Eintragung Bedenken, weil die Gründungsprüfer erklären oder weil es offensichtlich ist, daß der Nachgründungsbericht unrichtig oder unvollständig ist oder den gesetzlichen Vorschriften nicht entspricht oder daß die für die zu erwerbenden Vermögensgegenstände gewährte Vergütung unangemessen hoch ist, so kann das Gericht die Eintragung ablehnen.

(8) Bei der Eintragung genügt die Bezugnahme auf die eingereichten Urkunden. In die Bekanntmachung der Eintragung sind aufzunehmen der Tag des Vertragsabschlusses und der Zustimmung der Hauptversammlung sowie der zu erwerbende Vermögensgegenstand, die Person, von der die Gesellschaft ihn erwirbt, und die zu gewährende Vergütung.

(9) Vorstehende Vorschriften gelten nicht, wenn der Erwerb der Vermögensgegenstände den Gegen-

shall explain it at the beginning of the deliberations. It shall be attached to the minutes.

(3) Prior to the resolution of the shareholders' meeting, the supervisory board shall examine the agreement and make a written report (post-formation report). § 32, paragraphs 2 and 3, concerning the formation report, shall apply to the post-formation report.

(4) In addition, an audit shall be made by one or more auditors of the formation before the resolution is adopted. § 33, paragraphs 3 to 5, §§ 34 and 35, concerning the audit of the formation, shall apply *mutatis mutandis*.

(5) The shareholders' resolution shall require a majority of no less than three-fourths of the stated capital represented when the resolution is adopted. If the agreement was entered into within the first year after registration of the company in the Commercial Register, the majority voting for approval must also represent no less than one-fourth of the total stated capital. The articles of incorporation may, in lieu of these majorities, specify higher capital majorities and establish additional requirements.

(6) After approval by the shareholders, the managing board shall file an application to record the agreement in the Commercial Register. The application shall be accompanied by the original, a duplicate original, or a certified copy of the agreement, together with the post-formation report and the report of the auditors of the formation, along with the relevant documents.

(7) The court may deny the application for registration on the grounds that registration would be objectionable because the auditors of the formation state, or because it is apparent, that the post-formation report is inaccurate or incomplete or does not comply with the statutory provisions, or that the consideration for the assets to be acquired is unreasonably high.

(8) Upon registration, reference to the documents filed shall be sufficient. The publication of the registration shall specify the date the agreement was executed and approval of the shareholders given as well as the asset to be acquired, the person from whom the company is to acquire it, and the consideration.

(9) The foregoing provisions shall be inapplicable if it is the purpose of the enterprise to

§ 52

engage in the acquisition of such assets or if the assets are acquired in the course of a judicial foreclosure.

(10) An agreement described in paragraph 1 hereof shall not be invalid, irrespective of whether it was executed within the two-year period from the date of registration of the company in the Commercial Register or thereafter, merely because a contract entered into by the incorporators concerning the same subject matter is invalid as against the company pursuant to § 27, paragraph 2.

stand des Unternehmens bildet oder wenn sie in der Zwangsvollstreckung erworben werden.

(10) Ein Vertrag nach Absatz 1 ist, gleichviel ob er vor oder nach Ablauf von zwei Jahren seit der Eintragung der Gesellschaft in das Handelsregister geschlossen ist, nicht deshalb unwirksam, weil ein Vertrag der Gründer über denselben Gegenstand nach § 27 Abs. 2 der Gesellschaft gegenüber unwirksam ist.

§ 53
Damage Claims in Case of
Post-Formation Acquisitions

§§ 46, 47, and 49 to 51, relating to claims for damage sustained by the company, shall apply *mutatis mutandis* to post-formation acquisitions. Instead of the incorporators the members of the managing board and of the supervisory board shall be liable. They shall act with the care of a diligent and prudent executive. To the extent that it is there provided that periods of limitation are to run from the date of registration of the company in the Commercial Register, the date of registration of the post-formation agreement shall be used instead.

§ 53
Ersatzansprüche bei der Nachgründung

Für die Nachgründung gelten die §§ 46, 47, 49 bis 51 über die Ersatzansprüche der Gesellschaft sinngemäß. An die Stelle der Gründer treten die Mitglieder des Vorstands und des Aufsichtsrats. Sie haben die Sorgfalt eines ordentlichen und gewissenhaften Geschäftsleiters anzuwenden. Soweit Fristen mit der Eintragung der Gesellschaft in das Handelsregister beginnen, tritt an deren Stelle die Eintragung des Vertrags über die Nachgründung.

Part Three

Legal Relationships of the
Company and of the Shareholders

Dritter Teil
Rechtsverhältnisse der Gesellschaft
und der Gesellschafter

§ 54
Principal Obligation of the Shareholders

(1) The obligation of the shareholders to effect contributions shall be limited by the par value of the shares plus any premium.

(2) Unless the articles of incorporation provide for the contribution of assets, the shareholders shall pay in the par value of the shares plus any premium.

(3) The amount called in prior to the application to record the company may be put at the

§ 54
Hauptverpflichtung der Aktionäre

(1) Die Verpflichtung der Aktionäre zur Leistung der Einlagen wird durch den Nennbetrag oder den höheren Ausgabebetrag der Aktien begrenzt.

(2) Soweit nicht in der Satzung Sacheinlagen festgesetzt sind, haben die Aktionäre den Nennbetrag oder den höheren Ausgabebetrag der Aktien einzuzahlen.

(3) Der vor der Anmeldung der Gesellschaft eingeforderte Betrag kann nur in gesetzlichen Zah-

lungsmitteln, in von der Deutschen Bundesbank bestätigten Schecks, durch Gutschrift auf ein Konto im Inland bei der Deutschen Bundesbank oder einem Kreditinstitut oder auf ein Postscheckkonto der Gesellschaft oder des Vorstands zu seiner freien Verfügung eingezahlt werden. Forderungen des Vorstands aus diesen Einzahlungen gelten als Forderungen der Gesellschaft.

free disposal of the company only in the form of legal tender, in checks certified by the Deutsche Bundesbank, or by transfer to an account maintained in Germany with the Deutsche Bundesbank or another bank, or to a postal checking account of the company or of the managing board. Claims of the managing board to the monies so deposited shall be deemed to be claims of the company.

§ 55
Nebenverpflichtungen der Aktionäre

(1) Ist die Übertragung der Aktien an die Zustimmung der Gesellschaft gebunden, so kann die Satzung Aktionären die Verpflichtung auferlegen, neben den Einlagen auf das Grundkapital wiederkehrende, nicht in Geld bestehende Leistungen zu erbringen. Dabei hat sie zu bestimmen, ob die Leistungen entgeltlich oder unentgeltlich zu erbringen sind. Die Verpflichtung und der Umfang der Leistungen sind in den Aktien und Zwischenscheinen anzugeben.

(2) Die Satzung kann Vertragsstrafen für den Fall festsetzen, daß die Verpflichtung nicht oder nicht gehörig erfüllt wird.

§ 55
Other Obligations of the Shareholders

(1) The articles of incorporation of a company the transfer of whose shares is contingent upon the company's consent may impose an obligation upon the shareholders to render recurring performances, other than the payment of money, in addition to contributions to the capital. In this event, the articles of incorporation shall specify whether or not such performances shall be compensated. The share and interim certificates shall refer to this obligation and the extent of such performances.

(2) The articles of incorporation may provide for penalties in the event that the obligation is not met or not met properly.

§ 56
Aktienübernahme für Rechnung der Gesellschaft oder durch ein abhängiges oder in Mehrheitsbesitz stehendes Unternehmen

(1) Wer als Gründer oder Zeichner oder in Ausübung eines bei einer bedingten Kapitalerhöhung eingeräumten Umtausch- oder Bezugsrechts eine Aktie für Rechnung der Gesellschaft oder eines abhängigen oder in Mehrheitsbesitz stehenden Unternehmens übernommen hat, kann sich nicht darauf berufen, daß er die Aktie nicht für eigene Rechnung übernommen hat. Er haftet ohne Rücksicht auf Vereinbarungen mit der Gesellschaft oder dem abhängigen oder in Mehrheitsbesitz stehenden Unternehmen auf die volle Einlage. Bevor er die Aktie für eigene Rechnung übernommen hat, stehen ihm keine Rechte aus der Aktie zu.

(2) Ein abhängiges Unternehmen darf keine Aktien der herrschenden Gesellschaft, ein in Mehrheitsbesitz stehendes Unternehmen keine Aktien der

§ 56
Acquisition of Shares for the Account of the Company or through a Controlled or Majority-Owned Enterprise

(1) No one who as incorporator, subscriber, or in the exercise of an option to convert or to subscribe to new shares issued in connection with a conditional capital increase has acquired a share for the account of the company or a controlled enterprise or majority-owned enterprise may assert that he did not acquire such share for his own account. Such person shall be liable for payment in full of the subscription price without regard to any agreements with the company or with the controlled or majority-owned enterprise. Until he acquires the share for his own account, he shall have none of the rights of a shareholder.

(2) A controlled enterprise may not act as incorporator or subscriber or exercise a right to convert or to subscribe to new shares issued in connection

§ 56

with a conditional capital increase to acquire shares of the controlling company, nor may a majority-owned enterprise act in such capacity to acquire shares in the company owning the majority interest. A violation of this provision shall not render such acquisition invalid.

an ihm mit Mehrheit beteiligten Gesellschaft als Gründer oder Zeichner oder in Ausübung eines bei einer bedingten Kapitalerhöhung eingeräumten Umtausch- oder Bezugsrechts übernehmen. Durch einen Verstoß gegen diese Vorschrift wird die Übernahme nicht unwirksam.

§ 57
No Repayment of Capital, No Payment of Interest on Contributions

§ 57
Keine Rückgewähr, keine Verzinsung der Einlagen

(1) Contributions may not be repaid to the shareholders. The payment of the purchase price in the case of a permissible acquisition of its own shares by the company shall not be considered a return of contributions.

(1) Den Aktionären dürfen die Einlagen nicht zurückgewährt werden. Als Rückgewähr von Einlagen gilt nicht die Zahlung des Erwerbspreises beim zulässigen Erwerb eigener Aktien.

(2) Interest shall be neither promised nor paid to the shareholders.

(2) Den Aktionären dürfen Zinsen weder zugesagt noch ausgezahlt werden.

(3) For the period required for the start-up of the enterprise until the commencement of its full operations, interest in a specified amount may be promised to the shareholders in the original articles of incorporation. The articles of incorporation shall specify the final date at which such payment of interest shall cease.

(3) Für den Zeitraum, den die Vorbereitung des Unternehmens bis zum Anfang des vollen Betriebs erfordert, können den Aktionären in der ursprünglichen Satzung Zinsen von bestimmter Höhe zugesagt werden. Die Satzung muß den Zeitpunkt bezeichnen, mit dem die Entrichtung von Zinsen spätestens aufhört.

§ 58
Disposition of Net Profit for the Year

§ 58
Verwendung des Jahresüberschusses

(1) Only in the event that the shareholders' meeting establishes the annual financial statements may the articles of incorporation provide that amounts from the net profit for the year shall be allocated to free reserves. The amount allocated to free reserves pursuant to such a provision in the articles of incorporation may not exceed one-half of the net profit for the year. Amounts required to be allocated to the statutory reserve and loss carry-forward shall first be deducted from the net profit for the year.

(1) Die Satzung kann nur für den Fall, daß die Hauptversammlung den Jahresabschluß feststellt, bestimmen, daß Beträge aus dem Jahresüberschuß in freie Rücklagen einzustellen sind. Auf Grund einer solchen Satzungsbestimmung kann höchstens die Hälfte des Jahresüberschusses in freie Rücklagen eingestellt werden. Dabei sind Beträge, die in die gesetzliche Rücklage einzustellen sind, und ein Verlustvortrag vorab vom Jahresüberschuß abzuziehen.

(2) In the event that the managing board and the supervisory board establish the annual financial statements, they may allocate a portion of the net profit for the year, not to exceed one-half thereof, to free reserves. The articles of incorporation may authorize the managing board and the supervisory board to allocate an amount in excess of one-half of the net profit for the year. The managing board and the supervisory board may not, however, on the basis of such a provision

(2) Stellen Vorstand und Aufsichtsrat den Jahresabschluß fest, so können sie einen Teil des Jahresüberschusses, höchstens jedoch die Hälfte, in freie Rücklagen einstellen. Die Satzung kann Vorstand und Aufsichtsrat zur Einstellung eines größeren Teils als der Hälfte des Jahresüberschusses ermächtigen. Auf Grund einer solchen Satzungsbestimmung

dürfen Vorstand und Aufsichtsrat keine Beträge in freie Rücklagen einstellen, wenn die freien Rücklagen die Hälfte des Grundkapitals übersteigen oder soweit sie nach der Einstellung die Hälfte übersteigen würden. Absatz 1 Satz 3 gilt sinngemäß.

(3) Die Hauptversammlung kann im Beschluß über die Verwendung des Bilanzgewinns weitere Beträge in offene Rücklagen einstellen oder als Gewinn vortragen. Sie kann ferner, wenn die Satzung sie hierzu ermächtigt, auch eine andere Verwendung als nach Satz 1 oder als die Verteilung unter die Aktionäre beschließen.

(4) Die Aktionäre haben Anspruch auf den Bilanzgewinn, soweit er nicht nach Gesetz oder Satzung, durch Hauptversammlungsbeschluß nach Absatz 3 oder als zusätzlicher Aufwand auf Grund des Gewinnverwendungsbeschlusses von der Verteilung unter die Aktionäre ausgeschlossen ist.

(5) Vor Auflösung der Gesellschaft darf unter die Aktionäre nur der Bilanzgewinn verteilt werden.

in the articles of incorporation, allocate such amounts to the free reserves if such free reserves exceed or, after allocation, would exceed one-half of the stated capital. Paragraph 1, third sentence, shall apply *mutatis mutandis.*

(3) The shareholders may in their resolution on the disposition of retained earnings allocate additional amounts to free reserves or carry them forward as profit. They may also, if authorized to do so in the articles of incorporation, adopt a resolution that the profits shall be used in some manner other than that provided for in the first sentence hereof or other than for distribution to the shareholders.

(4) The shareholders shall be entitled to the retained earnings to the extent that such earnings are not excluded from distribution to the shareholders by law or by the articles of incorporation, or by a shareholders' resolution to paragraph 3 hereof, or if such earnings are not excluded from distribution to shareholders as an additional expenditure pursuant to a resolution on the disposition of earnings.

(5) Prior to dissolution of the company only the retained earnings may be distributed to the shareholders.

§ 59
Abschlagszahlung auf den Bilanzgewinn

(1) Die Satzung kann den Vorstand ermächtigen, nach Ablauf des Geschäftsjahrs auf den voraussichtlichen Bilanzgewinn einen Abschlag an die Aktionäre zu zahlen.

(2) Der Vorstand darf einen Abschlag nur zahlen, wenn ein vorläufiger Abschluß für das vergangene Geschäftsjahr einen Jahresüberschuß ergibt. Als Abschlag darf höchstens die Hälfte des Betrags gezahlt werden, der von dem Jahresüberschuß nach Abzug der Beträge verbleibt, die nach Gesetz oder Satzung in offene Rücklagen einzustellen sind. Außerdem darf der Abschlag nicht die Hälfte des vorjährigen Bilanzgewinns übersteigen.

(3) Die Zahlung eines Abschlags bedarf der Zustimmung des Aufsichtsrats.

§ 59
Advance Payment on Retained Earnings

(1) The articles of incorporation may authorize the managing board to distribute to the shareholders after the close of the fiscal year an advance payment on the expected retained earnings.

(2) The managing board may pay out such an advance only if a preliminary financial statement for the past fiscal year shows a net profit. The amount distributed as advance payment shall not exceed one-half of the net profit for the year after deducting therefrom the amounts to be allocated to disclosed reserves pursuant to law or the articles of incorporation. Moreover, the advance payment may not exceed one-half of the retained earnings of the preceding year.

(3) The distribution of an advance payment shall require the approval of the supervisory board.

§ 59

§ 60
Distribution of Profit

(1) The shareholders shall participate in the profit in proportion to the par value of their shares.

(2) If contributions to the stated capital have not been rendered in the same proportion on all shares, the shareholders shall first receive out of the distributable profit an amount of four percent of their contributions. If the profit is insufficient to make such payment, the distributable amount shall be determined on the basis of an appropriately lower percentage. Contributions made during the course of the fiscal year shall be taken into account in proportion to the time elapsed since the contribution was made.

(3) The articles of incorporation may provide for some other method of profit distribution.

§ 61
Compensation for Other Performances

For recurring performances which the shareholders are required to render in addition to their contributions to the stated capital pursuant to the articles of incorporation, a consideration not exceeding the value of such performances may be paid irrespective of whether or not the balance sheet shows retained earnings.

§ 62
Liability of Shareholders upon Receipt of Prohibited Payments

(1) The shareholders shall return to the company payments received from it contrary to the provisions of this Act. If such amounts were received in the form of distributions of profit or interest, they are liable only if they knew that they were not entitled to such payments, or if their lack of knowledge was due to gross negligence. In case of a contest as to whether the requirements of the second sentence hereof are met, the shareholders shall bear the burden of proof.

(2) The company's claims may also be enforced by the company's creditors if they cannot demand payment from the company. If the company's assets have been subjected to bankruptcy proceedings, the receiver in bankruptcy shall, dur-

§ 60
Gewinnverteilung

(1) Die Anteile der Aktionäre am Gewinn bestimmen sich nach dem Verhältnis der Aktiennennbeträge.

(2) Sind die Einlagen auf das Grundkapital nicht auf alle Aktien in demselben Verhältnis geleistet, so erhalten die Aktionäre aus dem verteilbaren Gewinn vorweg einen Betrag von vier vom Hundert der geleisteten Einlagen. Reicht der Gewinn dazu nicht aus, so bestimmt sich der Betrag nach einem entsprechend niedrigeren Satz. Einlagen, die im Laufe des Geschäftsjahrs geleistet wurden, werden nach dem Verhältnis der Zeit berücksichtigt, die seit der Leistung verstrichen ist.

(3) Die Satzung kann eine andere Art der Gewinnverteilung bestimmen.

§ 61
Vergütung von Nebenleistungen

Für wiederkehrende Leistungen, zu denen Aktionäre nach der Satzung neben den Einlagen auf das Grundkapital verpflichtet sind, darf eine den Wert der Leistungen nicht übersteigende Vergütung ohne Rücksicht darauf gezahlt werden, ob ein Bilanzgewinn ausgewiesen wird.

§ 62
Haftung der Aktionäre beim Empfang verbotener Leistungen

(1) Die Aktionäre haben der Gesellschaft Leistungen, die sie entgegen den Vorschriften dieses Gesetzes von ihr empfangen haben, zurückzugewähren. Haben sie Beträge als Gewinnanteile oder Zinsen bezogen, so besteht die Verpflichtung nur, wenn sie wußten oder infolge grober Fahrlässigkeit nicht wußten, daß sie zum Bezuge nicht berechtigt waren. Ist streitig, ob die Voraussetzungen des Satzes 2 vorliegen, so trifft die Beweislast die Aktionäre.

(2) Der Anspruch der Gesellschaft kann auch von den Gläubigern der Gesellschaft geltend gemacht werden, soweit sie von dieser keine Befriedigung erlangen können. Ist über das Vermögen der Gesellschaft das Konkursverfahren eröffnet, so übt wäh-

rend dessen Dauer der Konkursverwalter das Recht der Gesellschaftsgläubiger gegen die Aktionäre aus.

(3) Die Ansprüche nach diesen Vorschriften verjähren in fünf Jahren seit dem Empfang der Leistung.

§ 63
Folgen nicht rechtzeitiger Einzahlung

(1) Die Aktionäre haben die Einlagen nach Aufforderung durch den Vorstand einzuzahlen. Die Aufforderung ist, wenn die Satzung nichts anderes bestimmt, in den Gesellschaftsblättern bekanntzumachen.

(2) Aktionäre, die den eingeforderten Betrag nicht rechtzeitig einzahlen, haben ihn vom Eintritt der Fälligkeit an mit fünf vom Hundert für das Jahr zu verzinsen. Die Geltendmachung eines weiteren Schadens ist nicht ausgeschlossen.

(3) Für den Fall nicht rechtzeitiger Einzahlung kann die Satzung Vertragsstrafen festsetzen.

§ 64
Ausschluß säumiger Aktionäre

(1) Aktionären, die den eingeforderten Betrag nicht rechtzeitig einzahlen, kann eine Nachfrist mit der Androhung gesetzt werden, daß sie nach Fristablauf ihrer Aktien und der geleisteten Einzahlungen für verlustig erklärt werden.

(2) Die Nachfrist muß dreimal in den Gesellschaftsblättern bekanntgemacht werden. Die erste Bekanntmachung muß mindestens drei Monate, die letzte mindestens einen Monat vor Fristablauf ergehen. Zwischen den einzelnen Bekanntmachungen muß ein Zeitraum von mindestens drei Wochen liegen. Ist die Übertragung der Aktien an die Zustimmung der Gesellschaft gebunden, so genügt an Stelle der öffentlichen Bekanntmachung die einmalige Einzelaufforderung an die säumigen Aktionäre; dabei muß eine Nachfrist gewährt werden, die mindestens einen Monat seit dem Empfang der Aufforderung beträgt.

(3) Aktionäre, die den eingeforderten Betrag trotzdem nicht zahlen, werden durch Bekanntmachung in den Gesellschaftsblättern ihrer Aktien und der geleisteten Einzahlungen zugunsten der Gesellschaft für verlustig erklärt. In der Bekannt-

ing the pendency of the proceedings, exercise the rights of the company's creditors against the shareholders.

(3) The claims under these provisions shall be barred after the expiration of five years from receipt of the payment.

§ 63
Consequences of Delayed Payment of Contributions

(1) The shareholders shall be required to pay in their contributions upon a call by the managing board. This request shall be published in the publications designated in the company's articles of incorporation unless the articles of incorporation provide otherwise.

(2) Shareholders who fail to make timely payment of the amount called in shall be required to pay interest thereon from the due date at five percent per annum. This shall not preclude an action for further damages.

(3) The articles of incorporation may provide for penalties for late payment.

§ 64
Expulsion of Defaulting Shareholders

(1) Shareholders who fail to make timely payment of the amounts called in may be given additional time, with the warning that upon expiration of this period their shares and any payments made thereon shall be declared forfeited.

(2) The additional period of time shall be published three times in the publications designated in the company's articles of incorporation. The first publication shall take place no later than three months, and the last no later than one month, prior to the expiration of this period. There must be an interval of at least three weeks between the publications. If the transfer of the shares is subject to the approval of the company, in lieu of a public announcement, a single notice addressed to the defaulting shareholders shall be sufficient; in this event, a grace period of no less than one month from the date of receipt of the notice shall be granted.

(3) Shareholders who nevertheless fail to pay the amount called in shall, by means of an announcement in the publications designated in the company's articles of incorporation, be declared to have forfeited in favor of the company

their shares and any payments made. The announcement shall specify the shares declared to be forfeited along with their distinctive markings.

machung sind die für verlustig erklärten Aktien mit ihren Unterscheidungsmerkmalen anzugeben.

(4) In lieu of the old share certificates, new ones shall be issued, which shall specify the amount uncollected in addition to any partial payments made. The shareholder expelled shall be liable to the company for any losses it may sustain with respect to this amount or any amounts subsequently called in.

(4) An Stelle der alten Urkunden werden neue ausgegeben; diese haben außer den geleisteten Teilzahlungen den rückständigen Betrag anzugeben. Für den Ausfall der Gesellschaft an diesem Betrag oder an den später eingeforderten Beträgen haftet ihr der ausgeschlossene Aktionär.

§ 65
Obligation to Pay of Predecessors in Interest

§ 65
Zahlungspflicht der Vormänner

(1) Each predecessor of the expelled shareholder, if such predecessor has been recorded in the stock register, shall be liable to the company for the payment of the amount uncollected to the extent that it cannot be collected from his successors. The company shall inform the immediate predecessor of any call for payment addressed to a former shareholder. If payment has not been received within one month from the call for payment and the notice to the predecessor, it shall be presumed that it is not forthcoming. A new certificate shall be issued upon payment of the amount uncollected.

(1) Jeder im Aktienbuch verzeichnete Vormann des ausgeschlossenen Aktionärs ist der Gesellschaft zur Zahlung des rückständigen Betrags verpflichtet, soweit dieser von seinen Nachmännern nicht zu erlangen ist. Von der Zahlungsaufforderung an einen früheren Aktionär hat die Gesellschaft seinen unmittelbaren Vormann zu benachrichtigen. Daß die Zahlung nicht zu erlangen ist, wird vermutet, wenn sie nicht innerhalb eines Monats seit der Zahlungsaufforderung und der Benachrichtigung des Vormanns eingegangen ist. Gegen Zahlung des rückständigen Betrags wird die neue Urkunde ausgehändigt.

(2) Each predecessor shall be liable for payment only with respect to amounts called in within two years. This period shall be computed from the date on which the transfer of the share is reported for recording in the company's stock register.

(2) Jeder Vormann ist nur zur Zahlung der Beträge verpflichtet, die binnen zwei Jahren eingefordert werden. Die Frist beginnt mit dem Tage, an dem die Übertragung der Aktie zum Aktienbuch der Gesellschaft angemeldet wird.

(3) If payment of the amount uncollected cannot be obtained from the predecessors, the company shall promptly sell the share at its official exchange quotation through a broker or, if there is no exchange quotation, by means of public auction. If a favorable result cannot be expected from an auction at the company's domicile, the share shall be sold at some other appropriate place. The time, place and object of the auction shall be publicly announced. The expelled shareholder and his predecessors shall be notified separately; such notification is not required if it would be impracticable. The publication and the notification shall be effected no less than two weeks prior to the auction.

(3) Ist die Zahlung des rückständigen Betrags von Vormännern nicht zu erlangen, so hat die Gesellschaft die Aktie unverzüglich zum amtlichen Börsenpreis durch Vermittlung eines Kursmaklers und beim Fehlen eines Börsenpreises durch öffentliche Versteigerung zu verkaufen. Ist von der Versteigerung am Sitz der Gesellschaft kein angemessener Erfolg zu erwarten, so ist die Aktie an einem geeigneten Ort zu verkaufen. Zeit, Ort und Gegenstand der Versteigerung sind öffentlich bekanntzumachen. Der ausgeschlossene Aktionär und seine Vormänner sind besonders zu benachrichtigen; die Benachrichtigung kann unterbleiben, wenn sie untunlich ist. Bekanntmachung und Benachrichtigung müssen mindestens zwei Wochen vor der Versteigerung ergehen.

§ 66

**Keine Befreiung der Aktionäre
von ihren Leistungspflichten**

(1) Die Aktionäre und ihre Vormänner können von ihren Leistungspflichten nach den §§ 54 und 65 nicht befreit werden. Gegen eine Forderung der Gesellschaft nach den §§ 54 und 65 ist die Aufrechnung nicht zulässig.

(2) Absatz 1 gilt entsprechend für die Verpflichtung zur Rückgewähr von Leistungen, die entgegen den Vorschriften dieses Gesetzes empfangen sind, für die Ausfallhaftung des ausgeschlossenen Aktionärs sowie für die Schadenersatzpflicht des Aktionärs wegen nicht gehöriger Leistung einer Sacheinlage.

(3) Durch eine ordentliche Kapitalherabsetzung oder durch eine Kapitalherabsetzung durch Einziehung von Aktien können die Aktionäre von der Verpflichtung zur Leistung von Einlagen befreit werden, durch eine ordentliche Kapitalherabsetzung jedoch höchstens in Höhe des Betrags, um den das Grundkapital herabgesetzt worden ist.

§ 66
No Waiver of Shareholders' Obligation to Perform

(1) The shareholders and their predecessors cannot be relieved of their obligations to render performance pursuant to §§ 54 and 65. A set-off against the claims of the company pursuant to §§ 54 and 65 shall be ineffective.

(2) Paragraph 1 hereof shall apply, *mutatis mutandis,* to the obligation to return any contributions received in violation of the provisions of this Act, to the liability for non-collection of the expelled shareholder, and to the liability of a shareholder for insufficient performance with respect to a contribution of assets.

(3) The shareholders may be relieved of the obligation to render contributions by means of an ordinary capital reduction or a reduction of capital by redemption of shares; however, in the case of an ordinary capital reduction, only up to the amount by which the stated capital has been reduced.

§ 67

Eintragung im Aktienbuch

(1) Namensaktien sind unter Bezeichnung des Inhabers nach Namen, Wohnort und Beruf in das Aktienbuch der Gesellschaft einzutragen.

(2) Im Verhältnis zur Gesellschaft gilt als Aktionär nur, wer als solcher im Aktienbuch eingetragen ist.

(3) Ist jemand nach Ansicht der Gesellschaft zu Unrecht als Aktionär in das Aktienbuch eingetragen worden, so kann die Gesellschaft die Eintragung nur löschen, wenn sie vorher die Beteiligten von der beabsichtigten Löschung benachrichtigt und ihnen eine angemessene Frist zur Geltendmachung eines Widerspruchs gesetzt hat. Widerspricht ein Beteiligter innerhalb der Frist, so hat die Löschung zu unterbleiben.

(4) Diese Vorschriften gelten sinngemäß für Zwischenscheine.

(5) Jedem Aktionär ist auf Verlangen Einsicht in das Aktienbuch zu gewähren.

§ 67
Recording in Stock Register

(1) Registered shares shall be recorded in the company's stock register, designating the holder by name, residence, and occupation.

(2) In relation to the company, only such persons as are registered in the stock register shall be considered as shareholders.

(3) In the event that, in the opinion of the company, a person was wrongly registered as a shareholder in the stock register, the company may cancel the entry only if it previously informed the parties concerned of the intended cancellation and granted them a reasonable period of time to raise objections. If a party concerned raises objections within such time limit, the cancellation may not be made.

(4) These provisions shall apply, *mutatis mutandis,* to interim certificates.

(5) Each shareholder shall be permitted to inspect the stock register upon request.

§ **67**

§ 68

Transfer of Registered Shares.
Transfer Entries in the Stock Register

(1) Registered shares may be transferred by endorsement. Articles 12, 13 and 16 of the *Wechselgesetz* shall apply, *mutatis mutandis* to the form of the endorsement, the proof of ownership in the holder and his obligation to surrender possession.

(2) The articles of incorporation may make the transfer subject to the consent of the company. Such consent is given by the managing board. However, the articles of incorporation may provide that a resolution by the supervisory board or the shareholders' meeting is required for such consent. The articles of incorporation may specify the reasons for which the consent may be refused.

(3) The company shall be notified of any transfer of a registered share to another party. The share certificate shall be presented and evidence of the transfer shall be given. The company shall record the transfer in the stock register.

(4) The company shall be required to examine the regularity of the chain of endorsements and declarations of assignment, but not the signatures.

(5) These provisions shall apply, *mutatis mutandis,* to interim certificates.

§ 68

Übertragung von Namensaktien.
Umschreibung im Aktienbuch

(1) Namensaktien können durch Indossament übertragen werden. Für die Form des Indossaments, den Rechtsausweis des Inhabers und seine Verpflichtung zur Herausgabe gelten sinngemäß Artikel 12, 13 und 16 des Wechselgesetzes.

(2) Die Satzung kann die Übertragung an die Zustimmung der Gesellschaft binden. Die Zustimmung erteilt der Vorstand. Die Satzung kann jedoch bestimmen, daß der Aufsichtsrat oder die Hauptversammlung über die Erteilung der Zustimmung beschließt. Die Satzung kann die Gründe bestimmen, aus denen die Zustimmung verweigert werden darf.

(3) Geht die Namensaktie auf einen anderen über, so ist dies bei der Gesellschaft anzumelden. Die Aktie ist vorzulegen und der Übergang nachzuweisen. Die Gesellschaft vermerkt den Übergang im Aktienbuch.

(4) Die Gesellschaft ist verpflichtet, die Ordnungsmäßigkeit der Reihe der Indossamente und der Abtretungserklärungen, aber nicht die Unterschriften zu prüfen.

(5) Diese Vorschriften gelten sinngemäß für Zwischenscheine.

§ 69

Rights in Common to a Share

(1) If several parties are entitled to a share, they may exercise the rights conferred by the share only through a common representative.

(2) They shall be jointly and severally liable for any performances to be rendered on the share.

(3) For declarations with legal effect by the company to the shareholder, it shall suffice, in the event that the parties in interest have not designated to the company a common representative, to address such declarations to one of the parties in interest. In the case of a plurality of heirs of a shareholder, this shall apply only to such declarations as are effected after the expiration of one month from the date of succession.

§ 69

Rechtsgemeinschaft an einer Aktie

(1) Steht eine Aktie mehreren Berechtigten zu, so können sie die Rechte aus der Aktie nur durch einen gemeinschaftlichen Vertreter ausüben.

(2) Für die Leistungen auf die Aktie haften sie als Gesamtschuldner.

(3) Hat die Gesellschaft eine Willenserklärung dem Aktionär gegenüber abzugeben, so genügt, wenn die Berechtigten der Gesellschaft keinen gemeinschaftlichen Vertreter benannt haben, die Abgabe der Erklärung gegenüber einem Berechtigten. Bei mehreren Erben eines Aktionärs gilt dies nur für Willenserklärungen, die nach Ablauf eines Monats seit dem Anfall der Erbschaft abgegeben werden.

§ 70

Berechnung der Aktienbesitzzeit

Ist die Ausübung von Rechten aus der Aktie davon abhängig, daß der Aktionär während eines bestimmten Zeitraums Inhaber der Aktie gewesen ist, so steht dem Eigentum ein Anspruch auf Übereignung gegen ein Kreditinstitut gleich. Die Eigentumszeit eines Rechtsvorgängers wird dem Aktionär zugerechnet, wenn er die Aktie unentgeltlich, von seinem Treuhänder, als Gesamtrechtsnachfolger, bei Auseinandersetzung einer Gemeinschaft oder bei einer Bestandsübertragung nach § 14 des Gesetzes über die Beaufsichtigung der privaten Versicherungsunternehmungen und Bausparkassen erworben hat.

§ 71

Erwerb eigener Aktien

(1) Die Gesellschaft darf eigene Aktien nur erwerben,

1. wenn der Erwerb notwendig ist, um einen schweren Schaden von der Gesellschaft abzuwenden,

2. wenn die Aktien den Arbeitnehmern der Gesellschaft zum Erwerb angeboten werden sollen,

3. wenn der Erwerb geschieht, um Aktionäre nach § 305 Abs. 2 oder § 320 Abs. 5 abzufinden,

4. wenn auf die Aktien der Nennbetrag oder der höhere Ausgabebetrag voll geleistet ist und der Erwerb unentgeltlich geschieht oder die Gesellschaft mit dem Erwerb eine Einkaufskommission ausführt,

5. durch Gesamtrechtsnachfolge oder

6. auf Grund eines Beschlusses der Hauptversammlung zur Einziehung nach den Vorschriften über die Herabsetzung des Grundkapitals.

Der Gesamtnennbetrag der zu den Zwecken nach Nummern 1 bis 3 erworbenen Aktien darf jedoch zusammen mit dem Betrag anderer Aktien der Gesellschaft, die die Gesellschaft oder ein abhängiges oder ein in ihrem Mehrheitsbesitz stehendes Unternehmen oder ein für Rechnung der Gesellschaft oder eines abhängigen oder eines in ihrem Mehrheitsbesitz stehenden Unternehmens bereits zu diesen Zwecken erworben hat und noch besitzt, zehn vom Hundert des Grundkapitals nicht übersteigen.

(2) Ein Verstoß gegen Absatz 1 macht den Erwerb eigener Aktien nur unwirksam, wenn auf sie der Nennbetrag oder der höhere Ausgabebetrag noch nicht voll geleistet ist. Ein schuldrechtliches

§ 70

Computation of Period of Share Ownership

Where the exercise of rights attributable to a share is dependent on the shareholder's holding of such share for a certain period of time, the right to demand transfer of title from a bank shall be considered equivalent to ownership. The period of ownership of a predecessor shall be attributed to the shareholder if he has acquired the share gratuitously or from his trustee, or as a successor in interest, or upon partition of a community of interest, or by virtue of an assignment pursuant to § 14 of the *Gesetz über die Beaufsichtigung der privaten Versicherungsunternehmungen und Bausparkassen.*

§ 71

Acquisition of Own Shares by the Company

(1) The company may acquire its own shares only in the following instances:

1. if the acquisition is necessary to avoid a serious injury to the company,

2. if such shares are to be offered to the company's employees for acquisition by them,

3. if the purpose of the acquisition is to indemnify shareholders pursuant to § 305, paragraph 2, or § 320, paragraph 5,

4. if the par value of the shares plus any premium has been paid in full and if such acquisition is gratuitous or undertaken by the company in the execution of a purchaser's order,

5. through a succession in interest, or

6. pursuant to a shareholders' resolution for redemption in accordance with the provisions concerning reduction of the stated capital.

The total par value of the shares acquired for the purposes specified in Nos. 1 to 3 hereof, together with the amount of other shares of the company already acquired for such purposes and still held by the company or by a controlled enterprise or a majority-owned enterprise, or by another party for the account of the company or a controlled enterprise or a majority-owned enterprise, shall, however, in no event exceed ten percent of the stated capital.

(2) A violation of paragraph 1 hereof shall render the acquisition of the company's own shares invalid only if the par value plus any premium has not been paid in full. The agree-

ment underlying the acquisition of its own shares shall be invalid to the extent that the acquisition violates paragraph 1 hereof.

(3) The acceptance by a company of its own shares as a pledge shall be tantamount to an acquisition of its own shares. However, a bank may accept its own shares as a pledge up to the total par value specified in paragraph 1, second sentence, hereof; such shares shall be added to the shares that have been pledged to the company for the purposes specified in paragraph 1, Nos. 1 to 3, hereof.

(4) A controlled enterprise may acquire shares of the controlling company or accept them as a pledge, and a majority-owned enterprise may acquire shares of the majority-owning company or accept them as a pledge, only to the extent that the controlling or the majority-owning company could do so pursuant to paragraph 1, Nos. 1 to 5, and paragraph 3, second sentence, hereof. A violation of the preceding sentence does not render the acquisition or the pledge of the shares invalid; however, the agreement underlying the unlawful acquisition or an unlawful pledge shall be void.

(5) A transaction between the company or a controlled or majority-owned enterprise and another whereby the latter is entitled or obligated to acquire or to accept as a pledge the company's own shares for the account of the company, the controlled enterprise, or the majority-owned enterprise shall be void to the extent that the acquisition or the acceptance as a pledge of the shares by the company, the controlled enterprise, or the majority-owned enterprise violates paragraphs 1, 3 and 4 hereof.

(6) The company shall not be entitled to the rights of a shareholder with respect to its own shares. The same shall apply with respect to shares held by another for the account of the company.

§ 72

Cancellation of Certificates

(1) In the event that a share certificate or an interim certificate has been lost or destroyed, the certificate may be invalidated by means of the cancellation proceeding pursuant to the Code of Civil Procedure. § 799, paragraph 2, and § 800 of the Civil Code shall apply *mutatis mutandis*.

§ 72

Geschäft über den Erwerb eigener Aktien ist nichtig, soweit der Erwerb gegen Absatz 1 verstößt.

(3) Dem Erwerb eigener Aktien steht es gleich, wenn eigene Aktien als Pfand genommen werden. Jedoch darf ein Kreditinstitut eigene Aktien bis zu dem in Absatz 1 Satz 2 bestimmten Gesamtnennbetrag als Pfand nehmen; sie rechnen zu den Aktien, die zu den Zwecken nach Absatz 1 Nr. 1 bis 3 als Pfand genommen sind.

(4) Ein abhängiges Unternehmen darf Aktien der herrschenden Gesellschaft, ein im Mehrheitsbesitz stehendes Unternehmen Aktien der an ihm mit Mehrheit beteiligten Gesellschaft nur erwerben oder als Pfand nehmen, soweit dies der herrschenden oder mit Mehrheit beteiligten Gesellschaft nach Absatz 1 Nr. 1 bis 5, Absatz 3 Satz 2 gestattet wäre. Ein Verstoß gegen Satz 1 macht den Erwerb oder die Inpfandnahme der Aktien nicht unwirksam; jedoch ist das schuldrechtliche Geschäft über einen verbotswidrigen Erwerb oder eine verbotswidrige Inpfandnahme nichtig.

(5) Ein Rechtsgeschäft zwischen der Gesellschaft oder einem abhängigen oder in ihrem Mehrheitsbesitz stehenden Unternehmen und einem anderen, nach dem dieser berechtigt oder verpflichtet sein soll, eigene Aktien der Gesellschaft für Rechnung der Gesellschaft oder des abhängigen oder des in ihrem Mehrheitsbesitz stehenden Unternehmens zu erwerben oder als Pfand zu nehmen, ist nichtig, soweit der Erwerb oder die Inpfandnahme der Aktien durch die Gesellschaft oder das abhängige oder das in ihrem Mehrheitsbesitz stehende Unternehmen gegen die Absätze 1, 3 und 4 verstößt.

(6) Aus eigenen Aktien stehen der Gesellschaft keine Rechte zu. Gleiches gilt für Aktien, die einem anderen für Rechnung der Gesellschaft gehören.

§ 72

Kraftloserklärung von Aktien im Aufgebotsverfahren

(1) Ist eine Aktie oder ein Zwischenschein abhanden gekommen oder vernichtet, so kann die Urkunde im Aufgebotsverfahren nach der Zivilprozeßordnung für kraftlos erklärt werden. § 799 Abs. 2 und § 800 des Bürgerlichen Gesetzbuchs gelten sinngemäß.

(2) Sind Gewinnanteilscheine auf den Inhaber ausgegeben, so erlischt mit der Kraftloserklärung der Aktie oder des Zwischenscheins auch der Anspruch aus den noch nicht fälligen Gewinnanteilscheinen.

(3) Die Kraftloserklärung einer Aktie nach §§ 73 oder 226 steht der Kraftloserklärung der Urkunde nach Absatz 1 nicht entgegen.

(2) In the event that coupons are issued to bearer, the rights attributable to coupons which have not as yet matured shall expire upon the cancellation of the share certificate or the interim certificate.

(3) The cancellation of a share certificate pursuant to § 73 or 226 shall not bar the cancellation of the share certificate pursuant to paragraph 1 hereof.

§ 73
Kraftloserklärung von Aktien durch die Gesellschaft

(1) Ist der Inhalt von Aktienurkunden durch eine Veränderung der rechtlichen Verhältnisse unrichtig geworden, so kann die Gesellschaft die Aktien, die trotz Aufforderung nicht zur Berichtigung oder zum Umtausch bei ihr eingereicht sind, mit Genehmigung des Gerichts für kraftlos erklären. Beruht die Unrichtigkeit auf einer Änderung des Nennbetrags der Aktien, so können sie nur dann für kraftlos erklärt werden, wenn der Nennbetrag zur Herabsetzung des Grundkapitals herabgesetzt ist. Namensaktien können nicht deshalb für kraftlos erklärt werden, weil die Bezeichnung des Aktionärs unrichtig geworden ist. Gegen die Entscheidung des Gerichts ist die sofortige Beschwerde zulässig; eine Anfechtung der Entscheidung, durch die die Genehmigung erteilt wird, ist ausgeschlossen.

(2) Die Aufforderung, die Aktien einzureichen, hat die Kraftloserklärung anzudrohen und auf die Genehmigung des Gerichts hinzuweisen. Die Kraftloserklärung kann nur erfolgen, wenn die Aufforderung in der in § 64 Abs. 2 für die Nachfrist vorgeschriebenen Weise bekanntgemacht worden ist. Die Kraftloserklärung geschieht durch Bekanntmachung in den Gesellschaftsblättern. In der Bekanntmachung sind die für kraftlos erklärten Aktien so zu bezeichnen, daß sich aus der Bekanntmachung ohne weiteres ergibt, ob eine Aktie für kraftlos erklärt ist.

(3) An Stelle der für kraftlos erklärten Aktien sind neue Aktien auszugeben und dem Berechtigten auszuhändigen oder, wenn ein Recht zur Hinterlegung besteht, zu hinterlegen. Die Aushändigung oder Hinterlegung ist dem Gericht anzuzeigen.

§ 73
Cancellation of Certificates by the Company

(1) If the content of share certificates has become incorrect through a change in legal circumstances, the company may, with the permission of the court, cancel any share certificates which, in spite of a notice to this effect, have not been turned over to it for correction or exchange. If the incorrectness relates to a change in the par value of the shares, the certificates may be cancelled only if the par value has been reduced to effect a capital reduction. Registered shares may not be cancelled merely because the designation of the shareholder has become incorrect. The decision of the court may be appealed; however, a decision granting permission to cancel the certificate is not subject to appeal.

(2) The notice to surrender share certificates shall contain a warning to the effect that they will be cancelled and shall refer to the permission of the court. The cancellation may be issued only if notice has been given in the manner provided for in § 64, paragraph 2, for the grace period. The cancellation shall become effective upon publication in the publications designated in the company's articles of incorporation. The shares cancelled shall be designated in the publication in such a manner that it will be clearly indicated in the publication whether a specific share certificate has been cancelled.

(3) In lieu of the share certificates cancelled, new share certificates shall be issued and delivered to the person entitled thereto or, if the company has a right to deposit them with the court, they shall be so deposited. The court shall be notified of the delivery or the deposit.

§ 73

(4) To the extent that shares are consolidated to effect a capital reduction, §226 shall be applicable.

§74
New Certificates in Lieu of Damaged or Defaced Share or Interim Certificates

If a share certificate or an interim certificate has been damaged or defaced in such a manner that the certificate is no longer suitable for circulation, the party entitled thereto may request the company to issue a new certificate against delivery of the old one, if the essential content and the distinctive markings of the certificate are still recognizable with certainty. Such party shall bear the expenses and advance same.

§75
New Dividend Coupons

New dividend coupons shall not be issued to the holder of the renewal coupon if the holder of the share certificate or of the interim certificate opposes the issuance; they shall be issued to the holder of the share certificate or the interim certificate upon presentation of the principal instrument.

Part Four
Constitution of the Stock Corporation

First Division
Managing Board

§76
Directing the Stock Corporation

(1) The managing board is charged with the personal responsibility of directing the company.

(2) The managing board may consist of one or several persons. In the case of companies having a stated capital of more than three million

§ 74

---

(4) Soweit zur Herabsetzung des Grundkapitals Aktien zusammengelegt werden, gilt § 226.

§ 74
Neue Urkunden an Stelle beschädigter oder verunstalteter Aktien oder Zwischenscheine

Ist eine Aktie oder ein Zwischenschein so beschädigt oder verunstaltet, daß die Urkunde zum Umlauf nicht mehr geeignet ist, so kann der Berechtigte, wenn der wesentliche Inhalt und die Unterscheidungsmerkmale der Urkunde noch sicher zu erkennen sind, von der Gesellschaft die Erteilung einer neuen Urkunde gegen Aushändigung der alten verlangen. Die Kosten hat er zu tragen und vorzuschießen.

§ 75
Neue Gewinnanteilscheine

Neue Gewinnanteilscheine dürfen an den Inhaber des Erneuerungsscheins nicht ausgegeben werden, wenn der Besitzer der Aktie oder des Zwischenscheins der Ausgabe widerspricht; sie sind dem Besitzer der Aktie oder des Zwischenscheins auszuhändigen, wenn er die Haupturkunde vorlegt.

Vierter Teil
Verfassung der Aktiengesellschaft

Erster Abschnitt
Vorstand

§ 76
Leitung der Aktiengesellschaft

(1) Der Vorstand hat unter eigener Verantwortung die Gesellschaft zu leiten.

(2) Der Vorstand kann aus einer oder mehreren Personen bestehen. Bei Gesellschaften mit einem Grundkapital von mehr als drei Millionen Deutsche

Mark hat er aus mindestens zwei Personen zu bestehen, es sei denn, die Satzung bestimmt, daß er aus einer Person besteht. Die Vorschriften über die Bestellung eines Arbeitsdirektors bleiben unberührt.

(3) Mitglied des Vorstands kann nur eine natürliche, unbeschränkt geschäftsfähige Person sein.

§ 77
Geschäftsführung

(1) Besteht der Vorstand aus mehreren Personen, so sind sämtliche Vorstandsmitglieder nur gemeinschaftlich zur Geschäftsführung befugt. Die Satzung oder die Geschäftsordnung des Vorstands kann Abweichendes bestimmen; es kann jedoch nicht bestimmt werden, daß ein oder mehrere Vorstandsmitglieder Meinungsverschiedenheiten im Vorstand gegen die Mehrheit seiner Mitglieder entscheiden.

(2) Der Vorstand kann sich eine Geschäftsordnung geben, wenn nicht die Satzung den Erlaß der Geschäftsordnung dem Aufsichtsrat übertragen hat oder der Aufsichtsrat eine Geschäftsordnung für den Vorstand erläßt. Die Satzung kann Einzelfragen der Geschäftsordnung bindend regeln. Beschlüsse des Vorstands über die Geschäftsordnung müssen einstimmig gefaßt werden.

§ 78
Vertretung

(1) Der Vorstand vertritt die Gesellschaft gerichtlich und außergerichtlich.

(2) Besteht der Vorstand aus mehreren Personen, so sind, wenn die Satzung nichts anderes bestimmt, sämtliche Vorstandsmitglieder nur gemeinschaftlich zur Vertretung der Gesellschaft befugt. Ist eine Willenserklärung gegenüber der Gesellschaft abzugeben, so genügt die Abgabe gegenüber einem Vorstandsmitglied.

(3) Die Satzung kann auch bestimmen, daß einzelne Vorstandsmitglieder allein oder in Gemeinschaft mit einem Prokuristen zur Vertretung der Gesellschaft befugt sind. Dasselbe kann der Aufsichtsrat bestimmen, wenn die Satzung ihn hierzu ermächtigt hat. Absatz 2 Satz 2 gilt in diesen Fällen sinngemäß.

German marks, it shall consist of no less than two persons, unless the articles of incorporation specify that it shall consist of one person. The provisions concerning the appointment of a manager representing the employees are not affected hereby.

(3) Only a natural person with full legal capacity can be a member of the managing board.

§ 77
Management

(1) If the managing board consists of several persons, the members of the managing board shall manage the company jointly. The articles of incorporation or the rules of procedure of the managing board may provide otherwise; however, they may not provide that one or several members of the managing board shall, in case of a difference of opinion within the board, be able to overrule the majority of its members.

(2) The managing board may establish rules of procedure, unless the articles of incorporation provide that such rules shall be established by the supervisory board, or unless the supervisory board has in fact established such rules for the managing board. The articles of incorporation may contain binding provisions on specific questions relating to the rules of procedure. Resolutions of the managing board concerning the rules of procedure require unanimity.

§ 78
Representation

(1) The managing board shall represent the company both in and out of court.

(2) If the managing board consists of several persons, all members of the managing board shall represent the company jointly, unless the articles of incorporation provide otherwise. If declarations with legal effect are to be addressed to the company, it shall be sufficient to address them to a member of the managing board.

(3) The articles of incorporation may also provide that individual members of the managing board can represent the company alone or together with a *Prokurist*. The same provision may be made by the supervisory board if the articles of incorporation authorize it to do so. Paragraph 2, second sentence, hereof shall apply in such cases *mutatis mutandis*.

§ 78

(4) Members of the managing board authorized to represent the company jointly may authorize individual members to carry out specified transactions or specified types of transactions. The same shall apply, *mutatis mutandis*, if an individual member of the managing board is empowered to represent the company together with a *Prokurist*.

(4) Zur Gesamtvertretung befugte Vorstandsmitglieder können einzelne von ihnen zur Vornahme bestimmter Geschäfte oder bestimmter Arten von Geschäften ermächtigen. Dies gilt sinngemäß, wenn ein einzelnes Vorstandsmitglied in Gemeinschaft mit einem Prokuristen zur Vertretung der Gesellschaft befugt ist.

§ 79
Signature by Members of Managing Board

Members of the managing board shall sign for the company by adding their own signatures to the name of the company or to the designation "managing board."

§ 79
Zeichnung durch Vorstandsmitglieder

Vorstandsmitglieder zeichnen für die Gesellschaft, indem sie der Firma der Gesellschaft oder der Benennung des Vorstands ihre Namensunterschrift hinzufügen.

§ 80
Names on Business Correspondence

All business correspondence directed to a specific addressee shall list all of the members of the managing board and the chairman of the supervisory board by their family names and at least one of their full given names and shall state the company's domicile. The chairman of the managing board shall be designated as such. This designation shall not be required in the case of communications or reports customarily made on printed forms, in which only the details relevant to the specific case need be inserted.

§ 80
Namensangabe

Auf allen Geschäftsbriefen, die an einen bestimmten Empfänger gerichtet werden, müssen alle Vorstandsmitglieder und der Vorsitzende des Aufsichtsrats mit dem Familiennamen und mindestens einem ausgeschriebenen Vornamen sowie der Sitz der Gesellschaft angegeben werden. Der Vorsitzende des Vorstands ist als solcher zu bezeichnen. Der Angabe bedarf es nicht bei Mitteilungen oder Berichten, für die üblicherweise Vordrucke verwendet werden, in denen lediglich die im Einzelfall erforderlichen besonderen Angaben eingefügt zu werden brauchen.

§ 81
Change in Managing Board and in Powers of Representation of Its Members

(1) Any change in the managing board or in the power of representation of a member of the managing board, as well as any provision made by the supervisory board pursuant to § 78, paragraph 3, second sentence, shall be submitted by the managing board for recording in the Commercial Register.

§ 81
Änderung des Vorstands und der Vertretungsbefugnis seiner Mitglieder

(1) Jede Änderung des Vorstands oder der Vertretungsbefugnis eines Vorstandsmitglieds sowie eine Anordnung des Aufsichtsrats nach § 78 Abs. 3 Satz 2 hat der Vorstand zur Eintragung in das Handelsregister anzumelden.

(2) To the application for registration shall be attached the original or a certified copy of the documents concerning such change or provision, to be submitted to the court at the company's domicile.

(2) Der Anmeldung sind die Urkunden über die Änderung oder Anordnung in Urschrift oder öffentlich beglaubigter Abschrift für das Gericht des Sitzes der Gesellschaft beizufügen.

(3) New members of the managing board must deposit their signatures with the court.

(3) Die neuen Vorstandsmitglieder haben ihre Namensunterschrift zur Aufbewahrung beim Gericht zu zeichnen.

§ 82

**Beschränkungen der Vertretungs-
und Geschäftsführungsbefugnis**

(1) Die Vertretungsbefugnis des Vorstands kann nicht beschränkt werden.

(2) Im Verhältnis der Vorstandsmitglieder zur Gesellschaft sind diese verpflichtet, die Beschränkungen einzuhalten, die im Rahmen der Vorschriften über die Aktiengesellschaft die Satzung, der Aufsichtsrat, die Hauptversammlung und die Geschäftsordnungen des Vorstands und des Aufsichtsrats für die Geschäftsführungsbefugnis getroffen haben.

§ 83

**Vorbereitung und Ausführung
von Hauptversammlungsbeschlüssen**

(1) Der Vorstand ist auf Verlangen der Hauptversammlung verpflichtet, Maßnahmen, die in die Zuständigkeit der Hauptversammlung fallen, vorzubereiten. Das gleiche gilt für die Vorbereitung und den Abschluß von Verträgen, die nur mit Zustimmung der Hauptversammlung wirksam werden. Der Beschluß der Hauptversammlung bedarf der Mehrheiten, die für die Maßnahmen oder für die Zustimmung zu dem Vertrag erforderlich sind.

(2) Der Vorstand ist verpflichtet, die von der Hauptversammlung im Rahmen ihrer Zuständigkeit beschlossenen Maßnahmen auszuführen.

§ 84

Bestellung und Abberufung des Vorstands

(1) Vorstandsmitglieder bestellt der Aufsichtsrat auf höchstens fünf Jahre. Eine wiederholte Bestellung oder Verlängerung der Amtszeit, jeweils für höchstens fünf Jahre, ist zulässig. Sie bedarf eines erneuten Aufsichtsratsbeschlusses, der frühestens ein Jahr vor Ablauf der bisherigen Amtszeit gefaßt werden kann. Nur bei einer Bestellung auf weniger als fünf Jahre kann eine Verlängerung der Amtszeit ohne neuen Aufsichtsratsbeschluß vorgesehen werden, sofern dadurch die gesamte Amtszeit nicht mehr als fünf Jahre beträgt. Dies gilt sinngemäß für

§ 82

Restrictions on Power of Representation and Management

(1) The power of the managing board to represent the company cannot be limited.

(2) As between the company and the members of the managing board, the latter shall be required to comply with the restrictions on the power of management which, in accordance with the provisions governing the stock corporation, are prescribed by the articles of incorporation, by the supervisory board, by the shareholders, or by the rules of procedure of the managing board and of the supervisory board.

§ 83

Preparation and Implementation of Shareholders' Resolutions

(1) The managing board shall, at the request of the shareholders' meeting, be required to prepare any measures that are within the competence of the shareholders' meeting. The same shall apply with respect to the preparation and execution of agreements which require the approval of the shareholders' meeting to be valid. The relevant shareholders' resolution shall require the majorities necessary for such measures or for the approval of such agreements.

(2) The managing board shall be required to implement any measures adopted by the shareholders within their sphere of competence.

§ 84

Appointment and Dismissal of Managing Board

(1) The members of the managing board shall be appointed by the supervisory board for periods not exceeding five years. Reappointment or extension of their term of office for a maximum of five years is permissible. This shall require a further resolution of the supervisory board, which may be adopted no earlier than one year prior to the expiration of the preceding term of office. An extension of the term of office may be provided without a further resolution of the supervisory board only in case of an appointment for less than five years and only if the entire term does not thereby aggregate more than five years. The same shall apply, *mutatis mutandis,* for the employment contract, which may, however,

provide that in the event of an extension of the term of office, it shall continue in effect until the end of such term.

(2) If several persons are appointed members of the managing board, the supervisory board may designate one member to serve as chairman of the managing board.

(3) The supervisory board may revoke the appointment of any member of the managing board and the designation of the chairman of the managing board for compelling reasons. Such reasons are, in particular, gross breach of duty, inability to conduct the business of the company properly, or vote of no-confidence of the shareholders' meeting, unless such vote is based on obviously arbitrary grounds. This shall also apply to the initial managing board appointed by the supervisory board. The revocation shall be effective until such time as a final decision holding it invalid is rendered. Rights under an employment contract shall be governed by the general provisions of the law.

(4) The provisions concerning the special majorities required for a resolution by the supervisory board appointing a labor director or revoking the appointment of such director shall not be affected hereby.

§ 85
Appointment by the Court

(1) If the managing board lacks a necessary member, the court shall, in urgent cases, appoint such member upon application of a party in interest. This decision can be appealed.

(2) The office of the court-appointed member of the managing board shall terminate as soon as the vacancy is filled.

(3) A court-appointed member of the managing board shall be entitled to reimbursement for reasonable cash expenditures and remuneration for his services. If the court-appointed member of the managing board and the company cannot agree, the court shall determine such expenditures and remuneration. The decision of the court can be appealed. It shall not be subject to further appeal. The final decision shall be enforceable in accordance with the provisions of the Code of Civil Procedure.

§ 85

den Anstellungsvertrag; er kann jedoch vorsehen, daß er für den Fall einer Verlängerung der Amtszeit bis zu deren Ablauf weitergilt.

(2) Werden mehrere Personen zu Vorstandsmitgliedern bestellt, so kann der Aufsichtsrat ein Mitglied zum Vorsitzenden des Vorstands ernennen.

(3) Der Aufsichtsrat kann die Bestellung zum Vorstandsmitglied und die Ernennung zum Vorsitzenden des Vorstands widerrufen, wenn ein wichtiger Grund vorliegt. Ein solcher Grund ist namentlich grobe Pflichtverletzung, Unfähigkeit zur ordnungsmäßigen Geschäftsführung oder Vertrauensentzug durch die Hauptversammlung, es sei denn, daß das Vertrauen aus offenbar unsachlichen Gründen entzogen worden ist. Dies gilt auch für den vom ersten Aufsichtsrat bestellten Vorstand. Der Widerruf ist wirksam, bis seine Unwirksamkeit rechtskräftig festgestellt ist. Für die Ansprüche aus dem Anstellungsvertrag gelten die allgemeinen Vorschriften.

(4) Die Vorschriften über die besonderen Mehrheitserfordernisse für einen Aufsichtsratsbeschluß über die Bestellung eines Arbeitsdirektors oder den Widerruf seiner Bestellung bleiben unberührt.

§ 85
Bestellung durch das Gericht

(1) Fehlt ein erforderliches Vorstandsmitglied, so hat in dringenden Fällen das Gericht auf Antrag eines Beteiligten das Mitglied zu bestellen. Gegen die Entscheidung ist die sofortige Beschwerde zulässig.

(2) Das Amt des gerichtlich bestellten Vorstandsmitglieds erlischt in jedem Fall, sobald der Mangel behoben ist.

(3) Das gerichtlich bestellte Vorstandsmitglied hat Anspruch auf Ersatz angemessener barer Auslagen und auf Vergütung für seine Tätigkeit. Einigen sich das gerichtlich bestellte Vorstandsmitglied und die Gesellschaft nicht, so setzt das Gericht die Auslagen und die Vergütung fest. Gegen die Entscheidung ist die sofortige Beschwerde zulässig. Die weitere Beschwerde ist ausgeschlossen. Aus der rechtskräftigen Entscheidung findet die Zwangsvollstreckung nach der Zivilprozeßordnung statt.

§ 86

Gewinnbeteiligung der Vorstandsmitglieder

(1) Den Vorstandsmitgliedern kann für ihre Tätigkeit eine Beteiligung am Gewinn gewährt werden. Sie soll in der Regel in einem Anteil am Jahresgewinn der Gesellschaft ,bestehen.

(2) Wird den Vorstandsmitgliedern ein Anteil am Jahresgewinn der Gesellschaft gewährt, so berechnet sich der Anteil nach dem Jahresüberschuß, vermindert um einen Verlustvortrag aus dem Vorjahr und um die Beträge, die nach Gesetz oder Satzung aus dem Jahresüberschuß in offene Rücklagen einzustellen sind. Entgegenstehende Festsetzungen sind nichtig.

§ 87

Grundsätze für die Bezüge der Vorstandsmitglieder

(1) Der Aufsichtsrat hat bei der Festsetzung der Gesamtbezüge des einzelnen Vorstandsmitglieds (Gehalt, Gewinnbeteiligungen, Aufwandsentschädigungen, Versicherungsentgelte, Provisionen und Nebenleistungen jeder Art) dafür zu sorgen, daß die Gesamtbezüge in einem angemessenen Verhältnis zu den Aufgaben des Vorstandsmitglieds und zur Lage der Gesellschaft stehen. Dies gilt sinngemäß für Ruhegehalt, Hinterbliebenenbezüge und Leistungen verwandter Art.

(2) Tritt nach der Festsetzung eine so wesentliche Verschlechterung in den Verhältnissen der Gesellschaft ein, daß die Weitergewährung der in Absatz 1 Satz 1 aufgeführten Bezüge eine schwere Unbilligkeit für die Gesellschaft sein würde, so ist der Aufsichtsrat, im Fall des § 85 Abs. 3 das Gericht auf Antrag des Aufsichtsrats, zu einer angemessenen Herabsetzung berechtigt. Durch eine Herabsetzung wird der Anstellungsvertrag im übrigen nicht berührt. Das Vorstandsmitglied kann jedoch seinen Anstellungsvertrag für den Schluß des nächsten Kalendervierteljahrs mit einer Kündigungsfrist von sechs Wochen kündigen.

(3) Wird über das Vermögen der Gesellschaft das Konkursverfahren eröffnet und kündigt der Konkursverwalter den Anstellungsvertrag eines Vor-

§ 86

Profit Sharing by Members of the Managing Board

(1) Members of the managing board may, for their services, be granted the right to participate in the profit. Such participation shall, as a rule, consist of a portion of the company's profit for the year.

(2) If the members of the managing board have been granted the right to participate in the company's profit for the year, their share shall be computed by reference to the net profit for the year, reduced by the loss carry-forward from the preceding year and any amounts which, pursuant to the law or the articles of incorporation, must be allocated out of the profit for the year to disclosed reserves. Provisions to the contrary shall be void.

§ 87

Rules for Compensating Managing Board Members

(1) The supervisory board in fixing the total compensation of any member of the managing board (salary, profit sharing, allowance for expenses, insurance, commissions, and additional compensation of any kind), shall see to it that such total compensation bears a reasonable relationship to the functions of the member of the managing board and to the condition of the company. The same shall apply, *mutatis mutandis,* to pensions of the member or his survivors and similar payments.

(2) If, after the total compensation has been fixed, the company's condition deteriorates to such an extent that further payment of the compensation referred to in paragraph 1, first sentence, hereof would create a substantial hardship for the company, the supervisory board or, in the case of § 85, paragraph 3, the court upon request of the supervisory board shall have the power to order an appropriate reduction. Such reduction shall not affect the other provisions of the employment contract. The member of the managing board may, however, terminate his employment contract as of the end of the next following calendar quarter upon six weeks' notice.

(3) If an order subjecting the assets of the company to bankruptcy proceedings has been issued and the receiver in bankruptcy elects to terminate

§ 87

the employment contract of a member of the managing board, such member shall be entitled to compensation for any damage arising from the termination of the employment relationship only for the two years following such termination of the employment relationship. The same shall apply if an order subjecting the company's assets to proceedings for the avoidance of bankruptcy has been issued and the company terminates the employment contract.

standsmitglieds, so kann es Ersatz für den Schaden, der ihm durch die Aufhebung des Dienstverhältnisses entsteht, nur für zwei Jahre seit dem Ablauf des Dienstverhältnisses verlangen. Gleiches gilt, wenn über die Gesellschaft das gerichtliche Vergleichsverfahren eröffnet wird und die Gesellschaft den Anstellungsvertrag kündigt.

§ 88
Non-competition Clause

(1) Absent the approval of the supervisory board, the members of the managing board may neither engage in a trade or business nor enter into any business transactions which are within the company's line of business, for their own account or for the account of others. Moreover, absent such approval, they may not be members of the managing board or managers or general partners of another commercial enterprise. The approval of the supervisory board must be limited to a specific type of trade or business, specific companies, or specific types of business transactions.

(2) If a member of the managing board violates this prohibition, the company may claim damages. In lieu thereof it may require the member to carry out a transaction entered into for the member's account as one entered into for the account of the company, and to transfer to it the compensation received for transactions entered into for the account of another, or to assign his rights to such compensation.

(3) The company's claims shall be barred after the expiration of three months from the date on which the other members of the managing board and the members of the supervisory board obtained knowledge of the acts giving rise to the claim for damages. Irrespective of such knowledge, these claims shall be barred after the expiration of five years from the date on which they arose.

§ 88
Wettbewerbsverbot

(1) Die Vorstandsmitglieder dürfen ohne Einwilligung des Aufsichtsrats weder ein Handelsgewerbe betreiben noch im Geschäftszweig der Gesellschaft für eigene oder fremde Rechnung Geschäfte machen. Sie dürfen ohne Einwilligung auch nicht Mitglied des Vorstands oder Geschäftsführer oder persönlich haftender Gesellschafter einer anderen Handelsgesellschaft sein. Die Einwilligung des Aufsichtsrats kann nur für bestimmte Handelsgewerbe oder Handelsgesellschaften oder für bestimmte Arten von Geschäften erteilt werden.

(2) Verstößt ein Vorstandsmitglied gegen dieses Verbot, so kann die Gesellschaft Schadenersatz fordern. Sie kann statt dessen von dem Mitglied verlangen, daß es die für eigene Rechnung gemachten Geschäfte als für Rechnung der Gesellschaft eingegangen gelten läßt und die aus Geschäften für fremde Rechnung bezogene Vergütung herausgibt oder seinen Anspruch auf die Vergütung abtritt.

(3) Die Ansprüche der Gesellschaft verjähren in drei Monaten seit dem Zeitpunkt, in dem die übrigen Vorstandsmitglieder und die Aufsichtsratsmitglieder von der zum Schadenersatz verpflichtenden Handlung Kenntnis erlangen. Sie verjähren ohne Rücksicht auf diese Kenntnis in fünf Jahren seit ihrer Entstehung.

§ 89
Loans Granted to Members of Managing Board

(1) The company may extend loans or credit to members of its managing board only pursuant to a resolution of the supervisory board. Such

§ 89
Kreditgewährung an Vorstandsmitglieder

(1) Die Gesellschaft darf ihren Vorstandsmitgliedern Kredit nur auf Grund eines Beschlusses des Aufsichtsrats gewähren. Der Beschluß kann nur für

bestimmte Kreditgeschäfte oder Arten von Kreditgeschäften und nicht für länger als drei Monate im voraus gefaßt werden. Er hat die Verzinsung und Rückzahlung des Kredits zu regeln. Der Gewährung eines Kredits steht die Gestattung einer Entnahme gleich, die über die dem Vorstandsmitglied zustehenden Bezüge hinausgeht, namentlich auch die Gestattung der Entnahme von Vorschüssen auf Bezüge. Dies gilt nicht für Kredite, die ein Monatsgehalt nicht übersteigen.

(2) Die Gesellschaft darf ihren Prokuristen und zum gesamten Geschäftsbetrieb ermächtigten Handlungsbevollmächtigten Kredit nur mit Einwilligung des Aufsichtsrats gewähren. Eine herrschende Gesellschaft darf Kredite an gesetzliche Vertreter, Prokuristen oder zum gesamten Geschäftsbetrieb ermächtigte Handlungsbevollmächtigte eines abhängigen Unternehmens nur mit Einwilligung ihres Aufsichtsrats, eine abhängige Gesellschaft darf Kredite an gesetzliche Vertreter, Prokuristen oder zum gesamten Geschäftsbetrieb ermächtigte Handlungsbevollmächtigte des herrschenden Unternehmens nur mit Einwilligung des Aufsichtsrats des herrschenden Unternehmens gewähren. Absatz 1 Satz 2 bis 5 gilt sinngemäß.

(3) Absatz 2 gilt auch für Kredite an den Ehegatten oder an ein minderjähriges Kind eines Vorstandsmitglieds, eines anderen gesetzlichen Vertreters, eines Prokuristen oder eines zum gesamten Geschäftsbetrieb ermächtigten Handlungsbevollmächtigten. Er gilt ferner für Kredite an einen Dritten, der für Rechnung dieser Personen oder für Rechnung eines Vorstandsmitglieds, eines anderen gesetzlichen Vertreters, eines Prokuristen oder eines zum gesamten Geschäftsbetrieb ermächtigten Handlungsbevollmächtigten handelt.

(4) Ist ein Vorstandsmitglied, ein Prokurist oder ein zum gesamten Geschäftsbetrieb ermächtigter Handlungsbevollmächtigter zugleich gesetzlicher Vertreter oder Mitglied des Aufsichtsrats einer anderen juristischen Person oder Gesellschafter einer Personenhandelsgesellschaft, so darf die Gesellschaft der juristischen Person oder der Personenhandelsgesellschaft Kredit nur mit Einwilligung des Aufsichtsrats gewähren, Absatz 1 Satz 2 und 3 gilt sinngemäß. Dies gilt nicht, wenn die juristische Person oder die Personenhandelsgesellschaft mit der Gesellschaft verbunden ist oder wenn der Kredit für

resolution must be limited to specific credit transactions or types of credit transactions, and for no more than three months in advance. The resolution shall specify the interest and the conditions of repayment of the principal. The permission to withdraw funds in excess of the salary and other compensation to which the member of the managing board is entitled, in particular also the permission to withdraw advances on such compensation, shall be treated in the same manner as the granting of a loan. This shall not apply to loans not exceeding one month's salary.

(2) The company may extend loans and credit to its *Prokuristen* and to such of its agents whose powers to bind the company extend to its business as a whole only with the approval of the supervisory board. A controlling company may extend loans or credit to the legal representatives, *Prokuristen*, or such of its agents of a controlled company whose powers to bind the company extend to the business as a whole only with the approval of its supervisory board, and a controlled company may extend loans to the legal representatives, *Prokuristen*, or such of its agents whose powers to bind the company extend to its business as a whole only with the approval of the supervisory board of the controlling company. Paragraph 1, second to fifth sentences, hereof shall apply *mutatis mutandis*.

(3) Paragraph 2 hereof shall also apply to loans or credit extended to the spouse or minor child of a member of the managing board, of other legal representatives, *Prokuristen*, or agents whose powers to bind the company extend to its business as a whole. It shall apply, moreover, to loans or credit extended to any third party acting for the account of such persons, or for the account of a member of the managing board, other legal representative, a *Prokurist*, or an agent whose powers to bind the company extend to its business as a whole.

(4) If any member of the managing board, a *Prokurist*, or an agent whose powers to bind the company extend to its business as a whole is also a legal representative or member of the supervisory board of another legal entity or member of a business partnership, the company may extend credit or a loan to such legal entity or partnership only with the approval of the supervisory board. Paragraph 1, second and third sentences, hereof shall apply *mutatis mutandis*. This shall not apply where the legal entity or business partner-

§ 89

ship is related to the company or if the loan or credit is extended for the payment for goods which the company sells to such legal entity or business partnership.

die Bezahlung von Waren gewährt wird, welche die Gesellschaft der juristischen Person oder der Personenhandelsgesellschaft liefert.

(5) Loans or credit extended contrary to the provisions of paragraphs 1 to 4 hereof shall be repaid immediately, notwithstanding any agreements to the contrary, unless the supervisory board approves them subsequently.

(5) Wird entgegen den Absätzen 1 bis 4 Kredit gewährt, so ist der Kredit ohne Rücksicht auf entgegenstehende Vereinbarungen sofort zurückzugewähren, wenn nicht der Aufsichtsrat nachträglich zustimmt.

(6) If the company is a bank, the provisions of the *Gesetz über das Kreditwesen* shall apply in lieu of paragraphs 1 to 5 hereof.

(6) Ist die Gesellschaft ein Kreditinstitut, so gelten an Stelle der Absätze 1 bis 5 die Vorschriften des Gesetzes über das Kreditwesen.

§ 90
Reports to Supervisory Board

(1) The managing board shall report to the supervisory board on
1. the prospective business policy and other fundamental questions concerning the future conduct of the company's business;
2. the profitability of the company, particularly with respect to the return on the company's capital;
3. the business transacted, particularly the turnover and the condition of the company;
4. transactions that may substantially affect the profitability or liquidity of the company.

Furthermore, the chairman of the supervisory board shall be notified of other important events; an important event shall be deemed to exist also in the case of a business transaction of a related enterprise of which the managing board has obtained knowledge and which may substantially affect the condition of the company.

§ 90
Berichte an den Aufsichtsrat

(1) Der Vorstand hat dem Aufsichtsrat zu berichten über
1. die beabsichtigte Geschäftspolitik und andere grundsätzliche Fragen der künftigen Geschäftsführung;
2. die Rentabilität der Gesellschaft, insbesondere die Rentabilität des Eigenkapitals;
3. den Gang der Geschäfte, insbesondere den Umsatz, und die Lage der Gesellschaft;
4. Geschäfte, die für die Rentabilität oder Liquidität der Gesellschaft von erheblicher Bedeutung sein können.

Außerdem ist dem Vorsitzenden des Aufsichtsrats aus sonstigen wichtigen Anlässen zu berichten; als wichtiger Anlaß ist auch ein dem Vorstand bekanntgewordener geschäftlicher Vorgang bei einem verbundenen Unternehmen anzusehen, der auf die Lage der Gesellschaft von erheblichem Einfluß sein kann.

(2) The reports required by paragraph 1, first sentence, Nos. 1 to 4, hereof shall be submitted as follows:
1. the reports required by No. 1, at least once a year, unless a change in the circumstances or novel questions require an immediate report;
2. the reports required by No. 2, at the meeting of the supervisory board at which the annual financial statements are discussed;
3. the reports required by No. 3, regularly, at least quarter-annually;
4. the reports required by No. 4, if possible timely enough to permit the supervisory board to comment on them before such transactions are carried out.

(2) Die Berichte nach Absatz 1 Satz 1 Nr. 1 bis 4 sind wie folgt zu erstatten:
1. die Berichte nach Nummer 1 mindestens einmal jährlich, wenn nicht Änderungen der Lage oder neue Fragen eine unverzügliche Berichterstattung gebieten;
2. die Berichte nach Nummer 2 in der Sitzung des Aufsichtsrats, in der über den Jahresabschluß verhandelt wird;
3. die Berichte nach Nummer 3 regelmäßig, mindestens vierteljährlich;
4. die Berichte nach Nummer 4 möglichst so rechtzeitig, daß der Aufsichtsrat vor Vornahme der Geschäfte Gelegenheit hat, zu ihnen Stellung zu nehmen.

(3) The supervisory board may at any time request the managing board to report on matters

(3) Der Aufsichtsrat kann vom Vorstand jederzeit einen Bericht verlangen über Angelegenheiten der

Gesellschaft, über ihre rechtlichen und geschäftlichen Beziehungen zu verbundenen Unternehmen sowie über geschäftliche Vorgänge bei diesen Unternehmen, die auf die Lage der Gesellschaft von erheblichem Einfluß sein können. Auch ein einzelnes Mitglied kann einen Bericht, jedoch nur an den Aufsichtsrat, verlangen; lehnt der Vorstand die Berichterstattung ab, so kann der Bericht nur verlangt werden, wenn ein anderes Aufsichtsratsmitglied das Verlangen unterstützt.

(4) Die Berichte haben den Grundsätzen einer gewissenhaften und getreuen Rechenschaft zu entsprechen.

(5) Jedes Aufsichtsratsmitglied hat das Recht, von den Berichten Kenntnis zu nehmen. Soweit die Berichte schriftlich erstattet worden sind, sind sie auch jedem Aufsichtsratsmitglied auf Verlangen auszuhändigen, soweit der Aufsichtsrat nichts anderes beschlossen hat. Der Vorsitzende des Aufsichtsrats hat die Aufsichtsratsmitglieder über die Berichte nach Absatz 1 Satz 2 spätestens in der nächsten Aufsichtsratssitzung zu unterrichten.

§ 91

Buchführung

Der Vorstand hat dafür zu sorgen, daß die erforderlichen Handelsbücher geführt werden.

§ 92

Vorstandspflichten bei Verlust, Überschuldung oder Zahlungsunfähigkeit

(1) Ergibt sich bei Aufstellung der Jahresbilanz oder einer Zwischenbilanz oder ist bei pflichtmäßigem Ermessen anzunehmen, daß ein Verlust in Höhe der Hälfte des Grundkapitals besteht, so hat der Vorstand unverzüglich die Hauptversammlung einzuberufen und ihr dies anzuzeigen.

(2) Wird die Gesellschaft zahlungsunfähig, so hat der Vorstand ohne schuldhaftes Zögern, spätestens aber drei Wochen nach Eintritt der Zahlungsunfähigkeit, die Eröffnung des Konkursverfahrens oder des gerichtlichen Vergleichsverfahrens zu beantragen. Dies gilt sinngemäß, wenn das Vermögen der Gesellschaft nicht mehr die Schulden deckt. Der Antrag ist nicht schuldhaft verzögert, wenn der Vorstand die Eröffnung des gerichtlichen Vergleichsverfahrens mit der Sorgfalt eines ordentlichen und gewissenhaften Geschäftsleiters betreibt.

concerning the company, its legal and business relationships with related enterprises, and business transactions of such enterprises which may substantially affect the condition of the company. Any member of the supervisory board may also request such a report, although only for submission to the entire supervisory board; if the managing board refuses to render it, the report can be requested only if another member of the supervisory board seconds the request.

(4) The reports shall conform to the principles of a conscientious and true account.

(5) Each member of the supervisory board shall have the right to review the reports. To the extent that the reports have been submitted in written form, they shall be made available to any member of the supervisory board upon his request, absent a resolution of the supervisory board to the contrary. The chairman of the supervisory board shall inform its members of the reports provided for in paragraph 1, second sentence, hereof no later than the next following meeting of the supervisory board

§ 91

Accounting

The managing board shall cause the required books of account to be kept.

§ 92

Duties of Managing Board in Case of Loss, Excess of Liabilities over Assets, or Insolvency

(1) If it appears upon preparation of the annual balance sheet or an interim balance sheet, or if upon proper consideration it must be assumed, that the company has incurred a loss amounting to one-half of the stated capital, the managing board shall without delay call a shareholders' meeting and report this fact to it.

(2) If the company becomes insolvent, the managing board shall, without undue delay and no later than three weeks after the insolvency arose, file a petition with the court to order bankruptcy proceedings or composition proceedings. The same shall apply, *mutatis mutandis*, if the company's liabilities exceed its assets. The petition shall not be deemed to have been unduly delayed if the managing board proceeds to initiate the composition proceedings with the care of a diligent and prudent executive.

(3) After the company has become insolvent or its liabilities exceed its assets, the managing board may not make any payments. This shall not apply with respect to payments which, although made after such time, are in accordance with the standard of care of a diligent and prudent executive.

§ 93
Duty of Care and Liability of Members of Managing Board

(1) In managing the company, the members of the managing board shall act with the care of a diligent and prudent executive. They shall not reveal any confidential information and secrets of the company, in particular business and trade secrets which have become known to them in connection with their activities as members of the managing board.

(2) Members of the managing board who breach their duties shall be jointly and severally liable to the company for the redress of any damage resulting therefrom. In case of a contest as to whether they acted with the care of a diligent and prudent executive, they shall bear the burden of proof.

(3) The members of the managing board shall be liable for redress in particular if, contrary to this Act,

1. capital contributions are repaid to the shareholders;
2. interest is paid, or profits are distributed, to the shareholders;
3. the company's own shares or those of another company have been subscribed to, acquired, taken as a pledge, or cancelled;
4. share certificates are issued before the full amount of the par value plus any premium has been paid in;
5. the company's assets are distributed;
6. payments are made after the company has become insolvent or its liabilities exceed its assets;
7. payments are made to the members of the supervisory board;
8. credit or loans are extended;
9. in the event of a conditional capital increase, preemptive shares are issued for a purpose other than that stated or prior to payment in full of the consideration to be rendered.

(4) The members of the managing board shall not be liable to the company if a transaction is

(3) Nachdem die Zahlungsunfähigkeit der Gesellschaft eingetreten ist oder sich ihre Überschuldung ergeben hat, darf der Vorstand keine Zahlungen leisten. Dies gilt nicht von Zahlungen, die auch nach diesem Zeitpunkt mit der Sorgfalt eines ordentlichen und gewissenhaften Geschäftsleiters vereinbar sind.

§ 93
Sorgfaltspflicht und Verantwortlichkeit der Vorstandsmitglieder

(1) Die Vorstandsmitglieder haben bei ihrer Geschäftsführung die Sorgfalt eines ordentlichen und gewissenhaften Geschäftsleiters anzuwenden. Über vertrauliche Angaben und Geheimnisse der Gesellschaft, namentlich Betriebs- oder Geschäftsgeheimnisse, die ihnen durch ihre Tätigkeit im Vorstand bekanntgeworden sind, haben sie Stillschweigen zu bewahren.

(2) Vorstandsmitglieder, die ihre Pflichten verletzen, sind der Gesellschaft zum Ersatz des daraus entstehenden Schadens als Gesamtschuldner verpflichtet. Ist streitig, ob sie die Sorgfalt eines ordentlichen und gewissenhaften Geschäftsleiters angewandt haben, so trifft sie die Beweislast.

(3) Die Vorstandsmitglieder sind namentlich zum Ersatz verpflichtet, wenn entgegen diesem Gesetz

1. Einlagen an die Aktionäre zurückgewährt werden,
2. den Aktionären Zinsen oder Gewinnanteile gezahlt werden,
3. eigene Aktien der Gesellschaft oder einer anderen Gesellschaft gezeichnet, erworben, als Pfand genommen oder eingezogen werden,
4. Aktien vor der vollen Leistung des Nennbetrags oder des höheren Ausgabebetrags ausgegeben werden,
5. Gesellschaftsvermögen verteilt wird,
6. Zahlungen geleistet werden, nachdem die Zahlungsunfähigkeit der Gesellschaft eingetreten ist oder sich ihre Überschuldung ergeben hat,
7. Vergütungen an Aufsichtsratsmitglieder gewährt werden,
8. Kredit gewährt wird,
9. bei der bedingten Kapitalerhöhung außerhalb des festgesetzten Zwecks oder vor der vollen Leistung des Gegenwerts Bezugsaktien ausgegeben werden.

* (4) Der Gesellschaft gegenüber tritt die Ersatzpflicht nicht ein, wenn die Handlung auf einem

gesetzmäßigen Beschluß der Hauptversammlung beruht. Dadurch, daß der Aufsichtsrat die Handlung gebilligt hat, wird die Ersatzpflicht nicht ausgeschlossen. Die Gesellschaft kann erst drei Jahre nach der Entstehung des Anspruchs und nur dann auf Ersatzansprüche verzichten oder sich über sie vergleichen, wenn die Hauptversammlung zustimmt und nicht eine Minderheit, deren Anteile zusammen den zehnten Teil des Grundkapitals erreichen, zur Niederschrift Widerspruch erhebt. Die zeitliche Beschränkung gilt nicht, wenn der Ersatzpflichtige zahlungsunfähig ist und sich zur Abwendung oder Beseitigung des Konkursverfahrens mit seinen Gläubigern vergleicht.

(5) Der Ersatzanspruch der Gesellschaft kann auch von den Gläubigern der Gesellschaft geltend gemacht werden, soweit sie von dieser keine Befriedigung erlangen können. Dies gilt jedoch in anderen Fällen als denen des Absatzes 3 nur dann, wenn die Vorstandsmitglieder die Sorgfalt eines ordentlichen und gewissenhaften Geschäftsleiters gröblich verletzt haben; Absatz 2 Satz 2 gilt sinngemäß. Den Gläubigern gegenüber wird die Ersatzpflicht weder durch einen Verzicht oder Vergleich der Gesellschaft noch dadurch aufgehoben, daß die Handlung auf einem Beschluß der Hauptversammlung beruht. Ist über das Vermögen der Gesellschaft das Konkursverfahren eröffnet, so übt während dessen Dauer der Konkursverwalter das Recht der Gläubiger gegen die Vorstandsmitglieder aus.

(6) Die Ansprüche aus diesen Vorschriften verjähren in fünf Jahren.

§ 94
Stellvertreter von Vorstandsmitgliedern

Die Vorschriften für die Vorstandsmitglieder gelten auch für ihre Stellvertreter.

Zweiter Abschnitt
Aufsichtsrat

§ 95
Zahl der Aufsichtsratsmitglieder

Der Aufsichtsrat besteht aus drei Mitgliedern. Die Satzung kann eine bestimmte höhere Zahl fest-

based on a lawful shareholders' resolution. Liability shall not, however, be precluded by the fact that the supervisory board has approved the transaction. The company can waive or compromise the right to demand redress only after the expiration of three years from the date on which such right arose and then only upon approval of the shareholders and if a minority whose combined holdings amount to no less than one-tenth of the stated capital does not have its objection recorded in the minutes. This time limit shall not apply if the party liable is insolvent and enters into a composition with its creditors to avert or terminate bankruptcy proceedings.

(5) The company's claim for damages can also be asserted by its creditors to the extent that they cannot obtain satisfaction from the company. However, in cases other than those specified in paragraph 3 hereof, this shall apply only if the members of the managing board grossly breached their duty to act with the care of a diligent and prudent executive; paragraph 2, second sentence, hereof shall apply *mutatis mutandis*. With respect to creditors, this liability shall not be barred by a waiver or compromise on the part of the company nor by the fact that the transaction is based on a shareholders' resolution. If an order subjecting the assets of the company to bankruptcy proceedings has been issued, the receiver in bankruptcy shall exercise the rights of the creditors against the members of the managing board during the pendency of such proceedings.

(6) The claims arising out of these provisions shall be barred after the expiration of five years.

§ 94
Substitutes for Members of Managing Board

The provisions concerning the members of the managing board shall also apply to their substitutes.

Second Division
Supervisory Board

§ 95
Number of Members of Supervisory Board

The supervisory board shall have three members. The articles of incorporation may provide for a specified higher number. Such number must be divisible by three. The maximum number of members of the supervisory board shall be, in the case of companies with a stated capital of

up to 3,000,000 German marks, nine,
more than 3,000,000 German marks, fifteen,
more than 20,000,000 German marks,
    twenty-one.

The above provisions shall not affect contrary provisions contained in the *Gesetz über die Mitbestimmung der Arbeitnehmer in den Aufsichtsräten und Vorständen der Unternehmen des Bergbaus und der Eisen und Stahl erzeugenden Industrie* of May 21, 1951 (*Bundesgesetzbl.* I, page 347) – the *Mitbestimmungsgesetz* – and the *Gesetz zur Ergänzung des Gesetzes über die Mitbestimmung der Arbeitnehmer in den Aufsichtsräten und Vorständen der Unternehmen des Bergbaus und der Eisen und Stahl erzeugenden Industrie* of August 7, 1956 (*Bundesgesetzbl.* I, page 707) – the *Mitbestimmungsergänzungsgesetz.*

§ 96
Composition of Supervisory Board

(1) The supervisory board shall be composed, in the case of companies subject to § 76, paragraph 1, of the *Betriebsverfassungsgesetz*, of members representing the shareholders and the employees,

in the case of companies subject to the *Mitbestimmungsgesetz*, of members representing the shareholders and the employees and of other members,

in the case of companies subject to §§ 5 to 13 of the *Mitbestimmungsergänzungsgesetz*, of members representing the shareholders and the employees and of one additional member,

in the case of all other companies, only of members of the supervisory board representing the shareholders.

(2) The supervisory board may be composed pursuant to statutory provisions other than those applied previously only if, pursuant to § 97 or § 98, the statutory provisions indicated in the announcement of the managing board or those designated in the decision of the court are applicable.

§ 97
Announcement Concerning Composition of Supervisory Board

(1) If the managing board is of the opinion that the composition of the supervisory board

§ 96

---

setzen. Die Zahl muß durch drei teilbar sein. Die Höchstzahl der Aufsichtsratsmitglieder beträgt bei Gesellschaften mit einem Grundkapital

bis zu   3 000 000 Deutsche Mark   neun,
von mehr als 3 000 000 Deutsche Mark fünfzehn,
von mehr als 20 000 000 Deutsche Mark einund-
                                zwanzig.

Durch die vorstehenden Vorschriften werden hiervon abweichende Vorschriften des Gesetzes über die Mitbestimmung der Arbeitnehmer in den Aufsichtsräten und Vorständen der Unternehmen des Bergbaus und der Eisen und Stahl erzeugenden Industrie vom 21. Mai 1951 (Bundesgesetzbl. I S. 347) — Mitbestimmungsgesetz — und des Gesetzes zur Ergänzung des Gesetzes über die Mitbestimmung der Arbeitnehmer in den Aufsichtsräten und Vorständen der Unternehmen des Bergbaus und der Eisen und Stahl erzeugenden Industrie vom 7. August 1956 (Bundesgesetzbl. I S. 707) — Mitbestimmungsergänzungsgesetz — nicht berührt.

§ 96
Zusammensetzung des Aufsichtsrats

(1) Der Aufsichtsrat setzt sich zusammen

bei Gesellschaften, für die § 76 Abs. 1 des Betriebsverfassungsgesetzes gilt, aus Aufsichtsratsmitgliedern der Aktionäre und der Arbeitnehmer,

bei Gesellschaften, für die das Mitbestimmungsgesetz gilt, aus Aufsichtsratsmitgliedern der Aktionäre und der Arbeitnehmer und aus weiteren Mitgliedern,

bei Gesellschaften, für die die §§ 5 bis 13 des Mitbestimmungsergänzungsgesetzes gelten, aus Aufsichtsratsmitgliedern der Aktionäre und der Arbeitnehmer und aus einem weiteren Mitglied,

bei den übrigen Gesellschaften nur aus Aufsichtsratsmitgliedern der Aktionäre.

(2) Nach anderen als den zuletzt angewandten gesetzlichen Vorschriften kann der Aufsichtsrat nur zusammengesetzt werden, wenn nach § 97 oder nach § 98 die in der Bekanntmachung des Vorstands oder in der gerichtlichen Entscheidung angegebenen gesetzlichen Vorschriften anzuwenden sind.

§ 97
Bekanntmachung über die Zusammensetzung des Aufsichtsrats

(1) Ist der Vorstand der Ansicht, daß der Aufsichtsrat nicht nach den für ihn maßgebenden gesetz-

lichen Vorschriften zusammengesetzt ist, so hat er dies unverzüglich in den Gesellschaftsblättern und gleichzeitig durch Aushang in sämtlichen Betrieben der Gesellschaft und ihrer Konzernunternehmen bekanntzumachen. In der Bekanntmachung sind die nach Ansicht des Vorstands maßgebenden gesetzlichen Vorschriften anzugeben. Es ist darauf hinzuweisen, daß der Aufsichtsrat nach diesen Vorschriften zusammengesetzt wird, wenn nicht Antragsberechtigte nach § 98 Abs. 2 innerhalb eines Monats nach der Bekanntmachung im Bundesanzeiger das nach § 98 Abs. 1 zuständige Gericht anrufen.

(2) Wird das nach § 98 Abs. 1 zuständige Gericht nicht innerhalb eines Monats nach der Bekanntmachung im Bundesanzeiger angerufen, so ist der neue Aufsichtsrat nach den in der Bekanntmachung des Vorstands angegebenen gesetzlichen Vorschriften zusammenzusetzen. Die Bestimmungen der Satzung über die Zusammensetzung des Aufsichtsrats, über die Zahl der Aufsichtsratsmitglieder sowie über die Wahl, Abberufung und Entsendung von Aufsichtsratsmitgliedern treten mit der Beendigung der ersten Hauptversammlung, die nach Ablauf der Anrufungsfrist einberufen wird, spätestens sechs Monate nach Ablauf dieser Frist insoweit außer Kraft, als sie den nunmehr anzuwendenden gesetzlichen Vorschriften widersprechen. Mit demselben Zeitpunkt erlischt das Amt der bisherigen Aufsichtsratsmitglieder. Eine Hauptversammlung, die innerhalb der Frist von sechs Monaten stattfindet, kann an Stelle der außer Kraft tretenden Satzungsbestimmungen mit einfacher Stimmenmehrheit neue Satzungsbestimmungen beschließen.

(3) Solange ein gerichtliches Verfahren nach §§ 98, 99 anhängig ist, kann eine Bekanntmachung über die Zusammensetzung des Aufsichtsrats nicht erfolgen.

§ 98

Gerichtliche Entscheidung über die Zusammensetzung des Aufsichtsrats

(1) Ist streitig oder ungewiß, nach welchen gesetzlichen Vorschriften der Aufsichtsrat zusammen-

does not comply with the applicable statutory provisions, it shall promptly announce this fact in the publications designated in the company's articles of incorporation and, at the same time, by a notice exhibited in all of the plants of the company and of its related enterprises. The announcement shall specify the statutory provisions which, in the opinion of the managing board, are applicable. Reference shall be made to the fact that the supervisory board will be composed pursuant to such provisions unless the parties entitled to make the application pursuant to § 98, paragraph 2, apply to the court having jurisdiction pursuant to § 98, paragraph 1, within one month from the date of publication of the announcement in the *Bundesanzeiger*.

(2) If no application has been made to the court having jurisdiction pursuant to § 98, paragraph 1, within one month from the date of publication of the announcement in the *Bundesanzeiger*, a new supervisory board shall be composed in accordance with the statutory provisions specified in the announcement of the managing board. The provisions of the articles of incorporation concerning the composition of the supervisory board, the number of supervisory board members, as well as the election, dismissal, and delegation of supervisory board members, shall become ineffective to the extent that they conflict with the statutory provisions which thereupon become applicable, as of the adjournment of the first shareholders' meeting called after the expiration of this period, but no later than six months from the expiration of this period. As of that same time, the term of office of the previous members of the supervisory board shall expire. A meeting of shareholders, which shall take place within the six-month period, may, by simple majority, adopt new provisions to replace the provisions in the articles of incorporation which become ineffective.

(3) As long as judicial proceedings pursuant to §§ 98 and 99 are pending, no announcement concerning the composition of the supervisory board may be made.

§ 98

Judicial Decision on Composition of Supervisory Board

(1) In the event of a contest or uncertainty regarding the statutory provisions to be applied

§ 98

in the composition of the supervisory board, the district court (civil chamber) of the district in which the company is domiciled shall have exclusive jurisdiction to adjudicate this matter upon application. The state government may, by decree, delegate the jurisdiction to render such a decision for several judicial districts to a particular district court, if such delegation would serve to ensure the uniform application of the law. The state government may confer this power upon the ministry of justice of such state.

(2) The parties entitled to make the application are:
1. the managing board,
2. each member of the supervisory board,
3. each shareholder,
4. the works council of each of the company's plants,
5. the works council of any other plant, the employees of which participate personally or through electors in the election of members of the company's supervisory board, pursuant to the statutory provisions whose application is contested or uncertain,
6. at least ten percent or one hundred of the employees who participate personally or through electors in the election of the members of the company's supervisory board pursuant to the statutory provisions whose application is contested or uncertain,
7. central union organizations which, pursuant to the statutory provisions whose application is contested or uncertain, would have the right to nominate or delegate representatives to the supervisory board.

(3) Paragraphs 1 and 2 hereof shall apply, *mutatis mutandis*, if there is a contest as to whether the annual auditor has correctly ascertained the relevant turnover ratio pursuant to § 3 of the *Mitbestimmungsergänzungsgesetz.*

(4) If the composition of the supervisory board does not comply with the decision of the court, the new supervisory board shall be composed in accordance with the statutory provisions specified in such decision. § 97, paragraph 2, shall apply *mutatis mutandis*, except that the six-month period shall be computed from the date the decision becomes final.

§ 99

Procedure

(1) The procedure shall be governed by the *Reichsgesetz über die Angelegenheiten der frei-*

§ 99

---

zusetzen ist, so entscheidet darüber auf Antrag ausschließlich das Landgericht (Zivilkammer), in dessen Bezirk die Gesellschaft ihren Sitz hat. Die Landesregierung kann die Entscheidung durch Rechtsverordnung für die Bezirke mehrerer Landgerichte einem der Landgerichte übertragen, wenn dies der Sicherung einer einheitlichen Rechtsprechung dient. Die Landesregierung kann die Ermächtigung auf die Landesjustizverwaltung übertragen.

(2) Antragsberechtigt sind
1. der Vorstand,
2. jedes Aufsichtsratsmitglied,
3. jeder Aktionär,
4. der Betriebsrat jedes Betriebs der Gesellschaft,
5. der Betriebsrat jedes anderen Betriebs, dessen Arbeitnehmer nach den gesetzlichen Vorschriften, deren Anwendung streitig oder ungewiß ist, selbst oder durch Wahlmänner an der Wahl von Aufsichtsratsmitgliedern der · Gesellschaft teilnehmen,
6. mindestens ein Zehntel oder einhundert der Arbeitnehmer, die nach den gesetzlichen Vorschriften, deren Anwendung streitig oder ungewiß ist, selbst oder durch Wahlmänner an der Wahl von Aufsichtsratsmitgliedern der Gesellschaft teilnehmen,
7. Spitzenorganisationen der Gewerkschaften, die nach den gesetzlichen Vorschriften, deren Anwendung streitig oder ungewiß ist, ein Vorschlags- oder Entsendungsrecht hätten.

(3) Die Absätze 1 und 2 gelten sinngemäß, wenn streitig ist, ob der Abschlußprüfer das nach § 3 des Mitbestimmungsergänzungsgesetzes maßgebliche Umsatzverhältnis richtig ermittelt hat.

(4) Entspricht die Zusammensetzung des Aufsichtsrats nicht der gerichtlichen Entscheidung, so ist der neue Aufsichtsrat nach den in der Entscheidung angegebenen gesetzlichen Vorschriften zusammenzusetzen. § 97 Abs. 2 gilt sinngemäß mit der Maßgabe, daß die Frist von sechs Monaten mit dem Eintritt der Rechtskraft beginnt.

§ 99

Verfahren

(1) Auf das Verfahren ist das Reichsgesetz über die Angelegenheiten der freiwilligen Gerichtsbar-

keit anzuwenden, soweit in den Absätzen 2 bis 5 nichts anderes bestimmt ist.

(2) Das Landgericht hat den Antrag in den Gesellschaftsblättern bekanntzumachen. Der Vorstand und jedes Aufsichtsratsmitglied sowie die nach § 98 Abs. 2 antragsberechtigten Betriebsräte und Spitzenorganisationen sind zu hören.

(3) Das Landgericht entscheidet durch einen mit Gründen versehenen Beschluß. Gegen die Entscheidung findet die sofortige Beschwerde statt. Sie kann nur auf eine Verletzung des Gesetzes gestützt werden; die §§ 550, 551, 561, 563 der Zivilprozeßordnung gelten sinngemäß. Die Beschwerde kann nur durch Einreichung einer von einem Rechtsanwalt unterzeichneten Beschwerdeschrift eingelegt werden. Über sie entscheidet das Oberlandesgericht. § 28 Abs. 2 und 3 des Reichsgesetzes über die Angelegenheiten der freiwilligen Gerichtsbarkeit gilt entsprechend. Die weitere Beschwerde ist ausgeschlossen. Die Landesregierung kann durch Rechtsverordnung die Entscheidung über die Beschwerde für die Bezirke mehrerer Oberlandesgerichte einem der Oberlandesgerichte oder dem Obersten Landesgericht übertragen, wenn dies der Sicherung einer einheitlichen Rechtsprechung dient. Die Landesregierung kann die Ermächtigung auf die Landesjustizverwaltung übertragen.

(4) Das Gericht hat seine Entscheidung dem Antragsteller und der Gesellschaft zuzustellen. Es hat sie ferner ohne Gründe in den Gesellschaftsblättern bekanntzumachen. Die Beschwerde steht jedem nach § 98 Abs. 2 Antragsberechtigten zu. Die Beschwerdefrist beginnt mit der Bekanntmachung der Entscheidung im Bundesanzeiger, für den Antragsteller und die Gesellschaft jedoch nicht vor der Zustellung der Entscheidung.

(5) Die Entscheidung wird erst mit der Rechtskraft wirksam. Sie wirkt für und gegen alle. Der Vorstand hat die rechtskräftige Entscheidung unverzüglich zum Handelsregister einzureichen.

(6) Für die Kosten des Verfahrens gilt die Kostenordnung. Für das Verfahren des ersten Rechtszugs wird das Vierfache der vollen Gebühr erhoben. Für den zweiten Rechtszug wird die gleiche Gebühr erhoben; dies gilt auch dann, wenn die Beschwerde Erfolg hat. Wird der Antrag oder die Beschwerde zurückgenommen, bevor es zu einer Entscheidung

willigen Gerichtsbarkeit, unless paragraphs 2 to 5 hereof provide otherwise.

(2) The district court shall publish the application in the publications designated in the company's articles of incorporation. The managing board and each member of the supervisory board, as well as the works councils and the central union organizations entitled to make the application pursuant to § 98, paragraph 2, shall be heard.

(3) The district court shall render its decision by a decree containing a reasoned opinion. The decision of the court can be appealed. The appeal may be based only on a violation of the law; §§ 550, 551, 561, and 563 of the Code of Civil Procedure shall apply *mutatis mutandis.* The appeal can be taken only by filing a notice of appeal, which must be signed by an attorney-at-law. The court of appeal shall have jurisdiction to decide the appeal. § 28, paragraphs 2 and 3, of the *Reichsgesetz über die Angelegenheiten der freiwilligen Gerichtsbarkeit* shall apply *mutatis mutandis.* The decision shall not be subject to further appeal. The state government may, by decree, delegate the jurisdiction to adjudicate such appeals for the circuits of several courts of appeal to a specific court of appeal or to the highest court of appeal if such delegation would serve to ensure the uniform application of the law. The state government may confer this power upon the ministry of justice of such state.

(4) The court shall serve its decision on the applicant and on the company. It shall publish its decision, without the opinion, in the publications designated in the company's articles of incorporation. Any party entitled to make the application pursuant to § 98, paragraph 2, may appeal the decision. The period for filing an appeal shall begin with the date of publication of the decision in the *Bundesanzeiger;* however, as to the applicant and the company it does not begin to run until the decision is served on them.

(5) The decision shall not have any effect before it becomes final. It shall be binding on all persons. The managing board shall promptly file the final decision with the Commercial Register.

(6) The costs of the proceedings shall be determined by reference to the *Kostenordnung.* In the proceedings before the court of first instance, four times the amount of one full court fee shall be assessed. In the proceedings before the court of second instance, the same court fee shall be assessed; this also applies if the appeal is suc-

§ 99

cessful. If the application or the appeal is withdrawn before a decision is rendered, the court fees shall be reduced by one-half. The value of the subject matter in issue shall be determined ex officio. It shall be fixed in accordance with § 30, paragraph 2, of the *Kostenordnung*, provided that such value shall generally be deemed to amount to one hundred thousand German marks. No advances on costs shall be assessed. The company shall be liable for the costs. The costs may, however, be assessed in whole or in part against the applicant if fairness so requires. The parties shall not be entitled to reimbursement for their expenses.

kommt, so ermäßigt sich die Gebühr auf die Hälfte. Der Geschäftswert ist von Amts wegen festzusetzen. Er bestimmt sich nach § 30 Abs. 2 der Kostenordnung mit der Maßgabe, daß der Wert regelmäßig auf einhunderttausend Deutsche Mark anzunehmen ist. Kostenvorschüsse werden nicht erhoben. Schuldner der Kosten ist die Gesellschaft. Die Kosten können jedoch ganz oder zum Teil dem Antragsteller auferlegt werden, wenn dies der Billigkeit entspricht. Kosten der Beteiligten werden nicht erstattet.

§ 100
Personal Requirements for Membership on Supervisory Board

(1) Only a natural person with full legal capacity can be a member of the supervisory board.

(2) The following may not be members of a supervisory board:
1. a person who already is a member of the supervisory board of ten commercial companies or mining companies which are required by law to have a supervisory board,
2. a legal representative of an enterprise controlled by the company, or
3. a legal representative of another corporation or mining company whose supervisory board has a member who is also a member of the managing board of the company.

In determining the maximum number pursuant to the first sentence, No. 1, hereof, no account shall be taken of a maximum of five memberships on other supervisory boards which a legal representative (or, in the case of a sole proprietorship, the owner) of the controlling enterprise of an affiliated group of companies has in commercial companies and mining companies which are part of the group and which are required by law to have a supervisory board.

(3) The *Betriebsverfassungsgesetz*, the *Mitbestimmungsgesetz*, and the *Mitbestimmungsergänzungsgesetz* shall apply with respect to the additional personal requirements for membership on the supervisory board of members representing the employees and the additional members.

§ 100
Persönliche Voraussetzungen für Aufsichtsratsmitglieder

(1) Mitglied des Aufsichtsrats kann nur eine natürliche, unbeschränkt geschäftsfähige Person sein.

(2) Mitglied des Aufsichtsrats kann nicht sein, wer
1. bereits in zehn Handelsgesellschaften oder bergrechtlichen Gewerkschaften, die gesetzlich einen Aufsichtsrat zu bilden haben, Aufsichtsratsmitglied ist,
2. gesetzlicher Vertreter eines von der Gesellschaft abhängigen Unternehmens ist, oder
3. gesetzlicher Vertreter einer anderen Kapitalgesellschaft oder bergrechtlichen Gewerkschaft ist, deren Aufsichtsrat ein Vorstandsmitglied der Gesellschaft angehört.

Auf die Höchstzahl nach Satz 1 Nr. 1 sind bis zu fünf Aufsichtsratssitze nicht anzurechnen, die ein gesetzlicher Vertreter (beim Einzelkaufmann der Inhaber) des herrschenden Unternehmens eines Konzerns in zum Konzern gehörenden Handelsgesellschaften und bergrechtlichen Gewerkschaften, die gesetzlich einen Aufsichtsrat zu bilden haben, inne hat.

(3) Die anderen persönlichen Voraussetzungen der Aufsichtsratsmitglieder der Arbeitnehmer sowie der weiteren Mitglieder bestimmen sich nach dem Betriebsverfassungsgesetz, dem Mitbestimmungsgesetz und dem Mitbestimmungsergänzungsgesetz.

§ 100

(4) Die Satzung kann persönliche Voraussetzungen nur für Aufsichtsratsmitglieder fordern, die von der Hauptversammlung ohne Bindung an Wahlvorschläge gewählt oder auf Grund der Satzung in den Aufsichtsrat entsandt werden.

(4) The articles of incorporation may specify personal requirements only for such members of the supervisory board as can be freely elected by the shareholders without being subject to binding nominations or as are delegated to the supervisory board pursuant to the articles of incorporation.

§ 101
Bestellung der Aufsichtsratsmitglieder

(1) Die Mitglieder des Aufsichtsrats werden von der Hauptversammlung gewählt, soweit sie nicht in den Aufsichtsrat zu entsenden oder als Aufsichtsratsmitglieder der Arbeitnehmer nach dem Betriebsverfassungsgesetz oder dem Mitbestimmungsergänzungsgesetz zu wählen sind. An Wahlvorschläge ist die Hauptversammlung nur gemäß §§ 6 und 8 des Mitbestimmungsgesetzes gebunden.

(2) Ein Recht, Mitglieder in den Aufsichtsrat zu entsenden, kann, soweit es nicht Spitzenorganisationen der Gewerkschaften nach dem Mitbestimmungsergänzungsgesetz zusteht, nur durch die Satzung und nur für bestimmte Aktionäre oder für die jeweiligen Inhaber bestimmter Aktien begründet werden. Inhabern bestimmter Aktien kann das Entsendungsrecht nur eingeräumt werden, wenn die Aktien auf Namen lauten und ihre Übertragung an die Zustimmung der Gesellschaft gebunden ist. Die Aktien der Entsendungsberechtigten gelten nicht als eine besondere Gattung. Die Entsendungsrechte können insgesamt höchstens für ein Drittel der sich aus dem Gesetz oder der Satzung ergebenden Zahl der Aufsichtsratsmitglieder der Aktionäre eingeräumt werden.

(3) Stellvertreter von Aufsichtsratsmitgliedern können nicht bestellt werden. Jedoch kann für jedes Aufsichtsratsmitglied mit Ausnahme des weiteren Mitglieds, das nach dem Mitbestimmungsgesetz oder dem Mitbestimmungsergänzungsgesetz auf Vorschlag der übrigen Aufsichtsratsmitglieder gewählt wird, ein Ersatzmitglied bestellt werden, das Mitglied des Aufsichtsrats wird, wenn das Aufsichtsratsmitglied vor Ablauf seiner Amtszeit wegfällt. Das Ersatzmitglied kann nur gleichzeitig mit dem Aufsichtsratsmitglied bestellt werden. Auf seine Be-

§ 101
Appointment of Members of Supervisory Board

(1) The members of the supervisory board shall be elected by the shareholders unless they are to be delegated to the supervisory board or are to be elected as members representing the employees pursuant to the *Betriebsverfassungsgesetz* or the *Mitbestimmungsergänzungsgesetz*. The shareholders shall be subject to binding nominations only pursuant to §§ 6 and 8 of the *Mitbestimmungsgesetz*.

(2) The power to delegate members to the supervisory board, except where the central union organizations have such power pursuant to the *Mitbestimmungsergänzungsgesetz*, must be specified in the articles of incorporation, and can be granted only to specific shareholders or the holders of specific shares. The power to delegate may be reserved to the holders of specific shares only if such shares are in registered form and if their transfer requires the approval of the company. The shares of the persons to whom such power is reserved shall not be considered as a separate class of shares. The power to delegate may be reserved with respect to no more than one-third of the total number of members of the supervisory board representing the shareholders, as such number is determined by law or by the articles of incorporation.

(3) Substitutes for members of the supervisory board may not be appointed. However, a substitute member, who shall serve as a member of the supervisory board in the event that a member ceases to function prior to the expiration of his term of office, may be appointed for each member of the supervisory board, with the exception of the additional member to be elected upon the proposal of the remaining members of the supervisory board pursuant to the *Mitbestimmungsgesetz* or the *Mitbestimmungsergänzungsgesetz*. The substitute member must be appointed at the same time as the principal member of the supervisory board. The provisions regarding

§ 101

membership on the supervisory board shall apply to his appointment, as well as to the nullity and voidability of such appointment.

stellung sowie die Nichtigkeit und Anfechtung sei-ner Bestellung sind die für das Aufsichtsratsmit-glied geltenden Vorschriften anzuwenden.

§ 102
Term of Office of Supervisory Board Members

(1) The members of the supervisory board may not be appointed for a period of time extend-ing beyond the adjournment of the shareholders' meeting which adopts the resolutions concern-ing the ratification of acts of management for the fourth fiscal year following the beginning of the term of office. The fiscal year in which the term of office begins shall not be taken into account.

(2) The term of office of a substitute member shall terminate no later than at the end of the term of office of the supervisory board member whom he replaces.

§ 102
Amtszeit der Aufsichtsratsmitglieder

(1) Aufsichtsratsmitglieder können nicht für län-gere Zeit als bis zur Beendigung der Hauptversamm-lung bestellt werden, die über die Entlastung für das vierte Geschäftsjahr nach dem Beginn der Amtszeit beschließt. Das Geschäftsjahr, in dem die Amtszeit beginnt, wird nicht mitgerechnet.

(2) Das Amt des Ersatzmitglieds erlischt späte-stens mit Ablauf der Amtszeit des weggefallenen Aufsichtsratsmitglieds.

§ 103
Dismissal of Members of Supervisory Board

(1) Members of the supervisory board elected by the shareholders other than those elected pur-suant to binding nominations may be dismissed by them before the expiration of their term of office. The resolution shall require a majority of no less than three-fourths of the votes cast. The articles of incorporation may provide for a different majority and establish additional requirements.

(2) A supervisory board member who is dele-gated to the supervisory board pursuant to the articles of incorporation may be dismissed at any time by the person entitled to delegate him and be replaced by another. If the requirements set forth in the articles of incorporation concern-ing the power of delegation are no longer met, the shareholders may dismiss the delegated member by a simple majority of votes.

(3) The court shall dismiss a supervisory board member upon the application of the supervisory board whenever there is a compelling reason relating to such person. The supervisory board shall adopt the resolution concerning such appli-cation by simple majority. If the supervisory board member has been delegated to the super-visory board pursuant to the articles of incorpo-ration, shareholders whose combined holdings amount to no less than one-tenth of the stated

§ 103
Abberufung der Aufsichtsratsmitglieder

(1) Aufsichtsratsmitglieder, die von der Haupt-versammlung ohne Bindung an einen Wahlvor-schlag gewählt worden sind, können von ihr vor Ablauf der Amtszeit abberufen werden. Der Be-schluß bedarf einer Mehrheit, die mindestens drei Viertel der abgegebenen Stimmen umfaßt. Die Sat-zung kann eine andere Mehrheit und weitere Er-fordernisse bestimmen.

(2) Ein Aufsichtsratsmitglied, das auf Grund der Satzung in den Aufsichtsrat entsandt ist, kann von dem Entsendungsberechtigten jederzeit abberufen und durch ein anderes ersetzt werden. Sind die in der Satzung bestimmten Voraussetzungen des Ent-sendungsrechts weggefallen, so kann die Hauptver-sammlung das entsandte Mitglied mit einfacher Stimmenmehrheit abberufen.

(3) Das Gericht hat auf Antrag des Aufsichtsrats ein Aufsichtsratsmitglied abzuberufen, wenn in des-sen Person ein wichtiger Grund vorliegt. Der Auf-sichtsrat beschließt über die Antragstellung mit ein-facher Mehrheit. Ist das Aufsichtsratsmitglied auf Grund der Satzung in den Aufsichtsrat entsandt worden, so können auch Aktionäre, deren Anteile

zusammen den zehnten Teil des Grundkapitals oder den Nennbetrag von zwei Millionen Deutsche Mark erreichen, den Antrag stellen. Gegen die Entscheidung ist die sofortige Beschwerde zulässig.

(4) Für die Abberufung der Aufsichtsratsmitglieder, die weder von der Hauptversammlung ohne Bindung an einen Wahlvorschlag gewählt worden sind noch auf Grund der Satzung in den Aufsichtsrat entsandt sind, gelten außer Absatz 3 das Betriebsverfassungsgesetz, das Mitbestimmungsgesetz und das Mitbestimmungsergänzungsgesetz.

(5) Für die Abberufung eines Ersatzmitglieds gelten die Vorschriften über die Abberufung des Aufsichtsratsmitglieds, für das es bestellt ist.

§ 104
Bestellung durch das Gericht

(1) Gehört dem Aufsichtsrat die zur Beschlußfähigkeit nötige Zahl von Mitgliedern nicht an, so hat ihn das Gericht auf Antrag des Vorstands, eines Aufsichtsratsmitglieds oder eines Aktionärs auf diese Zahl zu ergänzen. Der Vorstand ist verpflichtet, den Antrag unverzüglich zu stellen, es sei denn, daß die rechtzeitige Ergänzung vor der nächsten Aufsichtsratssitzung zu erwarten ist. Hat der Aufsichtsrat auch aus Aufsichtsratsmitgliedern der Arbeitnehmer zu bestehen, so können auch den Antrag stellen

1. der Betriebsrat jedes Betriebs der Gesellschaft,
2. der Betriebsrat jedes anderen Betriebs, dessen Arbeitnehmer selbst oder durch Wahlmänner an der Wahl teilnehmen,
3. mindestens ein Zehntel oder einhundert der Arbeitnehmer, die selbst oder durch Wahlmänner an der Wahl teilnehmen,
4. Spitzenorganisationen der Gewerkschaften, die das Recht haben, Aufsichtsratsmitglieder der Arbeitnehmer vorzuschlagen oder zu entsenden.

Gegen die Entscheidung ist die sofortige Beschwerde zulässig.

(2) Gehören dem Aufsichtsrat länger als drei Monate weniger Mitglieder als die durch Gesetz oder Satzung festgesetzte Zahl an, so hat ihn das Gericht auf Antrag auf diese Zahl zu ergänzen. In dringenden Fällen hat das Gericht auf Antrag den Aufsichtsrat auch vor Ablauf der Frist zu ergänzen.

capital, or the par value of which amounts to no less than two million German marks, may likewise make such application. The decision of the court can be appealed.

(4) In addition to paragraph 3 of the *Betriebsverfassungsgesetz,* the *Mitbestimmungsgesetz* and the *Mitbestimmungsergänzungsgesetz* shall apply to the dismissal of such members of the supervisory board as have neither been freely elected by the shareholders without being subject to binding nominations nor been delegated to the supervisory board pursuant to the articles of incorporation.

(5) The provisions for the dismissal of a member of the supervisory board shall be equally applicable to the dismissal of a substitute member.

§ 104
Appointment by the Court

(1) If the supervisory board does not have the number of members necessary to form a quorum, the court shall augment it to reach such number, upon application by the managing board, by a member of the supervisory board, or by a shareholder. The managing board is required to present such application promptly, unless it can be expected that this quorum will be reached in time before the next following meeting of the supervisory board. If the supervisory board must also contain members representing the employees, the following parties shall also be entitled to make such application:

1. the works council of each of the company's plants,
2. the works council of any other plant, the employees of which participate in the election personally or through electors,
3. at least ten percent or one hundred of the employees who participate in the election personally or through electors,
4. central union organizations entitled to nominate or to delegate members of the supervisory board representing the employees.

The decision of the court can be appealed.

(2) If for more than three months the supervisory board has fewer members than the number specified in this Act or in the articles of incorporation, the court shall, upon application, augment it to reach such number. In urgent cases, the court shall, upon application, augment the supervisory board even before the expiration of

§ 104

this period. The right to make such an application shall be subject to paragraph 1 hereof. The decision of the court can be appealed.

Das Antragsrecht bestimmt sich nach Absatz 1. Gegen die Entscheidung ist die sofortige Beschwerde zulässig.

(3) Paragraph 2 hereof shall apply to a supervisory board in which the employees have a right to be represented pursuant to the *Mitbestimmungsgesetz* or the *Mitbestimmungsergänzungsgesetz*, subject to the following provisions:

(3) Absatz 2 ist auf einen Aufsichtsrat, in dem die Arbeitnehmer ein Mitbestimmungsrecht nach dem Mitbestimmungsgesetz oder dem Mitbestimmungsergänzungsgesetz haben, mit der Maßgabe anzuwenden,

1. the court may not augment the supervisory board with respect to the additional member, to be elected pursuant to the statutes referred to, upon the proposal of the other members of the supervisory board,

2. an urgent case shall always be deemed to exist if the supervisory board, apart from the additional member referred to in No. 1, above, does not have the full number of members required pursuant to the law or the articles of incorporation.

1. daß das Gericht den Aufsichtsrat hinsichtlich des weiteren Mitglieds, das nach diesen Gesetzen auf Vorschlag der übrigen Aufsichtsratmitglieder gewählt wird, nicht ergänzen kann,

2. daß es stets ein dringender Fall ist, wenn dem Aufsichtsrat, abgesehen von dem in Nummer 1 genannten weiteren Mitglied, nicht alle Mitglieder angehören, aus denen er nach Gesetz oder Satzung zu bestehen hat.

(4) If the supervisory board must also contain members representing the employees, the court shall augment the board's membership in such a way as to yield the numerical proportion required for the composition of the board. If membership on the supervisory board is to be augmented to enable it to adopt a resolution, the above shall apply only to the extent that the number of members required to enable the board to adopt a resolution makes it possible to keep this proportion. If a member of the supervisory board who must meet specific personal requirements pursuant to this Act or the articles of incorporation is to be replaced, the supervisory board member appointed by the court must also meet these requirements. In the event of replacement of a member of the supervisory board with respect to whose election a central union organization or the works council would have a right of nomination, the court shall consider the nominations of these organizations unless an overriding interest of the company or of the public would bar the appointment of the person nominated; the same shall apply if the member of the supervisory board is to be elected by electors with respect to joint nominations by the works councils of the enterprises of a group of companies for which such electors are to be elected.

(4) Hat der Aufsichtsrat auch aus Aufsichtsratmitgliedern der Arbeitnehmer zu bestehen, so hat das Gericht ihn so zu ergänzen, daß das für seine Zusammensetzung maßgebende zahlenmäßige Verhältnis hergestellt wird. Wenn der Aufsichtsrat zur Herstellung seiner Beschlußfähigkeit ergänzt wird, gilt dies nur, soweit die zur Beschlußfähigkeit nötige Zahl der Aufsichtsratmitglieder die Wahrung dieses Verhältnisses möglich macht. Ist ein Aufsichtsratmitglied zu ersetzen, das nach Gesetz oder Satzung in persönlicher Hinsicht besonderen Voraussetzungen entsprechen muß, so muß auch das vom Gericht bestellte Aufsichtsratmitglied diesen Voraussetzungen entsprechen. Ist ein Aufsichtsratmitglied zu ersetzen, bei dessen Wahl eine Spitzenorganisation der Gewerkschaften oder die Betriebsräte ein Vorschlagsrecht hätten, so soll das Gericht Vorschläge dieser Stellen berücksichtigen, soweit nicht überwiegende Belange der Gesellschaft oder der Allgemeinheit der Bestellung des Vorgeschlagenen entgegenstehen; das gleiche gilt, wenn das Aufsichtsratmitglied durch Wahlmänner zu wählen wäre, für gemeinsame Vorschläge der Betriebsräte der Konzernunternehmen, in denen Wahlmänner zu wählen sind.

(5) The term of office of the court-appointed member of the supervisory board shall terminate, in any event, as soon as the vacancy has been filled.

(5) Das Amt des gerichtlich bestellten Aufsichtsratmitglieds erlischt in jedem Fall, sobald der Mangel behoben ist.

§ 104

(6) Das gerichtlich bestellte Aufsichtsratsmitglied hat Anspruch auf Ersatz angemessener barer Auslagen und, wenn den Aufsichtsratsmitgliedern der Gesellschaft eine Vergütung gewährt wird, auf Vergütung für seine Tätigkeit. Auf Antrag des Aufsichtsratsmitglieds setzt das Gericht die Auslagen und die Vergütung fest. Gegen die Entscheidung ist die sofortige Beschwerde zulässig. Die weitere Beschwerde ist ausgeschlossen. Aus der rechtskräftigen Entscheidung findet die Zwangsvollstreckung nach der Zivilprozeßordnung statt.

§ 105

Unvereinbarkeit der Zugehörigkeit zum Vorstand und zum Aufsichtsrat

(1) Ein Aufsichtsratsmitglied kann nicht zugleich Vorstandsmitglied, dauernd Stellvertreter von Vorstandsmitgliedern, Prokurist oder zum gesamten Geschäftsbetrieb ermächtigter Handlungsbevollmächtigter der Gesellschaft sein.

(2) Nur für einen im voraus begrenzten Zeitraum, höchstens für ein Jahr, kann der Aufsichtsrat einzelne seiner Mitglieder zu Stellvertretern von fehlenden oder behinderten Vorstandsmitgliedern bestellen. Eine wiederholte Bestellung oder Verlängerung der Amtszeit ist zulässig, wenn dadurch die Amtszeit insgesamt ein Jahr nicht übersteigt. Während ihrer Amtszeit als Stellvertreter von Vorstandsmitgliedern können die Aufsichtsratsmitglieder keine Tätigkeit als Aufsichtsratsmitglied ausüben. Das Wettbewerbsverbot des § 88 gilt für sie nicht.

§ 106

Bekanntmachung der Änderungen im Aufsichtsrat

Der Vorstand hat jeden Wechsel der Aufsichtsratsmitglieder unverzüglich in den Gesellschaftsblättern bekanntzumachen und die Bekanntmachung zum Handelsregister einzureichen.

§ 107

Innere Ordnung des Aufsichtsrats

(1) Der Aufsichtsrat hat nach näherer Bestimmung der Satzung aus seiner Mitte einen Vorsitzenden und mindestens einen Stellvertreter zu wählen. Der

(6) A court-appointed member of the supervisory board shall be entitled to reimbursement for reasonable cash expenditures and, where remuneration is granted to the members of the company's supervisory board, to remuneration for his services. The court shall determine such expenditures and remuneration upon application of the supervisory board member. The decision of the court can be appealed. It shall not be subject to further appeal. The final decision shall be enforceable in accordance with the provisions of the Code of Civil Procedure.

§ 105

Incompatibility of Membership on Managing Board with Membership on Supervisory Board

(1) A member of the supervisory board may not at the same time be a member of the managing board, a permanent substitute for any member of the managing board, a *Prokurist*, or an agent whose powers to bind the company extend to the business as a whole.

(2) The supervisory board may appoint, for a period of time limited in advance, but not to exceed one year, one or more of its members to act as substitutes for members of the managing board who are absent or unable to attend. A reappointment or extension of their terms of office is permissible provided that the aggregate term of each does not exceed one year. During their terms of office as substitutes for members of the managing board, such members of the supervisory board may not act as members of the supervisory board. The provisions of § 88 prohibiting competition shall not apply to them.

§ 106

Publication of Changes in Supervisory Board

The managing board shall promptly announce any change in the membership of the supervisory board in the publications designated in the company's articles of incorporation and shall file such announcement with the Commercial Register.

§ 107

Organization of Supervisory Board

(1) The supervisory board shall, subject to more specific provisions in the articles of incorporation, elect from among its members a chair-

man and at least one vice chairman. The managing board shall report to the Commercial Register who has been so elected. The vice chairman shall have the rights and duties of the chairman only if the latter is unable to attend.

(2) Minutes of the meetings of the supervisory board shall be kept, which the chairman shall sign. The minutes shall indicate the place and time of the meeting, the participants, the items on the agenda, the essential content of the deliberations, and the resolutions adopted by the supervisory board. Non-compliance with the first or second sentence hereof shall not render a resolution invalid. Each member of the supervisory board shall receive, on request, a copy of the minutes of the meeting.

(3) The supervisory board may appoint from among its members one or more committees, in particular in order to prepare its deliberations and resolutions, or in order to supervise the implementation of its resolutions. Neither the duties referred to in paragraph 1, first sentence, hereof, § 59, paragraph 3, § 77, paragraph 2, first sentence, § 84, paragraph 1, first and third sentences, paragraph 2, and paragraph 3, first sentence, § 111, paragraph 3, §§ 171, 314, paragraphs 2 and 3, and § 331, paragraph 3, third sentence, nor resolutions to the effect that certain types of transactions require approval by the supervisory board, may be delegated to a committee for adoption of resolutions by it in lieu of the supervisory board.

§ 108
Resolutions of the Supervisory Board

(1) Action taken by the supervisory board shall be in the form of a resolution.

(2) The quorum required for a resolution by the supervisory board may be specified in the articles of incorporation unless it is provided for by statute. If the quorum is specified neither in a statute nor in the articles of incorporation, the supervisory board may adopt a resolution only if at least half of the total membership required by statute or the articles of incorporation participates in its adoption. In any event, at least three members must participate in the vote on a resolution. There may be a quorum even though the supervisory board is composed of fewer persons than required by statute or the articles of incorporation, and even though the numerical pro-

Vorstand hat zum Handelsregister anzumelden, wer gewählt ist. Der Stellvertreter hat nur dann die Rechte und Pflichten des Vorsitzenden, wenn dieser behindert ist.

(2) Über die Sitzungen des Aufsichtsrats ist eine Niederschrift anzufertigen, die der Vorsitzende zu unterzeichnen hat. In der Niederschrift sind der Ort und der Tag der Sitzung, die Teilnehmer, die Gegenstände der Tagesordnung, der wesentliche Inhalt der Verhandlungen und die Beschlüsse des Aufsichtsrats anzugeben. Ein Verstoß gegen Satz 1 oder Satz 2 macht einen Beschluß nicht unwirksam. Jedem Mitglied des Aufsichtsrats ist auf Verlangen eine Abschrift der Sitzungsniederschrift auszuhändigen.

(3) Der Aufsichtsrat kann aus seiner Mitte einen oder mehrere Ausschüsse bestellen, namentlich, um seine Verhandlungen und Beschlüsse vorzubereiten oder die Ausführung seiner Beschlüsse zu überwachen. Die Aufgaben nach Absatz 1 Satz 1, § 59 Abs. 3, § 77 Abs. 2 Satz 1, § 84 Abs. 1 Satz 1 und 3, Abs. 2 und Abs. 3 Satz 1, § 111 Abs. 3, §§ 171, 314 Abs. 2 und 3 und § 331 Abs. 3 Satz 3 sowie Beschlüsse, daß bestimmte Arten von Geschäften nur mit Zustimmung des Aufsichtsrats vorgenommen werden dürfen, können einem Ausschuß nicht an Stelle des Aufsichtsrats zur Beschlußfassung überwiesen werden.

§ 108
Beschlußfassung des Aufsichtsrats

(1) Der Aufsichtsrat entscheidet durch Beschluß.

(2) Die Beschlußfähigkeit des Aufsichtsrats kann, soweit sie nicht gesetzlich geregelt ist, durch die Satzung bestimmt werden. Ist sie weder gesetzlich noch durch die Satzung geregelt, so ist der Aufsichtsrat nur beschlußfähig, wenn mindestens die Hälfte der Mitglieder, aus denen er nach Gesetz oder Satzung insgesamt zu bestehen hat, an der Beschlußfassung teilnimmt. In jedem Fall müssen mindestens drei Mitglieder an der Beschlußfassung teilnehmen. Der Beschlußfähigkeit steht nicht entgegen, daß dem Aufsichtsrat weniger Mitglieder als die durch Gesetz oder Satzung festgesetzte Zahl angehören, auch wenn das für seine Zusammen-

setzung maßgebende zahlenmäßige Verhältnis nicht gewahrt ist.

(3) Abwesende Aufsichtsratsmitglieder können dadurch an der Beschlußfassung des Aufsichtsrats und seiner Ausschüsse teilnehmen, daß sie schriftliche Stimmabgaben überreichen lassen. Die schriftlichen Stimmabgaben können durch andere Aufsichtsratsmitglieder überreicht werden. Sie können auch durch Personen, die nicht dem Aufsichtsrat angehören, übergeben werden, wenn diese nach § 109 Abs. 3 zur Teilnahme an der Sitzung berechtigt sind.

(4) Schriftliche, telegrafische oder fernmündliche Beschlußfassungen des Aufsichtsrats oder eines Ausschusses sind nur zulässig, wenn kein Mitglied diesem Verfahren widerspricht.

§ 109

Teilnahme an Sitzungen des Aufsichtsrats und seiner Ausschüsse

(1) An den Sitzungen des Aufsichtsrats und seiner Ausschüsse sollen Personen, die weder dem Aufsichtsrat noch dem Vorstand angehören, nicht teilnehmen. Sachverständige und Auskunftspersonen können zur Beratung über einzelne Gegenstände zugezogen werden.

(2) Aufsichtsratsmitglieder, die dem Ausschuß nicht angehören, können an den Ausschußsitzungen teilnehmen, wenn der Vorsitzende des Aufsichtsrats nichts anderes bestimmt.

(3) Die Satzung kann zulassen, daß an den Sitzungen des Aufsichtsrats und seiner Ausschüsse Personen, die dem Aufsichtsrat nicht angehören, an Stelle von verhinderten Aufsichtsratsmitgliedern teilnehmen können, wenn diese sie hierzu schriftlich ermächtigt haben.

(4) Abweichende gesetzliche Vorschriften bleiben unberührt.

§ 110

Einberufung des Aufsichtsrats

(1) Jedes Aufsichtsratsmitglied oder der Vorstand kann unter Angabe des Zwecks und der Gründe verlangen, daß der Vorsitzende des Aufsichtsrats unverzüglich den Aufsichtsrat einberuft. Die Sitzung muß binnen zwei Wochen nach der Einberufung stattfinden.

(2) Wird einem Verlangen, das von mindestens zwei Aufsichtsratsmitgliedern oder vom Vorstand

portion required for its composition does not exist.

(3) Members of the supervisory board who are not present may participate in the resolutions of the supervisory board and of its committees by having written votes delivered to the meeting. The written votes may be delivered by other members of the supervisory board. They may also be delivered by persons who are not members of the supervisory board, if such persons are entitled to participate in the meeting pursuant to § 109, paragraph 3.

(4) Resolutions of the supervisory board or of one of its committees may be adopted in writing, by cable, or by telephone only if none of the members objects to such procedure.

§ 109
Attendance at Meetings of Supervisory Board and Its Committees

(1) Persons who are not members of either the supervisory board or the managing board may not attend the meetings of the supervisory board and its committees. Experts and consultants may be called in for advice on specific subjects.

(2) Members of the supervisory board who are not members of a committee may attend the meetings of such committee unless the chairman of the supervisory board rules to the contrary.

(3) The articles of incorporation may permit persons who are not members of the supervisory board to attend the meetings of the supervisory board and its committees in lieu of members of the supervisory board who are unable to attend, provided that they have written authorization from such members.

(4) The foregoing shall not affect any contrary statutory provisions.

§ 110
Calling Meetings of Supervisory Board

(1) Each member of the supervisory board or the managing board may, upon stating the purpose and reasons therefor, request that the chairman of the supervisory board promptly call a meeting of the supervisory board. The meeting must take place within two weeks from the date it is called.

(2) In the event of non-compliance with a request to this effect made by at least two members

§ 110

of the supervisory board or by the managing board, the parties making such request may call a meeting of the supervisory board upon stating these facts.

(3) A meeting of the supervisory board should, as a rule, be called once every three months; it must be called once every six months.

§ 111
Duties and Rights of Supervisory Board

(1) The supervisory board shall supervise the management of the company.

(2) The supervisory board may inspect and examine the company's books and records, as well as its assets, in particular, cash, securities, and stocks of goods on hand. It may also authorize individual members or, with respect to specific tasks, special experts, to make such inspection or examination.

(3) The supervisory board shall call a shareholders' meeting whenever required in the interest of the company. A simple majority shall suffice to adopt a resolution to this effect.

(4) Managerial functions cannot be delegated to the supervisory board. However, the articles of incorporation or the supervisory board may provide that specific types of transactions may be undertaken only with its approval. If the supervisory board refuses to grant such approval, the managing board may ask that such approval be submitted to a shareholders' resolution. A shareholders' resolution in favor of the approval shall require a majority of at least three-fourths of the votes cast. The articles of incorporation may neither provide for a different majority nor establish additional requirements.

(5) The members of the supervisory board may not delegate their duties to others.

§ 112
Representation of Company in Dealings with Members of Managing Board

In dealings with members of the managing board, the supervisory board shall represent the company both in and out of court.

§ 113
Remuneration of Members of Supervisory Board

(1) The members of the supervisory board may be paid a remuneration for their services.

geäußert ist, nicht entsprochen, so können die Antragsteller unter Mitteilung des Sachverhalts selbst den Aufsichtsrat einberufen.

(3) Der Aufsichtsrat soll in der Regel einmal im Kalendervierteljahr, er muß einmal im Kalenderhalbjahr einberufen werden.

§ 111
Aufgaben und Rechte des Aufsichtsrats

(1) Der Aufsichtsrat hat die Geschäftsführung zu überwachen.

(2) Der Aufsichtsrat kann die Bücher und Schriften der Gesellschaft sowie die Vermögensgegenstände, namentlich die Gesellschaftskasse und die Bestände an Wertpapieren und Waren, einsehen und prüfen. Er kann damit auch einzelne Mitglieder oder für bestimmte Aufgaben besondere Sachverständige beauftragen.

(3) Der Aufsichtsrat hat eine Hauptversammlung einzuberufen, wenn das Wohl der Gesellschaft es fordert. Für den Beschluß genügt die einfache Mehrheit.

(4) Maßnahmen der Geschäftsführung können dem Aufsichtsrat nicht übertragen werden. Die Satzung oder der Aufsichtsrat kann jedoch bestimmen, daß bestimmte Arten von Geschäften nur mit seiner Zustimmung vorgenommen werden dürfen. Verweigert der Aufsichtsrat seine Zustimmung, so kann der Vorstand verlangen, daß die Hauptversammlung über die Zustimmung beschließt. Der Beschluß, durch den die Hauptversammlung zustimmt, bedarf einer Mehrheit, die mindestens drei Viertel der abgegebenen Stimmen umfaßt. Die Satzung kann weder eine andere Mehrheit noch weitere Erfordernisse bestimmen.

(5) Die Aufsichtsratsmitglieder können ihre Aufgaben nicht durch andere wahrnehmen lassen.

§ 112
Vertretung der Gesellschaft gegenüber Vorstandsmitgliedern

Vorstandsmitgliedern gegenüber vertritt der Aufsichtsrat die Gesellschaft gerichtlich und außergerichtlich.

§ 113
Vergütung der Aufsichtsratsmitglieder

(1) Den Aufsichtsratsmitgliedern kann für ihre Tätigkeit eine Vergütung gewährt werden. Sie kann

in der Satzung festgesetzt oder von der Hauptversammlung bewilligt werden. Sie soll in einem angemessenen Verhältnis zu den Aufgaben der Aufsichtsratsmitglieder und zur Lage der Gesellschaft
stehen. Ist die Vergütung in der Satzung festgesetzt,
so kann die Hauptversammlung eine Satzungsänderung, durch welche die Vergütung herabgesetzt
wird, mit einfacher Stimmenmehrheit beschließen.

(2) Den Mitgliedern des ersten Aufsichtsrats kann
nur die Hauptversammlung eine Vergütung für ihre
Tätigkeit bewilligen. Der Beschluß kann erst in der
Hauptversammlung gefaßt werden, die über die
Entlastung der Mitglieder des ersten Aufsichtsrats
beschließt.

(3) Wird den Aufsichtsratsmitgliedern ein Anteil
am Jahresgewinn der Gesellschaft gewährt, so berechnet sich der Anteil nach dem Bilanzgewinn, vermindert um einen Betrag von mindestens vier vom
Hundert der auf den Nennbetrag der Aktien geleisteten Einlagen. Entgegenstehende Festsetzungen
sind nichtig.

§ 114

Verträge mit Aufsichtsratsmitgliedern

(1) Verpflichtet sich ein Aufsichtsratsmitglied
außerhalb seiner Tätigkeit im Aufsichtsrat durch
einen Dienstvertrag, durch den ein Arbeitsverhältnis
nicht begründet wird, oder durch einen Werkvertrag
gegenüber der Gesellschaft zu einer Tätigkeit höherer Art, so hängt die Wirksamkeit des Vertrags
von der Zustimmung des Aufsichtsrats ab.

(2) Gewährt die Gesellschaft auf Grund eines
solchen Vertrags dem Aufsichtsratsmitglied eine
Vergütung, ohne daß der Aufsichtsrat dem Vertrag
zugestimmt hat, so hat das Aufsichtsratsmitglied die
Vergütung zurückzugewähren, es sei denn, daß der
Aufsichtsrat den Vertrag genehmigt. Ein Anspruch
des Aufsichtsratsmitglieds gegen die Gesellschaft
auf Herausgabe der durch die geleistete Tätigkeit
erlangten Bereicherung bleibt unberührt; der Anspruch kann jedoch nicht gegen den Rückgewähr-
anspruch aufgerechnet werden.

Such remuneration may be specified in the articles of incorporation or authorized by a shareholders' resolution. It shall be commensurate
with the duties of the members of the supervisory board and with the condition of the company. If the remuneration is specified in the
articles of incorporation, the shareholders may,
by simple majority, amend the articles of incorporation to reduce the remuneration.

(2) The members of the initial supervisory
board may be granted a remuneration for their
services only by the shareholders. A resolution
to this effect may not be adopted prior to the
shareholders' meeting which adopts the resolution concerning the release from responsibility
of the members of the initial supervisory board.

(3) If any portion of the company's profit for
the year is granted to the members of the supervisory board, such portion shall be computed by
reference to the retained earnings, reduced by
an amount of no less than four percent of the contributions rendered on the par value of the
shares. Any provisions to the contrary shall be
void.

§ 114

**Agreements with Members
of Supervisory Board**

(1) In the event that a member of the supervisory board, in addition to his activities on the
supervisory board, undertakes to render professional services for the company in accordance
with an agreement for services which does not
create an employer-employee relationship, or
in accordance with an agreement to produce a
given result, such agreement shall be binding
only if approved by the supervisory board.

(2) If the company in accordance with such an
agreement grants a remuneration to the member
of the supervisory board without the prior approval of the supervisory board, the member
shall return such remuneration unless the supervisory board subsequently approves the agreement. The foregoing shall not affect any claim
for unjust enrichment that the supervisory board
member may have against the company because
of the services rendered; such claim may not,
however, be set off against the company's claim
for repayment of the remuneration.

§ 114

§ 115
Extension of Credit and Loans to Members of Supervisory Board

(1) The company may extend credit or make loans to members of its supervisory board only with the approval of the supervisory board. A controlling company may extend credit or make loans to members of the supervisory board of a controlled enterprise only with the approval of its supervisory board; a controlled company may extend credit or make loans to members of the supervisory board of the controlling enterprise only with the approval of the supervisory board of the controlling enterprise. The approval may be granted only for specific credit transactions or types of credit transactions and for no longer than three months in advance. The resolution approving such transactions shall specify the interest and the method of repayment of the principal. If the supervisory board member carries on a business as sole proprietor, such approval shall not be necessary if the credit or loan is extended to pay for merchandise which the company furnishes to such sole proprietorship.

(2) Paragraph 1 hereof shall also apply with respect to credit or loans extended to a spouse or minor child of a member of the supervisory board or to any third party acting for the account of such persons or for the account of a member of the supervisory board.

(3) If a member of the supervisory board is also a legal representative of another legal entity or a member of a business partnership, the company may extend credit or loans to such legal entity or business partnership only with the approval of the supervisory board; paragraph 1, third and fourth sentences, hereof shall apply *mutatis mutandis*. This shall not apply if the legal entity or business partnership is related to the company or if the credit or loans are extended to pay for merchandise furnished by the company to such legal entity or business partnership.

(4) Credit or loans extended in violation of the provisions of paragraphs 1 to 3 hereof shall be repaid immediately, notwithstanding any agreements to the contrary, unless the supervisory board approves them subsequently.

(5) If the company is a bank, the provisions of the *Gesetz über das Kreditwesen* shall apply in lieu of paragraphs 1 to 4 hereof.

§ 115
Kreditgewährung an Aufsichtsratsmitglieder

(1) Die Gesellschaft darf ihren Aufsichtsratsmitgliedern Kredit nur mit Einwilligung des Aufsichtsrats gewähren. Eine herrschende Gesellschaft darf Kredite an Aufsichtsratsmitglieder eines abhängigen Unternehmens nur mit Einwilligung ihres Aufsichtsrats, eine abhängige Gesellschaft darf Kredite an Aufsichtsratsmitglieder des herrschenden Unternehmens nur mit Einwilligung des Aufsichtsrats des herrschenden Unternehmens gewähren. Die Einwilligung kann nur für bestimmte Kreditgeschäfte oder Arten von Kreditgeschäften und nicht für länger als drei Monate im voraus erteilt werden. Der Beschluß über die Einwilligung hat die Verzinsung und Rückzahlung des Kredits zu regeln. Betreibt das Aufsichtsratsmitglied ein Handelsgewerbe als Einzelkaufmann, so ist die Einwilligung nicht erforderlich, wenn der Kredit für die Bezahlung von Waren gewährt wird, welche die Gesellschaft seinem Handelsgeschäft liefert.

(2) Absatz 1 gilt auch für Kredite an den Ehegatten oder an ein minderjähriges Kind eines Aufsichtsratsmitglieds und für Kredite an einen Dritten, der für Rechnung dieser Personen oder für Rechnung eines Aufsichtsratsmitglieds handelt.

(3) Ist ein Aufsichtsratsmitglied zugleich gesetzlicher Vertreter einer anderen juristischen Person oder Gesellschafter einer Personenhandelsgesellschaft, so darf die Gesellschaft der juristischen Person oder der Personenhandelsgesellschaft Kredit nur mit Einwilligung des Aufsichtsrats gewähren; Absatz 1 Satz 3 und 4 gilt sinngemäß. Dies gilt nicht, wenn die juristische Person oder die Personenhandelsgesellschaft mit der Gesellschaft verbunden ist oder wenn der Kredit für die Bezahlung von Waren gewährt wird, welche die Gesellschaft der juristischen Person oder der Personenhandelsgesellschaft liefert.

(4) Wird entgegen den Absätzen 1 bis 3 Kredit gewährt, so ist der Kredit ohne Rücksicht auf entgegenstehende Vereinbarungen sofort zurückzugewähren, wenn nicht der Aufsichtsrat nachträglich zustimmt.

(5) Ist die Gesellschaft ein Kreditinstitut, so gelten an Stelle der Absätze 1 bis 4 die Vorschriften des Gesetzes über das Kreditwesen.

§ 116

**Sorgfaltspflicht und Verantwortlichkeit
der Aufsichtsratsmitglieder**

Für die Sorgfaltspflicht und Verantwortlichkeit der Aufsichtsratsmitglieder gilt § 93 über die Sorgfaltspflicht und Verantwortlichkeit der Vorstandsmitglieder sinngemäß.

Dritter Abschnitt

Benutzung des Einflusses auf die Gesellschaft

§ 117

Schadenersatzpflicht

(1) Wer vorsätzlich unter Benutzung seines Einflusses auf die Gesellschaft ein Mitglied des Vorstands oder des Aufsichtsrats, einen Prokuristen oder einen Handlungsbevollmächtigten dazu bestimmt, zum Schaden der Gesellschaft oder ihrer Aktionäre zu handeln, ist der Gesellschaft zum Ersatz des ihr daraus entstehenden Schadens verpflichtet. Er ist auch den Aktionären zum Ersatz des ihnen daraus entstehenden Schadens verpflichtet, soweit sie, abgesehen von einem Schaden, der ihnen durch Schädigung der Gesellschaft zugefügt worden ist, geschädigt worden sind.

(2) Neben ihm haften als Gesamtschuldner die Mitglieder des Vorstands und des Aufsichtsrats, wenn sie unter Verletzung ihrer Pflichten gehandelt haben. Ist streitig, ob sie die Sorgfalt eines ordentlichen und gewissenhaften Geschäftsleiters angewandt haben, so trifft sie die Beweislast. Der Gesellschaft und auch den Aktionären gegenüber tritt die Ersatzpflicht der Mitglieder des Vorstands und des Aufsichtsrats nicht ein, wenn die Handlung auf einem gesetzmäßigen Beschluß der Hauptversammlung beruht. Dadurch, daß der Aufsichtsrat die Handlung gebilligt hat, wird die Ersatzpflicht nicht ausgeschlossen.

(3) Neben ihm haftet ferner als Gesamtschuldner, wer durch die schädigende Handlung einen Vorteil erlangt hat, sofern er die Beeinflussung vorsätzlich veranlaßt hat.

(4) Für die Aufhebung der Ersatzpflicht gegenüber der Gesellschaft gilt sinngemäß § 93 Abs. 4 Satz 3 und 4.

§ 116

**Duty of Care and Liability of Members
of Supervisory Board**

§ 93, relating to the duty of care and the liability of the members of the managing board, shall apply, *mutatis mutandis*, to the duty of care and liability of the members of the supervisory board.

Third Division

Abuse of Influence on the Company

§ 117

Liability for Damages

(1) Any person who, by using his influence on the company, intentionally causes a member of the managing board or a member of the supervisory board, a *Prokurist*, or an agent whose powers to bind the company extend to the business as a whole to act to the detriment of the company or its shareholders shall be liable to the company for any damage resulting therefrom. Such person shall also be liable to the shareholders for damage resulting from such act to the extent that they have sustained damage other than that caused to them by virtue of the fact that the company has been injured.

(2) Together with such person, the members of the managing board and of the supervisory board shall be jointly and severally liable if they acted in violation of their duties. In case of a contest as to whether they acted with the care of a diligent and prudent executive, they shall bear the burden of proof. Members of the managing board and of the supervisory board shall not be liable to the company or to the shareholders if their action was based on a lawful shareholders' resolution. Liability for damages shall not be precluded by the fact that the supervisory board has approved such action.

(3) In addition to such person, anyone who gained an advantage by virtue of the action which caused the damage shall be jointly and severally liable, provided that he intentionally caused such abuse of influence.

(4) § 93, paragraph 4, third and fourth sentences, shall apply *mutatis mutandis* with respect to the grounds precluding liability to the company.

(5) The company's claim for damages may also be asserted by the creditors of the company to the extent that they cannot obtain satisfaction from the company. As far as the creditors of the company are concerned, the liability for damages shall be barred neither by a waiver or compromise effected by the company nor by the fact that the act was based upon a shareholders' resolution. If an order subjecting the assets of the company to bankruptcy proceedings has been issued, the receiver in bankruptcy shall exercise the rights of the creditors during the pendency of such proceedings.

(6) The claims arising out of these provisions shall be barred after the expiration of five years.

(7) The above provisions shall not apply if the member of the managing board or of the supervisory board, a *Prokurist*, or an agent whose powers to bind the company extend to the business as a whole was induced to take the action causing the injury by

1. the exercise of voting rights at the shareholders' meeting,
2. the exercise of the power of direction pursuant to a control agreement, or
3. the exercise of the powers of direction of a principal company (§ 319) which has integrated the company.

Fourth Division

Shareholders' Meeting

First Subdivision
Rights of Shareholders

§ 118
General Provisions

(1) The shareholders shall exercise their rights with respect to corporate matters in the shareholders' meeting unless the law provides otherwise.

(2) The members of the managing board and of the supervisory board shall attend the shareholders' meetings.

§ 119
Rights of the Shareholders

(1) The shareholders shall by resolution decide all matters expressly provided for by law and in the articles of incorporation, in particular,

(5) Der Ersatzanspruch der Gesellschaft kann auch von den Gläubigern der Gesellschaft geltend gemacht werden, soweit sie von dieser keine Befriedigung erlangen können. Den Gläubigern gegenüber wird die Ersatzpflicht weder durch einen Verzicht oder Vergleich der Gesellschaft noch dadurch aufgehoben, daß die Handlung auf einem Beschluß der Hauptversammlung beruht. Ist über das Vermögen der Gesellschaft das Konkursverfahren eröffnet, so übt während dessen Dauer der Konkursverwalter das Recht der Gläubiger aus.

(6) Die Ansprüche aus diesen Vorschriften verjähren in fünf Jahren.

(7) Diese Vorschriften gelten nicht, wenn das Mitglied des Vorstands oder des Aufsichtsrats, der Prokurist oder der Handlungsbevollmächtigte durch Ausübung

1. des Stimmrechts in der Hauptversammlung,
2. der Leitungsmacht auf Grund eines Beherrschungsvertrags oder
3. der Leitungsmacht einer Hauptgesellschaft (§ 319), in die die Gesellschaft eingegliedert ist,

zu der schädigenden Handlung bestimmt worden ist.

Vierter Abschnitt
Hauptversammlung

Erster Unterabschnitt
Rechte der Hauptversammlung

§ 118
Allgemeines

(1) Die Aktionäre üben ihre Rechte in den Angelegenheiten der Gesellschaft in der Hauptversammlung aus, soweit das Gesetz nichts anderes bestimmt.

(2) Die Mitglieder des Vorstands und des Aufsichtsrats sollen an der Hauptversammlung teilnehmen.

§ 119
Rechte der Hauptversammlung

(1) Die Hauptversammlung beschließt in den im Gesetz und in der Satzung ausdrücklich bestimmten Fällen, namentlich über

1. die Bestellung der Mitglieder des Aufsichtsrats, soweit sie nicht in den Aufsichtsrat zu entsenden oder als Aufsichtsratsmitglieder der Arbeitnehmer nach dem Betriebsverfassungsgesetz oder dem Mitbestimmungsergänzungsgesetz zu wählen sind;
2. die Verwendung des Bilanzgewinns;
3. die Entlastung der Mitglieder des Vorstands und des Aufsichtsrats;
4. die Bestellung der Abschlußprüfer;
5. Satzungsänderungen;
6. Maßnahmen der Kapitalbeschaffung und der Kapitalherabsetzung;
7. die Bestellung von Prüfern zur Prüfung von Vorgängen bei der Gründung oder der Geschäftsführung;
8. die Auflösung der Gesellschaft.

(2) Über Fragen der Geschäftsführung kann die Hauptversammlung nur entscheiden, wenn der Vorstand es verlangt.

§ 120
Entlastung

(1) Die Hauptversammlung beschließt alljährlich in den ersten acht Monaten des Geschäftsjahrs über die Entlastung der Mitglieder des Vorstands und über die Entlastung der Mitglieder des Aufsichtsrats. Über die Entlastung eines einzelnen Mitglieds ist gesondert abzustimmen, wenn die Hauptversammlung es beschließt oder eine Minderheit es verlangt, deren Anteile zusammen den zehnten Teil des Grundkapitals oder den Nennbetrag von zwei Millionen Deutsche Mark erreichen.

(2) Durch die Entlastung billigt die Hauptversammlung die Verwaltung der Gesellschaft durch die Mitglieder des Vorstands und des Aufsichtsrats. Die Entlastung enthält keinen Verzicht auf Ersatzansprüche.

(3) Die Verhandlung über die Entlastung soll mit der Verhandlung über die Verwendung des Bilanzgewinns verbunden werden. Der Vorstand hat den Jahresabschluß, den Geschäftsbericht und den Bericht des Aufsichtsrats der Hauptversammlung vorzulegen. Für die Auslegung dieser Vorlagen und

1. the appointment of the members of the supervisory board, unless such members are required to be delegated to the supervisory board or to be elected members of the supervisory board as representatives of the employees pursuant to the *Betriebsverfassungsgesetz* or the *Mitbestimmungsergänzungsgesetz;*
2. the disposition of the retained earnings shown in the balance sheet;
3. the annual release from responsibility of the members of the managing board and of the supervisory board;
4. the appointment of the annual auditors;
5. amendments to the articles of incorporation;
6. measures to acquire and reduce capital;
7. the appointment of auditors for the examination of transactions upon formation or of transactions of the management;
8. the dissolution of the company.

(2) The shareholders' meeting may adopt resolutions concerning questions relating to the management of the company only if so requested by the managing board.

§ 120
Release from Responsibility

(1) The shareholders' meeting shall annually, within the first eight months of the fiscal year, adopt a resolution concerning the release from responsibility of the members of the managing board and of the members of the supervisory board. A specific member shall be released from responsibility by separate vote if the shareholders adopt a resolution to this effect or if a request to this effect is made by a minority whose combined holdings amount to no less than one-tenth of the stated capital or a par value of two million German marks.

(2) By their release the shareholders approve the conduct of the company's management by the members of the managing board and of the supervisory board. Release does not, however, imply a waiver of claims for damages.

(3) The deliberations concerning release shall be combined with the deliberations concerning the disposition of the retained earnings. The managing board shall present to the shareholders' meeting the annual financial statements, the business report, and the report of the supervisory board. § 175, paragraph 2, shall apply,

§ 120

mutatis mutandis, to the exhibition of these documents and the distribution of copies thereof.

für die Erteilung von Abschriften gilt § 175 Abs. 2 sinngemäß.

Second Subdivision
Calling of Shareholders' Meeting

§ 121
General Provisions

(1) A shareholders' meeting shall be called in all cases provided for by law or the articles of incorporation, or whenever a meeting is required in the interest of the company.

(2) The shareholders' meeting shall be called by the managing board pursuant to a board resolution requiring a simple majority of votes. Persons recorded in the Commercial Register as members of the managing board shall be deemed to have the requisite authority. The right of other parties to call a shareholders' meeting pursuant to the law or the articles of incorporation shall not be affected hereby.

(3) Notice of the meeting shall be published in the publications designated in the company's articles of incorporation. It shall set forth the name and the domicile of the company, the time and place of the shareholders' meeting, and the conditions under which persons may attend the shareholders' meeting and exercise the right to vote.

(4) Unless the articles of incorporation provide otherwise, the shareholders' meeting shall take place at the company's domicile. If the company's shares are admitted for trading on a German stock exchange, the shareholders' meeting may also be held at the place where the exchange is domiciled, unless the articles of incorporation provide otherwise.

§ 122
Calling of Meeting at Request of a Minority

(1) A shareholders' meeting shall be called if shareholders whose combined holdings equal or exceed one-twentieth of the stated capital request such meeting in writing, stating the purpose and the reasons for such meeting; such request shall be addressed to the managing board. The articles of incorporation may provide that the right to request the calling of a shareholders' meeting shall depend on the ownership of a lesser portion of the stated capital.

Zweiter Unterabschnitt
Einberufung der Hauptversammlung

§ 121
Allgemeines

(1) Die Hauptversammlung ist in den durch Gesetz oder Satzung bestimmten Fällen sowie dann einzuberufen, wenn das Wohl der Gesellschaft es fordert.

(2) Die Hauptversammlung wird durch den Vorstand einberufen, der darüber mit einfacher Mehrheit beschließt. Personen, die in das Handelsregister als Vorstand eingetragen sind, gelten als befugt. Das auf Gesetz oder Satzung beruhende Recht anderer Personen, die Hauptversammlung einzuberufen, bleibt unberührt.

(3) Die Einberufung ist in den Gesellschaftsblättern bekanntzumachen. Sie muß die Firma, den Sitz der Gesellschaft, Zeit und Ort der Hauptversammlung und die Bedingungen angeben, von denen die Teilnahme an der Hauptversammlung und die Ausübung des Stimmrechts abhängen.

(4) Wenn die Satzung nichts anderes bestimmt, soll die Hauptversammlung am Sitz der Gesellschaft stattfinden. Sind die Aktien der Gesellschaft an einer deutschen Börse zum amtlichen Handel zugelassen, so kann, wenn die Satzung nichts anderes bestimmt, die Hauptversammlung auch am Sitz der Börse stattfinden.

§ 122
Einberufung auf Verlangen einer Minderheit

(1) Die Hauptversammlung ist einzuberufen, wenn Aktionäre, deren Anteile zusammen den zwanzigsten Teil des Grundkapitals erreichen, die Einberufung schriftlich unter Angabe des Zwecks und der Gründe verlangen; das Verlangen ist an den Vorstand zu richten. Die Satzung kann das Recht, die Einberufung der Hauptversammlung zu verlangen, an den Besitz eines geringeren Anteils am Grundkapital knüpfen.

(2) In gleicher Weise können Aktionäre, deren Anteile zusammen den zwanzigsten Teil des Grundkapitals oder den Nennbetrag von einer Million Deutsche Mark erreichen, verlangen, daß Gegenstände zur Beschlußfassung einer Hauptversammlung bekanntgemacht werden.

(3) Wird dem Verlangen nicht entsprochen, so kann das Gericht die Aktionäre, die das Verlangen gestellt haben, ermächtigen, die Hauptversammlung einzuberufen oder den Gegenstand bekanntzumachen. Zugleich kann das Gericht den Vorsitzenden der Versammlung bestimmen. Auf die Ermächtigung muß bei der Einberufung oder Bekanntmachung hingewiesen werden. Gegen die Entscheidung ist die sofortige Beschwerde zulässig.

(4) Die Gesellschaft trägt die Kosten der Hauptversammlung und im Fall des Absatzes 3 auch die Gerichtskosten, wenn das Gericht dem Antrag stattgegeben hat.

§ 123

Einberufungsfrist

(1) Die Hauptversammlung ist mindestens einen Monat vor dem Tage der Versammlung einzuberufen.

(2) Die Satzung kann die Teilnahme an der Hauptversammlung oder die Ausübung des Stimmrechts davon abhängig machen, daß die Aktien bis zu einem bestimmten Zeitpunkt vor der Versammlung hinterlegt werden, ferner davon, daß sich die Aktionäre vor der Versammlung anmelden. Sieht die Satzung eine solche Bestimmung vor, so tritt für die Berechnung der Einberufungsfrist an die Stelle des Tages der Versammlung der Tag, bis zu dessen Ablauf die Aktien zu hinterlegen sind oder sich die Aktionäre vor der Versammlung anmelden müssen.

(3) Hängt nach der Satzung die Teilnahme an der Hauptversammlung oder die Ausübung des Stimmrechts davon ab, daß die Aktien bis zu einem bestimmten Zeitpunkt vor der Versammlung hinterlegt werden, so genügt es, wenn sie nicht später als am zehnten Tage vor der Versammlung hinterlegt werden. Die Hinterlegung bei einem Notar oder bei einer Wertpapiersammelbank ist ausreichend.

(4) Hängt nach der Satzung die Teilnahme an der Hauptversammlung oder die Ausübung des Stimmrechts davon ab, daß sich die Aktionäre vor der Versammlung anmelden, so genügt es, wenn sie

(2) Similarly, shareholders whose combined holdings amount to no less than one-twentieth of the stated capital or a par value of one million German marks can request the announcement of specific items, to be submitted to decision by the shareholders' meeting.

(3) In case of non-compliance with such request, the court may authorize the shareholders who made the request to call a shareholders' meeting or to announce such item. At the same time, the court may appoint a person to preside over such shareholders' meeting. The notice of the meeting or the announcement shall refer to such authorization. The decision of the court can be appealed.

(4) The company shall bear the expenses of the shareholders' meeting and, in the case referred to in paragraph 3 hereof, also the court costs, if the court granted the application.

§ 123

Period of Notice of Meeting

(1) The shareholders' meeting shall be called no later than one month prior to the day of the meeting.

(2) The articles of incorporation may make attendance at the shareholders' meeting or the exercise of the right to vote subject to the deposit of the shares by a specified date prior to the meeting, and also to the requirement that the shareholders announce their intention to attend before the meeting. If the articles of incorporation contain such a provision, the period of notice shall be computed by reference to the date by which the shares must be deposited or by which the shareholders must give notice of their intention to attend, rather than by reference to the date of the meeting.

(3) If, pursuant to the articles of incorporation, attendance at the shareholders' meeting or the exercise of the right to vote is subject to the deposit of the shares by a specified time prior to the meeting, it shall suffice if they are deposited no later than the tenth day before the meeting. Deposit of the shares with a notary or with a *Wertpapiersammelbank* shall be sufficient.

(4) If, pursuant to the articles of incorporation, attendance at the shareholders' meeting or the exercise of the right to vote depends upon the shareholders' announcement of their intention to

attend, it shall suffice if such announcement is made no later than the third day before the meeting.

§ 124

Publication of the Agenda

(1) The agenda of a shareholders' meeting shall be published in the publications designated in the company's articles of incorporation at the time the meeting is called. If a minority, after the shareholders' meeting is called, requests announcements of additional items to be submitted for resolution of the shareholders, it shall suffice if these items are published within ten days from the date the shareholders' meeting is called.

(2) If the agenda includes the election of members of the supervisory board, the announcement shall designate the statutory provisions that are to govern the composition of the supervisory board and indicate whether the shareholders are required to accept binding nominations. If the shareholders' meeting is to adopt a resolution concerning an amendment of the articles of incorporation or an agreement which requires the approval of the shareholders, the text of the proposed amendment or the essential content of the agreement shall be published.

(3) With respect to each item on the agenda concerning which the shareholders are to adopt a resolution, the managing board and the supervisory board shall make proposals in the announcement of the agenda regarding the resolution to be adopted; however, with respect to the election of members of the supervisory board and of auditors, only the supervisory board shall make such proposals. This shall not apply if the shareholders are required to accept binding nominations in electing members of the supervisory board, pursuant to § 6 of the *Mitbestimmungsgesetz*, or if the subject of the resolution was put on the agenda at the request of a minority. Proposals for the election of supervisory board members or auditors shall state their names, occupation, and residence.

(4) Resolutions may not be adopted with regard to items on the agenda that have not been duly announced. No such announcement shall, however, be required in order to adopt a resolution on a motion to call a shareholders' meeting made at the meeting, or to adopt a resolution on a motion which concerns items on the agenda, or to discuss matters without adopting a resolution.

§ 124

sich nicht später als am dritten Tage vor der Versammlung anmelden.

§ 124

Bekanntmachung der Tagesordnung

(1) Die Tagesordnung der Hauptversammlung ist bei der Einberufung in den Gesellschaftsblättern bekanntzumachen. Hat die Minderheit nach der Einberufung der Hauptversammlung die Bekanntmachung von Gegenständen zur Beschlußfassung der Hauptversammlung verlangt, so genügt es, wenn diese Gegenstände binnen zehn Tagen nach der Einberufung der Hauptversammlung bekanntgemacht werden.

(2) Steht die Wahl von Aufsichtsratsmitgliedern auf der Tagesordnung, so ist in der Bekanntmachung anzugeben, nach welchen gesetzlichen Vorschriften sich der Aufsichtsrat zusammensetzt, und ob die Hauptversammlung an Wahlvorschläge gebunden ist. Soll die Hauptversammlung über eine Satzungsänderung oder über einen Vertrag beschließen, der nur mit Zustimmung der Hauptversammlung wirksam wird, so ist auch der Wortlaut der vorgeschlagenen Satzungsänderung oder der wesentliche Inhalt des Vertrags bekanntzumachen.

(3) Zu jedem Gegenstand der Tagesordnung, über den die Hauptversammlung beschließen soll, haben der Vorstand und der Aufsichtsrat, zur Wahl von Aufsichtsratsmitgliedern und Prüfern nur der Aufsichtsrat, in der Bekanntmachung der Tagesordnung Vorschläge zur Beschlußfassung zu machen. Dies gilt nicht, wenn die Hauptversammlung bei der Wahl von Aufsichtsratsmitgliedern nach § 6 des Mitbestimmungsgesetzes an Wahlvorschläge gebunden ist, oder wenn der Gegenstand der Beschlußfassung auf Verlangen einer Minderheit auf die Tagesordnung gesetzt worden ist. Der Vorschlag zur Wahl von Aufsichtsratsmitgliedern oder Prüfern hat deren Namen, Beruf und Wohnort anzugeben.

(4) Über Gegenstände der Tagesordnung, die nicht ordnungsgemäß bekanntgemacht sind, dürfen keine Beschlüsse gefaßt werden. Zur Beschlußfassung über den in der Versammlung gestellten Antrag auf Einberufung einer Hauptversammlung, zu Anträgen, die zu Gegenständen der Tagesordnung gestellt werden, und zu Verhandlungen ohne Beschlußfassung bedarf es keiner Bekanntmachung.

§ 125

Mitteilungen für die Aktionäre und an Aufsichtsratsmitglieder

(1) Der Vorstand hat binnen zwölf Tagen nach der Bekanntmachung der Einberufung der Hauptversammlung im Bundesanzeiger den Kreditinstituten und den Vereinigungen von Aktionären, die in der letzten Hauptversammlung Stimmrechte für Aktionäre ausgeübt oder die die Mitteilung verlangt haben, die Einberufung der Hauptversammlung, die Bekanntmachung der Tagesordnung und etwaige Anträge und Wahlvorschläge von Aktionären einschließlich des Namens des Aktionärs, der Begründung und einer etwaigen Stellungnahme der Verwaltung mitzuteilen.

(2) Die gleiche Mitteilung hat der Vorstand den Aktionären zu übersenden, die

1. eine Aktie bei der Gesellschaft hinterlegt haben,
2. es nach der Bekanntmachung der Einberufung der Hauptversammlung im Bundesanzeiger verlangen oder
3. als Aktionär im Aktienbuch der Gesellschaft eingetragen sind und deren Stimmrechte in der letzten Hauptversammlung nicht durch ein Kreditinstitut ausgeübt worden sind.

(3) Jedes Aufsichtsratsmitglied kann verlangen, daß ihm der Vorstand die gleichen Mitteilungen übersendet.

(4) Jeder Aktionär, der eine Aktie bei der Gesellschaft hinterlegt oder als Aktionär im Aktienbuch der Gesellschaft eingetragen ist, und jedes Aufsichtsratsmitglied kann verlangen, daß der Vorstand ihm die in der Hauptversammlung gefaßten Beschlüsse schriftlich mitteilt.

§ 126

Anträge von Aktionären

(1) Anträge von Aktionären brauchen nach § 125 nur mitgeteilt zu werden, wenn der Aktionär binnen einer Woche nach der Bekanntmachung der Einberufung der Hauptversammlung im Bundesanzeiger der Gesellschaft einen Gegenantrag mit Begründung übersandt und dabei mitgeteilt hat, er wolle in der Versammlung einem Vorschlag des Vorstands und des Aufsichtsrats widersprechen und die anderen Aktionäre veranlassen, für seinen Gegenantrag zu stimmen.

(2) Ein Gegenantrag und dessen Begründung brauchen nicht mitgeteilt zu werden,

§ 125

Communications to Shareholders and to Members of Supervisory Board

(1) Within twelve days from the date of publication of the notice of meeting in the *Bundesanzeiger*, the managing board shall communicate to the banks and any associations of shareholders which exercised voting rights for shareholders at the last shareholders' meeting, or which requested such communication, the notice of the shareholders' meeting, the publication of the agenda, and any motions and nominations for election made by shareholders, including the name of the shareholder, the reasons given therefor, and any comments of management.

(2) The managing board shall send the same communication to shareholders who

1. deposited a share with the company,
2. made a request to this effect after publication of the notice of meeting in the *Bundesanzeiger*, or
3. are recorded as shareholders in the company's stock register if their right to vote was not exercised by a bank in the preceding shareholders' meeting.

(3) Each member of the supervisory board can request that the managing board send him the same communication.

(4) Each shareholder who has deposited a share with the company or is recorded in the company's stock register, and each member of the supervisory board, can request that the managing board inform him in writing of the resolutions adopted by the shareholders.

§ 126

Motions Made by Shareholders

(1) Motions made by shareholders are required to be communicated in accordance with § 125 only if the shareholder has, within one week from the date of publication of the notice of the shareholders' meeting in the *Bundesanzeiger*, transmitted to the company a countermotion, stating the grounds for such countermotion and stating that at the shareholders' meeting he intends to oppose a proposal made by the managing board or the supervisory board and to induce the other shareholders to vote in favor of his countermotion.

(2) A countermotion and the grounds on which it is based need not be communicated

1. if communication would render the managing board criminally liable,
2. if such countermotion would result in a shareholders' resolution that would be illegal or violate the articles of incorporation,
3. if the grounds contain statements which, in essential points, are obviously false or misleading or if they contain defamatory statements,
4. if the shareholder's countermotion, based on the same facts, was already announced with respect to a shareholders' meeting of the company pursuant to § 125,
5. if the same countermotion made by the shareholder based on essentially the same grounds had already been presented, within the past five years, to at least two shareholders' meetings of the company in accordance with § 125 and if at such shareholders' meetings less than one-twentieth of the stated capital represented voted in favor of it,
6. if the shareholder indicates that he will not attend the shareholders' meeting and will not be represented, or
7. if within the past two years the shareholder, in two shareholders' meetings, failed to make or cause to be made a countermotion communicated by him.

A statement of grounds consisting of more than one hundred words need not be communicated.

(3) If several shareholders make countermotions relating to the same subject of a resolution, the managing board may combine such countermotions and the statements of grounds given therefor.

§ 127

Nominations by Shareholders

§ 126 shall apply, *mutatis mutandis*, to the nomination by a shareholder for the election of supervisory board members or of annual auditors. Such nominations need not state reasons. Moreover, the managing board need not communicate the nominations if they fail to set forth the details required by § 124, paragraph 3, third sentence.

§ 128

Duty of Banks and Shareholders' Protective Associations to Forward Communications

(1) If shareholders have deposited shares of the company with a bank, such bank shall promptly forward to them any communications pursuant to § 125, paragraph 1.

§ 127

---

1. soweit sich der Vorstand durch die Mitteilung strafbar machen würde,
2. wenn der Gegenantrag zu einem gesetz- oder satzungswidrigen Beschluß der Hauptversammlung führen würde,
3. wenn die Begründung in wesentlichen Punkten offensichtlich falsche oder irreführende Angaben oder wenn sie Beleidigungen enthält,
4. wenn ein auf denselben Sachverhalt gestützter Gegenantrag des Aktionärs bereits zu einer Hauptversammlung der Gesellschaft nach § 125 mitgeteilt worden ist,
5. wenn derselbe Gegenantrag des Aktionärs mit wesentlich gleicher Begründung in den letzten fünf Jahren bereits zu mindestens zwei Hauptversammlungen der Gesellschaft nach § 125 mitgeteilt worden ist und in der Hauptversammlung weniger als der zwanzigste Teil des vertretenen Grundkapitals für ihn gestimmt hat,
6. wenn der Aktionär zu erkennen gibt, daß er an der Hauptversammlung nicht teilnehmen und sich nicht vertreten lassen wird, oder
7. wenn der Aktionär in den letzten zwei Jahren in zwei Hauptversammlungen einen von ihm mitgeteilten Gegenantrag nicht gestellt hat oder nicht hat stellen lassen.

Die Begründung braucht nicht mitgeteilt zu werden, wenn sie insgesamt mehr als einhundert Worte beträgt.

(3) Stellen mehrere Aktionäre zu demselben Gegenstand der Beschlußfassung Gegenanträge, so kann der Vorstand die Gegenanträge und ihre Begründungen zusammenfassen.

§ 127

Wahlvorschläge von Aktionären

Für den Vorschlag eines Aktionärs zur Wahl von Aufsichtsratsmitgliedern oder von Abschlußprüfern gilt § 126 sinngemäß. Der Wahlvorschlag braucht nicht begründet zu werden. Der Vorstand braucht den Wahlvorschlag auch dann nicht mitzuteilen, wenn der Vorschlag nicht die Angaben nach § 124 Abs. 3 Satz 3 enthält.

§ 128

Weitergabe der Mitteilungen durch Kreditinstitute und Vereinigungen von Aktionären

(1) Verwahrt ein Kreditinstitut für Aktionäre Aktien der Gesellschaft, so hat es die Mitteilungen nach § 125 Abs. 1 unverzüglich an sie weiterzugeben.

(2) Beabsichtigt das Kreditinstitut, in der Hauptversammlung das Stimmrecht für Aktionäre auszuüben oder ausüben zu lassen, so hat es dem Aktionär außerdem eigene Vorschläge für die Ausübung des Stimmrechts zu den einzelnen Gegenständen der Tagesordnung mitzuteilen. Bei den Vorschlägen hat sich das Kreditinstitut vom Interesse des Aktionärs leiten zu lassen. Das Kreditinstitut hat den Aktionär ferner um Erteilung von Weisungen für die Ausübung des Stimmrechts zu bitten und darauf hinzuweisen, daß es, wenn der Aktionär nicht rechtzeitig eine andere Weisung erteilt, das Stimmrecht entsprechend seinen nach Satz 1 mitgeteilten Vorschlägen ausüben werde. Das Kreditinstitut hat der Bitte um Erteilung von Weisungen ein Formblatt beizufügen, durch dessen Ausfüllung der Aktionär Weisungen für die Ausübung des Stimmrechts zu den einzelnen Gegenständen der Tagesordnung erteilen kann. Gehört ein Vorstandsmitglied des Kreditinstituts dem Aufsichtsrat der Gesellschaft oder ein Vorstandsmitglied der Gesellschaft dem Aufsichtsrat des Kreditinstituts an, so hat das Kreditinstitut auch dies mitzuteilen.

(2) If the bank intends to exercise or to have exercised for shareholders the right to vote in a shareholders' meeting, it shall also inform the shareholder of its own proposals regarding the exercise of the right to vote with respect to each item on the agenda. Concerning such proposals, the bank shall be guided by the interest of the shareholder. The bank shall also request from the shareholder instructions for the exercise of the right to vote and shall point out the fact that it will exercise the right to vote in accordance with its proposals communicated to the shareholder pursuant to the first sentence hereof, absent timely instructions by the shareholder to the contrary. The bank shall attach a form to its request for instructions by completion of which the shareholder may give instructions for the exercise of the right to vote with respect to each item on the agenda. If a member of the bank's managing board is also a member of the company's supervisory board, or if a member of the company's managing board is a member of the bank's supervisory board, the bank shall inform the shareholder of this fact.

(3) Soweit ein Aktionär nach Einberufung der Hauptversammlung dem Kreditinstitut zu den einzelnen Gegenständen der Tagesordnung schriftlich Weisungen für die Ausübung des Stimmrechts erteilt hat, braucht das Kreditinstitut keine eigenen Vorschläge nach Absatz 2 mitzuteilen und den Aktionär nicht um Erteilung von Weisungen zu bitten.

(3) If a shareholder, after notice of the shareholders' meeting has been given, has issued written instructions to the bank regarding the exercise of the right to vote on each item on the agenda, the bank need not furnish information concerning its own proposals pursuant to paragraph 2 hereof, or ask the shareholder for instructions.

(4) Die Verpflichtung des Kreditinstituts zum Ersatz eines aus der Verletzung der Absätze 1 oder 2 entstehenden Schadens kann im voraus weder ausgeschlossen noch beschränkt werden.

(4) The liability of a bank for any damage caused by a violation of paragraph 1 or 2 hereof can be neither waived nor limited in advance.

(5) Gehören einer Vereinigung von Aktionären Aktionäre der Gesellschaft als Mitglieder an, so hat die Vereinigung die Mitteilungen nach § 125 Abs. 1 an diese Mitglieder auf deren Verlangen unverzüglich weiterzugeben. Im übrigen gelten die Absätze 2 bis 4 für Vereinigungen von Aktionären entsprechend.

(5) If shareholders of the company are members of a shareholders' protective association, such association shall promptly forward to these members upon their request the communications specified in § 125, paragraph 1. In other respects, paragraphs 2 to 4 hereof shall apply, *mutatis mutandis*, to shareholders' protective associations.

(6) Der Bundesminister der Justiz wird ermächtigt, im Einvernehmen mit dem Bundesminister für Wirtschaft durch Rechtsverordnung
1. ein Formblatt für die Erteilung von Weisungen durch den Aktionär vorzuschreiben, das die

(6) The Federal Minister of Justice, in consultation with the Federal Minister of Economics, is authorized to issue decrees

1. prescribing a form for the issuance of instructions by shareholders which the banks and

§ 128

the shareholders' protective associations are required to attach to their request for instructions pursuant to paragraph 2, third sentence, hereof,

2. providing that the company shall reimburse the banks and the shareholders' protective associations for the expense of making copies of the communications and for sending them to shareholders or to members. A lump-sum amount may be fixed to cover the expenses for each notice required by paragraph 1 hereof.

The decree shall not require approval by the Bundesrat.

Third Subdivision

Minutes of Meeting.

Right to Information

§ 129

List of Participants

(1) In the shareholders' meeting a list of the shareholders present or represented, and of the representatives of shareholders, shall be prepared. Such list shall state the name and residence of each shareholder as well as the amount and the class of shares represented by each.

(2) If a bank or any person referred to in § 135, paragraph 9, has been authorized to exercise the right to vote and if such authorized party exercises the right to vote on behalf of an undisclosed principal, the amount and the class of shares for which it received such authorization shall be specified separately for recording in such list. The names of shareholders who have given proxies need not be stated.

(3) A person who has been authorized by a shareholder to exercise the right to vote, in his own name, shares which he does not own shall state the amount and the class of these shares separately for purposes of recording in the list. This shall also apply for registered shares where the person authorized is recorded in the stock register as owner of such shares.

(4) The list shall be exhibited for inspection by all participants prior to the first vote. It shall be signed by the chairman.

§ 130

Minutes

(1) Each shareholders' resolution shall be recorded in the minutes of the meeting, which

Kreditinstitute und die Vereinigungen von Aktionären ihrer Bitte um Weisungen nach Absatz 2 Satz 3 beizufügen haben,

2. vorzuschreiben, daß die Gesellschaft den Kreditinstituten und den Vereinigungen von Aktionären die Aufwendungen für die Vervielfältigung der Mitteilungen und für ihre Übersendung an die Aktionäre oder an ihre Mitglieder zu ersetzen hat. Zur Abgeltung der Aufwendungen kann für jedes Schreiben nach Absatz 1 ein Pauschbetrag festgesetzt werden.

Die Rechtsverordnung bedarf nicht der Zustimmung des Bundesrates.

Dritter Unterabschnitt

Verhandlungsniederschrift.
Auskunftsrecht

§ 129

Verzeichnis der Teilnehmer

(1) In der Hauptversammlung ist ein Verzeichnis der erschienenen oder vertretenen Aktionäre und der Vertreter von Aktionären mit Angabe ihres Namens und Wohnorts sowie des Betrags der von jedem vertretenen Aktien unter Angabe ihrer Gattung aufzustellen.

(2) Sind einem Kreditinstitut oder einer in § 135 Abs. 9 bezeichneten Person Vollmachten zur Ausübung des Stimmrechts erteilt worden und übt der Bevollmächtigte das Stimmrecht im Namen dessen, den es angeht, aus, so sind der Betrag und die Gattung der Aktien, für die ihm Vollmachten erteilt worden sind, zur Aufnahme in das Verzeichnis gesondert anzugeben. Die Namen der Aktionäre, welche Vollmachten erteilt haben, brauchen nicht angegeben zu werden.

(3) Wer von einem Aktionär ermächtigt ist, im eigenen Namen das Stimmrecht für Aktien auszuüben, die ihm nicht gehören, hat den Betrag und die Gattung dieser Aktien zur Aufnahme in das Verzeichnis gesondert anzugeben. Dies gilt auch für Namensaktien, als deren Aktionär der Ermächtigte im Aktienbuch eingetragen ist.

(4) Das Verzeichnis ist vor der ersten Abstimmung zur Einsicht für alle Teilnehmer auszulegen. Es ist vom Vorsitzenden zu unterzeichnen.

§ 130

Niederschrift

(1) Jeder Beschluß der Hauptversammlung ist durch eine über die Verhandlung gerichtlich oder

notariell aufgenommene Niederschrift zu beurkunden. Gleiches gilt für jedes Verlangen einer Minderheit nach § 120 Abs. 1 Satz 2, §§ 137 und 147 Abs. 1.

(2) In der Niederschrift sind der Ort und der Tag der Verhandlung, der Name des Richters oder Notars sowie die Art und das Ergebnis der Abstimmung und die Feststellung des Vorsitzenden über die Beschlußfassung anzugeben.

(3) Das Verzeichnis der Teilnehmer an der Versammlung sowie die Belege über die Einberufung sind der Niederschrift als Anlagen beizufügen. Die Belege über die Einberufung brauchen nicht beigefügt zu werden, wenn sie unter Angabe ihres Inhalts in der Niederschrift aufgeführt werden.

(4) Die Niederschrift ist von dem Richter oder Notar zu unterschreiben. Die Zuziehung von Zeugen ist nicht nötig.

(5) Unverzüglich nach der Versammlung hat der Vorstand eine öffentlich beglaubigte Abschrift der Niederschrift und ihrer Anlagen zum Handelsregister einzureichen.

§ 131
Auskunftsrecht des Aktionärs

(1) Jedem Aktionär ist auf Verlangen in der Hauptversammlung vom Vorstand Auskunft über Angelegenheiten der Gesellschaft zu geben, soweit sie zur sachgemäßen Beurteilung des Gegenstands der Tagesordnung erforderlich ist. Die Auskunftspflicht erstreckt sich auch auf die rechtlichen und geschäftlichen Beziehungen der Gesellschaft zu einem verbundenen Unternehmen.

(2) Die Auskunft hat den Grundsätzen einer gewissenhaften und getreuen Rechenschaft zu entsprechen.

(3) Der Vorstand darf die Auskunft verweigern,
1. soweit die Erteilung der Auskunft nach vernünftiger kaufmännischer Beurteilung geeignet ist, der Gesellschaft oder einem verbundenen Unternehmen einen nicht unerheblichen Nachteil zuzufügen;
2. soweit sie sich auf steuerliche Wertansätze oder die Höhe einzelner Steuern bezieht;
3. über den Unterschied zwischen dem Wert, mit dem Gegenstände in der Jahresbilanz angesetzt worden sind, und einem höheren Wert dieser Gegenstände, es sei denn, daß die Hauptversammlung den Jahresabschluß feststellt;

shall be in the form of a judicial or notarial record. The same shall apply to each request made by a minority pursuant to § 120, paragraph 1, second sentence, and §§ 137 and 147, paragraph 1.

(2) The minutes shall set forth the place and the date of the meeting, the name of the judge or the notary, as well as the nature and the result of the voting, and the determination made by the chairman regarding the resolution.

(3) The list of participants at the meeting as well as the documents concerning the notice of the shareholders' meeting shall be attached to the minutes. The documents concerning such notice need not be attached if a statement of its content is entered in the minutes.

(4) The minutes shall be signed by the judge or the notary. The presence of witnesses is not required.

(5) After the shareholders' meeting the managing board shall promptly file a certified copy of the minutes and of the attachments thereto with the Commercial Register.

§ 131
Shareholder's Right to Information

(1) Each shareholder shall, upon request made at the shareholders' meeting to the managing board, be furnished information on matters affecting the company, to the extent that such information is required to permit proper evaluation of any item on the agenda. The duty to furnish information shall also apply to the company's legal and business dealings with a related enterprise.

(2) The information shall comply with the principles of a conscientious and true account.

(3) The managing board may refuse to furnish information
1. to the extent that such information is, according to reasonable business judgment, likely to expose the company or a related enterprise to a not inconsiderable detriment;
2. to the extent that it relates to tax valuations or amounts of specific taxes;
3. concerning the difference between the valuation of assets for purposes of the annual financial statements and the higher market value of such assets, unless the shareholders' meeting establishes the annual financial statements;

4. the methods of valuation and depreciation, to the extent that setting forth such methods in the business report is sufficient to convey the clearest possible picture of the company's financial and earnings position; this shall not apply if the shareholders' meeting establishes the annual financial statements;
5. if furnishing such information would render the managing board criminally liable.

The information may not be refused on any other grounds.

(4) If a shareholder by virtue of his status as a shareholder has been furnished information outside of a shareholders' meeting, such information shall also be furnished to any other shareholder, upon his request, at the shareholders' meeting, even though such information is not necessary to permit a proper evaluation of any item on the agenda. The managing board may not refuse to furnish such information pursuant to paragraph 3, first sentence, Nos. 1 to 4, hereof.

(5) If a shareholder is denied any information, such shareholder can request that his question and the reason for the refusal of the information be recorded in the minutes of the meeting.

§ 132
Judicial Decision on the Right to Information

(1) The district court of the district in which the company is domiciled shall have exclusive jurisdiction to determine, upon application, whether the managing board is required to furnish information. If the district court has a commercial division, such division rather than the civil division shall have jurisdiction. The state government may, by decree, delegate jurisdiction over such decisions for several judicial districts to a particular district court, if such delegation would serve to ensure the uniform application of the law. The state government may confer this power upon the ministry of justice of such state.

(2) Entitled to make the application shall be any shareholder who has not been furnished the information he requested and, if a resolution was adopted on the item of the agenda to which the information related, each shareholder who appeared at the meeting and had his objections to the resolution recorded in the minutes. The application shall be filed within two weeks after the shareholders' meeting at which the information was refused.

§ 132

---

4. über die Bewertungs- und Abschreibungsmethoden, soweit die Angabe dieser Methoden im Geschäftsbericht zur Vermittlung eines möglichst sicheren Einblicks in die Vermögens- und Ertragslage der Gesellschaft ausreicht; dies gilt nicht, wenn die Hauptversammlung den Jahresabschluß feststellt;
5. soweit sich der Vorstand durch die Erteilung der Auskunft strafbar machen würde.

Aus anderen Gründen darf die Auskunft nicht verweigert werden.

(4) Ist einem Aktionär wegen seiner Eigenschaft als Aktionär eine Auskunft außerhalb der Hauptversammlung gegeben worden, so ist sie jedem anderen Aktionär auf dessen Verlangen in der Hauptversammlung zu geben, auch wenn sie zur sachgemäßen Beurteilung des Gegenstands der Tagesordnung nicht erforderlich ist. Der Vorstand darf die Auskunft nicht nach Absatz 3 Satz 1 Nr. 1 bis 4 verweigern.

(5) Wird einem Aktionär eine Auskunft verweigert, so kann er verlangen, daß seine Frage und der Grund, aus dem die Auskunft verweigert worden ist, in die Niederschrift über die Verhandlung aufgenommen werden.

§ 132
Gerichtliche Entscheidung über das Auskunftsrecht

(1) Ob der Vorstand die Auskunft zu geben hat, entscheidet auf Antrag ausschließlich das Landgericht, in dessen Bezirk die Gesellschaft ihren Sitz hat. Ist bei dem Landgericht eine Kammer für Handelssachen gebildet, so entscheidet diese an Stelle der Zivilkammer. Die Landesregierung kann die Entscheidung durch Rechtsverordnung für die Bezirke mehrerer Landgerichte einem der Landgerichte übertragen, wenn dies der Sicherung einer einheitlichen Rechtsprechung dient. Die Landesregierung kann die Ermächtigung auf die Landesjustizverwaltung übertragen.

(2) Antragsberechtigt ist jeder Aktionär, dem die verlangte Auskunft nicht gegeben worden ist, und, wenn über den Gegenstand der Tagesordnung, auf den sich die Auskunft bezog, Beschluß gefaßt worden ist, jeder in der Hauptversammlung erschienene Aktionär, der in der Hauptversammlung Widerspruch zur Niederschrift erklärt hat. Der Antrag ist binnen zwei Wochen nach der Hauptversammlung zu stellen, in der die Auskunft abgelehnt worden ist.

(3) § 99 Abs. 1, Abs. 3 Satz 1, 2, 4 bis 9 und Abs. 5 Satz 1 und 3 gilt sinngemäß. Die sofortige Beschwerde findet nur statt, wenn das Landgericht sie in der Entscheidung für zulässig erklärt. Es soll sie nur zulassen, wenn dadurch die Klärung einer Rechtsfrage von grundsätzlicher Bedeutung zu erwarten ist.

(4) Wird dem Antrag stattgegeben, so ist die Auskunft auch außerhalb der Hauptversammlung zu geben. Aus der Entscheidung findet die Zwangsvollstreckung nach den Vorschriften der Zivilprozeßordnung statt.

(5) Für die Kosten des Verfahrens gilt die Kostenordnung. Für das Verfahren des ersten Rechtszugs wird das Doppelte der vollen Gebühr erhoben. Für den zweiten Rechtszug wird die gleiche Gebühr erhoben; dies gilt auch dann, wenn die Beschwerde Erfolg hat. Wird der Antrag oder die Beschwerde zurückgenommen, bevor es zu einer Entscheidung oder einer vom Gericht vermittelten Einigung kommt, so ermäßigt sich die Gebühr auf die Hälfte. Der Geschäftswert ist von Amts wegen festzusetzen. Er bestimmt sich nach § 30 Abs. 2 der Kostenordnung mit der Maßgabe, daß der Wert regelmäßig auf zehntausend Deutsche Mark anzunehmen ist. Das mit dem Verfahren befaßte Gericht bestimmt nach billigem Ermessen, welchem Beteiligten die Kosten des Verfahrens aufzuerlegen sind.

Vierter Unterabschnitt

Stimmrecht

§ 133

Grundsatz der einfachen Stimmenmehrheit

(1) Die Beschlüsse der Hauptversammlung bedürfen der Mehrheit der abgegebenen Stimmen (einfache Stimmenmehrheit), soweit nicht Gesetz oder Satzung eine größere Mehrheit oder weitere Erfordernisse bestimmen.

(2) Für Wahlen kann die Satzung andere Bestimmungen treffen.

§ 134

Stimmrecht

(1) Das Stimmrecht wird nach Aktiennennbeträgen ausgeübt. Für den Fall, daß einem Aktionär mehrere Aktien gehören, kann die Satzung das

(3) § 99, paragraph 1, paragraph 3, first, second, and fourth to ninth sentences, and paragraph 5, first and third sentences, shall apply *mutatis mutandis*. The decision is subject to appeal only if the district court in its decision grants leave to appeal. It shall grant such leave only if it can be expected that the appeal will settle a legal question of fundamental importance.

(4) If the application is granted, the information must be furnished even outside a shareholders' meeting. The decision shall be enforceable in accordance with the provisions of the Code of Civil Procedure.

(5) The costs of the proceedings shall be determined by reference to the *Kostenordnung*. In the proceedings before the court of first instance, twice the amount of one full court fee shall be assessed. In the proceedings before the court of second instance, the same court fee shall be assessed; this also applies if the appeal is successful. If the application or the appeal is withdrawn before a decision is rendered or a judicial settlement is reached, the court fees shall be reduced by one-half. The value of the subject matter in issue shall be determined ex officio. It shall be fixed in accordance with § 30, paragraph 2, of the *Kostenordnung*, provided that such value shall generally be deemed to amount to ten thousand German marks. The court adjudicating the matter shall in its best judgment determine which of the parties is to bear the costs of the proceedings.

Fourth Subdivision
Voting Rights

§ 133
Principle of Simple Majority Vote

(1) Shareholders' resolutions shall require a majority of the votes cast (simple majority), unless the law or the articles of incorporation provide for a greater majority or establish additional requirements.

(2) For elections, the articles of incorporation may establish different rules.

§ 134
Voting Rights

(1) The voting rights shall be exercised on the basis of the total par value of the shares held. In the event that one shareholder holds several

shares, the articles of incorporation may limit the voting rights by providing for a maximum total par value or a graduated scale. The articles of incorporation may also provide that shares held by another for the account of a shareholder shall be added to the shares belonging to the shareholder. Where the shareholder is an enterprise, the articles of incorporation may provide further that shares belonging to an enterprise controlled by it or controlling it or affiliated with it in a group, or held by a third party for the account of any such enterprises, shall be added to the shares belonging to the shareholder. It shall not be permissible to provide for such limitations to apply only to specific shareholders. The limitations shall not be taken into account in the computation of any capital majority required by law or by the articles of incorporation.

(2) The voting rights shall commence as soon as the contribution is rendered in full. The articles of incorporation may provide that the voting rights shall commence when the statutory minimum contribution or a higher minimum contribution specified in the articles of incorporation is rendered on the share. In this event the payment of the minimum contribution shall confer one vote; where higher contributions are rendered, the proportion of votes shall be measured by the amount of the contributions made. If the articles of incorporation do not provide that the right to vote commences before the contribution is rendered in full, and if full contribution has not been rendered on any of the shares, the votes shall be counted in proportion to the amounts paid in; in this event payment of the minimum contribution shall confer one vote. In such cases, fractions of votes shall be taken into account only to the extent that together they amount to full votes in the hands of any shareholder entitled to vote. The articles of incorporation may not contain provisions pursuant to this paragraph whose applicability is restricted to specific shareholders or to specific classes of shares.

(3) The voting rights may be exercised by proxy. It shall be necessary and sufficient that the power of attorney be in writing. The power of attorney shall be presented to the company and shall be kept by it.

§ 134

Stimmrecht durch Festsetzung eines Höchstbetrags oder von Abstufungen beschränken. Die Satzung kann außerdem bestimmen, daß zu den Aktien, die dem Aktionär gehören, auch die Aktien rechnen, die einem anderen für seine Rechnung gehören. Für den Fall, daß der Aktionär ein Unternehmen ist, kann sie ferner bestimmen, daß zu den Aktien, die ihm gehören, auch die Aktien rechnen, die einem von ihm abhängigen oder ihn beherrschenden oder einem mit ihm konzernverbundenen Unternehmen oder für Rechnung solcher Unternehmen einem Dritten gehören. Die Beschränkungen können nicht für einzelne Aktionäre angeordnet werden. Bei der Berechnung einer nach Gesetz oder Satzung erforderlichen Kapitalmehrheit bleiben die Beschränkungen außer Betracht.

(2) Das Stimmrecht beginnt mit der vollständigen Leistung der Einlage. Die Satzung kann bestimmen, daß das Stimmrecht beginnt, wenn auf die Aktie die gesetzliche oder höhere satzungsmäßige Mindesteinlage geleistet ist. In diesem Fall gewährt die Leistung der Mindesteinlage eine Stimme; bei höheren Einlagen richtet sich das Stimmenverhältnis nach der Höhe der geleisteten Einlagen. Bestimmt die Satzung nicht, daß das Stimmrecht vor der vollständigen Leistung der Einlage beginnt, und ist noch auf keine Aktie die Einlage vollständig geleistet, so richtet sich das Stimmenverhältnis nach der Höhe der geleisteten Einlagen; dabei gewährt die Leistung der Mindesteinlage eine Stimme. Bruchteile von Stimmen werden in diesen Fällen nur berücksichtigt, soweit sie für den stimmberechtigten Aktionär volle Stimmen ergeben. Die Satzung kann Bestimmungen nach diesem Absatz nicht für einzelne Aktionäre oder für einzelne Aktiengattungen treffen.

(3) Das Stimmrecht kann durch einen Bevollmächtigten ausgeübt werden. Für die Vollmacht ist die schriftliche Form erforderlich und genügend. Die Vollmachtsurkunde ist der Gesellschaft vorzulegen und bleibt in ihrer Verwahrung.

(4) Die Form der Ausübung des Stimmrechts richtet sich nach der Satzung.

§ 135

Ausübung des Stimmrechts durch Kreditinstitute und geschäftsmäßig Handelnde

(1) Ein Kreditinstitut darf das Stimmrecht für Inhaberaktien, die ihm nicht gehören, nur ausüben oder ausüben lassen, wenn es schriftlich bevollmächtigt ist. In der eigenen Hauptversammlung darf das bevollmächtigte Kreditinstitut das Stimmrecht auf Grund der Vollmacht nur ausüben, soweit der Aktionär eine ausdrückliche Weisung zu den einzelnen Gegenständen der Tagesordnung erteilt hat.

(2) Die Vollmacht darf nur einem bestimmten Kreditinstitut und nur für längstens fünfzehn Monate erteilt werden. Sie ist jederzeit widerruflich. Die Vollmachtsurkunde muß bei der Erteilung der Vollmacht vollständig ausgefüllt sein und darf keine anderen Erklärungen enthalten. Sie soll das Datum der Ausstellung enthalten. Die Frist in Satz 1 beginnt spätestens mit dem Tage der Ausstellung.

(3) Das bevollmächtigte Kreditinstitut darf Personen, die nicht seine Angestellten sind, nur unterbevollmächtigen, wenn die Vollmacht eine Unterbevollmächtigung ausdrücklich gestattet und das bevollmächtigte Kreditinstitut am Ort der Hauptversammlung keine Niederlassung hat. Gleiches gilt für eine Übertragung der Vollmacht durch das bevollmächtigte Kreditinstitut.

(4) Auf Grund der Vollmacht kann das Kreditinstitut das Stimmrecht unter Benennung des Aktionärs in dessen Namen ausüben. Wenn es die Vollmacht bestimmt, kann das Kreditinstitut das Stimmrecht auch im Namen dessen, den es angeht, ausüben. Übt das Kreditinstitut das Stimmrecht unter Benennung des Aktionärs in dessen Namen aus, ist die Vollmachtsurkunde der Gesellschaft vorzulegen und von dieser zu verwahren. Übt es das Stimmrecht im Namen dessen, den es angeht, aus, genügt zum Nachweis seiner Stimmberechtigung gegenüber der Gesellschaft die Erfüllung der in der Satzung für die Ausübung des Stimmrechts vorgesehenen Erfordernisse; enthält die Satzung darüber keine Bestimmungen, genügt die Vorlegung der Aktien oder einer Bescheinigung über die Hinterlegung der Aktien bei einem Notar oder einer Wertpapiersammelbank.

(4) The form for the exercise of the voting rights shall be subject to the provisions of the articles of incorporation.

§ 135

Exercise of Voting Rights by Banks and Professional Agents

(1) A bank may, directly or through another, vote bearer shares which it does not own only if it has a written power of attorney authorizing it to do so. At its own shareholders' meetings, the bank so authorized may vote as proxy only to the extent that the shareholder has given express instructions with respect to the items on the agenda.

(2) A power of attorney may be granted only to a specific bank and only for a period of time not exceeding fifteen months. It may be revoked at any time. The document conferring the power of attorney shall be completely filled in at the time the power is given and may not contain any other provisions. It shall set forth the date of execution. The period of time specified in the first sentence hereof shall be computed from the date of execution.

(3) The authorized bank may delegate its powers to persons other than its employees only if the power of attorney expressly permits such delegation and if the authorized bank does not maintain an office at the place where the shareholders' meeting is held. The same shall apply to a transfer of the power of attorney by the authorized bank.

(4) By virtue of the power of attorney, the bank may, upon stating the name of the shareholder, vote in his name. The bank may also vote on behalf of an undisclosed principal if the power of attorney so provides. If the bank votes in the name of the shareholder and names him, the power of attorney shall be presented to the company and kept by it. If it votes on behalf of an undisclosed principal, compliance with the requirements contained in the articles of incorporation for the exercise of the voting rights shall be sufficient to establish its voting rights as far as the company is concerned; if the articles of incorporation do not contain any such provisions, the presentation of the share certificates or of a voucher evidencing the deposit of the shares with a notary or a *Wertpapiersammelbank* shall be sufficient.

§ 135

(5) If the shareholder has not given the bank instructions concerning the exercise of the voting rights, the bank shall exercise the voting rights in accordance with its own proposals reported to the shareholders pursuant to § 128, paragraph 2, unless the bank may assume under the circumstances that the shareholder would approve a different exercise of the voting rights upon full knowledge of the facts.

(5) Hat der Aktionär dem Kreditinstitut keine Weisung für die Ausübung des Stimmrechts erteilt, so hat das Kreditinstitut das Stimmrecht entsprechend seinen eigenen, den Aktionären nach § 128 Abs. 2 mitgeteilten Vorschlägen auszuüben, es sei denn, daß das Kreditinstitut den Umständen nach annehmen darf, daß der Aktionär bei Kenntnis der Sachlage die abweichende Ausübung des Stimmrechts billigen würde.

(6) The validity of any vote cast shall not be affected by any violation of paragraph 1, second sentence, or paragraphs 2, 3 and 5 hereof.

(6) Die Wirksamkeit der Stimmabgabe wird durch einen Verstoß gegen Absatz 1 Satz 2, Absätze 2, 3 und 5 nicht beeinträchtigt.

(7) A bank may vote registered shares it does not own despite any entry listing it as the shareholder in the stock register, only pursuant to a written authorization and, if the bank is not listed as the holder of such shares, only in the name of the shareholder, whom it must name, and pursuant to a written power of attorney. Paragraph 1, second sentence, and paragraphs 2, 3 and 5 hereof shall apply to the authorization or the power of attorney and, in the case of a power of attorney, also paragraph 4, third sentence. In addition, paragraph 6 hereof shall be applicable.

(7) Ein Kreditinstitut darf das Stimmrecht für Namensaktien, die ihm nicht gehören, als deren Aktionär es aber im Aktienbuch eingetragen ist, nur auf Grund einer schriftlichen Ermächtigung, wenn es nicht als deren Aktionär eingetragen ist, nur unter Benennung des Aktionärs in dessen Namen auf Grund einer schriftlichen Vollmacht ausüben. Auf die Ermächtigung oder Vollmacht sind Absatz 1 Satz 2, Absätze 2, 3 und 5, auf die Vollmacht außerdem Absatz 4 Satz 3 anzuwenden. Im übrigen gilt Absatz 6.

(8) If the bank, in exercising the voting rights, deviates from an instruction of the shareholder or, if the shareholder has not given any instructions, deviates from its own proposal as communicated to the shareholder in accordance with § 128, paragraph 2, it shall inform the shareholder of this deviation and state the reasons therefor.

(8) Ist das Kreditinstitut bei der Ausübung des Stimmrechts von einer Weisung des Aktionärs oder, wenn der Aktionär keine Weisung erteilt hat, von seinem eigenen, dem Aktionär nach § 128 Abs. 2 mitgeteilten Vorschlag abgewichen, so hat es dies dem Aktionär mitzuteilen und die Gründe anzugeben.

(9) Paragraphs 1 to 8 hereof shall apply, *mutatis mutandis*, to the exercise of the voting rights by
1. shareholders' protective associations,
2. executives and employees of a bank if shares not owned by them have been entrusted to the bank for deposit,
3. persons who professionally solicit from shareholders the exercise of the voting rights at shareholders' meetings.
This shall not apply if the person seeking to vote is a legal representative or spouse of the shareholder or is related to him directly or by marriage within the fourth degree.

(9) Die Absätze 1 bis 8 gelten sinngemäß für die Ausübung des Stimmrechts durch
1. Vereinigungen von Aktionären,
2. Geschäftsleiter und Angestellte eines Kreditinstituts, wenn die ihnen nicht gehörenden Aktien dem Kreditinstitut zur Verwahrung anvertraut sind,
3. Personen, die sich geschäftsmäßig gegenüber Aktionären zur Ausübung des Stimmrechts in der Hauptversammlung erbieten.
Dies gilt nicht, wenn derjenige, der das Stimmrecht ausüben will, gesetzlicher Vertreter oder Ehegatte des Aktionärs oder mit ihm bis zum vierten Grade verwandt oder verschwägert ist.

(10) A bank shall be required to accept the order of a shareholder to exercise the voting right at the shareholders' meeting if it has shares of the company on deposit for the shareholder and if it has solicited from shareholders of the

(10) Ein Kreditinstitut ist verpflichtet, den Auftrag eines Aktionärs zur Ausübung des Stimmrechts in einer Hauptversammlung anzunehmen, wenn es für den Aktionär Aktien der Gesellschaft verwahrt und sich gegenüber Aktionären der Gesellschaft zur

§ 135

Ausübung des Stimmrechts in derselben Hauptversammlung erboten hat. Die Verpflichtung besteht nicht, wenn das Kreditinstitut am Ort der Hauptversammlung keine Niederlassung hat und der Aktionär die Übertragung der Vollmacht auf oder die Unterbevollmächtigung von Personen, die nicht Angestellte des Kreditinstituts sind, nicht gestattet hat.

(11) Die Verpflichtung des Kreditinstituts zum Ersatz eines aus der Verletzung der Absätze 1 bis 3, 5, 7, 8 oder 10 entstehenden Schadens kann im voraus weder ausgeschlossen noch beschränkt werden.

§ 136

Ausschluß des Stimmrechts

(1) Niemand kann für sich oder für einen anderen das Stimmrecht ausüben, wenn darüber Beschluß gefaßt wird, ob er zu entlasten oder von einer Verbindlichkeit zu befreien ist oder ob die Gesellschaft gegen ihn einen Anspruch geltend machen soll. Für Aktien, aus denen der Aktionär nach Satz 1 das Stimmrecht nicht ausüben kann, kann das Stimmrecht auch nicht durch einen anderen ausgeübt werden.

(2) Das Stimmrecht kann nicht ausgeübt werden für Aktien, die der Gesellschaft oder einem abhängigen Unternehmen oder einem anderen für Rechnung der Gesellschaft oder eines abhängigen Unternehmens gehören.

(3) Ein Vertrag, durch den sich ein Aktionär verpflichtet, nach Weisung der Gesellschaft, des Vorstands oder des Aufsichtsrats der Gesellschaft oder nach Weisung eines abhängigen Unternehmens das Stimmrecht auszuüben, ist nichtig. Ebenso ist ein Vertrag nichtig, durch den sich ein Aktionär verpflichtet, für die jeweiligen Vorschläge des Vorstands oder des Aufsichtsrats der Gesellschaft zu stimmen.

§ 137

Abstimmung über Wahlvorschläge von Aktionären

Hat ein Aktionär einen Vorschlag zur Wahl von Aufsichtsratsmitgliedern nach § 127 gemacht und beantragt er in der Hauptversammlung die Wahl des von ihm Vorgeschlagenen, so ist über seinen Antrag vor dem Vorschlag des Aufsichtsrats zu beschließen, wenn es eine Minderheit der Aktionäre verlangt, deren Anteile zusammen den zehnten Teil des vertretenen Grundkapitals erreichen.

company the right to vote at the same shareholders' meeting. The bank shall not be under such obligation if it has no branch at the place where the shareholders' meeting is held and the shareholder has refused to permit the transfer of the power of attorney or the delegation thereof to third persons who are not employees of the bank.

(11) The liability of a bank for any damage caused by a violation of paragraphs 1 to 3, 5, 7, 8 or 10 hereof can be neither waived nor limited in advance.

§ 136

Suspension of Voting Rights

(1) No one may exercise the voting rights for himself or for another on a resolution concerning ratification of his acts or his release from an obligation, or assertion by the company of a claim against him. Shares which the shareholder may not vote pursuant to the first sentence hereof may not be voted by another.

(2) The voting rights may not be exercised with respect to shares owned by the company or a controlled enterprise or another for the account of the company or a controlled enterprise.

(3) An agreement whereby a shareholder obligates himself to exercise the voting rights in accordance with the instructions of the company, the company's managing board or supervisory board, or of a controlled enterprise, shall be void. An agreement whereby a shareholder obligates himself to vote in favor of whatever proposals the company's managing board or supervisory board may make shall likewise be void.

§ 137

Voting on Nominations by Shareholders

If a shareholder has nominated a person to be elected as a member of the supervisory board pursuant to § 127 and at the shareholders' meeting moves for the election of the person nominated by him, a resolution on this motion shall be acted upon before acting on a nomination made by the supervisory board, if a minority of shareholders whose combined holdings amount to no less than one-tenth of the stated capital represented at the meeting so requests.

§ 137

Fifth Subdivision

Separate Resolutions

§ 138
Separate Shareholders' Meeting. Separate Voting

Where this Act or the articles of incorporation provide for separate resolutions by certain shareholders, such resolutions shall be passed either in a separate meeting of these shareholders or by means of a separate vote, unless the law provides otherwise. The provisions concerning shareholders' meetings shall apply to the calling of and attendance at separate meetings, as well as to the right of information; the provisions concerning shareholders' resolutions shall apply, *mutatis mutandis*, to separate resolutions. If shareholders entitled to participate in the voting on a separate resolution request the calling of a separate meeting or the announcement of an item to be voted on separately, it shall suffice if the holdings which entitle them to participate in the voting on the separate resolution together equal or exceed one-tenth of all of the shares entitled to vote on a separate resolution.

Sixth Subdivision

Non-voting Preferred Shares

§ 139
Nature

(1) Shares entitled to cumulative preferred distributions may be denied the right to vote (non-voting preferred shares).

(2) Non-voting preferred shares may be issued only up to a total par value equal to the total par value of all other shares.

§ 140
Rights of Holders of Preferred Shares

(1) Non-voting preferred shares shall confer the same rights as those enjoyed by the other shareholders, except the right to vote.

(2) In the event that the preferred distribution is not paid or is not paid in full in any year and,

Fünfter Unterabschnitt

Sonderbeschluß

§ 138
Gesonderte Versammlung. Gesonderte Abstimmung

In diesem Gesetz oder in der Satzung vorgeschriebene Sonderbeschlüsse gewisser Aktionäre sind entweder in einer gesonderten Versammlung dieser Aktionäre oder in einer gesonderten Abstimmung zu fassen, soweit das Gesetz nichts anderes bestimmt. Für die Einberufung der gesonderten Versammlung und die Teilnahme an ihr sowie für das Auskunftsrecht gelten die Bestimmungen über die Hauptversammlung, für die Sonderbeschlüsse die Bestimmungen über Hauptversammlungsbeschlüsse sinngemäß. Verlangen Aktionäre, die an der Abstimmung über den Sonderbeschluß teilnehmen können, die Einberufung einer gesonderten Versammlung oder die Bekanntmachung eines Gegenstands zur gesonderten Abstimmung, so genügt es, wenn ihre Anteile, mit denen sie an der Abstimmung über den Sonderbeschluß teilnehmen können, zusammen den zehnten Teil der Anteile erreichen, aus denen bei der Abstimmung über den Sonderbeschluß das Stimmrecht ausgeübt werden kann.

Sechster Unterabschnitt

Vorzugsaktien ohne Stimmrecht

§ 139
Wesen

(1) Für Aktien, die mit einem nachzuzahlenden Vorzug bei der Verteilung des Gewinns ausgestattet sind, kann das Stimmrecht ausgeschlossen werden (Vorzugsaktien ohne Stimmrecht).

(2) Vorzugsaktien ohne Stimmrecht dürfen nur bis zu einem Gesamtnennbetrag in Höhe des Gesamtnennbetrags der anderen Aktien ausgegeben werden.

§ 140
Rechte der Vorzugsaktionäre

(1) Die Vorzugsaktien ohne Stimmrecht gewähren mit Ausnahme des Stimmrechts die jedem Aktionär aus der Aktie zustehenden Rechte.

(2) Wird der Vorzugsbetrag in einem Jahr nicht oder nicht vollständig gezahlt und der Rückstand im

§ 138

nächsten Jahr nicht neben dem vollen Vorzug dieses Jahres nachgezahlt, so haben die Vorzugsaktionäre das Stimmrecht, bis die Rückstände nachgezahlt sind. In diesem Fall sind die Vorzugsaktien auch bei der Berechnung einer nach Gesetz oder Satzung erforderlichen Kapitalmehrheit zu berücksichtigen.

(3) Soweit die Satzung nichts anderes bestimmt, entsteht dadurch, daß der Vorzugsbetrag in einem Jahr nicht oder nicht vollständig gezahlt wird, noch kein durch spätere Beschlüsse über die Gewinnverteilung bedingter Anspruch auf den rückständigen Vorzugsbetrag.

§ 141
Aufhebung oder Beschränkung des Vorzugs

(1) Ein Beschluß, durch den der Vorzug aufgehoben oder beschränkt wird, bedarf zu seiner Wirksamkeit der Zustimmung der Vorzugsaktionäre.

(2) Ein Beschluß über die Ausgabe von Vorzugsaktien, die bei der Verteilung des Gewinns oder des Gesellschaftsvermögens den Vorzugsaktien ohne Stimmrecht vorgehen oder gleichstehen, bedarf gleichfalls der Zustimmung der Vorzugsaktionäre. Der Zustimmung bedarf es nicht, wenn die Ausgabe bei Einräumung des Vorzugs oder, falls das Stimmrecht später ausgeschlossen wurde, bei der Ausschließung ausdrücklich vorbehalten worden war und das Bezugsrecht der Vorzugsaktionäre nicht ausgeschlossen wird.

(3) Über die Zustimmung haben die Vorzugsaktionäre in einer gesonderten Versammlung einen Sonderbeschluß zu fassen. Er bedarf einer Mehrheit, die mindestens drei Viertel der abgegebenen Stimmen umfaßt Die Satzung kann weder eine andere Mehrheit noch weitere Erfordernisse bestimmen. Wird in dem Beschluß über die Ausgabe von Vorzugsaktien, die bei der Verteilung des Gewinns oder des Gesellschaftsvermögens den Vorzugsaktien ohne Stimmrecht vorgehen oder gleichstehen, das Bezugsrecht der Vorzugsaktionäre auf den Bezug solcher Aktien ganz oder zum Teil ausgeschlossen, so gilt für den Sonderbeschluß § 186 Abs. 3 bis 5 sinngemäß.

(4) Ist der Vorzug aufgehoben, so gewähren die Aktien das Stimmrecht.

in the next following year, such arrears are not added to the full preferred distribution for that year, the holders of preferred shares shall be entitled to vote until the arrears have been paid. In this event the preferred shares shall also be taken into account in computing any capital majority required by law or the articles of incorporation.

(3) Unless the articles of incorporation provide otherwise, non-payment or payment of less than the full preferred distribution in any year shall not give rise to an enforceable claim, conditioned on later resolutions concerning the distribution of profits, for payment of the arrears in preferred distributions.

§ 141
Cancellation or Restriction of Preference

(1) A resolution cancelling or restricting a preference shall, in order to be effective, require the consent of the preferred shareholders.

(2) A resolution to issue preferred shares which, upon distribution of the profits or assets of the company, have preference over or are treated the same as outstanding non-voting preferred shares shall likewise require the consent of the preferred shareholders. Such consent shall not be required if the issuance was expressly reserved when the preference was granted or, if the right to vote was later eliminated, upon such elimination, and if the preemptive right of the preferred shareholders to subscribe to new shares is not excluded.

(3) Preferred shareholders shall, in a separate meeting, pass a separate resolution on such consent. This resolution shall require a majority of at least three-fourths of the votes cast. The articles of incorporation may neither provide for a different majority nor establish additional requirements. § 186, paragraphs 3 to 5, shall apply, *mutatis mutandis*, with respect to such separate resolution if the resolution concerning the issuance of preferred shares with preference over or rights equal to outstanding non-voting preferred shares upon distribution of profits or assets of the company partially or wholly eliminates the preemptive rights of the preferred shareholders to subscribe to such new shares.

(4) The shares shall confer voting rights if the preference is cancelled.

§ 141

Seventh Subdivision	Siebenter Unterabschnitt

Seventh Subdivision

Special Audits.

Assertion of Claims for Damages

§ 142

Appointment of Special Auditors

(1) To audit transactions in connection with the formation or the conduct of the management of the company and also, in particular, in connection with measures to acquire or reduce capital, the shareholders may, by simple majority, appoint auditors (special auditors). On such a resolution, a member of the managing board or of the supervisory board may vote neither for himself nor for another if the audit is to cover transactions relating to the approval of acts of a member of the managing board or of the supervisory board or the institution of legal proceedings between the company and a member of the managing board or of the supervisory board. The voting rights of a member of the managing board or of the supervisory board barred from voting pursuant to the second sentence hereof may not be exercised through another.

(2) If the shareholders reject a motion to appoint special auditors to examine a transaction relating to the formation or a transaction relating to the company's management which occurred within the past five years, the court shall appoint such special auditors on the application of shareholders whose combined holdings amount to no less than one-tenth of the stated capital or the total par value of which amounts to no less than two million German marks, provided that there are facts which would justify the suspicion that, in connection with such transaction, there were improprieties or gross violations of the law or of the articles of incorporation. The parties making the application shall deposit their shares until a decision on the application is rendered and shall make a showing that they have been holders of the shares for no less than three months prior to the date of the shareholders' meeting. For purposes of such showing, an affidavit executed before a judge or a notary shall suffice.

(3) Paragraphs 1 and 2 hereof shall not apply to transactions which may be the subject of a special audit pursuant to § 258.

(4) If the shareholders have appointed special auditors, the court, on the application of shareholders whose combined holdings amount to no

Siebenter Unterabschnitt

Sonderprüfung.

Geltendmachung von Ersatzansprüchen

§ 142

Bestellung der Sonderprüfer

(1) Zur Prüfung von Vorgängen bei der Gründung oder der Geschäftsführung, namentlich auch bei Maßnahmen der Kapitalbeschaffung und Kapitalherabsetzung, kann die Hauptversammlung mit einfacher Stimmenmehrheit Prüfer (Sonderprüfer) bestellen. Bei der Beschlußfassung kann ein Mitglied des Vorstands oder des Aufsichtsrats weder für sich noch für einen anderen mitstimmen, wenn die Prüfung sich auf Vorgänge erstrecken soll, die mit der Entlastung eines Mitglieds des Vorstands oder des Aufsichtsrats oder der Einleitung eines Rechtsstreits zwischen der Gesellschaft und einem Mitglied des Vorstands oder des Aufsichtsrats zusammenhängen. Für ein Mitglied des Vorstands oder des Aufsichtsrats, das nach Satz 2 nicht mitstimmen kann, kann das Stimmrecht auch nicht durch einen anderen ausgeübt werden.

(2) Lehnt die Hauptversammlung einen Antrag auf Bestellung von Sonderprüfern zur Prüfung eines Vorgangs bei der Gründung oder eines nicht über fünf Jahre zurückliegenden Vorgangs bei der Geschäftsführung ab, so hat das Gericht auf Antrag von Aktionären, deren Anteile zusammen den zehnten Teil des Grundkapitals oder den Nennbetrag von zwei Millionen Deutsche Mark erreichen, Sonderprüfer zu bestellen, wenn Tatsachen vorliegen, die den Verdacht rechtfertigen, daß bei dem Vorgang Unredlichkeiten oder grobe Verletzungen des Gesetzes oder der Satzung vorgekommen sind. Die Antragsteller haben die Aktien bis zur Entscheidung über den Antrag zu hinterlegen und glaubhaft zu machen, daß sie seit mindestens drei Monaten vor dem Tage der Hauptversammlung Inhaber der Aktien sind. Zur Glaubhaftmachung genügt eine eidesstattliche Versicherung vor einem Gericht oder Notar.

(3) Die Absätze 1 und 2 gelten nicht für Vorgänge, die Gegenstand einer Sonderprüfung nach § 258 sein können.

(4) Hat die Hauptversammlung Sonderprüfer bestellt, so hat das Gericht auf Antrag von Aktionären, deren Anteile zusammen den zehnten Teil des

Grundkapitals oder den Nennbetrag von zwei Millionen Deutsche Mark erreichen, einen anderen Sonderprüfer zu bestellen, wenn dies aus einem in der Person des bestellten Sonderprüfers liegenden Grund geboten erscheint, insbesondere, wenn der bestellte Sonderprüfer nicht die für den Gegenstand der Sonderprüfung erforderlichen Kenntnisse hat, oder wenn Besorgnis der Befangenheit oder Bedenken gegen seine Zuverlässigkeit bestehen. Der Antrag ist binnen zwei Wochen seit dem Tage der Hauptversammlung zu stellen.

(5) Das Gericht hat außer den Beteiligten auch den Aufsichtsrat und im Fall des Absatzes 4 den von der Hauptversammlung bestellten Sonderprüfer zu hören. Gegen die Entscheidung ist die sofortige Beschwerde zulässig.

(6) Die vom Gericht bestellten Sonderprüfer haben Anspruch auf Ersatz angemessener barer Auslagen und auf Vergütung für ihre Tätigkeit. Die Auslagen und die Vergütung setzt das Gericht fest. Gegen die Entscheidung ist die sofortige Beschwerde zulässig. Die weitere Beschwerde ist ausgeschlossen. Aus der rechtskräftigen Entscheidung findet die Zwangsvollstreckung nach der Zivilprozeßordnung statt.

§ 143

Auswahl der Sonderprüfer

(1) Als Sonderprüfer sollen, wenn der Gegenstand der Sonderprüfung keine anderen Kenntnisse fordert, nur bestellt werden
1. Personen, die in der Buchführung ausreichend vorgebildet und erfahren sind;
2. Prüfungsgesellschaften, von deren gesetzlichen Vertretern mindestens einer in der Buchführung ausreichend vorgebildet und erfahren ist.

(2) Sonderprüfer kann nicht sein, wer
1. Mitglied des Vorstands oder des Aufsichtsrats oder Angestellter der zu prüfenden Gesellschaft ist oder in den letzten drei Jahren vor seiner Bestellung oder während der Zeit war, in der sich der zu prüfende Vorgang ereignet hat;
2. gesetzlicher Vertreter oder Mitglied des Aufsichtsrats einer juristischen Person, Gesellschafter einer Personengesellschaft oder Inhaber eines Unternehmens ist, sofern die juristische Person, die Personengesellschaft oder das Einzelunternehmen mit der zu prüfenden Gesellschaft verbunden ist;

less than one-tenth of the stated capital or the total par value of which amounts to no less than two million German marks, shall appoint some other special auditor if this appears necessary for reasons relating to the person appointed as special auditor, particularly if the special auditor appointed does not have the requisite expertise concerning the subject of the special audit, or if there is reason to doubt his impartiality or to question his reliability. The application shall be made within two weeks from the date of the shareholders' meeting.

(5) In addition to the persons concerned, the court shall also hear the supervisory board and, in the case of paragraph 4 hereof, the special auditor appointed by the shareholders. The decision of the court can be appealed.

(6) The special auditors appointed by the court shall be entitled to reimbursement for their reasonable cash expenditures and remuneration for their services. The expenditures and the remuneration shall be determined by the court. The decision of the court can be appealed. It shall not be subject to further appeal. The final decision shall be enforceable in accordance with the provisions of the Code of Civil Procedure.

§ 143

Selection of Special Auditors

(1) Unless the subject of the special audit requires a different expertise, only the following may be appointed as special auditors:
1. persons who are sufficiently trained and experienced in accounting;
2. auditing firms at least one of whose legal representatives is sufficiently trained and experienced in accounting.

(2) The following may not act as special auditor:
1. a person who is or who was, within the last three years prior to his appointment, or during the time when the transaction subject to the audit occurred, a member of the managing board or of the supervisory board or an employee of the company to be audited;
2. a legal representative or a member of the supervisory board of a legal entity, a member of a partnership or owner of a sole proprietorship, if such legal entity, partnership or sole proprietorship is related to the company to be audited;

§ 143

3. an employee of an enterprise related to the company to be audited.

(3) An auditing firm may not act as special auditor:

1. if it or an enterprise related to it is related to the company to be audited;
2. if a legal representative of an auditing firm which is a legal entity or a partner of an auditing firm could not act as special auditor pursuant to paragraph 2 hereof;
3. if a member of the supervisory board of the auditing firm could not be special auditor pursuant to paragraph 2, No. 1, hereof.

§ 144
Liability of Special Auditors

§ 168, concerning the liability of the annual auditors, shall apply *mutatis mutandis*.

§ 145
Rights of Special Auditors. Audit Report

(1) The managing board is required to permit the special auditors to examine the company's books and records as well as its assets, in particular the company's cash position and the securities and goods on hand.

(2) The special auditors may request from the members of the managing board and from the supervisory board any information and proof necessary for a thorough examination of any transactions.

(3) The special auditors shall have the rights pursuant to paragraph 2 hereof also against any member of an affiliated group of companies and against any controlled or controlling enterprise.

(4) The special auditors shall make a written report on the result of the audit. The audit report shall even include facts which, upon becoming public knowledge, are likely to expose the company or a related enterprise to a not inconsiderable detriment, provided that the knowledge of such facts is necessary for the evaluation of the transaction examined by the shareholders. The special auditors shall sign the report and promptly present it to the managing board and the Commercial Register at the company's domicile. The managing board shall, upon request, furnish a copy of the audit report to any shareholder. The managing board shall submit the report to the supervisory board and publish it as

3. Angestellter eines Unternehmens ist, das mit der zu prüfenden Gesellschaft verbunden ist.

(3) Eine Prüfungsgesellschaft kann nicht Sonderprüfer sein,

1. wenn sie oder ein mit ihr verbundenes Unternehmen mit der zu prüfenden Gesellschaft verbunden ist;
2. wenn bei Prüfungsgesellschaften, die juristische Personen sind, ein gesetzlicher Vertreter, bei anderen Prüfungsgesellschaften ein Gesellschafter nach Absatz 2 nicht Sonderprüfer sein könnte;
3. wenn ein Aufsichtsratsmitglied der Prüfungsgesellschaft nach Absatz 2 Nr. 1 nicht Sonderprüfer sein könnte.

§ 144
Verantwortlichkeit der Sonderprüfer

§ 168 über die Verantwortlichkeit der Abschlußprüfer gilt sinngemäß.

§ 145
Rechte der Sonderprüfer. Prüfungsbericht

(1) Der Vorstand hat den Sonderprüfern zu gestatten, die Bücher und Schriften der Gesellschaft sowie die Vermögensgegenstände, namentlich die Gesellschaftskasse und die Bestände an Wertpapieren und Waren, zu prüfen.

(2) Die Sonderprüfer können von den Mitgliedern des Vorstands und des Aufsichtsrats alle Aufklärungen und Nachweise verlangen, welche die sorgfältige Prüfung der Vorgänge notwendig macht.

(3) Die Sonderprüfer haben die Rechte nach Absatz 2 auch gegenüber einem Konzernunternehmen sowie gegenüber einem abhängigen oder herrschenden Unternehmen.

(4) Die Sonderprüfer haben über das Ergebnis der Prüfung schriftlich zu berichten. Auch Tatsachen, deren Bekanntwerden geeignet ist, der Gesellschaft oder einem verbundenen Unternehmen einen nicht unerheblichen Nachteil zuzufügen, müssen in den Prüfungsbericht aufgenommen werden, wenn ihre Kenntnis zur Beurteilung des zu prüfenden Vorgangs durch die Hauptversammlung erforderlich ist. Die Sonderprüfer haben den Bericht zu unterzeichnen und unverzüglich dem Vorstand und zum Handelsregister des Sitzes der Gesellschaft einzureichen. Auf Verlangen hat der Vorstand jedem Aktionär eine Abschrift des Prüfungsberichts zu erteilen. Der Vorstand hat den Bericht dem Aufsichtsrat vorzulegen und bei der Einberufung der nächsten Haupt-

versammlung als Gegenstand der Tagesordnung bekanntzumachen.

an item of the agenda when the next shareholders' meeting is called.

§ 146
Kosten

Bestellt das Gericht Sonderprüfer, so trägt die Gesellschaft unbeschadet eines ihr nach den Vorschriften des bürgerlichen Rechts zustehenden Ersatzanspruchs die Gerichtskosten und die Kosten der Prüfung.

§ 146
Expenses

If special auditors are appointed by the court, the company shall bear the court costs and expenses of the audit, without prejudice to any right to reimbursement it may have pursuant to the rules of private law.

§ 147
Geltendmachung von Ersatzansprüchen

(1) Die Ersatzansprüche der Gesellschaft aus der Gründung gegen die nach den §§ 46 bis 48, 53 verpflichteten Personen oder aus der Geschäftsführung gegen die Mitglieder des Vorstands und des Aufsichtsrats oder aus § 117 müssen geltend gemacht werden, wenn es die Hauptversammlung mit einfacher Stimmenmehrheit beschließt oder es eine Minderheit verlangt, deren Anteile zusammen den zehnten Teil des Grundkapitals erreichen. Das Verlangen der Minderheit ist nur zu berücksichtigen, wenn glaubhaft gemacht wird, daß die Aktionäre, die die Minderheit bilden, seit mindestens drei Monaten vor dem Tage der Hauptversammlung Inhaber der Aktien sind. Zur Glaubhaftmachung genügt eine eidesstattliche Versicherung vor einem Gericht oder einem Notar.

(2) Der Ersatzanspruch soll binnen sechs Monaten seit dem Tage der Hauptversammlung geltend gemacht werden.

(3) Zur Geltendmachung des Ersatzanspruchs kann die Hauptversammlung besondere Vertreter bestellen. Hat die Hauptversammlung die Geltendmachung des Ersatzanspruchs beschlossen oder eine Minderheit sie verlangt, so hat das Gericht (§ 14) auf Antrag von Aktionären, deren Anteile zusammen den zehnten Teil des Grundkapitals oder den Nennbetrag von zwei Millionen Deutsche Mark erreichen, als Vertreter der Gesellschaft zur Geltendmachung des Ersatzanspruchs andere als die nach §§ 78, 112 oder nach Satz 1 zur Vertretung der Gesellschaft berufenen Personen zu bestellen, wenn ihm dies für eine gehörige Geltendmachung zweckmäßig erscheint. Gegen die Entscheidung ist die sofortige Beschwerde zulässig. Die gerichtlich bestellten Vertreter können von der Gesellschaft den Ersatz angemessener barer Auslagen und eine Vergütung für

§ 147
Assertion of Claims for Damages

(1) Damage claims of the company relating to its formation against persons liable pursuant to §§ 46 to 48 and 53, or relating to its management against the members of the managing board and of the supervisory board, or those resulting from § 117 must be asserted if the shareholders by simple majority adopt a resolution to this effect or if a minority whose combined holdings amount to no less than one-tenth of the stated capital so requests. The request of a minority shall be acted upon only if a showing is made that the shareholders composing such minority have held the shares for at least three months prior to the date of the shareholders' meeting. For purposes of such showing, an affidavit executed before a judge or a notary shall suffice.

(2) Any action for damages must be brought within six months from the date of the shareholders' meeting.

(3) The shareholders may appoint special representatives to assert the claim for damages. If the shareholders adopt a resolution to assert the claim for damages or if a minority so requests, the court (§ 14), upon application of shareholders whose combined holdings amount to no less than one-tenth of the stated capital or a par value of two million German marks, shall appoint as representatives of the company for the purpose of asserting the claim for damages persons other than those authorized to represent the company pursuant to §§ 78, 112, or the first sentence hereof, if the court deems that this would serve to assure that the claims are properly asserted. The decision of the court can be appealed. The court-appointed representatives may request from the company reimbursement for their reasonable cash expenditures and remuneration for their

§ 147

services. The expenditures and the remuneration shall be determined by the court. The decision of the court can be appealed. It is not subject to further appeal. The final decision shall be enforceable in accordance with the provisions of the Code of Civil Procedure.

(4) If a minority has requested the assertion of the claim for damages, and if the company has become liable for payment of the costs of the action because it was defeated, wholly or partially, in such litigation, the minority shall be obligated to reimburse the company for these costs. If the company is defeated entirely in the action, the minority shall also be obligated to reimburse the company for the court costs incurred by the company in connection with the appointment of special representatives pursuant to paragraph 3, second and fourth sentences, hereof, and for the cash expenditures and remuneration of the special representatives.

ihre Tätigkeit verlangen. Die Auslagen und die Vergütung setzt das Gericht fest. Gegen die Entscheidung ist die sofortige Beschwerde zulässig. Die weitere Beschwerde ist ausgeschlossen. Aus der rechtskräftigen Entscheidung findet die Zwangsvollstreckung nach der Zivilprozeßordnung statt.

(4) Hat eine Minderheit die Geltendmachung des Ersatzanspruchs verlangt und hat die Gesellschaft, weil sie im Rechtsstreit ganz oder teilweise unterlegen ist, Kosten des Rechtsstreits zu tragen, so ist die Minderheit der Gesellschaft zur Erstattung dieser Kosten verpflichtet. Ist die Gesellschaft ganz unterlegen, so ist die Minderheit der Gesellschaft auch zur Erstattung der Gerichtskosten, die der Gesellschaft durch die Bestellung besonderer Vertreter nach Absatz 3 Satz 2 und 4 entstanden sind, sowie der baren Auslagen und der Vergütung der besonderen Vertreter verpflichtet.

Part Five

Annual Statements.
Disposition of Retained Earnings

First Division

Preparation of Annual Financial Statements and Business Report

§ 148
Preparation by Managing Board

The managing board shall, within the first three months of each fiscal year, prepare the balance sheet and the profit and loss statement (annual financial statements), as well as the business report for the preceding fiscal year, and submit them to the annual auditors.

§ 149
Content of Annual Financial Statements

(1) The annual financial statements shall conform with proper accounting principles. They shall be prepared in a clear and informative manner and must, subject to the rules concerning valuation, permit as accurate as possible a picture of the financial and earnings position of the company.

§ 148

Fünfter Teil
Rechnungslegung. Gewinnverwendung

Erster Abschnitt
Aufstellung des Jahresabschlusses und des Geschäftsberichts

§ 148
Aufstellung durch den Vorstand

Der Vorstand hat in den ersten drei Monaten des Geschäftsjahrs für das vergangene Geschäftsjahr die Jahresbilanz und die Gewinn- und Verlustrechnung (Jahresabschluß) sowie den Geschäftsbericht aufzustellen und den Abschlußprüfern vorzulegen.

§ 149
Inhalt des Jahresabschlusses

(1) Der Jahresabschluß hat den Grundsätzen ordnungsmäßiger Buchführung zu entsprechen. Er ist klar und übersichtlich aufzustellen und muß im Rahmen der Bewertungsvorschriften einen möglichst sicheren Einblick in die Vermögens- und Ertragslage der Gesellschaft geben.

(2) Soweit in den folgenden Vorschriften nichts anderes bestimmt ist, sind die Vorschriften des Vierten Abschnitts des Ersten Buchs des Handelsgesetzbuchs über Handelsbücher anzuwenden.

§ 150
Gesetzliche Rücklage

(1) Es ist eine gesetzliche Rücklage zu bilden.

(2) In diese sind außer den Beträgen, deren Einstellung in die gesetzliche Rücklage für den Fall der Kapitalherabsetzung nach den §§ 232, 237 Abs. 5 oder nach anderen Vorschriften vorgeschrieben ist, einzustellen

1. der zwanzigste Teil des um einen Verlustvortrag aus dem Vorjahr geminderten Jahresüberschusses, bis die Rücklage den zehnten oder den in der Satzung bestimmten höheren Teil des Grundkapitals erreicht;
2. der Betrag, der bei der Ausgabe von Aktien einschließlich von Bezugsaktien über den Nennbetrag der Aktien hinaus erzielt wird;
3. der Betrag, der bei der Ausgabe von Wandelschuldverschreibungen über ihren Rückzahlungsbetrag hinaus erzielt wird;
4. der Betrag von Zuzahlungen, die Aktionäre gegen Gewährung eines Vorzugs für ihre Aktien leisten.

(3) Übersteigt die gesetzliche Rücklage nicht den zehnten oder den in der Satzung bestimmten höheren Teil des Grundkapitals, so darf sie nur verwandt werden

1. zum Ausgleich eines Jahresfehlbetrags, soweit er nicht durch einen Gewinnvortrag aus dem Vorjahr gedeckt ist und nicht durch Auflösung freier Rücklagen ausgeglichen werden kann;
2. zum Ausgleich eines Verlustvortrags aus dem Vorjahr, soweit er nicht durch einen Jahresüberschuß gedeckt ist und nicht durch Auflösung freier Rücklagen ausgeglichen werden kann.

(4) Übersteigt die gesetzliche Rücklage den zehnten oder den in der Satzung bestimmten höheren Teil des Grundkapitals, so darf der übersteigende Betrag verwandt werden

1. zum Ausgleich eines Jahresfehlbetrags, soweit er nicht durch einen Gewinnvortrag aus dem Vorjahr gedeckt ist;
2. zum Ausgleich eines Verlustvortrags aus dem Vorjahr, soweit er nicht durch einen Jahresüberschuß gedeckt ist;

(2) Unless otherwise specified in the following provisions, the provisions of Part Four of Book One of the Commercial Code, concerning books and records of commercial enterprises, shall be applicable.

§ 150
Statutory Reserve

(1) A statutory reserve shall be created.

(2) In addition to the amounts to be set aside in the event of a reduction of capital as required by §§ 232, 237, paragraph 5, or other provisions, the following shall be allocated to the statutory reserve:

1. one-twentieth of the net profit for the year, reduced by any losses carried forward from the preceding year until the reserve reaches one-tenth of the stated capital or any higher percentage specified in the articles of incorporation;
2. any premium derived from the issuance of shares, including preemptive shares, in excess of their par value;
3. any premium derived from the issuance of convertible bonds in excess of the amount for which they can be redeemed;
4. any premium paid by shareholders in consideration of preferential rights granted with respect to their shares.

(3) If the statutory reserve does not exceed one-tenth or such higher portion of the stated capital as may be specified in the articles of incorporation, it may be used only

1. to offset a loss in any fiscal year to the extent that it is not covered by retained earnings of the preceding year and cannot be covered by the release of free reserves;
2. to offset a loss carried forward from the preceding year, to the extent that it is not covered by net profits of the present fiscal year and cannot be covered by the release of free reserves.

(4) If the statutory reserve exceeds one-tenth or such higher portion of the stated capital as may be specified in the articles of incorporation, the amount in excess may be used

1. to offset a loss in any fiscal year to the extent that it is not covered by retained earnings of the preceding year;
2. to offset a loss carried forward from the preceding year to the extent that it is not covered by net profits of the present fiscal year;

§ 150

3. to effect a capital increase out of the company's surplus pursuant to §§ 207 to 220.

Statutory reserves may not be used in accordance with Nos. 1 and 2 hereof if, at the same time, free reserves are released to effect a distribution of profits.

§ 151
Classification of Annual Balance Sheet

(1) The annual balance sheet shall, without prejudice to a further classification, specifically set forth the following items, unless the type of business involved requires a different classification, in which event such classification must be at least as detailed as that shown herein:

On the assets side:
I. Outstanding subscriptions to stated capital; amount of such subscriptions called in:
II. Fixed assets:
  A. Tangible and intangible fixed assets:
    1. real property and rights deemed to be real property with office buildings, plants, and other improvements;
    2. real property and rights deemed to be real property with residential buildings;
    3. unimproved real property and rights deemed to be real property;
    4. buildings on real property owned by third parties and not encompassed by No. 1 or 2 hereof;
    5. machinery and equipment;
    6. production and office equipment;
    7. facilities under construction and installment payments for such facilities;
    8. franchises, industrial property rights and similar rights, as well as licenses under such rights.
  B. Long-term investments:
    1. securities in related companies;
    2. securities considered fixed assets and not encompassed by No. 1 hereof;
    3. loans not maturing for four years;

    portion of such loans secured by encumbrances on real property:
III. Current assets:
  A. Inventories:
    1. raw materials, maintenance materials and supplies;

---

3. zur Kapitalerhöhung aus Gesellschaftsmitteln nach §§ 207 bis 220.

Die Verwendung nach Nummern 1 und 2 ist nicht zulässig, wenn gleichzeitig freie Rücklagen zur Gewinnausschüttung aufgelöst werden.

§ 151
Gliederung der Jahresbilanz

(1) In der Jahresbilanz sind, wenn der Geschäftszweig keine abweichende Gliederung bedingt, die gleichwertig sein muß, unbeschadet einer weiteren Gliederung folgende Posten gesondert auszuweisen:

Auf der Aktivseite:
I. Ausstehende Einlagen auf das Grundkapital; davon eingefordert:
II. Anlagevermögen:
  A. Sachanlagen und immaterielle Anlagewerte:
    1. Grundstücke und grundstücksgleiche Rechte mit Geschäfts-, Fabrik- und anderen Bauten;
    2. Grundstücke und grundstücksgleiche Rechte mit Wohnbauten;
    3. Grundstücke und grundstücksgleiche Rechte ohne Bauten;
    4. Bauten auf fremden Grundstücken, die nicht zu Nummer 1 oder 2 gehören;
    5. Maschinen und maschinelle Anlagen;
    6. Betriebs- und Geschäftsausstattung;
    7. Anlagen im Bau und Anzahlungen auf Anlagen;
    8. Konzessionen, gewerbliche Schutzrechte und ähnliche Rechte sowie Lizenzen an solchen Rechten.
  B. Finanzanlagen:
    1. Beteiligungen;
    2. Wertpapiere des Anlagevermögens, die nicht zu Nummer 1 gehören;
    3. Ausleihungen mit einer Laufzeit von mindestens vier Jahren;
    davon durch Grundpfandrechte gesichert:
III. Umlaufvermögen:
  A. Vorräte:
    1. Roh-, Hilfs- und Betriebsstoffe;

2. unfertige Erzeugnisse;
3. fertige Erzeugnisse, Waren.

B. Andere Gegenstände des Umlaufvermögens:
1. geleistete Anzahlungen, soweit sie nicht zu II A Nr. 7 gehören;
2. Forderungen aus Lieferungen und Leistungen;
   davon mit einer Restlaufzeit von mehr als einem Jahr:
3. Wechsel;
   davon bundesbankfähig:
4. Schecks;
5. Kassenbestand, Bundesbank- und Postscheckguthaben;
6. Guthaben bei Kreditinstituten;
7. Wertpapiere, die nicht zu Nummer 3, 4, 8 oder 9 oder zu II B gehören;
8. eigene Aktien unter Angabe ihres Nennbetrags;
9. Anteile an einer herrschenden oder an der Gesellschaft mit Mehrheit beteiligten Kapitalgesellschaft oder bergrechtlichen Gewerkschaft unter Angabe ihres Nennbetrags, bei Kuxen ihrer Zahl;
10. Forderungen an verbundene Unternehmen;
11. Forderungen aus Krediten, die
    a) unter § 89,
    b) unter § 115
    fallen;
12. sonstige Vermögensgegenstände.

IV. Rechnungsabgrenzungsposten

V. Bilanzverlust

Auf der Passivseite:

I. Grundkapital

II. Offene Rücklagen:
1. gesetzliche Rücklage;
2. andere Rücklagen (freie Rücklagen).

III. Wertberichtigungen

IV. Rückstellungen:
1. Pensionsrückstellungen;
2. andere Rückstellungen.

V. Verbindlichkeiten mit einer Laufzeit von mindestens vier Jahren:
1. Anleihen;
   davon durch Grundpfandrechte gesichert:
2. Verbindlichkeiten gegenüber Kreditinstituten;
   davon durch Grundpfandrechte gesichert:

2. work in process;
3. finished goods, merchandise.

B. Other current assets:
1. advance payments other than those encompassed by II A, No. 7;
2. accounts receivable from sales and services;
   portion thereof due after more than one year:
3. notes receivable;
   portion thereof eligible for discounting with the Bundesbank:
4. checks;
5. cash on hand and on deposit with the Bundesbank and in postal checking account;
6. other bank accounts;
7. securities not classified under No. 3, 4, 8, or 9, or II B hereof;
8. treasury shares, stating their total par value;
9. securities in a controlling company, or a corporation or mining company owning a majority interest in the company, stating their total par value or, in the case of mining certificates, their total number;
10. accounts receivable from related enterprises;
11. accounts receivable from loans qualifying under
    a) § 89,
    b) § 115;
12. other assets.

IV. Deferred charges

V. Losses

On the liabilities side:

I. Stated capital

II. Disclosed reserves:
1. statutory reserves;
2. other reserves (free reserves).

III. Reserves for decline in value of fixed assets.

IV. Reserves for expenses:
1. reserves for pensions;
2. other reserves.

V. Liabilities not maturing for four years:
1. loans;
   portion of such loans secured by encumbrances on real property:
2. liabilities to banks;
   portion of such liabilities secured by encumbrances on real property:

§ 151

3. other liabilities;

portion of such liabilities secured by encumbrances on real property:

Of the items listed under Nos. 1 to 3, the following are due prior to the expiration of four years:

VI. Other liabilities:
1. accounts payable for goods and services;
2. liabilities arising from the acceptance of drafts and the issuance of promissory notes;
3. liabilities to banks and not encompassed by V hereof;
4. advances from customers;
5. accounts payable to related enterprises;
6. other liabilities.

VII. Deferred income

VIII. Retained earnings

(2) A company not having items falling within one of these classifications need not list such classification.

(3) If an item could be listed under several classifications, the classification under which it is listed shall contain a reference to the other possible classifications to which it could belong, if this is necessary for the preparation of a clear and informative annual balance sheet. As a rule, accounts receivable from and accounts payable to related enterprises shall be identified as such; if they are listed under different classifications, this fact shall be noted. Treasury shares and securities in a corporation or mining company which controls or owns a majority interest in the company may not be listed under other classifications.

(4) Reserves for depreciation, for decline in value, and for expenses, and allocations to special accounts which in part constitute reserves shall be provided in the annual balance sheet. The same applies to withdrawals from disclosed reserves and allocations to disclosed reserves required by law or the articles of incorporation, or effected by the managing board and the supervisory board pursuant to § 58, paragraph 2. The excess of assets over liabilities (retained earnings) or the excess of liabilities over assets (accumulated losses) shall be listed without further breakdown and separately at the end of the annual balance sheet.

(5) Unless such items must be entered as a liability, the annual balance sheet shall list separately the full amount of

§ 151

---

3. sonstige Verbindlichkeiten;

davon durch Grundpfandrechte gesichert:

Von Nummern 1 bis 3 sind vor Ablauf von vier Jahren fällig:

VI. Andere Verbindlichkeiten:
1. Verbindlichkeiten aus Lieferungen und Leistungen;
2. Verbindlichkeiten aus der Annahme gezogener Wechsel und der Ausstellung eigener Wechsel;
3. Verbindlichkeiten gegenüber Kreditinstituten, soweit sie nicht zu V gehören;
4. erhaltene Anzahlungen;
5. Verbindlichkeiten gegenüber verbundenen Unternehmen;
6. sonstige Verbindlichkeiten.

VII. Rechnungsabgrenzungsposten

VIII. Bilanzgewinn

(2) Sind unter einen Posten fallende Gegenstände bei einer Gesellschaft nicht vorhanden, so braucht der Posten nicht aufgeführt zu werden.

(3) Fällt ein Gegenstand unter mehrere Posten, so ist bei dem Posten, unter dem er ausgewiesen wird, die Mitzugehörigkeit zu den anderen Posten zu vermerken, wenn dies zur Aufstellung einer klaren und übersichtlichen Jahresbilanz nötig ist. Forderungen und Verbindlichkeiten gegenüber verbundenen Unternehmen sind in der Regel als solche auszuweisen; werden sie unter anderen Posten ausgewiesen, so muß diese Eigenschaft vermerkt werden. Eigene Aktien und Anteile an einer herrschenden oder mit Mehrheit beteiligten Kapitalgesellschaft oder bergrechtlichen Gewerkschaft dürfen nicht unter anderen Posten aufgeführt werden.

(4) Abschreibungen, Wertberichtigungen, Rückstellungen und Einstellungen in Sonderposten mit Rücklageanteil sind bereits in der Jahresbilanz vorzunehmen. Gleiches gilt für Entnahmen aus offenen Rücklagen sowie für Einstellungen in offene Rücklagen, die nach Gesetz oder Satzung vorzunehmen sind oder die Vorstand und Aufsichtsrat auf Grund des § 58 Abs. 2 vornehmen. Der Überschuß der Aktivposten über die Passivposten (Bilanzgewinn) oder der Überschuß der Passivposten über die Aktivposten (Bilanzverlust) ist am Schluß der Jahresbilanz ungeteilt und gesondert auszuweisen.

(5) In der Jahresbilanz sind, sofern sie nicht auf der Passivseite auszuweisen sind, in voller Höhe gesondert zu vermerken

1. Verbindlichkeiten aus der Begebung und Übertragung von Wechseln;
2. Verbindlichkeiten aus Bürgschaften, Wechsel- und Scheckbürgschaften;
3. Verbindlichkeiten aus Gewährleistungsverträgen;
4. Haftung aus der Bestellung von Sicherheiten für fremde Verbindlichkeiten.

Sie sind auch dann zu vermerken, wenn ihnen gleichwertige Rückgriffsforderungen gegenüberstehen. Besteht die Verbindlichkeit oder die Haftung gegenüber verbundenen Unternehmen, so ist dies bei den einzelnen Vermerken unter Angabe des Betrags anzugeben.

1. liabilities arising out of the drawing and endorsement of notes;
2. liabilities arising out of suretyships, and guaranties of notes and checks;
3. liabilities arising out of warranties;
4. liability arising out of collateral furnished to secure third parties.

These items shall be listed even though they may be offset by equivalent rights of recourse. If such liabilities or guaranties to related enterprises exist, this fact shall be mentioned in the relevant notes, specifying the amount.

§ 152

Vorschriften zu einzelnen Posten der Jahresbilanz

(1) Beim Anlagevermögen sind nur die Gegenstände auszuweisen, die am Abschlußstichtag bestimmt sind, dauernd dem Geschäftsbetrieb der Gesellschaft zu dienen. Die Zugänge und Abgänge, die Zuschreibungen, die für das Geschäftsjahr gemachten Abschreibungen sowie die Umbuchungen sind bei den einzelnen Posten des Anlagevermögens gesondert aufzuführen.

(2) Als Beteiligung gelten im Zweifel Anteile an einer Kapitalgesellschaft, deren Nennbeträge insgesamt den vierten Teil des Nennkapitals dieser Gesellschaft erreichen, sowie Kuxe einer bergrechtlichen Gewerkschaft, deren Zahl insgesamt den vierten Teil der Kuxe dieser Gewerkschaft erreicht.

(3) Beim Grundkapital sind die Gesamtnennbeträge der Aktien jeder Gattung gesondert anzugeben. Bedingtes Kapital ist mit dem Nennbetrag zu vermerken. Bestehen Mehrstimmrechtsaktien, so sind beim Grundkapital die Gesamtstimmenzahl der Mehrstimmrechtsaktien und die der übrigen Aktien zu vermerken.

(4) Bei den offenen Rücklagen sind gesondert aufzuführen
1. die Beträge, die die Hauptversammlung aus dem Bilanzgewinn des Vorjahrs eingestellt hat,
2. die Beträge, die aus dem Jahresüberschuß des Geschäftsjahrs eingestellt werden,
3. die Beträge, die für das Geschäftsjahr entnommen werden.

(5) Werden auf der Passivseite Posten ausgewiesen, die auf Grund steuerlicher Vorschriften erst bei ihrer Auflösung zu versteuern sind, so sind

§ 152

Rules Concerning Specific Items of the Annual Balance Sheet

(1) Only such assets shall be included as fixed assets which as of the closing date of the annual financial statements are designed to serve the company's business permanently. Additions and disposals, appreciations, depreciation made or provided for during the fiscal year, as well as reclassifications, shall be listed separately under the classification concerning fixed assets to which they relate.

(2) Equity interests in a corporation, the total par value of which amounts to no less than one-fourth of the stated capital of such company, as well as shares of a mining company, the total number of which amounts to no less than one-fourth of the total shares in such mining company, shall, in case of doubt, be considered as equity interests.

(3) Under stated capital, the total par value of shares of each class shall be stated separately. Conditional capital shall be shown by reference to its total par value. In the case of shares with multiple voting rights, the reference to the stated capital shall indicate the total number of votes of the shares having multiple voting rights and the total number of votes of the other shares.

(4) With respect to disclosed reserves, the following shall be stated separately:
1. amounts allocated by the shareholders from the retained earnings of the preceding year,
2. amounts allocated from the net profit for the fiscal year,
3. amounts withdrawn during the fiscal year.

(5) If items are shown on the liabilities side which, under the tax laws, are taxable only when they are liquidated, such items shall be listed on

§ 152

the liabilities side separately from the disclosed reserves, referring to the provisions pursuant to which they were established, under "II a, special items which in part constitute reserves."

(6) Reserves for decline in value may be made only for tangible assets, securities in related enterprises, and other securities considered fixed assets, and in the form of overall provisions for the general risk of collection of the accounts receivable. The provisions relating to individual items shall be itemized separately in a manner corresponding to paragraph 1, second sentence, hereof; the overall provision shall be shown as "overall provision for accounts receivable."

(7) Reserves may be established for potential liabilities and for anticipated losses from pending transactions. Reserves may also be established for
1. expenditures for maintenance or waste removal deferred from the present fiscal year to the following fiscal year;
2. warranties which are extended without legal obligation.
Such reserves shall be listed separately by stating their purpose in detail. Reserves may not be established for other purposes. The item "reserve for pensions" shall specify reserves for current pensions and for vested rights to future pension payments.

(8) Receivables may not be offset against liabilities, nor may uninvoiced sales and services be offset against down payments, nor rights in real property against encumbrances on real property. Special reserves, reserves for decline in value, and reserves for expenses may not be listed as liabilities.

(9) The following only may be designated as deferred items:
1. On the assets side, payments made prior to the closing date of the annual financial statements, to the extent that they constitute expenses attributable to a certain period of time after such date;
2. On the liabilities side, payments received prior to the closing date of the annual financial statements, to the extent that they constitute income attributable to a certain period of time after such date.

§ 153

Valuation of Fixed Assets

(1) Fixed assets shall be listed at the cost of acquisition or production reduced by deprecia-

---

diese Posten gesondert von den offenen Rücklagen unter Angabe der Vorschriften, nach denen sie gebildet sind, auf der Passivseite unter „II a Sonderposten mit Rücklageanteil" auszuweisen.

(6) Wertberichtigungen dürfen nur zu Sachanlagen, zu Beteiligungen und zu Wertpapieren des Anlagevermögens sowie als Pauschalwertberichtigung wegen des allgemeinen Kreditrisikos zu Forderungen vorgenommen werden. Die auf die einzelnen Posten entfallenden Wertberichtigungen sind in einer Absatz 1 Satz 2 entsprechenden Gliederung gesondert, die Pauschalwertberichtigung ist als „Pauschalwertberichtigung zu Forderungen" auszuweisen.

(7) Rückstellungen dürfen für ungewisse Verbindlichkeiten und für drohende Verluste aus schwebenden Geschäften gebildet werden. Ferner dürfen Rückstellungen gebildet werden für
1. im Geschäftsjahr unterlassene Aufwendungen für Instandhaltung oder Abraumbeseitigung, die im folgenden Geschäftsjahr nachgeholt werden;
2. Gewährleistungen, die ohne rechtliche Verpflichtung erbracht werden;
diese Rückstellungen sind unter näherer Bezeichnung ihres Zwecks gesondert auszuweisen. Für andere Zwecke dürfen keine Rückstellungen gebildet werden. Unter dem Posten „Pensionsrückstellungen" sind die Rückstellungen für laufende Pensionen und die für Anwartschaften auf Pensionen auszuweisen.

(8) Forderungen dürfen nicht mit Verbindlichkeiten, nicht abgerechnete Leistungen nicht mit Anzahlungen, Grundstücksrechte nicht mit Grundstückslasten verrechnet werden. Rücklagen, Wertberichtigungen und Rückstellungen dürfen nicht als Verbindlichkeiten aufgeführt werden.

(9) Als Rechnungsabgrenzungsposten dürfen nur ausgewiesen werden
1. auf der Aktivseite Ausgaben vor dem Abschlußstichtag, soweit sie Aufwand für eine bestimmte Zeit nach diesem Tag darstellen;
2. auf der Passivseite Einnahmen vor dem Abschlußstichtag, soweit sie Ertrag für eine bestimmte Zeit nach diesem Tag darstellen.

§ 153

Wertansätze der Gegenstände des Anlagevermögens

(1) Gegenstände des Anlagevermögens sind zu den Anschaffungs- oder Herstellungskosten vermin-

dert um Abschreibungen oder Wertberichtigungen nach § 154 anzusetzen. Zugänge sind mit den Anschaffungs- oder Herstellungskosten aufzuführen.

(2) Bei der Berechnung der Herstellungskosten dürfen in angemessenem Umfang Abnutzungen und sonstige Wertminderungen sowie angemessene Teile der Betriebs- und Verwaltungskosten eingerechnet werden, die auf den Zeitraum der Herstellung entfallen; Vertriebskosten gelten nicht als Betriebs- und Verwaltungskosten.

(3) Für immaterielle Anlagewerte darf ein Aktivposten nur angesetzt werden, wenn sie entgeltlich erworben wurden.

(4) Die Aufwendungen für die Gründung und Kapitalbeschaffung (§§ 182 bis 221) dürfen nicht als Aktivposten eingesetzt werden. Die Kosten der Ingangsetzung des Geschäftsbetriebs der Gesellschaft dürfen unter die Posten des Anlagevermögens aufgenommen werden. Der Betrag ist gesondert auszuweisen und in jedem folgenden Geschäftsjahr zu mindestens einem Fünftel durch Abschreibungen zu tilgen.

(5) Für den Geschäfts- oder Firmenwert darf kein Aktivposten eingesetzt werden. Übersteigt jedoch die für die Übernahme eines Unternehmens bewirkte Gegenleistung die Werte der einzelnen Vermögensgegenstände des Unternehmens im Zeitpunkt der Übernahme, so darf der Unterschied unter die Posten des Anlagevermögens aufgenommen werden. Der Betrag ist gesondert auszuweisen und in jedem folgenden Geschäftsjahr zu mindestens einem Fünftel durch Abschreibungen zu tilgen.

§ 154

Abschreibungen. Wertberichtigungen

(1) Bei den Gegenständen des Anlagevermögens, deren Nutzung zeitlich begrenzt ist, sind die Anschaffungs- oder Herstellungskosten um planmäßige Abschreibungen oder Wertberichtigungen zu vermindern. Der Plan muß die Anschaffungs- oder Herstellungskosten nach einer den Grundsätzen ordnungsmäßiger Buchführung entsprechenden Abschreibungsmethode auf die Geschäftsjahre verteilen, in denen der Gegenstand voraussichtlich genutzt werden kann.

(2) Ohne Rücksicht darauf, ob ihre Nutzung zeitlich begrenzt ist, können bei Gegenständen des Anlagevermögens außerplanmäßige Abschreibungen oder Wertberichtigungen vorgenommen werden, um die Gegenstände

1. mit dem niedrigeren Wert, der ihnen am Abschlußstichtag beizulegen ist, oder
2. mit dem niedrigeren Wert, der für Zwecke der Steuern vom Einkommen und vom Ertrag für zulässig gehalten wird,

tion or reserves for decline in value pursuant to § 154. Additions shall be valued at the cost of acquisition or production.

(2) In determining the cost of production, to a reasonable extent wear and tear and other factors diminishing the value, as well as reasonable portions of the operating and administrative overhead attributable to the period of production, may be taken into account; selling expenses shall not be deemed to be operating and administrative overhead.

(3) Intangible assets may be listed only if such assets were acquired for a consideration.

(4) Expenses of formation and acquisition of capital (§§ 182 to 221) may not be listed as assets. Expenses for the start-up of operations of the business may be included under fixed assets. The amount thereof shall be listed separately and at least one-fifth of such amount shall be amortized in each subsequent fiscal year.

(5) The value of the business or its good will may not be listed as an asset. However, if the consideration for the acquisition of an enterprise exceeds the total value of the individual assets of such enterprise at the time of the acquisition, the difference may be listed as a fixed asset. The amount thereof shall be listed separately and at least one-fifth of such amount shall be amortized in each subsequent fiscal year.

§ 154

Depreciation. Reserve for Decline in Value

(1) The cost of acquisition or production of fixed assets whose usefulness is limited in time shall be amortized by scheduled depreciation or reserve for decline in value. The schedule shall spread the cost of acquisition or production over the fiscal years during which the asset can be expected to be used, in accordance with a method of depreciation compatible with proper accounting principles.

(2) Irrespective of whether their usefulness is limited in time, fixed assets may be subject to extraordinary depreciation or to reserves for decline in value in order to list them

1. at the lower value attributed to them on the closing date of the annual financial statements, or
2. at such lower value deemed proper for purposes of the taxes on corporate income and on business profit.

§ 154

Such depreciation or reserve for decline in value shall be made in the case of a foreseeable permanent diminution of value. The lower valuation may be retained even when the reasons for the extraordinary depreciation or reserve for decline in value no longer exist.

anzusetzen; sie sind vorzunehmen bei einer voraussichtlich dauernden Wertminderung. Der niedrigere Wertansatz darf beibehalten werden, auch wenn die Gründe der außerplanmäßigen Abschreibung oder Wertberichtigung nicht mehr bestehen.

§ 155
Valuation of Current Assets

(1) Current assets shall be valued at their cost of acquisition or production unless a lower valuation is required by paragraph 2 hereof or is permissible pursuant to paragraphs 3 and 4 hereof. § 153, paragraph 2, shall apply in determining the cost of production. For the valuation of similar items of inventory, it may be presumed, to the extent compatible with proper accounting principles, that the items first or last acquired or produced are used or disposed of first, or in some other definite sequence.

(2) If the cost of acquisition or production is higher than the value determined by reference to the price quoted on an exchange or the market price as of the closing date of the annual financial statements, the assets shall be listed at such value. If no quoted exchange or market price can be ascertained, and the cost of acquisition or production exceeds the value to be attributed to such items as of the closing date of the annual financial statements, the assets shall be listed at such value.

(3) Current assets may be listed at a lower value than the value determined by reference to paragraph 1 or 2 hereof, if such lower valuation
1. is, according to reasonable business judgment, necessary in order to avoid changes in the valuation of these assets in the near future because of fluctuations in value, or
2. is considered permissible for purposes of tax on corporate income and on business profit.

(4) The lower valuation pursuant to paragraph 2 or 3 hereof may be retained even where the underlying reason for it no longer exists.

§ 156
Valuation of Liabilities

(1) The stated capital shall be stated at its nominal value.

(2) Liabilities shall be stated at the amount repayable; liabilities for annuity payments, at their present value.

§ 155
Wertansätze der Gegenstände des Umlaufvermögens

(1) Die Gegenstände des Umlaufvermögens sind zu den Anschaffungs- oder Herstellungskosten anzusetzen, soweit nicht ein niedrigerer Wertansatz nach Absatz 2 geboten oder nach den Absätzen 3 und 4 zulässig ist. Für die Berechnung der Herstellungskosten gilt § 153 Abs. 2. Soweit es den Grundsätzen ordnungsmäßiger Buchführung entspricht, kann für den Wertansatz gleichartiger Gegenstände des Vorratsvermögens unterstellt werden, daß die zuerst oder daß die zuletzt angeschafften oder hergestellten Gegenstände zuerst oder in einer sonstigen bestimmten Folge verbraucht oder veräußert worden sind.

(2) Sind die Anschaffungs- oder Herstellungskosten höher als der Wert, der sich aus dem Börsen- oder Marktpreis am Abschlußstichtag ergibt, so ist dieser Wert anzusetzen. Ist ein Börsen- oder Marktpreis nicht festzustellen und übersteigen die Anschaffungs- oder Herstellungskosten den Wert, der den Gegenständen am Abschlußstichtag beizulegen ist, so ist dieser Wert anzusetzen.

(3) Die Gegenstände des Umlaufvermögens dürfen mit einem niedrigeren Wert als dem Wert nach Absatz 1 oder Absatz 2 angesetzt werden, soweit der niedrigere Wertansatz
1. bei vernünftiger kaufmännischer Beurteilung notwendig ist, um zu verhindern, daß in der nächsten Zukunft der Wertansatz dieser Gegenstände auf Grund von Wertschwankungen geändert werden muß oder
2. für Zwecke der Steuern vom Einkommen und vom Ertrag für zulässig gehalten wird.

(4) Ein niedrigerer Wertansatz nach den Absätzen 2 oder 3 darf beibehalten werden, auch wenn seine Gründe nicht mehr bestehen.

§ 156
Ansätze von Passivposten

(1) Das Grundkapital ist zum Nennbetrag anzusetzen.

(2) Verbindlichkeiten sind zu ihrem Rückzahlungsbetrag, Rentenverpflichtungen zu ihrem Barwert anzusetzen.

(3) Ist der Rückzahlungsbetrag von Verbindlichkeiten oder Anleihen höher als der Ausgabebetrag, so darf der Unterschied unter die Rechnungsabgrenzungsposten der Aktivseite aufgenommen werden. Der Betrag ist gesondert auszuweisen und durch planmäßige jährliche Abschreibungen, die auf die gesamte Laufzeit verteilt werden dürfen, zu tilgen.

(4) Rückstellungen sind nur in Höhe des Betrags anzusetzen, der nach vernünftiger kaufmännischer Beurteilung notwendig ist.

§ 157

Gliederung der Gewinn- und Verlustrechnung

(1) In der Gewinn- und Verlustrechnung sind, wenn der Geschäftszweig keine abweichende Gliederung bedingt, die gleichwertig sein muß, unbeschadet einer weiteren Gliederung folgende Posten in Staffelform gesondert auszuweisen:

1. Umsatzerlöse
2. Erhöhung oder Verminderung des Bestands an fertigen und unfertigen Erzeugnissen
3. andere aktivierte Eigenleistungen
4. Gesamtleistung
5. Aufwendungen für Roh-, Hilfs- und Betriebsstoffe sowie für bezogene Waren
6. Rohertrag/Rohaufwand
7. Erträge aus Gewinngemeinschaften, Gewinnabführungs- und Teilgewinnabführungsverträgen
8. Erträge aus Beteiligungen
9. Erträge aus den anderen Finanzanlagen
10. sonstige Zinsen und ähnliche Erträge
11. Erträge aus dem Abgang von Gegenständen des Anlagevermögens und aus Zuschreibungen zu Gegenständen des Anlagevermögens
12. Erträge aus der Herabsetzung der Pauschalwertberichtigung zu Forderungen

(3) If the amount necessary to repay liabilities or loans exceeds the consideration received, the difference may be listed as a deferred charge on the assets side. This amount shall be listed separately and shall be amortized by scheduled annual deductions, which may be spread over the entire term of the obligation.

(4) Reserves shall be stated only in the amount considered necessary according to reasonable business judgment.

§ 157

Classification of Profit and Loss Statement

(1) The profit and loss statement shall, without prejudice to a further classification, specifically set forth the following profit and loss items in columnar form, unless the type of business involved requires a different classification, in which event such classification must be at least as detailed as that shown herein:

1. gross income from sales and services
2. increase or decrease in inventory of finished goods and work in process
3. other capitalized assets produced by the company
4. total production
5. cost of raw materials, maintenance materials, and supplies, and of goods purchased
6. gross profit/gross costs
7. income from pooling of profits and from agreements to transfer profits in whole or in part
8. income from securities in related companies
9. income from other securities
10. other interest and similar income
11. gain from disposal of fixed assets and write-up of fixed assets
12. income from a reduction of overall provision for uncollectible accounts receivable

13. income from reduction or dissolution of reserves ....
14. other income ....
    of which extraordinary ....
15. income from agreements to absorb the company's losses ....

———— ————

....

16. wages and salaries ....
17. social security taxes ....
18. old-age benefits and cost of social assistance ....
19. depreciation and amortization of tangible and intangible fixed assets ....
20. depreciation and reserve for decline in value of equity investments, except for amounts entered in the overall provision for uncollectible accounts receivable ....
21. write-offs due to decline in value or disposal of current assets, excluding inventories (§ 151, paragraph 1, assets III B) and those already covered by the overall provision for uncollectible accounts receivable ....
22. losses from disposal of fixed assets ....
23. interest and similar expenses ....
24. taxes
    a) on corporate income, on business profit, and on assets ....
    b) other taxes ....

————

25. charge resulting from agreements to assume losses ....
26. other expenses ....
27. income transferred pursuant to pooling of profits arrangements and agreements to transfer profits in whole or in part ....

§ 157

13. Erträge aus der Auflösung von Rückstellungen ....
14. sonstige Erträge ....
    davon außerordentliche ......
15. Erträge aus Verlustübernahme ....
    ....
16. Löhne und Gehälter ....
17. soziale Abgaben ....
18. Aufwendungen für Altersversorgung und Unterstützung
19. Abschreibungen und Wertberichtigungen auf Sachanlagen und immaterielle Anlagewerte ....
20. Abschreibungen und Wertberichtigungen auf Finanzanlagen mit Ausnahme des Betrags, der in die Pauschalwertberichtigung zu Forderungen eingestellt ist
21. Verluste aus Wertminderungen oder dem Abgang von Gegenständen des Umlaufvermögens außer Vorräten (§ 151 Abs. 1 Aktivseite III B) und Einstellung in die Pauschalwertberichtigung zu Forderungen
22. Verluste aus dem Abgang von Gegenständen des Anlagevermögens ....
23. Zinsen und ähnliche Aufwendungen ....
24. Steuern
    a) vom Einkommen, vom Ertrag und vom Vermögen ....
    b) sonstige ....
25. Aufwendungen aus Verlustübernahme ....
26. sonstige Aufwendungen ....
27. auf Grund einer Gewinngemeinschaft, eines Gewinnabführungs- und eines Teilgewinnabführungsvertrags abgeführte Gewinne ....

————

28. Jahresüberschuß/Jahresfehl-
betrag

29. Gewinnvortrag/Verlust-
vortrag aus dem Vorjahr

30. Entnahmen aus offenen
Rücklagen
    a) aus der gesetzlichen
    Rücklage
    b) aus freien Rücklagen

31. Einstellungen aus dem
Jahresüberschuß in offene
Rücklagen
    a) in die gesetzliche Rücklage
    b) in freie Rücklagen

32. Bilanzgewinn/Bilanzverlust

28. net profit/net loss for the
year

29. profit/loss carried forward
from previous fiscal year

30. reduction of disclosed
reserves
    a) from statutory reserves
    b) from free reserves

31. Allocations from annual
profit to disclosed re-
serves
    a) to statutory reserves
    b) to free reserves

32. retained earnings/accu-
mulated losses

(2) Sind unter einen Posten fallende Aufwendungen oder Erträge bei einer Gesellschaft nicht ange-
fallen, so braucht der Posten nicht ausgewiesen zu
werden.

(3) Werden Aufwendungen oder Erträge unter
einem anderen Posten ausgewiesen als gleichartige
Aufwendungen oder Erträge für das vorausgegangene Geschäftsjahr, so ist dies unter Angabe des auf sie entfallenden Betrags in der Gewinn- und Verlustrechnung zu vermerken.

(4) Sind am Abschlußstichtag keine Aktien der
Gesellschaft an einer deutschen Börse zum amtlichen Handel zugelassen oder in den geregelten
Freiverkehr einbezogen und ist auch nicht die Zulassung von Aktien zum amtlichen Handel an einer
deutschen Börse beantragt, so brauchen die Posten
unter Absatz 1 Nr. 1 bis 5 nicht gesondert ausgewiesen zu werden, wenn
1. die Bilanzsumme drei Millionen Deutsche Mark
nicht übersteigt oder
2. die Gesellschaft eine Familiengesellschaft ist und
die Bilanzsumme zehn Millionen Deutsche Mark
nicht übersteigt; als Familiengesellschaften gelten
solche Aktiengesellschaften, deren Aktionär
eine einzelne natürliche Person ist oder deren
Aktionäre natürliche Personen sind, die untereinander im Sinne von § 10 Nr. 2 bis 5 des Steuer-
anpassungsgesetzes vom 16. Oktober 1934 (Reichs-

(2) A company not having income or expense
items falling within one of these classifications
need not list such classification.

(3) If expenses or income is listed in a classification different from that under which similar
expenses or income was listed in the profit and
loss statement for the preceding fiscal year, this
fact shall be noted in the profit and loss statement
together with the relevant amounts.

(4) If, at the closing date of the annual financial
statements, shares of the company are not listed
on a German stock exchange or admitted for
trading over the counter, and if no application
for listing of the shares on a German stock exchange has been filed, the entries in the classifications referred to in paragraph 1, Nos. 1 to 5,
hereof need not be stated separately, provided
that
1. the total amount of the balance sheet on the
assets or on the liabilities side does not exceed
three million German marks, or
2. the company is family-owned and the total
amount of the balance sheet on the assets or
on the liabilities side does not exceed ten
million German marks; a stock corporation
shall be deemed to be a family-owned company if its sole shareholder is a natural person
or if its shareholders are natural persons who
are related to each other directly or by marriage within the purview of § 10, Nos. 2 to 5,

§ 157

of the *Steueranpassungsgesetz* of October 16, 1934 (*Reichsgesetzblatt* I, p. 925).

If a family-owned company avails itself of the election pursuant to the first sentence hereof, each shareholder may request that the profit and loss statement be submitted to him at the annual shareholders' meeting at which the profit and loss statement is discussed, in the form it would have without the application of the first sentence hereof.

§ 158

Rules Concerning Specific Items of Profit and Loss Statement

(1) In the case of enterprises whose business is the production or manufacture of goods or the sale of merchandise, only income derived from the production, manufacture or sale of such goods or merchandise shall be listed as gross income from sales and services.

(2) The gross income from sales and services shall be shown as the amount remaining after deduction of discounts and refunds; other amounts may not be deducted.

(3) From the income resulting from an agreement to transfer profit in whole or in part, there shall be deducted any contractual payment to outside shareholders; if such payment exceeds this income, the difference shall be listed among the charges resulting from agreements to assume losses (§ 157, paragraph 1, No. 25). Other amounts may not be deducted.

(4) To be listed as taxes shall be all amounts owed by the company as a taxpayer.

(5) Allocations to statutory reserves pursuant to § 150, paragraph 2, Nos. 2 to 4, or § 237, paragraph 5, shall not be listed as amounts which, according to the law or the articles of incorporation, are required to be allocated to statutory reserves from the net profit for the year.

(6) Income resulting from the liquidation of special accounts which, in part, constitute reserves (§ 152, paragraph 5) shall be listed separately as a special item to be inserted between items No. 13 and No. 14; allocations to special accounts which, in part, constitute reserves shall be listed separately as a special item to be inserted between items No. 25 and No. 26.

§ 159

Notation Regarding Pension Payments

The annual financial statements shall indicate in a note the amount of any pension payments

gesetzbl. I S. 925) verwandt oder verschwägert sind.

Macht eine Familiengesellschaft von der Befugnis nach Satz 1 Gebrauch, so kann jeder Aktionär verlangen, daß ihm in der Hauptversammlung über den Jahresabschluß die Gewinn- und Verlustrechnung in der Form vorgelegt wird, die sie ohne Anwendung des Satzes 1 hätte.

§ 158

Vorschriften zu einzelnen Posten der Gewinn- und Verlustrechnung

(1) Bei Unternehmen, deren Geschäftszweig in der Erzeugung oder Fertigung von Gegenständen oder im Vertrieb von Waren besteht, sind als Umsatzerlöse nur die Erlöse aus der Erzeugung, Fertigung oder Lieferung dieser Gegenstände oder Waren auszuweisen.

(2) Die Umsatzerlöse sind nach Abzug von Preisnachlässen und zurückgewährten Entgelten auszuweisen; andere Beträge dürfen nicht abgesetzt werden.

(3) Von dem Ertrag aus einem Gewinnabführungs- oder Teilgewinnabführungsvertrag ist ein vertraglich zu leistender Ausgleich für außenstehende Gesellschafter abzusetzen; übersteigt dieser den Ertrag, so ist der übersteigende Betrag unter den Aufwendungen aus Verlustübernahme (§ 157 Abs. 1 Nr. 25) auszuweisen. Andere Beträge dürfen nicht abgesetzt werden.

(4) Als Steuern sind die Beträge auszuweisen, die die Gesellschaft als Steuerschuldner zu entrichten hat.

(5) Einstellungen in die gesetzliche Rücklage nach § 150 Abs. 2 Nr. 2 bis 4 oder § 237 Abs. 5 sind nicht als Beträge auszuweisen, die nach Gesetz oder Satzung aus dem Jahresüberschuß in die gesetzliche Rücklage einzustellen sind.

(6) Erträge aus der Auflösung von Sonderposten mit Rücklageanteil (§ 152 Abs. 5) sind in einem zwischen den Posten Nummer 13 und Nummer 14, Einstellungen in Sonderposten mit Rücklageanteil in einem zwischen den Posten Nummer 25 und Nummer 26 einzufügenden Posten gesondert auszuweisen.

§ 159

Vermerk der Pensionszahlungen

Im Jahresabschluß sind der Betrag der im Geschäftsjahr geleisteten Pensionszahlungen ein-

§ 158

schließlich der Zahlungen an rechtlich selbständige Versorgungskassen und in Vom-Hundert-Sätzen dieses Betrags die in jedem der folgenden fünf Geschäftsjahre voraussichtlich zu leistenden Zahlungen zu vermerken.

§ 160

Inhalt des Geschäftsberichts

(1) Im Geschäftsbericht sind der Geschäftsverlauf und die Lage der Gesellschaft darzulegen. Zu berichten ist auch über Vorgänge von besonderer Bedeutung, die nach dem Schluß des Geschäftsjahrs eingetreten sind.

(2) Im Geschäftsbericht ist ferner der Jahresabschluß zu erläutern. Dabei sind die Bewertungs- und Abschreibungsmethoden so vollständig anzugeben, wie es zur Vermittlung eines möglichst sicheren Einblicks in die Vermögens- und Ertragslage der Gesellschaft erforderlich ist; auf die Angabe dieser Methoden im Geschäftsbericht für ein früheres Geschäftsjahr, das nicht weiter zurückliegt als das dritte vorausgegangene Geschäftsjahr, kann Bezug genommen werden. In jedem Geschäftsbericht sind zu den einzelnen Posten des Anlagevermögens die Abschreibungen und Wertberichtigungen anzugeben, die auf Zugänge des Geschäftsjahrs gemacht worden sind. In jedem Geschäftsbericht sind ferner Abweichungen des Jahresabschlusses von dem letzten Jahresabschluß, die die Vergleichbarkeit mit dem letzten Jahresabschluß beeinträchtigen, namentlich wesentliche Änderungen der Bewertungs- und Abschreibungsmethoden einschließlich der Vornahme außerplanmäßiger Abschreibungen oder Wertberichtigungen zu erörtern; dabei brauchen Einzelheiten nicht angegeben zu werden. Wird infolge von Änderungen der Bewertungs- und Abschreibungsmethoden einschließlich der Vornahme außerplanmäßiger Abschreibungen oder Wertberichtigungen ein Jahresüberschuß oder Jahresfehlbetrag ausgewiesen, der um mehr als zehn vom Hundert unter oder über dem Betrag liegt, der ohne die Änderung auszuweisen wäre, so ist der Unterschiedsbetrag anzugeben, wenn er einhalb vom Hundert des Grundkapitals übersteigt.

(3) In jedem Geschäftsbericht sind Angaben zu machen über

1. Bestand und Zugang an Aktien, die ein Aktionär für Rechnung der Gesellschaft oder eines abhängigen oder eines im Mehrheitsbesitz der Gesellschaft stehenden Unternehmens oder ein abhängiges oder im Mehrheitsbesitz der Gesellschaft stehendes Unternehmen als Gründer oder Zeichner oder in Ausübung eines bei einer bedingten Kapitalerhöhung eingeräumten Umtausch- oder Bezugsrechts übernommen hat; sind solche Aktien im Geschäftsjahr verwertet worden, so ist auch über die Verwertung unter

made during the fiscal year, including payments to legally separate pension funds, and the payments, in percentages of this amount, expected to be made in each of the following five fiscal years.

§ 160
Content of Business Report

(1) The business report shall contain a business analysis and status report of the company. Events of particular significance which took place after the close of the fiscal year shall also be reported.

(2) The business report shall also comment on the annual financial statements. In this connection, the methods of valuation and depreciation must be described as fully as necessary to permit as accurate as possible a picture of the financial and earnings position of the company; the explanation of such methods in a business report for a prior fiscal year not further removed than the third preceding year may be incorporated by reference. Each business report shall specify the reserves for depreciation and for decline in value of fixed assets acquired during the fiscal year. Each business report shall further discuss in the annual financial statements such deviations from the last annual financial statements as tend to impair comparison with such last annual financial statements, in particular, substantial changes in the valuation and depreciation methods, including extraordinary depreciation or reserves for decline in value; particulars need not be set forth. If as a result of a change in the valuation and depreciation method, including extraordinary depreciation or reserves for decline in value, a net profit or loss for the year is shown which is more than ten percent above or below the amount that would be shown without such change, such difference shall be shown if it exceeds one-half of one percent of the stated capital.

(3) Each business report shall contain statements concerning

1. the number of shares held and acquired by a shareholder for the account of the company or of an enterprise controlled or majority-owned by the company, or of an enterprise controlled or majority-owned by the company as incorporator or subscriber or, in the case of a conditional capital increase, in the exercise of a preemptive right to exchange or to subscribe; if such shares were sold during

§ **160**

the fiscal year, the sale shall also be reported, stating the amount and the disposition of the proceeds;

2. the number of the company's own shares which it, or an enterprise controlled or majority-owned by the company, or another for the account of the company or an enterprise controlled or majority-owned by the company, has acquired or accepted as a pledge; if such shares were acquired or sold during the fiscal year, the acquisition or sale shall also be reported, stating the consideration for the acquisition or sale and the use of the proceeds;

3. the existence of an interlocking interest, naming the other enterprise;

4. shares issued in connection with a conditional capital increase during the fiscal year;

5. the authorized capital;

6. debentures, rights from bonus certificates and similar rights, stating which of these were newly created during the fiscal year;

7. suretyships not reflected in the annual financial statements, including guaranties for the company's own liabilities;

8. the total compensation (salary, profit participation, perquisites, insurance, commissions, and any other benefits) paid to the members of the managing board, of the supervisory board and of any advisory board or similar body, in each instance specifically designating the body concerned. In such total compensation, remuneration which is not paid out but is converted into rights of a different nature or used to augment other rights shall be included. In addition to the compensation attributable to the fiscal year, other compensation shall be set forth if it was granted during the fiscal year and was not shown in any prior business report. If members of the company's managing board receive compensation from related enterprises for services rendered to the company or for services as legal representatives or employees of the related enterprises, such compensation shall be listed separately;

9. the total compensation (indemnities, pensions, payments to survivors, and payments of a similar nature) paid to former members of the managing board and their survivors. No. 8, second and third sentences, shall apply *mutatis mutandis*. If former members of the company's managing board or their survivors also receive indemnities or pen-

§ 160

Angabe des Erlöses und die Verwendung des Erlöses zu berichten;

2. Bestand an eigenen Aktien der Gesellschaft, die sie, ein abhängiges oder im Mehrheitsbesitz der Gesellschaft stehendes Unternehmen oder ein anderer für Rechnung der Gesellschaft oder eines abhängigen oder eines im Mehrheitsbesitz der Gesellschaft stehenden Unternehmens erworben oder als Pfand genommen hat; sind solche Aktien im Geschäftsjahr erworben oder veräußert worden, so ist auch über den Erwerb oder die Veräußerung unter Angabe des Erwerbs- oder Veräußerungspreises und über die Verwendung des Erlöses zu berichten;

3. das Bestehen einer wechselseitigen Beteiligung unter Angabe des Unternehmens;

4. Aktien, die bei bedingter Kapitalerhöhung im Geschäftsjahr bezogen worden sind;

5. das genehmigte Kapital;

6. Genußrechte, Rechte aus Besserungsscheinen und ähnliche Rechte unter Angabe der im Geschäftsjahr neu entstandenen;

7. aus der Jahresbilanz nicht ersichtliche Haftungsverhältnisse einschließlich der Bestellung von Sicherheiten für eigene Verbindlichkeiten;

8. die Gesamtbezüge (Gehälter, Gewinnbeteiligungen, Aufwandsentschädigungen, Versicherungsentgelte, Provisionen und Nebenleistungen jeder Art) der Mitglieder des Vorstands, des Aufsichtsrats und eines Beirats oder einer ähnlichen Einrichtung jeweils gesondert unter Bezeichnung der einzelnen Einrichtung. In die Gesamtbezüge sind auch Bezüge einzurechnen, die nicht ausgezahlt, sondern in Ansprüche anderer Art umgewandelt oder zur Erhöhung anderer Ansprüche verwandt werden. Außer den Bezügen für das Geschäftsjahr sind die weiteren Bezüge anzugeben, die im Geschäftsjahr gewährt, bisher aber in keinem Geschäftsbericht angegeben worden sind. Erhalten Mitglieder des Vorstands der Gesellschaft von verbundenen Unternehmen für ihre Tätigkeit für die Gesellschaft oder für ihre Tätigkeit als gesetzliche Vertreter oder Angestellte der verbundenen Unternehmen Bezüge. so sind diese Bezüge gesondert anzugeben;

9. die Gesamtbezüge (Abfindungen, Ruhegehälter, Hinterbliebenenbezüge und Leistungen verwandter Art) der früheren Mitglieder des Vorstands und ihrer Hinterbliebenen. Nummer 8 Satz 2 und 3 gilt sinngemäß. Erhalten frühere Mitglieder des Vorstands der Gesellschaft oder ihre Hinterbliebenen auch von verbundenen

Unternehmen Abfindungen oder Ruhegehälter, so sind diese Bezüge gesondert anzugeben;

10. die rechtlichen und geschäftlichen Beziehungen zu verbundenen Unternehmen mit Sitz im Inland, ferner über geschäftliche Vorgänge bei diesen Unternehmen, die auf die Lage der Gesellschaft von erheblichem Einfluß sein können;

11. das Bestehen einer Beteiligung an der Gesellschaft, die ihr nach § 20 Abs. 1 oder 4 mitgeteilt worden ist; dabei ist anzugeben, wem die Beteiligung gehört und ob sie den vierten Teil aller Aktien der Gesellschaft übersteigt oder eine Mehrheitsbeteiligung (§ 16 Abs. 1) ist.

(4) Der Bericht hat den Grundsätzen einer gewissenhaften und getreuen Rechenschaft zu entsprechen. Die Berichterstattung hat insoweit zu unterbleiben, wie es für das Wohl der Bundesrepublik Deutschland oder eines ihrer Länder erforderlich ist. Bei der Berichterstattung nach Absatz 3 Nr. 7 und 10 brauchen Einzelheiten insoweit nicht angegeben zu werden, als nach vernünftiger kaufmännischer Beurteilung damit gerechnet werden muß, daß durch die Angaben der Gesellschaft oder einem verbundenen Unternehmen erhebliche Nachteile entstehen. Werden auf Grund von Satz 3 Angaben nicht gemacht, so ist im Geschäftsbericht unter Anführung der Nummer, nach der sie erforderlich sind, anzugeben, daß für Angaben nach dieser Nummer von der Schutzklausel nach Satz 3 Gebrauch gemacht worden ist.

(5) Im Geschäftsbericht sind alle Mitglieder des Vorstands und des Aufsichtsrats, auch die im Geschäftsjahr oder nachher ausgeschiedenen, mit dem Familiennamen und mindestens einem ausgeschriebenen Vornamen anzugeben. Der Vorsitzende des Aufsichtsrats, seine Stellvertreter und ein etwaiger Vorsitzender des Vorstands sind als solche zu bezeichnen.

§ 161

Formblätter für den Jahresabschluß

(1) Der Bundesminister der Justiz wird ermächtigt, im Einvernehmen mit dem Bundesminister für Wirtschaft und den sonst für den Geschäftszweig der Gesellschaft zuständigen Bundesministern durch Rechtsverordnung Formblätter vorzuschreiben oder andere Vorschriften für die Gliederung des Jahresabschlusses zu erlassen, wenn der Geschäftszweig eine von § 151 Abs. 1, 2 und 5, §§ 152, 157 Abs. 1

sions from related enterprises, such compensation shall be listed separately;

10. the legal and business dealings with related enterprises domiciled in Germany; in addition, the transactions of such enterprises which are apt to affect the condition of the company substantially;

11. the existence of an equity interest in the company, which has been reported to it pursuant to § 20, paragraph 1 or 4; in this connection it must be stated who owns such interest and whether it exceeds one-fourth of all the shares of the company, or whether it constitutes a majority interest (§ 16, paragraph 1).

(4) The report shall comply with the principles of a true and conscientious accounting. To the extent that the welfare of the Federal Republic of Germany or one of its States necessitates omissions, there shall be no reporting. Upon reporting pursuant to paragraph 3, Nos. 7 and 10, hereof, details need not be stated to the extent that the exercise of reasonable business judgment would suggest that such statements will result in a substantial detriment to the company or a related enterprise. If statements are omitted by virtue of the third sentence hereof, the business report shall state that the escape clause of the third sentence has been invoked with respect to such statement and indicate the number pursuant to which such statement would otherwise be required.

(5) In the business report, all members of the managing board and of the supervisory board, including those who ceased to be members during or after the close of the fiscal year, must be listed by their family name and at least one fully written-out given name. The chairman of the supervisory board, his deputies, and the chairman of the managing board, if any, shall be designated as such.

§ 161

Forms for Annual Financial Statements

(1) The Federal Minister of Justice, in consultation with the Federal Minister of Economics and such other Ministers of the Federal Republic of Germany as have jurisdiction over the type of business conducted by the company, is hereby authorized to prescribe forms by decree or to issue other rules concerning the classification of the annual financial statements, provided that the pertinent type of business requires a classification different from that specified in § 151,

§ **161**

paragraphs 1, 2, and 5, §§ 152, 157, paragraphs 1 and 2, and § 158. Such a decree shall not require the assent of the Bundesrat (Federal Council).

(2) If a company is engaged in several lines of business and if the annual financial statements for them require a classification in keeping with different provisions applicable to such classification, the company shall structure its annual financial statements in accordance with the classification prescribed for one of its lines of business and supplement it as needed to comply with the classification prescribed for its other lines of business.

und 2, § 158 abweichende Gliederung des Jahresabschlusses bedingt. Die Rechtsverordnung bedarf nicht der Zustimmung des Bundesrates.

(2) Hat eine Gesellschaft mehrere Geschäftszweige und bedingen diese die Gliederung des Jahresabschlusses nach verschiedenen Gliederungsvorschriften, so hat die Gesellschaft den Jahresabschluß nach der für einen ihrer Geschäftszweige vorgeschriebenen Gliederung aufzustellen und nach der für ihre anderen Geschäftszweige vorgeschriebenen Gliederung zu ergänzen.

Second Division

Examination of Annual Financial Statements

First Subdivision

Audit by Annual Auditors

Zweiter Abschnitt

Prüfung des Jahresabschlusses

Erster Unterabschnitt

Prüfung durch Abschlußprüfer

§ 162

Subject and Scope of Audit

(1) The annual financial statements together with the accounting and the business report shall be audited by one or more professional auditors (annual auditors). The annual financial statements may not be established unless there has been an audit.

(2) The audit of the annual financial statements shall extend to the question of whether the provisions of the law and of the articles of incorporation concerning the annual financial statement have been observed. The business report shall be examined to determine whether § 160, paragraphs 2 to 5, has been observed and whether other statements in the business report might give an erroneous impression of the condition of the company.

(3) In the event that the managing board, after having received the audit report (§ 166), should amend the annual financial statements or the business report, the annual auditors shall again audit the annual financial statements and the business report to the extent required by such amendments. Paragraph 1, second sentence, hereof shall apply *mutatis mutandis*. A previously issued certification shall become invalid.

§ 162

Gegenstand und Umfang der Prüfung

(1) Der Jahresabschluß ist unter Einbeziehung der Buchführung und des Geschäftsberichts durch einen oder mehrere sachverständige Prüfer (Abschlußprüfer) zu prüfen. Hat keine Prüfung stattgefunden, so kann der Jahresabschluß nicht festgestellt werden.

(2) Die Prüfung des Jahresabschlusses hat sich darauf zu erstrecken, ob die Bestimmungen des Gesetzes und der Satzung über den Jahresabschluß beachtet sind. Der Geschäftsbericht ist darauf zu prüfen, ob § 160 Abs. 2 bis 5 beachtet ist und ob die sonstigen Angaben im Geschäftsbericht nicht eine falsche Vorstellung von der Lage der Gesellschaft erwecken.

(3) Ändert der Vorstand den Jahresabschluß oder den Geschäftsbericht, nachdem ihm der Prüfungsbericht (§ 166) vorgelegt worden ist, so haben die Abschlußprüfer den Jahresabschluß und den Geschäftsbericht erneut zu prüfen, soweit es die Änderung fordert. Absatz 1 Satz 2 gilt entsprechend. Ein bereits erteilter Bestätigungsvermerk ist unwirksam.

§ 163

Appointment of Annual Auditors

(1) The annual auditors shall be elected by the shareholders. They shall be elected prior

§ 163

Bestellung der Abschlußprüfer

(1) Die Abschlußprüfer werden von der Hauptversammlung gewählt. Sie sollen jeweils vor Ab-

lauf des Geschäftsjahrs gewählt werden, auf das sich ihre Prüfungstätigkeit erstreckt. Der Vorstand hat den gewählten Prüfern unverzüglich den Prüfungsauftrag zu erteilen.

(2) Auf Antrag des Vorstands, des Aufsichtsrats oder von Aktionären, deren Anteile zusammen den zehnten Teil des Grundkapitals oder den Nennbetrag von zwei Millionen Deutsche Mark erreichen, hat das Gericht nach Anhörung der Beteiligten und des gewählten Prüfers einen anderen Abschlußprüfer zu bestellen, wenn dies aus einem in der Person des gewählten Prüfers liegenden Grund geboten erscheint, insbesondere wenn Besorgnis der Befangenheit besteht. Der Antrag ist binnen zwei Wochen seit dem Tage der Hauptversammlung zu stellen. Ihn kann nur stellen, wer gegen die Auswahl der Abschlußprüfer Widerspruch zur Niederschrift erklärt hat. Stellen Aktionäre den Antrag, so haben sie glaubhaft zu machen, daß sie seit mindestens drei Monaten vor dem Tage der Hauptversammlung Inhaber der Aktien sind. Zur Glaubhaftmachung genügt eine eidesstattliche Versicherung vor einem Gericht oder einem Notar. Gegen die Entscheidung ist die sofortige Beschwerde zulässig.

(3) Hat die Hauptversammlung bis zum Ablauf des Geschäftsjahrs keine Abschlußprüfer gewählt, so hat auf Antrag des Vorstands, des Aufsichtsrats oder eines Aktionärs das Gericht die Abschlußprüfer zu bestellen. Gleiches gilt, wenn ein gewählter Prüfer die Annahme des Prüfungsauftrags abgelehnt hat, weggefallen ist oder am rechtzeitigen Abschluß der Prüfung verhindert ist und die Hauptversammlung keinen anderen Prüfer gewählt hat. Der Vorstand ist verpflichtet, den Antrag zu stellen. Gegen die Entscheidung des Gerichts findet die sofortige Beschwerde statt; die Bestellung der Abschlußprüfer ist unanfechtbar.

(4) Die vom Gericht bestellten Abschlußprüfer haben Anspruch auf Ersatz angemessener barer Auslagen und auf Vergütung für ihre Tätigkeit. Die Auslagen und die Vergütung setzt das Gericht fest. Gegen die Entscheidung ist die sofortige Beschwerde zulässig. Die weitere Beschwerde ist ausgeschlossen. Aus der rechtskräftigen Entscheidung findet die Zwangsvollstreckung nach der Zivilprozeßordnung statt.

(5) Die Wahl zum Abschlußprüfer kann die Hauptversammlung bis zur Vorlegung des Prüfungsberichts an den Vorstand widerrufen; vor dem Widerruf ist dem Abschlußprüfer Gelegenheit zur Stellungnahme vor der Hauptversammlung zu geben. Dies gilt auch für die von den Gründern

to the expiration of the fiscal year to which their auditing activities extend. The managing board shall promptly instruct the auditors elected to proceed with their audit.

(2) Upon application of the managing board, the supervisory board, or shareholders whose combined holdings amount to no less than one-tenth of the stated capital or a par value of two million German marks, the court, after hearing the parties concerned and the auditor elected, shall appoint another annual auditor if this appears warranted for reasons relating to the person of the annual auditor elected, particularly if his impartiality is in doubt. The application shall be made within two weeks from the date of the shareholders' meeting. Such application may be made only by a person who had his objection to the selection of the annual auditors recorded in the minutes. If shareholders make the application, they shall make a showing that they were shareholders for at least three months prior to the date of the shareholders' meeting. For purposes of such showing, an affidavit executed before a judge or notary shall suffice. The decision of the court can be appealed.

(3) If no annual auditors are elected by the shareholders before the end of the fiscal year, the court shall appoint the annual auditors upon application by the managing board, the supervisory board, or any shareholder. The same shall apply if the auditor elected refuses to accept the appointment or is no longer available or is prevented from completing the audit in time, and the shareholders have not elected another auditor. The managing board has the duty to make such application. The decision of the court can be appealed; however, the appointment of the annual auditors shall be final.

(4) The annual auditors appointed by the court shall be entitled to reimbursement for their reasonable cash expenditures and remuneration for their services. The amount of such expenditures and remuneration shall be determined by the court. The decision of the court can be appealed. It shall not be subject to further appeal. The final decision shall be enforceable in accordance with the provisions of the Code of Civil Procedure.

(5) The election of an annual auditor may be revoked by the shareholders at any time before submission of the audit report to the managing board; before such revocation, the annual auditor shall be given an opportunity to be heard in a shareholders' meeting. The same shall apply to

§ 163

the annual auditors appointed by the incorpora-tors; in the event that the election of the latter is revoked, the annual auditors for the first full or partial fiscal year shall be elected by the share-holders. If the court has appointed an auditor, it may revoke the appointment upon application by the managing board. The decision of the court can be appealed. An annual auditor whose ap-pointment has been revoked shall report the results of the portion of his audit which is com-pleted. The report shall be subject to § 166. The managing board shall, without delay, submit the report to the supervisory board. Each member of the supervisory board shall have the right to inspect the report. A copy of the report shall also be furnished to each member of the supervisory board upon his request, unless the supervisory board has decided otherwise by resolution.

bestellten Abschlußprüfer; wird deren Wahl wider-rufen, so werden die Abschlußprüfer für das erste Voll- oder Rumpfgeschäftsjahr von der Hauptver-sammlung gewählt. Hat das Gericht den Prüfer bestellt, so kann es auf Antrag des Vorstands die Bestellung widerrufen. Gegen die Entscheidung ist die sofortige Beschwerde zulässig. Der abberufene Abschlußprüfer hat über das Ergebnis seiner bishe-rigen Prüfung zu berichten. Für den Bericht gilt § 166. Der Vorstand hat den Bericht unverzüglich dem Aufsichtsrat vorzulegen. Jedes Aufsichtsrats-mitglied hat das Recht, von dem Bericht Kenntnis zu nehmen. Der Bericht ist auch jedem Aufsichtsrats-mitglied auf Verlangen auszuhändigen, soweit der Aufsichtsrat nichts anderes beschlossen hat.

§ 164
Selection of Annual Auditors

(1) Only certified public accountants and firms of certified public accountants may act as annual auditors.

(2) The following may not act as annual auditors:

1. persons who are or, within the last three years prior to their appointment, were members of the managing board or of the supervisory board, or employees of the company to be audited;
2. legal representatives or members of the super-visory board of a legal entity, members of a partnership or owners of a sole proprietorship, if such legal entity, partnership, or sole pro-prietorship is related to the company to be audited;
3. employees of an enterprise related to the company to be audited.

(3) A firm of certified public accountants may not act as annual auditors

1. if it or any enterprise related to it is related to the company to be audited;
2. if a legal representative of an auditing firm which is a legal entity, or a partner of an audit-ing firm, could not act as annual auditor pur-suant to paragraph 2 hereof;
3. if a member of the supervisory board of an auditing firm could not act as annual auditor pursuant to paragraph 2, No. 1, hereof.

§ 164
Auswahl der Abschlußprüfer

(1) Nur Wirtschaftsprüfer und Wirtschaftsprü-fungsgesellschaften können Abschlußprüfer sein.

(2) Ein Wirtschaftsprüfer kann nicht Abschluß-prüfer sein, wenn er

1. Mitglied des Vorstands oder des Aufsichtsrats oder Angestellter der zu prüfenden Gesellschaft ist oder in den letzten drei Jahren vor seiner Bestellung war;
2. gesetzlicher Vertreter oder Mitglied des Auf-sichtsrats einer juristischen Person, Gesellschafter einer Personengesellschaft oder Inhaber eines Unternehmens ist, sofern die juristische Person, die Personengesellschaft oder das Einzelunter-nehmen mit der zu prüfenden Gesellschaft ver-bunden ist;
3. Angestellter eines Unternehmens ist, das mit der zu prüfenden Gesellschaft verbunden ist.

(3) Eine Wirtschaftsprüfungsgesellschaft kann nicht Abschlußprüfer sein,

1. wenn sie oder ein mit ihr verbundenes Unter-nehmen mit der zu prüfenden Gesellschaft ver-bunden ist;
2. wenn bei Wirtschaftprüfungsgesellschaften, die juristische Personen sind, ein gesetzlicher Ver-treter, bei anderen Wirtschaftsprüfungsgesell-schaften ein Gesellschafter nach Absatz 2 nicht Abschlußprüfer sein könnte;
3. wenn ein Aufsichtsratsmitglied der Wirtschafts-prüfungsgesellschaft nach Absatz 2 Nr. 1 nicht Abschlußprüfer sein könnte.

§ 165

Auskunftsrecht

(1) Der Vorstand hat den Abschlußprüfern zu gestatten, die Bücher und Schriften der Gesellschaft sowie die Vermögensgegenstände, namentlich die Gesellschaftskasse und die Bestände an Wertpapieren und Waren, zu prüfen.

(2) Die Abschlußprüfer können vom Vorstand alle Aufklärungen und Nachweise verlangen, welche für eine sorgfältige Prüfung notwendig sind.

(3) Soweit es die Vorbereitung der Abschlußprüfung fordert, haben die Prüfer diese Rechte auch schon vor Aufstellung des Jahresabschlusses.

(4) Soweit es für eine sorgfältige Prüfung notwendig ist, haben die Abschlußprüfer die Rechte nach den Absätzen 2 und 3 auch gegenüber einem Konzernunternehmen sowie gegenüber einem abhängigen oder herrschenden Unternehmen.

§ 166

Prüfungsbericht

(1) Die Abschlußprüfer haben über das Ergebnis der Prüfung schriftlich zu berichten. Im Bericht ist besonders festzustellen, ob die Buchführung, der Jahresabschluß und der Geschäftsbericht, soweit er den gesetzlichen Vorschriften entsprechen und ob der Vorstand die verlangten Aufklärungen und Nachweise erbracht hat. Die Posten des Jahresabschlusses sind aufzugliedern und ausreichend zu erläutern.

(2) Stellen die Abschlußprüfer bei Wahrnehmung ihrer Aufgaben Tatsachen fest, die den Bestand des Unternehmens gefährden oder seine Entwicklung wesentlich beeinträchtigen können oder die schwerwiegende Verstöße des Vorstands gegen Gesetz oder Satzung erkennen lassen, so haben sie auch darüber zu berichten.

(3) Die Abschlußprüfer haben den Bericht zu unterzeichnen und dem Vorstand vorzulegen.

§ 167

Bestätigungsvermerk

(1) Sind nach dem abschließenden Ergebnis der Prüfung keine Einwendungen zu erheben, so haben die Abschlußprüfer dies durch folgenden Vermerk zum Jahresabschluß zu bestätigen:

Die Buchführung, der Jahresabschluß und der Geschäftsbericht entsprechen nach meiner (unserer) pflichtmäßigen Prüfung Gesetz und Satzung.

§ 165

Right to Information

(1) The managing board must permit the annual auditors to inspect the company's books and records, as well as its assets, in particular the cash and the securities and goods on hand.

(2) The annual auditors may request from the managing board any information and proof required for a careful audit.

(3) To the extent required for the completion of the annual audit, the auditors shall have these rights even before the preparation of the annual financial statements.

(4) To the extent that a careful audit so requires, the annual auditors shall exercise the rights specified in paragraphs 2 and 3 hereof with respect to any enterprise of an affiliated group of companies and with respect to any controlled or controlling enterprise.

§ 166

Annual Audit Report

(1) The annual auditors shall make a written report on the results of the audit. The report shall specify, in particular, whether the accounting, the annual financial statements, and the business report, insofar as it explains the annual financial statements, comply with the statutory provisions and whether the managing board has furnished the information and proof requested. The items shown in the annual financial statements shall be analyzed and adequately explained.

(2) If the annual auditors, in the performance of their duties, discover facts which could jeopardize the standing of the enterprise or substantially impair its development, or facts which tend to indicate gross violations of the law or the articles of incorporation on the part of the managing board, they shall include such matters in their report.

(3) The annual auditors shall sign the report and present it to the managing board.

§ 167

Certification

(1) If, according to the final results of the audit, there are no objections, the annual auditors shall so state by means of the following certification of the annual financial statements:
The accounting, the annual financial statements, and the business report which I/we have duly examined comply with the law and the articles of incorporation.

§ 167

(2) If there are objections, the annual auditors shall qualify or refuse the certification.

(3) The annual auditors shall sign the certification, stating the place and date. The certification shall also be made part of the audit report.

§ 168
Liability of Annual Auditors

(1) The annual auditors, their assistants, and the legal representatives of any auditing firm participating in the audit shall make their audit conscientiously and impartially, and shall maintain secrecy. They may not make unauthorized use of any trade or business secrets they have learned in connection with their activities. Whoever intentionally or negligently violates his duties shall be liable to the company, as well as to any affiliated group of companies or controlling or controlled enterprise which has been injured, for any damage arising from such violation. If more than one person was involved, they shall be liable jointly and severally.

(2) The liability of persons who acted negligently shall be limited to five hundred thousand German marks per audit. The same shall apply if more than one person participated in the audit or if several acts giving rise to liability were committed, and irrespective of whether other parties involved acted intentionally.

(3) Where an auditing firm acts as annual auditor, the obligation of secrecy shall extend also to the supervisory board and the members of the supervisory board of such firm.

(4) The liability for damages specified in these provisions can be neither waived nor limited by contract.

(5) Claims arising from these provisions shall be barred after the expiration of five years.

§ 169
Disputes between Company and Annual Auditors

(1) Any disputes between the annual auditors and the company relating to the interpretation of the provisions concerning the annual financial statements and the business report shall be decided, upon application by an annual auditor or the managing board, by the court having jurisdiction pursuant to § 132, paragraph 1.

(2) § 99, paragraph 1, paragraph 3, first, second and fourth to ninth sentences, and paragraph 5, first sentence, shall apply *mutatis mutandis.*

§ 168

---

(2) Sind Einwendungen zu erheben, so haben die Abschlußprüfer die Bestätigung einzuschränken oder zu versagen.

(3) Die Abschlußprüfer haben den Bestätigungsvermerk mit Angabe von Ort und Tag zu unterzeichnen. Der Bestätigungsvermerk ist auch in den Prüfungsbericht aufzunehmen.

§ 168
Verantwortlichkeit der Abschlußprüfer

(1) Die Abschlußprüfer, ihre Gehilfen und die bei der Prüfung mitwirkenden gesetzlichen Vertreter einer Prüfungsgesellschaft sind zur gewissenhaften und unparteiischen Prüfung und zur Verschwiegenheit verpflichtet. Sie dürfen nicht unbefugt Geschäfts- und Betriebsgeheimnisse verwerten, die sie bei ihrer Tätigkeit erfahren haben. Wer vorsätzlich oder fahrlässig seine Pflichten verletzt, ist der Gesellschaft und, wenn ein Konzernunternehmen oder ein herrschendes oder abhängiges Unternehmen geschädigt worden ist, auch diesem zum Ersatz des daraus entstehenden Schadens verpflichtet. Mehrere Personen haften als Gesamtschuldner.

(2) Die Ersatzpflicht von Personen, die fahrlässig gehandelt haben, beschränkt sich auf fünfhunderttausend Deutsche Mark für eine Prüfung. Dies gilt auch, wenn an der Prüfung mehrere Personen beteiligt gewesen oder mehrere zum Ersatz verpflichtende Handlungen begangen worden sind, und ohne Rücksicht darauf, ob andere Beteiligte vorsätzlich gehandelt haben.

(3) Die Verpflichtung zur Verschwiegenheit besteht, wenn eine Prüfungsgesellschaft Abschlußprüfer ist, auch gegenüber dem Aufsichtsrat und den Mitgliedern des Aufsichtsrats der Prüfungsgesellschaft.

(4) Die Ersatzpflicht nach diesen Vorschriften kann durch Vertrag weder ausgeschlossen noch beschränkt werden.

(5) Die Ansprüche aus diesen Vorschriften verjähren in fünf Jahren.

§ 169
Meinungsverschiedenheiten zwischen Gesellschaft und Abschlußprüfern

(1) Bei Meinungsverschiedenheiten zwischen den Abschlußprüfern und der Gesellschaft über die Auslegung der Bestimmungen über den Jahresabschluß und den Geschäftsbericht entscheidet auf Antrag eines Abschlußprüfers oder des Vorstands das nach § 132 Abs. 1 zuständige Gericht.

(2) § 99 Abs. 1, Abs. 3 Satz 1, 2, 4 bis 9 und Abs. 5 Satz 1 gilt sinngemäß. Die sofortige Beschwerde findet nur statt, wenn das Landgericht sie in der

Entscheidung für zulässig erklärt. Es soll sie nur zulassen, wenn dadurch die Klärung einer Rechtsfrage von grundsätzlicher Bedeutung zu erwarten ist.

(3) Für die Kosten des Verfahrens gilt die Kostenordnung. Für das Verfahren des ersten Rechtszugs wird das Doppelte der vollen Gebühr erhoben. Für den zweiten Rechtszug wird die gleiche Gebühr erhoben; dies gilt auch dann, wenn die Beschwerde Erfolg hat. Wird der Antrag oder die Beschwerde zurückgenommen, bevor es zu einer Entscheidung kommt, so ermäßigt sich die Gebühr auf die Hälfte. Der Geschäftswert ist von Amts wegen festzusetzen. Er bestimmt sich nach § 30 Abs. 2 der Kostenordnung. Der Abschlußprüfer ist zur Leistung eines Kostenvorschusses nicht verpflichtet. Schuldner der Kosten ist die Gesellschaft. Die Kosten können jedoch ganz oder zum Teil dem Abschlußprüfer auferlegt werden, wenn dies der Billigkeit entspricht.

Zweiter Unterabschnitt

Prüfung durch den Aufsichtsrat

§ 170

Vorlage an den Aufsichtsrat

(1) Unverzüglich nach Eingang des Prüfungsberichts der Abschlußprüfer hat der Vorstand den Jahresabschluß, den Geschäftsbericht und den Prüfungsbericht dem Aufsichtsrat vorzulegen.

(2) Zugleich hat der Vorstand dem Aufsichtsrat den Vorschlag vorzulegen, den er der Hauptversammlung für die Verwendung des Bilanzgewinns machen will. Der Vorschlag ist, sofern er keine abweichende Gliederung bedingt, wie folgt zu gliedern:

1. Verteilung an die Aktionäre ....
2. Einstellung in offene Rücklagen ....
3. Gewinnvortrag ....
4. zusätzlicher Aufwand bei Beschlußfassung nach dem Vorschlag des Vorstands ....
5. Bilanzgewinn ....

(3) Jedes Aufsichtsratsmitglied hat das Recht, von den Vorlagen Kenntnis zu nehmen. Die Vorlagen sind auch jedem Aufsichtsratsmitglied auf Verlangen auszuhändigen, soweit der Aufsichtsrat nichts anderes beschlossen hat.

The decision is subject to appeal only if the district court in its decision grants leave to appeal. It shall grant such leave only if it can be expected that the appeal will settle a legal question of fundamental importance.

(3) The costs of the proceedings shall be determined by reference to the *Kostenordnung*. In the proceedings before the court of first instance, twice the amount of one full court fee shall be assessed. In the proceedings before the court of second instance, the same court fee shall be assessed; this also applies if the appeal is successful. If the application or the appeal is withdrawn before a decision is rendered, the court fees shall be reduced by one-half. The value of the subject matter in issue shall be determined ex officio. It shall be fixed in accordance with § 30, paragraph 2, of the *Kostenordnung*. Annual auditors shall not be required to pay advances on costs. The company shall be liable for the costs. The costs may, however, be assessed, in whole or in part, against the annual auditor if fairness so requires.

Second Subdivision

Examination by Supervisory Board

§ 170

Submission to the Supervisory Board

(1) Upon receipt of the audit report of the annual auditors, the managing board shall promptly submit the annual financial statements, the business report, and the audit report to the supervisory board.

(2) At the same time, the managing board shall submit to the supervisory board the proposal for the disposition of the retained earnings which it intends to present to the shareholders' meeting. Unless such proposal requires a different classification, it shall be in the following form:

1. Distributions to the shareholders ......
2. Transfer to disclosed reserves ......
3. Earnings carried forward ......
4. Additional expenses in the event of a resolution adopting the proposal of the managing board ......
5. Retained earnings as shown in the balance sheet ......

(3) Each member of the supervisory board shall have the right to inspect the statements submitted. Copies shall also be furnished upon request to each member of the supervisory board, unless the supervisory board has, by resolution, decided otherwise.

§ 170

§ 171
Examination by Supervisory Board

(1) The supervisory board shall examine the annual financial statements, the business report, and the proposal for the disposition of the retained earnings as shown in the balance sheet. If so requested by the supervisory board, the annual auditors will participate in its deliberations concerning these statements.

(2) The supervisory board shall make a written report on the results of the audit to the shareholders' meeting. In its report, the supervisory board shall also state in what manner and to what extent it has examined the conduct of the company's affairs during the fiscal year. Furthermore, it shall comment on the results of the audit of the annual financial statements by the annual auditors. At the conclusion of the report, the supervisory board shall state whether, on the basis of the final result of its examination, there are any objections, and whether it approves the annual financial statements prepared by the managing board.

(3) The supervisory board shall submit its report to the managing board within one month from the date of receipt of the statements submitted to it. If the report is not submitted to the managing board within this period, the managing board shall promptly specify an additional period of not more than one month within which the supervisory board must submit its report. If the report is not submitted to the managing board prior to the expiration of such additional period of time, the annual financial statements shall be deemed not to have been approved by the supervisory board.

Third Division

Establishing Annual Financial Statements. Disposition of Retained Earnings

First Subdivision

Establishing Annual Financial Statements

§ 172
Establishment by Managing Board and Supervisory Board

If the annual financial statements are approved by the supervisory board, they shall be considered to have been established, unless the

§ 171

---

§ 171
Prüfung durch den Aufsichtsrat

(1) Der Aufsichtsrat hat den Jahresabschluß, den Geschäftsbericht und den Vorschlag für die Verwendung des Bilanzgewinns zu prüfen. Auf Verlangen des Aufsichtsrats haben die Abschlußprüfer an seinen Verhandlungen über diese Vorlagen teilzunehmen.

(2) Der Aufsichtsrat hat über das Ergebnis der Prüfung schriftlich an die Hauptversammlung zu berichten. In dem Bericht hat der Aufsichtsrat auch mitzuteilen, in welcher Art und in welchem Umfang er die Geschäftsführung der Gesellschaft während des Geschäftsjahrs geprüft hat. Er hat ferner zu dem Ergebnis der Prüfung des Jahresabschlusses durch die Abschlußprüfer Stellung zu nehmen. Am Schluß des Berichts hat der Aufsichtsrat zu erklären, ob nach dem abschließenden Ergebnis seiner Prüfung Einwendungen zu erheben sind und ob er den vom Vorstand aufgestellten Jahresabschluß billigt.

(3) Der Aufsichtsrat hat seinen Bericht innerhalb eines Monats, nachdem ihm die Vorlagen zugegangen sind, dem Vorstand zuzuleiten. Wird der Bericht dem Vorstand nicht innerhalb der Frist zugeleitet, hat der Vorstand dem Aufsichtsrat unverzüglich eine weitere Frist von nicht mehr als einem Monat zu setzen. Wird der Bericht dem Vorstand nicht vor Ablauf der weiteren Frist zugeleitet, gilt der Jahresabschluß als vom Aufsichtsrat nicht gebilligt.

Dritter Abschnitt

Feststellung des Jahresabschlusses. Gewinnverwendung

Erster Unterabschnitt

Feststellung des Jahresabschlusses

§ 172
Feststellung durch Vorstand und Aufsichtsrat

Billigt der Aufsichtsrat den Jahresabschluß, so ist dieser festgestellt, sofern nicht Vorstand und Aufsichtsrat beschließen, die Feststellung des Jahresabschlusses der Hauptversammlung zu überlassen. Die Beschlüsse des Vorstands und des Aufsichtsrats sind in den Bericht des Aufsichtsrats an die Hauptversammlung aufzunehmen.

§ 173
Feststellung durch die Hauptversammlung

(1) Haben Vorstand und Aufsichtsrat beschlossen, die Feststellung des Jahresabschlusses der Hauptversammlung zu überlassen, oder hat der Aufsichtsrat den Jahresabschluß nicht gebilligt, so stellt die Hauptversammlung den Jahresabschluß fest.

(2) Auf den Jahresabschluß sind §§ 149 bis 159, 161 anzuwenden. Die Hauptversammlung darf bei der Feststellung des Jahresabschlusses nur die Beträge in offene Rücklagen einstellen, die nach Gesetz oder Satzung in offene Rücklagen einzustellen sind.

(3) Ändert die Hauptversammlung den vom Vorstand aufgestellten Jahresabschluß, so haben die Abschlußprüfer ihn erneut zu prüfen, soweit es die Änderung fordert. Ein bereits erteilter Bestätigungsvermerk ist unwirksam. Vor der erneuten Prüfung gefaßte Beschlüsse der Hauptversammlung über die Feststellung des Jahresabschlusses und die Gewinnverwendung werden erst wirksam, wenn auf Grund der erneuten Prüfung ein hinsichtlich der Änderungen uneingeschränkter Bestätigungsvermerk erteilt worden ist. Sie werden nichtig, wenn nicht binnen zwei Wochen seit der Beschlußfassung ein hinsichtlich der Änderungen uneingeschränkter Bestätigungsvermerk erteilt wird.

Zweiter Unterabschnitt
Gewinnverwendung

§ 174

(1) Die Hauptversammlung beschließt über die Verwendung des Bilanzgewinns. Sie ist hierbei an den festgestellten Jahresabschluß gebunden.

(2) In dem Beschluß ist die Verwendung des Bilanzgewinns im einzelnen darzulegen, namentlich sind anzugeben
1. der Bilanzgewinn;
2. der an die Aktionäre auszuschüttende Betrag;

---

managing board and the supervisory board by resolution decide that the annual financial statements shall be established by the shareholders. The resolutions of the managing board and the supervisory board shall be included in the report of the supervisory board to the shareholders.

§ 173
Establishment by Shareholders

(1) If the managing board and the supervisory board have by resolution decided that the establishment of the annual financial statements shall be left to the shareholders, or if the supervisory board failed to approve the annual financial statements, the shareholders shall establish the annual financial statements.

(2) §§ 149 to 159 and § 161 shall apply to the annual financial statements. The shareholders, when establishing the annual financial statements, may allocate to disclosed reserves only such amounts as are required by law or the articles of incorporation to be allocated to disclosed reserves.

(3) In the event the shareholders amend the annual financial statements prepared by the managing board, the annual auditors shall re-audit them to the extent that such re-audit is necessitated by the amendments. A previously issued certification shall become invalid. Shareholders' resolutions on the establishment of the annual financial statements and the disposition of profits which were adopted prior to the second audit shall become effective only upon issuance of a new unqualified certification which is based on the second audit. They shall become void unless within two weeks after the resolution is adopted a certification is given which is unqualified as far as the amendments are concerned.

Second Subdivision
Disposition of Retained Earnings

§ 174

(1) The shareholders shall decide by resolution on the disposition of the retained earnings. In so doing, they shall be bound by the annual financial statements as established.

(2) The resolution shall specify in detail the disposition of the retained earnings; in particular, the following shall be set forth:
1. the retained earnings;
2. the amount to be distributed to the shareholders;

3. the amounts to be transferred to disclosed reserves;
4. earnings carried forward;
5. the additional expenses incurred as a result of the resolution.

(3) The resolution shall not be deemed to effect an amendment of the annual financial statements as established.

Third Subdivision

Ordinary Shareholders' Meeting

§ 175

Calling of Meeting

(1) Upon receipt of the report of the supervisory board, the managing board shall promptly call a shareholders' meeting in order to present to the shareholders the annual financial statements as established and to adopt a resolution on the disposition of the retained earnings. The shareholders' meeting shall be called within the first eight months of the fiscal year.

(2) The annual financial statements, the business report, the report of the supervisory board and the proposal of the managing board concerning the disposition of the retained earnings shall be exhibited on the company's premises for inspection by the shareholders, beginning with the date on which the meeting is called. Each shareholder shall, upon request, promptly be furnished a copy of these documents.

(3) If it is up to the shareholders to establish the annual financial statements, paragraphs 1 and 2 hereof shall apply, *mutatis mutandis*, with respect to the calling of the shareholders' meeting for the purpose of establishing the annual financial statements and with respect to the exhibition of the documents, as well as the distribution of copies. The establishment of the annual financial statements and the disposition of the retained earnings shall be discussed together.

(4) Upon the calling of the shareholders' meeting to which the annual financial statements as established are to be submitted or, if it is up to the shareholders to establish the annual financial statements, upon the calling of the shareholders' meeting which is to establish the annual financial statements, the managing board and the supervisory board shall be bound by the explanations concerning the annual financial statements con-

3. die in offene Rücklagen einzustellenden Beträge;
4. ein Gewinnvortrag;
5. der zusätzliche Aufwand auf Grund des Beschlusses.

(3) Der Beschluß führt nicht zu einer Änderung des festgestellten Jahresabschlusses.

Dritter Unterabschnitt

Ordentliche Hauptversammlung

§ 175

Einberufung

(1) Unverzüglich nach Eingang des Berichts des Aufsichtsrats hat der Vorstand die Hauptversammlung zur Entgegennahme des festgestellten Jahresabschlusses und zur Beschlußfassung über die Verwendung eines Bilanzgewinns einzuberufen. Die Hauptversammlung hat in den ersten acht Monaten des Geschäftsjahrs stattzufinden.

(2) Der Jahresabschluß, der Geschäftsbericht, der Bericht des Aufsichtsrats und der Vorschlag des Vorstands für die Verwendung des Bilanzgewinns sind von der Einberufung an in dem Geschäftsraum der Gesellschaft zur Einsicht der Aktionäre auszulegen. Auf Verlangen ist jedem Aktionär unverzüglich eine Abschrift der Vorlagen zu erteilen.

(3) Hat die Hauptversammlung den Jahresabschluß festzustellen, so gelten für die Einberufung der Hauptversammlung zur Feststellung des Jahresabschlusses und für die Auslegung der Vorlagen und die Erteilung von Abschriften die Absätze 1 und 2 sinngemäß. Die Verhandlungen über die Feststellung des Jahresabschlusses und über die Verwendung des Bilanzgewinns sollen verbunden werden.

(4) Mit der Einberufung der Hauptversammlung zur Entgegennahme des festgestellten Jahresabschlusses oder, wenn die Hauptversammlung den Jahresabschluß festzustellen hat, der Hauptversammlung zur Feststellung des Jahresabschlusses sind Vorstand und Aufsichtsrat an die in dem Bericht des Aufsichtsrats enthaltenen Erklärungen

über den Jahresabschluß (§§ 172, 173 Abs. 1) gebunden.

tained in the report of the supervisory board (§§ 172 and 173, paragraph 1).

§ 176
Vorlagen. Anwesenheit der Abschlußprüfer

(1) Der Vorstand hat der Hauptversammlung die in § 175 Abs. 2 angegebenen Vorlagen vorzulegen. Zu Beginn der Verhandlung soll der Vorstand seine Vorlagen, der Vorsitzende des Aufsichtsrats den Bericht des Aufsichtsrats erläutern. Der Vorstand soll dabei auch zu einem ausgewiesenen Bilanzverlust Stellung nehmen.

(2) Die Abschlußprüfer haben an den Verhandlungen über die Feststellung des Jahresabschlusses teilzunehmen. Sie sind nicht verpflichtet, einem Aktionär Auskunft zu erteilen.

§ 176
Documents. Presence of Annual Auditors

(1) The managing board shall submit to the shareholders' meeting the documents referred to in § 175, paragraph 2. At the beginning of the meeting, the managing board shall explain the papers it submits, and the chairman of the supervisory board shall explain the report of the supervisory board. In this connection, the managing board shall also comment on any losses shown in the balance sheet.

(2) The annual auditors shall participate in the deliberations concerning the establishment of the annual financial statements. They are not required to furnish information to any shareholder.

Vierter Abschnitt
Bekanntmachung des Jahresabschlusses

Fourth Division
Publication of Annual Financial Statements

§ 177
Einreichung des Jahresabschlusses und des Geschäftsberichts zum Handelsregister. Bekanntmachung des Jahresabschlusses

(1) Der Vorstand hat unverzüglich nach der Hauptversammlung über den Jahresabschluß den festgestellten Jahresabschluß mit Bestätigungsvermerk und den Geschäftsbericht nebst dem Bericht des Aufsichtsrats (§ 171 Abs. 2) zum Handelsregister des Sitzes der Gesellschaft einzureichen. Der dem eingereichten Jahresabschluß beigefügte Bestätigungsvermerk muß von den Abschlußprüfern unterschrieben sein. Haben die Abschlußprüfer die Bestätigung des Jahresabschlusses versagt, so muß dies auf dem eingereichten Jahresabschluß vermerkt, der Vermerk von den Abschlußprüfern unterschrieben sein.

(2) Der Vorstand hat unverzüglich nach der Hauptversammlung über den Jahresabschluß den festgestellten Jahresabschluß in den Gesellschaftsblättern bekanntzumachen und die Bekanntmachung zum Handelsregister des Sitzes der Gesellschaft einzureichen.

§ 177
Filing of Annual Financial Statements and Business Report with the Commercial Register. Publication of Annual Financial Statements

(1) After the shareholders' meeting on the annual financial statements, the managing board shall promptly file the annual financial statements as established, accompanied by the certification and the business report, together with the report of the supervisory board (§ 171, paragraph 2), with the Commercial Register at the company's domicile. The certification accompanying the annual financial statements filed must be signed by the annual auditors. If the annual auditors have refused to certify the annual financial statements, this fact shall be noted on the annual financial statements filed, and the notation signed by the annual auditors.

(2) After the shareholders' meeting on the annual financial statements, the managing board shall promptly publish the annual financial statements as established in the publications designated in the company's articles of incorporation and file the publication with the Commercial Register at the company's domicile.

§ 177

(3) The court shall examine whether the annual financial statements filed comply with paragraph 1 hereof, whether they were published, and whether the publication meets the requirements of § 178, paragraph 1. It shall also examine whether the annual financial statements are clearly void. However, the court need not examine whether the annual financial statements and the business report comply with the provisions of the law and of the articles of incorporation.

§ 178

Form and Content of Publication of Annual Financial Statements and Business Report

(1) In connection with all publications and reproductions of the annual financial statements provided for by law or by the articles of incorporation, the following rules shall be observed:

1. The annual financial statements shall be reproduced fully and accurately, together with the entire text of the certification; if the annual auditors have refused to certify them, this fact shall be mentioned in a special notation to the annual financial statements;

2. the items shown in the balance sheet and the profit and loss statement must be arranged one below the other in such a manner that each item, with the pertinent amount expressed in figures, is entered on a separate line;

3. the shareholders' resolution on the disposition of the retained earnings, together with the statements pursuant to § 174, paragraph 2, must be set forth;

4. each member of the managing board and of the supervisory board in office at the time the publication or reproduction is made shall be listed by his family name and at least one full given name; the chairmen of the managing board and of the supervisory board shall be designated as such.

(2) If the annual financial statements are not reproduced in full in any publications and reproductions other than those required by law or by the articles of incorporation, it shall expressly be noted in a heading on the annual financial statements that they are not the full annual financial statements. The certification may not be attached. However, it shall be stated whether the annual auditors have certified the complete annual financial statements or whether they have refused or qualified the certification. It shall also

§ 178

---

(3) Das Gericht hat zu prüfen, ob der eingereichte Jahresabschluß dem Absatz 1 entspricht, ob er bekanntgemacht worden ist und ob die Bekanntmachung dem § 178 Abs. 1 entspricht. Es hat ferner zu prüfen, ob der Jahresabschluß offensichtlich nichtig ist. Im übrigen braucht es nicht zu prüfen, ob der Jahresabschluß und der Geschäftsbericht den Bestimmungen des Gesetzes und der Satzung entsprechen.

§ 178

Form und Inhalt der Bekanntmachung des Jahresabschlusses und des Geschäftsberichts

(1) Bei allen Veröffentlichungen und Vervielfältigungen des Jahresabschlusses, die durch das Gesetz oder die Satzung vorgeschrieben sind, sind die folgenden Vorschriften einzuhalten:

1. Der Jahresabschluß ist vollständig und richtig mit dem vollen Wortlaut des Bestätigungsvermerks wiederzugeben; haben die Abschlußprüfer die Bestätigung versagt, so ist hierauf in einem besonderen Vermerk zum Jahresabschluß hinzuweisen;

2. die in der Bilanz und in der Gewinn- und Verlustrechnung ausgewiesenen Posten müssen in der Weise untereinandergesetzt werden, daß jeder Posten mit dem dazugehörigen, in Ziffern ausgedrückten Betrag eine besondere Zeile erhält;

3. der Beschluß der Hauptversammlung über die Verwendung des Bilanzgewinns mit den Angaben nach § 174 Abs. 2 ist mitzuteilen;

4. alle im Zeitpunkt der Veröffentlichung oder Vervielfältigung im Amt befindlichen Mitglieder des Vorstands und des Aufsichtsrats sind mit dem Familiennamen und mindestens einem ausgeschriebenen Vornamen anzugeben; die Vorsitzenden des Vorstands und des Aufsichtsrats sind als solche zu bezeichnen.

(2) Wird der Jahresabschluß in Veröffentlichungen und Vervielfältigungen, die nicht durch das Gesetz oder die Satzung vorgeschrieben sind, nicht vollständig wiedergegeben, so ist in einer Überschrift zum Jahresabschluß ausdrücklich darauf hinzuweisen, daß es sich nicht um den vollständigen Jahresabschluß handelt. Der Bestätigungsvermerk darf nicht beigefügt werden. Es ist jedoch anzugeben, ob die Abschlußprüfer den vollständigen Jahresabschluß bestätigt haben oder ob sie die Bestätigung eingeschränkt oder versagt haben. Ferner

ist anzugeben, in welcher Nummer des Bundes-anzeigers der vollständige Jahresabschluß bekannt-gemacht worden ist.

(3) Absatz 1 Nr. 1 und Absatz 2 Satz 1 bis 3 gelten sinngemäß für Veröffentlichungen und Vervielfälti-gungen des Geschäftsberichts.

Sechster Teil

Satzungsänderung. Maßnahmen der Kapitalbeschaffung und Kapitalherabsetzung

Erster Abschnitt

Satzungsänderung

§ 179
Beschluß der Hauptversammlung

(1) Jede Satzungsänderung bedarf eines Beschlus-ses der Hauptversammlung. Die Befugnis zu Ände-rungen, die nur die Fassung betreffen, kann die Hauptversammlung dem Aufsichtsrat übertragen.

(2) Der Beschluß der Hauptversammlung bedarf einer Mehrheit, die mindestens drei Viertel des bei der Beschlußfassung vertretenen Grundkapitals um-faßt. Die Satzung kann eine andere Kapitalmehrheit, für eine Änderung des Gegenstands des Unterneh-mens jedoch nur eine größere Kapitalmehrheit bestimmen. Sie kann weitere Erfordernisse auf-stellen.

(3) Soll das bisherige Verhältnis mehrerer Gat-tungen von Aktien zum Nachteil einer Gattung geändert werden, so bedarf der Beschluß der Haupt-versammlung zu seiner Wirksamkeit der Zustim-mung der benachteiligten Aktionäre. Über die Zu-stimmung haben die benachteiligten Aktionäre einen Sonderbeschluß zu fassen. Für diesen gilt Absatz 2.

§ 180
Zustimmung der betroffenen Aktionäre

(1) Ein Beschluß, der Aktionären Nebenverpflich-tungen auferlegt, bedarf zu seiner Wirksamkeit der Zustimmung aller betroffenen Aktionäre.

(2) Gleiches gilt für einen Beschluß, durch den die Übertragung von Namensaktien oder Zwi-

be stated in which issue of the *Bundesanzeiger* the complete annual financial statements were published.

(3) Paragraph 1, No. 1, and paragraph 2, first to third sentences, hereof shall apply, *mutatis mutandis*, to publications and reproductions of the business report.

Part Six

Amendment of Articles of Incorporation. Measures to Acquire and Reduce Capital

First Division

Amendment of Articles of Incorporation

§ 179
Shareholders' Resolution

(1) Any amendment of the articles of incor-poration shall require a shareholders' resolution. The power to make amendments which merely concern the wording of the articles of incorpo-ration may be delegated by the shareholders to the supervisory board.

(2) The shareholders' resolution shall require a majority of no less than three-fourths of the stated capital represented when the resolution is adopted. The articles of incorporation may pro-vide for a different capital majority; however, for a change of the purpose of the enterprise, the capital majority can only be a higher one. The articles of incorporation may establish additional requirements.

(3) A shareholders' resolution changing the existing proportion of several classes of shares to the disadvantage of one class shall, in order to be valid, require the approval of the shareholders adversely affected. The shareholders shall adopt a separate resolution concerning such approval. Paragraph 2 hereof shall apply to such resolution.

§ 180
Approval of Shareholders Affected

(1) A resolution imposing other obligations upon shareholders shall, in order to be valid, re-quire the approval of all shareholders affected.

(2) The same shall apply to a resolution pur-suant to which the transfer of registered shares or

interim certificates is made dependent on the approval of the company.

§ 181
Registration of Amendment of Articles of Incorporation

(1) The managing board shall file an application to record the amendment of the articles of incorporation in the Commercial Register. If the amendment of the articles of incorporation requires governmental authorization, the application shall be accompanied by the instrument evidencing such authorization.

(2) Unless the amendment refers to the subject matter dealt with in § 39, reference to the documents filed with the court shall be sufficient for purposes of recording. If an amendment concerns provisions the content of which must be published, the content of the amendment shall likewise be published.

(3) The amendment shall become effective only upon registration in the Commercial Register at the company's domicile.

Second Division
Measures to Acquire Capital

First Subdivision
Capital Increase Against Contributions

§ 182
Prerequisites

(1) A resolution to increase the stated capital against contributions shall require a majority of no less than three-fourths of the stated capital represented when the resolution is adopted. The articles of incorporation may provide for a different capital majority; however, for the issuance of non-voting preferred shares, the capital majority can only be a higher one. The articles of incorporation may establish additional requirements. The capital increase may be effected only by issuing new shares.

(2) If there are several classes of shares, the shareholders' resolution shall, in order to be valid, require the approval of the shareholders of each class. The shareholders of each class shall adopt a separate resolution authorizing such approval. Paragraph 1 hereof shall apply to such resolution.

schenscheinen an die Zustimmung der Gesellschaft gebunden wird.

§ 181
Eintragung der Satzungsänderung

(1) Der Vorstand hat die Satzungsänderung zur Eintragung in das Handelsregister anzumelden. Bedarf die Satzungsänderung staatlicher Genehmigung, so ist der Anmeldung die Genehmigungsurkunde beizufügen.

(2) Soweit nicht die Änderung Angaben nach § 39 betrifft, genügt bei der Eintragung die Bezugnahme auf die beim Gericht eingereichten Urkunden. Betrifft eine Änderung Bestimmungen, die ihrem Inhalt nach bekanntzumachen sind, so ist auch die Änderung ihrem Inhalt nach bekanntzumachen.

(3) Die Änderung wird erst wirksam, wenn sie in das Handelsregister des Sitzes der Gesellschaft eingetragen worden ist.

Zweiter Abschnitt
Maßnahmen der Kapitalbeschaffung

Erster Unterabschnitt
Kapitalerhöhung gegen Einlagen

§ 182
Voraussetzungen

(1) Eine Erhöhung des Grundkapitals gegen Einlagen kann nur mit einer Mehrheit beschlossen werden, die mindestens drei Viertel des bei der Beschlußfassung vertretenen Grundkapitals umfaßt. Die Satzung kann eine andere Kapitalmehrheit, für die Ausgabe von Vorzugsaktien ohne Stimmrecht jedoch nur eine größere Kapitalmehrheit bestimmen. Sie kann weitere Erfordernisse aufstellen. Die Kapitalerhöhung kann nur durch Ausgabe neuer Aktien ausgeführt werden.

(2) Sind mehrere Gattungen von Aktien vorhanden, so bedarf der Beschluß der Hauptversammlung zu seiner Wirksamkeit der Zustimmung der Aktionäre jeder Gattung. Über die Zustimmung haben die Aktionäre jeder Gattung einen Sonderbeschluß zu fassen. Für diesen gilt Absatz 1.

§ 181

(3) Sollen die neuen Aktien für einen höheren Betrag als den Nennbetrag ausgegeben werden, so ist der Mindestbetrag, unter dem sie nicht ausgegeben werden sollen, im Beschluß über die Erhöhung des Grundkapitals festzusetzen.

(4) Das Grundkapital soll nicht erhöht werden, solange ausstehende Einlagen auf das bisherige Grundkapital noch erlangt werden können. Für Versicherungsgesellschaften kann die Satzung etwas anderes bestimmen. Stehen Einlagen in verhältnismäßig unerheblichem Umfang aus, so hindert dies die Erhöhung des Grundkapitals nicht.

§ 183
Kapitalerhöhung mit Sacheinlagen

(1) Wird eine Sacheinlage gemacht, so müssen ihr Gegenstand, die Person, von der die Gesellschaft den Gegenstand erwirbt, und der Nennbetrag der bei der Sacheinlage zu gewährenden Aktien im Beschluß über die Erhöhung des Grundkapitals festgesetzt werden. Der Beschluß darf nur gefaßt werden, wenn die Einbringung von Sacheinlagen und die Festsetzungen nach Satz 1 ausdrücklich und ordnungsgemäß (§ 124 Abs. 1) bekanntgemacht worden sind.

(2) Ohne diese Festsetzung sind Verträge über Sacheinlagen und die Rechtshandlungen zu ihrer Ausführung der Gesellschaft gegenüber unwirksam. Ist die Durchführung der Erhöhung des Grundkapitals eingetragen, so wird die Gültigkeit der Kapitalerhöhung durch diese Unwirksamkeit nicht berührt. Der Aktionär ist verpflichtet, den Nennbetrag oder den höheren Ausgabebetrag der Aktien einzuzahlen. Die Unwirksamkeit kann durch Satzungsänderung nicht geheilt werden, nachdem der Durchführung der Erhöhung des Grundkapitals in das Handelsregister eingetragen worden ist.

§ 184
Anmeldung des Beschlusses

(1) Der Vorstand und der Vorsitzende des Aufsichtsrats haben den Beschluß über die Erhöhung des Grundkapitals zur Eintragung in das Handelsregister anzumelden.

(2) In der Anmeldung ist anzugeben, welche Einlagen auf das bisherige Grundkapital noch nicht geleistet sind und warum sie nicht erlangt werden können.

(3) Hat das Gericht Zweifel, ob der Wert der Sacheinlage den Nennbetrag der dafür zu gewährenden Aktien erreicht, so hat eine Prüfung durch einen oder mehrere Prüfer stattzufinden. § 33 Abs. 3 bis 5,

(3) If the new shares are to be issued at a premium, the minimum amount below which they may not be issued shall be stated in the resolution authorizing the capital increase.

(4) The stated capital shall not be increased as long as contributions outstanding on the present stated capital can still be obtained. In the case of insurance companies, the articles of incorporation may provide otherwise. Where the contributions still outstanding are relatively minor, this shall not prevent a capital increase.

§ 183
Capital Increase Against Contributions of Assets

(1) Where assets are contributed, their nature, the person from whom the company acquires them, and the par value of the shares to be issued against such contribution of assets shall be stated in the resolution authorizing the capital increase. The resolution may be adopted only after the contribution of assets and the statements pursuant to the first sentence hereof have been published explicitly and in proper form (§ 124, paragraph 1).

(2) Absent such statement, agreements regarding contributions of assets and the transactions designed to consummate them shall be invalid as against the company. Once the consummation of the capital increase is recorded, the effectiveness of the capital increase shall not be affected by such invalidity. The shareholders concerned shall be obligated to pay in the par value of the shares plus any premium. The invalidity cannot be cured by amending the articles of incorporation once the consummation of the capital increase has been recorded in the Commercial Register.

§ 184
Application to Record Resolution

(1) The managing board and the chairman of the supervisory board shall file an application to record the resolution authorizing the capital increase in the Commercial Register.

(2) The application shall state what contributions to the former stated capital have not been rendered and why they cannot be obtained.

(3) If the court is in doubt as to whether the value of the assets contributed equals the par value of the shares to be issued therefor, an audit by one or more auditors shall be ordered. § 33,

§ 184

paragraphs 3 to 5, § 34, paragraphs 2 and 3, and § 35 shall apply *mutatis mutandis*. The court shall refuse registration if the value of the assets contributed is less than the par value of the shares to be issued therefor, unless the difference is negligible.

§ 34 Abs. 2 und 3, § 35 gelten sinngemäß. Das Gericht hat die Eintragung abzulehnen, wenn der Wert der Sacheinlage nicht unwesentlich hinter dem Nennbetrag der dafür zu gewährenden Aktien zurückbleibt.

§ 185
Subscription to New Shares

(1) Subscription to the new shares shall be effected by means of a written declaration (certificate of subscription), which shall describe the equity interest by setting forth the number, the par value and, if several classes are issued, the class of the shares. The certificate of subscription shall be executed in duplicate. It shall contain the following:

1. the date on which the resolution authorizing the capital increase was adopted;
2. the amount for which the shares were issued, the amount of payments specified, as well as the extent of any other obligations;
3. the particulars required in the event of a capital increase against contributions of assets and, if several classes are issued, the total par value of each class of shares;
4. the date on which the subscription loses its binding effect for failure to record the consummation of the capital increase, if such consummation has not been recorded by that time.

(2) Certificates of subscription which do not contain these statements in full, or which contain limitations on the obligation of the subscriber other than the reservation specified in paragraph 1, No. 4, hereof shall be void.

(3) Once the consummation of the capital increase has been recorded, the subscriber cannot assert the fact that the certificate of subscription was void or that it was not binding if, on the basis of such certificate, he has exercised rights or fulfilled obligations as a shareholder.

(4) Any limitation not contained in the certificate of subscription shall be invalid as against the company.

§ 185
Zeichnung der neuen Aktien

(1) Die Zeichnung der neuen Aktien geschieht durch schriftliche Erklärung (Zeichnungsschein), aus der die Beteiligung nach der Zahl, dem Nennbetrag und, wenn mehrere Gattungen ausgegeben werden, der Gattung der Aktien hervorgehen muß. Der Zeichnungsschein soll doppelt ausgestellt werden. Er hat zu enthalten

1. den Tag, an dem die Erhöhung des Grundkapitals beschlossen worden ist;
2. den Ausgabebetrag der Aktien, den Betrag der festgesetzten Einzahlungen sowie den Umfang von Nebenverpflichtungen;
3. die bei einer Kapitalerhöhung mit Sacheinlagen vorgesehenen Festsetzungen und, wenn mehrere Gattungen ausgegeben werden, den Gesamtnennbetrag einer jeden Aktiengattung;
4. den Zeitpunkt, an dem die Zeichnung unverbindlich wird, wenn nicht bis dahin die Durchführung der Erhöhung des Grundkapitals eingetragen ist.

(2) Zeichnungsscheine, die diese Angaben nicht vollständig oder die außer dem Vorbehalt in Absatz 1 Nr. 4 Beschränkungen der Verpflichtung des Zeichners enthalten, sind nichtig.

(3) Ist die Durchführung der Erhöhung des Grundkapitals eingetragen, so kann sich der Zeichner auf die Nichtigkeit oder Unverbindlichkeit des Zeichnungsscheins nicht berufen, wenn er auf Grund des Zeichnungsscheins als Aktionär Rechte ausgeübt oder Verpflichtungen erfüllt hat.

(4) Jede nicht im Zeichnungsschein enthaltene Beschränkung ist der Gesellschaft gegenüber unwirksam.

§ 186
Preemptive Rights

(1) Each shareholder shall be entitled, upon his request, to subscribe to the new shares in proportion to his existing interest. A period of no less than two weeks may be specified for the exercise of the subscription rights.

§ 186
Bezugsrecht

(1) Jedem Aktionär muß auf sein Verlangen ein seinem Anteil an dem bisherigen Grundkapital entsprechender Teil der neuen Aktien zugeteilt werden. Für die Ausübung des Bezugsrechts kann eine Frist von mindestens zwei Wochen bestimmt werden.

§ 185

(2) Der Vorstand hat den Ausgabebetrag und zugleich eine nach Absatz 1 bestimmte Frist in den Gesellschaftsblättern bekanntzumachen.

(3) Das Bezugsrecht kann ganz oder zum Teil nur im Beschluß über die Erhöhung des Grundkapitals ausgeschlossen werden. In diesem Fall bedarf der Beschluß neben den in Gesetz oder Satzung für die Kapitalerhöhung aufgestellten Erfordernissen einer Mehrheit, die mindestens drei Viertel des bei der Beschlußfassung vertretenen Grundkapitals umfaßt. Die Satzung kann eine größere Kapitalmehrheit und weitere Erfordernisse bestimmen.

(4) Ein Beschluß, durch den das Bezugsrecht ganz oder zum Teil ausgeschlossen wird, darf nur gefaßt werden, wenn die Ausschließung ausdrücklich und ordnungsgemäß (§ 124 Abs. 1) bekanntgemacht worden ist.

(5) Als Ausschluß des Bezugsrechts ist es nicht anzusehen, wenn nach dem Beschluß die neuen Aktien von einem Kreditinstitut mit der Verpflichtung übernommen werden sollen, sie den Aktionären zum Bezug anzubieten. Der Vorstand hat das Bezugsangebot des Kreditinstituts unter Angabe des für die Aktien zu leistenden Entgelts und einer für die Annahme des Angebots gesetzten Frist in den Gesellschaftsblättern bekanntzumachen; gleiches gilt, wenn die neuen Aktien von einem anderen als einem Kreditinstitut mit der Verpflichtung übernommen werden sollen, sie den Aktionären zum Bezug anzubieten.

§ 187
Zusicherung von Rechten auf den Bezug neuer Aktien

(1) Rechte auf den Bezug neuer Aktien können nur unter Vorbehalt des Bezugsrechts der Aktionäre zugesichert werden.

(2) Zusicherungen vor dem Beschluß über die Erhöhung des Grundkapitals sind der Gesellschaft gegenüber unwirksam.

§ 188
Anmeldung und Eintragung der Durchführung

(1) Der Vorstand und der Vorsitzende des Aufsichtsrats haben die Durchführung der Erhöhung des Grundkapitals zur Eintragung in das Handelsregister anzumelden.

(2) The managing board shall publish in the publications designated in the company's articles of incorporation the consideration for which the new shares are issued, together with the period of time referred to in paragraph 1 hereof.

(3) Preemptive rights may be eliminated, in whole or in part, only in the resolution to increase the stated capital. In this event, the resolution shall require, in addition to the requirements for a capital increase specified by law or in the articles of incorporation, a majority of no less than three-fourths of the stated capital represented when the resolution is adopted. The articles of incorporation may provide for a higher capital majority and establish additional requirements.

(4) A resolution eliminating preemptive rights in whole or in part may be adopted only if such elimination has been published explicitly and in proper form (§ 124, paragraph 1).

(5) Preemptive rights shall not be deemed to have been eliminated if, pursuant to the resolution, the new shares are to be acquired by a bank subject to the obligation to offer them to the shareholders. The managing board shall publish the bank's offer in the publications designated in the company's articles of incorporation, setting forth the consideration payable for the shares and the period of time specified for the acceptance of the offer; the same shall apply if the new shares are to be acquired by a party other than a bank subject to the obligation to offer them to the shareholders.

§ 187
Offers of Rights to Subscribe to New Shares

(1) Rights to subscribe to new shares may be offered only subject to the preemptive rights of the shareholders.

(2) Offers made prior to the resolution to increase the stated capital shall be invalid as against the company.

§ 188
Application to Record and Registration of Capital Increase

(1) The managing board and the chairman of the supervisory board shall file an application to record the consummation of the capital increase in the Commercial Register.

§ 188

(2) § 36, paragraph 2, and § 37, paragraph 1, shall apply, *mutatis mutandis*, to this application. Payment may not be effected by crediting an account maintained by the managing board.

(3) For the records of the court at the company's domicile, the application shall be accompanied by the following:

1. the duplicates of the subscription certificates and a list of subscribers, signed by the managing board, which shall designate the shares issued to each of them and the amounts paid thereon;

2. if a capital increase is effected by contributions of assets, the agreements underlying the statements required by § 183 or executed to implement such statements, as well as the certification to the effect that the report has been filed with the examiner for the Chamber of Industry and Commerce;

3. an account of the expenses the company will incur through the issuance of the new shares;

4. if the capital increase requires governmental authorization, the instrument evidencing such authorization.

(4) If the court is in doubt as to whether the value of the assets contributed equals the par value of the shares to be issued therefor, an audit by one or more auditors shall be ordered. § 33, paragraphs 3 to 5, § 34, paragraphs 2 and 3, and § 35 shall apply *mutatis mutandis*. The court shall refuse registration if the value of the assets contributed is less than the par value of the shares to be issued therefor, unless the difference is negligible.

(5) The application and registration of the consummation of the capital increase may be combined with the application and registration of the resolution authorizing the increase.

(6) An original, duplicate original, or certified copy of the documents filed shall be kept in the court records.

§ 189

Effective Date of Capital Increase

The capital increase shall become effective upon registration of the consummation of the capital increase.

§ 190

Publication

The publication of the registration (§ 188) shall, in addition to the content of the registra-

§ 189

---

(2) Für die Anmeldung gelten sinngemäß § 36 Abs. 2 und § 37 Abs. 1. Durch Gutschrift auf ein Konto des Vorstands kann die Einzahlung nicht geleistet werden.

(3) Der Anmeldung sind für das Gericht des Sitzes der Gesellschaft beizufügen

1. die Zweitschriften der Zeichnungsscheine und ein vom Vorstand unterschriebenes Verzeichnis der Zeichner, das die auf jeden entfallenden Aktien und die auf sie geleisteten Einzahlungen angibt;

2. bei einer Kapitalerhöhung mit Sacheinlagen die Verträge, die den Festsetzungen nach § 183 zugrunde liegen oder zu ihrer Ausführung geschlossen worden sind, sowie die Bescheinigung, daß der Bericht der Prüfer der Industrie- und Handelskammer eingereicht worden ist;

3. eine Berechnung der Kosten, die für die Gesellschaft durch die Ausgabe der neuen Aktien entstehen werden;

4. wenn die Erhöhung des Grundkapitals der staatlichen Genehmigung bedarf, die Genehmigungsurkunde.

(4) Hat das Gericht Zweifel, ob der Wert der Sacheinlage den Nennbetrag der dafür zu gewährenden Aktien erreicht, so hat eine Prüfung durch einen oder mehrere Prüfer stattzufinden. § 33 Abs. 3 bis 5, § 34 Abs. 2 und 3, § 35 gelten sinngemäß. Das Gericht hat die Eintragung abzulehnen, wenn der Wert der Sacheinlage nicht unwesentlich hinter dem Nennbetrag der dafür zu gewährenden Aktien zurückbleibt.

(5) Anmeldung und Eintragung der Durchführung der Erhöhung des Grundkapitals können mit Anmeldung und Eintragung des Beschlusses über die Erhöhung verbunden werden.

(6) Die eingereichten Schriftstücke werden beim Gericht in Urschrift, Ausfertigung oder öffentlich beglaubigter Abschrift aufbewahrt.

§ 189

Wirksamwerden der Kapitalerhöhung

Mit der Eintragung der Durchführung der Erhöhung des Grundkapitals ist das Grundkapital erhöht.

§ 190

Bekanntmachung

In die Bekanntmachung der Eintragung (§ 188) sind außer deren Inhalt der Ausgabebetrag der Ak-

tien und die bei einer Kapitalerhöhung mit Sacheinlagen vorgesehenen Festsetzungen aufzunehmen.
Bei der Bekanntmachung dieser Festsetzungen genügt die Bezugnahme auf die beim Gericht eingereichten Urkunden.

tion, set forth the amount for which the shares
are issued and the information required for a
capital increase effected by contributions of
assets. For purposes of the publication of such
statements, reference to the documents filed
with the court shall be sufficient.

§ 191
Verbotene Ausgabe von Aktien
und Zwischenscheinen

Vor der Eintragung der Durchführung der Erhöhung des Grundkapitals können die neuen
Anteilsrechte nicht übertragen, neue Aktien und
Zwischenscheine nicht ausgegeben werden. Die vorher ausgegebenen neuen Aktien und Zwischenscheine sind nichtig. Für den Schaden aus der Ausgabe sind die Ausgeber den Inhabern als Gesamtschuldner verantwortlich.

§ 191
Prohibited Issuance of Share Certificates
and Interim Certificates

The new equity interests may not be transferred, and new share certificates and interim
certificates may not be issued, prior to registration of the consummation of the capital increase.
New share certificates and interim certificates
issued prior thereto shall be void. The issuers
shall be jointly and severally liable to the holders
for any damage arising from such issuance.

Zweiter Unterabschnitt

Bedingte Kapitalerhöhung

Second Subdivision
Conditional Capital Increase

§ 192
Voraussetzungen

(1) Die Hauptversammlung kann eine Erhöhung
des Grundkapitals beschließen, die nur so weit
durchgeführt werden soll, wie von einem Umtausch-
oder Bezugsrecht Gebrauch gemacht wird, das die
Gesellschaft auf die neuen Aktien (Bezugsaktien)
einräumt (bedingte Kapitalerhöhung).

(2) Die bedingte Kapitalerhöhung soll nur zu
folgenden Zwecken beschlossen werden:
1. zur Gewährung von Umtausch- oder Bezugsrechten an Gläubiger von Wandelschuldverschreibungen;
2. zur Vorbereitung des Zusammenschlusses mehrerer Unternehmen;
3. zur Gewährung von Bezugsrechten an Arbeitnehmer der Gesellschaft zum Bezug neuer Aktien
gegen Einlage von Geldforderungen, die den
Arbeitnehmern aus einer ihnen von der Gesellschaft eingeräumten Gewinnbeteiligung zustehen.

(3) Der Nennbetrag des bedingten Kapitals darf
die Hälfte des Grundkapitals, das zur Zeit der Beschlußfassung über die bedingte Kapitalerhöhung
vorhanden ist, nicht übersteigen.

(4) Ein Beschluß der Hauptversammlung, der dem
Beschluß über die bedingte Kapitalerhöhung entgegensteht, ist nichtig.

(5) Die folgenden Vorschriften über das Bezugsrecht gelten sinngemäß für das Umtauschrecht.

§ 192
Prerequisites

(1) The shareholders may decide by resolution to increase the stated capital only to the extent that conversion or subscription rights
granted by the company with respect to new
shares (preemptive shares) are exercised (conditional capital increase).

(2) A resolution authorizing a conditional
capital increase shall be adopted only for the
following purposes:
1. to grant conversion or subscription rights to
the holders of convertible bonds;
2. to initiate a combination of several enterprises;
3. to grant to employees of the company rights
to subscribe to new shares to be paid for by
contributing rights to receive payments to
which such employees are entitled under a
profit-sharing arrangement with the company.

(3) The par value of the conditional capital
may not exceed one-half of the stated capital
existing at the time the resolution authorizing
the conditional capital increase is adopted.

(4) A shareholders' resolution which would be
contrary to the resolution authorizing the conditional capital increase shall be void.

(5) The provisions concerning subscription
rights set forth below shall apply, *mutatis mutandis*, to conversion rights.

§ 192

§ 193
Requirements for the Resolution

(1) The resolution authorizing the conditional capital increase shall require a majority of no less than three-fourths of the stated capital represented when the resolution is adopted. The articles of incorporation may provide for a higher capital majority and establish additional requirements. § 182, paragraph 2, and § 187, paragraph 2, shall apply.

(2) The resolution shall also set forth the following:

1. the purpose of the conditional capital increase;
2. the persons entitled to subscribe;
3. the amount for which the shares are issued or the basis for the computation of such amount.

§ 194
Conditional Capital Increase Involving Contributions of Assets

(1) If assets are contributed, their nature, the person from whom the company acquires the assets, and the par value of the shares to be issued for such contribution of assets shall be stated in the resolution authorizing the conditional capital increase. The surrender of bonds in exchange for the new shares shall not be deemed to be a contribution of assets. The resolution may be adopted only after the contribution of assets has been published explicitly and in proper form (§ 124, paragraph 1).

(2) Absent such statement, agreements regarding contributions of assets and the transactions designed to implement them shall be invalid as against the company. Once the new shares have been issued, the effectiveness of the conditional capital increase shall not be affected by such invalidity. The shareholders concerned shall be obligated to pay in the par value of the new shares plus any premium. The invalidity cannot be cured by amending the articles of incorporation once the new shares have been issued.

(3) Paragraphs 1 and 2 hereof shall not apply to contributions in the form of rights to receive payments to which employees of the company are entitled under a profit-sharing arrangement with the company.

§ 195
Application to Record the Resolution

(1) The managing board and the chairman of the supervisory board shall file an application to

§ 193

§ 193
Erfordernisse des Beschlusses

(1) Der Beschluß über die bedingte Kapitalerhöhung bedarf einer Mehrheit, die mindestens drei Viertel des bei der Beschlußfassung vertretenen Grundkapitals umfaßt. Die Satzung kann eine größere Kapitalmehrheit und weitere Erfordernisse bestimmen. § 182 Abs. 2 und § 187 Abs. 2 gelten.

(2) Im Beschluß müssen auch festgestellt werden
1. der Zweck der bedingten Kapitalerhöhung;
2. der Kreis der Bezugsberechtigten;
3. der Ausgabebetrag oder die Grundlagen, nach denen dieser Betrag errechnet wird.

§ 194
Bedingte Kapitalerhöhung mit Sacheinlagen

(1) Wird eine Sacheinlage gemacht, so müssen ihr Gegenstand, die Person, von der die Gesellschaft den Gegenstand erwirbt, und der Nennbetrag der bei der Sacheinlage zu gewährenden Aktien im Beschluß über die bedingte Kapitalerhöhung festgesetzt werden. Als Sacheinlage gilt nicht die Hingabe von Schuldverschreibungen im Umtausch gegen Bezugsaktien. Der Beschluß darf nur gefaßt werden, wenn die Einbringung von Sacheinlagen ausdrücklich und ordnungsgemäß (§ 124 Abs. 1) bekanntgemacht worden ist.

(2) Ohne diese Festsetzung sind Verträge über Sacheinlagen und die Rechtshandlungen zu ihrer Ausführung der Gesellschaft gegenüber unwirksam. Sind die Bezugsaktien ausgegeben, so wird die Gültigkeit der bedingten Kapitalerhöhung durch diese Unwirksamkeit nicht berührt. Der Aktionär ist verpflichtet, den Nennbetrag oder den höheren Ausgabebetrag der Bezugsaktien einzuzahlen. Die Unwirksamkeit kann durch Satzungsänderung nicht geheilt werden, nachdem die Bezugsaktien ausgegeben worden sind.

(3) Die Absätze 1 und 2 gelten nicht für die Einlage von Geldforderungen, die Arbeitnehmern der Gesellschaft aus einer ihnen von der Gesellschaft eingeräumten Gewinnbeteiligung zustehen.

§ 195
Anmeldung des Beschlusses

(1) Der Vorstand und der Vorsitzende des Aufsichtsrats haben den Beschluß über die bedingte

Kapitalerhöhung zur Eintragung in das Handelsregister anzumelden.

(2) Der Anmeldung sind für das Gericht des Sitzes der Gesellschaft beizufügen

1. bei einer bedingten Kapitalerhöhung mit Sacheinlagen die Verträge, die den Festsetzungen nach § 194 zugrunde liegen oder zu ihrer Ausführung geschlossen worden sind;
2. eine Berechnung der Kosten, die für die Gesellschaft durch die Ausgabe der Bezugsaktien entstehen werden;
3. wenn die Kapitalerhöhung der staatlichen Genehmigung bedarf, die Genehmigungsurkunde.

(3) Hat das Gericht Zweifel, ob der Wert der Sacheinlage den Nennbetrag der dafür zu gewährenden Aktien erreicht, so hat eine Prüfung durch einen oder mehrere Prüfer stattzufinden. § 33 Abs. 3 bis 5, § 34 Abs. 2 und 3, § 35 gelten sinngemäß. Das Gericht hat die Eintragung abzulehnen, wenn der Wert der Sacheinlage nicht unwesentlich hinter dem Nennbetrag der dafür zu gewährenden Aktien zurückbleibt.

(4) Die eingereichten Schriftstücke werden beim Gericht in Urschrift, Ausfertigung oder öffentlich beglaubigter Abschrift aufbewahrt.

§ 196
Bekanntmachung der Eintragung

In die Bekanntmachung der Eintragung des Beschlusses über die bedingte Kapitalerhöhung sind außer deren Inhalt die Feststellungen nach § 193 Abs. 2 und die nach § 194 bei der Einbringung von Sacheinlagen vorgesehenen Festsetzungen aufzunehmen. Für die Festsetzungen nach § 194 genügt die Bezugnahme auf die beim Gericht eingereichten Urkunden.

§ 197
Verbotene Aktienausgabe

Vor der Eintragung des Beschlusses über die bedingte Kapitalerhöhung können die Bezugsaktien nicht ausgegeben werden. Ein Anspruch des Bezugsberechtigten entsteht vor diesem Zeitpunkt nicht. Die vorher ausgegebenen Bezugsaktien sind nichtig. Für den Schaden aus der Ausgabe sind die Ausgeber den Inhabern als Gesamtschuldner verantwortlich.

record the resolution authorizing the conditional capital increase in the Commercial Register.

(2) For the records of the court at the company's domicile, the application shall be accompanied by the following:

1. in the event the conditional capital increase is effected by contributions of assets, the agreements underlying the statements required by § 194 or executed to implement such statements;
2. an account of the expenses the company will incur through the issuance of the new shares;
3. if the capital increase requires governmental authorization, the instrument evidencing such authorization.

(3) If the court is in doubt as to whether the value of the assets contributed equals the par value of the shares to be issued therefor, an audit by one or more auditors shall be ordered. § 33, paragraphs 3 to 5, § 34, paragraphs 2 and 3, and § 35 shall apply *mutatis mutandis*. The court shall refuse registration if the value of the assets contributed is less than the par value of the shares to be issued therefor, unless the difference is negligible.

(4) An original, duplicate original, or certified copy of the documents filed shall be kept in the court records.

§ 196
Publication of Registration

The publication of the registration of the resolution authorizing the conditional capital increase shall, in addition to the content of the registration, set forth the statements required by § 193, paragraph 2, and the statements required for the contribution of assets pursuant to § 194. For the statements required by § 194, reference to the documents filed with the court shall be sufficient.

§ 197
Prohibited Issuance of Shares

Preemptive shares may not be issued before the resolution authorizing the conditional capital increase has been recorded. Prior to such time, those entitled to subscribe have no enforceable rights. Preemptive shares issued prior to such time shall be void. The issuers shall be jointly and severally liable to the holders for any damage arising from such issuance.

§ 198
Declaration of Exercise of Preemptive Rights

(1) The right to subscribe shall be exercised by a written declaration. Such declaration (declaration of exercise of preemptive rights) shall be executed in duplicate. It shall describe the equity interest by setting forth the number, the par value and, if several classes are issued, the class of the shares, the statements required by § 193, paragraph 2, the statements required for contributions of assets pursuant to § 194, as well as the date on which the resolution authorizing the conditional capital increase was adopted.

(2) The declaration of the exercise of preemptive rights shall have the same effect as a declaration to subscribe. Declarations of the exercise of preemptive rights whose content does not comply with paragraph 1 hereof, or which contain limitations on the liability of the person making such a declaration, shall be void.

(3) If new shares are issued in spite of the fact that the declaration of the exercise of preemptive rights is void, the person making such declaration cannot assert such nullity if, on the basis of such declaration, he has exercised rights or fulfilled obligations as a shareholder.

(4) Any restriction not contained in the declaration of the exercise of preemptive rights shall be invalid as against the company.

§ 199
Issuance of the New Shares

(1) The managing board may issue the new shares only in pursuance of the purpose stated in the resolution authorizing the conditional capital increase and after full payment of the consideration specified in the resolution.

(2) The managing board may issue new shares in exchange for convertible bonds only if the difference between the price for which the convertible bonds surrendered for exchange are issued and the higher par value of the new shares to be issued therefor is offset by such free reserves as may be used for this purpose or by an additional payment by the person entitled to the exchange. This shall not apply if the total amount for which the convertible bonds are issued equals or exceeds the total par value of the new shares.

§ 198

§ 198
Bezugserklärung

(1) Das Bezugsrecht wird durch schriftliche Erklärung ausgeübt. Die Erklärung (Bezugserklärung) soll doppelt ausgestellt werden. Sie hat die Beteiligung nach der Zahl, dem Nennbetrag und, wenn mehrere Gattungen ausgegeben werden, der Gattung der Aktien, die Feststellungen nach § 193 Abs. 2, die nach § 194 bei der Einbringung von Sacheinlagen vorgesehenen Festsetzungen sowie den Tag anzugeben, an dem der Beschluß über die bedingte Kapitalerhöhung gefaßt worden ist.

(2) Die Bezugserklärung hat die gleiche Wirkung wie eine Zeichnungserklärung. Bezugserklärungen, deren Inhalt nicht dem Absatz 1 entspricht oder die Beschränkungen der Verpflichtung des Erklärenden enthalten, sind nichtig.

(3) Werden Bezugsaktien ungeachtet der Nichtigkeit einer Bezugserklärung ausgegeben, so kann sich der Erklärende auf die Nichtigkeit nicht berufen, wenn er auf Grund der Bezugserklärung als Aktionär Rechte ausgeübt oder Verpflichtungen erfüllt hat.

(4) Jede nicht in der Bezugserklärung enthaltene Beschränkung ist der Gesellschaft gegenüber unwirksam.

§ 199
Ausgabe der Bezugsaktien

(1) Der Vorstand darf die Bezugsaktien nur in Erfüllung des im Beschluß über die bedingte Kapitalerhöhung festgesetzten Zwecks und nicht vor der vollen Leistung des Gegenwerts ausgeben, der sich aus dem Beschluß ergibt.

(2) Der Vorstand darf Bezugsaktien gegen Wandelschuldverschreibungen nur ausgeben, wenn der Unterschied zwischen dem Ausgabebetrag der zum Umtausch eingereichten Schuldverschreibungen und dem höheren Nennbetrag der für sie zu gewährenden Bezugsaktien aus einer freien Rücklage, soweit sie zu diesem Zweck verwandt werden kann, oder durch Zuzahlung des Umtauschberechtigten gedeckt ist. Dies gilt nicht, wenn der Gesamtbetrag, zu dem die Schuldverschreibungen ausgegeben sind, den Gesamtnennbetrag der Bezugsaktien erreicht oder übersteigt.

§ 200

Wirksamwerden der bedingten Kapitalerhöhung

Mit der Ausgabe der Bezugsaktien ist das Grundkapital erhöht.

§ 201

Anmeldung der Ausgabe von Bezugsaktien

(1) Der Vorstand hat innerhalb eines Monats nach Ablauf des Geschäftsjahrs zur Eintragung in das Handelsregister anzumelden, in welchem Umfang im abgelaufenen Geschäftsjahr Bezugsaktien ausgegeben worden sind.

(2) Der Anmeldung sind für das Gericht des Sitzes der Gesellschaft die Zweitschriften der Bezugserklärungen und ein vom Vorstand unterschriebenes Verzeichnis der Personen, die das Bezugsrecht ausgeübt haben, beizufügen. Das Verzeichnis hat die auf jeden Aktionär entfallenden Aktien und die auf sie gemachten Einlagen anzugeben.

(3) In der Anmeldung hat der Vorstand zu erklären, daß die Bezugsaktien nur in Erfüllung des im Beschluß über die bedingte Kapitalerhöhung festgesetzen Zwecks und nicht vor der vollen Leistung des Gegenwerts ausgegeben worden sind, der sich aus dem Beschluß ergibt.

(4) Die eingereichten Schriftstücke werden beim Gericht in Urschrift, Ausfertigung oder öffentlich beglaubigter Abschrift aufbewahrt.

Dritter Unterabschnitt

Genehmigtes Kapital

§ 202

Voraussetzungen

(1) Die Satzung kann den Vorstand für höchstens fünf Jahre nach Eintragung der Gesellschaft ermächtigen, das Grundkapital bis zu einem bestimmten Nennbetrag (genehmigtes Kapital) durch Ausgabe neuer Aktien gegen Einlagen zu erhöhen.

(2) Die Ermächtigung kann auch durch Satzungsänderung für höchstens fünf Jahre nach Eintragung der Satzungsänderung erteilt werden. Der Beschluß der Hauptversammlung bedarf einer Mehrheit, die mindestens drei Viertel des bei der Beschlußfassung vertretenen Grundkapitals umfaßt. Die Satzung

§ 200

Effective Date of Conditional Capital Increase

The capital increase shall become effective upon issuance of the new shares.

§ 201

Application to Record Issuance of Preemptive Shares

(1) Within one month after the end of the fiscal year, the managing board shall file an application to record in the Commercial Register the extent to which preemptive shares were issued during the preceding fiscal year.

(2) For the records of the court at the company's domicile, the application shall be accompanied by duplicates of the declarations to exercise preemptive rights and a list, signed by the managing board, of the persons who exercised their preemptive rights. Such list shall show the shares issued to each shareholder and the contributions made thereon.

(3) In the application, the managing board shall state that the preemptive shares were issued solely in pursuance of the purpose stated in the resolution authorizing the conditional capital increase and after full payment of the consideration specified in the resolution.

(4) An original, duplicate original, or certified copy of the documents filed shall be kept in the court records.

Third Subdivision

Authorized Capital

§ 202

Prerequisites

(1) The articles of incorporation may authorize the managing board, for a maximum period of five years from the date of the company's registration, to increase the stated capital up to a specified nominal amount (authorized capital) by issuing new shares against contributions.

(2) An amendment of the articles of incorporation may also provide for such authorization, to be effective for a maximum of five years from the date of registration of such amendment. The shareholders' resolution adopting the amendment shall require a majority of no less than three-fourths of the stated capital represented when the resolution is adopted. The articles of incorporation may provide for a higher capital

§ 202

majority and establish additional requirements. § 182, paragraph 2, shall apply.

(3) The nominal value of the authorized capital may not exceed one-half of the stated capital existing at the time the authorization is granted. The new shares may be issued only with the approval of the supervisory board.

(4) The articles of incorporation may also provide that the new shares are to be issued to employees of the company.

§ 203
Issuance of New Shares

(1) Unless the following provisions require a different result, §§ 185 to 191, relating to a capital increase against contributions, shall apply, *mutatis mutandis*, to the issuance of the new shares. The authorization to issue new shares contained in the articles of incorporation shall be substituted for the resolution authorizing the capital increase.

(2) The authorization may provide that the managing board shall have the power to abrogate preemptive rights. § 186, paragraph 4, shall apply, *mutatis mutandis*, if an authorization to this effect is contained in an amendment to the articles of incorporation.

(3) New shares shall not be issued as long as contributions outstanding on the present stated capital can still be obtained. In the case of insurance companies, the articles of incorporation may provide otherwise. Where contributions still outstanding are relatively minor, this shall not prevent the issuance of the new shares. The first application to record the implementation of the capital increase shall specify what contributions to the previous stated capital have not been made and why they cannot be obtained.

(4) Paragraph 3, first and fourth sentences, hereof shall not apply if the shares are issued to employees of the company.

§ 204
Conditions for Issuance of Shares

(1) To the extent that the authorization contains no such provisions, the managing board shall decide what rights are granted by the shares and the conditions for their issuance. The decision of the managing board shall require the approval of the supervisory board; the same shall apply to the decision of the managing board pursuant to § 203, paragraph 2, to abrogate preemptive rights.

kann eine größere Kapitalmehrheit und weitere Erfordernisse bestimmen. § 182 Abs. 2 gilt.

(3) Der Nennbetrag des genehmigten Kapitals darf die Hälfte des Grundkapitals, das zur Zeit der Ermächtigung vorhanden ist, nicht übersteigen. Die neuen Aktien sollen nur mit Zustimmung des Aufsichtsrats ausgegeben werden.

(4) Die Satzung kann auch vorsehen, daß die neuen Aktien an Arbeitnehmer der Gesellschaft ausgegeben werden.

§ 203
Ausgabe der neuen Aktien

(1) Für die Ausgabe der neuen Aktien gelten sinngemäß, soweit sich aus den folgenden Vorschriften nichts anderes ergibt, §§ 185 bis 191 über die Kapitalerhöhung gegen Einlagen. An die Stelle des Beschlusses über die Erhöhung des Grundkapitals tritt die Ermächtigung der Satzung zur Ausgabe neuer Aktien.

(2) Die Ermächtigung kann vorsehen, daß der Vorstand über den Ausschluß des Bezugsrechts entscheidet. Wird eine Ermächtigung, die dies vorsieht, durch Satzungsänderung erteilt, so gilt § 186 Abs. 4 sinngemäß.

(3) Die neuen Aktien sollen nicht ausgegeben werden, solange ausstehende Einlagen auf das bisherige Grundkapital noch erlangt werden können. Für Versicherungsgesellschaften kann die Satzung etwas anderes bestimmen. Stehen Einlagen in verhältnismäßig unerheblichem Umfang aus, so hindert dies die Ausgabe der neuen Aktien nicht. In der ersten Anmeldung der Durchführung der Erhöhung des Grundkapitals ist anzugeben, welche Einlagen auf das bisherige Grundkapital noch nicht geleistet sind und warum sie nicht erlangt werden können.

(4) Absatz 3 Satz 1 und 4 gilt nicht, wenn die Aktien an Arbeitnehmer der Gesellschaft ausgegeben werden.

§ 204
Bedingungen der Aktienausgabe

(1) Über den Inhalt der Aktienrechte und die Bedingungen der Aktienausgabe entscheidet der Vorstand, soweit die Ermächtigung keine Bestimmungen enthält. Die Entscheidung des Vorstands bedarf der Zustimmung des Aufsichtsrats; gleiches gilt für die Entscheidung des Vorstands nach § 203 Abs. 2 über den Ausschluß des Bezugsrechts.

(2) Sind Vorzugsaktien ohne Stimmrecht vorhanden, so können Vorzugsaktien, die bei der Verteilung des Gewinns oder des Gesellschaftsvermögens ihnen vorgehen oder gleichstehen, nur ausgegeben werden, wenn die Ermächtigung es vorsieht.

(3) Weist ein Jahresabschluß, der mit einem uneingeschränkten Bestätigungsvermerk versehen ist, einen Jahresüberschuß aus, so können Aktien an Arbeitnehmer der Gesellschaft auch in der Weise ausgegeben werden, daß die auf sie zu leistende Einlage aus dem Teil des Jahresüberschusses gedeckt wird, den nach § 58 Abs. 2 Vorstand und Aufsichtsrat in freie Rücklagen einstellen könnten. Für die Ausgabe der neuen Aktien gelten die Vorschriften über eine Kapitalerhöhung gegen Bareinlagen, ausgenommen § 188 Abs. 2. Der Anmeldung der Durchführung der Erhöhung des Grundkapitals ist außerdem der festgestellte Jahresabschluß mit Bestätigungsvermerk beizufügen. Die Anmeldenden haben ferner die Erklärung nach § 210 Abs. 1 Satz 2 abzugeben.

§ 205
Ausgabe gegen Sacheinlagen

(1) Gegen Sacheinlagen dürfen Aktien nur ausgegeben werden, wenn die Ermächtigung es vorsieht.

(2) Der Gegenstand der Sacheinlage, die Person, von der die Gesellschaft den Gegenstand erwirbt, und der Nennbetrag der bei der Sacheinlage zu gewährenden Aktien sind, wenn sie nicht in der Ermächtigung festgesetzt sind, vom Vorstand festzusetzen und in den Zeichnungsschein aufzunehmen. Der Vorstand soll die Entscheidung nur mit Zustimmung des Aufsichtsrats treffen.

(3) Ohne die vorgeschriebene Festsetzung sind Verträge über Sacheinlagen und die Rechtshandlungen zu ihrer Ausführung der Gesellschaft gegenüber unwirksam. Gleiches gilt, wenn die Festsetzung des Vorstands nicht in den Zeichnungsschein aufgenommen ist. Ist die Durchführung der Erhöhung des Grundkapitals eingetragen, so wird die Gültigkeit der Kapitalerhöhung durch diese Unwirksamkeit nicht berührt. Der Aktionär ist verpflichtet, den Nennbetrag oder den höheren Ausgabebetrag der Aktien einzuzahlen. Die Unwirksamkeit kann durch Satzungsänderung nicht geheilt werden, nachdem die Durchführung der Erhöhung des Grundkapitals in das Handelsregister eingetragen worden ist.

(4) Die Absätze 2 und 3 gelten nicht für die Einlage von Geldforderungen, die Arbeitnehmern der

(2) If non-voting preferred shares are outstanding, preferred shares with priority over or equal to them with respect to the distribution of profits or the company's assets may be issued only if the authorization so provides.

(3) If the annual financial statements contain an unqualified certification and show a net profit for the year, shares may also be issued to employees of the company in such a manner that the contributions to be rendered thereon are paid from that part of the net profit for the year which the managing board and the supervisory board could, pursuant to § 58, paragraph 2, allocate to free reserves. With respect to the issuance of new shares, the provisions concerning capital increases for contributions in cash shall apply, except for § 188, paragraph 2. The application to record the consummation of the capital increase shall also be accompanied by the approved annual financial statements, to which a certification is attached. The applicants shall also make the declaration pursuant to § 210, paragraph 1, second sentence.

§ 205
Issuance for Assets

(1) Shares may be issued for assets only if the authorization so provides.

(2) Unless specified in the authorization, the nature of the assets, the person from whom the company acquires such assets, and the par value of the shares to be issued for the assets shall be specified by the managing board and entered in the subscription certificate. The managing board may make this determination only with the consent of the supervisory board.

(3) Absent the prescribed determination, agreements regarding contributions of assets and transactions to implement them shall be invalid as against the company. The same shall apply if the determination of the managing board has not been entered in the subscription certificate. Once the consummation of the capital increase has been recorded, the effectiveness of the capital increase shall not be affected by such invalidity. The shareholders concerned shall be obligated to pay in the par value of the shares plus any premium. The invalidity cannot be cured by amending the articles of incorporation once the consummation of the capital increase has been recorded in the Commercial Register.

(4) Paragraphs 2 and 3 hereof shall not apply to contributions in the form of rights to receive

payment to which employees of the company are entitled under a profit-sharing arrangement with the company.

§ 206
Agreements on Contributions of Assets Prior to Registration of the Company

If, prior to the registration of the company, agreements are entered into pursuant to which contributions to the authorized capital shall be in the form of assets, the articles of incorporation shall contain the statements prescribed for an issuance of shares against assets. In this case, § 27, paragraphs 2 and 4, §§ 32 to 35, 37, paragraph 2, Nos. 2, 4 and 5, § 38, paragraph 2, and § 49, concerning the formation of the company, shall apply *mutatis mutandis*. The managing board shall be substituted for the incorporators, and registration of the consummation of the capital increase shall be substituted for the application and registration of the company.

Fourth Subdivision
Capital Increase Out of Retained Earnings

§ 207
Prerequisites

(1) The shareholders may decide by resolution to increase the stated capital by converting disclosed reserves into stated capital.

(2) § 182, paragraph 1, first, second, and fourth sentences, and § 184, paragraph 1, shall apply, *mutatis mutandis*, to the resolution and to the application to record the resolution.

(3) A resolution authorizing the increase may be adopted only after the annual financial statements for the fiscal year last preceding the resolution authorizing the capital increase (last annual financial statements) have been established.

(4) The resolution shall be based on a balance sheet.

§ 208
Convertible Reserves

(1) The reserves to be converted into stated capital must be shown as "disclosed reserves" in the last annual balance sheet, and, if the resolution is based on some other balance sheet, in the latter as well. Subject to paragraph 2 hereof, free reserves may be fully converted into stated capital; the statutory reserve, however, may be converted only to the extent that it exceeds one-tenth or such higher portion of the existing stated

§ 206

Gesellschaft aus einer ihnen von der Gesellschaft eingeräumten Gewinnbeteiligung zustehen.

§ 206
Verträge über Sacheinlagen vor Eintragung der Gesellschaft

Sind vor Eintragung der Gesellschaft Verträge geschlossen worden, nach denen auf das genehmigte Kapital eine Sacheinlage zu leisten ist, so muß die Satzung die Festsetzungen enthalten, die für eine Ausgabe gegen Sacheinlagen vorgeschrieben sind. Dabei gelten sinngemäß § 27 Abs. 2, 4, §§ 32 bis 35, 37 Abs. 2 Nr. 2, 4 und 5, § 38 Abs. 2, § 49 über die Gründung der Gesellschaft. An die Stelle der Gründer tritt der Vorstand und an die Stelle der Anmeldung und Eintragung der Gesellschaft die Anmeldung und Eintragung der Durchführung der Erhöhung des Grundkapitals.

Vierter Unterabschnitt
Kapitalerhöhung aus Gesellschaftsmitteln

§ 207
Voraussetzungen

(1) Die Hauptversammlung kann eine Erhöhung des Grundkapitals durch Umwandlung von offenen Rücklagen in Grundkapital beschließen.

(2) Für den Beschluß und für die Anmeldung des Beschlusses gelten § 182 Abs. 1 Satz 1, 2 und 4, § 184 Abs. 1 sinngemäß.

(3) Die Erhöhung kann erst beschlossen werden, nachdem der Jahresabschluß für das letzte vor der Beschlußfassung über die Kapitalerhöhung abgelaufene Geschäftsjahr (letzter Jahresabschluß) festgestellt ist.

(4) Dem Beschluß ist eine Bilanz zugrunde zu legen.

§ 208
Umwandlungsfähige Rücklagen

(1) Die Rücklagen, die in Grundkapital umgewandelt werden sollen, müssen in der letzten Jahresbilanz, wenn dem Beschluß eine andere Bilanz zugrunde gelegt wird, auch in dieser Bilanz, unter "Offene Rücklagen" ausgewiesen sein. Vorbehaltlich des Absatzes 2 können freie Rücklagen in voller Höhe, die gesetzliche Rücklage nur, soweit sie den zehnten oder den in der Satzung bestimmten

höheren Teil des bisherigen Grundkapitals übersteigt, in Grundkapital umgewandelt werden.

(2) Die Rücklagen können nicht umgewandelt werden, soweit in der zugrunde gelegten Bilanz ein Verlust, einschließlich eines Verlustvortrags, oder ein anderer Gegenposten zum Eigenkapital ausgewiesen ist. Sonderposten mit Rücklageanteil können nicht umgewandelt werden. Freie Rücklagen, die einem bestimmten Zweck zu dienen bestimmt sind, dürfen nur umgewandelt werden, soweit dies mit ihrer Zweckbestimmung vereinbar ist.

§ 209
Zugrunde gelegte Bilanz

(1) Dem Beschluß kann die letzte Jahresbilanz zugrunde gelegt werden, wenn die Jahresbilanz geprüft und der festgestellte Jahresbilanz mit dem uneingeschränkten Bestätigungsvermerk der Abschlußprüfer versehen ist und wenn ihr Stichtag höchstens acht Monate vor der Anmeldung des Beschlusses zur Eintragung in das Handelsregister liegt.

(2) Wird dem Beschluß nicht die letzte Jahresbilanz zugrunde gelegt, so muß die Bilanz den §§ 151 bis 156 entsprechen. Der Stichtag der Bilanz darf höchstens acht Monate vor der Anmeldung des Beschlusses zur Eintragung in das Handelsregister liegen.

(3) Die Bilanz muß durch einen oder mehrere Abschlußprüfer darauf geprüft werden, ob sie den §§ 151 bis 156 entspricht. Sie muß mit einem uneingeschränkten Bestätigungsvermerk versehen sein.

(4) Wenn die Hauptversammlung keine anderen Prüfer wählt, gelten die Prüfer als gewählt, die für die Prüfung des letzten Jahresabschlusses von der Hauptversammlung gewählt oder vom Gericht bestellt worden sind. Soweit sich aus der Besonderheit des Prüfungsauftrags nichts anderes ergibt, sind auf die Prüfung § 163 Abs. 1 Satz 3, §§ 164 bis 166, 167 Abs. 3, § 168 anzuwenden.

(5) Bei Versicherungsgesellschaften werden die Prüfer vom Aufsichtsrat bestimmt; Absatz 4 Satz 1 gilt sinngemäß. Soweit sich aus der Besonderheit des Prüfungsauftrags nichts anderes ergibt, sind auf die Prüfung §§ 57 bis 59 des Gesetzes über die Beaufsichtigung der privaten Versicherungsunternehmungen und Bausparkassen anzuwenden.

(6) Im Fall der Absätze 2 bis 5 gilt für die Auslegung der Bilanz und für die Erteilung von Abschriften § 175 Abs. 2 sinngemäß.

§ 210
Anmeldung und Eintragung des Beschlusses

(1) Der Anmeldung des Beschlusses zur Eintragung in das Handelsregister ist für das Gericht des

---

capital as may be specified in the articles of incorporation.

(2) The reserves may not be converted if losses are shown in the underlying balance sheet, including any loss carry-forwards, or if some other entry is offset against the capital. Special accounts which, in part, constitute reserves may not be converted. Free reserves earmarked for a special purpose may be converted only to the extent that this accords with their purpose.

§ 209
Underlying Balance Sheet

(1) The resolution may be based on the last annual balance sheet if it has been audited and the established balance sheet has been certified without qualification by the annual auditors, and if its closing date precedes the application to record the resolution in the Commercial Register by no more than eight months.

(2) If the resolution is not based on the last annual balance sheet, the underlying balance sheet must comply with §§ 151 to 156. The closing date of such balance sheet may not precede the application to record the resolution in the Commercial Register by more than eight months.

(3) One or more auditors shall ascertain whether the balance sheet complies with §§ 151 to 156. It must bear an unqualified certification.

(4) Unless the shareholders elect some other auditors, the auditors elected by the shareholders or appointed by the court to audit the last annual financial statements shall be deemed to have been elected. § 163, paragraph 1, third sentence, §§ 164 to 166, 167, paragraph 3, and § 168 shall apply to the audit, unless the peculiarities of the audit assignment require a different result.

(5) In the case of insurance companies, the auditors shall be appointed by the supervisory board; paragraph 4, first sentence, hereof shall apply *mutatis mutandis*. §§ 57 to 59 of the *Gesetz über die Beaufsichtigung der privaten Versicherungsunternehmungen und Bausparkassen* shall apply to the audit, unless the peculiarities of the audit assignment require a different result.

(6) In the cases referred to in paragraphs 2 to 5 hereof, § 175, paragraph 2, shall apply, *mutatis mutandis*, for the interpretation of the balance sheet and the copies to be furnished.

§ 210
Application to Record and Registration of Resolution

(1) For the records of the court at the company's domicile, the application to record the

resolution in the Commercial Register shall be accompanied by the balance sheet underlying the capital increase and bearing the certification, and, in the case of § 209, paragraphs 2 to 6, by the last annual balance sheet as well, unless it has already been filed. The applicants shall declare to the court that, to the best of their knowledge, there has been no decline in the company's assets between the closing date of the underlying balance sheet and the date the application is filed which would bar the capital increase if the resolution were adopted on the date the application is filed.

(2) The court may record the resolution only if the balance sheet underlying the capital increase has been prepared as of a closing date of no more than eight months prior to the date the application is filed, and if a declaration according to paragraph 1, second sentence, hereof has been made.

(3) The court need not examine whether the balance sheet complies with the statutory provisions.

(4) The entry concerning the resolution shall state that the increase in the capital was made out of the company's retained earnings.

(5) An original, duplicate original, or certified copy of the documents filed shall be kept in the court records.

§ 211
Effective Date of Capital Increase

(1) The capital increase shall become effective upon registration of the resolution authorizing the capital increase.

(2) The new shares shall be deemed to be fully paid in.

§ 212
Persons Deriving Rights from Capital Increase

The shareholders shall be entitled to the new shares in proportion to their interests in the existing stated capital. A shareholders' resolution to the contrary shall be void.

§ 213
Fractional Shares

(1) If a capital increase has the effect that an interest entitles its holder to only a fraction of a

Sitzes der Gesellschaft die der Kapitalerhöhung zugrunde gelegte Bilanz mit Bestätigungsvermerk, im Fall des § 209 Abs. 2 bis 6 außerdem die letzte Jahresbilanz, sofern sie noch nicht eingereicht ist, beizufügen. Die Anmeldenden haben dem Gericht gegenüber zu erklären, daß nach ihrer Kenntnis seit dem Stichtag der zugrunde gelegten Bilanz bis zum Tag der Anmeldung keine Vermögensminderung eingetreten ist, die der Kapitalerhöhung entgegenstünde, wenn sie am Tag der Anmeldung beschlossen worden wäre.

(2) Das Gericht darf den Beschluß nur eintragen, wenn die der Kapitalerhöhung zugrunde gelegte Bilanz auf einen höchstens acht Monate vor der Anmeldung liegenden Stichtag aufgestellt und eine Erklärung nach Absatz 1 Satz 2 abgegeben worden ist.

(3) Das Gericht braucht nicht zu prüfen, ob die Bilanzen den gesetzlichen Vorschriften entsprechen.

(4) Bei der Eintragung des Beschlusses ist anzugeben, daß es sich um eine Kapitalerhöhung aus Gesellschaftsmitteln handelt.

(5) Die eingereichten Schriftstücke werden beim Gericht in Urschrift, Ausfertigung oder öffentlich beglaubigter Abschrift aufbewahrt.

§ 211
Wirksamwerden der Kapitalerhöhung

(1) Mit der Eintragung des Beschlusses über die Erhöhung des Grundkapitals ist das Grundkapital erhöht.

(2) Die neuen Aktien gelten als voll eingezahlt.

§ 212
Aus der Kapitalerhöhung Berechtigte

Die neuen Aktien stehen den Aktionären im Verhältnis ihrer Anteile am bisherigen Grundkapital zu. Ein entgegenstehender Beschluß der Hauptversammlung ist nichtig.

§ 213
Teilrechte

(1) Führt die Kapitalerhöhung dazu, daß auf einen Anteil am bisherigen Grundkapital nur ein

Teil einer neuen Aktie entfällt, so ist dieses Teilrecht selbständig veräußerlich und vererblich.

(2) Die Rechte aus einer neuen Aktie einschließlich des Anspruchs auf Ausstellung einer Aktienurkunde können nur ausgeübt werden, wenn Teilrechte, die zusammen eine volle Aktie ergeben, in einer Hand vereinigt sind oder wenn sich mehrere Berechtigte, deren Teilrechte zusammen eine volle Aktie ergeben, zur Ausübung der Rechte zusammenschließen.

§ 214
Aufforderung an die Aktionäre

(1) Nach der Eintragung des Beschlusses über die Erhöhung des Grundkapitals hat der Vorstand unverzüglich die Aktionäre aufzufordern, die neuen Aktien abzuholen. Die Aufforderung ist in den Gesellschaftsblättern bekanntzumachen. In der Bekanntmachung ist anzugeben,

1. um welchen Betrag das Grundkapital erhöht worden ist,
2. in welchem Verhältnis auf die alten Aktien neue Aktien entfallen.

In der Bekanntmachung ist ferner darauf hinzuweisen, daß die Gesellschaft berechtigt ist, Aktien, die nicht innerhalb eines Jahres seit der Bekanntmachung der Aufforderung abgeholt werden, nach dreimaliger Androhung für Rechnung der Beteiligten zu verkaufen.

(2) Nach Ablauf eines Jahres seit der Bekanntmachung der Aufforderung hat die Gesellschaft den Verkauf der nicht abgeholten Aktien anzudrohen. Die Androhung ist dreimal in Abständen von mindestens einem Monat in den Gesellschaftsblättern bekanntzumachen. Die letzte Bekanntmachung muß vor dem Ablauf von achtzehn Monaten seit der Bekanntmachung der Aufforderung ergehen.

(3) Nach Ablauf eines Jahres seit der letzten Bekanntmachung der Androhung hat die Gesellschaft die nicht abgeholten Aktien für Rechnung der Beteiligten zum amtlichen Börsenpreis durch Vermittlung eines Kursmaklers und beim Fehlen eines Börsenpreises durch öffentliche Versteigerung zu verkaufen. § 226 Abs. 3 Satz 2 bis 6 gilt sinngemäß.

(4) Die Absätze 1 bis 3 gelten sinngemäß für Gesellschaften, die keine Aktienurkunden ausgegeben haben. Die Gesellschaften haben die Aktionäre aufzufordern, sich die neuen Aktien zuteilen zu lassen.

---

new share in the previous stated capital, such fractional share can be independently transferred and inherited.

(2) The rights deriving from a new share, including the right to receive a share certificate, can be exercised only if fractional shares which together form a whole share are owned by the same person, or if several of the parties whose fractional shares together form one whole share join to exercise these rights.

§ 214
Notice to the Shareholders

(1) After registration of the resolution authorizing the capital increase, the managing board shall promptly request the shareholders to call for the new share certificates. This request shall be published in the publications designated in the company's articles of incorporation. The publication shall state the following:

1. the amount by which the stated capital has been increased;
2. the proportion of new shares to be issued on the old shares.

The publication shall also make reference to the fact that the company, after three warnings, has the right to sell, for the account of the parties in interest, any shares not called for within one year from the date the request is published.

(2) After the expiration of one year from the date the request is published, the company shall issue a warning that the shares not called for will be sold. The warning shall be published in the publications designated in the company's articles of incorporation three times, at intervals of no less than one month. The last publication shall be made prior to the expiration of eighteen months from the date the request is published.

(3) After the expiration of one year from the last publication of the warning, the company shall sell the shares not called for, for the account of the parties in interest, through a broker at the official stock-exchange quotation and, if there is no stock-exchange quotation, by public auction. § 226, paragraph 3, second to sixth sentences, shall apply *mutatis mutandis*.

(4) Paragraphs 1 to 3 hereof shall apply, *mutatis mutandis*, to companies that have not issued share certificates. Such companies shall request the shareholders to accept the allotment of new shares.

§ 215
Treasury Shares. Shares Paid Up in Part

(1) Treasury shares shall participate in capital increases.

(2) Shares paid up in part shall participate in capital increases in proportion to their par value. With respect to such shares, the capital increase may be effected only by increasing the par value of the shares. If there are fully paid-up shares as well as shares paid up in part, with respect to the former a capital increase may be effected either by increasing the par value of the shares or by issuing new shares; the resolution authorizing the capital increase shall state the manner in which the increase is effected. To the extent that the capital is increased by increasing the par value of the shares, the increase shall be adjusted in such a way as to avoid allocation of amounts to any share which cannot be offset by increasing the par value of the shares.

§ 216
Protection of Rights of Shareholders and Third Parties

(1) The relationship as between the rights attributable to the shares shall not be affected by a capital increase. The issuance of new shares with multiple voting rights and the increase of voting rights of shares with multiple voting rights to comply with the first sentence hereof shall not require the permission specified in § 12, paragraph 2, second sentence.

(2) To the extent that specific rights in shares paid up in part, particularly the right to share in the profit and the right to vote, are determined by the contributions made on the shares, the shareholders shall, until the contributions still outstanding are paid in, have such rights, but only up to the amount of the contribution paid in, increased by the percentage of the capital increase determined by reference to the nominal value of the stated capital. If further contributions are made, these rights shall increase accordingly. In the case of § 271, paragraph 3, the amounts attributable to the increase shall be deemed to be paid up in full.

(3) The substance of contractual relationships of the company with third parties which are dependent on the company's distribution of profits, the nominal amount or the value of its shares or of its stated capital, or otherwise on the previously existing capital or profit ratios, shall not

§ 215
Eigene Aktien. Teileingezahlte Aktien

(1) Eigene Aktien nehmen an der Erhöhung des Grundkapitals teil.

(2) Teileingezahlte Aktien nehmen entsprechend ihrem Nennbetrag an der Erhöhung des Grundkapitals teil. Bei ihnen kann die Kapitalerhöhung nur durch Erhöhung des Nennbetrags der Aktien ausgeführt werden. Sind neben teileingezahlten Aktien volleingezahlte Aktien vorhanden, so kann bei diesen die Kapitalerhöhung durch Erhöhung des Nennbetrags der Aktien und durch Ausgabe neuer Aktien ausgeführt werden; der Beschluß über die Erhöhung des Grundkapitals muß die Art der Erhöhung angeben. Soweit die Kapitalerhöhung durch Erhöhung des Nennbetrags der Aktien ausgeführt wird, ist sie so zu bemessen, daß durch sie auf keine Aktie Beträge entfallen, die durch eine Erhöhung des Nennbetrags der Aktien nicht gedeckt werden können.

§ 216
Wahrung der Rechte der Aktionäre und Dritter

(1) Das Verhältnis der mit den Aktien verbundenen Rechte zueinander wird durch die Kapitalerhöhung nicht berührt. Die Ausgabe neuer Mehrstimmrechtsaktien und die Erhöhung des Stimmrechts von Mehrstimmrechtsaktien auf Grund des Satzes 1 bedürfen keiner Zulassung nach § 12 Abs. 2 Satz 2.

(2) Soweit sich einzelne Rechte teileingezahlter Aktien, insbesondere die Beteiligung am Gewinn oder das Stimmrecht, nach der auf die Aktie geleisteten Einlage bestimmen, stehen diese Rechte den Aktionären bis zur Leistung der noch ausstehenden Einlagen nur nach der Höhe der geleisteten Einlage, erhöht um den auf den Nennbetrag des Grundkapitals berechneten Hundertsatz der Erhöhung des Grundkapitals zu. Werden weitere Einzahlungen geleistet, so erweitern sich diese Rechte entsprechend. Im Fall des § 271 Abs. 3 gelten die Erhöhungsbeträge als voll eingezahlt.

(3) Der wirtschaftliche Inhalt vertraglicher Beziehungen der Gesellschaft zu Dritten, die von der Gewinnausschüttung der Gesellschaft, dem Nennbetrag oder Wert ihrer Aktien oder ihres Grundkapitals oder sonst von den bisherigen Kapital- oder

Gewinnverhältnissen abhängen, wird durch die Kapitalerhöhung nicht berührt. Gleiches gilt fü Nebenverpflichtungen der Aktionäre.

§ 217
Beginn der Gewinnbeteiligung

(1) Die neuen Aktien nehmen, wenn nichts anderes bestimmt ist, am Gewinn des ganzen Geschäftsjahrs teil, in dem die Erhöhung des Grundkapitals beschlossen worden ist.

(2) Im Beschluß über die Erhöhung des Grundkapitals kann bestimmt werden, daß die neuen Aktien bereits am Gewinn des letzten vor der Beschlußfassung über die Kapitalerhöhung abgelaufenen Geschäftsjahrs teilnehmen. In diesem Fall ist die Erhöhung des Grundkapitals zu beschließen, bevor über die Verwendung des Bilanzgewinns des letzten vor der Beschlußfassung abgelaufenen Geschäftsjahrs Beschluß gefaßt ist. Der Beschluß über die Erhöhung des Grundkapitals und der Beschluß über die Verwendung des Bilanzgewinns des letzten vor der Beschlußfassung über die Kapitalerhöhung abgelaufenen Geschäftsjahrs wird erst wirksam, wenn das Grundkapital erhöht ist. Der Beschluß über die Erhöhung des Grundkapitals und der Beschluß über die Verwendung des Bilanzgewinns des letzten vor der Beschlußfassung über die Kapitalerhöhung abgelaufenen Geschäftsjahrs sind nichtig, wenn der Beschluß über die Kapitalerhöhung nicht binnen drei Monaten nach der Beschlußfassung in das Handelsregister eingetragen worden ist. Der Lauf der Frist ist gehemmt, solange eine Anfechtungs- oder Nichtigkeitsklage rechtshängig ist oder eine zur Kapitalerhöhung beantragte staatliche Genehmigung noch nicht erteilt ist.

§ 218
Bedingtes Kapital

Bedingtes Kapital erhöht sich im gleichen Verhältnis wie das Grundkapital. Ist das bedingte Kapital zur Gewährung von Umtauschrechten an Gläubiger von Wandelschuldverschreibungen beschlossen worden, so ist zur Deckung des Unterschieds zwischen dem Ausgabebetrag der Schuldverschreibungen und dem höheren Gesamtnennbetrag der für sie zu gewährenden Bezugsaktien eine Sonderrücklage zu bilden, soweit nicht Zuzahlungen der Umtauschberechtigten vereinbart sind.

be affected by the capital increase. The same shall apply with respect to other obligations of the shareholders.

§ 217
Beginning of Profit Participation

(1) Unless otherwise provided, the new shares shall confer the right to participate in profits for the full fiscal year in which the resolution authorizing the capital increase was adopted.

(2) The resolution authorizing the capital increase may provide that the new shares shall confer the right to participate in profits for the fiscal year which ended prior to the resolution authorizing the capital increase. In this event, the resolution authorizing the capital increase shall be adopted before adoption of the resolution authorizing the disposition of the retained earnings of the fiscal year which ended prior to the date of the former resolution. The resolution authorizing the disposition of the retained earnings for the last fiscal year which ended prior to the resolution authorizing the capital increase shall become effective only upon consummation of the capital increase. The resolution authorizing the capital increase and the resolution authorizing the disposition of the retained earnings for the last fiscal year which ended prior to the date of the resolution authorizing the capital increase shall be void if the resolution authorizing the capital increase is not recorded in the Commercial Register within three months from the date it was adopted. This period shall be tolled for as long as an action to set aside the resolution or to declare it void is pending or a petition for governmental authorization of the capital increase has not yet been granted.

§ 218
Conditional Capital

Conditional capital shall increase in the same proportion as the stated capital. If conditional capital has been created for the purpose of granting conversion rights to creditors holding convertible bonds, a special reserve shall be formed to offset the difference between the amount for which the convertible bonds are issued and the higher total par value of the shares to be issued therefor, unless it is stipulated that the parties entitled to the conversion are required to make additional payments.

§ 218

§ 219
Prohibited Issuance of Share and Interim Certificates

New share certificates and interim certificates may not be issued before the resolution authorizing the capital increase has been recorded in the Commercial Register.

§ 219

Verbotene Ausgabe von Aktien und Zwischenscheinen

Vor der Eintragung des Beschlusses über die Erhöhung des Grundkapitals in das Handelsregister dürfen neue Aktien und Zwischenscheine nicht ausgegeben werden.

§ 220
Valuations

The cost of acquisition of the shares acquired prior to the capital increase and of the new shares allotted to them shall be deemed to be the amounts attributable to the particular shares if the acquisition cost of the shares acquired prior to the capital increase is prorated between such shares and the new shares issued for them on the basis of their respective par values. The additional shares may not be shown as newly acquired assets.

§ 220

Wertansätze

Als Anschaffungskosten der vor der Erhöhung des Grundkapitals erworbenen Aktien und der auf sie entfallenen neuen Aktien gelten die Beträge, die sich für die einzelnen Aktien ergeben, wenn die Anschaffungskosten der vor der Erhöhung des Grundkapitals erworbenen Aktien auf diese und auf die auf sie entfallenen neuen Aktien nach dem Verhältnis der Nennbeträge verteilt werden. Der Zuwachs an Aktien ist nicht als Zugang auszuweisen.

Fifth Subdivision
Convertible Bonds.
Profit Participation Bonds

Fünfter Unterabschnitt

Wandelschuldverschreibungen.
Gewinnschuldverschreibungen

§ 221

(1) Bonds which grant creditors a right of conversion or subscription to shares (convertible bonds) and bonds which link the rights of creditors to distributions to shareholders (dividend bonds) may be issued only pursuant to a shareholders' resolution. The resolution shall require a majority of no less than three-fourths of the stated capital represented when the resolution is adopted. The articles of incorporation may provide for a higher capital majority and establish additional requirements.

(2) Paragraph 1 hereof shall apply, *mutatis mutandis*, to the issuance of other types of debentures.

(3) The shareholders shall have preemptive rights to convertible bonds, profit participation bonds, and other types of debentures. § 186 shall apply *mutatis mutandis*.

§ 221

(1) Schuldverschreibungen, bei denen den Gläubigern ein Umtausch- oder Bezugsrecht auf Aktien eingeräumt wird (Wandelschuldverschreibungen), und Schuldverschreibungen, bei denen die Rechte der Gläubiger mit Gewinnanteilen von Aktionären in Verbindung gebracht werden (Gewinnschuldverschreibungen), dürfen nur auf Grund eines Beschlusses der Hauptversammlung ausgegeben werden. Der Beschluß bedarf einer Mehrheit, die mindestens drei Viertel des bei der Beschlußfassung vertretenen Grundkapitals umfaßt. Die Satzung kann eine andere Kapitalmehrheit und weitere Erfordernisse bestimmen. § 182 Abs. 2 gilt.

(2) Absatz 1 gilt sinngemäß für die Gewährung von Genußrechten.

(3) Auf Wandelschuldverschreibungen, Gewinnschuldverschreibungen und Genußrechte haben die Aktionäre ein Bezugsrecht. § 186 gilt sinngemäß.

Dritter Abschnitt

Maßnahmen der Kapitalherabsetzung

Erster Unterabschnitt

Ordentliche Kapitalherabsetzung

§ 222

Voraussetzungen

(1) Eine Herabsetzung des Grundkapitals kann nur mit einer Mehrheit beschlossen werden, die mindestens drei Viertel des bei der Beschlußfassung vertretenen Grundkapitals umfaßt. Die Satzung kann eine größere Kapitalmehrheit und weitere Erfordernisse bestimmen.

(2) Sind mehrere Gattungen von Aktien vorhanden, so bedarf der Beschluß der Hauptversammlung zu seiner Wirksamkeit der Zustimmung der Aktionäre jeder Gattung. Über die Zustimmung haben die Aktionäre jeder Gattung einen Sonderbeschluß zu fassen. Für diesen gilt Absatz 1.

(3) In dem Beschluß ist festzusetzen, zu welchem Zweck die Herabsetzung stattfindet, namentlich ob Teile des Grundkapitals zurückgezahlt werden sollen.

(4) Das Grundkapital kann herabgesetzt werden
1. durch Herabsetzung des Nennbetrags der Aktien;
2. durch Zusammenlegung der Aktien; diese ist nur zulässig, soweit der Mindestnennbetrag für Aktien nicht innegehalten werden kann.

Der Beschluß muß die Art der Herabsetzung angeben.

§ 223

Anmeldung des Beschlusses

Der Vorstand und der Vorsitzende des Aufsichtsrats haben den Beschluß über die Herabsetzung des Grundkapitals zur Eintragung in das Handelsregister anzumelden.

§ 224

Wirksamwerden der Kapitalherabsetzung

Mit der Eintragung des Beschlusses über die Herabsetzung des Grundkapitals ist das Grundkapital herabgesetzt.

§ 225

Gläubigerschutz

(1) Den Gläubigern, deren Forderungen begründet worden sind, bevor die Eintragung des Beschlusses bekanntgemacht worden ist, ist, wenn sie sich

Third Division
Measures to Reduce Capital

First Subdivision
Ordinary Capital Reduction

§ 222
Prerequisites

(1) A resolution to reduce the stated capital shall require a majority of no less than three-fourths of the stated capital represented when the resolution is adopted. The articles of incorporation may provide for a higher capital majority and establish additional requirements.

(2) If there are several classes of shares, the shareholders' resolution shall, in order to be valid, require the approval of the shareholders of each class. The shareholders of each class shall adopt a separate resolution authorizing such approval. Paragraph 1 hereof shall apply to such resolution.

(3) The resolution shall specify the purpose of the reduction, in particular whether part of the stated capital is to be repaid to shareholders.

(4) The stated capital may be reduced:
1. by reducing the par value of the shares;
2. by consolidating the shares; such consolidation shall be permissible only to the extent that the minimum par value of shares cannot be maintained.
The resolution must specify the manner in which the capital is reduced.

§ 223
Application to Record Resolution

The managing board and the chairman of the supervisory board shall file an application to record the resolution authorizing the capital reduction in the Commercial Register.

§ 224
Effective Date of Capital Reduction

The capital reduction shall become effective upon registration of the resolution authorizing the capital reduction.

§ 225
Protection of Creditors

(1) Creditors whose claims arose prior to the publication of the registration of the resolution shall be furnished security to the extent that

they cannot demand performance, provided that they make a request to this effect within six months from the date of publication. The creditors shall be advised of this right in the publication of the registration. The right to request security shall not be available to creditors who, in the event of bankruptcy, would have a claim to preferred satisfaction from a fund which was established by statute for their protection and which is subject to governmental supervision.

(2) Payments to shareholders in pursuance of the reduction of the stated capital may be made only after the expiration of six months from the date of publication of the registration and after satisfying or securing the creditors who made a timely request. Similarly, a waiver of the obligation of shareholders to make contributions shall not take effect before the above-mentioned time and before the creditors who made a timely request have been satisfied or secured.

(3) Creditors may request security irrespective of whether payments to shareholders are made in pursuance of the capital reduction.

§ 226
Cancellation of Share Certificates

(1) If, to consummate a capital reduction, shares are to be consolidated by exchanging or stamping share certificates or a similar procedure, the company may cancel any share certificates that have not been surrendered to it despite a request to this effect. The same shall apply with respect to share certificates surrendered which together do not reach the number required for replacement by new shares and were not put at the disposal of the company to be used for the account of the parties in interest.

(2) The notice requesting surrender of share certificates shall contain the warning that they may be cancelled. The cancellation may be effected only if such notice has been published in the manner provided for in § 64, paragraph 2, with respect to the grace period. The cancellation shall take effect upon publication in the publications designated in the company's articles of incorporation. This publication shall designate the share certificates cancelled in such a manner that the publication clearly indicates whether or not a specific share certificate has been cancelled.

(3) The new shares to be issued for the cancelled shares shall be sold by the company without delay, for the account of the parties in inter-

§ 226

binnen sechs Monaten nach der Bekanntmachung zu diesem Zweck melden, Sicherheit zu leisten, soweit sie nicht Befriedigung verlangen können. Die Gläubiger sind in der Bekanntmachung der Eintragung auf dieses Recht hinzuweisen. Das Recht, Sicherheitsleistung zu verlangen, steht Gläubigern nicht zu, die im Fall des Konkurses ein Recht auf vorzugsweise Befriedigung aus einer Deckungsmasse haben, die nach gesetzlicher Vorschrift zu ihrem Schutz errichtet und staatlich überwacht ist.

(2) Zahlungen an die Aktionäre dürfen auf Grund der Herabsetzung des Grundkapitals erst geleistet werden, nachdem seit der Bekanntmachung der Eintragung sechs Monate verstrichen sind und nachdem den Gläubigern, die sich rechtzeitig gemeldet haben, Befriedigung oder Sicherheit gewährt worden ist. Auch eine Befreiung der Aktionäre von der Verpflichtung zur Leistung von Einlagen wird nicht vor dem bezeichneten Zeitpunkt und nicht vor Befriedigung oder Sicherstellung der Gläubiger wirksam, die sich rechtzeitig gemeldet haben.

(3) Das Recht der Gläubiger, Sicherheitsleistung zu verlangen, ist unabhängig davon, ob Zahlungen an die Aktionäre auf Grund der Herabsetzung des Grundkapitals geleistet werden.

§ 226
Kraftloserklärung von Aktien

(1) Sollen zur Durchführung der Herabsetzung des Grundkapitals Aktien durch Umtausch, Abstempelung oder durch ein ähnliches Verfahren zusammengelegt werden, so kann die Gesellschaft die Aktien für kraftlos erklären, die trotz Aufforderung nicht bei ihr eingereicht worden sind. Gleiches gilt für eingereichte Aktien, welche die zum Ersatz durch neue Aktien nötige Zahl nicht erreichen und der Gesellschaft nicht zur Verwertung für Rechnung der Beteiligten zur Verfügung gestellt sind.

(2) Die Aufforderung, die Aktien einzureichen, hat die Kraftloserklärung anzudrohen. Die Kraftloserklärung kann nur erfolgen, wenn die Aufforderung in der in § 64 Abs. 2 für die Nachfrist vorgeschriebenen Weise bekanntgemacht worden ist. Die Kraftloserklärung geschieht durch Bekanntmachung in den Gesellschaftsblättern. In der Bekanntmachung sind die für kraftlos erklärten Aktien so zu bezeichnen, daß sich aus der Bekanntmachung ohne weiteres ergibt, ob eine Aktie für kraftlos erklärt ist.

(3) Die neuen Aktien, die an Stelle der für kraftlos erklärten Aktien auszugeben sind, hat die Gesellschaft unverzüglich für Rechnung der Beteiligten

zum amtlichen Börsenpreis durch Vermittlung eines Kursmaklers und beim Fehlen eines Börsenpreises durch öffentliche Versteigerung zu verkaufen. Ist von der Versteigerung am Sitz der Gesellschaft kein angemessener Erfolg zu erwarten, so sind die Aktien an einem geeigneten Ort zu verkaufen. Zeit, Ort und Gegenstand der Versteigerung sind öffentlich bekanntzumachen. Die Beteiligten sind besonders zu benachrichtigen; die Benachrichtigung kann unterbleiben, wenn sie untunlich ist. Bekanntmachung und Benachrichtigung müssen mindestens zwei Wochen vor der Versteigerung ergehen. Der Erlös ist den Beteiligten auszuzahlen oder, wenn ein Recht zur Hinterlegung besteht, zu hinterlegen.

est, through a broker at the official stock exchange quotation and, if no official stock exchange quotation is available, by public auction. If a satisfactory result cannot be expected from an auction at the company's domicile, the shares shall be sold at a suitable location. The time, place and object of the auction shall be made public. The parties in interest shall be given specific notice; however, such notice may be omitted if it is impracticable. The publication and the notice shall be effected no less than two weeks prior to the auction. The proceeds shall be paid over to the parties in interest or, if a right to deposit exists, be deposited.

§ 227
Anmeldung der Durchführung

(1) Der Vorstand hat die Durchführung der Herabsetzung des Grundkapitals zur Eintragung in das Handelsregister anzumelden.

(2) Anmeldung und Eintragung der Durchführung der Herabsetzung des Grundkapitals können mit Anmeldung und Eintragung des Beschlusses über die Herabsetzung verbunden werden.

§ 227
Application to Record Consummation

(1) The managing board shall file an application to record the consummation of the capital reduction in the Commercial Register.

(2) The application and registration of the consummation of the capital reduction may be combined with the application and registration of the resolution authorizing the capital reduction.

§ 228
Herabsetzung unter den Mindestnennbetrag

(1) Das Grundkapital kann unter den in § 7 bestimmten Mindestnennbetrag herabgesetzt werden, wenn dieser durch eine Kapitalerhöhung wieder erreicht wird, die zugleich mit der Kapitalherabsetzung beschlossen ist und bei der Sacheinlagen nicht festgesetzt sind.

(2) Die Beschlüsse sind nichtig, wenn sie und die Durchführung der Erhöhung nicht binnen sechs Monaten nach der Beschlußfassung in das Handelsregister eingetragen worden sind. Der Lauf der Frist ist gehemmt, solange eine Anfechtungs- oder Nichtigkeitsklage rechtshängig ist oder eine zur Kapitalherabsetzung oder Kapitalerhöhung beantragte staatliche Genehmigung noch nicht erteilt ist. Die Beschlüsse und die Durchführung der Erhöhung des Grundkapitals sollen nur zusammen in das Handelsregister eingetragen werden.

§ 228
Reduction Below Minimum Nominal Amount

(1) The stated capital may be reduced below the minimum nominal amount specified in § 7 if this amount can be restored by means of a capital increase which is adopted in the same resolution as the capital reduction and which does not call for contributions of assets.

(2) The resolutions shall be void unless they and the consummation of the increase are recorded in the Commercial Register within six months from the date they were adopted. The running of this period shall be tolled for as long as an action to set aside the resolutions or to declare them void is pending or a petition for governmental authorization of the capital reduction or capital increase has not been granted. The resolutions and the consummation of the capital increase shall always be recorded in the Commercial Register together.

Zweiter Unterabschnitt

Vereinfachte Kapitalherabsetzung

Second Subdivision

Simplified Capital Reduction

§ 229
Voraussetzungen

(1) Eine Herabsetzung des Grundkapitals, die dazu dienen soll, Wertminderungen auszugleichen, son-

§ 229
Prerequisites

(1) A capital reduction which has the purpose of offsetting a decline in the value of assets, of

§ 229

covering other losses, or of allocating amounts to the statutory reserve may be effected in simplified form. The resolution shall state that the reduction serves such purposes.

(2) The simplified capital reduction shall be permissible only after releasing the free reserves and such portion of the statutory reserve as exceeds ten percent of the stated capital remaining after the reduction. It shall not be permissible as long as there are retained earnings.

(3) § 222, paragraphs 1, 2 and 4, §§ 223, 224, and 226 to 228, concerning ordinary capital reductions, shall apply *mutatis mutandis.*

§ 230
Prohibited Payments to Shareholders

The amounts resulting from a release of disclosed reserves and from the capital reduction may be used neither to effect payments to shareholders nor to waive the shareholders' obligation to make contributions. They may be used only to offset a decline in the value of assets, to cover other losses, and to allocate amounts to the statutory reserve. However, the use for any one of these purposes is permissible, but only to the extent that the resolution states it to be the purpose of the reduction.

§ 231
Limited Allocation to Statutory Reserve

The amounts resulting from a release of free reserves or a capital reduction may be allocated to the statutory reserve only to the extent that such reserve does not exceed ten percent of the stated capital. In this connection, stated capital shall mean the nominal amount after the reduction, but no less than the minimum nominal amount specified in § 7. In determining the permissible amount, amounts to be allocated to the statutory reserve pursuant to § 150, paragraph 2, Nos. 2 to 4, following adoption of the resolution authorizing the capital reduction shall not be taken into account, even if payment thereof is based on a resolution adopted together with the resolution authorizing the capital reduction.

§ 232
Allocation of Amounts to Statutory Reserve in Case of Overestimated Losses

If, upon drawing up the annual balance sheet for the fiscal year in which the resolution au-

stige Verluste zu decken oder Beträge in die gesetzliche Rücklage einzustellen, kann in vereinfachter Form vorgenommen werden. Im Beschluß ist festzusetzen, daß die Herabsetzung zu diesen Zwecken stattfindet.

(2) Die vereinfachte Kapitalherabsetzung ist nur zulässig, nachdem der Teil der gesetzlichen Rücklage, der über zehn vom Hundert des nach der Herabsetzung verbleibenden Grundkapitals hinausgeht, und die freien Rücklagen vorweg aufgelöst sind. Sie ist nicht zulässig, solange ein Gewinnvortrag vorhanden ist.

(3) § 222 Abs. 1, 2 und 4, §§ 223, 224, 226 bis 228 über die ordentliche Kapitalherabsetzung gelten sinngemäß.

§ 230
Verbot von Zahlungen an die Aktionäre

Die Beträge, die aus der Auflösung der offenen Rücklagen und aus der Kapitalherabsetzung gewonnen werden, dürfen nicht zu Zahlungen an die Aktionäre und nicht dazu verwandt werden, die Aktionäre von der Verpflichtung zur Leistung von Einlagen zu befreien. Sie dürfen nur verwandt werden, um Wertminderungen auszugleichen, sonstige Verluste zu decken und Beträge in die gesetzliche Rücklage einzustellen. Auch eine Verwendung zu einem dieser Zwecke ist nur zulässig, soweit sie im Beschluß als Zweck der Herabsetzung angegeben ist.

§ 231
Beschränkte Einstellung in die gesetzliche Rücklage

Die Beträge, die aus der Auflösung der freien Rücklagen und aus der Kapitalherabsetzung gewonnen werden, dürfen in die gesetzliche Rücklage nur eingestellt werden, soweit diese zehn vom Hundert des Grundkapitals nicht übersteigt. Als Grundkapital gilt dabei der Nennbetrag, der sich durch die Herabsetzung ergibt, mindestens aber der in § 7 bestimmte Mindestnennbetrag. Bei der Bemessung der zulässigen Höhe bleiben Beträge, die in der Zeit nach der Beschlußfassung über die Kapitalherabsetzung nach § 150 Abs. 2 Nr. 2 bis 4 in die gesetzliche Rücklage einzustellen sind, auch dann außer Betracht, wenn ihre Zahlung auf einem Beschluß beruht, der zugleich mit dem Beschluß über die Kapitalherabsetzung gefaßt wird.

§ 232
Einstellung von Beträgen in die gesetzliche Rücklage bei zu hoch angenommenen Verlusten

Ergibt sich bei Aufstellung der Jahresbilanz für das Geschäftsjahr, in dem der Beschluß über die

§ 230

Kapitalherabsetzung gefaßt wurde, oder für eines der beiden folgenden Geschäftsjahre, daß Wertminderungen und sonstige Verluste in der bei der Beschlußfassung angenommenen Höhe tatsächlich nicht eingetreten oder ausgeglichen waren, so ist der Unterschiedsbetrag in die gesetzliche Rücklage einzustellen.

§ 233

Gewinnausschüttung. Gläubigerschutz

(1) Gewinn darf nicht ausgeschüttet werden, bevor die gesetzliche Rücklage zehn vom Hundert des Grundkapitals erreicht hat. Als Grundkapital gilt dabei der Nennbetrag, der sich durch die Herabsetzung ergibt, mindestens aber der in § 7 bestimmte Mindestnennbetrag.

(2) Die Zahlung eines Gewinnanteils von mehr als vier vom Hundert ist erst für ein Geschäftsjahr zulässig, das später als zwei Jahre nach der Beschlußfassung über die Kapitalherabsetzung beginnt. Dies gilt nicht, wenn die Gläubiger, deren Forderungen vor der Bekanntmachung der Eintragung des Beschlusses begründet worden waren, befriedigt oder sichergestellt sind, soweit sie sich binnen sechs Monaten nach der Bekanntmachung des Jahresabschlusses, auf Grund dessen die Gewinnverteilung beschlossen ist, zu diesem Zweck gemeldet haben. Einer Sicherstellung der Gläubiger bedarf es nicht, die im Fall des Konkurses ein Recht auf vorzugsweise Befriedigung aus einer Deckungsmasse haben, die nach gesetzlicher Vorschrift zu ihrem Schutz errichtet und staatlich überwacht ist. Die Gläubiger sind in der Bekanntmachung des Jahresabschlusses auf die Befriedigung oder Sicherstellung hinzuweisen.

(3) Die Beträge, die aus der Auflösung von offenen Rücklagen und aus der Kapitalherabsetzung gewonnen sind, dürfen auch nach diesen Vorschriften nicht als Gewinn ausgeschüttet werden.

§ 234

Rückwirkung der Kapitalherabsetzung

(1) Im Jahresabschluß für das letzte vor der Beschlußfassung über die Kapitalherabsetzung abgelaufene Geschäftsjahr können Grundkapital und offene Rücklagen in der Höhe ausgewiesen werden, in der sie nach der Kapitalherabsetzung bestehen sollen.

(2) In diesem Fall beschließt die Hauptversammlung über die Feststellung des Jahresabschlusses.

thorizing the capital reduction was adopted or for either of the two following fiscal years, it appears that a decline in value of assets or other losses did in fact not occur to the extent assumed when the resolution was adopted, or that it was offset, the amount of the difference shall be allocated to the statutory reserve.

§ 233

**Distribution of Profits.
Protection of Creditors**

(1) Profits may not be distributed before the statutory reserve reaches ten percent of the stated capital. Stated capital shall be deemed to mean the nominal amount resulting from the reduction, but no less than the minimum nominal amount specified in § 7.

(2) The distribution of a share of the profits in excess of four percent is permissible only for a fiscal year commencing later than two years after the date of the resolution authorizing the capital reduction. This shall not apply if creditors whose rights arose prior to the publication of the registration of the resolution are satisfied or furnished security, provided that they notified the company for this purpose within six months from the date of publication of the annual financial statements on the basis of which the distribution of profits was determined. No security shall be required with respect to creditors who, in the event of bankruptcy, would have a claim to preferred satisfaction from a fund which was established by statute for their protection and which is subject to governmental supervision. The creditors shall be advised of the right to such satisfaction or security in the publication of the annual financial statements.

(3) These provisions do not authorize a distribution as profits of amounts resulting from the release of disclosed reserves or from a capital reduction.

§ 234

Retroactive Effect of Capital Reduction

(1) In the annual financial statements for the fiscal year last preceding the year in which the resolution authorizing the capital reduction was adopted, the stated capital and disclosed reserves may be shown at the figures as they will be after the capital reduction.

(2) In this event, the shareholders shall adopt the resolution authorizing the establishment of

the annual financial statements. The resolution shall be adopted together with the resolution authorizing the capital reduction.

(3) These resolutions shall be void unless the resolution authorizing the capital reduction is recorded in the Commercial Register within three months from the date of its adoption. This period shall be tolled for as long as an action to set aside the resolution or to declare it void is pending or a petition for governmental authorization of the capital reduction has not yet been granted.

§ 235
Retroactive Effect of a Simultaneous Capital Increase

(1) If, in the case of § 234, a resolution to increase the stated capital is adopted simultaneously with the capital reduction, the annual financial statements may likewise show the capital increase as having been effected. This resolution may be adopted only if all new shares have been subscribed to, if no assets are to be contributed, and if payment on each share had been made at the time the application to record the consummation of the capital increase in accordance with § 188, paragraph 2, was filed. Evidence of the subscription and the payment shall be furnished to the judge or the notary recording the resolution authorizing the capital increase.

(2) All the aforementioned resolutions shall be void unless the resolutions authorizing the capital reduction and the capital increase and the consummation of the increase are recorded in the Commercial Register within three months from the date of their adoption. This period shall be tolled for as long as an action to set aside the resolution or to declare it void is pending or a petition for governmental authorization of the capital reduction or the capital increase has not been granted. The resolutions and the consummation of the capital increase shall always be recorded in the Commercial Register together.

§ 236
Publication

The publication of the annual financial statements pursuant to § 177, paragraph 2, may, in the case of § 234, be effected only after registration of the resolution authorizing the capital reduction; in the case of § 235, it may be effected only after the resolutions authorizing the capital reduction and capital increase and the consummation of the capital increase have been recorded.

Der Beschluß soll zugleich mit dem Beschluß über die Kapitalherabsetzung gefaßt werden.

(3) Die Beschlüsse sind nichtig, wenn der Beschluß über die Kapitalherabsetzung nicht binnen drei Monaten nach der Beschlußfassung in das Handelsregister eingetragen worden ist. Der Lauf der Frist ist gehemmt, solange eine Anfechtungs- oder Nichtigkeitsklage rechtshängig ist oder eine zur Kapitalherabsetzung beantragte staatliche Genehmigung noch nicht erteilt ist.

§ 235
Rückwirkung einer gleichzeitigen Kapitalerhöhung

(1) Wird im Fall des § 234 zugleich mit der Kapitalherabsetzung eine Erhöhung des Grundkapitals beschlossen, so kann auch die Kapitalerhöhung in dem Jahresabschluß als vollzogen berücksichtigt werden. Die Beschlußfassung ist nur zulässig, wenn die neuen Aktien gezeichnet, keine Sacheinlagen festgesetzt sind und wenn auf jede Aktie die Einzahlung geleistet ist, die nach § 188 Abs. 2 zur Zeit der Anmeldung der Durchführung der Kapitalerhöhung bewirkt sein muß. Die Zeichnung und die Einzahlung sind dem Richter oder dem Notar nachzuweisen, der den Beschluß über die Erhöhung des Grundkapitals beurkundet.

(2) Sämtliche Beschlüsse sind nichtig, wenn die Beschlüsse über die Kapitalherabsetzung und die Kapitalerhöhung und die Durchführung der Erhöhung nicht binnen drei Monaten nach der Beschlußfassung in das Handelsregister eingetragen worden sind. Der Lauf der Frist ist gehemmt, solange eine Anfechtungs- oder Nichtigkeitsklage rechtshängig ist oder eine zur Kapitalherabsetzung oder Kapitalerhöhung beantragte staatliche Genehmigung noch nicht erteilt ist. Die Beschlüsse und die Durchführung der Erhöhung des Grundkapitals sollen nur zusammen in das Handelsregister eingetragen werden.

§ 236
Bekanntmachung

Die Bekanntmachung des Jahresabschlusses nach § 177 Abs. 2 darf im Fall des § 234 erst nach Eintragung des Beschlusses über die Kapitalherabsetzung, im Fall des § 235 erst ergehen, nachdem die Beschlüsse über die Kapitalherabsetzung und Kapitalerhöhung und die Durchführung der Kapitalerhöhung eingetragen worden sind.

<table>
<tr>
<td>

Dritter Unterabschnitt

Kapitalherabsetzung durch Einziehung von Aktien

§ 237

Voraussetzungen

(1) Aktien können zwangsweise oder nach Erwerb durch die Gesellschaft eingezogen werden. Eine Zwangseinziehung ist nur zulässig, wenn sie in der ursprünglichen Satzung oder durch eine Satzungsänderung vor Übernahme oder Zeichnung der Aktien angeordnet oder gestattet war.

(2) Bei der Einziehung sind die Vorschriften über die ordentliche Kapitalherabsetzung zu befolgen. Für die Zahlung des Entgelts, das Aktionären bei einer Zwangseinziehung oder bei einem Erwerb von Aktien zum Zwecke der Einziehung gewährt wird, und für die Befreiung dieser Aktionäre von der Verpflichtung zur Leistung von Einlagen gilt § 225 Abs. 2 sinngemäß.

(3) Die Vorschriften über die ordentliche Kapitalherabsetzung brauchen nicht befolgt zu werden, wenn Aktien, auf die der Nennbetrag oder der höhere Ausgabebetrag voll geleistet ist,
1. der Gesellschaft unentgeltlich zur Verfügung gestellt oder
2. zu Lasten des Bilanzgewinns oder einer freien Rücklage, soweit sie zu diesem Zweck verwandt werden können, eingezogen werden.

(4) Auch in den Fällen des Absatzes 3 kann die Kapitalherabsetzung durch Einziehung nur von der Hauptversammlung beschlossen werden. Für den Beschluß genügt die einfache Stimmenmehrheit. Die Satzung kann eine größere Mehrheit und weitere Erfordernisse bestimmen. Im Beschluß ist der Zweck der Kapitalherabsetzung festzusetzen. Der Vorstand und der Vorsitzende des Aufsichtsrats haben den Beschluß zur Eintragung in das Handelsregister anzumelden.

(5) In den Fällen des Absatzes 3 ist in die gesetzliche Rücklage ein Betrag einzustellen, der dem Gesamtnennbetrag der eingezogenen Aktien gleichkommt.

(6) Soweit es sich um eine durch die Satzung angeordnete Zwangseinziehung handelt, bedarf es eines Beschlusses der Hauptversammlung nicht. In diesem Fall tritt für die Anwendung der Vorschriften über die ordentliche Kapitalherabsetzung an die Stelle des Hauptversammlungsbeschlusses die Entscheidung des Vorstands über die Einziehung.

</td>
<td>

Third Subdivision

Capital Reduction by Cancellation of Shares

§ 237

Prerequisites

(1) Shares may be cancelled by means of a compulsory redemption or after acquisition by the company. Compulsory redemption is permissible only if required by or permitted in the original articles of incorporation or in an amendment thereof before the acquisition or the subscription of the shares.

(2) The cancellation shall be subject to the provisions governing ordinary capital reductions. § 225, paragraph 2, shall apply, *mutatis mutandis*, with respect to the indemnity payment to be made to shareholders in connection with a compulsory redemption or an acquisition of shares for purposes of cancellation and with respect to the discharge of these shareholders from the obligation to make contributions.

(3) The provisions governing ordinary capital reductions need not be complied with if shares, with respect to which the par value plus any premium has been paid in full,
1. are returned to the company gratuitously, or
2. are cancelled by debiting the retained earnings or a free reserve, to the extent that they can be used for this purpose.

(4) In the case of paragraph 3 hereof, a capital reduction by means of a cancellation of shares shall likewise require a shareholders' resolution. A simple majority of votes shall suffice to adopt such resolution. The articles of incorporation may provide for a higher majority and establish additional requirements. The resolution shall specify the purpose of the capital reduction. The managing board and the chairman of the supervisory board shall file an application to record the resolution in the Commercial Register.

(5) In the case of paragraph 3 hereof, an amount equal to the total par value of the shares cancelled shall be allocated to the statutory reserve.

(6) In the case of a compulsory redemption required by the articles of incorporation, no shareholders' resolution shall be required. In this event, the resolution of the managing board authorizing the cancellation shall be substituted for the shareholders' resolution for purposes of the application of the provisions concerning an ordinary capital reduction.

</td>
</tr>
</table>

§ 237

§ 238
Effective Date of Capital Reduction

The reduction of the stated capital by the amount of the total par value of the shares cancelled shall become effective upon registration of the resolution or, in the case of a subsequent cancellation, upon such cancellation. In the case of a compulsory redemption required by the articles of incorporation, the capital reduction shall become effective upon such compulsory redemption, unless the shareholders adopt a resolution authorizing the capital reduction. Cancellation shall require an affirmative act of the company aimed at nullifying the rights deriving from specific shares.

§ 239
Application to Record Consummation

(1) The managing board shall file an application to record the consummation of the capital reduction in the Commercial Register. This shall also apply in the case of a compulsory redemption required by the articles of incorporation.

(2) The application and registration of the consummation of the capital reduction may be combined with the application and registration of the resolution authorizing the capital reduction.

Fourth Subdivision

Accounting Treatment of Capital Reduction

§ 240

The amount resulting from the capital reduction shall be shown separately in the profit and loss statement as "income from capital reduction," following the item "reduction of disclosed reserves." An allocation to the statutory reserve pursuant to § 229, paragraph 1, and § 232 shall be shown separately as "allocation to statutory reserve pursuant to provisions on simplified capital reduction." The business report shall explain whether and to what extent the amounts resulting from the capital reduction and the release of disclosed reserves are used

1. to offset a decline in the value of assets;
2. to offset other losses; or
3. for allocation to the statutory reserve.

§ 238

§ 238
Wirksamwerden der Kapitalherabsetzung

Mit der Eintragung des Beschlusses oder, wenn die Einziehung nachfolgt, mit der Einziehung ist das Grundkapital um den Gesamtnennbetrag der eingezogenen Aktien herabgesetzt. Handelt es sich um eine durch die Satzung angeordnete Zwangseinziehung, so ist, wenn die Hauptversammlung nicht über die Kapitalherabsetzung beschließt, das Grundkapital mit der Zwangseinziehung herabgesetzt. Zur Einziehung bedarf es einer Handlung der Gesellschaft, die auf Vernichtung der Rechte aus bestimmten Aktien gerichtet ist.

§ 239
Anmeldung der Durchführung

(1) Der Vorstand hat die Durchführung der Herabsetzung des Grundkapitals zur Eintragung in das Handelsregister anzumelden. Dies gilt auch dann, wenn es sich um eine durch die Satzung angeordnete Zwangseinziehung handelt.

(2) Anmeldung und Eintragung der Durchführung der Herabsetzung können mit Anmeldung und Eintragung des Beschlusses über die Herabsetzung verbunden werden.

Vierter Unterabschnitt
Ausweis der Kapitalherabsetzung

§ 240

Der aus der Kapitalherabsetzung gewonnene Betrag ist in der Gewinn- und Verlustrechnung als „Ertrag aus der Kapitalherabsetzung" gesondert, und zwar hinter dem Posten „Entnahmen aus offenen Rücklagen", auszuweisen. Eine Einstellung in die gesetzliche Rücklage nach § 229 Abs. 1 und § 232 ist als „Einstellung in die gesetzliche Rücklage nach den Vorschriften über die vereinfachte Kapitalherabsetzung" gesondert auszuweisen. Im Geschäftsbericht ist zu erläutern, ob und in welcher Höhe die aus der Kapitalherabsetzung und aus der Auflösung von offenen Rücklagen gewonnenen Beträge

1. zum Ausgleich von Wertminderungen,
2. zur Deckung von sonstigen Verlusten oder
3. zur Einstellung in die gesetzliche Rücklage

verwandt werden.

Siebenter Teil

Nichtigkeit
von Hauptversammlungsbeschlüssen
und des festgestellten Jahresabschlusses.
Sonderprüfung wegen unzulässiger
Unterbewertung

Erster Abschnitt

Nichtigkeit
von Hauptversammlungsbeschlüssen

Erster Unterabschnitt

Allgemeines

§ 241

Nichtigkeitsgründe

Ein Beschluß der Hauptversammlung ist außer in
den Fällen des § 192 Abs. 4, §§ 212, 217 Abs. 2, § 228
Abs. 2, § 234 Abs. 3 und § 235 Abs. 2 nur dann nichtig, wenn er

1. in einer Hauptversammlung gefaßt worden ist,
die nicht nach § 121 Abs. 2 und 3 einberufen
war, es sei denn, daß alle Aktionäre erschienen
oder vertreten waren,

2. nicht nach § 130 Abs. 1, 2 und 4 beurkundet ist,

3. mit dem Wesen der Aktiengesellschaft nicht zu
vereinbaren ist oder durch seinen Inhalt Vorschriften verletzt, die ausschließlich oder überwiegend zum Schutze der Gläubiger der Gesellschaft oder sonst im öffentlichen Interesse
gegeben sind,

4. durch seinen Inhalt gegen die guten Sitten verstößt,

5. auf Anfechtungsklage durch Urteil rechtskräftig
für nichtig erklärt worden ist,

6. nach § 144 Abs. 2 des Reichsgesetzes über die
Angelegenheiten der freiwilligen Gerichtsbarkeit
auf Grund rechtskräftiger Entscheidung als nichtig
gelöscht worden ist.

§ 242

Heilung der Nichtigkeit

(1) Die Nichtigkeit eines Hauptversammlungsbeschlusses, der entgegen § 130 Abs. 1, 2 und 4 nicht
oder nicht gehörig beurkundet worden ist, kann
nicht mehr geltend gemacht werden, wenn der Beschluß in das Handelsregister eingetragen worden
ist.

(2) Ist ein Hauptversammlungsbeschluß nach § 241
Nr. 1, 3 oder 4 nichtig, so kann die Nichtigkeit nicht
mehr geltend gemacht werden, wenn der Beschluß

Part Seven

Nullity of Shareholders' Resolutions and of Established Annual Financial Statements. Special Audit for Improper Understatement

First Division

Nullity

of Shareholders' Resolutions

First Subdivision

General Provisions

§ 241

Grounds for Nullity

Except for the cases referred to in § 192, paragraph 4, §§ 212, 217, paragraph 2, § 228, paragraph 2, § 234, paragraph 3, and § 235, paragraph
2, a shareholders' resolution shall be void only if

1. it was passed in a shareholders' meeting which
was not called pursuant to § 121, paragraphs
2 and 3, unless all of the shareholders were
present or represented;

2. it was not recorded in accordance with § 130,
paragraphs 1, 2, and 4;

3. it is inconsistent with the nature of a stock
corporation or its content violates provisions
that are designed exclusively or primarily to
protect the company's creditors or are otherwise in the public interest;

4. its content violates good morals;

5. it has been declared void by a final judgment
rendered in an action to set it aside;

6. it has been cancelled in accordance with
§ 144, paragraph 2, of the *Reichsgesetz über
die Angelegenheiten der freiwilligen Gerichtsbarkeit* as void pursuant to a final decision.

§ 242

Curing of Nullity

(1) The nullity of a shareholders' resolution
which, in violation of § 130, paragraphs 1, 2, and
4, was not recorded or was not recorded properly,
can no longer be asserted once the resolution
has been recorded in the Commercial Register.

(2) If a shareholders' resolution is void pursuant to § 241, No. 1, 3, or 4, such nullity can no
longer be asserted once the resolution has been

recorded in the Commercial Register and three years have elapsed. If, at the expiration of this period, an action is pending to have the shareholders' resolution declared void, this period shall be tolled until the action is terminated by a final decision or is settled in some other manner. The expiration of the period shall not preclude an ex officio cancellation of the resolution pursuant to § 144, paragraph 2, of the *Reichsgesetz über die Angelegenheiten der freiwilligen Gerichtsbarkeit*.

(3) Paragraph 2 shall apply, *mutatis mutandis*, if in the cases of § 217, paragraph 2, § 228, paragraph 2, § 234, paragraph 3, and § 235, paragraph 2, the necessary registrations were not effected within the time specified therefor.

§ 243
Grounds for Action to Set Aside

(1) An action to set aside a shareholders' resolution may be brought for violation of the law or of the articles of incorporation.

(2) The action to set aside may also be based on the fact that a shareholder, in the exercise of his right to vote, attempted to obtain special advantages for himself or for a third party to the detriment of the company or the other shareholders, and that the resolution is apt to further this purpose. This shall not apply if the resolution provides for appropriate compensation of the other shareholders for damage sustained by them.

(3) An action to set aside may not be based on a violation of § 128.

(4) If an action to set aside a shareholders' resolution is based on a refusal to furnish information, the fact that the majority adopting the resolution or individual shareholders declare or have declared that the refusal to furnish information did not influence their decision shall be immaterial.

§ 244
Ratification of Voidable Shareholders' Resolutions

The action to set aside a shareholders' resolution shall be barred after the shareholders' meeting ratifies the voidable resolution by a subsequent resolution and if no action to set it aside is brought against such subsequent resolution within the period provided for by law or if the action to set it aside is dismissed by a final decision. If the plaintiff has a legitimate interest in

in das Handelsregister eingetragen worden ist und seitdem drei Jahre verstrichen sind. Ist bei Ablauf der Frist eine Klage auf Feststellung der Nichtigkeit des Hauptversammlungsbeschlusses rechtshängig, so verlängert sich die Frist, bis über die Klage rechtskräftig entschieden ist oder sie sich auf andere Weise endgültig erledigt hat. Eine Löschung des Beschlusses von Amts wegen nach § 144 Abs. 2 des Reichsgesetzes über die Angelegenheiten der freiwilligen Gerichtsbarkeit wird durch den Zeitablauf nicht ausgeschlossen.

(3) Absatz 2 gilt entsprechend, wenn in den Fällen des § 217 Abs. 2, § 228 Abs. 2, § 234 Abs. 3 und § 235 Abs. 2 die erforderlichen Eintragungen nicht fristgemäß vorgenommen worden sind.

§ 243
Anfechtungsgründe

(1) Ein Beschluß der Hauptversammlung kann wegen Verletzung des Gesetzes oder der Satzung durch Klage angefochten werden.

(2) Die Anfechtung kann auch darauf gestützt werden, daß ein Aktionär mit der Ausübung des Stimmrechts für sich oder einen Dritten Sondervorteile zum Schaden der Gesellschaft oder der anderen Aktionäre zu erlangen suchte und der Beschluß geeignet ist, diesem Zweck zu dienen. Dies gilt nicht, wenn der Beschluß den anderen Aktionären einen angemessenen Ausgleich für ihren Schaden gewährt.

(3) Auf eine Verletzung des § 128 kann die Anfechtung nicht gestützt werden.

(4) Für eine Anfechtung, die auf die Verweigerung einer Auskunft gestützt wird, ist es unerheblich, daß die Hauptversammlung oder Aktionäre erklärt haben oder erklären, die Verweigerung der Auskunft habe ihre Beschlußfassung nicht beeinflußt.

§ 244
Bestätigung
anfechtbarer Hauptversammlungsbeschlüsse

Die Anfechtung kann nicht mehr geltend gemacht werden, wenn die Hauptversammlung den anfechtbaren Beschluß durch einen neuen Beschluß bestätigt hat und dieser Beschluß innerhalb der Anfechtungsfrist nicht angefochten oder die Anfechtung rechtskräftig zurückgewiesen worden ist. Hat der Kläger ein rechtliches Interesse, daß der anfechtbare

Beschluß für die Zeit bis zum Bestätigungsbeschluß für nichtig erklärt wird, so kann er die Anfechtung weiterhin mit dem Ziel geltend machen, den anfechtbaren Beschluß für diese Zeit für nichtig zu erklären.

having the voidable resolution declared void for the period prior to ratification by subsequent resolution, the action to set it aside may also be brought for the purpose of declaring the voidable resolution void for this period.

§ 245
Anfechtungsbefugnis

Zur Anfechtung ist befugt

1. jeder in der Hauptversammlung erschienene Aktionär, wenn er gegen den Beschluß Widerspruch zur Niederschrift erklärt hat;
2. jeder in der Hauptversammlung nicht erschienene Aktionär, wenn er zu der Hauptversammlung zu Unrecht nicht zugelassen worden ist oder die Versammlung nicht ordnungsgemäß einberufen oder der Gegenstand der Beschlußfassung nicht ordnungsgemäß bekanntgemacht worden ist;
3. im Fall des § 243 Abs. 2 jeder Aktionär;
4. der Vorstand;
5. jedes Mitglied des Vorstands und des Aufsichtsrats, wenn durch die Ausführung des Beschlusses Mitglieder des Vorstands oder des Aufsichtsrats eine strafbare Handlung oder eine Ordnungswidrigkeit begehen oder wenn sie ersatzpflichtig werden würden.

§ 245
Standing to Sue

The following may institute an action to set aside a shareholders' resolution:

1. any shareholder who appeared at the shareholders' meeting, if he had his protest against the resolution recorded in the minutes;
2. any shareholder who did not appear at the shareholders' meeting, if he was wrongfully refused admission to the shareholders' meeting or if the meeting was not duly called or the subject matter of the resolution was not duly published;
3. in the case of § 243, paragraph 2, every shareholder;
4. the managing board;
5. any member of the managing board and of the supervisory board if, by carrying out the resolution, members of the managing board or of the supervisory board would commit a criminal act or an offense, or if they would become liable for damages.

§ 246
Anfechtungsklage

(1) Die Klage muß innerhalb eines Monats nach der Beschlußfassung erhoben werden.

(2) Die Klage ist gegen die Gesellschaft zu richten. Die Gesellschaft wird durch Vorstand und Aufsichtsrat vertreten. Klagt der Vorstand oder ein Vorstandsmitglied, wird die Gesellschaft durch den Aufsichtsrat, klagt ein Aufsichtsratsmitglied, wird sie durch den Vorstand vertreten.

(3) Zuständig für die Klage ist ausschließlich das Landgericht, in dessen Bezirk die Gesellschaft ihren Sitz hat. Die mündliche Verhandlung findet nicht vor Ablauf der Monatsfrist des Absatzes 1 statt. Mehrere Anfechtungsprozesse sind zur gleichzeitigen Verhandlung und Entscheidung zu verbinden.

(4) Der Vorstand hat die Erhebung der Klage und den Termin zur mündlichen Verhandlung unverzüg-

§ 246
Action to Set Aside Shareholders' Resolution

(1) The action must be brought within one month from the date the resolution was adopted.

(2) The action shall be brought against the company. The company shall be represented by the managing board and the supervisory board. If the action is brought by the managing board or by a member of the managing board, the company shall be represented by the supervisory board; if the action is brought by a member of the supervisory board, it shall be represented by the managing board.

(3) The district court of the district in which the company is domiciled shall have exclusive jurisdiction to adjudicate the action. The hearing shall not be held before the expiration of the one-month period specified in paragraph 1 hereof. If several actions to set aside are pending, they shall be joined to be heard and decided together.

(4) The managing board shall promptly publish the pendency of the action and the date

set for the hearing in the publications designated in the company's articles of incorporation.

§ 247
Value of Subject Matter in Issue

(1) The value of the subject matter in issue shall be determined by the court in its discretion, taking into consideration all the circumstances of the particular case, especially the importance of the matter for the parties. However, the value may exceed one-tenth of the stated capital or, if one-tenth amounts to more than one million German marks, the amount of one million German marks, only to the extent that the importance of the matter for the plaintiff requires a higher valuation.

(2) If any party makes a showing that the assessment of court costs in accordance with the value of the subject matter in issue determined pursuant to paragraph 1 hereof would substantially jeopardize such party's financial condition, the court may order, upon the application of such party, that its obligation to pay the court costs shall be determined by reference to a portion of the value of the subject matter in issue appropriate to the party's financial condition. As a result of such order, the party favored shall likewise pay its attorney's fees only in accordance with this portion of the value of the subject matter in issue. To the extent that litigation expenses are assessed against it or assumed by it, it shall reimburse the opposing party for court costs paid by the latter and pay its attorney's fees only with respect to such portion of the value of the subject matter in issue. To the extent that fees are assessed against or assumed by the opposing party, the attorney for the party favored may collect his fees from the opposing party in accordance with the value of the subject matter in issue which applies to the opposing party.

(3) The application pursuant to paragraph 2 hereof may be made by a declaration recorded with the court clerk's office. It shall be filed before the hearing of the case. It may be made at a later date only if the value of the subject matter in issue as indicated or determined is increased by the court. Before rendering a decision on the application, the opposing party shall be heard.

§ 248
Effect of Judgment

To the extent that the resolution is declared invalid by a final judgment, such judgment shall

§ 247

gegen alle Aktionäre sowie die Mitglieder des Vorstands und des Aufsichtsrats, auch wenn sie nicht Partei sind. Der Vorstand hat das Urteil unverzüglich zum Handelsregister einzureichen. War der Beschluß in das Handelsregister eingetragen, so ist auch das Urteil einzutragen. Die Eintragung des Urteils ist in gleicher Weise wie die des Beschlusses bekanntzumachen.

be binding upon all shareholders as well as upon the members of the managing board and of the supervisory board even if they were not parties to the action. The managing board shall promptly file the judgment with the Commercial Register. If the resolution was recorded in the Commercial Register, the judgment shall likewise be recorded. Registration of the judgment shall be published in the same manner as the registration of the resolution.

§ 249

Nichtigkeitsklage

(1) Erhebt ein Aktionär, der Vorstand oder ein Mitglied des Vorstands oder des Aufsichtsrats Klage auf Feststellung der Nichtigkeit eines Hauptversammlungsbeschlusses gegen die Gesellschaft, so gelten § 246 Abs. 2, Abs. 3 Satz 1, Abs. 4, §§ 247 und 248 sinngemäß. Es ist nicht ausgeschlossen, die Nichtigkeit auf andere Weise als durch Erhebung der Klage geltend zu machen.

(2) Mehrere Nichtigkeitsprozesse sind zur gleichzeitigen Verhandlung und Entscheidung zu verbinden. Nichtigkeits- und Anfechtungsprozesse können verbunden werden.

§ 249

Action for Declaration of Nullity

(1) If a shareholder, the managing board, or a member of the managing board or of the supervisory board brings an action against the company to have a shareholders' resolution declared void, § 246, paragraph 2, paragraph 3, first sentence, paragraph 4, §§ 247 and 248 shall apply *mutatis mutandis*. The possibility of asserting such nullity in some manner other than by bringing an action shall not be precluded.

(2) If several actions for a declaration of nullity are pending, they shall be joined to be heard and decided together. Actions to set aside a shareholders' resolution and actions for a declaration of nullity may be joined.

Zweiter Unterabschnitt

Nichtigkeit bestimmter
Hauptversammlungsbeschlüsse

Second Subdivision
Nullity of Specific Shareholders' Resolutions

§ 250

Nichtigkeit der Wahl von Aufsichtsratsmitgliedern

(1) Die Wahl eines Aufsichtsratsmitglieds durch die Hauptversammlung ist außer im Falle des § 241 Nr. 1, 2 und 5 nur dann nichtig, wenn

1. der Aufsichtsrat unter Verstoß gegen § 96 Abs. 2, § 97 Abs. 2 Satz 1 oder § 98 Abs. 4 zusammengesetzt wird;

2. die Hauptversammlung, obwohl sie an Wahlvorschläge gebunden ist (§§ 6 und 8 des Mitbestimmungsgesetzes), eine nicht vorgeschlagene Person wählt;

3. durch die Wahl die gesetzliche Höchstzahl der Aufsichtsratsmitglieder überschritten wird (§ 95);

4. die gewählte Person nach § 100 Abs. 1 und 2 bei Beginn ihrer Amtszeit nicht Aufsichtsratsmitglied sein kann.

§ 250

Nullity of Election of Supervisory Board Members

(1) The election of a member of the supervisory board by the shareholders shall, except in the cases specified in § 241, Nos. 1, 2, and 5, be void only if

1. the supervisory board was composed in violation of § 96, paragraph 2, § 97, paragraph 2, first sentence, or § 98, paragraph 4;

2. the shareholders' meeting, despite the fact that it is subject to binding nominations (§§ 6 and 8 of the *Mitbestimmungsgesetz*), elected a person not nominated;

3. the election disregarded the statutory maximum number of members of the supervisory board (§ 95);

4. the person elected is barred by § 100, paragraphs 1 and 2, from becoming a member of the supervisory board when his term of office commences.

§ 250

(2) The works council of each of the company's plants, each union represented in the company's plants, and the union's central organization shall have the right to institute an action to have the election of a member of the supervisory board declared void.

(3) If a shareholder, the managing board, a member of the managing board or of the supervisory board, the works council of one of the company's plants, a union represented in the company's plants, or the union's central organization brings an action against the company to have the election of a member of the supervisory board declared void, § 246, paragraph 2, paragraph 3, first sentence, paragraph 4, §§ 247, 248, second sentence, and § 249, paragraph 2, shall apply *mutatis mutandis*. The possibility of asserting such nullity in some manner other than by bringing an action shall not be precluded.

(2) Für die Klage auf Feststellung, daß die Wahl eines Aufsichtsratsmitglieds nichtig ist, sind der Betriebsrat jedes Betriebs der Gesellschaft, jede in den Betrieben der Gesellschaft vertretene Gewerkschaft und deren Spitzenorganisation parteifähig.

(3) Erhebt ein Aktionär, der Vorstand, ein Mitglied des Vorstands oder des Aufsichtsrats, der Betriebsrat eines Betriebs der Gesellschaft, eine in den Betrieben der Gesellschaft vertretene Gewerkschaft oder deren Spitzenorganisation gegen die Gesellschaft Klage auf Feststellung, daß die Wahl eines Aufsichtsratsmitglieds nichtig ist, so gelten § 246 Abs. 2, Abs. 3 Satz 1, Abs. 4, §§ 247, 248 Satz 2 und § 249 Abs. 2 sinngemäß. Es ist nicht ausgeschlossen, die Nichtigkeit auf andere Weise als durch Erhebung der Klage geltend zu machen.

§ 251
Action to Set Aside Election of Supervisory Board Members

(1) An action to set aside the election of a member of the supervisory board by the shareholders may be brought on the ground of violation of the law or the articles of incorporation. If the shareholders are subject to binding nominations, the action to set aside the election may also be based on the fact that the nomination violated the law. § 243, paragraph 4, and § 244 shall apply.

(2) § 245, Nos. 1, 2, and 4, shall apply to the right to bring an action to set aside an election. An action to set aside the election of a member of the supervisory board elected in accordance with the *Mitbestimmungsgesetz* upon nomination made by the works council or a central union organization may also be brought by each works council of one of the company's plants, each union represented in the company's plants, or the union's central organization. An action to set aside the election of an additional member elected according to the *Mitbestimmungsgesetz* or the *Mitbestimmungsergänzungsgesetz* upon nomination made by the other members of the supervisory board may be brought by each member of the supervisory board.

(3) §§ 246, 247, and 248, second sentence, shall govern the procedure in an action to set aside an election.

§ 251

§ 251
Anfechtung der Wahl von Aufsichtsratsmitgliedern

(1) Die Wahl eines Aufsichtsratsmitglieds durch die Hauptversammlung kann wegen Verletzung des Gesetzes oder der Satzung durch Klage angefochten werden. Ist die Hauptversammlung an Wahlvorschläge gebunden, so kann die Anfechtung auch darauf gestützt werden, daß der Wahlvorschlag gesetzwidrig zustande gekommen ist. § 243 Abs. 4 und § 244 gelten.

(2) Für die Anfechtungsbefugnis gilt § 245 Nr. 1, 2 und 4. Die Wahl eines Aufsichtsratsmitglieds, das nach dem Mitbestimmungsgesetz auf Vorschlag der Betriebsräte oder einer Spitzenorganisation gewählt worden ist, kann auch von jedem Betriebsrat eines Betriebs der Gesellschaft, jeder in den Betrieben der Gesellschaft vertretene Gewerkschaft oder deren Spitzenorganisation angefochten werden. Die Wahl eines weiteren Mitglieds, das nach dem Mitbestimmungsgesetz oder dem Mitbestimmungsergänzungsgesetz auf Vorschlag der übrigen Aufsichtsratsmitglieder gewählt worden ist, kann auch von jedem Aufsichtsratsmitglied angefochten werden.

(3) Für das Anfechtungsverfahren gelten §§ 246, 247 und 248 Satz 2.

§ 252
Urteilswirkung

(1) Erhebt ein Aktionär, der Vorstand, ein Mitglied des Vorstands oder des Aufsichtsrats, der Betriebsrat eines Betriebs der Gesellschaft, eine in den Betrieben der Gesellschaft vertretene Gewerkschaft oder deren Spitzenorganisation gegen die Gesellschaft Klage auf Feststellung, daß die Wahl eines Aufsichtsratsmitglieds durch die Hauptversammlung nichtig ist, so wirkt ein Urteil, das die Nichtigkeit der Wahl rechtskräftig feststellt, für und gegen alle Aktionäre und Arbeitnehmer der Gesellschaft, die Mitglieder des Vorstands und des Aufsichtsrats, die Betriebsräte der Betriebe der Gesellschaft, die in den Betrieben der Gesellschaft vertretenen Gewerkschaften und deren Spitzenorganisationen, auch wenn sie nicht Partei sind.

(2) Wird die Wahl eines Aufsichtsratsmitglieds durch die Hauptversammlung durch rechtskräftiges Urteil für nichtig erklärt, so wirkt das Urteil für und gegen alle Aktionäre sowie die Mitglieder des Vorstands und Aufsichtsrats, auch wenn sie nicht Partei sind. Im Fall des § 251 Abs. 2 Satz 2 wirkt das Urteil auch für und gegen die nach dieser Vorschrift anfechtungsberechtigten Betriebsräte, Gewerkschaften und Spitzenorganisationen, auch wenn sie nicht Partei sind.

§ 252
Effect of Judgment

(1) If a shareholder, the managing board, a member of the managing board or of the supervisory board, the works council of one of the company's plants, a union represented in the company's plants, or the union's central organization brings an action against the company to have the election of a member of the supervisory board by the shareholders declared void, a final judgment holding the election void shall be binding on all shareholders and employees of the company, the members of the managing board and of the supervisory board, the works councils of the company's plants, the unions represented in the company's plants, and the unions' central organizations, even if they were not parties to the proceedings.

(2) If the election of a member of the supervisory board by the shareholders is held void by a final judgment, such judgment shall be binding upon all the shareholders as well as the members of the managing board and of the supervisory board, even if they were not parties to the proceedings. In the case of § 251, paragraph 2, second sentence, the final judgment shall also be binding upon the works councils, the unions, and the unions' central organizations having the right to bring an action to set aside an election pursuant to this provision, even though they were not parties to the proceedings.

§ 253
Nichtigkeit des Beschlusses über die Verwendung des Bilanzgewinns

(1) Der Beschluß über die Verwendung des Bilanzgewinns ist außer in den Fällen des § 173 Abs. 3, des § 217 Abs. 2 und des § 241 nur dann nichtig, wenn die Feststellung des Jahresabschlusses, auf dem er beruht, nichtig ist. Die Nichtigkeit des Beschlusses aus diesem Grunde kann nicht mehr geltend gemacht werden, wenn die Nichtigkeit der Feststellung des Jahresabschlusses nicht mehr geltend gemacht werden kann.

(2) Für die Klage auf Feststellung der Nichtigkeit gegen die Gesellschaft gilt § 249.

§ 253
Nullity of Resolution on Disposition of Retained Earnings

(1) The resolution concerning the disposition of retained earnings shall, except in the cases specified in § 173, paragraph 3, § 217, paragraph 2, and § 241, be void only if the establishment of the underlying annual financial statements is likewise void. The nullity of the resolution based on this ground may not be asserted once the nullity of the establishment of the annual financial statements can no longer be asserted.

(2) § 249 shall apply to an action against the company for a declaration of nullity.

§ 253

§ 254
Action to Set Aside Resolution on Disposition of Retained Earnings

(1) In addition to the grounds specified in § 243, an action to set aside the resolution concerning the disposition of retained earnings may also be brought if the shareholders allocate to reserves amounts from retained earnings that are not excluded from distribution to the shareholders by law or by the articles of incorporation, even though such allocation, according to reasonable business judgment, is not required to safeguard the company's viability and resiliency over a period of time for which the economic and financial requirements are foreseeable, and if, for this reason, earnings of no less than four percent of the stated capital, reduced by contributions not yet called in, cannot be distributed to the shareholders.

(2) §§ 244 to 248 shall apply to the action to set aside such resolutions. The statute of limitations for this action shall run from the date the resolution is adopted even if the annual financial statements must be reaudited pursuant to § 173, paragraph 3. An action to set aside such resolutions on the ground of excessively high allocations to reserves pursuant to paragraph 1 hereof may be brought only by shareholders whose combined holdings amount to no less than one-twentieth of the stated capital or a total par value of one million German marks.

§ 255
Action to Set Aside Capital Increase Against Contribution of Assets

(1) An action to set aside the resolution concerning a capital increase against contributions of assets may be brought in accordance with § 243.

(2) If the shareholders' preemptive rights to subscribe to new shares are abrogated in whole or in part, the action to set aside the resolution may also be based on the fact that the amount for which the shares are issued, as stated in the resolution authorizing the capital increase, or the minimum amount below which the new shares shall not be issued, is unreasonably low. This shall not apply if the new shares are to be acquired by a third party subject to the obligation to offer them to the shareholders.

(3) §§ 244 to 248 shall apply to the action to set aside the resolution.

§ 254

§ 254
Anfechtung des Beschlusses über die Verwendung des Bilanzgewinns

(1) Der Beschluß über die Verwendung des Bilanzgewinns kann außer nach § 243 auch angefochten werden, wenn die Hauptversammlung aus dem Bilanzgewinn Beträge in Rücklage stellt, die nicht nach Gesetz oder Satzung von der Verteilung unter die Aktionäre ausgeschlossen sind, obwohl die Einstellung bei vernünftiger kaufmännischer Beurteilung nicht notwendig ist, um die Lebens- und Widerstandsfähigkeit der Gesellschaft für einen hinsichtlich der wirtschaftlichen und finanziellen Notwendigkeiten übersehbaren Zeitraum zu sichern und dadurch unter die Aktionäre kein Gewinn in Höhe von mindestens vier vom Hundert des Grundkapitals abzüglich von noch nicht eingeforderten Einlagen verteilt werden kann.

(2) Für die Anfechtung gelten §§ 244 bis 248. Die Anfechtungsfrist beginnt auch dann mit der Beschlußfassung, wenn der Jahresabschluß nach § 173 Abs. 3 erneut zu prüfen ist. Zu einer Anfechtung wegen zu hoher Einstellung in Rücklagen nach Absatz 1 sind Aktionäre nur befugt, wenn ihre Anteile zusammen den zwanzigsten Teil des Grundkapitals oder den Nennbetrag von einer Million Deutsche Mark erreichen.

§ 255
Anfechtung der Kapitalerhöhung gegen Einlagen

(1) Der Beschluß über eine Kapitalerhöhung gegen Einlagen kann nach § 243 angefochten werden.

(2) Die Anfechtung kann, wenn das Bezugsrecht der Aktionäre ganz oder zum Teil ausgeschlossen worden ist, auch darauf gestützt werden, daß der sich aus dem Erhöhungsbeschluß ergebende Ausgabebetrag oder der Mindestbetrag, unter dem die neuen Aktien nicht ausgegeben werden sollen, unangemessen niedrig ist. Dies gilt nicht, wenn die neuen Aktien von einem Dritten mit der Verpflichtung übernommen werden sollen, sie den Aktionären zum Bezug anzubieten.

(3) Für die Anfechtung gelten §§ 244 bis 248.

Zweiter Abschnitt

Nichtigkeit
des festgestellten Jahresabschlusses

Second Division

Nullity of Established Annual Financial Statements

§ 256

Nichtigkeit

(1) Ein festgestellter Jahresabschluß ist außer in den Fällen des § 173 Abs. 3, § 234 Abs. 3 und § 235 Abs. 2 nichtig, wenn

1. er durch seinen Inhalt Vorschriften verletzt, die ausschließlich oder überwiegend zum Schutze der Gläubiger der Gesellschaft oder sonst im öffentlichen Interesse gegeben sind,
2. er nicht nach § 162 Abs. 1 und 3 geprüft worden ist,
3. er von Personen geprüft worden ist, die nicht zum Abschlußprüfer bestellt sind oder nach § 164 nicht Abschlußprüfer sein können,
4. bei seiner Feststellung die Bestimmungen des Gesetzes oder der Satzung über die Einstellung von Beträgen in offene Rücklagen oder über die Entnahme von Beträgen aus offenen Rücklagen verletzt worden sind.

(2) Ein von Vorstand und Aufsichtsrat festgestellter Jahresabschluß ist außer nach Absatz 1 nur nichtig, wenn der Vorstand oder der Aufsichtsrat bei seiner Feststellung nicht ordnungsgemäß mitgewirkt hat.

(3) Ein von der Hauptversammlung festgestellter Jahresabschluß ist außer nach Absatz 1 nur nichtig, wenn die Feststellung

1. in einer Hauptversammlung beschlossen worden ist, die nicht nach § 121 Abs. 2 und 3 einberufen war, es sei denn, daß alle Aktionäre erschienen oder vertreten waren,
2. nicht nach § 130 Abs. 1, 2 und 4 beurkundet ist,
3. auf Anfechtungsklage durch Urteil rechtskräftig für nichtig erklärt worden ist.

(4) Wegen Verstoßes gegen die Vorschriften über die Gliederung des Jahresabschlusses (§§ 151, 152, 157 bis 159) sowie wegen der Nichtbeachtung von Formblättern, nach denen der Jahresabschluß zu gliedern ist, ist der Jahresabschluß nur nichtig, wenn seine Klarheit und Übersichtlichkeit dadurch wesentlich beeinträchtigt sind. Eine wesentliche Beeinträchtigung liegt namentlich vor, wenn

§ 256

Nullity

(1) Established annual financial statements shall, in addition to the cases specified in § 173, paragraph 3, § 234, paragraph 3, and § 235, paragraph 2, be void if

1. their content violates provisions which are designed exclusively or primarily for the protection of the company's creditors or which are otherwise in the public interest,
2. they have not been audited pursuant to § 162, paragraphs 1 and 3,
3. they were audited by persons not appointed as annual auditors or persons precluded by § 164 from acting as annual auditors,
4. in connection with their establishment, the provisions of the law or of the articles of incorporation concerning the allocation of amounts to disclosed reserves or the withdrawal of amounts from disclosed reserves were violated.

(2) Annual financial statements established by the managing board and the supervisory board shall be void, in cases other than those referred to in paragraph 1 hereof, only if the managing board or the supervisory board did not duly participate in their establishment.

(3) Annual financial statements established by the shareholders shall be void, in cases other than those referred to in paragraph 1 hereof, if the establishment

1. was adopted in a shareholders' meeting which was not called in accordance with § 121, paragraphs 2 and 3, unless all of the shareholders appeared or were represented,
2. was not recorded in accordance with § 130, paragraphs 1, 2, and 4,
3. has been declared void by a final judgment rendered in an action to set it aside.

(4) The annual financial statements shall be void on the ground that the rules on the classification of the annual financial statements (§§ 151, 152, and 157 to 159) were violated or that the printed forms showing how the annual financial statements must be classified were not complied with, only if their clarity and comprehensibility are substantially impaired as a result. A substantial impairment exists, in particular, if

§ 256

1. in the balance sheet, § 152, paragraph 1, second sentence, and paragraphs 6 and 8, were not observed, or

2. in the profit and loss statement, the items specified in § 157, paragraph 1, Nos. 1 to 5, are not shown separately, despite the fact that the requirements set forth in § 157, paragraph 4, are not met, or if expenditures or income specified in § 157, paragraph 1, No. 7, 15, 24, 25, or 27, is not listed under such classifications.

(5) The annual financial statements shall be void for violation of the valuation provisions only if

1. items are overstated, or

2. items are understated, thus causing the company's financial and profit situation to be deliberately shown incorrectly or obscured.

Assets are overstated if they are stated at a higher value, and liabilities are overstated if they are stated at a lower amount, than permitted by §§ 153 to 156. Assets are understated if they are stated at a lower value, and liabilities are understated if they are stated at a higher amount, than permitted by §§ 153 to 156.

(6) Nullity pursuant to paragraph 1, Nos. 1, 3, and 4, paragraph 2, paragraph 3, Nos. 1 and 2, paragraphs 4 and 5, hereof, may not be asserted if, in the cases of paragraph 1, Nos. 3 and 4, paragraph 2, and paragraph 3, Nos. 1 and 2, hereof, six months, and in all other cases three years, have passed since the publication of the annual financial statements in the *Bundesanzeiger*. If, at the end of this period, an action is pending to have the annual financial statements declared void, this period shall be tolled until the action is terminated by a final decision or is settled in some other manner.

(7) § 249 shall apply, *mutatis mutandis*, to an action brought against the company for a declaration of nullity.

§ 257
Action to Set Aside Establishment of Annual Financial Statements by Shareholders

(1) An action to set aside the establishment of the annual financial statements by the shareholders may be brought pursuant to § 243. The action may not, however, be based on the ground that the content of the annual financial statements violates the law or the articles of incorporation.

(2) §§ 244 to 248 shall apply to such action. The statute of limitations for this action shall run from the date of the adoption of the resolution,

§ 257

---

1. in der Bilanz § 152 Abs. 1 Satz 2, Abs. 6 und 8 nicht beachtet ist, oder

2. in der Gewinn- und Verlustrechnung die Posten § 157 Abs. 1 Nr. 1 bis 5 nicht gesondert ausgewiesen sind, obgleich die Voraussetzungen des § 157 Abs. 4 nicht vorliegen, oder wenn Aufwendungen oder Erträge, die unter die Posten § 157 Abs. 1 Nr. 7, 15, 24, 25 oder 27 fallen, nicht unter diesen Posten ausgewiesen sind.

(5) Wegen Verstoßes gegen die Bewertungsvorschriften ist der Jahresabschluß nur nichtig, wenn

1. Posten überbewertet oder

2. Posten unterbewertet sind und dadurch die Vermögens- und Ertragslage der Gesellschaft vorsätzlich unrichtig wiedergegeben oder verschleiert wird.

Überbewertet sind Aktivposten, wenn sie mit einem höheren Wert, Passivposten, wenn sie mit einem niedrigeren Betrag angesetzt sind, als nach §§ 153 bis 156 zulässig ist. Unterbewertet sind Aktivposten, wenn sie mit einem niedrigeren Wert, Passivposten, wenn sie mit einem höheren Betrag angesetzt sind, als nach §§ 153 bis 156 zulässig ist.

(6) Die Nichtigkeit nach Absatz 1 Nr. 1, 3 und 4, Absatz 2, Absatz 3 Nr. 1 und 2, Absatz 4 und 5 kann nicht mehr geltend gemacht werden, wenn seit der Bekanntmachung des Jahresabschlusses im Bundesanzeiger in den Fällen des Absatzes 1 Nr. 3 und 4, des Absatzes 2 und des Absatzes 3 Nr. 1 und 2 sechs Monate, in den anderen Fällen drei Jahre verstrichen sind. Ist bei Ablauf der Frist eine Klage auf Feststellung der Nichtigkeit des Jahresabschlusses rechtshängig, so verlängert sich die Frist, bis über die Klage rechtskräftig entschieden ist oder sie sich auf andere Weise endgültig erledigt hat.

(7) Für die Klage auf Feststellung der Nichtigkeit gegen die Gesellschaft gilt § 249 sinngemäß.

§ 257
Anfechtung der Feststellung des Jahresabschlusses durch die Hauptversammlung

(1) Die Feststellung des Jahresabschlusses durch die Hauptversammlung kann nach § 243 angefochten werden. Die Anfechtung kann jedoch nicht darauf gestützt werden, daß der Inhalt des Jahresabschlusses gegen Gesetz oder Satzung verstößt.

(2) Für die Anfechtung gelten die §§ 244 bis 248. Die Anfechtungsfrist beginnt auch dann mit der

Beschlußfassung, wenn der Jahresabschluß nach § 173 Abs. 3 erneut zu prüfen ist.

even if the annual financial statements must be reaudited pursuant to § 173, paragraph 3.

Dritter Abschnitt

Sonderprüfung wegen unzulässiger Unterbewertung

§ 258

Bestellung der Sonderprüfer

(1) Besteht Anlaß für die Annahme, daß

1. in einem festgestellten Jahresabschluß bestimmte Posten nicht unwesentlich unterbewertet sind (§ 256 Abs. 5 Satz 3) oder

2. der Geschäftsbericht die Angaben nach § 160 Abs. 2 oder 3 nicht oder nicht vollständig enthält und der Vorstand in der Hauptversammlung die fehlenden Angaben, obwohl nach ihnen gefragt worden ist, nicht gemacht hat und die Aufnahme der Frage in die Niederschrift verlangt worden ist,

so hat das Gericht auf Antrag Sonderprüfer zu bestellen. Die Sonderprüfer haben die bemängelten Posten darauf zu prüfen, ob sie nicht unwesentlich unterbewertet sind. Sie haben den Geschäftsbericht darauf zu prüfen, ob die Angaben nach § 160 Abs. 2 und 3 nicht oder nicht vollständig gemacht worden sind und der Vorstand in der Hauptversammlung die fehlenden Angaben, obwohl nach ihnen gefragt worden ist, nicht gemacht hat und die Aufnahme der Frage in die Niederschrift verlangt worden ist.

(2) Der Antrag muß innerhalb eines Monats nach der Hauptversammlung über den Jahresabschluß gestellt werden. Dies gilt auch, wenn der Jahresabschluß nach § 173 Abs. 3 erneut zu prüfen ist. Er kann nur von Aktionären gestellt werden, deren Anteile zusammen den zwanzigsten Teil des Grundkapitals oder den Nennbetrag von einer Million Deutsche Mark erreichen. Die Antragsteller haben die Aktien bis zur Entscheidung über den Antrag zu hinterlegen und glaubhaft zu machen, daß sie seit mindestens drei Monaten vor dem Tage der Hauptversammlung Inhaber der Aktien sind. Zur Glaubhaftmachung genügt eine eidesstattliche Versicherung vor einem Gericht oder Notar.

(3) Vor der Bestellung hat das Gericht den Vorstand, den Aufsichtsrat und die Abschlußprüfer zu hören. Gegen die Entscheidung ist die sofortige Beschwerde zulässig.

Third Division

Special Audit for Improper Understating

§ 258

Appointment of Special Auditors

(1) If there is reason to believe that

1. in any established annual financial statements, certain items are not insubstantially understated (§ 256, paragraph 5, third sentence) or

2. the business report does not set forth the particulars pursuant to § 160, paragraph 2 or 3, or does not set them forth fully, and the managing board did not supply the missing particulars at the shareholders' meeting despite an inquiry and a request to record such inquiry in the minutes,

the court shall, upon application, appoint special auditors. The special auditors shall examine the contested items in order to determine whether they are not insubstantially understated. They shall examine the business report in order to determine whether the particulars required by § 160, paragraphs 2 and 3, were not set forth or were not set forth fully, and whether the managing board failed to supply the missing particulars at the shareholders' meeting despite an inquiry and a request to record such inquiry in the minutes.

(2) The application shall be made within one month from the date of the shareholders' meeting concerning the annual financial statements. The same shall apply even if the annual financial statements must be reaudited pursuant to § 173, paragraph 3. The application may be made only by shareholders whose combined holdings amount to no less than one-twentieth of the stated capital or a total par value of one million German marks. The parties making the application shall deposit their shares until a decision on their application is made and shall make a showing that they held the shares for no less than three months prior to the date of the shareholders' meeting. For purposes of such showing, an affidavit executed before a judge or notary shall suffice.

(3) The court shall hear the managing board, the supervisory board, and the annual auditors before appointing special auditors. The decision of the court can be appealed.

§ 258

(4) Only certified public accountants or firms of certified public accountants may act as special auditors pursuant to paragraph 1 hereof. § 164, paragraphs 2 and 3, shall apply, *mutatis mutandis*, to their selection. Annual auditors of the company and persons who had been annual auditors of the company within the last three years prior to their appointment cannot act as special auditors pursuant to paragraph 1 hereof.

(5) § 142, paragraph 6, concerning the reimbursement for reasonable cash expenditures and the remuneration of special auditors appointed by the court, § 145, paragraphs 1 to 3, concerning the rights of the special auditors, § 146, concerning the expenses of the special audit, and § 168, concerning the liability of the annual auditors, shall apply *mutatis mutandis*. The special auditors referred to in paragraph 1 hereof shall also have the rights set forth in § 145, paragraph 2, against the company's annual auditors.

§ 259
Audit Report. Concluding Statements

(1) The special auditors shall make a written report on the results of the audit. If the special auditors, in the performance of their duties, discover that items have been overstated (§ 256, paragraph 5, second sentence) or that the rules for the classification of the annual financial statements (§§ 151, 152, and 157 to 159) have been violated, or that printed forms have not been complied with, they shall report this also. § 145, paragraph 4, shall apply to the report *mutatis mutandis*.

(2) If the audit shows that the items contested are not insubstantially understated (§ 256, paragraph 5, third sentence), the special auditors shall set forth in a concluding statement at the end of their report

1. the minimum value of the particular asset and the maximum amount of the particular liability at which they should have been shown,
2. the amount by which the net profit for the year would have been increased if such values or amounts had been shown.

The special auditors shall base their opinion on the conditions prevailing at the closing date of the annual financial statements. To arrive at the values and amounts referred to in No. 1 hereof they shall use the method of valuation and depreciation used by the company in its last proper valuation of the items to be valued or similar items.

§ 259

---

(4) Sonderprüfer nach Absatz 1 können nur Wirtschaftsprüfer und Wirtschaftsprüfungsgesellschaften sein. Für die Auswahl gilt § 164 Abs. 2 und 3 sinngemäß. Die Abschlußprüfer der Gesellschaft und Personen, die in den letzten drei Jahren vor der Bestellung Abschlußprüfer der Gesellschaft waren, können nicht Sonderprüfer nach Absatz 1 sein.

(5) § 142 Abs. 6 über den Ersatz angemessener barer Auslagen und die Vergütung gerichtlich bestellter Sonderprüfer, § 145 Abs. 1 bis 3 über die Rechte der Sonderprüfer, § 146 über die Kosten der Sonderprüfung und § 168 über die Verantwortlichkeit der Abschlußprüfer gelten sinngemäß. Die Sonderprüfer nach Absatz 1 haben die Rechte nach § 145 Abs. 2 auch gegenüber den Abschlußprüfern der Gesellschaft.

§ 259
Prüfungsbericht.
Abschließende Feststellungen

(1) Die Sonderprüfer haben über das Ergebnis der Prüfung schriftlich zu berichten. Stellen die Sonderprüfer bei Wahrnehmung ihrer Aufgaben fest, daß Posten überbewertet sind (§ 256 Abs. 5 Satz 2), oder daß gegen die Vorschriften über die Gliederung des Jahresabschlusses (§§ 151, 152, 157 bis 159) verstoßen ist oder Formblätter nicht beachtet sind, so haben sie auch darüber zu berichten. Für den Bericht gilt § 145 Abs. 4 sinngemäß.

(2) Sind nach dem Ergebnis der Prüfung die bemängelten Posten nicht unwesentlich unterbewertet (§ 256 Abs. 5 Satz 3), so haben die Sonderprüfer am Schluß ihres Berichts in einer abschließenden Feststellung zu erklären,

1. zu welchem Wert die einzelnen Aktivposten mindestens und mit welchem Betrag die einzelnen Passivposten höchstens anzusetzen waren;
2. um welchen Betrag sich der Jahresüberschuß beim Ansatz dieser Werte oder Beträge erhöht hätte.

Die Sonderprüfer haben ihrer Beurteilung die Verhältnisse am Stichtag des Jahresabschlusses zugrunde zu legen. Sie haben für den Ansatz der Werte und Beträge nach Nummer 1 diejenige Bewertungs- und Abschreibungsmethode zugrunde zu legen, nach der die Gesellschaft die zu bewertenden Gegenstände oder vergleichbare Gegenstände zuletzt in zulässiger Weise bewertet hat.

(3) Sind nach dem Ergebnis der Prüfung die be-mängelten Posten nicht oder nur unwesentlich un-terbewertet (§ 256 Abs. 5 Satz 3), so haben die Son-derprüfer am Schluß ihres Berichts in einer ab-schließenden Feststellung zu erklären, daß nach ihrer pflichtmäßigen Prüfung und Beurteilung die bemängelten Posten nicht unzulässig unterbewertet sind.

(4) Hat nach dem Ergebnis der Prüfung der Ge-schäftsbericht die Angaben nach § 160 Abs. 2 oder 3 nicht oder nicht vollständig enthalten und der Vorstand in der Hauptversammlung die fehlenden Angaben, obwohl nach ihnen gefragt worden ist, nicht gemacht und ist die Aufnahme der Frage in die Niederschrift verlangt worden, so haben die Sonderprüfer am Schluß ihres Berichts in einer ab-schließenden Feststellung die fehlenden Angaben zu machen. Ist die Angabe von Änderungen von Bewertungs- oder Abschreibungsmethoden ein-schließlich der Vornahme außerplanmäßiger Ab-schreibungen oder Wertberichtigungen unterlassen worden, so ist in der abschließenden Feststellung auch der Betrag anzugeben, um den der Jahres-überschuß oder Jahresfehlbetrag ohne die Ände-rung, deren Angabe unterlassen wurde, höher oder niedriger gewesen wäre. Sind nach dem Ergebnis der Prüfung keine Angaben nach Satz 1 unterlassen worden, so haben die Sonderprüfer in einer ab-schließenden Feststellung zu erklären, daß nach ihrer pflichtmäßigen Prüfung und Beurteilung im Geschäftsbericht keine Angaben nach § 160 Abs. 2 oder 3 unterlassen worden sind.

(5) Der Vorstand hat die abschließenden Fest-stellungen der Sonderprüfer nach den Absätzen 2 bis 4 unverzüglich in den Gesellschaftsblättern be-kanntzumachen.

§ 260
Gerichtliche Entscheidung über die abschließenden Feststellungen der Sonderprüfer

(1) Gegen abschließende Feststellungen der Son-derprüfer nach § 259 Abs. 2 und 3 können die Ge-sellschaft oder Aktionäre, deren Anteile zusammen den zwanzigsten Teil des Grundkapitals oder den Nennbetrag von einer Million Deutsche Mark er-reichen, innerhalb eines Monats nach der Veröffent-lichung im Bundesanzeiger den Antrag auf Entschei-dung durch das nach § 132 Abs. 1 zuständige Ge-richt stellen. § 258 Abs. 2 Satz 4 und 5 gilt sinnge-mäß. Der Antrag muß auf Feststellung des Betrags

(3) If the audit indicates that the items con-tested are not undervalued or only insubstantially undervalued (§ 256, paragraph 5, third sentence), the special auditors shall declare in a concluding statement at the end of their report that, in their opinion and according to their audit carried out in compliance with their duties, the items con-tested are not improperly understated.

(4) If the result of the audit indicates that the business report does not or does not fully set forth the particulars required by § 160, paragraph 2 or 3, and the managing board did not at the shareholders' meeting supply the missing par-ticulars despite an inquiry concerning them and a request to record such inquiry in the minutes, the special auditors shall supply the missing particulars in a concluding statement at the end of their report. If changes in the methods of valu-ation or depreciation, including reserves for unscheduled depreciations or adjustments, were not reported, the concluding statement shall also specify the amount by which the net profit or loss for the year would have been higher or lower but for the unreported change. If the result of the audit shows that no particulars required by the first sentence hereof were missing, the special auditors shall declare in a concluding statement that, in their opinion and according to their audit carried out in compliance with their duties, none of the particulars required by § 160, paragraph 2 or 3, were unreported in the business report.

(5) The managing board shall without delay publish the concluding statements of the special auditors made pursuant to paragraphs 2 and 4 hereof in the publications designated in the com-pany's articles of incorporation.

§ 260
Judicial Decision on Concluding Statements of Special Auditors

(1) The company or shareholders whose com-bined holdings amount to no less than one-twentieth of the stated capital or a total par value of one million German marks may contest the concluding statements of the special auditors pursuant to § 259, paragraphs 2 and 3, by apply-ing for a decision of the court having jurisdiction pursuant to § 132, paragraph 1, within one month from publication in the *Bundesanzeiger*. § 258, paragraph 2, fourth and fifth sentences, shall

apply *mutatis mutandis.* The application shall request a determination of the minimum amount at which the assets designated in the application or the maximum amount of the liabilities designated in the application should have been stated. An application brought by the company may also request a determination to the effect that the annual financial statements did not contain the understatement found in the concluding statement of the special auditors.

(2) The court shall decide the application in accordance with its best opinion, with due regard for all the circumstances. § 259, paragraph 2, second and third sentences, shall be applied. To the extent that a full investigation of all relevant circumstances would involve considerable difficulties, the court shall estimate the values or amounts to be stated.

(3) § 99, paragraph 1, paragraph 2, first sentence, and paragraphs 3 and 5, shall apply *mutatis mutandis.* The court shall serve its decision on the company and, if the application pursuant to paragraph 1 was brought by the shareholders, also on them. In addition, the court shall publish it, without the opinion, in the publications designated in the company's articles of incorporation. The company and shareholders whose combined holdings amount to no less than one-twentieth of the stated capital or a total par value of one million German marks shall have the right to appeal. § 258, paragraph 2, fourth and fifth sentences, shall apply *mutatis mutandis.* The running of the time for bringing the appeal shall commence on the date of publication of the decision in the *Bundesanzeiger;* however, for the company and, if the application pursuant to paragraph 1 hereof was brought by shareholders, for such shareholders as well, this period shall not begin before service of the decision.

(4) The costs of the proceedings shall be determined by reference to the *Kostenordnung.* In the proceedings before the court of first instance, twice the amount of one full court fee shall be assessed. In the proceedings before the court of second instance, the same court fee shall be assessed; this applies even if the appeal is successful. If the application or the appeal is withdrawn before a decision is rendered, the court fees shall be reduced by one-half. The value of the subject matter in issue shall be determined ex officio. If the application is granted, the costs shall be assessed against the company; if not, they shall be assessed against the applicant. § 247 shall apply *mutatis mutandis.*

§ 260

---

gerichtet sein, mit dem die im Antrag zu bezeichnenden Aktivposten mindestens oder die im Antrag zu bezeichnenden Passivposten höchstens anzusetzen waren. Der Antrag der Gesellschaft kann auch auf Feststellung gerichtet sein, daß der Jahresabschluß die in der abschließenden Feststellung der Sonderprüfer festgestellten Unterbewertungen nicht enthielt.

(2) Über den Antrag entscheidet das Gericht unter Würdigung aller Umstände nach freier Überzeugung. § 259 Abs. 2 Satz 2 und 3 ist anzuwenden. Soweit die volle Aufklärung aller maßgebenden Umstände mit erheblichen Schwierigkeiten verbunden ist, hat das Gericht die anzusetzenden Werte oder Beträge zu schätzen.

(3) § 99 Abs. 1, Abs. 2 Satz 1, Abs. 3 und 5 gilt sinngemäß. Das Gericht hat seine Entscheidung der Gesellschaft und, wenn Aktionäre den Antrag nach Absatz 1 gestellt haben, auch diesen zuzustellen. Es hat sie ferner ohne Gründe in den Gesellschaftsblättern bekanntzumachen. Die Beschwerde steht der Gesellschaft und Aktionären zu, deren Anteile zusammen den zwanzigsten Teil des Grundkapitals oder den Nennbetrag von einer Million Deutsche Mark erreichen. § 258 Abs. 2 Satz 4 und 5 gilt sinngemäß. Die Beschwerdefrist beginnt mit der Bekanntmachung der Entscheidung im Bundesanzeiger, jedoch für die Gesellschaft und, wenn Aktionäre den Antrag nach Absatz 1 gestellt haben, auch für diese nicht vor der Zustellung der Entscheidung.

(4) Für die Kosten des Verfahrens gilt die Kostenordnung. Für das Verfahren des ersten Rechtszugs wird das Doppelte der vollen Gebühr erhoben. Für den zweiten Rechtszug wird die gleiche Gebühr erhoben; dies gilt auch dann, wenn die Beschwerde Erfolg hat. Wird der Antrag oder die Beschwerde zurückgenommen, bevor es zu einer Entscheidung kommt, so ermäßigt sich die Gebühr auf die Hälfte. Der Geschäftswert ist von Amts wegen festzusetzen. Die Kosten sind, wenn dem Antrag stattgegeben wird, der Gesellschaft, sonst dem Antragsteller aufzuerlegen. § 247 gilt sinngemäß.

§ 261

**Entscheidung über den Ertrag
auf Grund höherer Bewertung**

(1) Haben die Sonderprüfer in ihrer abschließenden Feststellung erklärt, daß Posten unterbewertet sind, und ist gegen diese Feststellung nicht innerhalb der in § 260 Abs. 1 bestimmten Frist der Antrag auf gerichtliche Entscheidung gestellt worden, so sind die Posten in dem ersten Jahresabschluß, der nach Ablauf dieser Frist aufgestellt wird, mit den von den Sonderprüfern festgestellten Werten oder Beträgen anzusetzen. Dies gilt nicht, soweit auf Grund veränderter Verhältnisse, namentlich bei Gegenständen, die der Abnutzung unterliegen, auf Grund der Abnutzung, nach §§ 153 bis 156 oder nach den Grundsätzen ordnungsmäßiger Buchführung für Aktivposten ein niedrigerer Wert oder für Passivposten ein höherer Betrag anzusetzen ist. In diesem Fall sind im Geschäftsbericht die Gründe anzugeben und in einer Sonderrechnung die Entwicklung des von den Sonderprüfern festgestellten Wertes oder Betrags auf den nach Satz 2 angesetzten Wert oder Betrag darzustellen. Sind die Gegenstände nicht mehr vorhanden, so ist darüber und über die Verwendung des Ertrags aus dem Abgang der Gegenstände im Geschäftsbericht zu berichten. Bei den einzelnen Posten der Jahresbilanz sind die Unterschiedsbeträge zu vermerken, um die auf Grund von Satz 1 und 2 Aktivposten zu einem höheren Wert oder Passivposten mit einem niedrigeren Betrag angesetzt worden sind. Die Summe der Unterschiedsbeträge ist auf der Passivseite der Bilanz nach dem Posten VIII und in der Gewinn- und Verlustrechnung nach dem Posten Nummer 32 als „Ertrag auf Grund höherer Bewertung gemäß dem Ergebnis der Sonderprüfung" gesondert auszuweisen.

(2) Hat das gemäß § 260 angerufene Gericht festgestellt, daß Posten unterbewertet sind, so gilt für den Ansatz der Posten in dem ersten Jahresabschluß, der nach Rechtskraft der gerichtlichen Entscheidung aufgestellt wird, Absatz 1 sinngemäß. Die Summe der Unterschiedsbeträge ist als „Ertrag auf Grund höherer Bewertung gemäß gerichtlicher Entscheidung" gesondert auszuweisen.

(3) Der Ertrag aus höherer Bewertung nach Absätzen 1 und 2 rechnet für die Anwendung der §§ 58 und 86 Abs. 2 nicht zum Jahresüberschuß. Über die Verwendung des Ertrags abzüglich der auf ihn zu entrichtenden Steuern entscheidet die Hauptversammlung, soweit nicht in dem Jahresabschluß ein Bilanzverlust ausgewiesen wird, der nicht durch offene Rücklagen gedeckt ist.

§ 261

**Decision on Income Based on
Higher Valuation**

(1) If the special auditors in their concluding statement declare that items are understated, and if no application for a judicial decision is brought to contest such statement within the period specified in § 260, paragraph 1, the items of the first annual financial statements prepared after the expiration of this period shall be stated at the values or amounts determined by the special auditors. This shall not apply to the extent that, because of changed conditions, in particular because of wear and tear in the case of assets that are subject to wear and tear, §§ 153 to 156 or proper accounting principles require that for assets a lower valuation or for liabilities a higher amount must be stated. In this event, the business report shall set forth the reasons therefor, and the change from the value or the amount determined by the special auditors to the value or amount stated according to the second sentence hereof shall be accounted for separately. If the company no longer has the assets, that fact and the use of the proceeds from the alienation of the assets shall be stated in the business report. Reference shall be made under the applicable items of the annual financial statements to the difference by which, pursuant to the first and second sentences hereof, assets are stated at a higher value or liabilities are stated at a lower amount. The total amount of the differences shall be stated separately in the annual balance sheet on the liabilities side following item VIII, and in the profit and loss statement, following item 32, as "income from higher valuation based on the result of the special audit."

(2) If the court to which an application was made in accordance with § 260 has determined that items are understated, paragraph 1 hereof shall apply, *mutatis mutandis*, to the valuation of the items in the first annual financial statements prepared after the date the decision of the court becomes final. The total amount of the differences shall be listed separately as "income from higher valuation based on judicial decision."

(3) The income from a higher valuation pursuant to paragraphs 1 and 2 hereof shall not be deemed to be net profit for the year in applying §§ 58 and 86, paragraph 2. The shareholders shall determine the disposition of the income, reduced by the taxes due thereon, unless the annual financial statements show accumulated losses not offset by disclosed reserves.

§ 261

Part Eight

Dissolution and Declaration of Nullity of the Company

First Division

Dissolution

First Subdivision

Grounds for Dissolution and Application to Record

§ 262

Grounds for Dissolution

(1) A stock corporation is dissolved

1. upon expiration of the period specified in the articles of incorporation;

2. by a shareholders' resolution; such resolution shall require a majority of no less than three-fourths of the stated capital represented when the resolution is adopted; the articles of incorporation may provide for a higher capital majority and establish additional requirements;

3. upon a court order subjecting the assets of the company to bankruptcy proceedings;

4. when an order rejecting a bankruptcy petition on the ground that the bankrupt's assets are insufficient to cover the costs of the proceedings becomes final.

(2) This division shall also apply if the stock corporation is dissolved for other reasons.

§ 263

Application to Record and Registration of Dissolution

The managing board shall file an application to record the dissolution of the company in the Commercial Register. This shall not apply in the case of an order subjecting the company's assets to bankruptcy proceedings or where a petition to order bankruptcy proceedings is rejected (§ 262, paragraph 1, Nos. 3 and 4). In these cases, the court shall record the dissolution and the grounds therefor ex officio.

Second Subdivision

Liquidation

§ 264

Duty to Liquidate

(1) After the company is dissolved, the company's assets shall be liquidated, except in the

Erster Unterabschnitt

Auflösungsgründe und Anmeldung

§ 262

Auflösungsgründe

(1) Die Aktiengesellschaft wird aufgelöst

1. durch Ablauf der in der Satzung bestimmten Zeit;

2. durch Beschluß der Hauptversammlung; dieser bedarf einer Mehrheit, die mindestens drei Viertel des bei der Beschlußfassung vertretenen Grundkapitals umfaßt; die Satzung kann eine größere Kapitalmehrheit und weitere Erfordernisse bestimmen;

3. durch die Eröffnung des Konkursverfahrens über das Vermögen der Gesellschaft;

4. mit der Rechtskraft des Beschlusses, durch den die Eröffnung des Konkursverfahrens mangels einer den Kosten des Verfahrens entsprechenden Konkursmasse abgelehnt wird.

(2) Dieser Abschnitt gilt auch, wenn die Aktiengesellschaft aus anderen Gründen aufgelöst wird.

§ 263

Anmeldung und Eintragung der Auflösung

Der Vorstand hat die Auflösung der Gesellschaft zur Eintragung in das Handelsregister anzumelden. Dies gilt nicht in den Fällen der Eröffnung und der Ablehnung der Eröffnung des Konkursverfahrens (§ 262 Abs. 1 Nr. 3 und 4). In diesen Fällen hat das Gericht die Auflösung und ihren Grund von Amts wegen einzutragen.

Zweiter Unterabschnitt

Abwicklung

§ 264

Notwendigkeit der Abwicklung

(1) Nach der Auflösung der Gesellschaft findet die Abwicklung statt, wenn nicht über das Vermögen

der Gesellschaft das Konkursverfahren eröffnet worden ist.

(2) Soweit sich aus diesem Unterabschnitt oder aus dem Zweck der Abwicklung nichts anderes ergibt, sind auf die Gesellschaft bis zum Schluß der Abwicklung die Vorschriften weiterhin anzuwenden, die für nicht aufgelöste Gesellschaften gelten.

§ 265
Abwickler

(1) Die Abwicklung besorgen die Vorstandsmitglieder als Abwickler.

(2) Die Satzung oder ein Beschluß der Hauptversammlung kann andere Personen als Abwickler bestellen. Auch eine juristische Person kann Abwickler sein.

(3) Auf Antrag des Aufsichtsrats oder einer Minderheit von Aktionären, deren Anteile zusammen den zwanzigsten Teil des Grundkapitals oder den Nennbetrag von einer Million Deutsche Mark erreichen, hat das Gericht bei Vorliegen eines wichtigen Grundes die Abwickler zu bestellen und abzuberufen. Die Aktionäre haben glaubhaft zu machen, daß sie seit mindestens drei Monaten Inhaber der Aktien sind. Zur Glaubhaftmachung genügt eine eidesstattliche Versicherung vor einem Gericht oder Notar. Gegen die Entscheidung ist die sofortige Beschwerde zulässig.

(4) Die gerichtlich bestellten Abwickler haben Anspruch auf Ersatz angemessener barer Auslagen und auf Vergütung für ihre Tätigkeit. Einigen sich der gerichtlich bestellte Abwickler und die Gesellschaft nicht, so setzt das Gericht die Auslagen und die Vergütung fest. Gegen die Entscheidung ist die sofortige Beschwerde zulässig. Die weitere Beschwerde ist ausgeschlossen. Aus der rechtskräftigen Entscheidung findet die Zwangsvollstreckung nach der Zivilprozeßordnung statt.

(5) Abwickler, die nicht vom Gericht bestellt sind, kann die Hauptversammlung jederzeit abberufen. Für die Ansprüche aus dem Anstellungsvertrag gelten die allgemeinen Vorschriften.

(6) Die Absätze 2 bis 5 gelten nicht für den Arbeitsdirektor. Seine Bestellung und Abberufung bestimmen sich nach den Vorschriften des Mitbestimmungsgesetzes oder des Mitbestimmungsergänzungsgesetzes.

§ 266
Anmeldung der Abwickler

(1) Die ersten Abwickler hat der Vorstand, jeden Wechsel der Abwickler haben diese zur Eintragung in das Handelsregister anzumelden. Ist über die Ver-

case of an order subjecting the company's assets to bankruptcy proceedings.

(2) Unless this subdivision or the purpose of the dissolution requires a different result, the provisions applicable to undissolved companies shall continue to apply to the company until the liquidation is terminated.

§ 265
Liquidators

(1) The members of the managing board shall carry out the liquidation as liquidators.

(2) The articles of incorporation or a shareholders' resolution may appoint other persons as liquidators. A legal entity may act as liquidator.

(3) The court shall appoint or dismiss the liquidators for a compelling reason upon application of the supervisory board or a minority of shareholders whose combined holdings amount to no less than one-twentieth of the stated capital or a total par value of one million German marks. The shareholders shall make a showing that they have held the shares for a period of no less than three months. For purposes of such showing, an affidavit executed before a judge or notary shall suffice. The decision of the court can be appealed.

(4) The liquidators appointed by the court shall be entitled to reimbursement for their reasonable cash expenditures and to remuneration for their services. In the event that a court-appointed liquidator and the company cannot reach agreement, such expenditures and remuneration shall be determined by the court. The decision of the court can be appealed; it shall not be subject to further appeal. The final decision shall be enforceable in accordance with the provisions of the Code of Civil Procedure.

(5) Liquidators other than those appointed by the court may be dismissed by the shareholders at any time. The rights they may have under employment contracts shall be governed by the general provisions of the law.

(6) Paragraphs 2 to 5 hereof shall not apply to the labor director. His appointment and dismissal shall be subject to the provisions of the *Mitbestimmungsgesetz* or the *Mitbestimmungsergänzungsgesetz*.

§ 266
Application to Record the Liquidators

(1) The managing board shall file an application to record the initial liquidators in the Commercial Register, and any change of liquidators

shall be filed by the latter for registration in the Commercial Register. If specific provision is made concerning the power of the liquidators to represent the company, such provision shall also be filed for registration.

(2) For the records of the court at the company's domicile, the application shall be accompanied by the original or certified copies of the documents concerning the appointment or dismissal of the liquidators as well as their powers to represent the company.

(3) The appointment or dismissal of liquidators by the court shall be recorded ex officio.

(4) The liquidators shall deposit their signatures with the court, unless they have already done so in their capacity as members of the managing board.

§ 267
Notice to Creditors

The liquidators shall give notice to the company's creditors requesting them to file their claims, which notice shall refer to the dissolution of the company. Such notice shall be published three times in the publications designated in the company's articles of incorporation.

§ 268
Duties of Liquidators

(1) The liquidators shall wind up pending business transactions, collect the receivables, convert the remaining assets into cash, and pay the creditors. To the extent required for winding-up purposes, they may also enter into new transactions.

(2) In all other respects the liquidators shall have, within the scope of their functions, the same rights and duties as the managing board. Like the managing board, they shall be subject to supervision by the supervisory board.

(3) They shall not be subject to the prohibition against competition specified in § 88.

(4) Any business correspondence directed to a specific addressee shall list all of the liquidators and the chairman of the supervisory board by their family names and at least one full given name as well as the company's domicile. This shall not be required in the case of information or reports for which printed forms with blank spaces for the details relevant in a specific case are customarily used.

tretungsbefugnis der Abwickler etwas bestimmt, so ist auch diese Bestimmung anzumelden.

(2) Der Anmeldung sind die Urkunden über die Bestellung oder Abberufung sowie über die Vertretungsbefugnis in Urschrift oder öffentlich beglaubigter Abschrift für das Gericht des Sitzes der Gesellschaft beizufügen.

(3) Die Bestellung oder Abberufung von Abwicklern durch das Gericht wird von Amts wegen eingetragen.

(4) Die Abwickler haben ihre Namensunterschrift zur Aufbewahrung beim Gericht zu zeichnen, wenn sie dies nicht schon als Vorstandsmitglieder getan haben.

§ 267
Aufruf der Gläubiger

Die Abwickler haben unter Hinweis auf die Auflösung der Gesellschaft die Gläubiger der Gesellschaft aufzufordern, ihre Ansprüche anzumelden. Die Aufforderung ist dreimal in den Gesellschaftsblättern bekanntzumachen.

§ 268
Pflichten der Abwickler

(1) Die Abwickler haben die laufenden Geschäfte zu beenden, die Forderungen einzuziehen, das übrige Vermögen in Geld umzusetzen und die Gläubiger zu befriedigen. Soweit es die Abwicklung erfordert, dürfen sie auch neue Geschäfte eingehen.

(2) Im übrigen haben die Abwickler innerhalb ihres Geschäftskreises die Rechte und Pflichten des Vorstands. Sie unterliegen wie dieser der Überwachung durch den Aufsichtsrat.

(3) Das Wettbewerbsverbot des § 88 gilt für sie nicht.

(4) Auf allen Geschäftsbriefen, die an einen bestimmten Empfänger gerichtet werden, müssen alle Abwickler und der Vorsitzende des Aufsichtsrats mit dem Familiennamen und mindestens einem ausgeschriebenen Vornamen sowie der Sitz der Gesellschaft angegeben werden. Der Angabe bedarf es nicht bei Mitteilungen oder Berichten, für die üblicherweise Vordrucke verwendet werden, in denen lediglich die im Einzelfall erforderlichen besonderen Angaben eingefügt zu werden brauchen.

§ 269

Vertretung durch die Abwickler

(1) Die Abwickler vertreten die Gesellschaft gerichtlich und außergerichtlich.

(2) Sind mehrere Abwickler bestellt, so sind, wenn die Satzung oder die sonst zuständige Stelle nichts anderes bestimmt, sämtliche Abwickler nur gemeinschaftlich zur Vertretung der Gesellschaft befugt. Ist eine Willenserklärung gegenüber der Gesellschaft abzugeben, so genügt die Abgabe gegenüber einem Abwickler.

(3) Die Satzung oder die sonst zuständige Stelle kann auch bestimmen, daß einzelne Abwickler allein oder in Gemeinschaft mit einem Prokuristen zur Vertretung der Gesellschaft befugt sind. Dasselbe kann der Aufsichtsrat bestimmen, wenn die Satzung oder ein Beschluß der Hauptversammlung ihn hierzu ermächtigt hat. Absatz 2 Satz 2 gilt in diesen Fällen sinngemäß.

(4) Zur Gesamtvertretung befugte Abwickler können einzelne von ihnen zur Vornahme bestimmter Geschäfte oder bestimmter Arten von Geschäften ermächtigen. Dies gilt sinngemäß, wenn ein einzelner Abwickler in Gemeinschaft mit einem Prokuristen zur Vertretung der Gesellschaft befugt ist.

(5) Die Vertretungsbefugnis der Abwickler kann nicht beschränkt werden.

(6) Abwickler zeichnen für die Gesellschaft, indem sie der Firma einen die Abwicklung andeutenden Zusatz und ihre Namensunterschrift hinzufügen.

§ 270

Eröffnungsbilanz. Jahresabschluß und Geschäftsbericht

(1) Die Abwickler haben für den Beginn der Abwicklung eine Bilanz (Eröffnungsbilanz) und einen die Eröffnungsbilanz erläuternden Bericht sowie für den Schluß jedes Jahres einen Jahresabschluß und einen Geschäftsbericht aufzustellen.

(2) Die Hauptversammlung beschließt über die Feststellung der Eröffnungsbilanz, des Jahresabschlusses und über die Entlastung der Abwickler und der Mitglieder des Aufsichtsrats. Für die Eröffnungsbilanz, den Jahresabschluß und den Geschäftsbericht gelten sinngemäß §§ 148, 149, 151, 152, 160, 161, 171, 175, 176 Abs. 1, §§ 177 und 178.

§ 269

Representation by Liquidators

(1) The liquidators shall represent the company both in and out of court.

(2) If several liquidators are appointed, they shall represent the company jointly, unless the articles of incorporation or the authority appointing the liquidators provides otherwise. If declarations with legal effect are to be addressed to the company, it shall be sufficient to address them to any one of the liquidators.

(3) The articles of incorporation or the authority appointing the liquidators may also provide that individual liquidators can represent the company alone or together with a *Prokurist*. The same provision may be made by the supervisory board if the articles of incorporation or a shareholders' resolution authorizes it to do so. In this event, paragraph 2, second sentence, hereof shall apply *mutatis mutandis*.

(4) Liquidators authorized to represent the company jointly may authorize individual liquidators to carry out specified transactions or specified types of transactions. The same shall apply, *mutatis mutandis*, if one of the liquidators is empowered to represent the company together with a *Prokurist*.

(5) The power of the liquidators to represent the company cannot be limited.

(6) The liquidators shall sign for the company by adding to the name of the company an affix indicating that the company is in liquidation, and their own signatures.

§ 270

Opening Balance Sheet.
Annual Financial Statements and Business Report

(1) The liquidators shall, at the beginning of the liquidation, prepare a balance sheet (opening balance sheet) and a report explaining the opening balance sheet, and, for each fiscal year, annual financial statements and a business report.

(2) The shareholders shall by resolution establish the opening balance sheet and the annual financial statements, and ratify the acts of the liquidators and the members of the supervisory board. §§ 148, 149, 151, 152, 160, 161, 171, 175, 176, paragraph 1, §§ 177 and 178 shall apply, *mutatis mutandis*, to the opening balance sheet, the annual financial statements, and the business report.

(3) §§ 153 to 158 and §§ 162 to 169, concerning the classifications of the profit and loss statement, the valuation of the items of the annual balance sheet, and the audit of the annual financial statements, shall not be applicable. The court may, however, for compelling reasons, order an audit of the opening balance sheet or of the annual financial statements; the decision of the court can be appealed. In this event, §§ 162 to 169, 171, paragraph 1, second sentence, and § 176, paragraph 2, concerning the audit of the annual financial statements, shall apply *mutatis mutandis.*

§ 271
Distribution of Assets

(1) Any assets of the company remaining after payment of the liabilities shall be distributed to the shareholders.

(2) The assets shall be distributed in proportion to the par value of the shares, unless there are shares granting different rights with respect to the distribution of the company's assets.

(3) If contributions to the stated capital were not rendered in the same proportion for all shares, the contributions paid in shall be returned and any surplus remaining shall be distributed in proportion to the par value of the shares. If the assets are insufficient to return the contributions, the shareholders shall bear the loss in proportion to the par value of their shares; contributions still outstanding shall be collected to the extent necessary.

§ 272
Protection of Creditors

(1) The assets may be distributed only after the expiration of one year from the date of the third publication of the notice to the creditors.

(2) In the event that a known creditor fails to respond, the amount owing him shall be deposited for his account, provided that a right to make such deposit exists.

(3) If any liability cannot be presently discharged or if it is contested, the assets may be distributed only if the creditor has been secured.

§ 273
Termination of Liquidation

(1) After the liquidation has been terminated and the final accounting has been rendered, the liquidators shall file an application to record the termination of the liquidation in the Commercial Register. The registration of the company shall be cancelled.

§ 271

---

(3) Die §§ 153 bis 158, 162 bis 169 über die Gliederung der Gewinn- und Verlustrechnung, über die Wertansätze in der Jahresbilanz und über die Prüfung des Jahresabschlusses gelten nicht. Das Gericht kann jedoch aus wichtigem Grund eine Prüfung der Eröffnungsbilanz oder des Jahresabschlusses anordnen; gegen die Entscheidung ist die sofortige Beschwerde zulässig. In diesem Fall gelten die §§ 162 bis 169, 171 Abs. 1 Satz 2, § 176 Abs. 2 über die Prüfung des Jahresabschlusses sinngemäß.

§ 271
Verteilung des Vermögens

(1) Das nach der Berichtigung der Verbindlichkeiten verbleibende Vermögen der Gesellschaft wird unter die Aktionäre verteilt.

(2) Das Vermögen ist nach dem Verhältnis der Aktiennennbeträge zu verteilen, wenn nicht Aktien mit verschiedenen Rechten bei der Verteilung des Gesellschaftsvermögens vorhanden sind.

(3) Sind die Einlagen auf das Grundkapital nicht auf alle Aktien in demselben Verhältnis geleistet, so werden die geleisteten Einlagen erstattet und ein Überschuß nach dem Verhältnis der Aktiennennbeträge verteilt. Reicht das Vermögen zur Erstattung der Einlagen nicht aus, so haben die Aktionäre den Verlust nach dem Verhältnis der Aktiennennbeträge zu tragen; die noch ausstehenden Einlagen sind, soweit nötig, einzuziehen.

§ 272
Gläubigerschutz

(1) Das Vermögen darf nur verteilt werden, wenn ein Jahr seit dem Tage verstrichen ist, an dem der Aufruf der Gläubiger zum drittenmal bekanntgemacht worden ist.

(2) Meldet sich ein bekannter Gläubiger nicht, so ist der geschuldete Betrag für ihn zu hinterlegen, wenn ein Recht zur Hinterlegung besteht.

(3) Kann eine Verbindlichkeit zur Zeit nicht berichtigt werden oder ist sie streitig, so darf das Vermögen nur verteilt werden, wenn dem Gläubiger Sicherheit geleistet ist.

§ 273
Schluß der Abwicklung

(1) Ist die Abwicklung beendet und die Schlußrechnung gelegt, so haben die Abwickler den Schluß der Abwicklung zur Eintragung in das Handelsregister anzumelden. Die Gesellschaft ist zu löschen.

(2) Die Bücher und Schriften der Gesellschaft sind an einem vom Gericht bestimmten sicheren Ort zur Aufbewahrung auf zehn Jahre zu hinterlegen.

(3) Das Gericht kann den Aktionären und den Gläubigern die Einsicht der Bücher und Schriften gestatten.

(4) Stellt sich nachträglich heraus, daß weitere Abwicklungsmaßnahmen nötig sind, so hat auf Antrag eines Beteiligten das Gericht die bisherigen Abwickler neu zu bestellen oder andere Abwickler zu berufen. § 265 Abs. 4 gilt.

(5) Gegen die Entscheidungen nach den Absätzen 2, 3 und 4 Satz 1 ist die sofortige Beschwerde zulässig.

§ 274
Fortsetzung einer aufgelösten Gesellschaft

(1) Ist eine Aktiengesellschaft durch Zeitablauf oder durch Beschluß der Hauptversammlung aufgelöst worden, so kann die Hauptversammlung, solange noch nicht mit der Verteilung des Vermögens unter die Aktionäre begonnen ist, die Fortsetzung der Gesellschaft beschließen. Der Beschluß bedarf einer Mehrheit, die mindestens drei Viertel des bei der Beschlußfassung vertretenen Grundkapitals umfaßt. Die Satzung kann eine größere Kapitalmehrheit und weitere Erfordernisse bestimmen.

(2) Gleiches gilt, wenn die Gesellschaft durch die Eröffnung des Konkursverfahrens aufgelöst, das Konkursverfahren aber auf Antrag der Gesellschaft eingestellt oder nach rechtskräftiger Bestätigung eines Zwangsvergleichs aufgehoben worden ist.

(3) Die Abwickler haben die Fortsetzung der Gesellschaft zur Eintragung in das Handelsregister anzumelden. Sie haben bei der Anmeldung nachzuweisen, daß noch nicht mit der Verteilung des Vermögens der Gesellschaft unter die Aktionäre begonnen worden ist.

(4) Der Fortsetzungsbeschluß wird erst wirksam, wenn er in das Handelsregister des Sitzes der Gesellschaft eingetragen worden ist.

Zweiter Abschnitt
Nichtigerklärung der Gesellschaft

§ 275
Klage auf Nichtigerklärung

(1) Enthält die Satzung nicht die nach § 23 Abs. 3 wesentlichen Bestimmungen oder ist eine dieser Be-

(2) The company's books and records shall be kept for ten years in a safe place to be specified by the court.

(3) The court may permit the shareholders and the creditors to inspect the books and records.

(4) If it later appears that additional measures of liquidation are necessary, the court, upon application of any party in interest, shall reappoint the former liquidators or appoint other liquidators. § 265, paragraph 4, shall apply.

(5) The decisions made pursuant to paragraphs 2, 3 and 4, first sentence, hereof can be appealed.

§ 274
Continuation of Dissolved Company

(1) If a stock corporation is dissolved by expiration of time or a resolution of the shareholders, the shareholders may adopt a resolution to continue the company as long as the distribution of its assets to the shareholders has not commenced. Such resolution shall require a majority of no less than three-fourths of the stated capital represented when the resolution is adopted. The articles of incorporation may provide for a higher capital majority and establish additional requirements.

(2) The same shall apply if the company was dissolved by an order subjecting the company's assets to bankruptcy proceedings, but such bankruptcy proceedings were discontinued on application by the company or terminated by a final judicial confirmation of a compulsory settlement with the creditors.

(3) The liquidators shall file an application to record the continuation of the company in the Commercial Register. Upon making such application they shall make a showing that the distribution of the company's assets to the shareholders has not commenced.

(4) The resolution to continue the company shall become effective upon its registration in the Commercial Register at the company's domicile.

Second Division
Declaration of Nullity of the Company

§ 275
Action for Declaration of Nullity

(1) If the articles of incorporation do not contain the essential provisions required by § 23,

paragraph 3, or if any one of these provisions is void, each shareholder and each member of the managing board and of the supervisory board may bring an action to have the company declared void. This action cannot be based on any other grounds.

(2) If the defect can be cured in accordance with § 276, the action may be brought only after a person entitled to bring such action has requested the company to cure the defect and the company has failed to comply with this request within three months.

(3) The action must be brought within three years from the date the company is registered. An ex officio cancellation of the company pursuant to § 144, paragraph 1, of the *Reichsgesetz über die Angelegenheiten der freiwilligen Gerichtsbarkeit* shall not be precluded by the expiration of this period.

(4) § 246, paragraphs 2 to 4, §§ 247, 248, first sentence, and § 249, paragraph 2, shall apply, *mutatis mutandis,* to the action. The managing board shall file a certified copy of the complaint and the final judgment with the Commercial Register. The nullity of the company pursuant to a final judgment shall be recorded.

§ 276
Curing of Defects

A defect in the provisions concerning the name or domicile of the company, the purpose of the enterprise, the composition of the managing board, or the manner in which notices of the company are to be published can be cured by amending the articles of incorporation in accordance with the law and the articles of incorporation.

§ 277
Effect of Registration of Nullity

(1) Once the nullity of a company pursuant to a final judgment or a decision of the court of registry is recorded in the Commercial Register, the company shall be liquidated in accordance with the provisions concerning liquidation in case of dissolution.

(2) The validity of transactions entered into in the name of the company shall not be affected by such nullity.

(3) The company's shareholders shall render contributions to the extent required to discharge liabilities incurred.

stimmungen nichtig, so kann jeder Aktionär und jedes Mitglied des Vorstands und des Aufsichtsrats darauf klagen, daß die Gesellschaft für nichtig erklärt werde. Auf andere Gründe kann die Klage nicht gestützt werden.

(2) Kann der Mangel nach § 276 geheilt werden, so kann die Klage erst erhoben werden, nachdem ein Klageberechtigter die Gesellschaft aufgefordert hat, den Mangel zu beseitigen, und sie binnen drei Monaten dieser Aufforderung nicht nachgekommen ist.

(3) Die Klage muß binnen drei Jahren nach Eintragung der Gesellschaft erhoben werden. Eine Löschung der Gesellschaft von Amts wegen nach § 144 Abs. 1 des Reichsgesetzes über die Angelegenheiten der freiwilligen Gerichtsbarkeit wird durch den Zeitablauf nicht ausgeschlossen.

(4) Für die Klage gelten § 246 Abs. 2 bis 4, §§ 247, 248 Satz 1, § 249 Abs. 2 sinngemäß. Der Vorstand hat eine beglaubigte Abschrift der Klage und das rechtskräftige Urteil zum Handelsregister einzureichen. Die Nichtigkeit der Gesellschaft auf Grund rechtskräftigen Urteils ist einzutragen.

§ 276
Heilung von Mängeln

Ein Mangel, der die Bestimmungen über die Firma oder den Sitz der Gesellschaft, den Gegenstand des Unternehmens, die Zusammensetzung des Vorstands oder die Form der Bekanntmachungen der Gesellschaft betrifft, kann unter Beachtung der Bestimmungen des Gesetzes und der Satzung über Satzungsänderungen geheilt werden.

§ 277
Wirkung der Eintragung der Nichtigkeit

(1) Ist die Nichtigkeit einer Gesellschaft auf Grund rechtskräftigen Urteils oder einer Entscheidung des Registergerichts in das Handelsregister eingetragen, so findet die Abwicklung nach den Vorschriften über die Abwicklung bei Auflösung statt.

(2) Die Wirksamkeit der im Namen der Gesellschaft vorgenommenen Rechtsgeschäfte wird durch die Nichtigkeit nicht berührt.

(3) Die Gesellschafter haben die Einlagen zu leisten, soweit es zur Erfüllung der eingegangenen Verbindlichkeiten nötig ist.

§ 276

Zweites Buch
Kommanditgesellschaft auf Aktien

Book Two
Partnership Limited by Shares

§ 278
Wesen der Kommanditgesellschaft auf Aktien

(1) Die Kommanditgesellschaft auf Aktien ist eine Gesellschaft mit eigener Rechtspersönlichkeit, bei der mindestens ein Gesellschafter den Gesellschaftsgläubigern unbeschränkt haftet (persönlich haftender Gesellschafter) und die übrigen an dem in Aktien zerlegten Grundkapital beteiligt sind, ohne persönlich für die Verbindlichkeiten der Gesellschaft zu haften (Kommanditaktionäre).

(2) Das Rechtsverhältnis der persönlich haftenden Gesellschafter untereinander und gegenüber der Gesamtheit der Kommanditaktionäre sowie gegenüber Dritten, namentlich die Befugnis der persönlich haftenden Gesellschafter zur Geschäftsführung und zur Vertretung der Gesellschaft, bestimmt sich nach den Vorschriften des Handelsgesetzbuchs über die Kommanditgesellschaft.

(3) Im übrigen gelten für die Kommanditgesellschaft auf Aktien, soweit sich aus den folgenden Vorschriften oder aus dem Fehlen eines Vorstands nichts anderes ergibt, die Vorschriften des Ersten Buchs über die Aktiengesellschaft sinngemäß.

§ 279
Firma

(1) Die Firma der Kommanditgesellschaft auf Aktien ist in der Regel dem Gegenstand des Unternehmens zu entnehmen. Sie muß die Bezeichnung „Kommanditgesellschaft auf Aktien" enthalten.

(2) Führt die Kommanditgesellschaft auf Aktien die Firma eines auf sie übergegangenen Handelsgeschäfts fort (§ 22 des Handelsgesetzbuchs), so muß sie die Bezeichnung „Kommanditgesellschaft auf Aktien" in die Firma aufnehmen.

§ 280
Feststellung der Satzung. Gründer

(1) Die Satzung muß von mindestens fünf Personen durch gerichtliche oder notarielle Beurkundung festgestellt werden. In der Urkunde sind der Nennbetrag, der Ausgabebetrag und, wenn mehrere Gattungen bestehen, die Gattung der Aktien anzugeben, die jeder Beteiligte übernimmt. Bevollmächtigte bedürfen einer gerichtlich oder notariell beglaubigten Vollmacht.

§ 278
Nature of Partnership Limited by Shares

(1) A partnership limited by shares is a company having separate legal personality with at least one member whose liability to the company's creditors is unlimited (general partner), and others who have an interest in the stated capital divided into shares and who are not personally liable for the obligations of the company (limited shareholders).

(2) The legal relationship of the general partners to each other and to the limited shareholders and third parties, in particular the power of the general partners to manage and to represent the company, shall be subject to the provisions of the Commercial Code concerning limited partnerships.

(3) In all other respects, the provisions of Book One concerning stock corporations shall apply, *mutatis mutandis*, to partnerships limited by shares, unless the following provisions or the lack of a managing board requires a different result.

§ 279
Name

(1) As a rule, the name of the partnership limited by shares shall be derived from the purpose of the enterprise. It must contain the designation *"Kommanditgesellschaft auf Aktien."*

(2) In the event that the partnership limited by shares retains the name of a business taken over by it (§ 22 of the Commercial Code), it must add the designation *"Kommanditgesellschaft auf Aktien"* to the name.

§ 280
Execution of Articles of Incorporation. Incorporators

(1) The articles of incorporation shall be executed by no less than five persons in the form of a judicial or notarial record. The instrument shall specify the par value of the shares, the amount for which they are issued and, if there are several classes of shares, the class of shares subscribed to by each participant. Attorneys-in-fact shall require a power of attorney certified by a judge or notary.

§ 280

(2) All general partners shall take part in the execution of the articles of incorporation. In addition, persons contributing, as limited shareholders, assets for shares shall take part in the execution.

(3) Incorporators of the company are those members who have executed the articles of incorporation.

§ 281
Content of Articles of Incorporation

(1) The articles of incorporation shall contain, in addition to the particulars set forth in § 23, paragraph 3, Nos. 1 to 4 and 6, the family name, given name, occupation, and residence of each general partner.

(2) Contributions made by the general partners, unless they become part of the stated capital, shall be specified in the articles of incorporation, stating the amount and nature thereof.

(3) § 26, paragraph 1, concerning preferences, shall apply to any preferences granted to general partners.

§ 282
Registration of General Partners

Upon registration of the company in the Commercial Register, the general partners shall be listed instead of members of the managing board. If the articles of incorporation contain special provisions concerning the power of the general partners to represent the company, such provisions shall also be recorded.

§ 283
General Partners

The provisions concerning the managing board of a stock corporation shall apply, *mutatis mutandis*, to the general partners with respect to the following:

1. the applications, filing, declarations and evidence to be presented to the Commercial Register, as well as the provisions concerning publications;
2. the audit of the formation;
3. the duty of care and liability;
4. the duties toward the supervisory board;
5. the permissibility of extending loans;
6. the calling of shareholders' meetings;
7. the special audit;

(2) Alle persönlich haftenden Gesellschafter müssen sich bei der Feststellung der Satzung beteiligen. Außer ihnen müssen die Personen mitwirken, die als Kommanditaktionäre Aktien gegen Einlagen übernehmen.

(3) Die Gesellschafter, die die Satzung festgestellt haben, sind die Gründer der Gesellschaft.

§ 281
Inhalt der Satzung

(1) Die Satzung muß außer den Festsetzungen nach § 23 Abs. 3 Nr. 1 bis 4 und 6 den Namen, Vornamen, Beruf und Wohnort jedes persönlich haftenden Gesellschafters enthalten.

(2) Vermögenseinlagen der persönlich haftenden Gesellschafter müssen, wenn sie nicht auf das Grundkapital geleistet werden, nach Höhe und Art in der Satzung festgesetzt werden.

(3) § 26 Abs. 1 über Sondervorteile gilt für alle besonderen Vorteile, die zugunsten eines persönlich haftenden Gesellschafters bedungen sind.

§ 282
Eintragung der persönlich haftenden Gesellschafter

Bei der Eintragung der Gesellschaft in das Handelsregister sind statt der Vorstandsmitglieder die persönlich haftenden Gesellschafter anzugeben. Enthält die Satzung besondere Bestimmungen über die Befugnis der persönlich haftenden Gesellschafter zur Vertretung der Gesellschaft, so sind auch diese Bestimmungen einzutragen.

§ 283
Persönlich haftende Gesellschafter

Für die persönlich haftenden Gesellschafter gelten sinngemäß die für den Vorstand der Aktiengesellschaft geltenden Vorschriften über

1. die Anmeldungen, Einreichungen, Erklärungen und Nachweise zum Handelsregister sowie über Bekanntmachungen;
2. die Gründungsprüfung;
3. die Sorgfaltspflicht und Verantwortlichkeit;
4. die Pflichten gegenüber dem Aufsichtsrat;
5. die Zulässigkeit einer Kreditgewährung;
6. die Einberufung der Hauptversammlung;
7. die Sonderprüfung;

8. die Geltendmachung von Ersatzansprüchen wegen der Geschäftsführung;
9. die Aufstellung und Vorlegung des Jahresabschlusses, des Geschäftsberichts und des Vorschlags für die Verwendung des Bilanzgewinns;
10. die Prüfung des Jahresabschlusses;
11. die Rechnungslegung im Konzern;
12. die Ausgabe von Aktien bei bedingter Kapitalerhöhung, bei genehmigtem Kapital und bei Kapitalerhöhung aus Gesellschaftsmitteln;
13. die Nichtigkeit und Anfechtung von Hauptversammlungsbeschlüssen;
14. den Antrag auf Eröffnung des Konkursverfahrens oder des gerichtlichen Vergleichsverfahrens

8. the assertion of claims for damages arising out of the conduct of the company's affairs;
9. the preparation and submission of the annual financial statements, the business report, and the proposal concerning the disposition of retained earnings;
10. the audit of the annual financial statements;
11. the accounting method used by an affiliated group of companies;
12. the issuance of shares in connection with a conditional capital increase, authorized capital, and capital increases out of retained earnings;
13. the nullity and voidability of shareholders' resolutions;
14. the petition to order bankruptcy proceedings or a judicial composition with creditors.

§ 284
Wettbewerbsverbot

(1) Ein persönlich haftender Gesellschafter darf ohne ausdrückliche Einwilligung der übrigen persönlich haftenden Gesellschafter und des Aufsichtsrats weder im Geschäftszweig der Gesellschaft für eigene oder fremde Rechnung Geschäfte machen noch Mitglied des Vorstands oder Geschäftsführer oder persönlich haftender Gesellschafter einer anderen gleichartigen Handelsgesellschaft sein. Die Einwilligung kann nur für bestimmte Arten von Geschäften oder für bestimmte Handelsgesellschaften erteilt werden.

(2) Verstößt ein persönlich haftender Gesellschafter gegen dieses Verbot, so kann die Gesellschaft Schadenersatz fordern. Sie kann statt dessen von dem Gesellschafter verlangen, daß er die für eigene Rechnung gemachten Geschäfte als für Rechnung der Gesellschaft eingegangen gelten läßt und die aus Geschäften für fremde Rechnung bezogene Vergütung herausgibt oder seinen Anspruch auf die Vergütung abtritt.

(3) Die Ansprüche der Gesellschaft verjähren in drei Monaten seit dem Zeitpunkt, in dem die übrigen persönlich haftenden Gesellschafter und die Aufsichtsratsmitglieder von der zum Schadenersatz verpflichtenden Handlung Kenntnis erlangen. Sie verjähren ohne Rücksicht auf diese Kenntnis in fünf Jahren seit ihrer Entstehung.

§ 285
Hauptversammlung

(1) In der Hauptversammlung haben die persönlich haftenden Gesellschafter nur ein Stimmrecht für

§ 284
Non-competition Clause

(1) Absent the express approval of the other general partners and of the supervisory board, a general partner may neither enter into any business transactions which are within the company's line of business for his own account or for the account of others nor be a member of the managing board or a manager or general partner of a similar enterprise. The approval must be limited to specific types of transactions or to specific commercial companies.

(2) If a general partner violates this prohibition, the company may claim damages. In lieu thereof, it may require the partner to carry out a transaction entered into for the partner's account as one made for the account of the company, and to transfer to it the compensation received for transactions entered into for the account of another, or to assign his rights to such compensation.

(3) The company's claim shall be barred after the expiration of three months from the date on which the other general partners and the members of the supervisory board obtained knowledge of the acts giving rise to the claim for damages. Irrespective of such knowledge, these claims shall be barred after the expiration of five years from the date on which they arose.

§ 285
Shareholders' Meeting

(1) In the shareholders' meeting the general partners may vote only shares which they own.

§ 285

They cannot exercise the right to vote either for themselves or for another in the case of resolutions concerning

1. the election and dismissal of the supervisory board;
2. the ratification of the acts of the general partners and of the members of the supervisory board;
3. the appointment of special auditors;
4. the assertion of claims for damages;
5. the waiver of claims for damages;
6. the election of annual auditors.

When such resolutions are adopted, the voting rights of the general partners may not be exercised by others.

(2) Resolutions of the shareholders shall require the approval of the general partners to the extent that they relate to matters which, in the case of a limited partnership, require the approval of the general partners and the limited partners. The exercise of powers of the limited shareholders or of a minority of limited shareholders in connection with the appointment of auditors and the assertion of claims by the company arising from the formation or management of the company shall not require the consent of the general partners.

(3) Resolutions of the shareholders which require the approval of the general partners shall not be filed with the Commercial Register before such approval is given. For resolutions that must be recorded in the Commercial Register, the approval shall be recorded in the minutes of the meeting or in an appendix to the minutes.

§ 286
Annual Financial Statements.
Business Report

(1) The shareholders shall by resolution establish the annual financial statements. Such resolutions shall require the approval of the general partners.

(2) The equity interests of the general partners shall be shown separately in the annual balance sheet following the item "stated capital." The losses allocable to the equity interest of a general partner for the fiscal year shall be deducted therefrom. To the extent that such losses exceed the equity interest, they shall be shown separately on the assets side, preceding the item "losses," as "share of loss of general partners offset by capital contributions." Loans qualifying

ihre Aktien. Sie können das Stimmrecht weder für sich noch für einen anderen ausüben bei Beschlußfassungen über

1. die Wahl und Abberufung des Aufsichtsrats;
2. die Entlastung der persönlich haftenden Gesellschafter und der Mitglieder des Aufsichtsrats;
3. die Bestellung von Sonderprüfern;
4. die Geltendmachung von Ersatzansprüchen;
5. den Verzicht auf Ersatzansprüche;
6. die Wahl von Abschlußprüfern.

Bei diesen Beschlußfassungen kann ihr Stimmrecht auch nicht durch einen anderen ausgeübt werden.

(2) Die Beschlüsse der Hauptversammlung bedürfen der Zustimmung der persönlich haftenden Gesellschafter, soweit sie Angelegenheiten betreffen, für die bei einer Kommanditgesellschaft das Einverständnis der persönlich haftenden Gesellschafter und der Kommanditisten erforderlich ist. Die Ausübung der Befugnisse, die der Hauptversammlung oder einer Minderheit von Kommanditaktionären bei der Bestellung von Prüfern und der Geltendmachung von Ansprüchen der Gesellschaft aus der Gründung oder der Geschäftsführung zustehen, bedarf nicht der Zustimmung der persönlich haftenden Gesellschafter.

(3) Beschlüsse der Hauptversammlung, die der Zustimmung der persönlich haftenden Gesellschafter bedürfen, sind zum Handelsregister erst einzureichen, wenn die Zustimmung vorliegt. Bei Beschlüssen, die in das Handelsregister einzutragen sind, ist die Zustimmung in der Verhandlungsniederschrift oder in einem Anhang zur Niederschrift zu beurkunden.

§ 286
Jahresabschluß. Geschäftsbericht

(1) Die Hauptversammlung beschließt über die Feststellung des Jahresabschlusses. Der Beschluß bedarf der Zustimmung der persönlich haftenden Gesellschafter.

(2) In der Jahresbilanz sind die Kapitalanteile der persönlich haftenden Gesellschafter nach dem Posten „Grundkapital" gesondert auszuweisen. Der auf den Kapitalanteil eines persönlich haftenden Gesellschafters für das Geschäftsjahr entfallende Verlust ist von dem Kapitalanteil abzuschreiben. Soweit der Verlust den Kapitalanteil übersteigt, ist er auf der Aktivseite vor dem Posten „Bilanzverlust" als „nicht durch Vermögenseinlagen gedeckter Verlustanteil persönlich haftender Gesellschafter" gesondert auszuweisen. Unter § 89 fallende Kredite, die die Gesellschaft persönlich haftenden Gesell-

schaftern, deren Ehegatten oder minderjährigen Kindern oder Dritten, die für Rechnung dieser Personen handeln, gewährt hat, sind auf der Aktivseite bei dem Posten III B Nr. 11 Buchstabe a unter „davon an persönlich haftende Gesellschafter und deren Angehörige" zu vermerken.

(3) In der Gewinn- und Verlustrechnung braucht der auf die Kapitalanteile der persönlich haftenden Gesellschafter entfallende Gewinn oder Verlust nicht gesondert ausgewiesen zu werden.

(4) § 160 Abs. 3 Nr. 8 und 9 gilt für die persönlich haftenden Gesellschafter mit der Maßgabe, daß der auf den Kapitalanteil eines persönlich haftenden Gesellschafters entfallende Gewinn nicht angegeben zu werden braucht.

§ 287
Aufsichtsrat

(1) Die Beschlüsse der Kommanditaktionäre führt der Aufsichtsrat aus, wenn die Satzung nichts anderes bestimmt.

(2) In Rechtsstreitigkeiten, die die Gesamtheit der Kommanditaktionäre gegen die persönlich haftenden Gesellschafter oder diese gegen die Gesamtheit der Kommanditaktionäre führen, vertritt der Aufsichtsrat die Kommanditaktionäre, wenn die Hauptversammlung keine besonderen Vertreter gewählt hat. Für die Kosten des Rechtsstreits, die den Kommanditaktionären zur Last fallen, haftet die Gesellschaft unbeschadet ihres Rückgriffs gegen die Kommanditaktionäre.

(3) Persönlich haftende Gesellschafter können nicht Aufsichtsratsmitglieder sein.

§ 288
Entnahmen
der persönlich haftenden Gesellschafter.
Kreditgewährung

(1) Entfällt auf einen persönlich haftenden Gesellschafter ein Verlust, der seinen Kapitalanteil übersteigt, so darf er keinen Gewinn auf seinen Kapitalanteil entnehmen. Er darf ferner keinen solchen Gewinnanteil und kein Geld auf seinen Kapitalanteil entnehmen, solange die Summe aus Bilanzverlust, nicht durch Einlagen gedeckten Verlustanteilen persönlich haftender Gesellschafter und Forderungen aus Krediten an persönlich haftende Gesellschafter und deren Angehörige die Summe aus Gewinnvortrag, offenen Rücklagen und Kapitalanteilen der persönlich haftenden Gesellschafter übersteigt.

(2) Solange die Voraussetzung von Absatz 1 Satz 2 vorliegt, darf die Gesellschaft keinen unter § 286 Abs. 2 Satz 4 fallenden Kredit gewähren. Ein

under § 89 extended by the company to general partners, their spouses or minor children, or to third parties acting for the account of such persons, shall be shown on the assets side under item III B No. 11 (a) as "portion thereof extended to general partners and their relatives."

(3) Profits or losses allocable to the equity interests of general partners need not be stated separately in the profit and loss statement.

(4) § 160, paragraph 3, Nos. 8 and 9, shall apply to the general partners, provided that the retained earnings allocable to the equity interest of a general partner need not be stated.

§ 287
Supervisory Board

(1) Unless the articles of incorporation provide otherwise, resolutions of the limited shareholders shall be carried out by the supervisory board.

(2) In case of legal action brought by the limited shareholders as a whole against the general partners, or by the latter against the limited shareholders as a whole, the supervisory board shall represent the limited shareholders unless the shareholders have elected special representatives. The company shall be liable for the cost of litigation assessed against the limited shareholders, notwithstanding its right of recourse against the limited shareholders.

(3) General partners cannot be members of the supervisory board.

§ 288
Withdrawals by General Partners.
Loans

(1) If losses in excess of his equity interest are allocable to a general partner, he may not withdraw profits on his equity interest. Moreover, he may not withdraw such profits or cash on his equity interest as long as the total of the accumulated losses, the share of losses of general partners not covered by contributions, and obligations arising from loans extended to general partners and their relatives exceed the total of retained earnings, disclosed reserves, and the equity of the general partners.

(2) As long as the conditions referred to in paragraph 1, second sentence, hereof exist, the company may not extend loans qualifying under § 286, paragraph 2, fourth sentence. A loan ex-

tended contrary to this provision shall be returned without delay, irrespective of any agreements to the contrary.

(3) The rights of general partners to remuneration for services rendered, where such remuneration is not dependent on profits, shall not be affected by these provisions. § 87, paragraph 2, first sentence, shall apply, *mutatis mutandis*, to a reduction of such remuneration.

§ 289
Dissolution

(1) The grounds for the dissolution of a partnership limited by shares and the withdrawal of one of several general partners from the company shall be subject to the provisions of the Commercial Code concerning limited partnerships, unless paragraphs 2 to 6 hereof provide otherwise.

(2) A company limited by shares shall be dissolved also by a final order dismissing the petition for the institution of bankruptcy proceedings, on the ground that the estate in bankruptcy is insufficient to cover the costs of the proceedings.

(3) The company shall not be dissolved by an order subjecting the assets of a limited shareholder to bankruptcy proceedings. The creditors of a limited shareholder shall not have the right to terminate the company.

(4) The termination of the company by the limited shareholders and their approval of the dissolution of the company shall require a shareholders' resolution. The same applies to the application for dissolution of the company by a court order. The resolution shall require a majority of no less than three-fourths of the stated capital represented when the resolution is adopted. The articles of incorporation may provide for a higher capital majority and establish additional requirements.

(5) Except in case of expulsion, general partners may withdraw from the company only if the articles of incorporation permit such withdrawal.

(6) An application to record the dissolution of the company and the withdrawal of a general partner in the Commercial Register must be filed by all of the general partners. § 143, paragraph 3, of the Commercial Code shall apply *mutatis mutandis*.

§ 289

trotzdem gewährter Kredit ist ohne Rücksicht auf entgegenstehende Vereinbarungen sofort zurückzugewähren.

(3) Ansprüche persönlich haftender Gesellschafter auf nicht vom Gewinn abhängige Tätigkeitsvergütungen werden durch diese Vorschriften nicht berührt. Für eine Herabsetzung solcher Vergütungen gilt § 87 Abs. 2 Satz 1 sinngemäß.

§ 289
Auflösung

(1) Die Gründe für die Auflösung der Kommanditgesellschaft auf Aktien und das Ausscheiden eines von mehreren persönlich haftenden Gesellschaftern aus der Gesellschaft richten sich, soweit in den Absätzen 2 bis 6 nichts anderes bestimmt ist, nach den Vorschriften des Handelsgesetzbuchs über die Kommanditgesellschaft.

(2) Die Kommanditgesellschaft auf Aktien wird auch mit der Rechtskraft des Beschlusses aufgelöst, durch den die Eröffnung des Konkursverfahrens mangels einer den Kosten des Verfahrens entsprechenden Konkursmasse abgelehnt wird.

(3) Durch die Eröffnung des Konkursverfahrens über das Vermögen eines Kommanditaktionärs wird die Gesellschaft nicht aufgelöst. Die Gläubiger eines Kommanditaktionärs sind nicht berechtigt, die Gesellschaft zu kündigen.

(4) Für die Kündigung der Gesellschaft durch die Kommanditaktionäre und für ihre Zustimmung zur Auflösung der Gesellschaft ist ein Beschluß der Hauptversammlung nötig. Gleiches gilt für den Antrag auf Auflösung der Gesellschaft durch gerichtliche Entscheidung. Der Beschluß bedarf einer Mehrheit, die mindestens drei Viertel des bei der Beschlußfassung vertretenen Grundkapitals umfaßt. Die Satzung kann eine größere Kapitalmehrheit und weitere Erfordernisse bestimmen.

(5) Persönlich haftende Gesellschafter können außer durch Ausschließung nur ausscheiden, wenn es die Satzung für zulässig erklärt.

(6) Die Auflösung der Gesellschaft und das Ausscheiden eines persönlich haftenden Gesellschafters ist von allen persönlich haftenden Gesellschaftern zur Eintragung in das Handelsregister anzumelden. § 143 Abs. 3 des Handelsgesetzbuchs gilt sinngemäß.

§ 290

Abwicklung

(1) Die Abwicklung besorgen alle persönlich haftenden Gesellschafter und eine oder mehrere von der Hauptversammlung gewählte Personen als Abwickler, wenn die Satzung nichts anderes bestimmt.

(2) Die Bestellung oder Abberufung von Abwicklern durch das Gericht kann auch jeder persönlich haftende Gesellschafter beantragen.

Drittes Buch

Verbundene Unternehmen

Erster Teil

Unternehmensverträge

Erster Abschnitt

Arten von Unternehmensverträgen

§ 291

Beherrschungsvertrag. Gewinnabführungsvertrag

(1) Unternehmensverträge sind Verträge, durch die eine Aktiengesellschaft oder Kommanditgesellschaft auf Aktien die Leitung ihrer Gesellschaft einem anderen Unternehmen unterstellt (Beherrschungsvertrag) oder sich verpflichtet, ihren ganzen Gewinn an ein anderes Unternehmen abzuführen (Gewinnabführungsvertrag). Als Vertrag über die Abführung des ganzen Gewinns gilt auch ein Vertrag, durch den eine Aktiengesellschaft oder Kommanditgesellschaft auf Aktien es übernimmt, ihr Unternehmen für Rechnung eines anderen Unternehmens zu führen.

(2) Stellen sich Unternehmen, die voneinander nicht abhängig sind, durch Vertrag unter einheitliche Leitung, ohne daß dadurch eines von ihnen von einem anderen vertragschließenden Unternehmen abhängig wird, so ist dieser Vertrag kein Beherrschungsvertrag.

(3) Leistungen der Gesellschaft auf Grund eines Beherrschungs- oder eines Gewinnabführungsvertrags gelten nicht als Verstoß gegen die §§ 57, 58 und 60.

§ 292

Andere Unternehmensverträge

(1) Unternehmensverträge sind ferner Verträge,

§ 290

Liquidation

(1) The liquidation shall be carried out by all of the general partners and one or more persons appointed as liquidators by the shareholders, unless the articles of incorporation provide otherwise.

(2) Each general partner may also request the appointment or dismissal of liquidators by the court.

Book Three

Related Enterprises

Part One

Enterprise Agreements

First Division

Types of Enterprise Agreements

§ 291

Control Agreement.

Agreement to Transfer Profit

(1) Enterprise agreements are agreements whereby a stock corporation or partnership limited by shares submits the company to management by another enterprise (control agreement) or undertakes to transfer all of its profit to another enterprise (agreement to transfer profit). An agreement whereby a stock corporation or a partnership limited by shares undertakes to conduct its business for the account of another enterprise shall also be deemed to be an agreement to transfer all of the profit.

(2) Where independent enterprises by agreement submit to a central management in such a manner that none of them becomes dependent on another contracting enterprise, such agreement shall not be deemed to be a control agreement.

(3) Payments made by a company pursuant to a control agreement or an agreement to transfer profit shall not be deemed to violate §§ 57, 58 and 60.

§ 292

Other Enterprise Agreements

(1) Agreements shall also be considered enterprise agreements if, pursuant thereto, a stock

corporation or a partnership limited by shares does any of the following:

1. undertakes to pool its profit or the profit of some of its plants, in whole or in part, with the profit of other enterprises or some of the plants of other enterprises for the purpose of sharing the pooled profits (pooling of profits),
2. undertakes to transfer part of its profit or the profit of some of its plants, in whole or in part, to another (agreement to transfer a portion of profit),
3. leases the entire enterprise to another or otherwise surrenders its operation to another (company lease agreement, company surrender agreement).

(2) A profit-sharing agreement with members of the managing board or of the supervisory board or with individual employees of the company, or an undertaking concerning the sharing of profit pursuant to agreements within the scope of the company's business or licensing agreements, shall not be deemed to be an agreement to transfer a portion of the profit.

(3) A company lease agreement or a company surrender agreement and the resolution whereby the shareholders have approved such agreement shall not be considered void as in violation of §§ 57, 58 and 60. The first sentence hereof shall not, however, preclude an action to set aside the resolution because of such violation.

Second Division

Execution, Amendment and Termination of Enterprise Agreements

§ 293

Shareholder Approval

(1) An enterprise agreement shall become effective only upon the approval of the shareholders. The resolution shall require a majority of no less than three-fourths of the stated capital represented when the resolution is adopted. The articles of incorporation may provide for a higher capital majority and establish additional requirements. The provisions of the law and of the articles of incorporation concerning the amendment of the articles of incorporation shall not apply to such resolution.

(2) If the other contracting party is a stock corporation or partnership limited by shares, a control agreement or an agreement to transfer profit

§ 293

durch die eine Aktiengesellschaft oder Kommanditgesellschaft auf Aktien

1. sich verpflichtet, ihren Gewinn oder den Gewinn einzelner ihrer Betriebe ganz oder zum Teil mit dem Gewinn anderer Unternehmen oder einzelner Betriebe anderer Unternehmen zur Aufteilung eines gemeinschaftlichen Gewinns zusammenzulegen (Gewinngemeinschaft),
2. sich verpflichtet, einen Teil ihres Gewinns oder den Gewinn einzelner ihrer Betriebe ganz oder zum Teil an einen anderen abzuführen (Teilgewinnabführungsvertrag),
3. den Betrieb ihres Unternehmens einem anderen verpachtet oder sonst überläßt (Betriebspachtvertrag, Betriebsüberlassungsvertrag).

(2) Ein Vertrag über eine Gewinnbeteiligung mit Mitgliedern von Vorstand und Aufsichtsrat oder mit einzelnen Arbeitnehmern der Gesellschaft sowie eine Abrede über eine Gewinnbeteiligung im Rahmen von Verträgen des laufenden Geschäftsverkehrs oder Lizenzverträgen ist kein Teilgewinnabführungsvertrag.

(3) Ein Betriebspacht- oder Betriebsüberlassungsvertrag und der Beschluß, durch den die Hauptversammlung dem Vertrag zugestimmt hat, sind nicht deshalb nichtig, weil der Vertrag gegen die §§ 57, 58 und 60 verstößt. Satz 1 schließt die Anfechtung des Beschlusses wegen dieses Verstoßes nicht aus.

Zweiter Abschnitt

Abschluß, Änderung und Beendigung von Unternehmensverträgen

§ 293

Zustimmung der Hauptversammlung

(1) Ein Unternehmensvertrag wird nur mit Zustimmung der Hauptversammlung wirksam. Der Beschluß bedarf einer Mehrheit, die mindestens drei Viertel des bei der Beschlußfassung vertretenen Grundkapitals umfaßt. Die Satzung kann eine größere Kapitalmehrheit und weitere Erfordernisse bestimmen. Auf den Beschluß sind die Bestimmungen des Gesetzes und der Satzung über Satzungsänderungen nicht anzuwenden.

(2) Ein Beherrschungs- oder ein Gewinnabführungsvertrag wird, wenn der andere Vertragsteil eine Aktiengesellschaft oder Kommanditgesellschaft

auf Aktien ist, nur wirksam, wenn auch die Hauptversammlung dieser Gesellschaft zustimmt. Für den Beschluß gilt Absatz 1 Satz 2 bis 4 sinngemäß.

(3) Der Vertrag bedarf der schriftlichen Form. Er ist von der Einberufung der Hauptversammlung an, die über die Zustimmung beschließen soll, in dem Geschäftsraum der Gesellschaft zur Einsicht der Aktionäre auszulegen. Auf Verlangen ist jedem Aktionär unverzüglich eine Abschrift zu erteilen. In der Hauptversammlung ist der Vertrag auszulegen. Der Vorstand hat ihn zu Beginn der Verhandlung zu erläutern. Der Niederschrift ist er als Anlage beizufügen.

(4) Jedem Aktionär ist auf Verlangen in der Hauptversammlung, die über die Zustimmung zu einem Beherrschungs- oder einem Gewinnabführungsvertrag beschließt, Auskunft auch über alle für den Vertragsschluß wesentlichen Angelegenheiten des Unternehmens zu geben, mit dem der Vertrag geschlossen werden soll.

§ 294

Eintragung. Wirksamwerden

(1) Der Vorstand der Gesellschaft hat das Bestehen und die Art des Unternehmensvertrags sowie den Namen des anderen Vertragsteils, bei Teilgewinnabführungsverträgen außerdem die Vereinbarung über die Höhe des abzuführenden Gewinns, zur Eintragung in das Handelsregister anzumelden. Der Anmeldung sind der Vertrag sowie, wenn er nur mit Zustimmung der Hauptversammlung des anderen Vertragsteils wirksam wird, die Niederschrift dieses Beschlusses und ihre Anlagen in Urschrift, Ausfertigung oder öffentlich beglaubigter Abschrift beizufügen.

(2) Der Vertrag wird erst wirksam, wenn sein Bestehen in das Handelsregister des Sitzes der Gesellschaft eingetragen worden ist.

§ 295

Änderung

(1) Ein Unternehmensvertrag kann nur mit Zustimmung der Hauptversammlung geändert werden. §§ 293, 294 gelten sinngemäß.

(2) Die Zustimmung der Hauptversammlung der Gesellschaft zu einer Änderung der Bestimmungen des Vertrags, die zur Leistung eines Ausgleichs an die außenstehenden Aktionäre der Gesellschaft oder zum Erwerb ihrer Aktien verpflichten, bedarf, um wirksam zu werden, eines Sonderbeschlusses der

shall become effective only if the shareholders of such company also approve it. Paragraph 1, second to fourth sentences, hereof shall apply, *mutatis mutandis*, to this resolution.

(3) The agreement must be in writing. It shall be exhibited on the company's premises for inspection by the shareholders, beginning with the date of the calling of the shareholders' meeting which is to decide on it. Each shareholder shall promptly, upon request, be furnished a copy. The agreement shall be exhibited at the shareholders' meeting. At the beginning of the deliberations, the managing board shall explain the agreement. It shall be attached to the minutes.

(4) At the shareholders' meeting in which the resolution approving a control agreement or an agreement to transfer profit is adopted, each shareholder shall, upon request, also be furnished information on such matters affecting the enterprise with which the agreement is to be concluded as are material to the making of the agreement.

§ 294

Registration. Effective Date

(1) The company's managing board shall file an application with the Commercial Register to record the existence and nature of the enterprise agreement, as well as the name of the other contracting party and, in the case of agreements to transfer a portion of the profit, also the stipulations concerning the amount of the profit to be transferred. The application shall be accompanied by the agreement and, if the agreement requires the approval of the shareholders of the other contracting party to become effective, the original, duplicate original or certified copy of the minutes of the resolution and its annexes.

(2) The agreement shall not become effective before its registration in the Commercial Register at the company's domicile.

§ 295

Amendment

(1) An enterprise agreement may be amended only with the approval of the shareholders. §§ 293 and 294 shall apply *mutatis mutandis*.

(2) The approval by the company's shareholders of an amendment of the provisions of the agreement which contain the obligation to compensate the company's outside shareholders or to acquire their shares shall require a separate resolution of the outside shareholders to become

§ 295

effective. § 293, paragraph 1, second and third sentences, shall apply to such separate resolution. In the meeting at which the resolution concerning the approval is adopted, each outside shareholder shall, upon request, also be furnished information on such matters affecting the other contracting party as are material to the amendment.

§ 296
Termination

(1) An enterprise agreement may be terminated by mutual accord only as of the end of the fiscal year or some other contractually agreed accounting period. Retroactive termination by mutual accord is not permitted. The termination must be in writing.

(2) An agreement which requires compensation of outside shareholders or purchase of their shares may be terminated by mutual accord only if the outside shareholders consent to such termination in a separate resolution. § 293, paragraph 1, second and third sentences, and § 295, paragraph 2, third sentence, shall apply, *mutatis mutandis*, to such separate resolution.

§ 297
Notice of Termination

(1) An enterprise agreement may be terminated for a compelling reason without giving the required advance notice. A compelling reason exists, in particular, if it can be expected that the other contracting party will probably not be able to perform its obligations under the agreement.

(2) Absent a compelling reason, the company's managing board may terminate an agreement which requires compensation of the company's outside shareholders or purchase of their shares only if the outside shareholders consent to such termination in a separate resolution. § 293, paragraph 1, second and third sentences, and § 295, paragraph 2, third sentence, shall apply, *mutatis mutandis*, to such separate resolution.

(3) The notice of termination must be in writing.

§ 298
Application and Registration

The company's managing board shall promptly file an application to record in the Commercial Register the termination of an enterprise agreement, the grounds for such termination, and the effective date thereof.

§ 296

außenstehenden Aktionäre. Für den Sonderbeschluß gilt § 293 Abs. 1 Satz 2 und 3. Jedem außenstehenden Aktionär ist auf Verlangen in der Versammlung, die über die Zustimmung beschließt, Auskunft auch über alle für die Änderung wesentlichen Angelegenheiten des anderen Vertragsteils zu geben.

§ 296
Aufhebung

(1) Ein Unternehmensvertrag kann nur zum Ende des Geschäftsjahrs oder des sonst vertraglich bestimmten Abrechnungszeitraums aufgehoben werden. Eine rückwirkende Aufhebung ist unzulässig. Die Aufhebung bedarf der schriftlichen Form.

(2) Ein Vertrag, der zur Leistung eines Ausgleichs an die außenstehenden Aktionäre oder zum Erwerb ihrer Aktien verpflichtet, kann nur aufgehoben werden, wenn die außenstehenden Aktionäre durch Sonderbeschluß zustimmen. Für den Sonderbeschluß gilt § 293 Abs. 1 Satz 2 und 3, § 295 Abs. 2 Satz 3 sinngemäß.

§ 297
Kündigung

(1) Ein Unternehmensvertrag kann aus wichtigem Grunde ohne Einhaltung einer Kündigungsfrist gekündigt werden. Ein wichtiger Grund liegt namentlich vor, wenn der andere Vertragsteil voraussichtlich nicht in der Lage sein wird, seine auf Grund des Vertrags bestehenden Verpflichtungen zu erfüllen.

(2) Der Vorstand der Gesellschaft kann einen Vertrag, der zur Leistung eines Ausgleichs an die außenstehenden Aktionäre der Gesellschaft oder zum Erwerb ihrer Aktien verpflichtet, ohne wichtigen Grund nur kündigen, wenn die außenstehenden Aktionäre durch Sonderbeschluß zustimmen. Für den Sonderbeschluß gilt § 293 Abs. 1 Satz 2 und 3, § 295 Abs. 2 Satz 3 sinngemäß.

(3) Die Kündigung bedarf der schriftlichen Form.

§ 298
Anmeldung und Eintragung

Der Vorstand der Gesellschaft hat die Beendigung eines Unternehmensvertrags, den Grund und den Zeitpunkt der Beendigung unverzüglich zur Eintragung in das Handelsregister anzumelden.

§ 299

Ausschluß von Weisungen

Auf Grund eines Unternehmensvertrags kann der Gesellschaft nicht die Weisung erteilt werden, den Vertrag zu ändern, aufrechtzuerhalten oder zu beendigen.

§ 299
Prohibited Instructions

An enterprise agreement cannot be used to give instructions to the company requiring it to amend, to continue, or to terminate such agreement.

Dritter Abschnitt

Sicherung der Gesellschaft und der Gläubiger

Third Division
Protection of the Company and Its Creditors

§ 300

Gesetzliche Rücklage

In die gesetzliche Rücklage sind an Stelle des in § 150 Abs. 2 Nr. 1 bestimmten Betrags einzustellen,

1. wenn ein Gewinnabführungsvertrag besteht, aus dem ohne die Gewinnabführung entstehenden, um einen Verlustvortrag aus dem Vorjahr geminderten Jahresüberschuß der Betrag, der erforderlich ist, um die gesetzliche Rücklage innerhalb der ersten fünf Geschäftsjahre, die während des Bestehens des Vertrags oder nach Durchführung einer Kapitalerhöhung beginnen, gleichmäßig auf den zehnten oder den in der Satzung bestimmten höheren Teil des Grundkapitals aufzufüllen, mindestens aber der in Nummer 2 bestimmte Betrag;

2. wenn ein Teilgewinnabführungsvertrag besteht, der Betrag, der nach § 150 Abs. 2 Nr. 1 aus dem ohne die Gewinnabführung entstehenden, um einen Verlustvortrag aus dem Vorjahr geminderten Jahresüberschuß in die gesetzliche Rücklage einzustellen wäre;

3. wenn ein Beherrschungsvertrag besteht, ohne daß die Gesellschaft auch zur Abführung ihres ganzen Gewinns verpflichtet ist, der zur Auffüllung der gesetzlichen Rücklage nach Nummer 1 erforderliche Betrag, mindestens aber der in § 150 Abs. 2 Nr. 1 oder, wenn die Gesellschaft verpflichtet ist, ihren Gewinn zum Teil abzuführen, der in Nummer 2 bestimmte Betrag.

§ 300
Statutory Reserve

In lieu of the amount specified in § 150, paragraph 2, No. 1, the following amounts shall be allocated to the statutory reserve:

1. where there is an agreement to transfer profit, an amount derived from the net profit for the year, including the profit to be transferred, reduced by any losses carried forward from the preceding year, as necessary to reach the statutory reserve, in equal portions, within the first five fiscal years beginning during the existence of the agreement or after the consummation of a capital increase, to one-tenth or such larger fraction of the stated capital as may be specified in the articles of incorporation, but no less than the amount specified in No. 2 hereof;

2. where there is an agreement to transfer a portion of the profit, the amount that would have to be allocated to the statutory reserve pursuant to § 150, paragraph 2, No. 1, from the net profit for the year, including the profit to be transferred, reduced by the loss carried forward from the preceding year;

3. where there is a control agreement which does not obligate the company to transfer all of its profit, the amount required to reach the statutory reserve pursuant to No. 1 hereof, but no less than the amount specified in § 150, paragraph 2, No. 1, or, where the company is obligated to transfer a portion of its profit, the amount specified in No. 2 hereof.

§ 301

Höchstbetrag der Gewinnabführung

Eine Gesellschaft kann, gleichgültig welche Vereinbarungen über die Berechnung des abzuführen-

§ 301
Maximum Amount of Profit Transferred

A company may, regardless of agreements on the computation of profit to be transferred, trans-

§ 301

fer as profit no more than the net profit for the year, exclusive of the profit to be transferred, reduced by the loss carry-forward from the preceding year and the amount to be allocated to the statutory reserve pursuant to § 300. If amounts have been allocated to free reserves during the existence of the agreement, such amounts can be withdrawn from the free reserves and transferred as profit.

§ 302
Assumption of Losses

(1) Where there is a control agreement or an agreement to transfer profit, the other contracting party shall offset any annual deficit which would otherwise arise during the existence of the agreement, to the extent that such deficit is not offset by the withdrawal of amounts allocated to free reserves during the existence of the agreement.

(2) In the event that a controlled company has leased or otherwise surrendered the operation of the enterprise to the controlling enterprise, such controlling enterprise shall offset any annual deficit which would otherwise arise during the existence of the agreement, to the extent that the consideration agreed upon is inadequate.

(3) The company may waive or compromise the right to demand compensation only after the expiration of three years from the date on which the registration of the termination of the agreement in the Commercial Register is deemed published pursuant to § 10 of the Commercial Code. This shall not apply if the party obligated to effect compensation is unable to pay its debts as they mature and enters into a composition with its creditors to avert or terminate bankruptcy proceedings. The waiver or the compromise shall be effective only if the outside shareholders consent to it by a separate resolution and a minority whose combined holdings amount to no less than one-tenth of the stated capital represented when the resolution is adopted does not have its objection recorded in the minutes of the meeting.

§ 303
Protection of Creditors

(1) Upon termination of a control agreement or an agreement to transfer profit, the other contracting party shall furnish security to the creditors of the company whose claims arose prior to the date on which the registration of the termination of the agreement in the Commercial Reg-

den Gewinns getroffen worden sind, als ihren Gewinn höchstens den ohne die Gewinnabführung entstehenden Jahresüberschuß, vermindert um einen Verlustvortrag aus dem Vorjahr und um den Betrag, der nach § 300 in die gesetzliche Rücklage einzustellen ist, abführen. Sind während der Dauer des Vertrags Beträge in freie Rücklagen eingestellt worden, so können diese Beträge den freien Rücklagen entnommen und als Gewinn abgeführt werden.

§ 302
Verlustübernahme

(1) Besteht ein Beherrschungs- oder ein Gewinnabführungsvertrag, so hat der andere Vertragsteil jeden während der Vertragsdauer sonst entstehenden Jahresfehlbetrag auszugleichen, soweit dieser nicht dadurch ausgeglichen wird, daß den freien Rücklagen Beträge entnommen werden, die während der Vertragsdauer in sie eingestellt worden sind.

(2) Hat eine abhängige Gesellschaft den Betrieb ihres Unternehmens dem herrschenden Unternehmen verpachtet oder sonst überlassen, so hat das herrschende Unternehmen jeden während der Vertragsdauer sonst entstehenden Jahresfehlbetrag auszugleichen, soweit die vereinbarte Gegenleistung das angemessene Entgelt nicht erreicht.

(3) Die Gesellschaft kann auf den Anspruch auf Ausgleich erst drei Jahre nach dem Tage, an dem die Eintragung der Beendigung des Vertrags in das Handelsregister nach § 10 des Handelsgesetzbuchs als bekanntgemacht gilt, verzichten oder sich über ihn vergleichen. Dies gilt nicht, wenn der Ausgleichspflichtige zahlungsunfähig ist und sich zur Abwendung oder Beseitigung des Konkursverfahrens mit seinen Gläubigern vergleicht. Der Verzicht oder Vergleich wird nur wirksam, wenn die außenstehenden Aktionäre durch Sonderbeschluß zustimmen und nicht eine Minderheit, deren Anteile zusammen den zehnten Teil des bei der Beschlußfassung vertretenen Grundkapitals erreichen, zur Niederschrift Widerspruch erhebt.

§ 303
Gläubigerschutz

(1) Endet ein Beherrschungs- oder ein Gewinnabführungsvertrag, so hat der andere Vertragsteil den Gläubigern der Gesellschaft, deren Forderungen begründet worden sind, bevor die Eintragung der Beendigung des Vertrags in das Handelsregister nach § 10 des Handelsgesetzbuchs als bekanntge-

macht gilt, Sicherheit zu leisten, wenn sie sich binnen sechs Monaten nach der Bekanntmachung der Eintragung zu diesem Zweck bei ihm melden. Die Gläubiger sind in der Bekanntmachung der Eintragung auf dieses Recht hinzuweisen.

(2) Das Recht, Sicherheitsleistung zu verlangen, steht Gläubigern nicht zu, die im Fall des Konkurses ein Recht auf vorzugsweise Befriedigung aus einer Deckungsmasse haben, die nach gesetzlicher Vorschrift zu ihrem Schutz errichtet und staatlich überwacht ist.

(3) Statt Sicherheit zu leisten, kann der andere Vertragsteil sich für die Forderung verbürgen. § 349 des Handelsgesetzbuchs über den Ausschluß der Einrede der Vorausklage ist nicht anzuwenden.

Vierter Abschnitt

Sicherung der außenstehenden Aktionäre bei Beherrschungs- und Gewinnabführungsverträgen

§ 304

Angemessener Ausgleich

(1) Ein Gewinnabführungsvertrag muß einen angemessenen Ausgleich für die außenstehenden Aktionäre durch eine auf die Aktiennennbeträge bezogene wiederkehrende Geldleistung (Ausgleichszahlung) vorsehen. Ein Beherrschungsvertrag muß, wenn die Gesellschaft nicht auch zur Abführung ihres ganzen Gewinns verpflichtet ist, den außenstehenden Aktionären als angemessenen Ausgleich einen bestimmten jährlichen Gewinnanteil nach der für die Ausgleichszahlung bestimmten Höhe garantieren. Von der Bestimmung eines angemessenen Ausgleichs kann nur abgesehen werden, wenn die Gesellschaft im Zeitpunkt der Beschlußfassung ihrer Hauptversammlung über den Vertrag keinen außenstehenden Aktionär hat.

(2) Als Ausgleichszahlung ist mindestens die jährliche Zahlung des Betrags zuzusichern, der nach der bisherigen Ertragslage der Gesellschaft und ihren künftigen Ertragsaussichten unter Berücksichtigung angemessener Abschreibungen und Wertberichtigungen, jedoch ohne Bildung freier Rücklagen, voraussichtlich als durchschnittlicher Gewinnanteil auf die einzelne Aktie verteilt werden könnte. Ist der andere Vertragsteil eine Aktiengesellschaft oder Kommanditgesellschaft auf Aktien, so kann als Ausgleichszahlung auch die Zahlung des Betrags

ister is deemed to be published in accordance with § 10 of the Commercial Code, provided that they make a request to this effect to such other contracting party within six months from the date on which the registration is published. The creditors shall be advised of this right in the publication of the registration.

(2) The right to request security shall not be available to creditors who, in the event of bankruptcy, would have a claim to preferred satisfaction from a fund which was established by statute for their protection and which is subject to governmental supervision.

(3) Instead of furnishing security, the other contracting party may elect to guarantee such claims. § 349 of the Commercial Code, which precludes the defense of exhaustion of remedies against the debtor, shall not be applicable.

Fourth Division

Protection of Outside Shareholders in Case of Control Agreements and Agreements to Transfer Profit

§ 304

Reasonable Compensation

(1) An agreement to transfer profit must provide for reasonable compensation for the outside shareholders by periodic payments based on the par value of the shares (compensation payments). Unless the company is obligated to transfer all of its profit, a control agreement must guarantee to the outside shareholders, as reasonable compensation, a specified annual profit distribution in the amount stipulated for the compensation payments. Only if at the time the shareholders' resolution concerning the agreement is adopted the company does not have any outside shareholders may the provision for reasonable compensation be omitted.

(2) As a minimum compensation, there shall be guaranteed annual payments in an amount which, in light of the company's past record of earnings and the prospects for its future profitability, could be expected to be distributed as an average dividend per share, taking into account appropriate depreciation and reserve for decline in value, exclusive, however, of free reserves. In the event that the other contracting party is a stock corporation or partnership limited by shares, compensation payments may also be effected by guaranteeing payments in the amount

of distributions made on shares of the other company, which shares must have at least a commensurate par value. The commensurate par value shall be determined by reference to the ratio in which, in case of a merger, each share of the company would be entitled to shares of the other company.

(3) An agreement which, contrary to paragraph 1 hereof, does not provide for any compensation shall be void. An action to set aside the resolution whereby the company's shareholders approved the agreement or any amendment within § 295, paragraph 2, may not be based on § 243, paragraph 2, or on the fact that the compensation specified in the agreement is inadequate. If the compensation specified in the agreement is inadequate, the court designated in § 306 shall determine, upon application, the contractual compensation to be paid, in which case the court shall, if the agreement provides for compensation to be calculated pursuant to paragraph 2, second sentence, hereof, determine the compensation in accordance with such provision.

(4) Each outside shareholder shall have the right to make such application. The application may be made only within two months from the date on which the registration in the Commercial Register of the existence of, or of an amendment, within § 295, paragraph 2, to, the agreement is deemed published in accordance with § 10 of the Commercial Code.

(5) If the compensation is determined by the court, the other contracting party may, without complying with the notice requirements, terminate the agreement within two months from the date on which the decision becomes final.

zugesichert werden, der auf Aktien der anderen Gesellschaft mit mindestens dem entsprechenden Nennbetrag jeweils als Gewinnanteil entfällt. Der entsprechende Nennbetrag bestimmt sich nach dem Verhältnis, in dem bei einer Verschmelzung auf eine Aktie der Gesellschaft Aktien der anderen Gesellschaft zu gewähren wären.

(3) Ein Vertrag, der entgegen Absatz 1 überhaupt keinen Ausgleich vorsieht, ist nichtig. Die Anfechtung des Beschlusses, durch den die Hauptversammlung der Gesellschaft dem Vertrag oder einer unter § 295 Abs. 2 fallenden Änderung des Vertrags zugestimmt hat, kann nicht auf § 243 Abs. 2 oder darauf gestützt werden, daß der im Vertrag bestimmte Ausgleich nicht angemessen ist. Ist der im Vertrag bestimmte Ausgleich nicht angemessen, so hat das in § 306 bestimmte Gericht auf Antrag den vertraglich geschuldeten Ausgleich zu bestimmen, wobei es, wenn der Vertrag einen nach Absatz 2 Satz 2 berechneten Ausgleich vorsieht, den Ausgleich nach dieser Vorschrift zu bestimmen hat.

(4) Antragsberechtigt ist jeder außenstehende Aktionär. Der Antrag kann nur binnen zwei Monaten seit dem Tage gestellt werden, an dem die Eintragung des Bestehens oder einer unter § 295 Abs. 2 fallenden Änderung des Vertrags im Handelsregister nach § 10 des Handelsgesetzbuchs als bekanntgemacht gilt.

(5) Bestimmt das Gericht den Ausgleich, so kann der andere Vertragsteil den Vertrag binnen zwei Monaten nach Rechtskraft der Entscheidung ohne Einhaltung einer Kündigungsfrist kündigen.

§ 305

Indemnity

(1) Aside from the obligation of compensation pursuant to § 304, a control agreement or an agreement to transfer profit must obligate the other contracting party to acquire, at the request of an outside shareholder, his shares against a reasonable indemnity to be specified in the agreement.

(2) The agreement shall provide for the following indemnity:

1. if the other contracting party is a stock corporation or a partnership limited by shares domiciled in Germany, which is not a controlled or

§ 305

Abfindung

(1) Außer der Verpflichtung zum Ausgleich nach § 304 muß ein Beherrschungs- oder ein Gewinnabführungsvertrag die Verpflichtung des anderen Vertragsteils enthalten, auf Verlangen eines außenstehenden Aktionärs dessen Aktien gegen eine im Vertrag bestimmte angemessene Abfindung zu erwerben.

(2) Als Abfindung muß der Vertrag,

1. wenn der andere Vertragsteil eine nicht abhängige und nicht in Mehrheitsbesitz stehende Aktiengesellschaft oder Kommanditgesellschaft auf

Aktien mit Sitz im Inland ist, die Gewährung eigener Aktien dieser Gesellschaft,

2. wenn der andere Vertragsteil eine abhängige oder in Mehrheitsbesitz stehende Aktiengesellschaft oder Kommanditgesellschaft auf Aktien und das herrschende Unternehmen eine Aktiengesellschaft oder Kommanditgesellschaft auf Aktien mit Sitz im Inland ist, entweder die Gewährung von Aktien der herrschenden oder mit Mehrheit beteiligten Gesellschaft oder eine Barabfindung,

3. in allen anderen Fällen eine Barabfindung vorsehen.

(3) Werden als Abfindung Aktien einer anderen Gesellschaft gewährt, so ist die Abfindung als angemessen anzusehen, wenn die Aktien in dem Verhältnis gewährt werden, in dem bei einer Verschmelzung auf eine andere Gesellschaft Aktien der anderen Gesellschaft zu gewähren wären, wobei Spitzenbeträge durch bare Zuzahlungen ausgeglichen werden können. Die angemessene Barabfindung muß die Vermögens- und Ertragslage der Gesellschaft im Zeitpunkt der Beschlußfassung ihrer Hauptversammlung über den Vertrag berücksichtigen.

(4) Die Verpflichtung zum Erwerb der Aktien kann befristet werden. Die Frist endet frühestens zwei Monate nach dem Tage, an dem die Eintragung des Bestehens des Vertrags im Handelsregister nach § 10 des Handelsgesetzbuchs als bekanntgemacht gilt. Ist ein Antrag auf Bestimmung des Ausgleichs oder der Abfindung durch das in § 306 bestimmte Gericht gestellt worden, so endet die Frist frühestens zwei Monate nach dem Tage, an dem die Entscheidung über den zuletzt beschiedenen Antrag im Bundesanzeiger bekanntgemacht worden ist.

(5) Die Anfechtung des Beschlusses, durch den die Hauptversammlung der Gesellschaft dem Vertrag oder einer unter § 295 Abs. 2 fallenden Änderung des Vertrags zugestimmt hat, kann nicht darauf gestützt werden, daß der Vertrag keine angemessene Abfindung vorsieht. Sieht der Vertrag überhaupt keine oder eine den Absätzen 1 bis 3 nicht entsprechende Abfindung vor, so hat das in § 306 bestimmte Gericht auf Antrag die vertraglich zu gewährende Abfindung zu bestimmen. Dabei hat es in den Fällen des Absatzes 2 Nr. 2, wenn der Vertrag die Gewährung von Aktien der herrschenden oder mit Mehrheit beteiligten Gesellschaft vorsieht, das Verhältnis, in dem diese Aktien zu gewähren sind, wenn der Vertrag nicht die Gewährung von Aktien der herrschenden oder mit Mehrheit beteiligten Gesellschaft vorsieht, die angemessene Barabfindung zu bestimmen. § 304 Abs. 4 und 5 gilt sinngemäß.

majority-owned enterprise, shares of such company,

2. if the other contracting party is a stock corporation or a partnership limited by shares which is controlled or majority-owned, and the controlling enterprise is a stock corporation or a partnership limited by shares domiciled in Germany, either shares of the controlling or of the majority-owning company, or cash,

3. in all other cases, cash.

(3) If shares of another company are given as indemnity, such indemnity shall be considered to be reasonable if the shares are issued in the same ratio in which, in case of a merger, each share of the company would be entitled to shares of the other company; fractional amounts may be compensated by cash payments. The reasonable cash indemnity shall take into account the company's financial condition and earnings at the time the resolution concerning the agreement is adopted by the shareholders.

(4) The obligation to acquire the shares may be made subject to a time limit. This time limit shall not expire earlier than two months from the date the registration of the existence of the agreement in the Commercial Register is deemed published in accordance with § 10 of the Commercial Code. If an application was made to the court designated in § 306 to determine the compensation or the indemnity, the time limit shall not expire earlier than two months from the date on which the decision on the application last decided was published in the *Bundesanzeiger*.

(5) An action to set aside the resolution whereby the company's shareholders approved the agreement or any amendment within § 295, paragraph 2, may not be based on the fact that the agreement does not provide for a reasonable indemnity. If the agreement does not provide for any indemnity, or if it provides for an indemnity which does not comply with paragraphs 1 to 3 hereof, the court designated in § 306 shall determine, upon application, the contractual indemnity to be paid. In this event, the court shall decide, in the cases set forth in paragraph 2, No. 2, if the agreement provides for the issuance of shares in the controlling company or in the majority-owning company, the ratio in which these shares are to be issued, or, if the agreement does not provide for shares in the controlling or in the majority-owning company, the reasonable cash indemnity. § 304, paragraphs 4 and 5, shall apply *mutatis mutandis*.

§ 305

§ 306
Procedure

(1) The district court of the district of domicile of the company whose outside shareholders are entitled to make the application shall have jurisdiction. § 132, paragraph 1, second to fourth sentences, shall be applicable.

(2) § 99, paragraph 1, paragraph 3, first, second, and fourth to ninth sentences, and paragraph 5, shall apply *mutatis mutandis*.

(3) The district court shall publish the application in the publications designated in the articles of incorporation of the company whose outside shareholders are entitled to make the application. Outside shareholders may still, within a period of two months from the date of such publication, make an independent application. The publication shall refer to this right.

(4) The district court shall hear the parties to the enterprise agreement. For such outside shareholders who are not applicants within the meaning of § 304, paragraph 4, or § 305, paragraph 5, or who have made independent applications pursuant to paragraph 3, second sentence, hereof, it shall appoint a common representative, who shall have the powers of a legal representative, to safeguard their rights. Where application is made to determine reasonable compensation and reasonable indemnity, the court shall appoint one common representative with respect to each application. No such appointment shall be required if the rights of the outside shareholders can be safeguarded in some other manner. The district court shall publish the appointment of the common representative in the publications designated in the company's articles of incorporation. The representative may request from the company reimbursement for his reasonable cash expenditures and remuneration for his services. The expenditures and the remuneration shall be determined by the district court. Upon request of the representative, the court may order the company to make advance payments. Execution on the assessment may issue in accordance with the provisions of the Code of Civil Procedure.

(5) The district court shall serve its decision on the parties to the enterprise agreement, on the applicants referred to in § 304, paragraph 4, and § 305, paragraph 5, on outside shareholders who made an independent application pursuant to paragraph 3, second sentence, hereof, and on the common representative, if such a representative was appointed.

§ 306

§ 306
Verfahren

(1) Zuständig ist das Landgericht, in dessen Bezirk die Gesellschaft, deren außenstehende Aktionäre antragsberechtigt sind, ihren Sitz hat. § 132 Abs. 1 Satz 2 bis 4 ist anzuwenden.

(2) § 99 Abs. 1, Abs. 3 Satz 1, 2, 4 bis 9, Abs. 5 gilt sinngemäß.

(3) Das Landgericht hat den Antrag in den Gesellschaftsblättern der Gesellschaft, deren außenstehende Aktionäre antragsberechtigt sind, bekanntzumachen. Außenstehende Aktionäre können noch binnen einer Frist von zwei Monaten nach dieser Bekanntmachung eigene Anträge stellen. Auf dieses Recht ist in der Bekanntmachung hinzuweisen.

(4) Das Landgericht hat die Vertragsteile des Unternehmensvertrags zu hören. Es hat den außenstehenden Aktionären, die nicht Antragsteller nach § 304 Abs. 4 oder § 305 Abs. 5 sind oder eigene Anträge nach Absatz 3 Satz 2 gestellt haben, zur Wahrung ihrer Rechte einen gemeinsamen Vertreter zu bestellen, der die Stellung eines gesetzlichen Vertreters hat. Werden die Festsetzung des angemessenen Ausgleichs und die Festsetzung der angemessenen Abfindung beantragt, so hat es für jeden Antrag einen gemeinsamen Vertreter zu bestellen. Die Bestellung kann unterbleiben, wenn die Wahrung der Rechte dieser außenstehenden Aktionäre auf andere Weise sichergestellt ist. Die Bestellung des gemeinsamen Vertreters hat das Landgericht in den Gesellschaftsblättern bekanntzumachen. Der Vertreter kann von der Gesellschaft den Ersatz angemessener barer Auslagen und eine Vergütung für seine Tätigkeit verlangen. Die Auslagen und die Vergütung setzt das Landgericht fest. Es kann der Gesellschaft auf Verlangen des Vertreters die Zahlung von Vorschüssen aufgeben. Aus der Festsetzung findet die Zwangsvollstreckung nach der Zivilprozeßordnung statt.

(5) Das Landgericht hat seine Entscheidung den Vertragsteilen des Unternehmensvertrags sowie den Antragstellern nach § 304 Abs. 4, § 305 Abs. 5, den außenstehenden Aktionären, die eigene Anträge nach Absatz 3 Satz 2 gestellt haben, und, wenn ein gemeinsamer Vertreter bestellt ist, diesem zuzustellen.

(6) Der Vorstand der Gesellschaft hat die rechtskräftige Entscheidung ohne Gründe in den Gesellschaftsblättern bekanntzumachen.

(7) Für die Kosten des Verfahrens gilt die Kostenordnung. Für das Verfahren des ersten Rechtszugs wird das Doppelte der vollen Gebühr erhoben. Für den zweiten Rechtszug wird die gleiche Gebühr erhoben; dies gilt auch dann, wenn die Beschwerde Erfolg hat. Wird der Antrag oder die Beschwerde zurückgenommen, bevor es zu einer Entscheidung kommt, so ermäßigt sich die Gebühr auf die Hälfte. Der Geschäftswert ist von Amts wegen festzusetzen. Er bestimmt sich nach § 30 Abs. 1 der Kostenordnung. Kostenvorschüsse werden nicht erhoben. Schuldner der Kosten sind die Vertragsteile des Unternehmensvertrags. Die Kosten können jedoch ganz oder zum Teil einem anderen Beteiligten auferlegt werden, wenn dies der Billigkeit entspricht.

§ 307
Vertragsbeendigung zur Sicherung außenstehender Aktionäre

Hat die Gesellschaft im Zeitpunkt der Beschlußfassung ihrer Hauptversammlung über einen Beherrschungs- oder Gewinnabführungsvertrag keinen außenstehenden Aktionär, so endet der Vertrag spätestens zum Ende des Geschäftsjahrs, in dem ein außenstehender Aktionär beteiligt ist.

Zweiter Teil
Leitungsmacht und Verantwortlichkeit bei Abhängigkeit von Unternehmen

Erster Abschnitt
Leitungsmacht und Verantwortlichkeit bei Bestehen eines Beherrschungsvertrags

§ 308
Leitungsmacht

(1) Besteht ein Beherrschungsvertrag, so ist das herrschende Unternehmen berechtigt, dem Vorstand der Gesellschaft hinsichtlich der Leitung der Gesellschaft Weisungen zu erteilen. Bestimmt der Vertrag nichts anderes, so können auch Weisungen

(6) The company's managing board shall publish the final decision, without an opinion, in the publications designated in the company's articles of incorporation.

(7) The costs of the proceedings shall be determined by reference to the *Kostenordnung*. In the proceedings before the court of first instance, twice the amount of one court fee shall be assessed. In the proceedings before the court of second instance, the same court fee shall be assessed; this also applies if the appeal is successful. If the application or the appeal is withdrawn before a decision is rendered, the court fee shall be reduced by one-half. The value of the subject matter in issue shall be determined ex officio. It shall be governed by § 30, paragraph 1, of the *Kostenordnung*. Advances on court costs shall not be required. The parties to the enterprise agreement shall be liable for the costs. However, the costs may be assessed, in whole or in part, against any other party in interest if fairness so requires.

§ 307
Termination of Agreement to Protect Outside Shareholders

If the company has no outside shareholders on the date when the resolution concerning the control agreement or the agreement to transfer profits is adopted by the shareholders, such agreement shall terminate no later than at the end of the fiscal year in which an outside shareholder acquired an interest.

Part Two
Power of Direction and Liability in Case of Controlled Enterprises

First Division
Power of Direction and Liability in Case of Control Agreement

§ 308
Power of Direction

(1) Where there is a control agreement, the controlling enterprise shall have the right to give instructions to the company's managing board concerning the management of the company. Unless the agreement provides otherwise, in-

structions may be given even if they are disadvantageous to the company, provided that they serve the interests of the controlling enterprise or of the affiliated group of enterprises of which it and the company are members.

(2) The managing board shall be required to follow the instructions given by the controlling enterprise. It shall not have the right to refuse compliance with an instruction on the ground that, in its opinion, such instruction does not serve the interests of the controlling enterprise or of the affiliated group of enterprises of which it and the company are members unless it is apparent that it does not serve such interests.

(3) If the managing board is instructed to enter into a transaction which requires the approval of the company's supervisory board, and if such approval is not granted within a reasonable period of time, the managing board shall notify the controlling enterprise of this fact. If after the notice is given the controlling enterprise repeats the instruction, the approval of the supervisory board shall no longer be required; if, however, the controlling enterprise has a supervisory board, the instruction may be repeated only with its approval.

§ 309
Liability of Legal Representatives of Controlling Enterprise

(1) Where there is a control agreement, the legal representatives (or, in the case of a sole proprietorship, the owner) of the controlling enterprise shall, in giving instructions to the company, apply the standard of care of a diligent and prudent executive.

(2) If such persons breach their duties they shall be jointly and severally liable to the company for the redress of any damage resulting therefrom. In case of a contest as to whether they acted with the care of a diligent and prudent executive, they shall bear the burden of proof.

(3) The company can waive or compromise the right to demand redress only after the expiration of three years from the date on which such right arose, and then only if the outside shareholders approve in a separate resolution and if a minority whose combined holdings amount to no less than one-tenth of the stated capital represented when the resolution is adopted does not have its objection recorded in the minutes. This time limit shall not apply if the party liable is insolvent and enters into a composition

erteilt werden, die für die Gesellschaft nachteilig sind, wenn sie den Belangen des herrschenden Unternehmens oder der mit ihm und der Gesellschaft konzernverbundenen Unternehmen dienen.

(2) Der Vorstand ist verpflichtet, die Weisungen des herrschenden Unternehmens zu befolgen. Er ist nicht berechtigt, die Befolgung einer Weisung zu verweigern, weil sie nach seiner Ansicht nicht den Belangen des herrschenden Unternehmens oder der mit ihm und der Gesellschaft konzernverbundenen Unternehmen dient, es sei denn, daß sie offensichtlich nicht diesen Belangen dient.

(3) Wird der Vorstand angewiesen, ein Geschäft vorzunehmen, das nur mit Zustimmung des Aufsichtsrats der Gesellschaft vorgenommen werden darf, und wird diese Zustimmung nicht innerhalb einer angemessenen Frist erteilt, so hat der Vorstand dies dem herrschenden Unternehmen mitzuteilen. Wiederholt das herrschende Unternehmen nach dieser Mitteilung die Weisung, so ist die Zustimmung des Aufsichtsrats nicht mehr erforderlich; die Weisung darf, wenn das herrschende Unternehmen einen Aufsichtsrat hat, nur mit dessen Zustimmung wiederholt werden.

§ 309
Verantwortlichkeit der gesetzlichen Vertreter des herrschenden Unternehmens

(1) Besteht ein Beherrschungsvertrag, so haben die gesetzlichen Vertreter (beim Einzelkaufmann der Inhaber) des herrschenden Unternehmens gegenüber der Gesellschaft bei der Erteilung von Weisungen an diese die Sorgfalt eines ordentlichen und gewissenhaften Geschäftsleiters anzuwenden.

(2) Verletzen sie ihre Pflichten, so sind sie der Gesellschaft zum Ersatz des daraus entstehenden Schadens als Gesamtschuldner verpflichtet. Ist streitig, ob sie die Sorgfalt eines ordentlichen und gewissenhaften Geschäftsleiters angewandt haben, so trifft sie die Beweislast.

(3) Die Gesellschaft kann erst drei Jahre nach der Entstehung des Anspruchs und nur dann auf Ersatzansprüche verzichten oder sich über sie vergleichen, wenn die außenstehenden Aktionäre durch Sonderbeschluß zustimmen und nicht eine Minderheit, deren Anteile zusammen den zehnten Teil des bei der Beschlußfassung vertretenen Grundkapitals erreichen, zur Niederschrift Widerspruch erhebt. Die zeitliche Beschränkung gilt nicht, wenn der Ersatzpflichtige zahlungsunfähig ist und sich zur Abwen-

dung oder Beseitigung des Konkursverfahrens mit seinen Gläubigern vergleicht.

(4) Der Ersatzanspruch der Gesellschaft kann auch von jedem Aktionär geltend gemacht werden. Der Aktionär kann jedoch nur Leistung an die Gesellschaft fordern. Der Ersatzanspruch kann ferner von den Gläubigern der Gesellschaft geltend gemacht werden, soweit sie von dieser keine Befriedigung erlangen können. Den Gläubigern gegenüber wird die Ersatzpflicht durch einen Verzicht oder Vergleich der Gesellschaft nicht ausgeschlossen. Ist über das Vermögen der Gesellschaft das Konkursverfahren eröffnet, so übt während dessen Dauer der Konkursverwalter das Recht der Aktionäre und Gläubiger, den Ersatzanspruch der Gesellschaft geltend zu machen, aus.

(5) Die Ansprüche aus diesen Vorschriften verjähren in fünf Jahren.

§ 310
Verantwortlichkeit der Verwaltungsmitglieder der Gesellschaft

(1) Die Mitglieder des Vorstands und des Aufsichtsrats der Gesellschaft haften neben dem Ersatzpflichtigen nach § 309 als Gesamtschuldner, wenn sie unter Verletzung ihrer Pflichten gehandelt haben. Ist streitig, ob sie die Sorgfalt eines ordentlichen und gewissenhaften Geschäftsleiters angewandt haben, so trifft sie die Beweislast.

(2) Dadurch, daß der Aufsichtsrat die Handlung gebilligt hat, wird die Ersatzpflicht nicht ausgeschlossen.

(3) Eine Ersatzpflicht der Verwaltungsmitglieder der Gesellschaft besteht nicht, wenn die schädigende Handlung auf einer Weisung beruht, die nach § 308 Abs. 2 zu befolgen war.

(4) § 309 Abs. 3 bis 5 ist anzuwenden.

Zweiter Abschnitt

Verantwortlichkeit bei Fehlen eines Beherrschungsvertrags

§ 311
Schranken des Einflusses

(1) Besteht kein Beherrschungsvertrag, so darf ein herrschendes Unternehmen seinen Einfluß nicht dazu benutzen, eine abhängige Aktiengesellschaft oder Kommanditgesellschaft auf Aktien zu veranlassen, ein für sie nachteiliges Rechtsgeschäft vorzunehmen oder Maßnahmen zu ihrem Nachteil zu treffen oder zu unterlassen, es sei denn, daß die Nachteile ausgeglichen werden.

with its creditors to avert or terminate bankruptcy proceedings.

(4) The company's claim for damages can also be asserted by any shareholder. A shareholder may, however, direct the demand for payment only to the company. The claim for damages can also be asserted by the company's creditors to the extent that they cannot obtain satisfaction from the company. With respect to creditors, this liability shall not be barred by a waiver or compromise on the part of the company. If an order subjecting the assets of the company to bankruptcy proceedings has been issued, the receiver in bankruptcy shall exercise, during the pendency of such proceedings, the right of the shareholders and creditors to assert the company's claim for damages.

(5) The claims arising out of these provisions shall be barred after the expiration of five years.

§ 310
Liability of Members of the Company's Management

(1) The members of the company's managing board and of the supervisory board shall be jointly and severally liable with the party liable pursuant to § 309, if they acted in violation of their duties. In case of a contest as to whether they acted with the care of a diligent and prudent executive, they shall bear the burden of proof.

(2) The liability for redress shall not be barred by the fact that the supervisory board had approved the transaction.

(3) The members of the company's management shall not be liable for damages if the act causing the damage is based on an instruction compliance with which was required by § 308, paragraph 2.

(4) § 309, paragraphs 3 to 5, shall be applicable.

Second Division
Liability in Absence of Control Agreement

§ 311
Limits of Influence

(1) Where there is no control agreement, a controlling enterprise may not use its influence to induce a controlled stock corporation or partnership limited by shares to enter into transactions disadvantageous to it or to take or refrain from taking measures to its disadvantage, unless compensation is granted for such disadvantage.

§ 311

(2) If the compensation is not in fact effected during the fiscal year, it shall be specified, no later than at the end of the fiscal year in which the disadvantage was caused to the controlled company, when and by means of what benefits the disadvantage will be compensated. The controlled company shall be granted a vested right to the benefits designed to effect such compensation.

(2) Ist der Ausgleich nicht während des Geschäftsjahrs tatsächlich erfolgt, so muß spätestens am Ende des Geschäftsjahrs, in dem der abhängigen Gesellschaft der Nachteil zugefügt worden ist, bestimmt werden, wann und durch welche Vorteile der Nachteil ausgeglichen werden soll. Auf die zum Ausgleich bestimmten Vorteile ist der abhängigen Gesellschaft ein Rechtsanspruch zu gewähren.

§ 312
Report of the Managing Board on Dealings with Related Enterprises

(1) Where there is no control agreement, the managing board of a controlled company shall, within the first three months of the fiscal year, prepare a report on the dealings of the company with related enterprises. This report shall set forth any transactions the company entered into in the preceding fiscal year with the controlling enterprise or with an enterprise related to the latter, or at the instance or in the interest of such enterprises, as well as all other measures it took or refrained from taking at the instance or in the interest of such enterprises in the preceding fiscal year. The report shall state the consideration given and received in the case of transactions, and, in the case of other measures, the reasons for such measures and the benefits and disadvantages resulting to the company. With respect to the compensation of disadvantages, the report shall state in detail by what means compensation was in fact effected during the fiscal year or to which benefits the company was given a vested right.

(2) The report shall comply with the principles of a conscientious and true account.

(3) At the conclusion of the report, the managing board shall state whether the company, under the circumstances known to it at the time the transaction was entered into or the measure was taken or foregone, had received a reasonable consideration in connection with each transaction, and whether the company was disadvantaged by the fact that a measure was taken or foregone. In the event of any disadvantage resulting to the company, the board shall also explain whether such disadvantage was compensated. This statement shall also be made part of the business report.

§ 312
Bericht des Vorstands über Beziehungen zu verbundenen Unternehmen

(1) Besteht kein Beherrschungsvertrag, so hat der Vorstand einer abhängigen Gesellschaft in den ersten drei Monaten des Geschäftsjahrs einen Bericht über die Beziehungen der Gesellschaft zu verbundenen Unternehmen aufzustellen. In dem Bericht sind alle Rechtsgeschäfte, welche die Gesellschaft im vergangenen Geschäftsjahr mit dem herrschenden Unternehmen oder einem mit ihm verbundenen Unternehmen oder auf Veranlassung oder im Interesse dieser Unternehmen vorgenommen hat, und alle anderen Maßnahmen, die sie auf Veranlassung oder im Interesse dieser Unternehmen im vergangenen Geschäftsjahr getroffen oder unterlassen hat, aufzuführen. Bei den Rechtsgeschäften sind Leistung und Gegenleistung, bei den Maßnahmen die Gründe der Maßnahme und deren Vorteile und Nachteile für die Gesellschaft anzugeben. Bei einem Ausgleich von Nachteilen ist im einzelnen anzugeben, wie der Ausgleich während des Geschäftsjahrs tatsächlich erfolgt ist, oder auf welche Vorteile der Gesellschaft ein Rechtsanspruch gewährt worden ist.

(2) Der Bericht hat den Grundsätzen einer gewissenhaften und getreuen Rechenschaft zu entsprechen.

(3) Am Schluß des Berichts hat der Vorstand zu erklären, ob die Gesellschaft nach den Umständen, die ihm in dem Zeitpunkt bekannt waren, in dem das Rechtsgeschäft vorgenommen oder die Maßnahme getroffen oder unterlassen wurde, bei jedem Rechtsgeschäft eine angemessene Gegenleistung erhielt und dadurch, daß die Maßnahme getroffen oder unterlassen wurde, nicht benachteiligt wurde. Wurde die Gesellschaft benachteiligt, so hat er außerdem zu erklären, ob die Nachteile ausgeglichen worden sind. Die Erklärung ist auch in den Geschäftsbericht aufzunehmen.

§ 313
Prüfung durch die Abschlußprüfer

(1) Der Bericht über die Beziehungen zu verbundenen Unternehmen ist gleichzeitig mit dem Jahresabschluß und dem Geschäftsbericht den Abschlußprüfern der Gesellschaft vorzulegen. Diese haben zu prüfen, ob

1. die tatsächlichen Angaben des Berichts richtig sind,

2. bei den im Bericht aufgeführten Rechtsgeschäften nach den Umständen, die im Zeitpunkt ihrer Vornahme bekannt waren, die Leistung der Gesellschaft nicht unangemessen hoch war; soweit sie dies war, ob die Nachteile ausgeglichen worden sind,

3. bei den im Bericht aufgeführten Maßnahmen keine Umstände für eine wesentlich andere Beurteilung als die durch den Vorstand sprechen.

§ 165 gilt sinngemäß.

(2) Die Abschlußprüfer haben über das Ergebnis der Prüfung schriftlich zu berichten. Stellen sie bei Wahrnehmung ihrer Aufgaben nach Absatz 1 und § 162 fest, daß der Bericht über die Beziehungen zu verbundenen Unternehmen unvollständig ist, so haben sie auch hierüber zu berichten. Die Abschlußprüfer haben ihren Bericht zu unterzeichnen und dem Vorstand vorzulegen.

(3) Sind nach dem abschließenden Ergebnis der Prüfung keine Einwendungen zu erheben, so haben die Abschlußprüfer dies durch folgenden Vermerk zum Bericht über die Beziehungen zu verbundenen Unternehmen zu bestätigen:

Nach meiner/unserer pflichtmäßigen Prüfung und. Beurteilung bestätige ich/bestätigen wir, daß

1. die tatsächlichen Angaben des Berichts richtig sind,

2. bei den im Bericht aufgeführten Rechtsgeschäften die Leistung der Gesellschaft nicht unangemessen hoch war oder Nachteile ausgeglichen worden sind,

3. bei den im Bericht aufgeführten Maßnahmen keine Umstände für eine wesentlich andere Beurteilung als die durch den Vorstand sprechen.

Führt der Bericht kein Rechtsgeschäft auf, so ist Nummer 2, führt er keine Maßnahme auf, so ist Nummer 3 des Vermerks fortzulassen. Haben die Abschlußprüfer bei keinem im Bericht aufgeführten Rechtsgeschäft festgestellt, daß die Leistung der Gesellschaft unangemessen hoch war, so ist Num-

§ 313
Audit by Annual Auditors

(1) The report on the dealings with related enterprises shall be submitted to the company's annual auditors together with the annual financial statements and the business report. Such auditors shall examine

1. whether the factual statements in the report are accurate,

2. with regard to the transactions set forth in the report, whether, according to the circumstances known at the time they were entered into, the consideration given by the company was not unreasonably high, and, if so, whether the resulting disadvantage was compensated,

3. with regard to the other measures set forth in the report, whether there are no circumstances which would call for an evaluation substantially different from that made by the managing board.

§ 165 shall apply *mutatis mutandis.*

(2) The annual auditors shall report on the results of the audit in writing. If, in the exercise of their duties in accordance with paragraph 1 hereof and § 162, they determine that the report on the dealings with related enterprises is incomplete, they shall also report this fact. The annual auditors shall sign their report and submit it to the managing board.

(3) If, according to the final results of the audit, there are no objections, the annual auditors shall so state by means of the following certification of the report on the dealings with related enterprises:

According to my/our due examination and opinion, I/we certify that

1. the factual statements in the report are accurate,

2. for the transactions set forth in the report, the consideration given by the company was not unreasonably high or resulting disadvantages were compensated,

3. with respect to the other measures set forth in the report there are no circumstances which would call for an evaluation substantially different from that made by the managing board.

If the report does not refer to any transaction, No. 2, and if it does not refer to any other measure, No. 3, of this certification shall be omitted. If the annual auditors, in connection with the transactions referred to in the report, have determined that the consideration given by the company was not unreasonably high, No. 2 of the certification shall be limited to a confirmation to this effect.

(4) If there are objections or if the annual auditors have determined that the report on the dealings with related enterprises is incomplete, they shall qualify or refuse the certification. If the managing board itself has stated that the company has suffered disadvantages in connection with specific transactions or other measures and that such disadvantages have not been compensated, this shall be stated in the certificatioɯ, and the certification shall be limited to the remaining transactions or other measures.

(5) The annual auditors shall sign the certification, stating the place and date. The certification shall also be made part of the audit report.

§ 314
Examination by the Supervisory Board

(1) The managing board shall submit the report on the dealings with related enterprises and the audit report of the annual auditors, together with the documents referred to in § 170, to the supervisory board. Each member of the supervisory board shall have the right to inspect such reports. Copies shall also be issued upon request to each member of the supervisory board, unless the supervisory board has, by resolution, decided otherwise.

(2) The supervisory board shall examine the report on the dealings with related enterprises and report on the results of the examination in its report to the shareholders' meeting (§ 171, paragraph 2). In this report it shall also comment on the results of the audit by the annual auditors of the report on the dealings with related enterprises. The certification by the annual auditors shall be made part of the report, and a refusal to give the certification shall be expressly mentioned.

(3) At the conclusion of the report, the supervisory board shall state whether, on the basis of the final result of its examination, there are any objections to the statement made by the managing board at the conclusion of the report on the dealings with related enterprises.

(4) The annual auditors shall, when so requested, participate in the deliberations of the supervisory board concerning the report on the dealings with related enterprises.

mer 2 des Vermerks auf diese Bestätigung zu, beschränken.

(4) Sind Einwendungen zu erheben oder haben die Abschlußprüfer festgestellt, daß der Bericht über die Beziehungen zu verbundenen Unternehmen unvollständig ist, so haben sie die Bestätigung einzuschränken oder zu versagen. Hat der Vorstand selbst erklärt, daß die Gesellschaft durch bestimmte Rechtsgeschäfte oder Maßnahmen benachteiligt worden ist, ohne daß die Nachteile ausgeglichen worden sind, so ist dies in dem Vermerk anzugeben und der Vermerk auf die übrigen Rechtsgeschäfte oder Maßnahmen zu beschränken.

(5) Die Abschlußprüfer haben den Bestätigungsvermerk mit Angabe von Ort und Tag zu unterzeichnen. Der Bestätigungsvermerk ist auch in den Prüfungsbericht aufzunehmen.

§ 314
Prüfung durch den Aufsichtsrat

(1) Der Vorstand hat den Bericht über die Beziehungen zu verbundenen Unternehmen und den Prüfungsbericht der Abschlußprüfer zusammen mit den in § 170 angegebenen Vorlagen dem Aufsichtsrat vorzulegen. Jedes Aufsichtsratsmitglied hat das Recht, von den Berichten Kenntnis zu nehmen. Die Berichte sind auch jedem Aufsichtsratsmitglied auf Verlangen auszuhändigen, soweit der Aufsichtsrat nichts anderes beschlossen hat.

(2) Der Aufsichtsrat hat den Bericht über die Beziehungen zu verbundenen Unternehmen zu prüfen und in seinem Bericht an die Hauptversammlung (§ 171 Abs. 2) über das Ergebnis der Prüfung zu berichten. Er hat in diesem Bericht ferner zu dem Ergebnis der Prüfung des Berichts über die Beziehungen zu verbundenen Unternehmen durch die Abschlußprüfer Stellung zu nehmen. Ein von den Abschlußprüfern erteilter Bestätigungsvermerk ist in den Bericht aufzunehmen, eine Versagung des Bestätigungsvermerks ausdrücklich mitzuteilen.

(3) Am Schluß des Berichts hat der Aufsichtsrat zu erklären, ob nach dem abschließenden Ergebnis seiner Prüfung Einwendungen gegen die Erklärung des Vorstands am Schluß des Berichts über die Beziehungen zu verbundenen Unternehmen zu erheben sind.

(4) An der Verhandlung des Aufsichtsrats über den Bericht über die Beziehungen zu verbundenen Unternehmen haben die Abschlußprüfer auf Verlangen teilzunehmen.

§ 315

Sonderprüfung

Auf Antrag eines Aktionärs hat das Gericht Sonderprüfer zur Prüfung der geschäftlichen Beziehungen der Gesellschaft zu dem herrschenden Unternehmen oder einem mit ihm verbundenen Unternehmen zu bestellen, wenn

1. die Abschlußprüfer den Bestätigungsvermerk zum Bericht über die Beziehungen zu verbundenen Unternehmen eingeschränkt oder versagt haben,

2. der Aufsichtsrat erklärt hat, daß Einwendungen gegen die Erklärung des Vorstands am Schluß des Berichts über die Beziehungen zu verbundenen Unternehmen zu erheben sind,

3. der Vorstand selbst erklärt hat, daß die Gesellschaft durch bestimmte Rechtsgeschäfte oder Maßnahmen benachteiligt worden ist, ohne daß die Nachteile ausgeglichen worden sind.

Gegen die Entscheidung ist die sofortige Beschwerde zulässig. Hat die Hauptversammlung zur Prüfung derselben Vorgänge Sonderprüfer bestellt, so kann jeder Aktionär den Antrag nach § 142 Abs. 4 stellen.

§ 316

Kein Bericht über Beziehungen zu verbundenen Unternehmen bei Gewinnabführungsvertrag

§§ 312 bis 315 gelten nicht, wenn zwischen der abhängigen Gesellschaft und dem herrschenden Unternehmen ein Gewinnabführungsvertrag besteht.

§ 317

Verantwortlichkeit des herrschenden Unternehmens und seiner gesetzlichen Vertreter

(1) Veranlaßt ein herrschendes Unternehmen eine abhängige Gesellschaft, mit der kein Beherrschungsvertrag besteht, ein für sie nachteiliges Rechtsgeschäft vorzunehmen oder zu ihrem Nachteil eine Maßnahme zu treffen oder zu unterlassen, ohne daß es den Nachteil bis zum Ende des Geschäftsjahrs tatsächlich ausgleicht oder der abhängigen Gesellschaft einen Rechtsanspruch auf einen zum Ausgleich bestimmten Vorteil gewährt, so ist es der Gesellschaft zum Ersatz des ihr daraus entstehenden Schadens verpflichtet. Es ist auch den Aktionären zum Ersatz des ihnen daraus entstehenden Schadens verpflichtet, soweit sie, abgesehen von einem Schaden, der ihnen durch Schädigung der Gesellschaft zugefügt worden ist, geschädigt worden sind.

(2) Die Ersatzpflicht tritt nicht ein, wenn auch ein ordentlicher und gewissenhafter Geschäftsleiter einer unabhängigen Gesellschaft das Rechtsgeschäft

§ 315

Special Audit

Upon the application of a shareholder, the court shall appoint special auditors for the purpose of auditing the company's business dealings with the controlling enterprise or with an enterprise related to the latter, if

1. the annual auditors have qualified or refused the certification of the report on the dealings with related enterprises,

2. the supervisory board has stated that there are objections to the statement made by the managing board at the conclusion of the report on the dealings with related enterprises,

3. the managing board itself has stated that the company has suffered disadvantages in connection with specific transactions or other measures, and that such disadvantages have not been compensated.

The decision of the court can be appealed. If the shareholders' meeting has appointed special auditors for the purpose of auditing the same facts, each shareholder shall be entitled to make the application pursuant to § 142, paragraph 4.

§ 316

No Report on Dealings with Related Enterprises in the Case of Agreement to Transfer Profit

§§ 312 to 315 shall not apply in the case of an agreement to transfer profit between the controlled company and the controlling enterprise.

§ 317

Liability of Controlling Enterprise and Its Legal Representatives

(1) If a controlling enterprise induces a controlled company with which it does not have a control agreement to enter into a transaction disadvantageous to it or to take or refrain from taking other measures to its disadvantage, and fails, before the end of the fiscal year, to compensate for such disadvantage or to grant a vested right to a benefit designed to effect such compensation, it shall be liable to the company for the damage the latter thereby incurs. It shall also be liable to the shareholders for any damage they incurred to the extent that they sustained damage other than that incurred by reason of the damage to the company.

(2) It shall not be liable if a diligent and prudent executive of an independent company

§ 317

would have entered into the transaction or taken or refrained from taking the other measure.

(3) In addition to the controlling enterprise, those of the legal representatives of such enterprise who induced the company to enter into the transaction or to take the measure shall be jointly and severally liable.

(4) § 309, paragraphs 3 to 5, shall apply *mutatis mutandis*.

§ 318
Liability of Company's Management

(1) The members of the company's managing board shall be jointly and severally liable with the parties liable pursuant to § 317 if they failed, in violation of their duties, to refer to the disadvantageous transaction or to the disadvantageous measure in the report on the dealings of the company with related enterprises, or if they failed to state that the company has suffered disadvantages in connection with the transaction or other measure and that such disadvantages have not been compensated. In case of a contest as to whether they acted with the care of a diligent and prudent executive, they shall bear the burden of proof.

(2) The members of the company's supervisory board shall be jointly and severally liable with the parties liable pursuant to § 317 if, with respect to the disadvantageous transaction or to the disadvantageous measure, they failed in violation of their duties to examine the report on the dealings with related enterprises and to report on the results of the examination to the shareholders' meeting (§ 314); paragraph 1, second sentence, hereof shall apply *mutatis mutandis*.

(3) There shall be no liability to the company or to the shareholders if the act was based on a lawful shareholders' resolution.

(4) § 309, paragraphs 3 to 5, shall apply *mutatis mutandis*.

Part Three
Integrated Companies

§ 319
Integration

(1) The shareholders of a stock corporation may adopt a resolution to integrate the company into another stock corporation domiciled in Germany (principal company) if all of the shares of the company are held by the prospective principal

---

vorgenommen oder die Maßnahme getroffen oder unterlassen hätte.

(3) Neben dem herrschenden Unternehmen haften als Gesamtschuldner die gesetzlichen Vertreter des Unternehmens, die die Gesellschaft zu dem Rechtsgeschäft oder der Maßnahme veranlaßt haben.

(4) § 309 Abs. 3 bis 5 gilt sinngemäß.

§ 318
Verantwortlichkeit der Verwaltungsmitglieder der Gesellschaft

(1) Die Mitglieder des Vorstands der Gesellschaft haften neben den nach § 317 Ersatzpflichtigen als Gesamtschuldner, wenn sie es unter Verletzung ihrer Pflichten unterlassen haben, das nachteilige Rechtsgeschäft oder die nachteilige Maßnahme in dem Bericht über die Beziehungen der Gesellschaft zu verbundenen Unternehmen aufzuführen oder anzugeben, daß die Gesellschaft durch das Rechtsgeschäft oder die Maßnahme benachteiligt wurde und der Nachteil nicht ausgeglichen worden war. Ist streitig, ob sie die Sorgfalt eines ordentlichen und gewissenhaften Geschäftsleiters angewandt haben, so trifft sie die Beweislast.

(2) Die Mitglieder des Aufsichtsrats der Gesellschaft haften neben den nach § 317 Ersatzpflichtigen als Gesamtschuldner, wenn sie hinsichtlich des nachteiligen Rechtsgeschäfts oder der nachteiligen Maßnahme ihre Pflicht, den Bericht über die Beziehungen zu verbundenen Unternehmen zu prüfen und über das Ergebnis der Prüfung an die Hauptversammlung zu berichten (§ 314), verletzt haben; Absatz 1 Satz 2 gilt sinngemäß.

(3) Der Gesellschaft und auch den Aktionären gegenüber tritt die Ersatzpflicht nicht ein, wenn die Handlung auf einem gesetzmäßigen Beschluß der Hauptversammlung beruht.

(4) § 309 Abs. 3 bis 5 gilt sinngemäß.

Dritter Teil
Eingegliederte Gesellschaften

§ 319
Eingliederung

(1) Die Hauptversammlung einer Aktiengesellschaft kann die Eingliederung der Gesellschaft in eine andere Aktiengesellschaft mit Sitz im Inland (Hauptgesellschaft) beschließen, wenn sich alle Aktien der Gesellschaft in der Hand der zukünftigen

Hauptgesellschaft befinden. Auf den Beschluß sind die Bestimmungen des Gesetzes und der Satzung über Satzungsänderungen nicht anzuwenden.

(2) Der Beschluß über die Eingliederung wird nur wirksam, wenn die Hauptversammlung der zukünftigen Hauptgesellschaft zustimmt. Der Beschluß über die Zustimmung bedarf einer Mehrheit, die mindestens drei Viertel des bei der Beschlußfassung vertretenen Grundkapitals umfaßt. Die Satzung kann eine größere Kapitalmehrheit und weitere Erfordernisse bestimmen. Absatz 1 Satz 2 ist anzuwenden. Jedem Aktionär ist auf Verlangen in der Hauptversammlung, die über die Zustimmung beschließt, Auskunft auch über alle im Zusammenhang mit der Eingliederung wesentlichen Angelegenheiten der einzugliedernden Gesellschaft zu geben.

(3) Der Vorstand der einzugliedernden Gesellschaft hat die Eingliederung und die Firma der Hauptgesellschaft zur Eintragung in das Handelsregister anzumelden. Bei der Anmeldung hat der Vorstand zu erklären, daß die Hauptversammlungsbeschlüsse innerhalb der Anfechtungsfrist nicht angefochten worden sind oder daß die Anfechtung rechtskräftig zurückgewiesen worden ist. Der Anmeldung sind die Niederschriften der Hauptversammlungsbeschlüsse und ihre Anlagen in Ausfertigung oder öffentlich beglaubigter Abschrift beizufügen.

(4) Mit der Eintragung der Eingliederung in das Handelsregister des Sitzes der Gesellschaft wird die Gesellschaft in die Hauptgesellschaft eingegliedert.

§ 320
Eingliederung durch Mehrheitsbeschluß

(1) Die Hauptversammlung einer Aktiengesellschaft kann die Eingliederung der Gesellschaft in eine andere Aktiengesellschaft mit Sitz im Inland auch dann beschließen, wenn sich Aktien der Gesellschaft im Gesamtnennbetrag von fünfundneunzig vom Hundert des Grundkapitals in der Hand der zukünftigen Hauptgesellschaft befinden. Eigene Aktien und Aktien, die einem anderen für Rechnung der Gesellschaft gehören, sind vom Grundkapital abzusetzen. Für die Eingliederung gelten außer § 319 Abs. 1 Satz 2, Abs. 2 bis 4 die Absätze 2 bis 7.

(2) Die Bekanntmachung der Eingliederung als Gegenstand der Tagesordnung ist nur ordnungsgemäß, wenn

company. The provisions of the law and of the articles of incorporation concerning the amendment of the articles of incorporation shall not apply to such resolution.

(2) The resolution concerning integration shall become effective only if approved by the shareholders of the prospective principal company. The resolution concerning such approval shall require a majority of no less than three-fourths of the stated capital represented when the resolution is adopted. The articles of incorporation may provide for a higher capital majority and establish additional requirements. Paragraph 1, second sentence, hereof shall be applicable. At the shareholders' meeting in which the resolution concerning the approval is adopted, each shareholder shall, upon request, also be furnished information on such matters affecting the company to be integrated as are material to the integration.

(3) The managing board of the company to be integrated shall file an application to record the integration and the name of the principal company in the Commercial Register. In making such application, the managing board shall state that no action to set aside the shareholders' resolutions has been instituted within the time provided therefor, or that an action to set them aside has been dismissed by a final decision. The application shall be accompanied by a duplicate original or certified copy of the minutes of the resolutions and their annexes.

(4) The integration of the company into the principal company shall not become effective before registration of the integration in the Commercial Register at the company's domicile.

§ 320
Integration by Majority Resolution

(1) The shareholders of a stock corporation may also adopt a resolution to integrate the company into another stock corporation domiciled in Germany if shares of the company with a total par value of ninety-five percent of the stated capital are held by the prospective principal company. Treasury shares and shares held by a third party for the account of the company shall be deducted from the stated capital. In addition to § 319, paragraph 1, second sentence, and paragraphs 2 to 4, such integration shall be governed by paragraphs 2 to 7 hereof.

(2) The announcement of the integration as an item of the agenda shall be considered as having been duly made only if

1. it contains the name and the domicile of the prospective principal company,
2. it is accompanied by a statement by the prospective principal company in which such company offers to the withdrawing shareholders, as indemnity for their shares, its own shares and, in the case of paragraph 5, third sentence, hereof, an additional cash payment.

No. 2 of the first sentence hereof shall also apply to the announcement by the prospective principal company.

(3) At the shareholders' meeting in which the resolution concerning the integration is adopted, each shareholder shall, upon request, also be furnished information on matters affecting the prospective principal company that are material to the integration.

(4) Any shares not already held by the principal company shall pass to it by operation of law upon registration of the integration in the Commercial Register. If share certificates were issued for such shares, they shall, until their transfer to the principal company, only confer rights to indemnity.

(5) The withdrawing shareholders shall be entitled to a reasonable indemnity. By way of indemnity, they shall receive shares of the principal company. If the principal company is a controlled company, the withdrawing shareholders shall receive, at their election, either shares of the principal company or a reasonable cash indemnity. If shares of the principal company are given as indemnity, such indemnity shall be considered to be reasonable if shares are issued in the same ratio in which, in the event of merger, each share of the company would be entitled to shares of the principal company; fractional amounts may be compensated by cash payments. The reasonable cash indemnity shall take into account the company's financial condition and earnings at the time the resolution concerning the integration is adopted by the shareholders. The cash indemnity and cash payments shall bear interest at the rate of five percent per annum from the date the registration of the integration is published; this shall not preclude claims for further damages.

(6) An action to set aside the resolution whereby the shareholders of the integrated company adopted the integration of the company may not be based on § 243, paragraph 2, or on the fact that the indemnity offered by the principal company pursuant to paragraph 2, No. 2, hereof is not reasonable. If the indemnity offered by the prin-

1. sie die Firma und den Sitz der zukünftigen Hauptgesellschaft enthält,
2. ihr eine Erklärung der zukünftigen Hauptgesellschaft beigefügt ist, in der diese den ausscheidenden Aktionären als Abfindung für ihre Aktien eigene Aktien, im Falle des Absatzes 5 Satz 3 außerdem eine Barabfindung anbietet.

Satz 1 Nr. 2 gilt auch für die Bekanntmachung der zukünftigen Hauptgesellschaft.

(3) Jedem Aktionär ist auf Verlangen in der Hauptversammlung, die über die Eingliederung beschließt, Auskunft auch über alle im Zusammenhang mit der Eingliederung wesentlichen Angelegenheiten der zukünftigen Hauptgesellschaft zu geben.

(4) Mit der Eintragung der Eingliederung in das Handelsregister gehen alle Aktien, die sich nicht in der Hand der Hauptgesellschaft befinden, auf diese über. Sind über diese Aktien Aktienurkunden ausgegeben, so verbriefen sie bis zu ihrer Aushändigung an die Hauptgesellschaft nur den Anspruch auf Abfindung.

(5) Die ausgeschiedenen Aktionäre haben Anspruch auf angemessene Abfindung. Als Abfindung sind ihnen eigene Aktien der Hauptgesellschaft zu gewähren. Ist die Hauptgesellschaft eine abhängige Gesellschaft, so sind den ausgeschiedenen Aktionären nach deren Wahl eigene Aktien der Hauptgesellschaft oder eine angemessene Barabfindung zu gewähren. Werden als Abfindung Aktien der Hauptgesellschaft gewährt, so ist die Abfindung als angemessen anzusehen, wenn die Aktien in dem Verhältnis gewährt werden, in dem bei einer Verschmelzung auf eine Aktie der Gesellschaft Aktien der Hauptgesellschaft zu gewähren wären, wobei Spitzenbeträge durch bare Zuzahlungen ausgeglichen werden können. Die angemessene Barabfindung muß die Vermögens- und Ertragslage der Gesellschaft im Zeitpunkt der Beschlußfassung ihrer Hauptversammlung über die Eingliederung berücksichtigen. Die Barabfindung sowie bare Zuzahlungen sind von der Bekanntmachung der Eintragung der Eingliederung an mit fünf vom Hundert jährlich zu verzinsen; die Geltendmachung eines weiteren Schadens ist nicht ausgeschlossen.

(6) Die Anfechtung des Beschlusses, durch den die Hauptversammlung der eingegliederten Gesellschaft die Eingliederung der Gesellschaft beschlossen hat, kann nicht auf § 243 Abs. 2 oder darauf gestützt werden, daß die von der Hauptgesellschaft nach Absatz 2 Nr. 2 angebotene Abfindung nicht angemessen ist. Ist die angebotene Abfindung nicht

§ 320

angemessen, so hat das in § 306 bestimmte Gericht auf Antrag die angemessene Abfindung zu bestimmen. Das gleiche gilt, wenn die Hauptgesellschaft eine Abfindung nicht oder nicht ordnungsgemäß angeboten hat und eine hierauf gestützte Anfechtungsklage innerhalb der Anfechtungsfrist nicht erhoben oder zurückgenommen ·oder rechtskräftig abgewiesen worden ist.

(7) Antragsberechtigt ist jeder ausgeschiedene Aktionär. Der Antrag kann nur binnen zwei Monaten nach dem Tage gestellt werden, an dem die Eintragung der Eingliederung in das Handelsregister nach § 10 des Handelsgesetzbuchs als bekanntgemacht gilt. Für das Verfahren gilt § 306 sinngemäß.

§ 321
Gläubigerschutz

(1) Den Gläubigern der eingegliederten Gesellschaft, deren Forderungen begründet worden sind, bevor die Eintragung der Eingliederung in das Handelsregister bekanntgemacht worden ist, ist, wenn sie sich binnen sechs Monaten nach der Bekanntmachung zu diesem Zweck melden, Sicherheit zu leisten, soweit sie nicht Befriedigung verlangen können. Die Gläubiger sind in der Bekanntmachung der Eintragung auf dieses Recht hinzuweisen.

(2) Das Recht, Sicherheitsleistung zu verlangen, steht Gläubigern nicht zu, die im Falle des Konkurses ein Recht auf vorzugsweise Befriedigung aus einer Deckungsmasse haben, die nach gesetzlicher Vorschrift zu ihrem Schutz errichtet und staatlich überwacht ist.

§ 322
Haftung der Hauptgesellschaft

(1) Von der Eingliederung an haftet die Hauptgesellschaft für die vor diesem Zeitpunkt begründeten Verbindlichkeiten der eingegliederten Gesellschaft den Gläubigern dieser Gesellschaft als Gesamtschuldner. Die gleiche Haftung trifft sie für alle Verbindlichkeiten der eingegliederten Gesellschaft, die nach der Eingliederung begründet werden. Eine entgegenstehende Vereinbarung ist Dritten gegenüber unwirksam.

(2) Wird die Hauptgesellschaft wegen einer Verbindlichkeit der eingegliederten Gesellschaft in Anspruch genommen, so kann sie Einwendungen, die nicht in ihrer Person begründet sind, nur insoweit geltend machen, als sie von der eingegliederten Gesellschaft erhoben werden können.

(3) Die Hauptgesellschaft kann die Befriedigung des Gläubigers verweigern, solange der eingeglie-

cipal company is not reasonable, the court designated in § 306 shall, upon application, determine a reasonable indemnity. The same shall apply if the principal company did not offer any indemnity or offered it improperly, and an action, based on this fact, to set the resolution aside was not brought within the period of time provided therefor, or was withdrawn or dismissed by a final decision.

(7) Each withdrawing shareholder shall be entitled to make such application. The application may be made only within two months from the date on which the registration of the integration in the Commercial Register is deemed published in accordance with § 10 of the Commercial Code. § 306 shall apply to the procedure *mutatis mutandis*.

§ 321
Protection of Creditors

(1) Creditors of the integrated company whose claims arose prior to the date on which the registration of the integration was published in the Commercial Register shall be furnished security provided that they make a request to this effect within six months from the date of publication, unless such creditors are entitled to payment. The creditors shall be advised of this right in the publication of the registration.

(2) The right to request security shall not be available to creditors who, in the event of bankruptcy, would have a claim to preferred satisfaction from a fund which was established by statute for their protection and which is subject to governmental supervision.

§ 322
Liability of Principal Company

(1) Subsequent to the integration, the principal company shall be jointly and severally liable to the creditors of the integrated company for any liabilities of the company which arose prior thereto. It shall also be liable for any liabilities of the integrated company which arise after the date of integration. An agreement to the contrary shall be invalid as against third parties.

(2) If a claim based on a liability of the integrated company is asserted against the principal company, the principal company may raise defenses other than those it has in its own right only to the extent that they could be raised by the integrated company.

(3) The principal company may refuse to satisfy a creditor as long as the integrated com-

pany has the right to rescind the transaction giving rise to the claim against it. The principal company shall have the same right as long as a creditor can obtain satisfaction by offsetting his claim against any matured claim of the integrated company.

(4) A writ of execution against the integrated company shall not entitle the creditor to obtain execution against the principal company.

derten Gesellschaft das Recht zusteht, das ihrer Verbindlichkeit zugrunde liegende Rechtsgeschäft anzufechten. Die gleiche Befugnis hat die Hauptgesellschaft, solange sich der Gläubiger durch Aufrechnung gegen eine fällige Forderung der eingegliederten Gesellschaft befriedigen kann.

(4) Aus einem gegen die eingegliederte Gesellschaft gerichteten vollstreckbaren Schuldtitel findet die Zwangsvollstreckung gegen die Hauptgesellschaft nicht statt.

§ 323
Power of Direction of Principal Company and Liability of Members of Managing Board

(1) The principal company shall have the right to give instructions to the managing board of the integrated company concerning the management of the company. § 308, paragraph 2, first sentence, and paragraph 3, and §§ 309 and 310 shall apply *mutatis mutandis*. §§ 311 to 318 shall not be applicable.

(2) Performances rendered by the integrated company to the principal company shall not be deemed in violation of §§ 57, 58, and 60.

§ 323
Leitungsmacht der Hauptgesellschaft und Verantwortlichkeit der Vorstandsmitglieder

(1) Die Hauptgesellschaft ist berechtigt, dem Vorstand der eingegliederten Gesellschaft hinsichtlich der Leitung der Gesellschaft Weisungen zu erteilen. § 308 Abs. 2 Satz 1, Abs. 3, §§ 309, 310 gelten sinngemäß. §§ 311 bis 318 sind nicht anzuwenden.

(2) Leistungen der eingegliederten Gesellschaft an die Hauptgesellschaft gelten nicht als Verstoß gegen die §§ 57, 58 und 60.

§ 324
Statutory Reserve. Transfer of Profit. Assumption of Losses

(1) The statutory provisions concerning the formation of a statutory reserve, its disposition, and the allocation of amounts to the statutory reserve shall not apply to integrated companies.

(2) §§ 293 to 296 and 298 to 303 shall not apply to an agreement to transfer profit, a pooling of profits, or to an agreement to transfer a portion of the profit between the integrated company and the principal company. The agreement, any amendment thereof, and its termination must be in writing. The amount transferred as profit may not exceed the retained earnings as determined without reference to the transfer of profit. The agreement shall terminate no later than at the end of the fiscal year in which the integration terminates.

(3) The principal company shall be required to offset any losses that may otherwise arise for the integrated company, to the extent that such losses exceed the amount of disclosed reserves.

§ 324
Gesetzliche Rücklage. Gewinnabführung. Verlustübernahme

(1) Die gesetzlichen Vorschriften über die Bildung einer gesetzlichen Rücklage, über ihre Verwendung und über die Einstellung von Beträgen in die gesetzliche Rücklage sind auf eingegliederte Gesellschaften nicht anzuwenden.

(2) Auf einen Gewinnabführungsvertrag, eine Gewinngemeinschaft oder einen Teilgewinnabführungsvertrag zwischen der eingegliederten Gesellschaft und der Hauptgesellschaft sind die §§ 293 bis 296, 298 bis 303 nicht anzuwenden. Der Vertrag, seine Änderung und seine Aufhebung bedürfen der schriftlichen Form. Als Gewinn kann höchstens der ohne die Gewinnabführung entstehende Bilanzgewinn abgeführt werden. Der Vertrag endet spätestens zum Ende des Geschäftsjahrs, in dem die Eingliederung endet.

(3) Die Hauptgesellschaft ist verpflichtet, jeden bei der eingegliederten Gesellschaft sonst entstehenden Bilanzverlust auszugleichen, soweit dieser den Betrag der offenen Rücklagen übersteigt.

§ 323

§ 325

**Keine Einreichung und Bekanntmachung
des Jahresabschlusses**

(1) § 177 über die Pflicht, den Jahresabschluß und den Geschäftsbericht zum Handelsregister einzureichen sowie den Jahresabschluß bekanntzumachen, gilt nicht, wenn die eingegliederte Gesellschaft in einen auf den Stichtag ihres Jahresabschlusses von der Hauptgesellschaft aufgestellten Konzernabschluß oder Teilkonzernabschluß einbezogen ist.

(2) Werden der Jahresabschluß und der Geschäftsbericht nicht zum Handelsregister eingereicht oder wird der Jahresabschluß nicht bekanntgemacht, so hat der Vorstand der eingegliederten Gesellschaft unverzüglich nach der Hauptversammlung der Hauptgesellschaft über den Jahresabschluß (§ 337 Abs. 2) den Konzernabschluß oder Teilkonzernabschluß mit Bestätigungsvermerk und den Konzerngeschäftsbericht oder Teilkonzerngeschäftsbericht zum Handelsregister einzureichen. § 338 Abs. 1 Satz 2 und 3 ist anzuwenden. Der Vorstand hat ferner die Bekanntmachung des Konzernabschlusses oder Teilkonzernabschlusses zum Handelsregister einzureichen.

(3) Das Gericht hat nur zu prüfen, ob der eingereichte Konzernabschluß oder Teilkonzernabschluß § 338 Abs. 1 Satz 2 und 3 entspricht und ob die Gesellschaft nach dem Konzerngeschäftsbericht oder Teilkonzerngeschäftsbericht in ihn einbezogen ist.

§ 326

**Auskunftsrecht der Aktionäre der
Hauptgesellschaft**

Jedem Aktionär der Hauptgesellschaft ist über Angelegenheiten der eingegliederten Gesellschaft ebenso Auskunft zu erteilen wie über Angelegenheiten der Hauptgesellschaft.

§ 327

Ende der Eingliederung

(1) Die Eingliederung endet

1. durch Beschluß der Hauptversammlung der eingegliederten Gesellschaft,

---

§ 325

No Filing or Publication of Annual Financial Statements

(1) § 177, concerning the duty to file the annual financial statements and the business report with the Commercial Register and to publish the annual financial statements, shall not apply if the integrated company is included in the consolidated financial statements or partial consolidated financial statements prepared by the principal company as of the closing date of the annual financial statements of the integrated company.

(2) If the annual financial statements and the business report are not filed with the Commercial Register or if the annual financial statements are not published, the managing board of the integrated company shall promptly, after the shareholders' meeting of the principal company on the annual financial statements (§ 337, paragraph 2), file with the Commercial Register the consolidated financial statements or partial consolidated financial statements together with the certification and the consolidated business report or partial consolidated business report. § 338, paragraph 1, second and third sentences, shall be applicable. The managing board shall also file the publication of the consolidated financial statements or partial consolidated financial statements with the Commercial Register.

(3) The court shall examine only whether the consolidated financial statements or the partial consolidated financial statements filed comply with § 338, paragraph 1, second and third sentences, and whether the company is included in such statements according to the consolidated business report or the partial consolidated business report.

§ 326

Right of Principal Company's Shareholders to Information

Any shareholder of the principal company shall be entitled to be furnished information on matters affecting the integrated company to the same extent as such shareholder is entitled to be furnished information on matters affecting the principal company.

§ 327

Termination of Integration

(1) The integration shall terminate

1. upon a resolution of the shareholders of the integrated company,

2. if the principal company ceases to be a stock corporation domiciled in Germany,

3. if the principal company no longer holds all of the shares of the integrated company,

4. upon dissolution of the principal company.

(2) Whenever the principal company no longer holds all of the shares of the integrated company, the principal company shall promptly report this fact in writing to the integrated company.

(3) The managing board of the formerly integrated company shall promptly file an application to record the termination of the integration, the grounds therefor, and the effective date thereof, in the Commercial Register at the company's domicile.

(4) Claims against the former principal company concerning liabilities of the formerly integrated company shall be barred after the expiration of five years from the date on which the registration of the termination of the integration in the Commercial Register is deemed published in accordance with § 10 of the Commercial Code, unless such claim against the formerly integrated company is subject to a shorter statute of limitations. If a creditor's claim becomes due after the date on which the registration of the termination of the integration in the Commercial Register is deemed published, the statute of limitations shall begin to run on the date on which the claim falls due.

Part Four
Interlocking Enterprises

§ 328
Restriction on Rights

(1) Where a stock corporation or a partnership limited by shares and another enterprise are interlocking enterprises, rights either of them may have by virtue of its holdings in the other may, as soon as one of the enterprises obtains knowledge of the existence of the interlocking interests or as soon as it receives the notice pursuant to § 20, paragraph 3, or § 21, paragraph 1, from the other enterprise, be exercised only up to a maximum of one-fourth of the total equity of the other enterprise. This shall not apply to the right to subscribe to new shares in connection with a capital increase out of surplus. § 16, paragraph 4, shall be applicable.

2. wenn die Hauptgesellschaft nicht mehr eine Aktiengesellschaft mit Sitz im Inland ist,

3. wenn sich nicht mehr alle Aktien der eingegliederten Gesellschaft in der Hand der Hauptgesellschaft befinden,

4. durch Auflösung der Hauptgesellschaft.

(2) Befinden sich nicht mehr alle Aktien der eingegliederten Gesellschaft in der Hand der Hauptgesellschaft, so hat die Hauptgesellschaft dies der eingegliederten Gesellschaft unverzüglich schriftlich mitzuteilen.

(3) Der Vorstand der bisher eingegliederten Gesellschaft hat das Ende der Eingliederung, seinen Grund und seinen Zeitpunkt unverzüglich zur Eintragung in das Handelsregister des Sitzes der Gesellschaft anzumelden.

(4) Die Ansprüche gegen die frühere Hauptgesellschaft aus Verbindlichkeiten der bisher eingegliederten Gesellschaft verjähren in fünf Jahren seit dem Tage, an dem die Eintragung des Endes der Eingliederung in das Handelsregister nach § 10 des Handelsgesetzbuchs als bekanntgemacht gilt, sofern nicht der Anspruch gegen die bisher eingegliederte Gesellschaft einer kürzeren Verjährung unterliegt. Wird der Anspruch des Gläubigers erst nach dem Tage, an dem die Eintragung des Endes der Eingliederung in das Handelsregister als bekanntgemacht gilt, fällig, so beginnt die Verjährung mit dem Zeitpunkt der Fälligkeit.

Vierter Teil
Wechselseitig beteiligte Unternehmen

§ 328
Beschränkung der Rechte

(1) Sind eine Aktiengesellschaft oder Kommanditgesellschaft auf Aktien und ein anderes Unternehmen wechselseitig beteiligte Unternehmen, so können, sobald dem einen Unternehmen das Bestehen der wechselseitigen Beteiligung bekannt geworden ist oder ihm das andere Unternehmen eine Mitteilung nach § 20 Abs. 3 oder § 21 Abs. 1 gemacht hat, Rechte aus den Anteilen, die ihm an dem anderen Unternehmen gehören, nur für höchstens den vierten Teil aller Anteile des anderen Unternehmens ausgeübt werden. Dies gilt nicht für das Recht auf neue Aktien bei einer Kapitalerhöhung aus Gesellschaftsmitteln. § 16 Abs. 4 ist anzuwenden.

§ 328

(2) Die Beschränkung des Absatzes 1 gilt nicht, wenn das Unternehmen seinerseits dem anderen Unternehmen eine Mitteilung nach § 20 Abs. 3 oder § 21 Abs. 1 gemacht hatte, bevor es von dem anderen Unternehmen eine solche Mitteilung erhalten hat und bevor ihm das Bestehen der wechselseitigen Beteiligung bekannt geworden ist.

(3) Sind eine Aktiengesellschaft oder Kommanditgesellschaft auf Aktien und ein anderes Unternehmen wechselseitig beteiligte Unternehmen, so haben die Unternehmen einander unverzüglich die Höhe ihrer Beteiligung und jede Änderung schriftlich mitzuteilen.

(2) The restriction set forth in paragraph 1 hereof shall not apply if the enterprise has, on its part, prior to the receipt of such notice from the other enterprise and before obtaining knowledge of the existence of the interlocking interests, given notice to the other enterprise pursuant to § 20, paragraph 3, or § 21, paragraph 1.

(3) Where a stock corporation or a partnership limited by shares and another enterprise are interlocking enterprises, each enterprise shall promptly notify the other in writing of the amount of its holdings and every change in such amount.

Fünfter Teil

Rechnungslegung im Konzern

Part Five

Accounting Treatment of Affiliated Group of Companies

§ 329
Aufstellung von Konzernabschlüssen und Konzerngeschäftsberichten

(1) Stehen in einem Konzern die Konzernunternehmen unter der einheitlichen Leitung einer Aktiengesellschaft oder Kommanditgesellschaft auf Aktien mit Sitz im Inland (Obergesellschaft), so hat der Vorstand der Obergesellschaft auf den Stichtag des Jahresabschlusses der Obergesellschaft eine Konzernbilanz und eine Konzern-Gewinn- und Verlustrechnung (Konzernabschluß) sowie einen Konzerngeschäftsbericht aufzustellen. Weichen die Stichtage der Jahresabschlüsse der in den Konzernabschluß einbezogenen Unternehmen voneinander ab, so kann der Konzernabschluß auch auf einen der anderen Stichtage aufgestellt werden, wenn dies der Klarheit und der Übersichtlichkeit des Konzernabschlusses dient. Der Konzernabschluß und der Konzerngeschäftsbericht sind in den ersten fünf Monaten nach dem Stichtag des Konzernabschlusses aufzustellen.

(2) In den Konzernabschluß ist jedes Konzernunternehmen mit Sitz im Inland einzubeziehen, dessen Anteile zu mehr als der Hälfte Konzernunternehmen gehören. Von der Einbeziehung kann abgesehen werden, wenn die Darstellung der Vermögens- und Ertragslage des Konzerns wegen der geringen Bedeutung des Konzernunternehmens dadurch nicht beeinträchtigt wird. Von ihr ist abzusehen, wenn sie den Aussagewert des Konzernabschlusses beeinträchtigen würde. Andere Kon-

§ 329
Preparation of Consolidated Financial Statements and Business Reports

(1) If enterprises which are members of an affiliated group of companies are subject to central management by a stock corporation or a partnership limited by shares having a domicile in Germany (parent company), the managing board of the parent company shall prepare, as of the closing date of the parent company's annual financial statements, a consolidated balance sheet and a consolidated profit and loss statement (consolidated financial statements), as well as a consolidated business report. If the closing dates for the annual financial statements of the enterprises included in the consolidated financial statements differ, the consolidated financial statements may also be prepared as of one of the other closing dates, if this serves to further the clarity and informative value of the consolidated financial statements. The consolidated financial statements and the consolidated business report shall be prepared within the first five months of the closing date for the consolidated financial statements.

(2) The consolidated financial statements shall include each group member which is domiciled in Germany and more than one-half of whose equity is held by other group members. A group member need not be included if the description of the financial and earnings position of the group is not affected because of the minor significance of such enterprise. A group member shall not be

included if inclusion would impair the value of the consolidated financial statements as a disclosure device. Other group members may be included in the consolidated financial statements; they must be included if they are domiciled in Germany and if their inclusion is required for a proper evaluation of the financial and earnings position of the group.

§ 330
Preparation of Partial Consolidated Financial Statements and Partial Consolidated Business Reports

(1) If enterprises which are members of an affiliated group of companies are subject to central management by an enterprise having a domicile (head office) in Germany, which enterprise is not a stock corporation or partnership limited by shares, and if the enterprise heading the group controls other enterprises of the group through one or more stock corporations or partnerships limited by shares that are domiciled in Germany, the managing boards of such stock corporations or partnerships limited by shares domiciled in Germany which are closest to the enterprise heading the group shall each prepare partial consolidated financial statements and a partial consolidated business report. §§ 329 and 331 to 338 shall apply, *mutatis mutandis*, to the partial consolidated financial statements and the partial consolidated business report. Partial consolidated financial statements and partial consolidated business reports need not be prepared if the enterprise heading the group renders an accounting in the manner in which a parent company is required to render an accounting pursuant to §§ 329 and 331 to 338.

(2) Paragraph 1, first and second sentences, hereof shall apply, *mutatis mutandis*, if the enterprise heading the group has its domicile (head office) abroad. The preparation of partial consolidated financial statements and partial consolidated business reports is not required if the enterprise heading the group publishes in the *Bundesanzeiger* consolidated financial statements prepared in accordance with the principles set forth in §§ 331 to 333 and audited by certified public accountants.

§ 331
Consolidated Balance Sheet

(1) The consolidated balance sheet shall consolidate the balance sheets of the parent com-

zernunternehmen können in den Konzernabschluß einbezogen werden; sie müssen einbezogen werden, wenn sie ihren Sitz im Inland haben und wenn ihre Einbeziehung zu einer anderen Beurteilung der Vermögens- oder Ertragslage des Konzerns führt.

§ 330
Aufstellung von Teilkonzernabschlüssen und Teilkonzerngeschäftsberichten

(1) Stehen in einem Konzern die Konzernunternehmen unter der einheitlichen Leitung eines Unternehmens mit Sitz (Hauptniederlassung) im Inland, das nicht die Rechtsform einer Aktiengesellschaft oder Kommanditgesellschaft auf Aktien hat, beherrscht aber die Konzernleitung über eine oder mehrere zum Konzern gehörende Aktiengesellschaften oder Kommanditgesellschaften auf Aktien mit Sitz im Inland andere Konzernunternehmen, so haben die Vorstände der Aktiengesellschaften oder Kommanditgesellschaften auf Aktien mit Sitz im Inland, die der Konzernleitung am nächsten stehen, je einen Teilkonzernabschluß und einen Teilkonzerngeschäftsbericht aufzustellen. Für den Teilkonzernabschluß und den Teilkonzerngeschäftsbericht gelten §§ 329, 331 bis 338 sinngemäß. Die Aufstellung von Teilkonzernabschlüssen und Teilkonzerngeschäftsberichten kann unterbleiben, wenn die Konzernleitung so Rechnung legt, wie eine Obergesellschaft nach §§ 329, 331 bis 338 Rechnung zu legen hat.

(2) Absatz 1 Satz 1 und 2 gilt entsprechend, wenn die Konzernleitung ihren Sitz (Hauptniederlassung) im Ausland hat. Die Aufstellung von Teilkonzernabschlüssen und Teilkonzerngeschäftsberichten kann unterbleiben, wenn die Konzernleitung einen Konzernabschluß im Bundesanzeiger bekanntmacht, der nach den Grundsätzen der §§ 331 bis 333 aufgestellt und von Wirtschaftsprüfern geprüft worden ist.

§ 331
Konzernbilanz

(1) In der Konzernbilanz sind die auf den Stichtag des Konzernabschlusses aufgestellten Bilanzen der

Obergesellschaft und der übrigen einbezogenen Unternehmen nach folgenden Grundsätzen zusammenzufassen:

1. An die Stelle der Anteile an den übrigen einbezogenen Unternehmen treten die Vermögensgegenstände und Verbindlichkeiten, die Sonderposten mit Rücklageanteil, Rückstellungen, Wertberichtigungen und Rechnungsabgrenzungsposten aus den Bilanzen dieser Unternehmen, und zwar, soweit nicht nach Absatz 2 ein niedrigerer Wert einzusetzen ist, mit den in diesen Bilanzen eingesetzten Werten;

2. für Anteile konzernfremder Gesellschafter an den übrigen einbezogenen Unternehmen ist in Höhe ihres Anteils an Kapital, offenen Rücklagen, Gewinn und Verlust ein „Ausgleichsposten für Anteile in Fremdbesitz" gesondert auszuweisen; der auf Gewinn und der auf Verlust entfallende Betrag ist gesondert anzugeben;

3. sind die Wertansätze der Anteile an den übrigen einbezogenen Unternehmen höher oder niedriger als der auf die Anteile entfallende Betrag des Kapitals und der offenen Rücklagen der Unternehmen, so ist der Unterschiedsbetrag gesondert auszuweisen;

4. Forderungen und Verbindlichkeiten zwischen den in den Konzernabschluß einbezogenen Unternehmen sind wegzulassen.

(2) Am Stichtag des Konzernabschlusses bei einem einbezogenen Unternehmen vorhandene Vermögensgegenstände, die ganz oder teilweise Lieferungen oder Leistungen anderer einbezogener Unternehmen darstellen, dürfen, wenn sie

1. ohne oder nach Bearbeitung oder Verarbeitung zur Weiterveräußerung bestimmt sind oder

2. außerhalb des üblichen Lieferungs- und Leistungsverkehrs erworben wurden,

in der Konzernbilanz höchstens zu dem Wert angesetzt werden, zu dem sie, wenn die einbezogenen Unternehmen auch rechtlich ein einziges Unternehmen bilden würden, in der auf den gleichen Stichtag aufgestellten Jahresbilanz dieses Unternehmens höchstens angesetzt werden dürften.

(3) Die in den Konzernabschluß einbezogenen Unternehmen sollen denselben Abschlußstichtag haben. Weicht der Stichtag des Jahresabschlusses eines einbezogenen Unternehmens von dem Stichtag des Konzernabschlusses ab, so ist ein Abschluß zugrunde zu legen, der auf den Stichtag des Konzernabschlusses für den Zeitraum aufgestellt ist,

pany and of the other included enterprises, prepared as of the closing date of the consolidated financial statements in accordance with the following principles:

1. for the equity interests in other included enterprises, there shall be substituted the assets and liabilities, the special accounts which in part constitute reserves, reserves for depreciation, reserves for decline in value, and deferred items as shown on the balance sheets of such enterprises in the amounts stated in these balance sheets unless lower amounts must be stated according to paragraph 2 hereof;

2. with respect to equity interests in the other included enterprises held by parties other than group members, an item entitled "adjustment for equity owned by outsiders" shall be listed separately, showing their participation in the equity, disclosed reserves, and profits and losses; the proportionate participation in profits and losses shall be stated separately;

3. if the equity interests in the other included enterprises are stated at amounts higher or lower than the proportionate amounts of capital and of disclosed reserves of such enterprises, the difference shall be listed separately;

4. accounts receivable and payable as between enterprises included in the consolidated financial statements shall be omitted.

(2) Assets of an included enterprise which, on the closing date of the consolidated financial statements, consist in whole or in part of sales or services of other included enterprises may be shown, for purposes of the consolidated balance sheet, if they

1. are designed to be resold, with or without further processing, or

2. were not acquired in the course of normal trading,

at an amount not in excess of that at which they could have been stated in the annual financial statements of the enterprise as of the same closing date if the included enterprises were in the legal form of a single enterprise.

(3) The enterprises included in the consolidated financial statements shall normally have the same closing date for their annual financial statements. If the closing date for the annual financial statements of an included enterprise differs from that of the consolidated financial statements, financial statements shall be used which cover the period ending as of the closing

date of the consolidated financial statements. If such group member has a supervisory board, these financial statements shall require the approval of such board.

(4) §§ 149, 151, paragraphs 1 to 3, 5, § 152, paragraph 1, first sentence, and paragraphs 2, 3, 5, and 7 to 9, shall apply to the consolidated balance sheets except where their nature requires otherwise. Inventories may be stated as one item.

auf den sich der Konzernabschluß erstreckt. Der Abschluß bedarf, wenn ein Aufsichtsrat vorgesehen ist, seiner Billigung.

(4) Auf die Konzernbilanz sind, soweit ihre Eigenart keine Abweichung bedingt, §§ 149, 151 Abs. 1 bis 3, 5, § 152 Abs. 1 Satz 1, Abs. 2, 3, 5, 7 bis 9 anzuwenden. Die Vorräte können in einem Posten ausgewiesen werden.

§ 332
Consolidated Profit and Loss Statement

(1) The consolidated profit and loss statement shall comprise the profit and loss statements of the parent company and of the other included enterprises prepared as of the closing date of the consolidated financial statements in accordance with the following rules:

1. Gross income from sales and services between the enterprises included in the consolidated financial statements (gross income from intercompany transactions) shall be stated separately from the gross income from sales and services from third parties, unless it is offset against the cost to the recipients of such sales and services or stated as increases or decreases in inventory or as other capitalized assets produced by the company;

2. other income from performances rendered between the enterprises included in the consolidated financial statements shall be offset against the cost to the recipient of such performances.

(2) § 331, paragraph 3, second and third sentences, shall apply *mutatis mutandis*.

(3) §§ 149, 157, paragraphs 1 and 2, and § 158, paragraphs 1 to 4, shall apply to consolidated profit and loss statements except where their nature requires otherwise. Reductions in disclosed reserves and allocations to disclosed reserves may be stated as one item. Retained earnings and accumulated losses attributable to outside shareholders shall be shown separately before the item "group retained earnings/group accumulated losses."

§ 332
Konzern-Gewinn- und Verlustrechnung

(1) In der Konzern-Gewinn- und Verlustrechnung sind die auf den Stichtag des Konzernabschlusses aufgestellten Gewinn- und Verlustrechnungen der Obergesellschaft und der übrigen einbezogenen Unternehmen nach folgenden Grundsätzen zusammenzufassen:

1. Bei den Umsatzerlösen sind die Erlöse aus Lieferungen und Leistungen zwischen den in den Konzernabschluß einbezogenen Unternehmen (Innenumsatzerlöse) getrennt von den Außenumsatzerlösen auszuweisen, wenn sie nicht mit den auf sie entfallenden Aufwendungen der Empfänger der Lieferungen und Leistungen verrechnet oder als Bestandsänderungen oder als andere aktivierte Eigenleistungen ausgewiesen werden;

2. andere Erträge aus Leistungen zwischen den in den Konzernabschluß einbezogenen Unternehmen sind mit den auf sie entfallenden Aufwendungen der Empfänger der Leistungen zu verrechnen.

(2) § 331 Abs. 3 Satz 2 und 3 gilt sinngemäß.

(3) Auf die Konzern-Gewinn- und Verlustrechnung sind, soweit ihre Eigenart keine Abweichung bedingt, §§ 149, 157 Abs. 1 und 2, § 158 Abs. 1 bis 4 anzuwenden. Die Entnahmen aus offenen Rücklagen und die Einstellungen in offene Rücklagen können je in einem Posten ausgewiesen werden. Der konzernfremden Gesellschaftern zustehende Gewinn und der auf sie entfallende Verlust sind vor dem Posten „Konzerngewinn / Konzernverlust" gesondert auszuweisen.

§ 333
Consolidated Profit and Loss Statement in Simplified Form

(1) A simplified form may be used for consolidated profit and loss statements if the gross income from sales and services between enter-

§ 333
Konzern-Gewinn- und Verlustrechnung in vereinfachter Form

(1) Für die Konzern-Gewinn- und Verlustrechnung kann eine vereinfachte Form verwandt werden, wenn die Erträge aus Lieferungen und Leistun-

gen zwischen den in den Konzernabschluß einbezogenen Unternehmen mit den auf sie entfallenden Aufwendungen der Empfänger der Lieferungen und Leistungen verrechnet oder als Bestandsänderungen oder als andere aktivierte Eigenleistungen ausgewiesen werden.

(2) Bei Verwendung der vereinfachten Form sind, wenn der wirtschaftliche Zweck des Konzerns keine abweichende Gliederung bedingt, die gleichwertig sein muß, unbeschadet einer weiteren Gliederung folgende Posten in Staffelform gesondert auszuweisen:

1. Außenumsatzerlöse
2. nicht gesondert auszuweisende Aufwendungen nach Verrechnung mit Bestandsänderungen und Eigenleistungen
3. Erträge aus Beteiligungen an nicht in den Konzernabschluß einbezogenen Unternehmen
4. Erträge aus den anderen Finanzanlagen
5. sonstige Zinsen und ähnliche Erträge
6. Erträge aus Zuschreibungen
7. Erträge aus der Auflösung von Rückstellungen
8. sonstige Erträge
9. Abschreibungen und Wertberichtigungen auf Sachanlagen und immaterielle Anlagewerte
10. Abschreibungen und Wertberichtigungen auf Finanzanlagen
11. Zinsen und ähnliche Aufwendungen
12. Steuern
    a) vom Einkommen, vom Ertrag und vom Vermögen
    b) sonstige

prises included in the consolidated financial statements is offset by their cost to the recipients of such sales and services or is stated as increases or decreases in inventory or as other capitalized assets produced by the company.

(2) Unless the nature of the group's business requires a different classification, in which event such classification must be equivalent to the one provided for herein, the use of a simplified form shall require listing of the following items in columnar form, without prejudice to a more detailed classification:

1. gross income from third parties ....
2. costs not required to be stated separately after setoff against increases or decreases in inventory and assets produced by the company ....
3. income from securities in related enterprises not included in the consolidated financial statements ....
4. income from other securities ....
5. other interest and similar income ....
6. income from appreciation of fixed assets ....
7. income from reduction or dissolution of reserves ....
8. other income ....
9. depreciation and reserves for decline in value of tangible and intangible fixed assets ....
10. depreciation and reserves for decline in value of equity investments ....
11. interest and similar expenses ....
12. taxes
    a) on corporate income, on business profit, and on net assets ....
    b) other taxes ....

13. charge resulting from as-
    sumption of losses of enter-
    prises not included in the
    consolidated financial state-
    ments ....

14. annual profit/annual loss ...   .

15. profit/loss carried forward
    from preceding fiscal year   ....

16. reduction of disclosed re-
    serves ....

17. allocations to disclosed
    reserves ....

18. outside shareholders' share
    in profit ....

19. outside shareholders' share
    in losses ....

20. group retained earnings/
    group accumulated losses   ....

13. Aufwendungen aus der Uber-
    nahme des Verlustes eines
    nicht in den Konzernabschluß
    einbezogenen Unternehmens ....

14. Jahresüberschuß/ Jahresfehl-
    betrag   ....

15. Gewinnvortrag / Verlustvor-
    trag aus dem Vorjahr

16. Entnahmen aus offenen Rück-
    lagen

17. Einstellungen in offene Rück-
    lagen

18. konzernfremden Gesellschaf-
    tern zustehender Gewinn   ....

19. auf konzernfremde Gesell-
    schafter entfallender Verlust ....

20. Konzerngewinn/Konzernver-
    lust

(3) In partial consolidated financial statements, profit which, pursuant to an agreement to transfer profit in whole or in part, is transferable to enterprises not included in the partial consolidated annual financial statements shall be listed separately before the item "annual profit/annual loss," and losses that must be assumed by an enterprise not included in the consolidated financial statements shall be listed separately following the item "other income."

(4) § 331, paragraph 3, second and third sentences, shall apply *mutatis mutandis.* § 157, paragraph 2, and § 158, paragraphs 1 to 4, shall be applicable.

(3) In einem Teilkonzernabschluß sind Gewinne, die auf Grund eines Gewinnabführungs- und eines Teilgewinnabführungsvertrags an nicht in den Teilkonzernabschluß einbezogene Unternehmen abzuführen sind, vor dem Posten „Jahresüberschuß/Jahresfehlbetrag", und Verluste, die von einem nicht in den Konzernabschluß einbezogenen Unternehmen zu übernehmen sind, nach dem Posten „sonstige Erträge" gesondert auszuweisen.

(4) § 331 Abs. 3 Satz 2 und 3 gilt sinngemäß. § 157 Abs. 2, § 158 Abs. 1 bis 4 ist anzuwenden.

§ 334
Consolidated Business Report

(1) Each member of the group of affiliated companies which is domiciled in Germany shall be listed separately in the consolidated business report. The enterprises having a German domicile which are included in the consolidated financial statements shall be designated. If enterprises domiciled abroad are included, this fact shall be stated. If enterprises domiciled in

§ 334
Konzerngeschäftsbericht

(1) Im Konzerngeschäftsbericht sind die zum Konzern gehörenden Unternehmen mit Sitz im Inland einzeln aufzuführen. Die in den Konzernabschluß einbezogenen Unternehmen mit Sitz im Inland sind zu bezeichnen. Die Einbeziehung von Unternehmen mit Sitz im Ausland ist anzugeben. Werden Unter-

nehmen mit Sitz im Inland, deren Anteile zu mehr als der Hälfte Konzernunternehmen gehören, nicht in den Konzernabschluß einbezogen, so ist dies näher zu begründen. Dem Konzerngeschäftsbericht sind auf den Stichtag des Konzernabschlusses aufgestellte Abschlüsse dieser Unternehmen beizufügen, sofern sie Aktiengesellschaften oder Kommanditgesellschaften auf Aktien sind.

(2) Im Konzerngeschäftsbericht sind der Geschäftsverlauf und die Lage des Konzerns und der in den Konzernabschluß einbezogenen Unternehmen darzulegen. Zu berichten ist auch über Vorgänge von besonderer Bedeutung, die nach dem Stichtag des Konzernabschlusses eingetreten sind. Sind bei Konzernunternehmen, die nicht in den Konzernabschluß einbezogen sind, größere Verluste entstanden oder zu erwarten, so ist dies anzugeben.

(3) Im Konzerngeschäftsbericht ist ferner der Konzernabschluß zu erläutern. Dabei sind auch wesentliche Abweichungen von dem letzten Konzernabschluß zu erörtern. In jedem Konzerngeschäftsbericht sind Angaben zu machen über
1. die Ursachen und den bilanzmäßigen Charakter eines nach § 331 Abs. 1 Nr. 3 ausgewiesenen Unterschiedsbetrags;
2. aus dem Konzernabschluß nicht ersichtliche Haftungsverhältnisse einschließlich der Bestellung von Sicherheiten für Verbindlichkeiten der in den Konzernabschluß einbezogenen Unternehmen;
3. die rechtlichen und geschäftlichen Beziehungen zu Unternehmen mit Sitz im Inland, die nicht zum Konzern gehören, aber mit einem Konzernunternehmen verbunden sind, ferner über geschäftliche Vorgänge bei diesen Unternehmen, die auf die Lage des Konzerns von erheblichem Einfluß sein können.

(4) Der Bericht hat den Grundsätzen einer gewissenhaften und getreuen Rechenschaft zu entsprechen. Die Berichterstattung hat insoweit zu unterbleiben, wie es für das Wohl der Bundesrepublik Deutschland oder eines ihrer Länder erforderlich ist. Bei der Berichterstattung nach Absatz 3 Nr. 2 und 3 brauchen Einzelheiten insoweit nicht angegeben zu werden, als nach vernünftiger kaufmännischer Beurteilung damit gerechnet werden muß, daß durch die Angaben der Gesellschaft oder einem verbundenen Unternehmen erhebliche Nachteile entstehen. Werden auf Grund von Satz 3 Angaben nicht gemacht, so ist im Geschäftsbericht unter Anführung

Germany more than one-half of the shares of which belong to group members are not included in the consolidated financial statements, a further explanation shall be required. The consolidated business report shall be accompanied by the annual financial statements of such enterprises prepared as of the closing date of the consolidated financial statements if such enterprises are stock corporations or partnerships limited by shares.

(2) The consolidated business report shall contain a business analysis of the group and of the enterprises included in the consolidated financial statements. Events of particular significance which took place after the closing date of the consolidated financial statements shall also be reported. If group members not included in the consolidated financial statements have sustained or can be expected to sustain considerable losses, this fact shall be stated.

(3) The consolidated business report shall also explain the consolidated financial statements. In this connection, substantial deviations from the last consolidated financial statements shall be explained. Each consolidated business report shall contain statements concerning
1. the reasons for and the accounting nature of a difference shown pursuant to § 331, paragraph 1, No. 3;
2. liabilities not shown in the consolidated financial statements, including guaranties for liabilities of the enterprises included in the consolidated financial statements;
3. the legal and business dealings with enterprises domiciled in Germany which are not group members but are related to an enterprise which is a group member, and concerning business transactions of such enterprises which are apt to affect the condition of the group.

(4) The report shall comply with the principles of a true and conscientious accounting. To the extent that the welfare of the Federal Republic of Germany or one of its States necessitates omissions, there shall be no reporting. Upon reporting pursuant to paragraph 3, Nos. 2 and 3, hereof, details need not be stated to the extent that the exercise of reasonable business judgment would suggest that such statements will result in a substantial detriment to the company or a related enterprise. If statements are omitted by virtue of the third sentence hereof, the business report shall state that the escape clause of the third sentence has been invoked with respect to such

§ 334

statement and indicate the number pursuant to which such statement would otherwise be required.

der Nummer, nach der sie erforderlich sind, anzugeben, daß für Angaben nach dieser Nummer von der Schutzklausel nach Satz 3 Gebrauch gemacht worden ist.

§ 335
Submission of Documents

(1) All group members shall promptly submit to the parent company their annual financial statements, business reports, and, if their annual financial statements have been audited, the audit reports, as well as a financial statement prepared as of the closing date of the consolidated financial statements if the closing date of their annual financial statements differs from that of the consolidated financial statements.

(2) The managing board of the parent company may request from each group member all explanations and proof required for the preparation of the consolidated financial statements and the consolidated business report.

§ 335
Einreichung von Unterlagen

(1) Alle Konzernunternehmen haben der Obergesellschaft ihre Jahresabschlüsse, Geschäftsberichte und, wenn eine Prüfung des Jahresabschlusses stattgefunden hat, ihre Prüfungsberichte sowie, wenn der Stichtag des Jahresabschlusses von dem Stichtag des Konzernabschlusses abweicht, einen auf den Stichtag des Konzernabschlusses aufgestellten Abschluß unverzüglich einzureichen.

(2) Der Vorstand der Obergesellschaft kann von jedem Konzernunternehmen alle Aufklärungen und Nachweise verlangen, welche die Aufstellung des Konzernabschlusses und des Konzerngeschäftsberichts fordert.

§ 336
Audit of Consolidated Financial Statements

(1) The consolidated financial statements, together with the consolidated business report, shall be audited by one or more professional auditors (auditors of the consolidated financial statements). Unless other auditors are appointed, the auditors appointed to audit the annual financial statements of the parent company, as of the closing date for which the consolidated financial statements are prepared, shall be deemed to have been appointed as auditors of the consolidated financial statements. If the closing date of the consolidated financial statements differs from that of the annual financial statements of the parent company, the auditors appointed for the audit of the annual financial statements of the parent company following the closing date of the consolidated financial statements shall be deemed to have been appointed, unless other auditors are appointed. §§ 163 and 164 shall apply to the appointment of such other auditors.

(2) The audit of the consolidated financial statements shall include an examination of whether the provisions concerning consolidated financial statements have been observed. The consolidated business report shall be examined to determine whether § 334, paragraphs 1, 3 and 4, have been observed and whether the other statements in the business report might give an erroneous impression of the condition of the

§ 336
Prüfung des Konzernabschlusses

(1) Der Konzernabschluß ist unter Einbeziehung des Konzerngeschäftsberichts durch einen oder mehrere sachverständige Prüfer (Konzernabschlußprüfer) zu prüfen. Als Konzernabschlußprüfer gelten, wenn keine anderen Prüfer bestellt werden, die Prüfer als bestellt, die für die Prüfung des Jahresabschlusses der Obergesellschaft bestellt worden sind, auf dessen Stichtag der Konzernabschluß aufgestellt wird. Weicht der Stichtag des Konzernabschlusses von dem Stichtag des Jahresabschlusses der Obergesellschaft ab, so gelten, wenn keine anderen Prüfer bestellt werden, die Prüfer als bestellt, die für die Prüfung des nächsten auf den Stichtag des Konzernabschlusses folgenden Jahresabschlusses der Obergesellschaft bestellt worden sind. Für die Bestellung der anderen Prüfer gelten §§ 163, 164.

(2) Die Prüfung des Konzernabschlusses hat sich darauf zu erstrecken, ob die Vorschriften über den Konzernabschluß beachtet sind. Der Konzerngeschäftsbericht ist darauf zu prüfen, ob § 334 Abs. 1, 3 und 4 beachtet ist und ob die sonstigen Angaben im Bericht nicht eine falsche Vorstellung

von der Lage des Konzerns und der Konzernunternehmen erwecken. § 169 gilt sinngemäß.

(3) Die Konzernabschlußprüfer haben auch die dem Konzernabschluß zugrunde gelegten Abschlüsse der in den Konzernabschluß einbezogenen Unternehmen darauf zu prüfen, ob sie den Grundsätzen ordnungsmäßiger Buchführung entsprechen. Dies gilt nicht für Abschlüsse, die nach §§ 162 bis 168 oder nach anderen gesetzlichen Vorschriften oder die ohne gesetzliche Verpflichtung nach den Grundsätzen der §§ 162, 164 bis 167 geprüft worden sind.

(4) Der Vorstand der Obergesellschaft hat den Konzernabschlußprüfern den Konzernabschluß und den Konzerngeschäftsbericht, die Jahresabschlüsse, Geschäftsberichte und Prüfungsberichte aller Konzernunternehmen sowie die ihm nach § 335 Abs. 1 eingereichten Abschlüsse vorzulegen. Die Konzernabschlußprüfer haben die Rechte nach § 165 bei allen Konzernunternehmen, die Rechte nach § 165 Abs. 2 bis 4 auch gegenüber den Abschlußprüfern der Konzernunternehmen.

(5) Die Konzernabschlußprüfer haben über das Ergebnis der Prüfung schriftlich zu berichten und den Bericht zu unterzeichnen. Der Bericht ist dem Vorstand der Obergesellschaft vorzulegen.

(6) Sind nach dem abschließenden Ergebnis der Prüfung keine Einwendungen zu erheben, so haben die Konzernabschlußprüfer dies durch folgenden Vermerk zum Konzernabschluß zu bestätigen:

Der Konzernabschluß und der Konzerngeschäftsbericht entsprechen nach meiner (unserer) pflichtmäßigen Prüfung den gesetzlichen Vorschriften.

Sind Einwendungen zu erheben, so haben die Konzernabschlußprüfer die Bestätigung einzuschränken oder zu versagen. Die Konzernabschlußprüfer haben den Bestätigungsvermerk mit Angabe von Ort und Tag zu unterzeichnen. Der Bestätigungsvermerk ist auch in den Prüfungsbericht aufzunehmen.

(7) Ändert der Vorstand der Obergesellschaft den Konzernabschluß oder den Konzerngeschäftsbericht, nachdem ihm der Prüfungsbericht vorgelegt worden ist, so haben die Konzernabschlußprüfer den Konzernabschluß und den Konzerngeschäfts-

group and the group members. § 169 shall apply *mutatis mutandis.*

(3) The auditors of the consolidated financial statements shall also examine the annual financial statements of the enterprises included in the consolidated financial statements, on which the consolidated financial statements are based, to determine whether they comply with the principles of proper accounting. This shall not apply to financial statements that have been audited in accordance with §§ 162 to 168 or other statutory provisions, or have been audited in accordance with the principles of §§ 162 and 164 to 167, even though these statements were not legally required to be so audited.

(4) The managing board of the parent company shall submit to the auditors of the consolidated financial statements the consolidated financial statements and the consolidated business report, the annual financial statements, business reports and audit reports of all of the group members, as well as the financial statements submitted to it pursuant to § 335, paragraph 1. The auditors of the consolidated annual financial statements shall have the rights specified in § 165, paragraphs 2 to 4, also as against the annual auditors of the group members.

(5) The auditors of the consolidated financial statements shall make a written report on the results of the audit and sign the report. The report shall be submitted to the managing board of the parent company.

(6) If, according to the final results of the audit, there are no objections, the auditors of the consolidated financial statements shall so state by means of the following certification of the consolidated financial statements:

The consolidated financial statements and the consolidated business report which I/we have duly examined comply with the statutory provisions.

If there are objections, the auditors of the consolidated financial statements shall qualify or refuse the certification. The auditors of the consolidated financial statements shall sign the certification, stating the place and date. The certification shall also be made part of the audit report.

(7) In the event that the managing board of the parent company, after having received the audit report, should amend the consolidated financial statements or the consolidated business report, the auditors of the consolidated financial statements shall again audit the consolidated financial

§ 336

statements and the consolidated business report to the extent required by such amendments. A previously issued certification shall become invalid.

(8) § 168, concerning the liability of the annual auditors, shall apply *mutatis mutandis*.

bericht erneut zu prüfen, soweit es die Änderung fordert. Ein bereits erteilter Bestätigungsvermerk ist unwirksam.

(8) § 168 über die Verantwortlichkeit der Abschlußprüfer gilt sinngemäß.

§ 337
Submission of Consolidated Financial Statements and Consolidated Business Report

§ 337
Vorlage des Konzernabschlusses und des Konzerngeschäftsberichts

(1) Upon receipt of the audit report of the auditors of the consolidated financial statements, the managing board of the parent company shall promptly submit the consolidated financial statements, the consolidated business report, and the audit report to the supervisory board of the parent company for its information. Each member of the supervisory board shall have the right to inspect the statements submitted. Copies shall also be furnished upon request to each member of the supervisory board, unless the supervisory board has, by resolution, decided otherwise.

(1) Unverzüglich nach Eingang des Prüfungsberichts der Konzernabschlußprüfer hat der Vorstand der Obergesellschaft den Konzernabschluß, den Konzerngeschäftsbericht und den Prüfungsbericht dem Aufsichtsrat der Obergesellschaft zur Kenntnisnahme vorzulegen. Jedes Aufsichtsratsmitglied hat das Recht, von den Vorlagen Kenntnis zu nehmen. Die Vorlagen sind auch jedem Aufsichtsratsmitglied auf Verlangen auszuhändigen, soweit der Aufsichtsrat nichts anderes beschlossen hat.

(2) If the consolidated financial statements were prepared as of the closing date of the annual financial statements of the parent company, the consolidated financial statements and the consolidated business report shall be submitted to the shareholders' meeting called to receive or to establish these annual financial statements. If the closing date of the consolidated financial statements differs from the closing date of the annual financial statements of the parent company, the consolidated financial statements and the consolidated business report shall be submitted to the shareholders' meeting called to receive or to establish the annual financial statements following the closing date of the consolidated financial statements.

(2) Ist der Konzernabschluß auf den Stichtag des Jahresabschlusses der Obergesellschaft aufgestellt, so sind der Konzernabschluß und der Konzerngeschäftsbericht der Hauptversammlung vorzulegen, die diesen Jahresabschluß entgegennimmt oder festzustellen hat. Weicht der Stichtag des Konzernabschlusses vom Stichtag des Jahresabschlusses der Obergesellschaft ab, so sind der Konzernabschluß und der Konzerngeschäftsbericht der Hauptversammlung vorzulegen, die den nächsten auf den Stichtag des Konzernabschlusses folgenden Jahresabschluß entgegennimmt oder festzustellen hat.

(3) § 175, paragraph 2, shall apply to the exhibition of the consolidated financial statements and the consolidated business report and the distribution of copies thereof; § 176, paragraph 1, shall apply to their submission to the shareholders' meeting and to the report of the managing board.

(3) Für die Auslegung des Konzernabschlusses und des Konzerngeschäftsberichts und für die Erteilung von Abschriften gilt § 175 Abs. 2, für die Vorlage an die Hauptversammlung und für die Berichterstattung des Vorstands § 176 Abs. 1.

(4) Die Auskunftspflicht des Vorstands der Obergesellschaft in der Hauptversammlung, der der Konzernabschluß und der Konzerngeschäftsbericht vorgelegt werden, erstreckt sich auch auf die Lage des Konzerns und der in den Konzernabschluß einbezogenen Unternehmen.

(4) The obligation of the managing board of the parent company to furnish information to the shareholders' meeting to which the consolidated financial statements and the consolidated business report are submitted shall also apply to the condition of the group and of the enterprises included in the consolidated financial statements.

§ 338
Bekanntmachung des Konzernabschlusses

§ 338
Publication of Consolidated Financial Statements

(1) Der Vorstand der Obergesellschaft hat unverzüglich nach der Hauptversammlung über den Jahresabschluß (§ 337 Abs. 2) den Konzernabschluß mit Bestätigungsvermerk und den Konzerngeschäftsbericht zum Handelsregister des Sitzes der Obergesellschaft einzureichen. Der dem eingereichten Konzernabschluß beigefügte Bestätigungsvermerk muß von den Konzernabschlußprüfern unterschrieben sein. Haben die Konzernabschlußprüfer die Bestätigung des Konzernabschlusses versagt, so muß dies auf dem eingereichten Konzernabschluß vermerkt, der Vermerk von den Konzernabschlußprüfern unterschrieben sein.

(1) After the shareholders' meeting on the consolidated financial statements (§ 337, paragraph 2), the managing board of the parent company shall promptly file the consolidated financial statements accompanied by the certification and the consolidated business report with the Commercial Register at the parent company's domicile. The certification accompanying the consolidated financial statements filed must be signed by the auditors of the consolidated financial statements. If the auditors of the consolidated financial statements have refused to certify the consolidated financial statements, this fact shall be noted on the consolidated financial statements filed and the notation signed by the auditors of the consolidated financial statements.

(2) Der Vorstand der Obergesellschaft hat den Konzernabschluß zusammen mit dem Jahresabschluß in den Gesellschaftsblättern der Obergesellschaft bekanntzumachen und die Bekanntmachung zum Handelsregister des Sitzes der Obergesellschaft einzureichen.

(2) The managing board of the parent company shall publish the consolidated financial statements, together with the annual financial statements, in the publications designated in the parent company's articles of incorporation and file the publication with the Commercial Register at the parent company's domicile.

(3) Das Gericht hat zu prüfen, ob der eingereichte Konzernabschluß dem Absatz 1 entspricht, ob er nach Absatz 2 bekanntgemacht worden ist und ob die Bekanntmachung dem Absatz 4 entspricht. Ob der Konzernabschluß und der Konzerngeschäftsbericht den gesetzlichen Vorschriften entsprechen, braucht es nicht zu prüfen.

(3) The court shall examine whether the consolidated financial statements filed comply with paragraph 1 hereof, whether they were published in accordance with paragraph 2 hereof, and whether the publication meets the requirements of paragraph 4 hereof. The court need not examine whether the consolidated financial statements and the consolidated business report comply with the statutory provisions.

(4) Für die Veröffentlichungen und Vervielfältigungen des Konzernabschlusses und des Konzerngeschäftsberichts gilt § 178 Abs. 1 Nr. 1 und 2, Abs. 2 und 3 sinngemäß.

(4) § 178, paragraph 1, Nos. 1 and 2, and paragraphs 2 and 3, shall apply *mutatis mutandis* to the publication and reproduction of the consolidated financial statements and the consolidated business report.

Book Four

Business Combination.
Transfer of Assets.
Transformation

Part One

Business Combination

First Division

Combination of Stock Corporations

§ 339
Nature of Business Combination

(1) Stock corporations may be combined without liquidation (business combination). The combination may be effected

1. by transferring all of the assets of one company (transferor company) to another company (transferee company) for shares of the latter company (merger);

2. by forming a new stock corporation to which all of the assets of each of the companies to be combined are transferred for shares of the new company (consolidation).

(2) A business combination is also permitted where the transferor company or one of the companies to be consolidated has been dissolved but the company could be continued by a resolution to this effect.

First Subdivision
Merger
§ 340
Shareholders' Resolutions

(1) The merger agreement shall become effective only upon the approval of the shareholders of each company.

(2) The resolution shall require a majority of no less than three-fourths of the stated capital represented when the resolution is adopted. The articles of incorporation may provide for a higher capital majority and establish additional requirements.

(3) The merger agreement shall be exhibited on the company's premises for inspection by the shareholders, beginning with the date on which the shareholders' meeting which is to decide on it is called. Each shareholder shall, upon request, promptly be furnished a copy. The agreement shall be exhibited at the shareholders'

§ 339

Viertes Buch

Verschmelzung. Vermögensübertragung. Umwandlung

Erster Teil

Verschmelzung

Erster Abschnitt
Verschmelzung von Aktiengesellschaften

§ 339
Wesen der Verschmelzung

(1) Aktiengesellschaften können ohne Abwicklung vereinigt (verschmolzen) werden. Die Verschmelzung kann erfolgen

1. durch Übertragung des Vermögens der Gesellschaft (übertragende Gesellschaft) als Ganzes auf eine andere Gesellschaft (übernehmende Gesellschaft) gegen Gewährung von Aktien dieser Gesellschaft (Verschmelzung durch Aufnahme);

2. durch Bildung einer neuen Aktiengesellschaft, auf die das Vermögen jeder der sich vereinigenden Gesellschaften als Ganzes gegen Gewährung von Aktien der neuen Gesellschaft übergeht (Verschmelzung durch Neubildung).

(2) Die Verschmelzung ist auch zulässig, wenn die übertragende Gesellschaft oder eine der sich vereinigenden Gesellschaften aufgelöst ist und die Fortsetzung der Gesellschaft beschlossen werden könnte.

Erster Unterabschnitt
Verschmelzung durch Aufnahme

§ 340
Beschlüsse der Hauptversammlungen

(1) Der Verschmelzungsvertrag wird nur wirksam, wenn die Hauptversammlung jeder Gesellschaft ihm zustimmt.

(2) Der Beschluß bedarf einer Mehrheit, die mindestens drei Viertel des bei der Beschlußfassung vertretenen Grundkapitals umfaßt. Die Satzung kann eine größere Kapitalmehrheit und weitere Erfordernisse bestimmen.

(3) Der Verschmelzungsvertrag ist von der Einberufung der Hauptversammlung an, die über die Zustimmung beschließen soll, in dem Geschäftsraum der Gesellschaft zur Einsicht der Aktionäre auszulegen. Auf Verlangen ist jedem Aktionär unverzüglich eine Abschrift zu erteilen. In der Haupt-

versammlung ist der Vertrag auszulegen. Der Vorstand hat ihn zu Beginn der Verhandlung zu erläuten. Der Niederschrift ist er als Anlage beizufügen.

(4) Jedem Aktionär ist auf Verlangen in der Hauptversammlung, die über die Verschmelzung beschließt, Auskunft auch über alle für die Verschmelzung wesentlichen Angelegenheiten der Gesellschaft zu geben, mit welcher der Verschmelzungsvertrag geschlossen werden soll.

§ 341
Verschmelzungsvertrag

(1) Der Verschmelzungsvertrag bedarf der gerichtlichen oder notariellen Beurkundung. § 310 des Bürgerlichen Gesetzbuchs gilt für ihn nicht.

(2) Soll die Wirkung des Verschmelzungsvertrags erst nach mehr als zehn Jahren eintreten, so können beide Teile den Vertrag nach zehn Jahren mit halbjähriger Frist kündigen. Gleiches gilt, wenn der Vertrag unter einer Bedingung geschlossen und diese binnen zehn Jahren nicht eingetreten ist. Die Kündigung ist stets nur zulässig für den Schluß des Geschäftsjahrs der Gesellschaft, der gegenüber die Kündigung erklärt wird.

§ 342
Anwendung der Vorschriften
über die Nachgründung

Wird der Verschmelzungsvertrag in den ersten zwei Jahren seit Eintragung der übernehmenden Gesellschaft in das Handelsregister geschlossen, so gilt § 52 Abs. 3, 4, 7 bis 9 über die Nachgründung sinngemäß. Dies gilt nicht, wenn der Gesamtnennbetrag der zu gewährenden Aktien den zehnten Teil des Grundkapitals dieser Gesellschaft nicht übersteigt. Wird zur Durchführung der Verschmelzung das Grundkapital erhöht, so ist der Berechnung das erhöhte Grundkapital zugrunde zu legen.

§ 343
Erhöhung des Grundkapitals
zur Durchführung der Verschmelzung

(1) Erhöht die übernehmende Gesellschaft zur Durchführung der Verschmelzung das Grundkapital, so sind § 182 Abs. 4, § 184 Abs. 2, §§ 185, 186, 187 Abs. 1, § 188 Abs. 2 und 3 Nr. 1 nicht anzuwenden. Dies gilt auch dann, wenn das Grundkapital durch Ausgabe neuer Aktien auf Grund der Ermächtigung nach § 202 erhöht wird. In diesem Fall ist außerdem § 203 Abs. 3 nicht anzuwenden.

meeting. At the beginning of the deliberations the managing board shall explain the agreement. It shall be attached to the minutes.

(4) At the shareholders' meeting in which the resolution concerning the merger is adopted, each shareholder shall, upon request, also be furnished information on such matters affecting the company with which the merger agreement is to be concluded as are material to the merger.

§ 341
Merger Agreement

(1) The merger agreement must be in the form of a judicial or notarial record. It shall not be subject to § 310 of the Civil Code.

(2) If the merger agreement is to take effect after a period of more than ten years, either party may terminate the agreement after the expiration of ten years by giving six months' notice. The same shall apply if the agreement was conditioned on an event that did not materialize within ten years. Termination shall be permissible only as of the end of the fiscal year of the company to which the notice of termination is directed.

§ 342
Applicability of Provisions Concerning
Post-Formation Acquisitions

If the merger agreement is executed within the first two years from the date on which the transferee company was recorded in the Commercial Register, § 52, paragraphs 3, 4, and 7 to 9, concerning post-formation acquisitions, shall apply *mutatis mutandis*. These provisions shall not, however, apply if the total par value of the shares to be issued does not exceed one-tenth of the stated capital of such company. If the stated capital is increased for purposes of consummating the merger, this ratio shall be determined by reference to the increased stated capital.

§ 343
Capital Increase to Consummate Merger

(1) If the transferee company increases its stated capital to consummate the merger, § 182, paragraph 4, § 184, paragraph 2, §§ 185, 186, 187, paragraph 1, and § 188, paragraphs 2 and 3, No. 1, shall not be applicable. Nor shall these provisions apply if the stated capital is increased by the issuance of new shares pursuant to the authorization referred to in § 202. In this event, § 203, paragraph 3, shall likewise be inapplicable.

§ 343

(2) In addition to the documents referred to in § 188, paragraph 3, Nos. 2 to 4, the application to record the merger shall be accompanied, for the records of the court at the company's domicile, by a duplicate original or certified copy of the merger agreement and the minutes of the resolutions authorizing the merger.

§ 344
Consummation of Merger

(1) The merger may be consummated without a capital increase to the extent that the transferee company holds shares of stock in the transferor company or has treasury shares.

(2) If the transferee company also makes cash payments, such payments shall not exceed one-tenth of the total par value of the shares issued by the transferee company.

§ 345
Application to Record Merger

(1) The managing board of each company shall file an application to record the merger in the Commercial Register at the domicile of their respective companies.

(2) In connection with the application, the managing board shall state that no action to set aside the resolutions authorizing the merger was brought within the period provided therefor by law or that an action to set aside has been dismissed by a final decision. The application shall be accompanied by duplicate originals or certified copies of the merger agreement, the minutes of the resolutions authorizing the merger and, if the merger requires governmental authorization, the instrument evidencing such authorization.

(3) The application filed with the Commercial Register at the transferor company's domicile shall also be accompanied by a balance sheet of the transferor company (final balance sheet). The provisions concerning the annual balance sheet and the audit of the annual balance sheet shall apply, *mutatis mutandis*, to this balance sheet. The balance sheet need not be published. The court of registry shall record the merger only if the balance sheet has been prepared as of a closing date of no more than eight months prior to the application.

§ 346
Registration of Merger

(1) The merger may not be recorded in the Commercial Register at the transferee company's

§ 344

---

(2) Der Anmeldung sind für das Gericht des Sitzes der Gesellschaft außer den Schriftstücken in § 188 Abs. 3 Nr. 2 bis 4 der Verschmelzungsvertrag und die Niederschriften der Verschmelzungsbeschlüsse in Ausfertigung oder öffentlich beglaubigter Abschrift beizufügen.

§ 344
Durchführung der Verschmelzung

(1) Die Verschmelzung kann ohne Erhöhung des Grundkapitals durchgeführt werden, soweit die übernehmende Gesellschaft Aktien der übertragenden Gesellschaft oder eigene Aktien besitzt.

(2) Leistet die übernehmende Gesellschaft bare Zuzahlungen, so dürfen diese nicht den zehnten Teil des Gesamtnennbetrags der gewährten Aktien der übernehmenden Gesellschaft übersteigen.

§ 345
Anmeldung der Verschmelzung

(1) Der Vorstand jeder Gesellschaft hat die Verschmelzung zur Eintragung in das Handelsregister des Sitzes seiner Gesellschaft anzumelden.

(2) Bei der Anmeldung hat der Vorstand zu erklären, daß die Verschmelzungsbeschlüsse innerhalb der Anfechtungsfrist nicht angefochten worden sind oder daß die Anfechtung rechtskräftig zurückgewiesen worden ist. Der Anmeldung sind in Ausfertigung oder öffentlich beglaubigter Abschrift der Verschmelzungsvertrag, die Niederschriften der Verschmelzungsbeschlüsse sowie, wenn die Verschmelzung der staatlichen Genehmigung bedarf, die Genehmigungsurkunde beizufügen.

(3) Der Anmeldung zum Handelsregister des Sitzes der übertragenden Gesellschaft ist ferner eine Bilanz der übertragenden Gesellschaft beizufügen (Schlußbilanz). Für diese Bilanz gelten die Vorschriften über die Jahresbilanz und über die Prüfung der Jahresbilanz sinngemäß. Sie braucht nicht bekanntgemacht zu werden. Das Registergericht darf die Verschmelzung nur eintragen, wenn die Bilanz auf einen höchstens acht Monate vor der Anmeldung liegenden Stichtag aufgestellt worden ist.

§ 346
Eintragung der Verschmelzung

(1) Die Verschmelzung darf in das Handelsregister des Sitzes der übernehmenden Gesellschaft

erst eingetragen werden, nachdem sie im Handelsregister des Sitzes der übertragenden Gesellschaft eingetragen worden ist. Wird zur Durchführung der Verschmelzung das Grundkapital der übernehmenden Gesellschaft erhöht, so darf die Verschmelzung nicht eingetragen werden, bevor die Durchführung der Erhöhung des Grundkapitals im Handelsregister eingetragen worden ist.

(2) Die übertragende Gesellschaft hat einen Treuhänder für den Empfang der zu gewährenden Aktien und der baren Zuzahlungen zu bestellen. Die Verschmelzung darf erst eingetragen werden, wenn der Treuhänder dem Gericht angezeigt hat, daß er im Besitz der Aktien und der baren Zuzahlungen ist.

(3) Mit der Eintragung der Verschmelzung in das Handelsregister des Sitzes der übertragenden Gesellschaft geht das Vermögen dieser Gesellschaft einschließlich der Verbindlichkeiten auf die übernehmende Gesellschaft über. Treffen dabei aus gegenseitigen Verträgen, die zur Zeit der Verschmelzung von keiner Seite vollständig erfüllt sind, Abnahme-, Lieferungs- oder ähnliche Verpflichtungen zusammen, die miteinander unvereinbar sind oder die erfüllen eine solche Unbilligkeit für die übernehmende Gesellschaft bedeuten würde, so bestimmt sich der Umfang der Verpflichtungen nach Billigkeit unter Würdigung der vertraglichen Rechte aller Beteiligten.

(4) Die übertragende Gesellschaft erlischt mit der Eintragung der Verschmelzung in das Handelsregister ihres Sitzes. Einer besonderen Löschung der übertragenden Gesellschaft bedarf es nicht. Mit der Eintragung der Verschmelzung werden die Aktionäre der übertragenden Gesellschaft Aktionäre der übernehmenden Gesellschaft.

(5) Der Mangel der gerichtlichen oder notariellen Beurkundung des Verschmelzungsvertrags wird durch die Eintragung geheilt.

(6) Das Gericht des Sitzes der übertragenden Gesellschaft hat von Amts wegen die bei ihm aufbewahrten Urkunden und anderen Schriftstücke nach der Eintragung der Verschmelzung dem Gericht des Sitzes der übernehmenden Gesellschaft zur Aufbewahrung zu übersenden.

(7) Für den Umtausch der Aktien der übertragenden Gesellschaft gilt § 73, bei Zusammenlegung von Aktien § 226 über die Kraftloserklärung von Aktien sinngemäß. Einer Genehmigung des Gerichts bedarf es nicht.

domicile before registration in the Commercial Register at the transferor company's domicile. If, for purposes of consummating the merger, the stated capital of the transferee company is increased, the merger may not be recorded before registration of the consummation of the capital increase in the Commercial Register.

(2) The transferor company shall appoint a trustee to accept the shares to be issued and the additional cash payment. The merger may not be recorded before the date on which the trustee notifies the court that he has obtained possession of the shares and the additional cash payment.

(3) Upon registration of the merger in the Commercial Register at the transferor company's domicile, all of the assets of that company together with its liabilities shall devolve to the transferee company. If in this connection obligations to purchase or sell or similar obligations arising out of bilateral agreements not fully performed by the parties thereto should coincide, and if such obligations conflict or if the performance thereof would entail substantial hardship for the transferee company, the scope of such obligations shall be adjusted equitably, with due consideration for the contractual rights of all of the parties involved.

(4) The transferor company shall cease to exist upon registration of the merger in the Commercial Register of its domicile. Specific cancellation of the transferor company is not required. The shareholders of the transferor company shall become shareholders of the transferee company upon registration of the merger.

(5) If the merger agreement was not properly recorded before a judge or a notary, such defect shall be cured by registration.

(6) After registration of the merger, the court at the transferor company's domicile shall ex officio forward the corporate instruments kept by it and other documentation for custody to the court at the transferee company's domicile.

(7) With respect to the exchange of the shares of the transferor company, § 73 shall apply, and, in the event of a consolidation of shares, § 226, concerning the cancellation of share certificates, shall apply, *mutatis mutandis*. The permission of the court is not required.

§ 347

Gläubigerschutz

(1) Den Gläubigern der übertragenden Gesellschaft ist, wenn sie sich binnen sechs Monaten nach

§ 347

Protection of Creditors

(1) Creditors of the transferor company shall be furnished security provided that they make a

request to this effect within six months from the date the registration of the merger is published in the Commercial Register at the transferor company's domicile, unless such creditors are entitled to payment. The creditors shall be advised of this right in the publication of the registration

(2) The right to request security shall not be available to creditors who, in the event of bankruptcy, would have a claim to preferred satisfaction out of a fund which was established by statute for their protection and which is subject to governmental supervision.

§ 348
Valuation of the Transferee Company

(1) For purposes of the transferee company's annual balance sheets, the amounts stated in the final balance sheet of the transferor company shall be deemed to be the cost of acquisition within the meaning of § 153, paragraph 1, and § 155, paragraph 1.

(2) If the stated capital of the transferee company was increased for purposes of consummating the merger, and if the total par value plus any premium for which the shares were issued as consideration for the transfer of the assets by the transferor company, including any additional cash payments, exceeds the amounts listed in the final balance sheet for the various assets, the difference may be listed under the applicable classifications as a fixed asset. The amount shall be listed separately and shall be written off within a maximum period of five years.

§ 349
Liability of Management of Transferor Company

(1) The members of the managing board and of the supervisory board of the transferor company shall be jointly and severally liable for any damage sustained by that company, its shareholders and creditors by reason of the merger. Members of these boards who, in connection with the examination of the financial condition of the companies and the conclusion of the merger agreement, complied with their duty to exercise due care shall not be liable.

(2) For purposes of such claims as well as any further claims pursuant to the general provisions of the law, on behalf of or against the transferor company by reason of the merger, the transferor company shall be deemed to continue in existence. To this extent, claims and liabilities shall not be extinguished by the merger.

§ 348

der Bekanntmachung der Eintragung der Verschmelzung in das Handelsregister des Sitzes der übertragenden Gesellschaft zu diesem Zweck melden, Sicherheit zu leisten, soweit sie nicht Befriedigung verlangen können. Die Gläubiger sind in der Bekanntmachung der Eintragung auf dieses Recht hinzuweisen.

(2) Das Recht, Sicherheitsleistung zu verlangen, steht Gläubigern nicht zu, die im Fall des Konkurses ein Recht auf vorzugsweise Befriedigung aus einer Deckungsmasse haben, die nach gesetzlicher Vorschrift zu ihrem Schutz errichtet und staatlich überwacht ist.

§ 348
Wertansätze der übernehmenden Gesellschaft

(1) Die in der Schlußbilanz der übertragenden Gesellschaft angesetzten Werte gelten für die Jahresbilanzen der übernehmenden Gesellschaft als Anschaffungskosten im Sinne der § 153 Abs. 1, § 155 Abs. 1.

(2) Ist das Grundkapital der übernehmenden Gesellschaft zur Durchführung der Verschmelzung erhöht worden und übersteigt der Gesamtnennbetrag oder der höhere Gesamtausgabebetrag der für die Veräußerung des Vermögens der übertragenden Gesellschaft gewährten Aktien zuzüglich barer Zuzahlungen die in der Schlußbilanz angesetzten Werte der einzelnen Vermögensgegenstände, so darf der Unterschied unter den Posten des Anlagevermögens aufgenommen werden. Der Betrag ist gesondert auszuweisen und in nicht mehr als fünf Jahren durch Abschreibungen zu tilgen.

§ 349
Schadenersatzpflicht der Verwaltungsträger der übertragenden Gesellschaft

(1) Die Mitglieder des Vorstands und des Aufsichtsrats der übertragenden Gesellschaft sind als Gesamtschuldner zum Ersatz des Schadens verpflichtet, den diese Gesellschaft, ihre Aktionäre und Gläubiger durch die Verschmelzung erleiden. Mitglieder, die bei der Prüfung der Vermögenslage der Gesellschaften und beim Abschluß des Verschmelzungsvertrags ihre Sorgfaltspflicht beobachtet haben, sind von der Ersatzpflicht befreit.

(2) Für diese Ansprüche sowie weitere Ansprüche, die sich für und gegen die übertragende Gesellschaft nach den allgemeinen Vorschriften auf Grund der Verschmelzung ergeben, gilt die übertragende Gesellschaft als fortbestehend. Forderungen und Verbindlichkeiten vereinigen sich insoweit durch die Verschmelzung nicht.

(3) Die Ansprüche aus Absatz 1 verjähren in fünf Jahren seit dem Tage, an dem die Eintragung der Verschmelzung in das Handelsregister des Sitzes der übertragenden Gesellschaft nach § 10 des Handelsgesetzbuchs als bekanntgemacht gilt.

(3) The claims referred to in paragraph 1 hereof shall be barred after the expiration of five years from the date on which the registration of the merger in the Commercial Register at the transferor company's domicile is deemed published in accordance with § 10 of the Commercial Code.

§ 350
Durchführung des Schadenersatzanspruchs

(1) Die Ansprüche nach § 349 Abs. 1 und 2 können nur durch einen besonderen Vertreter geltend gemacht werden. Das Gericht des Sitzes der übertragenden Gesellschaft hat einen Vertreter auf Antrag eines Aktionärs oder eines Gläubigers dieser Gesellschaft zu bestellen. Antragsberechtigt sind nur Aktionäre, die ihre Aktien bereits gegen Aktien der übernehmenden Gesellschaft umgetauscht haben, und nur Gläubiger, die von der übernehmenden Gesellschaft keine Befriedigung erlangen können. Gegen die Entscheidung ist die sofortige Beschwerde zulässig.

(2) Der Vertreter hat unter Hinweis auf den Zweck seiner Bestellung die Aktionäre und Gläubiger der übertragenden Gesellschaft aufzufordern, die Ansprüche nach § 349 Abs. 1 und 2 innerhalb einer angemessenen Frist, die mindestens einen Monat betragen soll, anzumelden. Die Aufforderung ist in den Gesellschaftsblättern der übertragenden Gesellschaft bekanntzumachen.

(3) Den Betrag, der aus der Geltendmachung der Ansprüche der übertragenden Gesellschaft erzielt wird, hat der Vertreter zur Befriedigung der Gläubiger der übertragenden Gesellschaft zu verwenden, soweit diese nicht durch die übernehmende Gesellschaft befriedigt oder sichergestellt sind. Der Rest wird unter die Aktionäre verteilt. Für die Verteilung gilt § 271 Abs. 2 und 3 sinngemäß. Gläubiger und Aktionäre, die sich nicht fristgemäß gemeldet haben, werden bei der Verteilung nicht berücksichtigt.

(4) Der besondere Vertreter hat Anspruch auf Ersatz angemessener barer Auslagen und auf Vergütung für seine Tätigkeit. Die Auslagen und die Vergütung setzt das Gericht fest. Es bestimmt nach den gesamten Verhältnissen des einzelnen Falls nach freiem Ermessen, in welchem Umfange die Auslagen und die Vergütung von beteiligten Aktionären und Gläubigern zu tragen sind. Gegen die Entscheidung ist die sofortige Beschwerde zulässig; die weitere Beschwerde ist ausgeschlossen. Aus der

§ 350
Institution of Action for Damages

(1) The claims referred to in § 349, paragraphs 1 and 2, may be asserted only by a special representative. The court at the transferor company's domicile shall, upon application by a shareholder or a creditor of such company, appoint such a representative. Only shareholders who have already exchanged their shares for shares of the transferee company, and only such creditors who are unable to obtain satisfaction from the transferee company, shall have the right to make such application. The decision of the court can be appealed.

(2) The representative shall request the shareholders and creditors of the transferor company to file any of the claims referred to in § 349, paragraphs 1 and 2, which they may have, within a reasonable period of time of no less than one month, which request shall refer to the reason for his appointment. The notice shall be published in the publications designated in the transferor company's articles of incorporation.

(3) Any amounts collected on claims of the transferor company shall be used by the representative to satisfy the transferor company's creditors to the extent that they have not been satisfied or secured by the transferee company. The remainder shall be distributed to the shareholders. § 271, paragraphs 2 and 3, shall apply, *mutatis mutandis*, to such distribution. Creditors and shareholders who failed to make timely presentation of their claims shall not be entitled to participate in the distribution.

(4) The special representative shall be entitled to reimbursement for reasonable cash expenditures and remuneration for his services. The expenditures and the remuneration shall be determined by the court. The court shall determine, in its discretion, taking into account all of the circumstances of the particular case, to what extent the expenditures and the remuneration shall be borne by the shareholders and creditors concerned. The decision of the court can be appealed; it shall not be subject to further appeal. The final decision shall be enforceable in accord-

ance with the provisions of the Code of Civil Procedure.

§ 351
Liability of Management of Transferee Company

The statute of limitations for damage claims against members of the managing board and of the supervisory board of the transferee company arising by virtue of the merger pursuant to §§ 93, 116, 117, 309, 310, 317 and 318 shall begin to run on the date on which the registration of the merger in the Commercial Register at the transferor company's domicile is deemed published in accordance with § 10 of the Commercial Code.

§ 352
Nullity of Transferor Company's Resolution to Merge

After the merger has been recorded in the Commercial Register at the transferor company's domicile, an action to have that company's resolution authorizing the merger declared void can be brought only against the transferee company.

Second Subdivision
Consolidation
§ 353

(1) §§ 340, 341, 344, paragraph 2, § 345, paragraphs 2 and 3, § 346, paragraphs 2, 5 to 7, §§ 347 to 350, and 352 shall apply, *mutatis mutandis*, to the combination of stock corporations by consolidation. Each of the companies to be consolidated shall be deemed to be a transferor company, and the new company to be the transferee.

(2) A resolution to consolidate may be adopted only after each of the companies to be consolidated has been recorded in the Commercial Register for two years.

(3) The articles of incorporation of the new company and the appointment of members to its supervisory board shall require the approval of the shareholders of the consolidating companies. § 124, paragraph 2, second sentence, paragraph 3, first and third sentences, and § 340, paragraph 2, shall apply *mutatis mutandis*.

(4) The provisions concerning formation contained in § 23, paragraph 3, and §§ 29, 30, paragraphs 1 and 4, §§ 31, 39, and 41, paragraph 1, shall apply, *mutatis mutandis*, to the formation of the new company. Particulars concerning preferences, expenses of formation, contribution of assets, and acquisition of assets upon formation,

rechtskräftigen Entscheidung findet die Zwangsvollstreckung nach der Zivilprozeßordnung statt.

§ 351
Schadenersatzpflicht der Verwaltungsträger der übernehmenden Gesellschaft

Die Verjährung der Ersatzansprüche, die sich nach §§ 93, 116, 117, 309, 310, 317 und 318 gegen die Mitglieder des Vorstands und des Aufsichtsrats der übernehmenden Gesellschaft auf Grund der Verschmelzung ergeben, beginnt mit dem Tage, an dem die Eintragung der Verschmelzung in das Handelsregister des Sitzes der übertragenden Gesellschaft nach § 10 des Handelsgesetzbuchs als bekanntgemacht gilt.

§ 352
Nichtigkeit des Verschmelzungsbeschlusses der übertragenden Gesellschaft

Nach Eintragung der Verschmelzung in das Handelsregister des Sitzes der übertragenden Gesellschaft ist eine Klage auf Feststellung der Nichtigkeit des Verschmelzungsbeschlusses dieser Gesellschaft gegen die übernehmende Gesellschaft zu richten.

Zweiter Unterabschnitt
Verschmelzung durch Neubildung
§ 353

(1) Bei Verschmelzung von Aktiengesellschaften durch Bildung einer neuen Aktiengesellschaft gelten sinngemäß §§ 340, 341, 344 Abs. 2, § 345 Abs. 2 und 3, § 346 Abs. 2, 5 bis 7, §§ 347 bis 350, 352. Jede der sich vereinigenden Gesellschaften gilt als übertragende und die neue Gesellschaft als übernehmende.

(2) Die Verschmelzung darf erst beschlossen werden, wenn jede der sich vereinigenden Gesellschaften bereits zwei Jahre im Handelsregister eingetragen ist.

(3) Die Satzung der neuen Gesellschaft und die Bestellung ihrer Aufsichtsratsmitglieder bedürfen der Zustimmung der Hauptversammlungen der sich vereinigenden Gesellschaften. § 124 Abs. 2 Satz 2, Abs. 3 Satz 1 und 3, § 340 Abs. 2 gelten sinngemäß.

(4) Für die Bildung der neuen Gesellschaft gelten die Gründungsvorschriften des § 23 Abs. 3 und der §§ 29, 30 Abs. 1 und 4, §§ 31, 39, 41 Abs. 1 sinngemäß. Festsetzungen über Sondervorteile, Gründungsaufwand, Sacheinlagen und Sachübernahmen, die in den Satzungen der sich vereinigenden Ge-

§ 351

sellschaften enthalten waren, sind in die Satzung der neuen Gesellschaft zu übernehmen. § 26 Abs. 4 und 5 über die Änderung und Beseitigung dieser Festsetzungen bleibt unberührt.

(5) Die Vorstände der sich vereinigenden Gesellschaften haben die neue Gesellschaft bei dem Gericht, in dessen Bezirk sie ihren Sitz hat, zur Eintragung in das Handelsregister anzumelden. Mit der Eintragung der neuen Gesellschaft geht das Vermögen der sich vereinigenden Gesellschaften einschließlich der Verbindlichkeiten auf die neue Gesellschaft über. Treffen dabei aus gegenseitigen Verträgen, die zur Zeit der Verschmelzung von keiner Seite vollständig erfüllt sind, Abnahme-, Lieferungs- oder ähnliche Verpflichtungen zusammen, die miteinander unvereinbar sind oder die beide zu erfüllen eine schwere Unbilligkeit für die übernehmende Gesellschaft bedeuten würde, so bestimmt sich der Umfang der Verpflichtungen nach Billigkeit unter Würdigung der vertraglichen Rechte aller Beteiligten.

(6) Mit der Eintragung der neuen Gesellschaft erlöschen die sich vereinigenden Gesellschaften. Einer besonderen Löschung der sich vereinigenden Gesellschaften bedarf es nicht. Mit der Eintragung werden die Aktionäre der sich vereinigenden Gesellschaften Aktionäre der neuen Gesellschaft.

(7) In die Bekanntmachung der Eintragung der neuen Gesellschaft sind außer deren Inhalt aufzunehmen:
1. die Festsetzungen nach § 23 Abs. 3 Nr. 5 und 6, §§ 24, 25 Satz 2, § 26;
2. Name, Beruf und Wohnort der Mitglieder des ersten Aufsichtsrats;
3. die Bestimmungen des Verschmelzungsvertrags über die Zahl und, wenn mehrere Gattungen bestehen, die Gattung der Aktien, welche die neue Gesellschaft den Aktionären der sich vereinigenden Gesellschaften gewährt, und über die Art und den Zeitpunkt der Zuteilung dieser Aktien.

Zugleich ist bekanntzumachen, daß die mit der Anmeldung eingereichten Schriftstücke bei dem Gericht eingesehen werden können.

(8) Der Vorstand der neuen Gesellschaft hat die Verschmelzung zur Eintragung in die Handelsregister der sich vereinigenden Gesellschaften anzumelden. Die Verschmelzung darf erst eingetragen werden, wenn die neue Gesellschaft eingetragen worden ist.

contained in the articles of incorporation of the companies to be consolidated, shall be incorporated in the articles of incorporation of the new company. § 26, paragraphs 4 and 5, concerning the amendment and deletion of such particulars, shall be applicable.

(5) The managing boards of the consolidating companies shall file an application to record the new company in the Commercial Register at the court of the district in which it is domiciled. Upon registration of the new company, all of the assets of the consolidating companies together with their liabilities shall devolve to the new company. If in this connection obligations to purchase or sell or similar obligations arising out of bilateral agreements not fully performed by the parties thereto should coincide, and if such obligations conflict or if the performance thereof would entail substantial hardship for the transferee company, the scope of such obligations shall be adjusted equitably, with due consideration for the contractual rights of all of the parties involved.

(6) The consolidating companies shall cease to exist upon registration of the new company. Specific cancellation of the consolidating companies is not required. The shareholders of the consolidating companies shall become shareholders of the new company upon its registration.

(7) In addition to the content of the registration, the publication of the registration of the new company shall contain the following:
1. the information required in § 23, paragraph 3, Nos. 5 and 6, §§ 24, 25, second sentence, and § 26;
2. the name, occupation and residence of each of the members of the initial supervisory board;
3. the provisions of the consolidation agreement concerning the number and, if there are several classes, the classes of shares issued by the new company to the shareholders of the consolidating companies, as well as the manner and the date of issuance of such shares.

At the same time, it shall be announced that the documents filed with the application for registration may be examined at the court.

(8) The managing board of the new company shall file an application to record the consolidation in the Commercial Register at the domiciles of the consolidating companies. The consolidation shall be recorded only after registration of the new company.

§ 353

Second Division

Combination of Partnerships Limited by Shares and of Partnerships Limited by Shares with Stock Corporations

§ 354

(1) Partnerships limited by shares may be combined with each other. A partnership limited by shares may also be combined with a stock corporation, or a stock corporation may be combined with a partnership limited by shares.

(2) §§ 339 to 353 shall apply, *mutatis mutandis*, to such business combinations. For the managing board of the stock corporation there shall be substituted the general partners of the partnership limited by shares.

Third Division

Merger of Limited Liability Company with Stock Corporation or Partnership Limited by Shares

§ 355

Merger of Limited Liability Company with Stock Corporation

(1) A limited liability company may be merged with a stock corporation by transferring all of the assets of the company to the stock corporation for shares of the latter.

(2) Unless a different result is required by paragraphs 3 and 4 hereof, § 339, paragraph 2, §§ 340, 341, 343 to 347, 351, and 352 shall apply, *mutatis mutandis*, to this merger. For the managing board and the shareholders of the transferor stock corporation there shall be substituted the managers and the quotaholders of the limited liability company.

(3) The quotaholders' resolution authorizing the merger shall require a majority of three-fourths of the votes cast. The articles of incorporation may provide for a higher majority and establish additional requirements. The resolution must be in the form of a judicial or notarial record.

(4) The resolution to merge may be adopted only after the stock corporation has been recorded in the Commercial Register for two years.

(5) The managers and, if there is a supervisory board, the members of the supervisory board of the limited liability company shall be jointly and severally liable for any damage sustained by that

§ 354

Zweiter Abschnitt

Verschmelzung von Kommanditgesellschaften auf Aktien sowie von Kommanditgesellschaften auf Aktien und Aktiengesellschaften

§ 354

(1) Kommanditgesellschaften auf Aktien können miteinander verschmolzen werden. Ebenso kann eine Kommanditgesellschaft auf Aktien mit einer Aktiengesellschaft oder eine Aktiengesellschaft mit einer Kommanditgesellschaft auf Aktien verschmolzen werden.

(2) Für die Verschmelzung gelten die §§ 339 bis 353 sinngemäß. An die Stelle des Vorstands der Aktiengesellschaft treten die persönlich haftenden Gesellschafter der Kommanditgesellschaft auf Aktien.

Dritter Abschnitt

Verschmelzung einer Gesellschaft mit beschränkter Haftung mit einer Aktiengesellschaft oder einer Kommanditgesellschaft auf Aktien

§ 355

Verschmelzung einer Gesellschaft mit beschränkter Haftung mit einer Aktiengesellschaft

(1) Eine Gesellschaft mit beschränkter Haftung kann mit einer Aktiengesellschaft durch Übertragung des Vermögens der Gesellschaft als Ganzes auf die Aktiengesellschaft gegen Gewährung von Aktien dieser Gesellschaft verschmolzen werden.

(2) Für die Verschmelzung gelten, soweit sich aus den Absätzen 3 und 4 nichts anderes ergibt, § 339 Abs. 2, §§ 340, 341, 343 bis 347, 351, 352 sinngemäß. An die Stelle des Vorstands und der Hauptversammlung der übertragenden Aktiengesellschaft treten die Geschäftsführer und die Versammlung der Gesellschafter der Gesellschaft mit beschränkter Haftung.

(3) Der Verschmelzungsbeschluß der Versammlung der Gesellschafter bedarf einer Mehrheit von drei Vierteln der abgegebenen Stimmen. Der Gesellschaftsvertrag kann eine größere Mehrheit und weitere Erfordernisse bestimmen. Der Beschluß muß gerichtlich oder notariell beurkundet werden.

(4) Die Verschmelzung darf erst beschlossen werden, wenn die Aktiengesellschaft bereits zwei Jahre im Handelsregister eingetragen ist.

(5) Die Geschäftsführer und, wenn ein Aufsichtsrat bestellt ist, die Aufsichtsratsmitglieder der Gesellschaft mit beschränkter Haftung sind als Gesamtschuldner zum Ersatz des Schadens verpflichtet,

den die Gesellschaft, ihre Mitglieder und Gläubiger durch die Verschmelzung erleiden. Geschäftsführer und Aufsichtsratsmitglieder, die bei der Prüfung der Vermögenslage der Gesellschaften und bei Abschluß des Verschmelzungsvertrags die Sorgfalt eines ordentlichen Geschäftsleiters angewandt haben, sind von der Ersatzpflicht befreit. § 349 Abs. 2 und 3, § 350 gelten sinngemäß.

§ 356
Verschmelzung einer Gesellschaft mit beschränkter Haftung mit einer Kommanditgesellschaft auf Aktien

(1) Eine Gesellschaft mit beschränkter Haftung kann mit einer Kommanditgesellschaft auf Aktien durch Übertragung des Vermögens der Gesellschaft als Ganzes auf die Kommanditgesellschaft auf Aktien gegen Gewährung von Aktien dieser Gesellschaft verschmolzen werden.

(2) Für die Verschmelzung gilt § 355 sinngemäß. An die Stelle des Vorstands der Aktiengesellschaft treten die persönlich haftenden Gesellschafter der Kommanditgesellschaft auf Aktien.

Vierter Abschnitt
Verschmelzung einer bergrechtlichen Gewerkschaft mit einer Aktiengesellschaft oder einer Kommanditgesellschaft auf Aktien

§ 357
Verschmelzung einer bergrechtlichen Gewerkschaft mit einer Aktiengesellschaft

(1) Eine bergrechtliche Gewerkschaft mit eigener Rechtspersönlichkeit kann mit einer Aktiengesellschaft durch Übertragung des Vermögens der Gewerkschaft als Ganzes auf die Aktiengesellschaft gegen Gewährung von Aktien dieser Gesellschaft verschmolzen werden.

(2) Für die Verschmelzung gelten, soweit sich aus den folgenden Vorschriften nichts anderes ergibt, § 339 Abs. 2, §§ 340 bis 347, 351, 352 sinngemäß. An die Stelle des Vorstands und der Hauptversammlung der übertragenden Aktiengesellschaft treten die gesetzlichen Vertreter der Gewerkschaft und die Gewerkenversammlung.

(3) Für den Beschluß nach § 340 Abs. 1 bedarf es bei der übertragenden Gewerkschaft einer Mehrheit von mindestens drei Vierteln aller Kuxe. Die Satzung kann eine größere Mehrheit und weitere Erfordernisse bestimmen. Der Beschluß muß gerichtlich oder notariell beurkundet werden. Er bedarf zu seiner Wirksamkeit der Bestätigung durch die Bergbehörde, die nach dem Bergrecht für die Bestä-

company, its quotaholders and its creditors by reason of the merger. Managers and members of the supervisory board who, in connection with the examination of the financial condition of the companies and the conclusion of the merger agreement, acted with the care of a prudent executive, shall not be liable. § 349, paragraphs 2 and 3, and § 350 shall apply *mutatis mutandis*.

§ 356
Merger of Limited Liability Company with Partnership Limited by Shares

(1) A limited liability company may be merged with a partnership limited by shares by transferring all of the assets of the company to the partnership limited by shares for shares of the latter.

(2) § 355 shall apply, *mutatis mutandis*, to this merger. For the managing board of the stock corporation there shall be substituted the general partners of the partnership limited by shares.

Fourth Division
Merger of Mining Company with Stock Corporation or Partnership Limited by Shares

§ 357
Merger of Mining Company with Stock Corporation

(1) A mining company having separate legal personality may be merged with a stock corporation by transferring all of the assets of the mining company to the stock corporation for shares of the latter.

(2) Unless a different result is required by the following provisions, § 339, paragraph 2, §§ 340 to 347, 351, and 352 shall apply, *mutatis mutandis*, to this merger. For the managing board and the shareholders of the transferor stock corporation there shall be substituted the legal representatives of the mining company and the mining company's shareholders.

(3) The resolution referred to in § 340, paragraph 1, shall require, in the case of the transferor mining company, a majority of no less than three-fourths of all of the mining company's shares. The articles of incorporation may provide for a higher majority and establish additional requirements. The resolution must be in the form of a judicial or notarial record. To be effective, it must be confirmed by the bureau of mines which, under mining law, is competent to confirm the

company's articles of incorporation. The bureau of mines may refuse to issue such confirmation only if issuance would be contrary to the public interest.

(4) If the mining company is not recorded in the Commercial Register, the merger shall likewise not be recorded in the Commercial Register at the mining company's domicile. In this event, the legal consequences of registration shall take effect when the merger is recorded in the Commercial Register at the transferee company's domicile.

(5) The legal representatives of the mining company and, if there is a supervisory board, the members of the supervisory board of the mining company shall be jointly and severally liable for any damage sustained by the mining company, its shareholders, and the mining company's creditors by reason of the merger. § 349, paragraph 1, second sentence, and paragraphs 2 and 3, and § 350 shall apply *mutatis mutandis.*

§ 358
Merger of Mining Company with Partnership Limited by Shares

(1) A mining company having separate legal personality may be merged with a partnership limited by shares by transferring all of the assets of the mining company to the partnership limited by shares for shares of the latter.

(2) § 357 shall apply, *mutatis mutandis*, to this merger. For the managing board of the stock corporation there shall be substituted the general partners of the partnership limited by shares.

Part Two
Transfer of Assets

§ 359
Transfer of Assets to Public Agencies

(1) A stock corporation or partnership limited by shares may transfer all of its assets, without liquidation, to the Federal Republic of Germany, a German state, a municipal association, or a municipality.

(2) § 339, paragraph 2, § 340, paragraphs 1 to 3, §§ 341, 345, 346, paragraphs 3, 4, first and second sentences, paragraph 5, §§ 347 to 350, 352, and, in the case of a transfer of the assets of a partnership limited by shares, § 354, paragraph 2, second sentence, shall apply *mutatis mutandis.*

tigung der Satzung zuständig ist. Die Bergbehörde darf die Bestätigung nur versagen, wenn das öffentliche Interesse entgegensteht.

(4) Ist die Gewerkschaft nicht in das Handelsregister eingetragen, so wird auch die Verschmelzung nicht in das Handelsregister des Sitzes der Gewerkschaft eingetragen. Die Rechtsfolgen der Eintragung treten in diesem Falle ein, wenn die Verschmelzung in das Handelsregister des Sitzes der übernehmenden Gesellschaft eingetragen ist.

(5) Die gesetzlichen Vertreter der Gewerkschaft und, wenn ein Aufsichtsrat bestellt ist, die Mitglieder des Aufsichtsrats der Gewerkschaft sind als Gesamtschuldner zum Ersatz des Schadens verpflichtet, den die Gewerkschaft, die Gewerken und die Gläubiger der Gewerkschaft durch die Verschmelzung erleiden. § 349 Abs. 1 Satz 2, Abs. 2 und 3, § 350 gelten sinngemäß.

§ 358
Verschmelzung einer bergrechtlichen Gewerkschaft mit einer Kommanditgesellschaft auf Aktien

(1) Eine bergrechtliche Gewerkschaft mit eigener Rechtspersönlichkeit kann mit einer Kommanditgesellschaft auf Aktien durch Übertragung des Vermögens der Gewerkschaft als Ganzes auf die Kommanditgesellschaft auf Aktien gegen Gewährung von Aktien dieser Gesellschaft verschmolzen werden.

(2) Für die Verschmelzung gilt § 357 sinngemäß. An die Stelle des Vorstands der Aktiengesellschaft treten die persönlich haftenden Gesellschafter der Kommanditgesellschaft auf Aktien.

Zweiter Teil
Vermögensübertragung

§ 359
Vermögensübertragung auf die öffentliche Hand

(1) Eine Aktiengesellschaft oder Kommanditgesellschaft auf Aktien kann ihr Vermögen als Ganzes ohne Abwicklung auf den Bund, ein Land, einen Gemeindeverband oder eine Gemeinde übertragen.

(2) Für die übertragende Gesellschaft gelten § 339 Abs. 2, § 340 Abs. 1 bis 3, §§ 341, 345, 346 Abs. 3, 4 Satz 1 und 2, Abs. 5, §§ 347 bis 350, 352 und bei der Übertragung des Vermögens einer Kommanditgesellschaft auf Aktien § 354 Abs. 2 Satz 2 sinngemäß.

§ 358

§ 360

Vermögensübertragung auf einen Versicherungsverein auf Gegenseitigkeit

(1) Eine Aktiengesellschaft, die den Betrieb von Versicherungsgeschäften zum Gegenstand hat, kann ihr Vermögen als Ganzes ohne Abwicklung auf einen Versicherungsverein auf Gegenseitigkeit übertragen.

(2) Für die Vermögensübertragung gelten, soweit sich aus den folgenden Vorschriften nichts anderes ergibt, § 339 Abs. 2, §§ 340, 341, 345, 346 Abs. 3, 4 Satz 1 und 2, Abs. 5, §§ 347 bis 352 sinngemäß.

(3) Der Beschluß der obersten Vertretung des Versicherungsvereins auf Gegenseitigkeit bedarf einer Mehrheit, die mindestens drei Viertel der abgegebenen Stimmen umfaßt. Die Satzung kann eine größere Mehrheit und weitere Erfordernisse bestimmen.

(4) Die übertragende Gesellschaft hat einen Treuhänder für den Empfang des Entgelts zu bestellen. Die Vermögensübertragung darf erst eingetragen werden, wenn der Treuhänder dem Gericht angezeigt hat, daß er im Besitz des Entgelts ist.

(5) Die Urkunden über die Genehmigung nach § 14 des Gesetzes über die Beaufsichtigung der privaten Versicherungsunternehmungen und Bausparkassen sind der Anmeldung der Vermögensübertragung zum Handelsregister beizufügen.

§ 361

Vermögensübertragung in anderer Weise

(1) Ein Vertrag, durch den sich eine Aktiengesellschaft oder eine Kommanditgesellschaft auf Aktien zur Übertragung des ganzen Gesellschaftsvermögens verpflichtet, ohne daß die Übertragung unter die §§ 339 bis 360 fällt, wird nur mit Zustimmung der Hauptversammlung wirksam. Der Beschluß bedarf einer Mehrheit, die mindestens drei Viertel des bei der Beschlußfassung vertretenen Grundkapitals umfaßt. Die Satzung kann eine größere Kapitalmehrheit und weitere Erfordernisse bestimmen. Für den Vertrag gilt § 341 Abs. 1.

(2) Der Vertrag ist von der Einberufung der Hauptversammlung an, die über die Zustimmung beschließen soll, in dem Geschäftsraum der Gesellschaft zur Einsicht der Aktionäre auszulegen. Auf Verlangen ist jedem Aktionär unverzüglich eine Abschrift zu erteilen. In der Hauptversammlung ist der Vertrag auszulegen. Der Vorstand hat ihn zu Beginn der Verhandlung zu erläutern. Die Niederschrift ist er als Anlage beizufügen.

§ 360
Transfer of Assets to Mutual Insurance Company

(1) A stock corporation engaged in the insurance business may, without liquidation, transfer all of its assets to a mutual insurance company.

(2) Unless a different result is required by the following provisions, § 339, paragraph 2, §§ 340, 341, 345, 346, paragraphs 3 and 4, first and second sentences, paragraph 5, and §§ 347 to 352 shall apply, *mutatis mutandis*, to this transfer of assets.

(3) The resolution of the voting members of the mutual insurance company shall require a majority of no less than three-fourths of the votes cast. The articles of incorporation may provide for a higher majority and establish additional requirements.

(4) The transferor company shall appoint a trustee to accept the consideration. The transfer of assets may not be recorded before the trustee notifies the court that he has obtained possession of the consideration.

(5) The documents concerning the authorization required by § 14 of the *Gesetz über die Beaufsichtigung der privaten Versicherungsunternehmungen und Bausparkassen* shall be attached to the application to record the transfer of assets in the Commercial Register.

§ 361
Other Transfers of Assets

(1) An agreement whereby a stock corporation or a partnership limited by shares undertakes to transfer all of its assets, if such transfer is not subject to the provisions of §§ 339 to 360, shall be valid only if approved by the shareholders. The resolution shall require a majority of no less than three-fourths of the stated capital represented when the resolution is adopted. The articles of incorporation may provide for a higher capital majority and establish additional requirements. § 341, paragraph 1, shall apply to such agreement.

(2) The agreement shall be exhibited on the company's premises for inspection by the shareholders beginning with the date on which the shareholders' meeting is called which is to decide on it. Each shareholder shall promptly, upon request, be furnished a copy. The agreement shall be exhibited at the shareholders' meeting. At the beginning of the deliberations the managing board shall explain the agreement. It shall be attached to the minutes.

(3) If, in connection with the transfer of the company's assets, a resolution to dissolve the company is adopted, §§ 264 to 273 shall apply. The application to register the dissolution of the company shall be accompanied by a duplicate original or certified copy of the agreement.

(3) Wird aus Anlaß der Übertragung des Gesellschaftsvermögens die Auflösung der Gesellschaft beschlossen, so gelten §§ 264 bis 273. Der Anmeldung der Auflösung der Gesellschaft ist der Vertrag in Ausfertigung oder öffentlich beglaubigter Abschrift beizufügen.

Part Three
Transformation

First Division

Transformation of Stock Corporation into Partnership Limited by Shares

Dritter Teil
Umwandlung

Erster Abschnitt

Umwandlung einer Aktiengesellschaft in eine Kommanditgesellschaft auf Aktien

§ 362
Prerequisites

(1) A stock corporation may be transformed into a partnership limited by shares.

(2) Such transformation shall require a shareholders' resolution and the association of at least one person as general partner. The resolution shall require a majority of no less than three-fourths of the stated capital represented when the resolution is adopted. The articles of incorporation may provide for a higher capital majority and establish additional requirements. The resolution shall specify the name of the company and any additional amendments of the articles of incorporation required to carry out the transformation. The act of associating as general partner must be in the form of a judicial or notarial record. At the same time, the general partners shall approve the amendments to the articles of incorporation.

(3) A balance sheet in which the company's assets and liabilities are stated at the value attributable to them as of the closing date of the balance sheet shall be submitted to the shareholders' meeting which is to adopt the resolution concerning the transformation. The balance sheet shall be prepared as of the closing date on which the general partners begin participation in the company's profits and losses. If this closing date is later than the date of the resolution concerning the transformation, the balance sheet shall be prepared as of a closing date which precedes the date of the resolution concerning the transformation by no more than six months. § 175, paragraph 2, shall apply *mutatis mutandis*. The balance sheet shall be attached to the minutes.

§ 362
Voraussetzungen

(1) Eine Aktiengesellschaft kann in eine Kommanditgesellschaft auf Aktien umgewandelt werden.

(2) Zur Umwandlung bedarf es eines Beschlusses der Hauptversammlung und des Beitritts mindestens eines persönlich haftenden Gesellschafters. Der Beschluß bedarf einer Mehrheit, die mindestens drei Viertel des bei der Beschlußfassung vertretenen Grundkapitals umfaßt. Die Satzung kann eine größere Kapitalmehrheit und weitere Erfordernisse bestimmen. Im Beschluß sind die Firma und die weiteren zur Durchführung der Umwandlung nötigen Satzungsänderungen festzusetzen. Der Beitritt der persönlich haftenden Gesellschafter bedarf gerichtlicher oder notarieller Beurkundung. Hierbei haben die persönlich haftenden Gesellschafter die Satzungsänderungen zu genehmigen.

(3) Der Hauptversammlung, die über die Umwandlung beschließen soll, ist eine Bilanz vorzulegen, in der die Vermögensgegenstände und Verbindlichkeiten der Gesellschaft mit dem Wert angesetzt sind, der ihnen am Bilanzstichtag beizulegen ist. Die Bilanz ist auf den Stichtag aufzustellen, von dem ab die persönlich haftenden Gesellschafter am Gewinn oder Verlust der Gesellschaft teilnehmen sollen. Liegt dieser Stichtag nach der Beschlußfassung über die Umwandlung, so ist die Bilanz auf einen höchstens sechs Monate vor der Beschlußfassung über die Umwandlung liegenden Stichtag aufzustellen. § 175 Abs. 2 gilt sinngemäß. Die Bilanz ist der Niederschrift als Anlage beizufügen.

(4) Für die Umwandlung gelten die §§ 32 bis 35, 38, 46 bis 51 sinngemäß. An die Stelle der Gründer treten die persönlich haftenden Gesellschafter.

(4) §§ 32 to 35, 38, and 46 to 51 shall apply to the transformation *mutatis mutandis*. For the incorporators there shall be substituted the general partners.

§ 363
Zusammensetzung des Aufsichtsrats der Kommanditgesellschaft auf Aktien

(1) Der Vorstand der Aktiengesellschaft hat vor der Umwandlung bekanntzumachen, nach welchen gesetzlichen Vorschriften nach seiner Ansicht der Aufsichtsrat der Kommanditgesellschaft auf Aktien zusammengesetzt sein muß. Die Bekanntmachung soll mindestens zwei Monate vor der Beschlußfassung über die Umwandlung erfolgen. § 97 Abs. 1, Abs. 2 Satz 1, §§ 98, 99 gelten sinngemäß.

(2) Wird das nach § 98 Abs. 1 zuständige Gericht fristgemäß angerufen oder ist keine Bekanntmachung erfolgt, muß der Aufsichtsrat der Kommanditgesellschaft auf Aktien bei der Umwandlung nach § 96 Abs. 1 dieses Gesetzes und § 76 Abs. 1 des Betriebsverfassungsgesetzes zusammengesetzt sein, es sei denn, daß der Aufsichtsrat der Aktiengesellschaft nur aus Aufsichtsratsmitgliedern der Aktionäre zusammengesetzt war.

(3) Der Umwandlung steht nicht entgegen, daß die Aufsichtsratsmitglieder der Arbeitnehmer noch nicht gewählt sind.

§ 363
Composition of Supervisory Board of Partnership Limited by Shares

(1) The managing board of the stock corporation shall, prior to the transformation, announce the statutory provisions which, in its opinion, are applicable to the composition of the supervisory board of the partnership limited by shares. This announcement shall be made no later than two months prior to the date on which the resolution concerning the transformation is to be adopted. § 97, paragraph 1, paragraph 2, first sentence, and §§ 98 and 99 shall apply *mutatis mutandis*.

(2) If a timely application is filed with the court having jurisdiction pursuant to § 98, paragraph 1, or if no announcement was made, the supervisory board of the partnership limited by shares must be composed, at the time of transformation, in accordance with § 96, paragraph 1, of this Act and § 76, paragraph 1, of the *Betriebsverfassungsgesetz*, unless the supervisory board of the stock corporation was composed exclusively of members representing the shareholders.

(3) The fact that the members of the supervisory board representing the employees have not yet been elected shall not bar the transformation.

§ 364
Anmeldung der Umwandlung

Zugleich mit dem Umwandlungsbeschluß sind die persönlich haftenden Gesellschafter zur Eintragung in das Handelsregister anzumelden. Die Urkunden über ihren Beitritt sind für das Gericht des Sitzes der Gesellschaft in Ausfertigung oder öffentlich beglaubigter Abschrift beizufügen.

§ 364
Application to Record Transformation

The application to record the resolution authorizing the transformation in the Commercial Register shall be filed together with the application to record the general partners. A duplicate original or certified copy of the documents concerning their association as general partners shall be attached for the records of the court at the company's domicile.

§ 365
Wirkung der Eintragung

Von der Eintragung der Umwandlung an besteht die Gesellschaft als Kommanditgesellschaft auf Aktien weiter. Die persönlich haftenden Gesellschafter haften den Gläubigern der Gesellschaft auch für die bereits bestehenden Verbindlichkeiten unbeschränkt.

§ 365
Effect of Registration

Following the registration of the transformation, the company shall exist as a partnership limited by shares. The general partners shall be personally liable to the creditors of the company for preexisting obligations.

§ 365

Second Division

Transformation of Partnership Limited by Shares into Stock Corporation

§ 366
Prerequisites

(1) A partnership limited by shares may, with the approval of all of the general partners, be transformed into a stock corporation by a shareholders' resolution.

(2) The resolution shall specify the name of the company, the composition of the managing board, and any additional amendments of the articles of incorporation necessary to carry out the transformation.

(3) A balance sheet shall be submitted to the shareholders' meeting which is to adopt the resolution concerning the transformation. If the settlement of the accounts of the general partners is to be determined by reference to a balance sheet prepared as of a closing date which precedes the date of the resolution concerning the transformation, that balance sheet shall be submitted; if not, then a balance sheet prepared as of a closing date which precedes the date of the resolution concerning the transformation by no more than six months, and in accordance with the principles applicable to the settlement with the general partners. § 175, paragraph 2, shall apply *mutatis mutandis*. The balance sheet shall be attached to the minutes.

(4) § 363 shall apply, *mutatis mutandis*, to the composition of the supervisory board of the stock corporation.

§ 367
Application to Record Transformation

The application to record the resolution authorizing the transformation in the Commercial Register shall be filed together with the application to record the members of the managing board. The original or a certified copy of the documents dealing with their appointment shall be attached for the records of the court at the company's domicile.

§ 368
Effect of Registration

Following the registration of the transformation, the company shall exist as a stock corporation. The general partners shall cease to be members of the company. They shall remain

Zweiter Abschnitt

Umwandlung einer Kommanditgesellschaft auf Aktien in eine Aktiengesellschaft

§ 366
Voraussetzungen

(1) Eine Kommanditgesellschaft auf Aktien kann durch Beschluß der Hauptversammlung unter Zustimmung aller persönlich haftenden Gesellschafter in eine Aktiengesellschaft umgewandelt werden.

(2) Im Beschluß sind die Firma, die Zusammensetzung des Vorstands und die weiteren zur Durchführung der Umwandlung nötigen Satzungsänderungen festzusetzen.

(3) Der Hauptversammlung, die über die Umwandlung beschließen soll, ist eine Bilanz vorzulegen. Soll für die Auseinandersetzung mit den persönlich haftenden Gesellschaftern eine Bilanz maßgebend sein, die auf einen vor der Beschlußfassung über die Umwandlung liegenden Stichtag aufgestellt ist, so ist diese Bilanz vorzulegen, sonst eine Bilanz, die auf einen höchstens sechs Monate vor der Beschlußfassung über die Umwandlung liegenden Zeitpunkt und nach den Grundsätzen aufzustellen ist, die für die Auseinandersetzung mit den persönlich haftenden Gesellschaftern vorgesehen sind. § 175 Abs. 2 gilt sinngemäß. Die Bilanz ist der Niederschrift als Anlage beizufügen.

(4) Für die Zusammensetzung des Aufsichtsrats der Aktiengesellschaft gilt § 363 sinngemäß.

§ 367
Anmeldung der Umwandlung

Zugleich mit dem Umwandlungsbeschluß sind die Vorstandsmitglieder zur Eintragung in das Handelsregister anzumelden. Die Urkunden über ihre Bestellung sind für das Gericht des Sitzes der Gesellschaft in Urschrift oder öffentlich beglaubigter Abschrift beizufügen.

§ 368
Wirkung der Eintragung

Von der Eintragung der Umwandlung an besteht die Gesellschaft als Aktiengesellschaft weiter. Die persönlich haftenden Gesellschafter scheiden aus der Gesellschaft aus. Ihre Haftung für die bis zur Eintragung entstandenen Verbindlichkeiten der Gesellschaft bleibt unberührt.

Dritter Abschnitt

Umwandlung einer Aktiengesellschaft in eine Gesellschaft mit beschränkter Haftung

§ 369
Voraussetzungen

(1) Eine Aktiengesellschaft kann durch Beschluß der Hauptversammlung in eine Gesellschaft mit beschränkter Haftung umgewandelt werden.

(2) Dem Umwandlungsbeschluß müssen alle Aktionäre zustimmen. Die Zustimmung eines Aktionärs, der in der Hauptversammlung nicht erschienen und nicht vertreten war, gilt als erteilt, wenn nicht der Aktionär binnen drei Monaten nach der Hauptversammlung der Gesellschaft schriftlich mitteilt, daß er die Zustimmung verweigert, und auf Verlangen der Gesellschaft nachweist, daß er von der Einberufung der Hauptversammlung an Inhaber der Aktie war. Die Verweigerung der Zustimmung kann nur binnen drei Monaten nach der Hauptversammlung durch schriftliche Erklärung zurückgenommen werden.

(3) Der Umwandlungsbeschluß bedarf abweichend von Absatz 2 nicht der Zustimmung aller Aktionäre, wenn die Umwandlung mit einer Mehrheit beschlossen wird, die mindestens neun Zehntel des Grundkapitals umfaßt, und die Gesellschaft im Zeitpunkt der Beschlußfassung weniger als fünfzig Aktionäre hat; dabei sind Aktionäre, die in der Hauptversammlung nicht erschienen und nicht vertreten sind, nur zu berücksichtigen, wenn sie sich binnen drei Monaten nach der Hauptversammlung schriftlich bei der Gesellschaft melden und auf deren Verlangen nachweisen, daß sie von der Einberufung der Hauptversammlung an Inhaber der Aktie waren. Bei der Berechnung der Kapitalmehrheit sind eigene Aktien und Aktien, aus denen nach § 71 Abs. 6 keine Rechte zustehen, vom Grundkapital abzusetzen. Die Satzung kann eine größere Kapitalmehrheit und weitere Erfordernisse bestimmen.

(4) Bei Gesellschaften, die nach Absatz 3 durch Mehrheitsbeschluß umgewandelt werden können, ist die Bekanntmachung der Umwandlung als Gegen-

liable for obligations of the company which arose prior to the registration.

Third Division

Transformation of Stock Corporation into Limited Liability Company

§ 369
Prerequisites

(1) A stock corporation may be transformed into a limited liability company by a shareholders' resolution.

(2) The resolution authorizing the transformation shall require the approval of all of the shareholders. A shareholder who was not present or represented at the shareholders' meeting shall be deemed to have approved the resolution unless such shareholder within three months from the date of the shareholders' meeting notifies the company in writing that he refuses to give his approval and, at the request of the company, furnishes evidence showing that he was a shareholder at and since the time the shareholders' meeting was called. The refusal to approve can be withdrawn only in writing within three months after the date of the shareholders' meeting.

(3) Notwithstanding paragraph 2 hereof, the resolution authorizing the transformation shall not require the approval of all of the shareholders if the transformation is authorized by a majority of no less than nine-tenths of the stated capital and if the company, on the date the resolution is adopted, has fewer than fifty shareholders; for this purpose, shareholders not present or represented at the shareholders' meeting shall be taken into account only if they notify the company in writing within three months from the date of the shareholders' meeting and, at the request of the company, furnish evidence showing that they were shareholders at and since the time the shareholders' meeting was called. In determining the capital majority, the company's treasury shares and shares whose rights the company may not exercise pursuant to § 71, paragraph 6, shall be deducted from the stated capital. The articles of incorporation may provide for a higher capital majority and establish additional requirements.

(4) For companies that may be transformed by a majority resolution pursuant to paragraph 3 hereof, the announcement of the transformation

as an item of the agenda shall be proper only if it is accompanied by a declaration of the company in which it offers to acquire for cash the quotas resulting from the transformation from any shareholders who have their objection to the transformation recorded in the minutes.

(5) The resolution shall state the name of the company and any additional amendments to the articles of incorporation required to carry out the transformation.

(6) The par value of the quotas may be stated at an amount different from the par value of the shares. It must amount to no less than five hundred German marks and be divisible by one hundred. The determination of a nominal value at an amount different from the par value of the shares shall require the approval of each shareholder who cannot acquire an interest corresponding to the aggregate par value of his shares. The approval must be in the form of a judicial or notarial record. Approval is not required to the extent that such difference is necessitated by the second sentence hereof.

§ 370
Composition of Supervisory Board of Limited Liability Company

(1) The managing board of the stock corporation shall, prior to the transformation, announce whether a supervisory board will be appointed for the limited liability company and the statutory provisions which, in its opinion, shall apply to the composition of the supervisory board. This announcement shall be made no later than two months prior to the date on which the resolution concerning the transformation is to be adopted. § 97, paragraph 1, paragraph 2, first sentence, and §§ 98 and 99 shall apply *mutatis mutandis.*

(2) If a timely application is filed with the court having jurisdiction pursuant to § 98, paragraph 1, or if no announcement was made, a supervisory board shall be appointed for the limited liability company at the time of the transformation, which board must be composed in accordance with the statutory provisions which previously applied to the supervisory board, unless the supervisory board of the stock corporation was composed exclusively of members representing the shareholders.

(3) The fact that the members of the supervisory board representing the employees have not yet been elected shall not bar the transformation.

§ 370

stand der Tagesordnung nur ordnungsgemäß, wenn ihr eine Erklärung der Gesellschaft beigefügt ist, in der diese den Aktionären, die gegen die Umwandlung Widerspruch zur Niederschrift erklären, anbietet, ihre durch die Umwandlung entstehenden Geschäftsanteile gegen eine Barabfindung zu erwerben.

(5) Im Beschluß sind die Firma und die weiteren zur Durchführung der Umwandlung nötigen Satzungsänderungen festzusetzen.

(6) Der Nennbetrag der Geschäftsanteile kann abweichend von dem Nennbetrag der Aktien festgesetzt werden. Er muß mindestens fünfhundert Deutsche Mark betragen und durch hundert teilbar sein. Wird der Nennbetrag abweichend von dem Nennbetrag der Aktien festgesetzt, so muß der Festsetzung jeder Aktionär zustimmen, der sich nicht dem Gesamtnennbetrag seiner Aktien entsprechend beteiligen kann. Die Zustimmung muß gerichtlich oder notariell beurkundet werden. Die Zustimmung ist nicht erforderlich, soweit die abweichende Festsetzung durch Satz 2 bedingt ist.

§ 370
Zusammensetzung des Aufsichtsrats der Gesellschaft mit beschränkter Haftung

(1) Der Vorstand der Aktiengesellschaft hat vor der Umwandlung bekanntzumachen, ob für die Gesellschaft mit beschränkter Haftung ein Aufsichtsrat gebildet werden soll und nach welchen gesetzlichen Vorschriften er nach seiner Ansicht der Aufsichtsrat zusammengesetzt sein muß. Die Bekanntmachung soll mindestens zwei Monate vor der Beschlußfassung über die Umwandlung erfolgen. § 97 Abs. 1, Abs. 2 Satz 1, §§ 98, 99 gelten sinngemäß.

(2) Wird das nach § 98 Abs. 1 zuständige Gericht fristgemäß angerufen oder ist keine Bekanntmachung erfolgt, muß bei der Umwandlung für die Gesellschaft mit beschränkter Haftung ein Aufsichtsrat gebildet werden und dieser nach den zuletzt auf den Aufsichtsrat der Aktiengesellschaft angewandten gesetzlichen Vorschriften zusammengesetzt sein, es sei denn, daß der Aufsichtsrat der Aktiengesellschaft nur aus Aufsichtsratsmitgliedern der Aktionäre zusammengesetzt war.

(3) Der Umwandlung steht nicht entgegen, daß die Aufsichtsratsmitglieder der Arbeitnehmer noch nicht gewählt sind.

§ 371

Anmeldung der Umwandlung

(1) Zugleich mit dem Umwandlungsbeschluß sind die Geschäftsführer zur Eintragung in das Handelsregister anzumelden. Der Anmeldung muß eine von dem Anmeldenden unterschriebene Liste der Gesellschafter beigefügt sein, aus der ihr Name, Vorname, Beruf und Wohnort sowie ihre Stammeinlagen zu ersehen sind. Soweit Aktionäre unbekannt sind, ist dies unter Bezeichnung der Aktienurkunde und des auf die Aktie entfallenden Geschäftsanteils anzugeben.

(2) Bei der Anmeldung einer nach § 369 Abs. 2 beschlossenen Umwandlung hat der Vorstand zu erklären, ob der Gesellschaft eine Mitteilung nach § 369 Abs. 2 Satz 2 fristgemäß zugegangen ist. Ist der Gesellschaft eine solche Mitteilung zugegangen, so hat der Vorstand ferner zu erklären, ob die Mitteilung fristgemäß zurückgenommen worden ist. Ist die Mitteilung nicht fristgemäß zurückgenommen worden, so hat der Vorstand die Umstände darzulegen, aus denen sich ergeben soll, daß der Aktionär den von der Gesellschaft verlangten Besitznachweis nicht erbracht hat.

(3) Bei der Anmeldung einer nach § 369 Abs. 3 beschlossenen Umwandlung hat der Vorstand zu erklären, wie viele Aktionäre in der Hauptversammlung erschienen oder vertreten waren und wie viele in der Hauptversammlung nicht erschienene und nicht vertretene Aktionäre sich fristgemäß gemeldet haben. Soweit erforderlich, hat der Vorstand die Umstände darzulegen, aus denen sich ergeben soll, daß ein Aktionär den von der Gesellschaft verlangten Besitznachweis nicht erbracht hat.

§ 371

Application to Record Transformation

(1) The application to record the resolution authorizing the transformation shall be filed together with the application to record the managers in the Commercial Register. The application shall be accompanied by a list of the quotaholders signed by the applicants, which shall set forth their last name, given name, occupation, and residence as well as the amounts of their equity interests. Where shareholders are unknown, this fact shall be stated, designating their share certificates and the quotas attributable to their shares.

(2) When filing the application to record a transformation authorized in accordance with § 369, paragraph 2, the managing board shall state whether the company received timely notification pursuant to § 369, paragraph 2, second sentence. If the company has received such notification, the managing board shall state further whether the notification was withdrawn in time. If the notification was not withdrawn in time, the managing board shall state the circumstances from which it could be inferred that the shareholder failed to comply with the company's request for evidence of contemporaneous ownership.

(3) When filing the application to record a transformation authorized in accordance with § 369, paragraph 3, the managing board shall state how many shareholders were present or represented at the shareholders' meeting and how many of the shareholders who were not present or represented at the shareholders' meeting notified the company within the period of time specified therefor. If necessary, the managing board shall state the circumstances from which it could be inferred that a shareholder failed to comply with the company's request for evidence of contemporaneous ownership.

§ 372

Wirkung der Eintragung

Von der Eintragung der Umwandlung an besteht die Gesellschaft als Gesellschaft mit beschränkter Haftung weiter. Das Grundkapital ist zum Stammkapital, die Aktien sind zu Geschäftsanteilen geworden. Die an einer Aktie bestehenden Rechte Dritter bestehen an dem an die Stelle tretenden Geschäftsanteil weiter.

§ 372

Effect of Registration

Following the registration of the transformation, the company shall exist as a limited liability company. The stated capital of the stock corporation shall become its stated capital, and the shares shall become quotas. Rights of third parties existing in a share shall subsist with respect to the quota replacing it.

§ 372

§ 373
Exchange of Shares

With respect to the exchange of shares for quotas, § 73, paragraphs 1 and 2, and, if a consolidation of shares is necessary, § 226. paragraphs 1 and 2, concerning the cancellation of shares, shall apply *mutatis mutandis*. Permission from the court is not required.

§ 374
Protection of Creditors

Creditors whose claims arose prior to the publication of the registration of the transformation shall be furnished security to the extent that they cannot demand performance, provided that they make a request to this effect within six months from the date of publication. The creditors shall be advised of this right in the publication of the registration.

§ 375
Dissenting Shareholders

(1) Each shareholder who had his objection to the transformation recorded in the minutes may, within a period of two months, request that the company acquire his quota for a reasonable cash indemnity; § 320, paragraph 5, fifth sentence, shall apply, *mutatis mutandis*, to the amount of the cash indemnity. The period of time shall be computed from the date on which the registration of the transformation in the Commercial Register is deemed published in accordance with § 10 of the Commercial Code. If an application was made to the court designated in § 306 to determine the cash indemnity, the period of time shall be calculated from the date the decision was published in the *Bundesanzeiger*. The cost of the transfer of the quota shall be borne by the company. § 33 of the *Gesetz betreffend die Gesellschaften mit beschränkter Haftung* shall not bar the acquisition of quotas pursuant to the first sentence hereof.

(2) An action to set aside the resolution authorizing the transformation may not be based on the fact that the cash indemnity offered by the company is not reasonable. If the cash indemnity offered is not reasonable, the court designated in § 306 shall, upon application, determine a reasonable cash indemnity. The same shall apply if the company did not offer any cash indemnity or offered it improperly, and an action, based on this fact, to set aside the resolution for this reason was not brought or was withdrawn or was dis-

§ 373

§ 373
Umtausch der Aktien

Für den Umtausch der Aktien gegen Geschäftsanteile gilt § 73 Abs. 1 und 2, bei Zusammenlegung von Aktien § 226 Abs. 1 über die Kraftloserklärung von Aktien sinngemäß. Einer Genehmigung des Gerichts bedarf es nicht.

§ 374
Gläubigerschutz

Den Gläubigern, deren Forderungen begründet worden sind, bevor die Eintragung der Umwandlung bekanntgemacht worden ist, ist, wenn sie sich binnen sechs Monaten nach der Bekanntmachung zu diesem Zweck melden, Sicherheit zu leisten, soweit sie nicht Befriedigung verlangen können. Die Gläubiger sind in der Bekanntmachung der Eintragung auf dieses Recht hinzuweisen.

§ 375
Widersprechende Gesellschafter

(1) Jeder Aktionär, der gegen die Umwandlung Widerspruch zur Niederschrift erklärt hat, kann binnen einer Frist von zwei Monaten verlangen, daß die Gesellschaft seinen Geschäftsanteil gegen eine angemessene Barabfindung erwirbt; für die Höhe der Barabfindung gilt § 320 Abs. 5 Satz 5 sinngemäß. Die Frist beginnt mit dem Tage, an dem die Eintragung der Umwandlung in das Handelsregister nach § 10 des Handelsgesetzbuchs als bekanntgemacht gilt. Ist ein Antrag auf Bestimmung der Barabfindung durch das in § 306 bestimmte Gericht gestellt worden, so beginnt die Frist mit dem Tage, an dem die Entscheidung im Bundesanzeiger bekanntgemacht worden ist. Die Kosten der Abtretung des Geschäftsanteils trägt die Gesellschaft. § 33 des Gesetzes betreffend die Gesellschaften mit beschränkter Haftung steht einem Erwerb von Geschäftsanteilen nach Satz 1 nicht entgegen.

(2) Die Anfechtung des Umwandlungsbeschlusses kann nicht darauf gestützt werden, daß die von der Gesellschaft angebotene Barabfindung nicht angemessen ist. Ist die angebotene Barabfindung nicht angemessen, so hat das in § 306 bestimmte Gericht auf Antrag die angemessene Barabfindung zu bestimmen. Das gleiche gilt, wenn die Gesellschaft eine Barabfindung nicht oder nicht ordnungsgemäß angeboten hat und eine hierauf gestützte Anfechtungsklage innerhalb der Anfechtungsfrist nicht er-

hoben oder zurückgenommen oder rechtskräftig abgewiesen worden ist.

(3) Antragsberechtigt ist jeder Aktionär, der gegen die Umwandlung Widerspruch zur Niederschrift erklärt hat. Der Antrag kann nur binnen zwei Monaten nach dem Tage gestellt werden, an dem die Eintragung der Umwandlung in das Handelsregister nach § 10 des Handelsgesetzbuchs als bekanntgemacht gilt. Ist gegen den Umwandlungsbeschluß eine Anfechtungsklage erhoben worden, so beginnt die Frist mit der rechtskräftigen Abweisung oder der Zurücknahme der Anfechtungsklage. Für das Verfahren gilt § 306 sinngemäß mit der Maßgabe, daß an die Stelle der Vertragsteile die Gesellschaft und an die Stelle der außenstehenden Aktionäre die Aktionäre treten, die gegen die Umwandlung Widerspruch zur Niederschrift erklärt haben.

(4) Durch Absatz 1 wird das Recht des Gesellschafters, seinen Geschäftsanteil anderweit zu veräußern, nicht berührt. Satzungsmäßige Verfügungsbeschränkungen stehen einer Veräußerung innerhalb der in Absatz 1 bestimmten Frist nicht entgegen.

missed by a final decision within the period of time specified therefor.

(3) Each shareholder who had his objection to the transformation recorded in the minutes shall be entitled to make such application. The application may be made only within two months from the date on which the registration of the transformation in the Commercial Register is deemed published in accordance with § 10 of the Commercial Code. If an action to set aside the resolution authorizing the transformation is brought, the period of time within which the action must be brought shall be computed from the date the action is dismissed by a final decision or from the date the action is withdrawn. § 306 shall apply, *mutatis mutandis*, to the procedure, except that for the contracting parties there shall be substituted the company and for the outside shareholders there shall be substituted the shareholders who had their objection to the transformation recorded in the minutes.

(4) The right of any quotaholder to dispose of his quota in some other manner shall not be affected by paragraph 1 hereof. Restrictions on transferability contained in the articles of incorporation shall not bar any transfer made within the period of time specified in paragraph 1 hereof.

Vierter Abschnitt

Umwandlung einer Gesellschaft mit beschränkter Haftung in eine Aktiengesellschaft

Fourth Division

Transformation of Limited Liability Company into Stock Corporation

§ 376
Voraussetzungen

(1) Eine Gesellschaft mit beschränkter Haftung kann durch Beschluß der Gesellschafterversammlung in eine Aktiengesellschaft umgewandelt werden.

(2) Die Vorschriften des Gesetzes betreffend die Gesellschaften mit beschränkter Haftung über Abänderungen des Gesellschaftsvertrags sind anzuwenden. Ist die Abtretung der Geschäftsanteile von der Genehmigung einzelner Gesellschafter abhängig, so bedarf der Umwandlungsbeschluß zu seiner Wirksamkeit ihrer Zustimmung. Sind Gesellschaftern außer der Leistung von Kapitaleinlagen noch andere Verpflichtungen gegenüber der Gesellschaft auferlegt und können diese wegen der einschränkenden Bestimmung des § 55 bei der Umwandlung nicht aufrechterhalten werden, so bedarf der Umwandlungsbeschluß zu seiner Wirksamkeit der Zustimmung dieser Gesellschafter.

§ 376
Prerequisites

(1) A limited liability company may be transformed into a stock corporation by a quotaholders' resolution.

(2) The provisions of the *Gesetz betreffend die Gesellschaften mit beschränkter Haftung* concerning amendments of the articles of association shall apply. If the transfer of quotas is dependent on the approval of particular quotaholders, the resolution authorizing the transformation, to be effective, requires their approval. If quotaholders have obligations toward the company in addition to the payment of capital contributions which, in view of the transformation, cannot continue to exist because of the restrictive provision of § 55, the resolution authorizing the transformation, to be effective, requires the approval of such quotaholders.

§ 376

(3) The resolution shall specify the name of the company and any additional amendments to the articles of association necessary to carry out the transformation. The quotaholders who voted for the transformation shall be listed in the minutes by name.

(4) If the par value of the shares is stated at an amount of more than fifty German marks and differs from the nominal value of the quotas, each shareholder who cannot acquire an interest corresponding to the aggregate nominal value of his quotas must approve the determination of the par value. The approval must be in the form of a judicial or notarial record. To this extent, § 17, paragraph 6, of the *Gesetz betreffend die Gesellschaften mit beschränkter Haftung*, concerning the prohibition against division of quotas, shall not be applicable.

§ 377
Composition of Supervisory Board of Stock Corporation

(1) § 363, paragraphs 1 and 3, shall apply *mutatis mutandis.*

(2) If a timely application is filed with the court having jurisdiction pursuant to § 98, paragraph 1, or if no announcement was made, and if the supervisory board of the limited liability company also included members representing the employees, the supervisory board of the stock corporation must be composed, at the time of the transformation, in accordance with the statutory provisions which previously applied to the supervisory board of the limited liability company. If the limited liability company did not have a supervisory board, or had a supervisory board on which there were no members representing the employees, the supervisory board of the stock corporation may be composed, at the time of the transformation, exclusively of members representing the shareholders.

§ 378
Examination of Formation and Liability of Quotaholders

(1) Unless the following provisions require a different result, §§ 26, 27, 32 to 35, 38, and 46 to 53 shall apply, *mutatis mutandis*, to the transformation; the quotaholders who voted for the transformation have the same standing as the incorporators.

(2) The report referred to in § 32 shall contain a business analysis of the limited liability company.

§ 377

---

(3) Im Beschluß sind die Firma und die weiteren zur Durchführung der Umwandlung nötigen Abänderungen des Gesellschaftsvertrags festzusetzen. Die Gesellschafter, die für die Umwandlung gestimmt haben, sind in der Niederschrift namentlich aufzuführen.

(4) Wird der Nennbetrag der Aktien auf einen höheren Betrag als fünfzig Deutsche Mark und abweichend vom Nennbetrag der Geschäftsanteile festgesetzt, so muß der Festsetzung jeder Gesellschafter zustimmen, der sich nicht dem Gesamtnennbetrag seiner Geschäftsanteile entsprechend beteiligen kann. Die Zustimmung muß gerichtlich oder notariell beurkundet werden. § 17 Abs. 6 des Gesetzes betreffend die Gesellschaften mit beschränkter Haftung über die Unzulässigkeit einer Teilung von Geschäftsanteilen gilt insoweit nicht.

§ 377
Zusammensetzung des Aufsichtsrats der Aktiengesellschaft

(1) § 363 Abs. 1 und 3 gilt sinngemäß.

(2) Wird das nach § 98 Abs. 1 zuständige Gericht fristgemäß angerufen oder ist keine Bekanntmachung erfolgt, und bestand der Aufsichtsrat der Gesellschaft mit beschränkter Haftung auch aus Aufsichtsratsmitgliedern der Arbeitnehmer, so muß der Aufsichtsrat der Aktiengesellschaft bei der Umwandlung nach den zuletzt auf den Aufsichtsrat der Gesellschaft mit beschränkter Haftung angewandten gesetzlichen Vorschriften zusammengesetzt sein. Bestand für die Gesellschaft mit beschränkter Haftung kein Aufsichtsrat oder ein Aufsichtsrat ohne Aufsichtsratsmitglieder der Arbeitnehmer, so kann der Aufsichtsrat der Aktiengesellschaft bei der Umwandlung nur aus Aufsichtsratsmitgliedern der Aktionäre zusammengesetzt werden.

§ 378
Gründungsprüfung und Verantwortlichkeit der Gesellschafter

(1) Für die Umwandlung gelten, soweit sich aus den folgenden Vorschriften nichts anderes ergibt, die §§ 26, 27, 32 bis 35, 38, 46 bis 53 sinngemäß; den Gründern stehen gleich die Gesellschafter, die für die Umwandlung gestimmt haben.

(2) Im Bericht nach § 32 sind der Geschäftsverlauf und die Lage der Gesellschaft mit beschränkter Haftung darzulegen.

(3) Die Prüfung durch einen oder mehrere Prüfer nach § 33 Abs. 2 hat in jedem Fall stattzufinden.

(4) Die Frist von zwei Jahren nach § 52 Abs. 1 wird von der Eintragung der Umwandlung in das Handelsregister gerechnet.

§ 379
Anmeldung der Umwandlung

Zugleich mit dem Umwandlungsbeschluß sind die Vorstandsmitglieder zur Eintragung in das Handelsregister anzumelden. Die Urkunden über ihre Bestellung sind für das Gericht des Sitzes der Gesellschaft in Urschrift oder öffentlich beglaubigter Abschrift beizufügen. Der Anmeldung sind ferner eine Liste mit Namen, Beruf und Wohnort der Mitglieder des Aufsichtsrats, die Prüfungsberichte der Mitglieder des Vorstands und des Aufsichtsrats sowie der Prüfer mit ihren urkundlichen Unterlagen, ferner die Bescheinigung beizufügen, daß der Bericht der Prüfer der Industrie- und Handelskammer eingereicht worden ist.

§ 380
Inhalt der Bekanntmachung der Eintragung

In die Bekanntmachung der Eintragung der Umwandlung sind außer deren Inhalt der Name, Beruf und Wohnort der Mitglieder des Aufsichtsrats aufzunehmen. § 40 Abs. 2 gilt sinngemäß.

§ 381
Wirkung der Eintragung

Von der Eintragung der Umwandlung an besteht die Gesellschaft als Aktiengesellschaft weiter. Das Stammkapital ist zum Grundkapital, die Geschäftsanteile sind zu Aktien geworden. Die an einem Geschäftsanteil bestehenden Rechte Dritter bestehen an der an die Stelle tretenden Aktie weiter.

§ 382
Umtausch der Geschäftsanteile

Für den Umtausch der Geschäftsanteile gegen Aktien gilt § 73, bei Zusammenlegung von Geschäftsanteilen § 226 über die Kraftloserklärung

---

(3) An examination by one or more auditors pursuant to § 33, paragraph 2, shall always be required.

(4) The two-year period referred to in § 52, paragraph 1, shall be computed from the date on which the transformation is recorded in the Commercial Register.

§ 379
Application to Record Transformation

The application to record the resolution authorizing the transformation in the Commercial Register shall be filed together with the application to record the members of the managing board. The original or a certified copy of the documents concerning their appointment shall be attached for the records of the court at the company's domicile. The application shall further be accompanied by a list containing the name, occupation, and residence of each of the members of the supervisory board, the examination reports of the members of the managing board and of the supervisory board as well as the report of the auditors, together with any documents pertaining thereto, as well as a confirmation to the effect that the report of the auditors has been filed with the Chamber of Industry and Commerce.

§ 380
Content of Publication of Registration

In addition to the content of the registration, the publication of the registration of the transformation shall contain the name, occupation and residence of each of the members of the supervisory board. § 40, paragraph 2, shall apply *mutatis mutandis.*

§ 381
Effect of Registration

Following the registration of the transformation, the company shall exist as a stock corporation. The stated capital of the limited liability company shall become its stated capital, and the quotas shall become shares. Rights of third parties existing in a quota shall subsist with respect to the share replacing it.

§ 382
Exchange of Quotas

With respect to the exchange of quotas for shares, § 73, and, if a consolidation of shares is necessary, § 226, concerning the cancellation of

§ 382

share certificates, shall apply *mutatis mutandis.* Permission from the court is not required.

von Aktien sinngemäß. Einer Genehmigung des Gerichts bedarf es nicht.

§ 383
Dissenting Quotaholders

(1) Each quotaholder who had his objection to the transformation recorded in the minutes may put his shares at the disposal of the company. The managing board may specify a period of time of no less than three months for this purpose. This period may be specified only after the transformation has been recorded. Each known shareholder shall be given special notice thereof; as to the others, the deadline shall be published three times in the publications designated in the company's articles of incorporation.

(2) The company shall promptly sell the shares put at its disposal, for the account of the shareholders, through a broker at the official stock exchange quotation, and, if no official stock exchange quotation is available, by public auction. § 226, paragraph 3, second to sixth sentences, shall apply *mutatis mutandis.*

(3) The right of any shareholder to dispose of his shares himself shall not be affected by paragraphs 1 and 2 hereof. Restrictions on transferability contained in the articles of incorporation shall not bar any transfer made within the period of time specified in paragraph 1 hereof.

§ 383
Widersprechende Gesellschafter

(1) Jeder Gesellschafter, der gegen die Umwandlung Widerspruch zur Niederschrift erklärt hat, kann seine Aktie der Gesellschaft zur Verfügung stellen. Der Vorstand kann den Aktionären hierfür eine Ausschlußfrist von mindestens drei Monaten setzen. Die Fristsetzung ist erst nach der Eintragung der Umwandlung zulässig. Sie ist einem bekannten Aktionär besonders mitzuteilen, sonst ist sie dreimal in den Gesellschaftsblättern bekanntzumachen.

(2) Die Gesellschaft hat die ihr zu Verfügung gestellten Aktien unverzüglich für Rechnung des Aktionärs zum amtlichen Börsenpreis durch Vermittlung eines Kursmaklers und beim Fehlen eines Börsenpreises durch öffentliche Versteigerung zu verkaufen. § 226 Abs. 3 Satz 2 bis 6 gilt sinngemäß.

(3) Durch die Absätze 1 und 2 wird das Recht des Aktionärs, seine Aktien selbst zu veräußern, nicht berührt. Satzungsmäßige Verfügungsbeschränkungen stehen einer Veräußerung innerhalb der in Absatz 1 bestimmten Frist nicht entgegen.

Fifth Division

Transformation of Mining Company into Stock Corporation

Fünfter Abschnitt

Umwandlung einer bergrechtlichen Gewerkschaft in eine Aktiengesellschaft

§ 384
Prerequisites

(1) A mining company having separate legal personality may be transformed into a stock corporation by a resolution of the mining company's shareholders.

(2) The resolution shall require a majority of no less than three-fourths of all of the mining company's shares. The articles of incorporation may provide for a higher majority and establish additional requirements. The resolution must be in the form of a judicial or notarial record. To be effective, it must be confirmed by the bureau of mines which, under mining law, is competent to confirm the company's articles of incorporation. The bureau of mines may refuse to issue such confirmation only if issuance would be contrary to the public interest.

§ 384
Voraussetzungen

(1) Eine bergrechtliche Gewerkschaft mit eigener Rechtspersönlichkeit kann durch Beschluß der Gewerkenversammlung in eine Aktiengesellschaft umgewandelt werden.

(2) Der Beschluß bedarf einer Mehrheit von mindestens drei Vierteln aller Kuxe. Die Satzung kann eine größere Mehrheit und weitere Erfordernisse bestimmen. Der Beschluß muß gerichtlich oder notariell beurkundet werden. Er bedarf zu seiner Wirksamkeit der Bestätigung durch die Bergbehörde, die für die Bestätigung der Satzung zuständig ist. Die Bergbehörde darf die Bestätigung nur versagen, wenn das öffentliche Interesse entgegensteht.

(3) Im Beschluß ist die Firma festzusetzen. Außerdem sind in ihm die weiteren zur Durchführung der Umwandlung nötigen Maßnahmen zu treffen. Die Gewerken, die für die Umwandlung gestimmt haben, sind in der Niederschrift namentlich aufzuführen.

(4) Der Nennbetrag des Grundkapitals darf das nach Abzug der Schulden verbleibende Vermögen der bergrechtlichen Gewerkschaft nicht übersteigen. Er muß mindestens einhunderttausend Deutsche Mark betragen.

(5) Wird der Nennbetrag der Aktie auf einen höheren Betrag als fünfzig Deutsche Mark und abweichend von dem Betrag festgesetzt, der von dem festgesetzten Grundkapital auf einen Kux entfällt, so muß der Festsetzung jeder Gewerke zustimmen, der sich nicht dem auf seine Kuxe entfallenden Gesamtbetrag entsprechend beteiligen kann. Die Zustimmung muß gerichtlich oder notariell beurkundet werden.

(6) Für die Zusammensetzung des Aufsichtsrats der Aktiengesellschaft gilt § 377 sinngemäß.

§ 385
Wirkung der Eintragung

(1) Von der Eintragung an besteht die Gewerkschaft als Aktiengesellschaft weiter. Die Kuxe sind zu Aktien geworden. Die an einem Kux bestehenden Rechte Dritter bestehen an der an die Stelle tretenden Aktie weiter.

(2) Im übrigen gelten die §§ 378 bis 380, 382 und 383 sinngemäß.

Sechster Abschnitt

Umwandlung einer Kommanditgesellschaft auf Aktien in eine Gesellschaft mit beschränkter Haftung

§ 386
Voraussetzungen

(1) Eine Kommanditgesellschaft auf Aktien kann durch Beschluß der Hauptversammlung unter Zustimmung aller persönlich haftenden Gesellschafter in eine Gesellschaft mit beschränkter Haftung umgewandelt werden.

(2) Der Hauptversammlung, die über die Umwandlung beschließen soll, ist eine Bilanz vorzulegen. Soll für die Auseinandersetzung mit den persönlich haftenden Gesellschaftern eine Bilanz maßgebend sein, die auf einen vor der Beschluß-

(3) The resolution shall specify the name of the company. It shall also provide for any additional measures required to implement the transformation. The mining company's shareholders who voted for the transformation shall be listed in the minutes by name.

(4) The amount of the stated capital shall not exceed the mining company's assets, after deduction of the liabilities. It shall amount to no less than one hundred thousand German marks.

(5) If the par value of any share is stated in an amount of more than fifty German marks and differs from the ratable amount of the stated capital as specified attributable to one mining company share, the determination of the par value shall require the approval of each mining company shareholder who cannot acquire an interest corresponding to the aggregate par value attributable to his shares in the mining company. The approval must be in the form of a judicial or notarial record.

(6) § 377 shall apply, *mutatis mutandis,* to the composition of the supervisory board of the stock corporation.

§ 385
Effect of Registration

(1) Following the registration, the mining company shall exist as a stock corporation. The mining company's shares shall become shares of the stock corporation. Rights of third parties existing in a mining company share shall subsist with respect to the share replacing it.

(2) §§ 378 to 380, 382 and 383 shall apply *mutatis mutandis.*

Sixth Division

Transformation of Partnership Limited by Shares into Limited Liability Company

§ 386
Prerequisites

(1) A partnership limited by shares may, with the approval of all of the general partners, be transformed into a limited liability company by a shareholders' resolution.

(2) A balance sheet shall be submitted to the shareholders' meeting which is to adopt the resolution concerning the transformation. If the settlement of the accounts of the general partners is to be determined by reference to a balance

sheet prepared as of a closing date which precedes the date of the resolution concerning the transformation, that balance sheet shall be submitted; if not, then a balance sheet prepared as of a closing date which precedes the date of the resolution concerning the transformation by no more than six months, and in accordance with the principles applicable to the settlement with the general partners. § 175, paragraph 2, shall apply *mutatis mutandis*. The balance sheet shall be attached to the minutes.

(3) § 370 shall apply, *mutatis mutandis*, to the composition of the supervisory board of the limited liability company.

fassung über die Umwandlung liegenden Stichtag aufgestellt ist, so ist diese Bilanz vorzulegen, sonst eine Bilanz, die auf einen höchstens sechs Monate vor der Beschlußfassung über die Umwandlung liegenden Zeitpunkt und nach den Grundsätzen aufzustellen ist, die für die Auseinandersetzung mit den persönlich haftenden Gesellschaftern vorgesehen sind. § 175 Abs. 2 gilt sinngemäß. Die Bilanz ist der Niederschrift als Anlage beizufügen.

(3) Für die Zusammensetzung des Aufsichtsrats der Gesellschaft mit beschränkter Haftung gilt § 370 sinngemäß.

§ 387
Effect of Registration

(1) Following the registration of the transformation, the company shall exist as a limited liability company. The stated capital of the stock corporation shall become its stated capital, and the shares shall become quotas. Rights of third parties existing in a share shall subsist with respect to the quota replacing it.

(2) The general partners shall cease to be members of the company. They shall remain liable for obligations of the company which arose prior to the registration.

§ 387
Wirkung der Eintragung

(1) Von der Eintragung der Umwandlung an besteht die Gesellschaft als Gesellschaft mit beschränkter Haftung weiter. Das Grundkapital ist zum Stammkapital, die Aktien sind zu Geschäftsanteilen geworden. Die an einer Aktie bestehenden Rechte Dritter bestehen an dem an die Stelle tretenden Geschäftsanteil weiter.

(2) Die persönlich haftenden Gesellschafter scheiden aus der Gesellschaft aus. Ihre Haftung für die bis zur Eintragung entstandenen Verbindlichkeiten der Gesellschaft bleibt unberührt.

§ 388
Application of Provisions on Transformation of Stock Corporation*

Unless the above provisions require a different result, the provisions concerning the transformation of a stock corporation into a limited liability company shall be applicable.

§ 388
Anwendbarkeit der Vorschriften über die Umwandlung in eine Aktiengesellschaft

Soweit sich aus den vorstehenden Vorschriften nichts anderes ergibt, sind die Vorschriften über die Umwandlung einer Aktiengesellschaft in eine Gesellschaft mit beschränkter Haftung anzuwenden.

Seventh Division

Transformation of Limited Liability Company into Partnership Limited by Shares

Siebenter Abschnitt

Umwandlung einer Gesellschaft mit beschränkter Haftung in eine Kommanditgesellschaft auf Aktien

§ 389
Prerequisites

(1) A limited liability company may be transformed into a partnership limited by shares.

(2) Such transformation shall require a quotaholders' resolution and the association of at least one person as a general partner. The act of

§ 389
Voraussetzungen

(1) Eine Gesellschaft mit beschränkter Haftung kann in eine Kommanditgesellschaft auf Aktien umgewandelt werden.

(2) Zur Umwandlung bedarf es eines Beschlusses der Gesellschafterversammlung und des Beitritts mindestens eines persönlich haftenden Gesellschaf-

---

° This heading reflects the meaning of the text instead of the literal translation of the German text.

ters. Der Beitritt muß gerichtlich oder notariell beurkundet werden. Hierbei haben die persönlich haftenden Gesellschafter die Satzungsänderungen zu genehmigen.

(3) Der Gesellschafterversammlung, die über die Umwandlung beschließen soll, ist eine Bilanz vorzulegen, in der die Vermögensgegenstände und Verbindlichkeiten der Gesellschaft mit dem Wert angesetzt sind, der ihnen am Bilanzstichtag beizulegen ist. Die Bilanz ist auf den Stichtag aufzustellen, von dem ab die persönlich haftenden Gesellschafter am Gewinn oder Verlust der Gesellschaft teilnehmen sollen. Liegt dieser Stichtag nach der Beschlußfassung über die Umwandlung, so ist die Bilanz auf einen höchstens sechs Monate vor der Beschlußfassung über die Umwandlung liegenden Stichtag aufzustellen. § 175 Abs. 2 gilt sinngemäß. Die Bilanz ist der Niederschrift als Anlage beizufügen.

(4) Für die Umwandlung gelten sinngemäß die §§ 26, 27, 32 bis 35, 38, 46 bis 53. An die Stelle der Gründer treten die Gesellschafter, die für die Umwandlung gestimmt haben, sowie die persönlich haftenden Gesellschafter. Die Frist von zwei Jahren nach § 52 Abs. 1 wird von der Eintragung der Umwandlung in das Handelsregister gerechnet.

(5) Für die Zusammensetzung des Aufsichtsrats der Kommanditgesellschaft auf Aktien gilt § 363 sinngemäß.

§ 390
Anmeldung der Umwandlung

Zugleich mit dem Umwandlungsbeschluß sind die persönlich haftenden Gesellschafter zur Eintragung in das Handelsregister anzumelden. Die Urkunden über ihren Beitritt sind für das Gericht des Sitzes der Gesellschaft in Ausfertigung oder öffentlich beglaubigter Abschrift beizufügen.

§ 391
Wirkung der Eintragung

Von der Eintragung der Umwandlung an besteht die Gesellschaft als Kommanditgesellschaft auf Aktien weiter. Das Stammkapital ist zum Grundkapital, die Geschäftsanteile sind zu Aktien geworden. Die an einem Geschäftsanteil bestehenden Rechte Dritter bestehen an der an die Stelle tretenden Aktie weiter. Die persönlich haftenden Gesellschafter haften den Gläubigern der Gesellschaft auch für die bereits bestehenden Verbindlichkeiten unbeschränkt.

associating as a general partner must be in the form of a judicial or notarial record. At the same time, the general partners shall approve the amendments to the articles of incorporation.

(3) A balance sheet in which the company's assets and liabilities are stated at the value attributable to them as of the closing date of the balance sheet shall be submitted to the quotaholders' meeting which is to adopt the resolution concerning the transformation. The balance sheet shall be prepared as of the closing date on which the general partners begin participation in the company's profits and losses. If this closing date is later than the date of the resolution concerning the transformation, the balance sheet shall be prepared as of a closing date which precedes the date of the resolution concerning the transformation by no more than six months. § 175, paragraph 2, shall apply *mutatis mutandis*. The balance sheet shall be attached to the minutes.

(4) §§ 26, 27, 32 to 35, 38, and 46 to 53 shall apply, *mutatis mutandis*, to the transformation. For the incorporators there shall be substituted the quotaholders who voted for the transformation and the general partners. The two-year period referred to in § 52, paragraph 1, shall be computed from the date the transformation is recorded in the Commercial Register.

(5) § 363 shall apply, *mutatis mutandis*, to the composition of the supervisory board of the partnership limited by shares.

§ 390
Application to Record Transformation

The application to record the resolution authorizing the transformation in the Commercial Register shall be filed together with the application to record the general partners. A duplicate original or certified copy of the documents concerning their association as general partners shall be attached for the record of the court at the company's domicile.

§ 391
Effect of Registration

Following the registration of the transformation, the company shall exist as a partnership limited by shares. The stated capital of the limited liability company shall become its stated capital, and the quotas shall become shares. Rights of third parties existing in a quota shall subsist with respect to the share replacing it. The general partners shall be personally liable to the creditors of the company for preexisting obligations.

§ 391

§ 392

Application of Provisions on Transformation into Stock Corporation

Unless the foregoing provisions or the fact that there is no managing board requires a different result, the provisions concerning the transformation of a limited liability company into a stock corporation shall apply *mutatis mutandis*.

Eighth Division

Transformation of Mining Company into Partnership Limited by Shares

§ 393

(1) A mining company having separate legal personality may be transformed into a partnership limited by shares.

(2) §§ 389 to 391 shall apply, *mutatis mutandis*, to the transformation, as shall the provisions concerning the transformation of a mining company into a stock corporation, except to the extent that such provisions or the fact that there is no managing board requires a different result.

(3) § 363 shall apply, *mutatis mutandis*, to the composition of the supervisory board of the partnership limited by shares.

Book Five

Special, Penal, and Final Provisions

Part One

Special Provisions on Participation of Political Entities

§ 394

Reports of Members of Supervisory Board

Members of the supervisory board elected or delegated to the supervisory board at the instance of political entities shall not be bound by a duty of secrecy with respect to any reports they are required to submit to such political entity. This shall not, however, apply to confidential information and secrets of the company, in particular, trade or business secrets, if knowledge thereof is not relevant to the purpose of such reports.

§ 392

§ 392

Anwendbarkeit der Vorschriften über die Umwandlung in eine Aktiengesellschaft

Soweit sich aus den vorstehenden Vorschriften oder aus dem Fehlen eines Vorstands nichts anderes ergibt, sind die Vorschriften über die Umwandlung einer Gesellschaft mit beschränkter Haftung in eine Aktiengesellschaft sinngemäß anzuwenden.

Achter Abschnitt

Umwandlung einer bergrechtlichen Gewerkschaft in eine Kommanditgesellschaft auf Aktien

§ 393

(1) Eine bergrechtliche Gewerkschaft mit eigener Rechtspersönlichkeit kann in eine Kommanditgesellschaft auf Aktien umgewandelt werden.

(2) Für die Umwandlung gelten die §§ 389 bis 391 und, soweit sich aus ihnen oder aus dem Fehlen eines Vorstands nichts anderes ergibt, die Vorschriften über die Umwandlung einer bergrechtlichen Gewerkschaft in eine Aktiengesellschaft sinngemäß.

(3) Für die Zusammensetzung des Aufsichtsrats der Kommanditgesellschaft auf Aktien gilt § 363 sinngemäß.

Fünftes Buch

Sonder-, Straf- und Schlußvorschriften

Erster Teil

Sondervorschriften bei Beteiligung von Gebietskörperschaften

§ 394

Berichte der Aufsichtsratsmitglieder

Aufsichtsratsmitglieder, die auf Veranlassung einer Gebietskörperschaft in den Aufsichtsrat gewählt oder entsandt worden sind, unterliegen hinsichtlich der Berichte, die sie der Gebietskörperschaft zu erstatten haben, keiner Verschwiegenheitspflicht. Für vertrauliche Angaben und Geheimnisse der Gesellschaft, namentlich Betriebs- oder Geschäftsgeheimnisse, gilt dies nicht, wenn ihre Kenntnis für die Zwecke der Berichte nicht von Bedeutung ist.

§ 395

Verschwiegenheitspflicht

(1) Personen, die damit betraut sind, die Beteiligungen einer Gebietskörperschaft zu verwalten oder für eine Gebietskörperschaft die Gesellschaft, die Betätigung der Gebietskörperschaft als Aktionär oder die Tätigkeit der auf Veranlassung der Gebietskörperschaft gewählten oder entsandten Aufsichtsratsmitglieder zu prüfen, haben über vertrauliche Angaben und Geheimnisse der Gesellschaft, namentlich Betriebs- oder Geschäftsgeheimnisse, die ihnen aus Berichten nach § 394 bekanntgeworden sind, Stillschweigen zu bewahren; dies gilt nicht für Mitteilungen im dienstlichen Verkehr.

(2) Bei der Veröffentlichung von Prüfungsergebnissen dürfen vertrauliche Angaben und Geheimnisse der Gesellschaft, namentlich Betriebs- oder Geschäftsgeheimnisse, nicht veröffentlicht werden.

Zweiter Teil

Gerichtliche Auflösung

§ 396

Voraussetzungen

(1) Gefährdet eine Aktiengesellschaft oder Kommanditgesellschaft auf Aktien durch gesetzwidriges Verhalten ihrer Verwaltungsträger das Gemeinwohl und sorgen der Aufsichtsrat und die Hauptversammlung nicht für eine Abberufung der Verwaltungsträger, so kann die Gesellschaft auf Antrag der zuständigen obersten Landesbehörde des Landes, in dem die Gesellschaft ihren Sitz hat, durch Urteil aufgelöst werden. Ausschließlich zuständig für die Klage ist das Landgericht, in dessen Bezirk die Gesellschaft ihren Sitz hat.

(2) Nach der Auflösung findet die Abwicklung nach den §§ 264 bis 273 statt. Den Antrag auf Abberufung oder Bestellung der Abwickler aus einem wichtigen Grund kann auch die in Absatz 1 Satz 1 bestimmte Behörde stellen.

§ 397

Anordnungen bei der Auflösung

Ist die Auflösungsklage erhoben, so kann das Gericht auf Antrag der in § 396 Abs. 1 Satz 1 bestimmten Behörde durch einstweilige Verfügung die nötigen Anordnungen treffen.

§ 395

Duty of Secrecy

(1) Persons who are in charge of the administration of equity interests held by a political entity, or who, on behalf of such political entity, are in charge of the examination of the company, the activities of the political entity in its capacity as shareholder, or the activities of members of the supervisory board elected or delegated at the instance of the political entity, shall not disclose any confidential information and secrets of the company, in particular, trade or business secrets of which they obtained knowledge by virtue of the reports referred to in § 394; this shall not, however, apply with respect to intergovernmental communications.

(2) The publication of the results of the examination shall not make public confidential information and secrets of the company, in particular, trade or business secrets.

Part Two

Judicial Dissolution

§ 396

Prerequisites

(1) If a stock corporation or partnership limited by shares, because of the unlawful conduct of its management, endangers the public welfare, and if the supervisory board and the shareholders do not cause the dismissal of the management, such company may, upon application of the competent highest governmental authority of the State *(Land)* in which the company is domiciled, be dissolved by judicial decision. The district court in whose district the company is domiciled shall have exclusive jurisdiction to adjudicate such actions.

(2) After dissolution, the company shall be liquidated in accordance with the provisions of §§ 264 to 273. The application for the dismissal or appointment of liquidators for a compelling reason may also be made by the authority referred to in paragraph 1, first sentence, hereof.

§ 397

Interim Measures
in Case of Dissolution

If an action for dissolution has been brought, the court may, on application of the authority referred to in § 396, paragraph 1, first sentence, take the necessary interim measures by means of preliminary injunctions.

§ 397

§ 398
Registration

The decisions of the court shall be reported to the court of registry. To the extent that such decisions concern legal relationships that are required to be recorded, that court shall record them in the Commercial Register.

§ 398
Eintragung

Die Entscheidungen des Gerichts sind dem Registergericht mitzuteilen. Dieses trägt sie, soweit sie eintragungspflichtige Rechtsverhältnisse betreffen, in das Handelsregister ein.

Part Three
Provisions Concerning Penalties and Fines.
Final Provisions

Dritter Teil
Straf- und Bußgeldvorschriften. Schlußvorschriften

§ 399
False Statements

(1) Whoever,

1. as incorporator or as member of the managing board or of the supervisory board, for purposes of registration of the company, concerning the subscription to shares, the payments effected on shares, the disposition of amounts paid in, the amount for which shares are issued, preferences, costs of formation, contributions of assets, and acquisitions of assets, or

2. as incorporator or as member of the managing board or of the supervisory board, in the report on the formation, in the report on post-formation acquisitions, or in the audit report, or

3. in the official publication provided for in § 47, No. 3, or

4. as member of the managing board or of the supervisory board, for purposes of the registration of a capital increase (§§ 182 to 206), concerning the collection of amounts payable on the existing stated capital, the subscription to or the collection of amounts payable on the new capital, the amount for which the shares were issued, the issuance of shares pursuant to preemptive rights, or concerning assets contributed, or

5. as liquidator, for purposes of the registration of the continuation of the company, in the statement to be submitted pursuant to § 274, paragraph 3,

makes false statements or fails to disclose material facts shall be punished by imprisonment for not more than three years or by a fine, or by both.

(2) Whoever, as member of the managing board or of the supervisory board, for purposes of the registration of a capital increase, falsely

§ 399
Falsche Angaben

(1) Mit Gefängnis bis zu drei Jahren und mit Geldstrafe oder mit einer dieser Strafen wird bestraft, wer

1. als Gründer oder als Mitglied des Vorstands oder des Aufsichtsrats zum Zweck der Eintragung der Gesellschaft über die Übernahme der Aktien, die Einzahlung auf Aktien, die Verwendung eingezahlter Beträge, den Ausgabebetrag der Aktien, über Sondervorteile, Gründungsaufwand, Sacheinlagen und Sachübernahmen,

2. als Gründer oder als Mitglied des Vorstands oder des Aufsichtsrats im Gründungsbericht, im Nachgründungsbericht oder im Prüfungsbericht,

3. in der öffentlichen Ankündigung nach § 47 Nr. 3,

4. als Mitglied des Vorstands oder des Aufsichtsrats zum Zweck der Eintragung einer Erhöhung des Grundkapitals (§§ 182 bis 206) über die Einbringung des bisherigen, die Zeichnung oder Einbringung des neuen Kapitals, den Ausgabebetrag der Aktien, die Ausgabe der Bezugsaktien oder über Sacheinlagen, oder

5. als Abwickler zum Zweck der Eintragung der Fortsetzung der Gesellschaft in dem nach § 274 Abs. 3 zu führenden Nachweis

falsche Angaben macht oder erhebliche Umstände verschweigt.

(2) Ebenso wird bestraft, wer als Mitglied des Vorstands oder des Aufsichtsrats zum Zweck der Eintragung einer Erhöhung des Grundkapitals die in

§ 210 Abs. 1 Satz 2 vorgeschriebene Erklärung oder als Mitglied des Vorstands zum Zweck der Eintragung einer Umwandlung der Gesellschaft in eine Gesellschaft mit beschränkter Haftung die in § 371 Abs. 2 Satz 1 oder 2 oder Abs. 3 Satz 1 vorgeschriebene Erklärung der Wahrheit zuwider abgibt.

issues the declaration required pursuant to § 210, paragraph 1, second sentence, or, as a member of the supervisory board, for purposes of the registration of a transformation of the company into a limited liability company, falsely issues the declaration required pursuant to § 371, paragraph 2, first or second sentence, or paragraph 3, first sentence, shall be punished in the same manner.

§ 400
Unrichtige Darstellung

Mit Gefängnis bis zu drei Jahren und mit Geldstrafe oder mit einer dieser Strafen wird bestraft, wer als Mitglied des Vorstands oder des Aufsichtsrats oder als Abwickler

1. die Verhältnisse der Gesellschaft einschließlich ihrer Beziehungen zu verbundenen Unternehmen in Darstellungen oder Übersichten über den Vermögensstand, in Vorträgen oder Auskünften in der Hauptversammlung unrichtig wiedergibt oder verschleiert,

2. die Verhältnisse eines Konzerns oder Teilkonzerns, für den die Gesellschaft einen Konzernabschluß oder Teilkonzernabschluß aufzustellen hat, in Darstellungen oder Übersichten über den Vermögensstand des Konzerns oder Teilkonzerns unrichtig wiedergibt oder verschleiert,

3. in Aufklärungen und Nachweisen, die nach den Vorschriften dieses Gesetzes einem Abschlußprüfer oder sonstigen Prüfer der Gesellschaft oder eines verbundenen Unternehmens oder einem Konzernabschlußprüfer zu geben sind, falsche Angaben macht oder die Verhältnisse der Gesellschaft oder des Konzerns unrichtig wiedergibt oder verschleiert, oder

4. im Geschäftsbericht, im Konzerngeschäftsbericht oder Teilkonzerngeschäftsbericht über die Gegenstände nach § 160 Abs. 3 oder § 334 Abs. 3 Nr. 1 bis 3 falsche Angaben macht oder erhebliche Umstände verschweigt.

§ 400
Misrepresentation

Whoever, as member of the managing board or of the supervisory board, or as liquidator,

1. in personal presentations or information furnished at the shareholders' meeting, falsely reflects or conceals the actual condition of the company, including its dealings with related enterprises, in statements or summaries concerning its assets, or

2. in presentations or summaries concerning the assets of the affiliated group of companies or partial affiliated group of companies, falsely reflects or conceals the actual condition of an affiliated group of companies or partial affiliated group of companies for which the company is required to prepare consolidated financial statements or partial consolidated financial statements, or

3. in disclosures or statements required to be rendered, pursuant to provisions of this Act, to an annual auditor or other auditor of the company or of a related enterprise, or to the annual auditor of consolidated financial statements, makes false statements about, or falsely reflects or conceals, the actual condition of the company or of the affiliated group of companies, or

4. in the business report, the consolidated business report, or the partial consolidated business report, makes false statements or fails to disclose material facts with respect to the items referred to in § 160, paragraph 3, or § 334, paragraph 3, Nos. 1 to 3,

shall be punished by imprisonment for not more than three years or by a fine, or by both.

§ 401
Pflichtverletzung bei Verlust, Überschuldung oder Zahlungsunfähigkeit

(1) Mit Gefängnis bis zu drei Jahren und mit Geldstrafe oder mit einer dieser Strafen wird bestraft, wer es

1. als Mitglied des Vorstands entgegen § 92 Abs. 1 unterläßt, bei einem Verlust in Höhe der Hälfte

§ 401
Violation of Duty in Case of Loss, Excess of Liabilities over Assets, or Insolvency

(1) Whoever,

1. as member of the managing board, in violation of § 92, paragraph 1, in the event of a loss

§ **401**

amounting to one-half of the stated capital, fails to call a shareholders' meeting and to notify it of this fact, or

2. as member of the managing board, in violation of § 92, paragraph 2, or as liquidator, in violation of § 268, paragraph 2, first sentence, in the event of insolvency or excess of liabilities over assets, fails to file a petition with the court to order bankruptcy proceedings or composition proceedings with the creditors,

shall be punished by imprisonment for not more than three years or by a fine, or by both.

(2) If such person acts negligently, he shall be punished by imprisonment for up to one year or by a fine, or by both.

des Grundkapitals die Hauptversammlung einzuberufen und ihr dies anzuzeigen, oder

2. als Mitglied des Vorstands entgegen § 92 Abs. 2 oder als Abwickler entgegen § 268 Abs. 2 Satz 1 unterläßt, bei Zahlungsunfähigkeit oder Uberschuldung die Eröffnung des Konkursverfahrens oder des gerichtlichen Vergleichsverfahrens zu beantragen.

(2) Handelt der Täter fahrlässig, so ist die Strafe Gefängnis bis zu einem Jahr und Geldstrafe oder eine dieser Strafen.

§ 402
False Issuance or Falsification of Certificates of Deposit

(1) Whoever falsely issues or falsifies certificates concerning the deposit of shares or interim certificates designed to evidence the right to vote in a shareholders' meeting or a separate meeting shall be punished by imprisonment for not more than three years or by a fine, or by both, provided that such act is not subject to more severe penalties under other criminal provisions concerning documents.

(2) The same penalties shall be imposed on whoever makes use of a false or falsified certificate of the kind referred to in paragraph 1 hereof for the purpose of exercising voting rights.

(3) The attempt shall be punishable.

§ 402
Falsche Ausstellung oder Verfälschung von Hinterlegungsbescheinigungen

(1) Wer über die Hinterlegung von Aktien oder Zwischenscheinen Bescheinigungen, die zum Nachweis des Stimmrechts in einer Hauptversammlung oder in einer gesonderten Versammlung dienen sollen, falsch ausstellt oder verfälscht, wird mit Gefängnis bis zu drei Jahren und mit Geldstrafe oder mit einer dieser Strafen bestraft, wenn die Tat nicht in anderen Vorschriften über Urkundenstraftaten mit schwererer Strafe bedroht ist.

(2) Ebenso wird bestraft, wer von einer falschen oder verfälschten Bescheinigung der in Absatz 1 bezeichneten Art zur Ausübung des Stimmrechts Gebrauch macht.

(3) Der Versuch ist strafbar.

§ 403
Violation of Duty to Report

(1) Whoever, as auditor or as assistant to an auditor, renders a false report on the results of an audit or fails to disclose material facts in the report shall be punished by imprisonment for not more than three years or by a fine, or by both.

(2) If such person acted for a consideration or with the intent of profiting himself or another, or of causing a detriment to another, the penalty shall be imprisonment. In addition, a fine may be imposed.

§ 403
Verletzung der Berichtspflicht

(1) Mit Gefängnis bis zu drei Jahren und mit Geldstrafe oder mit einer dieser Strafen wird bestraft, wer als Prüfer oder als Gehilfe eines Prüfers über das Ergebnis der Prüfung falsch berichtet oder erhebliche Umstände im Bericht verschweigt.

(2) Handelt der Täter gegen Entgelt oder in der Absicht, sich oder einen anderen zu bereichern oder einen anderen zu schädigen, so ist die Strafe Gefängnis. Daneben kann auf Geldstrafe erkannt werden.

§ 404
Violation of Duty of Secrecy

(1) Whoever unlawfully discloses a secret of the company, in particular a trade or business

§ 404
Verletzung der Geheimhaltungspflicht

(1) Mit Gefängnis bis zu einem Jahr und mit Geldstrafe oder mit einer dieser Strafen wird be-

straft, wer ein Geheimnis der Gesellschaft, namentlich ein Betriebs- oder Geschäftsgeheimnis, das ihm in seiner Eigenschaft als

1. Mitglied des Vorstands oder des Aufsichtsrats oder Abwickler,

2. Prüfer oder Gehilfe eines Prüfers

bekanntgeworden ist, unbefugt offenbart.

(2) Handelt der Täter gegen Entgelt oder in der Absicht, sich oder einen anderen zu bereichern oder einen anderen zu schädigen, so ist die Strafe Gefängnis bis zu zwei Jahren; daneben kann auf Geldstrafe erkannt werden. Ebenso wird bestraft, wer ein Geheimnis der in Absatz 1 bezeichneten Art, namentlich ein Betriebs- oder Geschäftsgeheimnis, das ihm unter den Voraussetzungen des Absatzes 1 bekanntgeworden ist, unbefugt verwertet.

(3) Die Tat wird nur auf Antrag der Gesellschaft verfolgt. Der Antrag kann zurückgenommen werden. Hat ein Mitglied des Vorstands oder ein Abwickler die Tat begangen, so ist der Aufsichtsrat, hat ein Mitglied des Aufsichtsrats die Tat begangen, so sind der Vorstand oder die Abwickler antragsberechtigt.

§ 405
Ordnungswidrigkeiten

(1) Ordnungswidrig handelt, wer als Mitglied des Vorstands oder des Aufsichtsrats oder als Abwickler

1. Namensaktien ausgibt, in denen der Betrag der Teilleistung nicht angegeben ist, oder Inhaberaktien ausgibt, bevor auf sie der Nennbetrag oder der höhere Ausgabebetrag voll geleistet ist,

2. Aktien oder Zwischenscheine ausgibt, bevor die Gesellschaft oder im Fall einer Kapitalerhöhung die Durchführung der Erhöhung des Grundkapitals oder im Fall einer bedingten Kapitalerhöhung oder einer Kapitalerhöhung aus Gesellschaftsmitteln der Beschluß über die bedingte Kapitalerhöhung oder die Kapitalerhöhung aus Gesellschaftsmitteln eingetragen ist,

3. Aktien oder Zwischenscheine ausgibt, die auf einen geringeren als den nach § 8 zulässigen Mindestnennbetrag lauten oder

4. vorsätzlich oder leichtfertig nicht für die Einhaltung der §§ 178, 330 Abs. 1 Satz 2, § 338 Abs. 4 über Form und Inhalt der Bekanntmachung des Jahresabschlusses und des Geschäftsberichts, des Konzernabschlusses und des Konzerngeschäfts-

secret, of which he obtained knowledge in his capacity as

1. member of the managing board or of the supervisory board, or as liquidator, or

2. auditor or assistant to an auditor,

shall be punished by imprisonment for not more than one year or by a fine, or by both.

(2) If such person acted for a consideration or with the intent of profiting himself or another, or of causing a detriment to another, the penalty shall be imprisonment for not more than two years; in addition, a fine may be imposed. The same penalty shall be imposed on anyone who unlawfully uses a secret of the kind referred to in paragraph 1 hereof, in particular a trade or business secret, of which he obtained knowledge under the circumstances referred to in paragraph 1 hereof.

(3) The act shall be prosecuted only upon complaint of the company. This complaint can be withdrawn. The complaint may be filed by the supervisory board if a member of the managing board or a liquidator committed the act, or, if a member of the supervisory board committed the act, by the managing board or by the liquidators.

§ 405
Violations

(1) A violation is committed by whoever, as member of the managing board or of the supervisory board, or as liquidator,

1. issues registered share certificates which fail to state the amount of partial contributions, or issues bearer share certificates before full payment of the par amount plus any premium,

2. issues share certificates or interim certificates before the company has been recorded, or, in the event of a capital increase, before consummation of the capital increase, or, in the event of a conditional capital increase or a capital increase out of surplus, before the resolution concerning the conditional capital increase or the capital increase out of surplus has been recorded,

3. issues share certificates or interim certificates of a lower minimum par value than that permissible pursuant to § 8, or

4. willfully or recklessly fails to ensure compliance with §§ 178, 330, paragraph 1, second sentence, and § 338, paragraph 4, concerning the form and content of the publication of the annual financial statements and the business report, the consolidated financial statements

§ 405

and the consolidated business report, or the partial consolidated financial statement and the partial consolidated business report.

(2) A violation is committed also by whoever, as shareholder or representative of a shareholder, fails to make or fails to make correctly the statements required to be included in the list of shareholders pursuant to § 129.

(3) A violation is committed further by whoever

1. uses share certificates of another whom he is not authorized to represent, without such party's permission, to exercise rights in a shareholders' meeting or in a separate meeting,

2. uses share certificates of another to exercise rights in an annual shareholders' meeting or in a separate meeting, which shares he obtained for this purpose by granting or promising special advantages,

3. permits the use of share certificates for the purpose described in No. 2 hereof against the granting or the promise of special advantages,

4. uses share certificates of another to exercise voting rights which he or the party he represents may not exercise pursuant to § 135,

5. furnishes share certificates to another for the exercise of voting rights which he or the party he represents may not exercise pursuant to § 20, paragraph 7, § 21, paragraph 4, § 134, paragraph 1, §§ 135, 136, 142, paragraph 1, second sentence, or § 285, paragraph 1, or uses such share certificates received from another to exercise voting rights,

6. demands, obtains a promise of, or accepts special advantages in consideration of his refraining from voting or for voting in a prescribed manner in a shareholders' meeting or in a separate meeting, or

7. offers, promises, or grants special advantages to another in consideration of the latter's refraining from voting or voting in a prescribed manner in a shareholders' meeting or in a separate meeting.

(4) A willful violation may be punished by a fine of not more than fifty thousand German marks; a reckless violation, by a fine of not more than twenty thousand German marks.

berichts sowie des Teilkonzernabschlusses und des Teilkonzerngeschäftsberichts sorgt.

(2) Ordnungswidrig handelt auch, wer als Aktionär oder als Vertreter eines Aktionärs die nach § 129 in das Verzeichnis aufzunehmenden Angaben nicht oder nicht richtig macht.

(3) Ordnungswidrig handelt ferner, wer

1. Aktien eines anderen, zu dessen Vertretung er nicht befugt ist, ohne dessen Einwilligung zur Ausübung von Rechten in der Hauptversammlung oder in einer gesonderten Versammlung benutzt,

2. zur Ausübung von Rechten in der Hauptversammlung oder in einer gesonderten Versammlung Aktien eines anderen benutzt, die er sich zu diesem Zweck durch Gewähren oder Versprechen besonderer Vorteile verschafft hat,

3. Aktien zu dem in Nummer 2 bezeichneten Zweck gegen Gewähren oder Versprechen besonderer Vorteile einem anderen überläßt,

4. Aktien eines anderen, für die er oder der von ihm Vertretene das Stimmrecht nach § 135 nicht ausüben darf, zur Ausübung des Stimmrechts benutzt,

5. Aktien, für die er oder der von ihm Vertretene das Stimmrecht nach § 20 Abs. 7, § 21 Abs. 4, § 134 Abs. 1, §§ 135, 136, 142 Abs. 1 Satz 2, § 285 Abs. 1 nicht ausüben darf, einem anderen zum Zweck der Ausübung des Stimmrechts überläßt oder solche ihm überlassene Aktien zur Ausübung des Stimmrechts benutzt,

6. besondere Vorteile als Gegenleistung dafür fordert, sich versprechen läßt oder annimmt, daß er bei einer Abstimmung in der Hauptversammlung oder in einer gesonderten Versammlung nicht oder in einem bestimmten Sinne stimme oder

7. besondere Vorteile als Gegenleistung dafür anbietet, verspricht oder gewährt, daß jemand bei einer Abstimmung in der Hauptversammlung oder in einer gesonderten Versammlung nicht oder in einem bestimmten Sinne stimme.

(4) Die vorsätzliche Ordnungswidrigkeit kann mit einer Geldbuße bis zu fünfzigtausend Deutsche Mark, die leichtfertige Ordnungswidrigkeit mit einer Geldbuße bis zu zwanzigtausend Deutsche Mark geahndet werden.

§ 406

Statute of Limitations for Violations

The prosecution of the violations specified in § 405 shall be barred after two years.

§ 406

Verjährung von Ordnungswidrigkeiten

Die Verfolgung der Ordnungswidrigkeiten nach § 405 verjährt in zwei Jahren.

§ 407

Ordnungsstrafen

(1) Vorstandsmitglieder oder Abwickler, die § 52 Abs. 2 Satz 2 und 3, § 73 Abs. 3 Satz 2, §§ 80, 90, 104 Abs. 1, § 111 Abs. 2, §§ 145, 148, 160 Abs. 5, § 163 Abs. 1, 3 und 5, §§ 165, 170, 171 Abs. 3, §§ 175, 214 Abs. 1, § 246 Abs. 4, § 259 Abs. 5, § 268 Abs. 4, § 270 Abs. 1, § 273 Abs. 2, § 293 Abs. 3 Satz 2 und 3, § 306 Abs. 6, § 312 Abs. 1, § 313 Abs. 1, § 314 Abs. 1, §§ 329, 330, 336 Abs. 4, § 337 Abs. 1, § 340 Abs. 3 Satz 1 und 2, § 361 Abs. 2 Satz 1 und 2 nicht befolgen, sind hierzu vom Registergericht durch Ordnungsstrafen anzuhalten; § 14 des Handelsgesetzbuchs bleibt unberührt. Die einzelne Strafe darf den Betrag von zehntausend Deutsche Mark nicht übersteigen.

(2) Die Anmeldungen zum Handelsregister nach den §§ 36, 45, 52, 181 Abs. 1, §§ 184, 188, 195, 210, 223, 237 Abs. 4, §§ 274, 294 Abs. 1, § 319 Abs. 3, § 345 Abs. 1, § 353 Abs. 5, §§ 364, 367, 371, 379, 390 werden durch Ordnungsstrafen nicht erzwungen. Für die Einreichung der der Zahl der Zweigniederlassungen entsprechenden Stückzahl der Anmeldungen verbleibt es bei § 14 des Handelsgesetzbuchs.

§ 408

Strafbarkeit persönlich haftender Gesellschafter einer Kommanditgesellschaft auf Aktien

Die §§ 399 bis 407 gelten sinngemäß für die Kommanditgesellschaft auf Aktien. Soweit sie Vorstandsmitglieder betreffen, gelten sie bei der Kommanditgesellschaft auf Aktien für die persönlich haftenden Gesellschafter.

§ 409

Geltung in Berlin

Dieses Gesetz gilt nach Maßgabe des § 13 Abs. 1 des Dritten Überleitungsgesetzes vom 4. Januar 1952 (Bundesgesetzbl. I S. 1) auch im Land Berlin. Rechtsverordnung, die auf Grund dieses Gesetzes erlassen werden, gelten im Land Berlin nach § 14 des Dritten Überleitungsgesetzes.

§ 410

Inkrafttreten

Dieses Gesetz tritt am 1. Januar 1966 in Kraft.

§ 407
Enforcement by Fines

(1) The court of registry shall, notwithstanding the provisions of § 14 of the Commercial Code, impose fines to ensure compliance against members of the managing board or against liquidators who fail to comply with § 52, paragraph 2, second and third sentences, § 73, paragraph 3, second sentence, §§ 80, 90, 104, paragraph 1, § 111, paragraph 2, §§ 145, 148, 160, paragraph 5, § 163, paragraphs 1, 3 and 5, §§ 165, 170, 171, paragraph 3, §§ 175, 214, paragraph 1, § 246, paragraph 4, § 259, paragraph 5, § 268, paragraph 4, § 270, paragraph 1, § 273, paragraph 2, § 293, paragraph 3, second and third sentences, § 306, paragraph 6, § 312, paragraph 1, § 313, paragraph 1, § 314, paragraph 1, §§ 329, 330, 336, paragraph 4, § 337, paragraph 1, § 340, paragraph 3, first and second sentences, and § 361, paragraph 2, first and second sentences. Each such fine shall not exceed the amount of ten thousand German marks.

(2) No such fines shall be imposed to compel the filing of applications with the Commercial Register pursuant to §§ 36, 45, 52, 181, paragraph 1, §§ 184, 188, 195, 210, 223, 237, paragraph 4, §§ 274, 294, paragraph 1, § 319, paragraph 3, § 345, paragraph 1, § 353, paragraph 5, §§ 364, 367, 371, 379, and 390. Regarding the submission of applications sufficient in number to equal the number of branches, § 14 of the Commercial Code shall apply.

§ 408
Criminal Liability of General Partners of Partnership Limited by Shares

§§ 399 to 407 shall apply, *mutatis mutandis*, to partnerships limited by shares. Insofar as these provisions refer to members of the managing board, they shall, in the case of partnerships limited by shares, apply to the general partners.

§ 409
Application in Berlin

This Act shall also be applicable in the territory of Berlin, in accordance with § 13, paragraph 1, of the *Drittes Überleitungsgesetz*, dated January 4, 1952 (*Bundesgesetzblatt* I, page 1). Ordinances issued pursuant to this Act shall also be applicable in the territory of Berlin in accordance with § 14 of the *Drittes Überleitungsgesetz*.

§ 410
Effective Date

This Act shall enter into effect on January 1, 1966.

§ 410

LAW INTRODUCING THE STOCK CORPORATION ACT

(Einführungsgesetz zum Aktiengesetz)

of September 6, 1965

Summary   *Page*

First Division.   Transitional Provisions (§§ 1-26) 274
Second Division.   Application of Provisions of Stock Corporation Act to
                         Enterprises Having Different Legal Form (§§ 27-28) . . 284
Third Division.   Repeal and Amendment of Statutes (§§ 29-44) 285
Fourth Division.   Final Provisions (§§ 45-46) 285

First Division

Transitional Provisions

§ 1

Stated Capital

§ 6 of the Stock Corporation Act shall not apply to stock corporations the nominal value of whose stated capital and shares was not expressed in German marks at the effective date of the Stock Corporation Act, nor to corporations which, after the effective date of the Stock Corporation Act and in accordance with § 2 of the *D-Markbilanzergänzungsgesetz* of December 28, 1950 (*Bundesgesetzblatt*, page 811), transferred their domicile to the territory in which the Stock Corporation Act is effective. The currency in which the stated capital and shares of such companies must be expressed shall be determined by reference to the special provisions applicable to such stock corporations.

§ 2

Minimum Amount of Stated Capital

In the case of stock corporations whose stated capital amounts to less than one hundred thousand German marks in consequence of the fact that they were subject to a revaluation pursuant to the *D-Markbilanzgesetz*, the stated capital as revalued shall be deemed to be the minimum nominal amount within the meaning of § 7 of the Stock Corporation Act. However, if the circumstances of such companies change substantially, in particular if such companies substantially alter their corporate purpose or their charter, such changes shall be recorded only if the stated capital is increased to one hundred thousand German marks before or at the time such changes are made.

§ 1

Erster Abschnitt

Übergangsvorschriften

§ 1

Grundkapital

§ 6 des Aktiengesetzes gilt nicht für Aktiengesellschaften, deren Grundkapital und Aktien beim Inkrafttreten des Aktiengesetzes nicht auf einen Nennbetrag in Deutscher Mark lauten, sowie für Aktiengesellschaften, die nach dem Inkrafttreten des Aktiengesetzes nach Maßgabe des § 2 des D-Markbilanzergänzungsgesetzes vom 28. Dezember 1950 (Bundesgesetzbl. S. 811) ihren Sitz in den Geltungsbereich des Aktiengesetzes verlegen. Die Währung, auf die ihr Grundkapital und ihre Aktien lauten müssen, bestimmt sich nach den für sie geltenden besonderen Vorschriften.

§ 2

Mindestnennbetrag des Grundkapitals

Für Aktiengesellschaften, deren Grundkapital infolge der Neufestsetzung nach dem für sie geltenden D-Markbilanzgesetz weniger als einhunderttausend Deutsche Mark beträgt, gilt das neu festgesetzte Grundkapital als Mindestnennbetrag im Sinne des § 7 des Aktiengesetzes. Ändern jedoch solche Gesellschaften ihre Verhältnisse wesentlich, nehmen sie namentlich eine wesentliche Änderung des Gegenstands des Unternehmens oder ihrer Verfassung vor, so sind diese Änderungen nur einzutragen, wenn das Grundkapital spätestens zugleich mit den Änderungen auf einhunderttausend Deutsche Mark erhöht wird.

§ 3
Mindestnennbetrag der Aktien

(1) Aktien dürfen nur noch nach § 8 des Aktiengesetzes ausgegeben werden.

(2) Ist ein Beschluß über eine Kapitalerhöhung aus Gesellschaftsmitteln vor dem Inkrafttreten des Aktiengesetzes in das Handelsregister eingetragen worden, so bleibt es bei §§ 6, 12 Abs. 2 des Gesetzes über die Kapitalerhöhung aus Gesellschaftsmitteln und über die Gewinn- und Verlustrechnung vom 23. Dezember 1959 (Bundesgesetzbl. I S. 789).

(3) § 8 des Aktiengesetzes gilt nicht für Aktien, die vor dem Inkrafttreten des Aktiengesetzes nach den bisher geltenden Vorschriften mit einem nach § 8 des Aktiengesetzes nicht zulässigen Nennbetrag ausgegeben worden sind. Bei Aktien mit einem nicht durch hundert teilbaren Nennbetrag kann eine Kapitalerhöhung aus Gesellschaftsmitteln auch durch Erhöhung des Nennbetrags dieser Aktien ausgeführt werden; dies gilt nicht für Aktien mit einem Nennbetrag von fünfzig Deutsche Mark.

(4) Soweit eine Kapitalerhöhung aus Gesellschaftsmitteln durch Erhöhung des Nennbetrags ausgeführt werden kann, können Aktien mit einem nicht durch hundert teilbaren Nennbetrag, deren Nennbetrag erhöht wird, auf jeden durch zehn teilbaren Nennbetrag gestellt werden; Aktien mit einem Nennbetrag von fünfzig Deutsche Mark können nur auf einen durch hundert teilbaren Betrag gestellt werden. Der Nennbetrag darf jedoch nicht, wenn er unter fünfzig Deutsche Mark gestellt ist, über fünfzig Deutsche Mark, sonst nicht über den nächsten durch hundert teilbaren Betrag hinaus erhöht werden. Satz 2 gilt nicht für teileingezahlte Aktien.

(5) Soweit Aktiengesellschaften Aktien mit Nennbeträgen unter fünfzig Deutsche Mark ausgegeben haben, gilt der Nennbetrag dieser Aktien als ihr Mindestnennbetrag im Sinne der Vorschriften über die Kapitalherabsetzung.

§ 4
Vereinigung von Aktien

(1) Aktien, die nicht auf fünfzig Deutsche Mark oder auf einen durch hundert teilbaren Betrag lauten, können zu Aktien, die auf fünfzig Deutsche Mark oder auf einen durch hundert teilbaren Betrag lauten, vereinigt werden. Die Vereinigung bedarf

§ 3
Minimum Par Value of Shares

(1) Henceforth, shares may not be issued except in compliance with § 8 of the Stock Corporation Act.

(2) If a resolution to increase capital out of surplus was recorded in the Commercial Register prior to the effective date of the Stock Corporation Act, §§ 6 and 12, paragraph 2, of the *Gesetz über die Kapitalerhöhung aus Gesellschaftsmitteln und über die Gewinn- und Verlustrechnung* of December 23, 1959 (*Bundesgesetzblatt* I, page 789) shall be applicable.

(3) § 8 of the Stock Corporation Act shall not apply to shares having a par value that would not be permissible pursuant to § 8 of the Stock Corporation Act, if such shares were issued prior to the effective date of the Stock Corporation Act in accordance with the provisions then in effect. In the case of shares having a par value that is not divisible by one hundred, a capital increase out of surplus may also be effected by an increase in the par value of such shares; this shall not apply to shares with a par value of fifty German marks.

(4) To the extent that a capital increase out of surplus can be effected by increasing the par value, shares having a par value not divisible by one hundred whose par value is increased may be issued at any par value divisible by ten; shares having a par value of fifty German marks may be issued only at a par value divisible by one hundred. The par value may not, however, be increased to more than fifty German marks if it is under fifty German marks and, if it is over, to more than the next higher amount divisible by one hundred. The second sentence hereof shall not apply to partially paid-in shares.

(5) Where corporations have issued shares having a par value of less than fifty German marks, the par value of such shares shall be deemed their minimum par value within the meaning of the provisions concerning capital reductions.

§ 4
Consolidation of Shares

(1) Shares not having a par value of fifty German marks or of an amount divisible by one hundred may be consolidated to form shares having a par value of fifty German marks or of an

§ 4

amount divisible by one hundred. Such consolidation shall require the approval of the shareholders concerned. §§ 73 and 226 of the Stock Corporation Act shall not be applicable.

(2) The provisions of the articles of incorporation required by § 23, paragraph 3, No. 4, of the Stock Corporation Act may not be amended until the shareholders concerned have approved the consolidation of their shares and, in the event that share certificates or interim certificates were issued, not before such certificates are returned to the company or to an agency designated by it for the exchange. The supervisory board may adopt the resolution effecting this amendment of the articles of incorporation.

(3) Shares having a higher par value may not be issued before the necessary amendment of the articles of incorporation has been recorded in the Commercial Register.

§ 5
Multiple Voting Rights

(1) Multiple voting rights lawfully created prior to the effective date of the Stock Corporation Act shall remain in effect.

(2) The shareholders may adopt a resolution to abolish or to limit such multiple voting rights. A resolution to this effect shall require a majority of no less than three-fourths of the stated capital represented when the resolution is adopted, but not a majority of the votes cast. A separate resolution of the holders of shares with multiple voting rights is not required. If such multiple voting rights were granted to a shareholder because, as compared to other shareholders, he has rendered or will render special contributions to the company in addition to his capital contribution, the company shall grant him a reasonable compensation. An action for such compensation must be brought within a two-month period. This period shall be computed from the date on which the registration of the amendment of the articles of incorporation in the Commercial Register is deemed to have been published in accordance with § 10 of the Commercial Code. If an action was brought to set aside the shareholders' resolution, the period shall be computed from the date when the decision dismissing the complaint becomes final or when the action is withdrawn.

§ 6
Interlocking Enterprises

(1) If, at the effective date of the Stock Corporation Act, a stock corporation and another

der Zustimmung der betroffenen Aktionäre. §§ 73 und 226 des Aktiengesetzes sind nicht anzuwenden.

(2) Die nach § 23 Abs. 3 Nr. 4 des Aktiengesetzes erforderlichen Bestimmungen der Satzung dürfen nicht geändert werden, ehe die betroffenen Aktionäre der Vereinigung ihrer Aktien zugestimmt haben und, falls Aktienurkunden oder Zwischenscheine ausgegeben sind, die Urkunden der Gesellschaft oder einer von ihr bezeichneten Stelle zum Umtausch eingereicht haben. Über diese Satzungsänderung kann der Aufsichtsrat beschließen.

(3) Die Aktien höheren Nennbetrags sollen nicht ausgegeben werden, ehe die notwendige Satzungsänderung in das Handelsregister eingetragen ist.

§ 5
Mehrstimmrechte

(1) Mehrstimmrechte, die vor dem Inkrafttreten des Aktiengesetzes rechtmäßig geschaffen worden sind, bleiben aufrechterhalten.

(2) Die Hauptversammlung kann beschließen, die Mehrstimmrechte zu beseitigen oder zu beschränken. Der Beschluß bedarf einer Mehrheit, die mindestens drei Viertel des bei der Beschlußfassung vertretenen Grundkapitals umfaßt, aber nicht der Mehrheit der abgegebenen Stimmen. Eines Sonderbeschlusses der Aktionäre mit Mehrstimmrechten bedarf es nicht. Sind die Mehrstimmrechte einem Aktionär gewährt worden, weil er im Verhältnis zu den anderen Aktionären neben der Einlage auf das Grundkapital besondere Leistun_ _ für die Gesellschaft erbracht hat oder erbringt, so hat ihm die Gesellschaft ein angemessenes Entgelt zu gewähren. Der Anspruch ist binnen zwei Monaten gerichtlich geltend zu machen. Die Frist beginnt mit dem Tage, an dem die Eintragung der Satzungsänderung in das Handelsregister nach § 10 des Handelsgesetzbuchs als bekanntgemacht gilt. Ist gegen den Beschluß der Hauptversammlung eine Anfechtungsklage erhoben worden, so beginnt die Frist mit der rechtskräftigen Abweisung oder der Zurücknahme der Anfechtungsklage.

§ 6
Wechselseitig beteiligte Unternehmen

(1) Sind eine Aktiengesellschaft und ein anderes Unternehmen bereits beim Inkrafttreten des Aktien-

gesetzes wechselseitig beteiligte Unternehmen, ohne daß die Voraussetzungen des § 19 Abs. 2 oder 3 des Aktiengesetzes vorliegen, und haben beide Unternehmen fristgemäß (§ 7) die Mitteilung nach § 20 Abs. 3 oder § 21 Abs. 1 des Aktiengesetzes gemacht, so gilt § 328 Abs. 1 und 2 des Aktiengesetzes für sie nicht.

(2) Solange die Unternehmen wechselseitig beteiligt sind und nicht die Voraussetzungen des § 19 Abs. 2 oder 3 des Aktiengesetzes vorliegen, gilt für die Ausübung der Rechte aus den Anteilen an dem anderen Unternehmen statt dessen folgendes:

1. Aus den Anteilen, die den Unternehmen beim Inkrafttreten des Aktiengesetzes gehört haben oder die auf diese Anteile bei einer Kapitalerhöhung aus Gesellschaftsmitteln entfallen, können alle Rechte ausgeübt werden.
2. Aus Anteilen, die bei einer Kapitalerhöhung gegen Einlagen auf Grund eines nach Nummer 1 bestehenden Bezugsrechts übernommen werden, können alle Rechte mit Ausnahme des Stimmrechts ausgeübt werden; das gleiche gilt für Anteile, die auf diese Anteile bei einer Kapitalerhöhung aus Gesellschaftsmitteln entfallen.
3. Aus anderen Anteilen können mit Ausnahme des Rechts auf neue Aktien bei einer Kapitalerhöhung aus Gesellschaftsmitteln keine Rechte ausgeübt werden.

(3) Hat nur eines der wechselseitig beteiligten Unternehmen fristgemäß (§ 7) die Mitteilung nach § 20 Abs. 3 oder § 21 Abs. 1 des Aktiengesetzes gemacht, so gilt § 328 Abs. 1 und 2 nicht für dieses Unternehmen.

§ 7
Mitteilungspflicht von Beteiligungen

Die Mitteilungspflichten nach §§ 20, 21 und 328 Abs. 3 des Aktiengesetzes gelten auch für Beteiligungen, die beim Inkrafttreten des Aktiengesetzes bestehen. Die Beteiligungen sind binnen eines Monats nach dem Inkrafttreten des Aktiengesetzes mitzuteilen.

§ 8
Gegenstand des Unternehmens

Entspricht bei Aktiengesellschaften, die beim Inkrafttreten des Aktiengesetzes in das Handelsregister eingetragen sind, die Satzungsbestimmung über den Gegenstand des Unternehmens nicht dem

---

enterprise already exist as interlocking enterprises and do not meet the requirements of § 19, paragraph 2 or 3, of the Stock Corporation Act, and if such enterprises have timely filed (§ 7) the information required by § 20, paragraph 3, or § 21, paragraph 1, of the Stock Corporation Act, § 328, paragraphs 1 and 2, of the Stock Corporation Act shall not apply to them.

(2) For as long as the enterprises are interlocking and the requirements of § 19, paragraph 2 or 3, of the Stock Corporation Act are not met, the following shall apply with regard to the exercise of the rights as a shareholder in the other enterprise:

1. All rights pertaining to shares owned by the enterprises at the effective date of the Stock Corporation Act or in shares thereafter issued for such shares as a result of a capital increase out of surplus may be freely exercised.
2. All rights, except the right to vote, pertaining to shares which were acquired by exercising preemptive rights as described in No. 1 hereof in connection with a capital increase against contributions may be freely exercised; the same shall apply with respect to shares thereafter issued for such shares as a result of a capital increase out of surplus.
3. Rights pertaining to all other shares may not be exercised, except the preemptive right to new shares in the case of a capital increase out of surplus.

(3) If only one of the interlocking enterprises has timely submitted (§ 7) the information required by § 20, paragraph 3, or § 21, paragraph 1, of the Stock Corporation Act, § 328, paragraphs 1 and 2, shall not apply to such enterprise.

§ 7
Duty to Report Equity Interests

The duties to report set forth in §§ 20, 21, and 328, paragraph 3, of the Stock Corporation Act shall also apply to equity interests existing at the effective date of the Stock Corporation Act. Such equity interests shall be reported within one month from the effective date of the Stock Corporation Act.

§ 8
Purpose of the Company

If, in the case of stock corporations recorded in the Commercial Register prior to the effective date of the Stock Corporation Act, the provisions in the articles of incorporation concerning the

§ 8

purpose of the enterprise do not comply with § 23, paragraph 3, No. 2, of the Stock Corporation Act, shareholders' resolutions amending the articles of incorporation shall be recorded only if, at the same time, the purpose clause is amended so as to conform it to § 23, paragraph 3, No. 2, of the Stock Corporation Act.

§ 9
Registered Shares

Stock corporations which issued registered shares prior to the effective date of the Stock Corporation Act and whose articles of incorporation do not state whether shares are to be issued as bearer or registered shares are required to amend their articles of incorporation so as to provide that the shares shall be in registered form. This amendment may be passed by the supervisory board. Other amendments to the articles of incorporation may be recorded in the Commercial Register only after the amendment to the articles of incorporation pursuant to the first sentence hereof has been recorded.

§ 10
Other Obligations of the Shareholders

§ 55, paragraph 1, second sentence, of the Stock Corporation Act shall not apply to stock corporations whose articles of incorporation already provided for other obligations on the part of shareholders prior to the effective date of the Stock Corporation Act. However, if such companies change their purpose or amend the provisions of the articles of incorporation relating to other obligations, such amendments shall be recorded only if, at the same time, it is specified expressly whether the obligations are to be performed gratuitously or for a consideration.

§ 11
Expulsion of Shareholders in Default

§ 64, paragraph 2, third sentence, of the Stock Corporation Act shall not apply if prior to the effective date of the Stock Corporation Act the first announcement had already appeared in the publications designated in the company's articles of incorporation and if compliance with that provision would prevent timely publication of the final announcement.

§ 12
Supervisory Board

(1) Provisions of the articles of incorporation concerning the number of members of the super-

§ 9

§ 23 Abs. 3 Nr. 2 des Aktiengesetzes, so sind Änderungen der Satzung durch die Hauptversammlung nur einzutragen, wenn zugleich die Satzungsbestimmung über den Gegenstand des Unternehmens an § 23 Abs. 3 Nr. 2 des Aktiengesetzes angepaßt wird.

§ 9
Namensaktien

Aktiengesellschaften, die vor dem Inkrafttreten des Aktiengesetzes Namensaktien ausgegeben haben und deren Satzung nichts darüber bestimmt, ob die Aktien als Inhaber- oder Namensaktien auszustellen sind, haben ihre Satzung dahin zu ergänzen, daß die Aktien Namensaktien sind. Die Satzungsergänzung kann der Aufsichtsrat beschließen. Andere Änderungen der Satzung sind in das Handelsregister erst einzutragen, wenn zuvor die Satzungsergänzung nach Satz 1 eingetragen worden ist.

§ 10
Nebenverpflichtungen der Aktionäre

§ 55 Abs. 1 Satz 2 des Aktiengesetzes gilt nicht für Aktiengesellschaften, die bereits beim Inkrafttreten des Aktiengesetzes in ihrer Satzung Nebenverpflichtungen der Aktionäre vorgesehen haben. Ändern jedoch solche Gesellschaften den Gegenstand des Unternehmens oder die Satzungsbestimmungen über die Nebenverpflichtungen, so sind diese Änderungen nur einzutragen, wenn zugleich bestimmt wird, ob die Leistungen entgeltlich oder unentgeltlich zu erbringen sind.

§ 11
Ausschluß säumiger Aktionäre

§ 64 Abs. 2 Satz 3 des Aktiengesetzes gilt nicht, wenn beim Inkrafttreten des Aktiengesetzes bereits die erste Bekanntmachung in den Gesellschaftsblättern ergangen ist und bei Einhaltung der Vorschrift die letzte Bekanntmachung nicht rechtzeitig ergehen könnte.

§ 12
Aufsichtsrat

(1) Bestimmungen der Satzung über die Zahl der Aufsichtsratsmitglieder und über Stellvertreter von

Aufsichtsratsmitgliedern treten, soweit sie mit den Vorschriften des Aktiengesetzes nicht vereinbar sind, mit Beendigung der Hauptversammlung außer Kraft, die über die Entlastung der Mitglieder des Aufsichtsrats für das am 31. Dezember 1965 endende oder laufende Geschäftsjahr abgehalten wird, spätestens mit Ablauf der in § 120 Abs. 1 des Aktiengesetzes für die Beschlußfassung über die Entlastung bestimmten Frist. Eine Hauptversammlung, die innerhalb dieser Frist stattfindet, kann an Stelle der außer Kraft tretenden Satzungsbestimmungen mit einfacher Stimmenmehrheit neue Satzungsbestimmungen beschließen.

(2) Treten Satzungsbestimmungen nach Absatz 1 Satz 1 außer Kraft, erlischt das Amt der Aufsichtsratsmitglieder oder der Stellvertreter von Aufsichtsratsmitgliedern mit dem in Absatz 1 genannten Zeitpunkt.

(3) § 100 Abs. 2 des Aktiengesetzes gilt für Personen, die beim Inkrafttreten des Aktiengesetzes Aufsichtsratsmitglied sind, mit der Maßgabe, daß sie den Aufsichtsratssitz bis zum Ablauf der jeweilig laufenden Amtszeit innehaben dürfen.

§ 13
Hauptversammlung. Auskunftsrecht

(1) Die Vorschriften des Aktiengesetzes über die Einberufung der Hauptversammlung einschließlich der Vorschriften über die in die Bekanntmachung der Tagesordnung aufzunehmenden oder ihr beizufügenden Angaben und Erklärungen gelten ohne Rücksicht auf den Zeitpunkt der Einberufung für alle Hauptversammlungen, die nach dem Inkrafttreten des Aktiengesetzes stattfinden.

(2) Bei Anwendung des § 126 Abs. 2 Nr. 5 und 7 sind nur Hauptversammlungen zu berücksichtigen, die nach dem Inkrafttreten des Aktiengesetzes stattfinden.

(3) § 132 des Aktiengesetzes gilt nur, wenn die Auskunft in einer Hauptversammlung verweigert worden ist, die nach dem Inkrafttreten des Aktiengesetzes stattgefunden hat.

§ 14
Rechnungslegung

(1) Die Vorschriften des Aktiengesetzes über die Rechnungslegung gelten erstmals für das nach dem

visory board and substitutes of supervisory board members shall become ineffective, to the extent that they conflict with the provisions of the Stock Corporation Act, upon the adjournment of the shareholders' meeting in which the acts of the members of the managing board for the fiscal year ending on or after December 31, 1965, are ratified, but no later than upon expiration of the period specified in § 120, paragraph 1, of the Stock Corporation Act for the resolution concerning such ratification. A shareholders' meeting held within such period may, by simple majority, adopt a resolution to substitute new provisions for the provisions becoming ineffective.

(2) If any provisions of the articles of incorporation become ineffective pursuant to paragraph 1, first sentence, hereof, the term of office of the members of the supervisory board or of representatives of members of the supervisory board shall terminate at the time specified in paragraph 1 hereof.

(3) § 100, paragraph 2, of the Stock Corporation Act shall apply to persons who are members of the supervisory board on the effective date of the Stock Corporation Act; provided, however, that such persons may remain members of the supervisory board until expiration of their current term of office.

§ 13
Shareholders' Meeting. Right to Information

(1) The provisions of the Stock Corporation Act concerning the calling of a shareholders' meeting, including the provisions concerning statements and information to be included in or attached to the publication of the agenda, shall apply, regardless of when the meeting is called, to all shareholders' meetings taking place after the effective date of the Stock Corporation Act.

(2) In applying § 126, paragraph 2, Nos. 5 and 7, only such shareholders' meetings shall be taken into account as take place after the effective date of the Stock Corporation Act.

(3) § 132 of the Stock Corporation Act shall apply only if the information was refused in a shareholders' meeting which took place after the effective date of the Stock Corporation Act.

§ 14
Accounting

(1) The provisions of the Stock Corporation Act concerning accounting shall first be applied

§ 14

to the fiscal year commencing after December 31, 1966. They may, however, be applied to a previous fiscal year. When they are not applied to a previous fiscal year, that fiscal year shall be governed by the former statutory provisions.

(2) If fixed assets were shown in the annual financial statements for the fiscal year ending on or after December 31, 1966, at a value lower than that permissible according to §§ 153 and 154 of the Stock Corporation Act, such lower valuation may be continued. § 154, paragraph 1, of the Stock Corporation Act shall apply in such case, provided that the lower valuation is reduced by scheduled depreciations or adjustments which take into account the probable remaining useful life.

(3) If current assets were stated in the annual financial statements for the fiscal year ending on or after December 31, 1966, at a value lower than that permissible according to § 155 of the Stock Corporation Act, such lower valuation may be continued to the extent that:

1. such valuation was required by § 133, No. 3, third and fourth sentences, of the Stock Corporation Act of January 30, 1937 (*Reichsgesetzblatt* I, page 107), or

2. such valuation was adopted for the reasons set forth in § 155, paragraph 3, of the Stock Corporation Act.

(4) To the extent that a lower valuation for current assets may not be continued under paragraph 3 hereof, the managing board and the supervisory board may, in preparing the annual financial statements for the fiscal year commencing after December 31, 1966, show the amount resulting from the difference between the value stated in the preceding annual financial statements and that which is required to be stated pursuant to paragraph 3 hereof, or pursuant to § 155 of the Stock Corporation Act, as free reserves; such amount shall not be considered as part of the net profit for the year for purposes of § 58, paragraph 2, and § 86, paragraph 2, of the Stock Corporation Act.

§ 15

Disposition of Net Profit for the Year.
Disposition of Retained Earnings

(1) The provisions of the Stock Corporation Act concerning the disposition of the net profit for the year and the disposition of the retained earnings, as well as those concerning the profit participation of members of the managing board

§ 15

31. Dezember 1966 beginnende Geschäftsjahr. Sie können auf ein früheres Geschäftsjahr angewandt werden. Werden sie auf ein früheres Geschäftsjahr nicht angewandt, bleibt es für das Geschäftsjahr bei den bisherigen gesetzlichen Vorschriften.

(2) Waren Gegenstände des Anlagevermögens im Jahresabschluß für das am 31. Dezember 1966 endende oder laufende Geschäftsjahr mit einem niedrigeren Wert angesetzt, als nach §§ 153, 154 des Aktiengesetzes zulässig ist, so darf der niedrigere Wertansatz beibehalten werden. § 154 Abs. 1 des Aktiengesetzes gilt in diesem Fall mit der Maßgabe, daß der niedrigere Wertansatz um planmäßige Abschreibungen oder Wertberichtigungen entsprechend der voraussichtlichen Restnutzungsdauer zu vermindern ist.

(3) Waren Gegenstände des Umlaufvermögens im Jahresabschluß für das am 31. Dezember 1966 endende oder laufende Geschäftsjahr mit einem niedrigeren Wert angesetzt, als nach § 155 des Aktiengesetzes zulässig ist, so darf der niedrigere Wertansatz insoweit beibehalten werden, als er

1. auf Grund des § 133 Nr. 3 Satz 3 und 4 des Aktiengesetzes vom 30. Januar 1937 (Reichsgesetzbl. I S. 107) angesetzt werden mußte oder

2. aus den Gründen des § 155 Abs. 3 des Aktiengesetzes angesetzt worden ist.

(4) Soweit nach Absatz 3 ein niedrigerer Wertansatz für Gegenstände des Umlaufvermögens nicht beibehalten werden darf, können Vorstand und Aufsichtsrat, wenn sie den Jahresabschluß für das nach dem 31. Dezember 1966 beginnende Geschäftsjahr feststellen, den Betrag, der sich aus dem Unterschied zwischen dem im letzten vorausgehenden Jahresabschluß angesetzten Wert und dem nach Absatz 3 oder nach § 155 des Aktiengesetzes anzusetzenden Wert ergibt, in freie Rücklagen einstellen; dieser Betrag rechnet für die Anwendung des § 58 Abs. 2, § 86 Abs. 2 des Aktiengesetzes nicht zum Jahresüberschuß.

§ 15

**Verwendung des Jahresüberschusses.
Gewinnverwendung**

(1) Die Vorschriften des Aktiengesetzes über die Verwendung des Jahresüberschusses und die Gewinnverwendung sowie über die Gewinnbeteiligung der Vorstands- und Aufsichtsratsmitglieder gelten erstmals für das nach dem 31. Dezember 1966 begin-

nende Geschäftsjahr. Satzungsbestimmungen über die Verwendung des Jahresüberschusses und die Gewinnbeteiligung der Aktionäre sowie der Vorstands- und Aufsichtsratsmitglieder, die von der Hauptversammlung, die über die Verwendung des Bilanzgewinns für das in Satz 1 bezeichnete Geschäftsjahr beschließt, vor der Beschlußfassung über die Verwendung des Bilanzgewinns beschlossen worden sind, sind anzuwenden, jedoch wird der Beschluß über die Verwendung des Bilanzgewinns erst mit der Eintragung der Satzungsänderung wirksam.

(2) Für frühere Geschäftsjahre bleibt es bei den bisherigen gesetzlichen Vorschriften und Satzungsbestimmungen.

§ 16
Lastenausgleichs-Vermögensabgabe

(1) In der Gewinn- und Verlustrechnung ist die Lastenausgleichs-Vermögensabgabe in einem zwischen den Posten Nummer 24 und Nummer 25 einzufügenden Posten „Lastenausgleichs-Vermögensabgabe" besonders auszuweisen. In der Konzern-Gewinn- und Verlustrechnung in vereinfachter Form ist ein entsprechender Posten zwischen den Posten Nummer 12 und Nummer 13 besonders auszuweisen.

(2) Bei einer Kapitalerhöhung aus Gesellschaftsmitteln kann eine in der Jahresbilanz ausdrücklich als „Rücklage für die Lastenausgleichs-Vermögensabgabe" bezeichnete Rücklage nicht in Grundkapital umgewandelt werden.

§§ 17-18 [nicht abgedruckt]

§ 19
Auswahl der Abschlußprüfer

Für die Anwendung des § 164 Abs. 3 Nr. 3 des Aktiengesetzes bleibt eine Mitgliedschaft im Aufsichtsrat der zu prüfenden Gesellschaft außer Betracht, wenn sie spätestens mit der Beendigung der ersten Hauptversammlung der zu prüfenden Gesellschaft, die nach dem Inkrafttreten des Aktiengesetzes stattfindet, endet.

§ 20
Streitwert

In Rechtsstreitigkeiten, auf die § 247 des Aktiengesetzes anzuwenden ist, richtet sich der Streitwert nach dem bisherigen Recht, wenn der Rechtsstreit vor dem Inkrafttreten des Aktiengesetzes anhängig

and of the supervisory board, shall first be applied to fiscal years commencing after December 31, 1966. Provisions of the articles of incorporation concerning the disposition of the net profit for the year and the profit participation of shareholders and of members of the managing board and of the supervisory board, which were adopted by shareholders in the meeting which adopted the resolution concerning the disposition of the retained earnings for the fiscal year referred to in the first sentence hereof, prior to the resolution concerning the disposition of such retained earnings, shall apply; however, the resolution concerning the disposition of the retained earnings shall take effect only after the amendment of the articles of incorporation is recorded.

(2) Prior fiscal years shall be governed by the former statutory provisions and the provisions of the articles of incorporation.

§16
Equalization of Burden Tax Levy

(1) The item "equalization of burden tax" shall be shown in the profit and loss statement between items No. 24 and No. 25. In the consolidated profit and loss statement in simplified form a corresponding item shall be shown between No. 12 and No. 13.

(2) In the case of a capital increase out of surplus, a reserve shown on the balance sheet under the item "reserve for equalization of burden tax" may not be converted into stated capital.

§§ 17-18 [omitted]

§ 19
Selection of Annual Auditors

For purposes of the application of § 164, paragraph 3, No. 3, of the Stock Corporation Act, the fact that a party is a member of the supervisory board of the company to be audited shall be disregarded if such membership terminates no later than the adjournment of the first shareholders' meeting of the company to be audited which takes place after the effective date of the Stock Corporation Act.

§ 20
Value of Subject Matter in Issue

In actions governed by § 247 of the Stock Corporation Act, the value of the subject matter in issue shall be determined in accordance with the former law, if the action was brought prior to the

effective date of the Stock Corporation Act. This
shall not apply to appellate proceedings if such
appeal was brought after the effective date of the
Stock Corporation Act.

geworden ist. Dies gilt nicht im Verfahren über eine
Berufung oder eine Revision, wenn das Rechtsmittel
nach dem Inkrafttreten des Aktiengesetzes eingelegt
worden ist.

§ 21
Curing of Nullity of Annual Financial Statements

§ 256, paragraph 6, of the Stock Corporation
Act, relating to the curing of nullity of annual
financial statements, shall also apply to annual
financial statements prepared prior to the effective date of the Stock Corporation Act; however,
the curing of nullity pursuant to § 256, paragraph
2, of the Stock Corporation Act shall be subject
to the former provisions. The periods specified
in § 256, paragraph 6, of the Stock Corporation
Act for annual financial statements prepared prior
to the effective date of the Stock Corporation Act
shall not begin to run prior to the effective date
of the Stock Corporation Act.

§ 22
Enterprise Agreements

(1) Enterprise agreements (§§ 291 and 292 of
the Stock Corporation Act) entered into prior to
the effective date of the Stock Corporation Act
shall be subject to §§ 295 to 303, 307 to 310, and
316 of the Stock Corporation Act as of the effective date of the Stock Corporation Act. The period
specified in § 300, No. 1, of the Stock Corporation Act during which the statutory reserve must
be replenished shall be computed from the first
day of the fiscal year commencing after December
31, 1965. However, § 300, Nos. 1 and 3, of the
Stock Corporation Act shall not apply if, on the
effective date of the Stock Corporation Act, the
other party to the agreement was required by
its articles of incorporation or by contract to use
its earnings for public purposes. In cases governed by the third sentence hereof, the amount
which would have to be allocated to the statutory
reserves pursuant to § 300 of the Stock Corporation Act in conjunction with the second sentence
hereof, if these provisions would have been applicable to the company, shall be allocated to
the statutory reserve no later than upon termination of the enterprise agreement or the obligation
referred to in the third sentence hereof. Should
the amounts allocated to free reserves during
the existence of the agreement not suffice to permit such allocation, the other party to the agreement shall make up the deficiency.

(2) The company's managing board shall, without delay, after the effective date of the Stock

§ 21
Heilung der Nichtigkeit von Jahresabschlüssen

§ 256 Abs. 6 des Aktiengesetzes über die Heilung
der Nichtigkeit von Jahresabschlüssen gilt auch für
Jahresabschlüsse, die vor dem Inkrafttreten des
Aktiengesetzes festgestellt worden sind; jedoch
bleibt es für die Heilung der Nichtigkeit nach § 256
Abs. 2 des Aktiengesetzes bei den bisherigen Vorschriften. Die in § 256 Abs. 6 des Aktiengesetzes bestimmten Fristen beginnen für Jahresabschlüsse, die
vor dem Inkrafttreten des Aktiengesetzes festgestellt worden sind, nicht vor dem Inkrafttreten des
Aktiengesetzes.

§ 22
Unternehmensverträge

(1) Für Unternehmensverträge (§§ 291, 292 des
Aktiengesetzes), die vor dem Inkrafttreten des
Aktiengesetzes geschlossen worden sind, gelten
§§ 295 bis 303, 307 bis 310, 316 des Aktiengesetzes
mit Wirkung vom Inkrafttreten des Aktiengesetzes.
Die in § 300 Nr. 1 des Aktiengesetzes bestimmte
Frist für die Auffüllung der gesetzlichen Rücklage
läuft vom Beginn des nach dem 31. Dezember 1965
beginnenden Geschäftsjahrs an. § 300 Nr. 1 und 3
des Aktiengesetzes gilt jedoch nicht, wenn der andere Vertragsteil beim Inkrafttreten des Aktiengesetzes auf Grund der Satzung oder von Verträgen
verpflichtet ist, seine Erträge für öffentliche Zwecke
zu verwenden. In die gesetzliche Rücklage ist im
Falle des Satzes 3 spätestens bei Beendigung des
Unternehmensvertrags oder der Verpflichtung nach
Satz 3 der Betrag einzustellen, der nach § 300 des
Aktiengesetzes in Verbindung mit Satz 2 in die gesetzliche Rücklage einzustellen gewesen wäre, wenn
diese Vorschriften für die Gesellschaft gegolten hätten. Reichen die während der Dauer des Vertrags in
freie Rücklagen eingestellten Beträge hierzu nicht
aus, hat der andere Vertragsteil den Fehlbetrag auszugleichen.

(2) Der Vorstand der Gesellschaft hat das Bestehen und die Art des Unternehmensvertrags sowie

den Namen des anderen Vertragsteils unverzüglich nach dem Inkrafttreten des Aktiengesetzes zur Eintragung in das Handelsregister anzumelden. Bei der Anmeldung ist das Datum des Beschlusses anzugeben, durch den die Hauptversammlung dem Vertrag zugestimmt hat. Bei Teilgewinnabführungsverträgen ist außerdem die Vereinbarung über die Höhe des abzuführenden Gewinns anzumelden.

§ 23
**Rechnungslegung im Konzern.
Bericht über die Beziehungen zu verbundenen Unternehmen**

(1) Konzernabschlüsse und Konzerngeschäftsberichte sowie Teilkonzernabschlüsse und Teilkonzerngeschäftsberichte sind erstmals auf den Stichtag des Jahresabschlusses aufzustellen, der für das Geschäftsjahr aufgestellt wird, das nach dem 31. Dezember 1966 beginnt.

(2) Ein Bericht über die Beziehungen zu verbundenen Unternehmen ist erstmals für das Geschäftsjahr aufzustellen, das nach dem 31. Dezember 1965 beginnt.

§ 24
Umwandlungen

(1) Die Vorschriften des Dritten Teils des Vierten Buchs des Aktiengesetzes gelten nicht für Umwandlungen, bei denen der Umwandlungsbeschluß vor dem Inkrafttreten des Aktiengesetzes gefaßt worden ist.

(2) Für diese Umwandlungen bleibt es bei den bisherigen Vorschriften. Jedoch kann jeder Aktionär, der seinen Geschäftsanteil der Gesellschaft nach § 268 des Aktiengesetzes vom 30. Januar 1937 zur Verfügung gestellt hat oder noch zur Verfügung stellen kann, statt dessen verlangen, daß die Gesellschaft seinen Geschäftsanteil gegen eine angemessene Barabfindung erwirbt, sofern der Geschäftsanteil nicht bereits vor dem Inkrafttreten des Aktiengesetzes verkauft worden ist. § 375 des Aktiengesetzes gilt sinngemäß mit der Maßgabe, daß die Fristen des § 375 frühestens mit dem Inkrafttreten des Aktiengesetzes beginnen.

§ 25 [nicht abgedruckt]

§ 26
Kommanditgesellschaften auf Aktien

Die Vorschriften dieses Abschnitts gelten sinngemäß für Kommanditgesellschaften auf Aktien.

Corporation Act, file an application to record the existence and the type of enterprise agreement, as well as the name of the other party thereto, in the Commercial Register. The application shall state the date of the resolution in which the shareholders approved the agreement. In the case of agreements to transfer a portion of the profits, the application must also set forth the amount of profits the parties agreed would be transferred.

§ 23
Accounting in an Affiliated Group of Companies. Report on Dealings with Related Enterprises

(1) Consolidated financial statements and consolidated business reports as well as partial consolidated financial statements and partial consolidated business reports shall first be prepared as of the closing date of the annual financial statements prepared for the fiscal year commencing after December 31, 1966.

(2) A report on dealings with related enterprises shall first be prepared for the fiscal year commencing after December 31, 1965.

§ 24
Transformations

(1) The provisions of Part Three of Book Four of the Stock Corporation Act shall not apply to transformations if the resolution to effect a transformation was adopted prior to the effective date of the Stock Corporation Act.

(2) Such transformations shall be subject to the provisions theretofore in effect. However, each shareholder who put his shares at the disposal of the company pursuant to § 268 of the Stock Corporation Act of January 30, 1937, or who still has a right to do so, may request instead that the company acquire his shares for an appropriate cash payment, to the extent that the shares have not already been sold prior to the effective date of the Stock Corporation Act. § 375 of the Stock Corporation Act shall apply, *mutatis mutandis*; provided, however, that the periods specified in § 375 shall not begin to run prior to the effective date of the Stock Corporation Act.

§ 25 [omitted]

§ 26
Partnerships Limited by Shares

The provisions of this division shall apply, *mutatis mutandis*, to partnerships limited by shares.

§ 26

Second Division

Application of Provisions of Stock Corporation Act to Enterprises Having a Different Legal Form

§ 27
Decision Concerning Composition of Supervisory Board

§ 96, paragraph 2, and §§ 97 to 99 of the Stock Corporation Act shall apply, *mutatis mutandis*, to limited liability companies and mining companies.

§ 28
Limited Liability Companies and Mining Companies Which Are Members of Affiliated Group of Companies

(1) If enterprises which are members of an affiliated group of companies are subject to central management by a limited liability company or mining company domiciled in Germany, such limited liability company or mining company shall be required to render annual statements in the same manner as a parent company (§ 329 of the Stock Corporation Act) if any of the enterprises of the affiliated group which, pursuant to § 329, paragraph 2, of the Stock Corporation Act, would have to be included in the consolidated financial statements has the legal form of a stock corporation or of a partnership limited by shares.

(2) If the enterprise leading the affiliated group is not required to render annual statements pursuant to the provisions of Part Five of Book Three of the Stock Corporation Act, but if it controls, through one or more limited liability companies or mining companies domiciled in Germany, other enterprises of the affiliated group which have the legal form of a stock corporation or partnership limited by shares, such limited liability companies or mining companies shall render annual statements in accordance with § 330 of the Stock Corporation Act in the same manner as a stock corporation or partnership limited by shares through which the enterprise leading the affiliated group controls other enterprises of the group.

(3) If legal representatives or liquidators of a limited liability company or of a mining company which is required by paragraph 1 or paragraph 2 hereof to render annual statements in accordance

§ 27

Zweiter Abschnitt
Anwendung aktienrechtlicher Vorschriften auf Unternehmen mit anderer Rechtsform

§ 27
Entscheidung über die Zusammensetzung des Aufsichtsrats

§ 96 Abs. 2, §§ 97 bis 99 des Aktiengesetzes gelten sinngemäß für Gesellschaften mit beschränkter Haftung und bergrechtliche Gewerkschaften.

§ 28
Gesellschaften mit beschränkter Haftung und bergrechtliche Gewerkschaften in Konzernen

(1) Stehen in einem Konzern die Konzernunternehmen unter der einheitlichen Leitung einer Gesellschaft mit beschränkter Haftung oder bergrechtlichen Gewerkschaft mit Sitz im Inland, so hat die Gesellschaft mit beschränkter Haftung oder die bergrechtliche Gewerkschaft wie eine Obergesellschaft (§ 329 des Aktiengesetzes) Rechnung zu legen, wenn ein Konzernunternehmen, das nach § 329 Abs. 2 des Aktiengesetzes in den Konzernabschluß einzubeziehen wäre, die Rechtsform einer Aktiengesellschaft oder Kommanditgesellschaft auf Aktien hat.

(2) Ist die Konzernleitung nicht verpflichtet, nach den Vorschriften des Fünften Teils des Dritten Buchs des Aktiengesetzes Rechnung zu legen, beherrscht sie aber über eine oder mehrere Gesellschaften mit beschränkter Haftung oder bergrechtliche Gewerkschaften mit Sitz im Inland andere Konzernunternehmen in der Rechtsform einer Aktiengesellschaft oder Kommanditgesellschaft auf Aktien, so haben die Gesellschaften mit beschränkter Haftung oder die bergrechtlichen Gewerkschaften wie eine Aktiengesellschaft oder Kommanditgesellschaft auf Aktien, über die die Konzernleitung andere Konzernunternehmen beherrscht, nach Maßgabe des § 330 des Aktiengesetzes Rechnung zu legen.

(3) Gesetzliche Vertreter oder Abwickler einer Gesellschaft mit beschränkter Haftung oder bergrechtlichen Gewerkschaft, die nach Absatz 1 oder 2 nach Maßgabe der §§ 329 oder 330 des Aktiengeset-

zes Rechnung zu legen hat, sind, wenn sie die Absätze 1 und 2 in Verbindung mit §§ 329, 330, 336 Abs. 4 und § 337 Abs. 1 des Aktiengesetzes nicht befolgen, hierzu vom Registergericht durch Ordnungsstrafen anzuhalten. Die einzelne Strafe darf den Betrag von zehntausend Deutsche Mark nicht übersteigen.

with § 329 or 330 of the Stock Corporation Act fail to comply with paragraph 1 or 2 hereof in conjunction with §§ 329, 330, 336, paragraph 4, and § 337, paragraph 1, of the Stock Corporation Act, they can be compelled to do so bv the court of registry by means of fines. The amount of each fine imposed may not exceed ten thousand German marks.

Dritter Abschnitt
Aufhebung und Änderung von Gesetzen

Third Division
Repeal and Amendment of Statutes

§ 29
Aktiengesetz von 1937

(1) Das Aktiengesetz vom 30. Januar 1937 (Reichsgesetzbl. I S. 107)[2]), die drei Durchführungsverordnungen zum Aktiengesetz vom 29. September 1937 (Reichsgesetzbl. I S. 1026)[3]), vom 19. November 1937 (Reichsgesetzbl. I S. 1300)[4]) und vom 21. Dezember 1938 (Reichsgesetzbl. I S. 1839)[4a]) sowie das Einführungsgesetz zum Aktiengesetz vom 30. Januar 1937 (Reichsgesetzbl. I S. 166)[5]) werden aufgehoben, soweit nicht einzelne Vorschriften nach diesem Gesetz weiter anzuwenden sind.

[2] Bundesgesetzbl. III 4121-1
[3] Bundesgesetzbl. III 4121-1-1
[4] Bundesgesetzbl. III 4121-1-2
[4a] Bundesgesetzbl. III 4121-1-3
[5] Bundesgesetzbl. III 4121-2

(2) Wo in anderen gesetzlichen Vorschriften auf die aufgehobenen Vorschriften oder auf die durch § 18 Abs. 1 des Einführungsgesetzes zum Aktiengesetz vom 30. Januar 1937 aufgehobenen Vorschriften des Handelsgesetzbuchs verwiesen ist, treten, soweit nichts anderes bestimmt ist, die entsprechenden Vorschriften des Aktiengesetzes an ihre Stelle.

§ 29
Stock Corporation Act of 1937

(1) The Stock Corporation Act of January 30, 1937 (*Reichsgesetzblatt* I, page 107), the three Ordinances Implementing the Stock Corporation Act of September 29, 1937 (*Reichsgesetzblatt* I, page 1026), November 19, 1937 (*Reichsgesetzblatt* I, page 1300), and December 21, 1938 (*Reichsgesetzblatt* I, page 1839), as well as the Law Introducing the Stock Corporation Act of January 30, 1937 (*Reichsgesetzblatt* I, page 166), are hereby repealed, unless particular provisions thereof remain applicable pursuant to provisions of this Act.

(2) Whenever other statutory provisions refer to the provisions repealed hereby or to the provisions of the Commercial Code repealed by § 18, paragraph 1, of the Law Introducing the Stock Corporation Act of January 30, 1937, the corresponding provisions of this Stock Corporation Act shall be substituted for such provisions, unless otherwise provided.

§§ 30-44 [nicht abgedruckt]

§§ 30-44 [omitted]

Vierter Abschnitt
Schlußvorschriften

Fourth Division
Final Provisions

§ 45
Geltung in Berlin

Dieses Gesetz gilt nach Maßgabe des § 13 Abs. 1 des Dritten Überleitungsgesetzes vom 4. Januar 1952 (Bundesgesetzbl. I S. 1) auch im Land Berlin.

§ 45
Applicability in Berlin

This Act shall also apply in the territory of Berlin pursuant to the provisions of § 13, paragraph 1, of the *Drittes überleitungsgesetz* of January 4, 1952 (*Bundesgesetzblatt* I, page 1).

§ 46
Inkrafttreten

Dieses Gesetz tritt am 1. Januar 1966 in Kraft.

§ 46
Effective Date

This Act shall enter into effect on January 1, 1966.

§ 46

GLOSSARY

An explanation of terms, concepts, and statutes not translated. For a discussion of the various corporate forms and key terminology, see the Introduction.

Betriebsverfassungsgesetz. — The Works Councils Act of October 11, 1952, [1952] 1 *Bundesgesetzblatt* 681. This statute enlarged the co-determination rights of labor by establishing works councils in all enterprises having more than five employees. Works councils have a voice in personnel and social questions, and, through economic committees *(Wirtschaftsausschüsse)*, also in economic matters.

Bundesanzeiger. — The *Bundesanzeiger* is the Official Gazette of the Federal Republic of Germany. It is divided into an "official part" and an "unofficial part." In the official part regulations and legal notices concerning such matters as trade agreements and import quotas are published; it also carries statistical information, such as the weekly financial statements of the Bundesbank. The unofficial part primarily reports legislative proposals and the status of bills in Parliament.

An important supplement to the *Bundesanzeiger* is the *Zentralhandelsregister-Beilage,* which reports all entries made by the Commercial Registers throughout Germany.

D-Markbilanzgesetz. — Short title for the *Gesetz über die Eröffnungsbilanz in Deutsche Mark und die Kapitalneufestsetzung* (Statute Concerning Initial Balance Sheets in German Marks and Conversion of Stated Capital) of August 21, 1949, [1949] *Wirtschaftsgesetzblatt* 279. This law required companies to express the stated capital in German marks and permitted stated capital below the statutory figure of the 1937 *Aktiengesetz.* It was amended by several *D-Markbilanzergänzungsgesetze.*

Drittes Überleitungsgesetz. — Statute of January 4, 1952, [1952] 1 *Bundesgesetzblatt* 1. In consequence of the 1944 Allied Protocol on zones of occupation and the administration of Berlin, the Potsdam Declaration and supplementary protocols, Berlin has a special status. "Greater Berlin" is referred to as a state *(Land)* in article 23 of the Constitution of the Federal Republic and in the Constitution of West Berlin. However, the Military Governors of the Western Powers and the Allied *Kommandantura* made reservations with respect to the power of the Federal Republic to legislate for Berlin. The Berlin legislature can, however, adopt federal statutes by its vote. The Stock Corporation Act was adopted by an Act of the Berlin House of Representatives on October 14, 1965, [1965] *Berlin Gesetz- und Verordnungsblatt* 1473.

Gesetz über das Kreditwesen. — Banking Law of July 10, 1961, [1961] 1 *Bundesgesetzblatt* 881.

Gesetz über die Beaufsichtigung der privaten Versicherungsunternehmen und Bausparkassen. — Statute concerning the Supervision of Private Insurance Companies and Building and Loan Associations of June 12, 1931, [1931] 1 *Reichsgesetzblatt* 315.

Gesetz über die Kapitalerhöhung aus Gesellschaftsmitteln und über die Gewinn- und Verlustrechnung. — Statute Concerning Capital Increases Out of Surplus and Profit and Loss Statements, of December 23, 1959, [1959] 1 *Bundesgesetzblatt* 789. This statute remains applicable to limited liability companies (Section 33 of the Law Introducing the Stock Corporation Act); however, it no longer applies to stock corporations and partnerships limited by shares, having been superseded by Sections 207-220 and 273, paragraph 3, of the Stock Corporation Act.

Gesetz über die Mitbestimmung der Arbeitnehmer in den Aufsichtsräten und Vorstanden der Unternehmen der Eisen- und Stahl erzeugenden Industrie (Mitbestimmungsgesetz). — Statute Concerning the Co-determination of Labor on Supervisory Boards and Managing Boards of Iron and Steel Producing Enterprises, of May 21, 1951, [1951] 1 *Bundesgesetzblatt* 347; *Gesetz zur Ergänzung des Gesetzes über die Mitbestimmung der Arbeitnehmer in den Aufsichtsräten und Vorständen der Unternehmen der Eisen- und Stahl erzeugenden Industrie (Mitbestimmungsergänzungsgesetz).* — Statute Amending and Extending the Co-determination Statute of August 7, 1956, [1956] 1 *Bundesgesetzblatt* 707.

Kostenordnung. — Short title for the *Gesetz über die Kosten in Angelegenheiten der freiwilligen Gerichtsbarkeit* (Statute on Costs in Matters of Non-contentious Jurisdiction), of July 26, 1957, [1957] 1 *Bundesgesetzblatt* 960. This statute sets forth the rules concerning the court costs in "non-contentious matters." See *"Reichsgesetz über die Angelegenheiten der freiwilligen Gerichtsbarkeit,"* below.

Prokurist. — An executive employee of an enterprise who holds a *Prokura*, that is, a broad power of attorney to represent the enterprise in matters within the normal scope of its business. The appointment of a *Prokurist* must be recorded in the Commercial Register. Restrictions on his statutory powers are invalid as against third parties. See generally Commercial Code, Sections 48-53.

An enterprise may also delegate powers to other employees. The appointment of such agents *(Handlungsbevollmächtigte)* cannot be recorded in the Commercial Register. The scope of their powers depends on their mandate, subject to the rules of civil and commercial law on apparent authority.

Reichsgesetz über die Angelegenheiten der freiwilligen Gerichtsbarkeit. — Statute Concerning Matters of Non-contentious Jurisdiction, of May 17, 1898, [1898] *Reichsgesetzblatt* 189, as amended. This statute sets forth the rules concerning matters which under German law are not adjudicated in an adversary proceeding and are not subject to the Code of Civil Procedure. This includes probate and guardianship, adoption of children, and matters handled by the official registers, in particular the Commercial Register. This register is kept and administered by the local courts *(Amtsgerichte).* See also *Kostenordnung.*

Wechselgesetz. — Statute Concerning Bills of Exchange, of June 21, 1933, [1934] 1 *Reichsgesetzblatt* 57.

Wertpapiersammelbank. — Banks commercially engaged in keeping and servicing securities deposited by customers. To engage in this business authorization by the Federal Minister of Justice acting with the consent of the Federal Minister of Economics is required. See generally *Gesetz über die Verwahrung und Anschaffung von Wertpapieren* (Law on Deposit and Acquisition of Securities) of February 4, 1937, [1937] 1 *Reichsgesetzblatt* 171.

INDEX

→ References are to section (§) numbers of the German Stock Corporation Act and the Law Introducing the Stock Corporation Act.

A

Abuse of influence on company ... 117

Accounting ... 148-178
. affiliated group of companies ... 329-338
. . transitional provisions ... 23 (Intro. Law)
. managing board responsibility ... 91
. transitional provisions ... 14 (Intro. Law)

Acquisitions, post-formation ... 52, 53

Affiliated group of companies
. accounting ... 329-338
. . transitional provisions ... 23 (Intro. Law)
. business reports, annual ... 329, 334
. defined ... 18
. limited liability companies and mining companies as members of ... 28 (Intro. Law)

Agreements between enterprises — see Enterprise agreements

Amendment of statutes ... 29 (Intro. Law)

Articles of incorporation
. amendment ... 179
. . approval by shareholders affected ... 180
. . registration ... 181
. execution ... 23
. partnership limited by shares ... 280, 281

Assets
. acquisition after registration of company ... 52
. contributed or acquired, to appear in articles of incorporation ... 27
. contribution of
. . delayed payment by shareholders ... 63
. . failure to pay amounts called in ... 64
. . liability of predecessor of expelled shareholder ... 65
. . prohibited payments on ... 57

Audit of annual financial statements ... 162-169
. consolidated statements ... 336, 337
. report ... 166

Audit, special ... 142-146
. dealings with related enterprises ... 315
. expenses ... 146
. report ... 145
. understated items in financial statements ... 259

Auditors, annual
. appointment ... 163
. appointment for first year ... 30
. disputes with company ... 169
. information, right to ... 165
. liability ... 168
. persons who may not act as auditors ... 164
. presence at shareholders' meeting ... 176
. remuneration ... 163
. report on dealings with related enterprises ... 313
. selection ... 164
. . transitional provision ... 19 (Intro. Law)
. violation of duty to report, penalty ... 403

Auditors of formation ... 33
. claims for damages by company against ... 51, 53
. liability ... 49, 53
. remuneration and expenses ... 35

Auditors, special
. appointment ... 142
. . understated items of financial statement ... 258
. liability ... 144
. requirements ... 143
. rights ... 145

B

Balance sheet
. assets, current, valuation of ... 155
. assets, fixed
. . depreciation, reserve for decline in value ... 154
. . valuation ... 153
. classification ... 151
. consolidated balance sheet ... 331
. liabilities, valuation of ... 156

→*References are to section (§) numbers of the German Stock Corporation Act*
and the Law Introducing the Stock Corporation Act.

Balance sheet — continued
. nullity ... 256
. preparation by managing board ... 148
. specific items, rules concerning ... 152

Bankruptcy
. creditors' claims against shareholders ... 62
. partnership limited by shares ... 289

Berlin
. applicability of Introductory Law ... 45 (Intro. Law)
. application of Stock Corporation Act ... 409

Bonds, issuance of ... 221

Branches
. companies domiciled abroad, registration of branches ... 44
. establishment, discontinuance ... 42
. existing branches, registration of ... 43

Business combinations — see Mergers and business combinations

Business correspondence, names to appear on ... 80

Business reports, annual
. affiliated group of companies ... 329, 334
. audit of consolidated reports ... 336
. content ... 160
. documents to be submitted to parent company ... 335
. filing with Commercial Register ... 177
. partial consolidated financial statements and business reports ... 330
. partnership limited by shares ... 286
. preparation by managing board ... 148
. publication, form and content ... 178
. submission to supervisory board of parent company and to shareholders' meeting ... 337

C

Capital increase ... 182-221
. against contributions ... 182-191
. . action to set aside resolution ... 255
. . application to record increase ... 188
. . audit of contributions ... 184
. . contributions of assets ... 183

Capital increase — continued
. against contributions — continued
. . effective date ... 189
. . offers of subscription rights to new shares ... 187
. . preemptive rights ... 186
. . prohibition against issuance of share certificates and interim certificates ... 191
. . publication of registration of capital increase ... 190
. . registration of increase ... 188
. . resolution, application to record ... 184
. . subscription to new shares ... 185
. . transfer of equity interests ... 191
. authorized capital ... 202-206
. . agreements on contributions of assets prior to registration of company ... 206
. . issuance of new shares ... 203, 204
. . . for assets ... 205
. bonds, issuance of ... 221
. conditional capital increase ... 192-201
. . contributions of assets, involving ... 194
. . effective date ... 200
. . issuance of new shares ... 199
. . . application to record ... 201
. . issuance of preemptive shares ... 197
. . preemptive rights, declaration of exercise of ... 198
. . publication of registration of resolution ... 196
. . resolution, application to record ... 195
. . resolution, requirements for ... 193
. merger, capital increase to consummate ... 343
. out of retained earnings ... 207-220
. . balance sheet on which based ... 209
. . conditional capital ... 218
. . effective date ... 211
. . fractional shares ... 213
. . issuance of share and interim certificates ... 219
. . notice to shareholders ... 214
. . profit participation, beginning of ... 217

→*References are to section (§) numbers of the German Stock Corporation Act and the Law Introducing the Stock Corporation Act.*

Capital increase — continued
. out of retained earnings — continued
. . reserves, convertible ... 208
. . resolution, application to record and registration of ... 210
. . shareholders and third parties, protection of ... 216
. . shareholders' rights ... 212
. . shares paid up in part ... 215
. . shares, treasury ... 215
. . valuation of shares ... 220
. simultaneous with reduction ... 235
Capital reduction ... 222-240
. accounting treatment ... 240
. cancellation of shares
. . consummation, application to record ... 239
. . effective date ... 238
. capital increase, simultaneous ... 235
. losses, covering of ... 229
. offsetting decline in value of assets ... 229
. ordinary ... 222-228
. . application to record ... 227
. . effective date ... 224
. . minimum nominal amount, reduction below ... 228
. . payments to shareholders ... 225
. . protection of creditors ... 225
. . resolution, application to record ... 223
. . share certificates, cancellation of ... 226
. simplified ... 229-236
. . distribution of profits ... 233
. . protection of creditors ... 233
. . publication ... 236
. . retroactive effect ... 234
. . shareholders, payments to and obligations of ... 230
. . simultaneous capital increase ... 235
. . statutory reserve, allocation of amounts to ... 231, 232
Capital, stated ... 6
. applicability of requirement that capital be expressed in German marks... 1 (Intro. Law)
. minimum amount below statutory re-

Capital, stated — continued
quirement because of revaluation ... 2 (Intro. Law)
. minimum nominal value ... 7
Claims for damages
. against incorporators or others ... 50, 53
. against management of transferor company in merger ... 349
. asserted by company in connection with formation or management ... 147
. post-formation acquisitions ... 53
. statute of limitations ... 51
. waiver and compromise ... 50
Combinations — see Mergers and business combinations
Consolidations — see also Mergers and business combinations ... 353
Control agreements — see Enterprise agreements
Controlled enterprise defined ... 17
Credit
. managing board members and *Prokurists* ... 89
. supervisory board members ... 115
Creditors, protection of
. capital reduction ... 225, 233
. enterprise agreements ... 303
. integration of company ... 321
. liquidation of company ... 272
. mergers ... 347
. transformation of stock corporation into limited liability company ... 374

D

Damage claims — see Claims for damages
Definitions
. affiliated group of companies ... 18
. controlled enterprise ... 17
. court ... 14
. incorporators ... 28
. interlocking enterprises ... 19
. partnership limited by shares ... 278
. related enterprises ... 15
. stock corporation ... 1
Directing the stock corporation ... 76

*→References are to section (§) numbers of the German Stock Corporation Act
and the Law Introducing the Stock Corporation Act.*

Disclosure requirements on acquisition of shares ... 20, 21

Disputes
. between company and annual auditors ... 169
. between incorporators and auditors of formation ... 35

Dissolution — see also Liquidation
. application to record and registration ... 263
. continuation of dissolved company ... 274
. grounds ... 262
. judicial decision ... 396
. . interim measures ... 397
. . preliminary injunction ... 397
. . registration of decision of court ... 398
. partnership limited by shares ... 289

Dividend coupons, issuance of ... 75

Domicile ... 5
. transfer ... 45

E

Effective date of Act ... 410, 46 (Intro. Law)

Enterprise agreements ... 291, 292
. amendment ... 295
. approval by shareholders ... 293
. company lease agreement ... 292
. company surrender agreement ... 292
. control agreements ... 291
. . liability of legal representatives of controlling enterprise ... 309
. . liability of members of company's management ... 310
. . power of direction ... 308
. creditors, protection of ... 303
. effective date ... 294
. losses, assumption of ... 302
. outside shareholders, protection of ... 304-307
. . compensation, reasonable ... 304
. . indemnity ... 305
. . procedure ... 306
. . termination of agreement ... 307

Enterprise agreements — continued
. pooling of profits ... 292
. profit-sharing ... 292
. prohibited instructions ... 299
. protection of company and creditors ... 300-303
. registration ... 294
. statutory reserve ... 300
. termination ... 296, 307
. . application and registration ... 298
. . notice ... 297
. transfer of portion of profit ... 292
. transfer of profit ... 291
. . maximum amount ... 301
. . relationship with related enterprises ... 316
. transitional provisions ... 22 (Intro. Law)

Equalization of burden tax levy, entry in profit and loss statement ... 16 (Intro. Law)

Equity interests existing on effective date of Act, duty to report ... 7 (Intro. Law)

Establishment of company ... 29

F

False statements ... 399

Falsification or false issuance of certificates, penalty ... 402

Financial statements, annual — see also Balance sheet, Business report, and Profit and loss statement
. action to set aside ... 257
. audit ... 162
. certification by annual auditors ... 167
. company engaged in several lines of business ... 161
. consolidated statements ... 329
. . audit ... 336
. . publication ... 338
. . submission to supervisory board of parent company and to shareholders' meeting ... 337
. content ... 149
. disputes between company and annual auditors ... 169

→References are to section (§) numbers of the German Stock Corporation Act
and the Law Introducing the Stock Corporation Act.

Financial statements, annual — continued
. documents to be submitted to parent company ... 335
. establishment
. . managing board and supervisory board ... 172
. . shareholders ... 173
. examination ... 162-171
. . by supervisory board ... 170, 171
. filing with Commercial Register ... 177
. forms prescribed by Federal Minister of Justice ... 161
. integrated companies ... 325
. nullity, grounds for ... 256
. . transitional provisions ... 21 (Intro. Law)
. partial consolidated financial statements and business reports ... 330
. partnership limited by shares ... 286
. pension payments, notation regarding ... 159
. preparation by managing board ... 148
. publication ... 177, 178
. report of supervisory board to shareholders' meeting and to managing board ... 171
. shareholders' meeting, calling of ... 175
. submission to supervisory board ... 170
. understating of items
. . appointment of special auditors ... 258
. . judicial decision on concluding statements of special auditors ... 260
. . judicial decision on income based on higher valuation ... 261
. . report and concluding statements of special audit ... 259

Fines and penalties ... 399-408

Formation of company ... 23-53
. acquisition or contribution of assets ... 27
. examination by auditor and members of managing and supervisory boards ... 33, 34
. expenses to appear in articles of incorporation ... 26
. report ... 32

I

Incorporators
. claims for damages by company against ... 51, 53
. definition ... 28
. false statements, penalty ... 399
. liability
. . formation of company ... 46
. . post-formation acquisitions ... 53
. number ... 2

Insolvency of company, managing board duties in case of ... 92

Integrated companies
. action to set aside integration resolution ... 320
. financial statements, annual ... 325
. indemnification of withdrawing shareholders ... 320
. liability of managing board of integrated company ... 323
. liability of principal company ... 322
. losses assumed by principal company ... 324
. power of direction of principal company ... 323
. principal company's shareholders' right to information ... 326
. procedure for integration ... 319, 320
. profit to be transferred by principal company ... 324
. protection of creditors ... 321
. reserve, statutory ... 324
. termination of integration ... 327

Interlocking enterprises ... 328
. defined ... 19
. transitional provisions ... 6 (Intro. Law)

J

Jurisdiction over company ... 14

L

Liability
. abuse of influence on company ... 117
. auditors, annual ... 168
. auditors of formation ... 49, 53
. auditors, special ... 144
. control agreements ... 309, 310
. incorporators ... 46
. integrated companies ... 322, 323
. managing board members ... 48, 93

→ *References are to section (§) numbers of the German Stock Corporation Act*
and the Law Introducing the Stock Corporation Act.

Liability — continued
. mergers ... 349, 351
. person acting for company before registration ... 41
. persons other than incorporators ... 47, 53
. related enterprises where no control agreement ... 311-318
. shareholders who received prohibited payments ... 62
. supervisory board members ... 48, 116

Limitation period for prosecution of violations ... 406

Limited liability companies
. affiliated group of companies, members of ... 28 (Intro. Law)
. supervisory board ... 27 (Intro. Law)

Liquidation — see also Dissolution
. balance sheet, opening ... 270
. books and records of company ... 273
. business report ... 270
. creditors
. . notice to ... 267
. . protection ... 272
. distribution of assets ... 271
. duty to liquidate ... 264
. financial statements, annual ... 270
. nullity of company ... 277
. partnership limited by shares ... 290
. termination ... 273

Liquidators — see also Liquidation ... 265
. application to record ... 266
. duties ... 268
. misrepresentation, penalty ... 400
. representation of company ... 269
. violation of duties ... 405

Loans
. general partners of partnership limited by shares ... 288
. managing board members and *Prokurists* ... 89
. supervisory board members ... 115

Loss incurred by company, managing board duties in case of ... 92

M

Majority-owned and majority-owning enterprises ... 16

Management of stock corporation ... 77
. restrictions on power to represent company ... 82

Managing board ... 76-94
. appointment ... 84
. . by court ... 85
. . initial board ... 30
. changes ... 81
. credit by company to members ... 89
. delegation of members' powers ... 78
. dismissal ... 84
. duties in case of loss, excess of liabilities over assets, or insolvency ... 92
. keeping of books of account ... 91
. loans to members by company ... 89
. members
. . attendance at shareholders' meetings ... 118
. . compensation ... 87
. . . competition with corporation prohibited ... 88
. . duty of care ... 93
. . false statements, penalty ... 399
. . liability ... 93
. . . abuse of influence ... 117
. . . control agreements ... 310
. . . formation of company ... 48
. . . post-formation acquisitions ... 53
. . misrepresentation, penalties ... 400
. . termination of contract in case of bankruptcy ... 87
. . violation of duties, penalty ... 401, 402, 404, 405
. membership incompatible with membership on supervisory board ... 105
. profit sharing ... 86
. reports to supervisory board ... 90
. representation power ... 82
. rules of procedure ... 77
. signature by members ... 79
. substitutes for members ... 94

Mergers and business combinations
. limited liability company with partnership limited by shares ... 356
. limited liability company with stock corporation ... 355
. mining company with partnership limited by shares ... 358
. mining company with stock corporation ... 357
. partnership limited by shares with stock corporation ... 354
. partnerships limited by shares combined ... 354

→*References are to section (§) numbers of the German Stock Corporation Act and the Law Introducing the Stock Corporation Act.*

Mergers and business combinations — continued
. stock corporations.
. . action for damages against transferor company ... 350
. application to record merger ... 345
. . capital increase to consummate merger ... 343
. . combination ... 339
. . consolidation ... 353
. . consummation of merger ... 344
. . liability of management of transferee company ... 351
. . liability of management of transferor company ... 349
. . merger agreement ... 341, 342
. . nullity of transferor company's resolution to merge ... 352
. . protection of creditors ... 347
. . registration of merger ... 346
. . shareholders' resolution on merger agreement ... 340
. . valuation of transferee company ... 348

Mining companies' supervisory board ... 27 (Intro. Law)

Misrepresentation ... 400

N

Name of stock corporation ... 4
Nullity of company
. action for declaration ... 275
. defect in provisions on name or domicile, curing of ... 276
. registration, effect of ... 277
. validity of transactions ... 277
Nullity of shareholders' resolutions — see Resolutions of shareholders

O

Obligations contracted prior to registration, assumption by company ... 41

P

Partnerships limited by shares
. articles of incorporation
. . content ... 281
. . execution ... 280
. bankruptcy ... 289
. business report ... 286
. defined ... 278
. dissolution ... 289

Partnerships limited by shares — continued
. financial statements, annual ... 286
. general partners ... 283
. . criminal liability ... 408
. . non-competition with firm ... 284
. . registration ... 282
. . withdrawal from company ... 289
. . withdrawal of profits ... 288
. incorporators ... 280
. liquidation ... 290
. loans to general partners ... 288
. name ... 279
. shareholders' meetings ... 285
. supervisory board ... 287
. transitional provisions ... 26 (Intro. Law)

Penalties and fines ... 399-408

Political entities, participation in company
. report of supervisory board ... 394
. secrecy obligation ... 395

Post-formation acquisitions ... 52
. claims for damages ... 53

Preferences to shareholders ... 26

Profit
. distribution to shareholders ... 60
. net profit for year, disposition of ... 58
. . transitional provisions ... 15 (Intro. Law)
. retained earnings
. . advance payment on ... 59
. . disposition of ... 174
. . . transitional provisions ... 15 (Intro. Law)
. transfer in case of integration of companies ... 324

Profit and loss statement
. classification ... 157
. consolidated statement for affiliated group of companies ... 332
. . simplified form ... 333
. preparation by managing board ... 148
. specific items, rules concerning ... 158

Prokurist
. authority to represent corporation ... 78
. loans from company ... 89

Publication of company announcements ... 25

→ *References are to section (§) numbers of the German Stock Corporation Act
and the Law Introducing the Stock Corporation Act.*

Purpose of stock corporation ... 3
. transitional provisions ... 8 (Intro. Law)

R

Recording of company
. application ... 36, 37
. . examination by court ... 38
. content of registration ... 39
. liability of person acting for company before registration ... 41
. publication of registration ... 40
. refusal by court ... 38
Registration of company — see Recording of company
Related enterprises ... 291-338
. control agreement absent
. . compensation for disadvantages to controlled enterprise ... 311
. . influence of controlling enterprise ... 311
. . liability
. . . controlled company's management ... 318
. . . controlling enterprise and its representatives ... 317
. . report of managing board of controlled company ... 312
. . . audit by annual auditors ... 313
. . . examination by supervisory board ... 314
. . special audit of dealings with related enterprises ... 315
. defined ... 15
. enterprise agreements — see also Enterprise agreements ... 291-307
. first reports on dealings with ... 23 (Intro. Law)
. integrated companies — see Integrated companies
. interlocking enterprises ... 328
Repeal of prior law ... 29 (Intro. Law)
Representation of stock corporation ... 78
. changes in powers of representation of managing board members ... 81
. supervisory board in dealings with managing board members ... 112
Reserve, statutory ... 150
. capital reduction, allocation of amounts resulting from ... 231, 232
. enterprise agreements ... 300
. integrated companies ... 324

Resolutions of shareholders
. action to have resolution declared void ... 249
. action to set resolution aside ... 243, 246
. . barred after ratification of voidable resolution ... 244
. . capital increase against contribution of assets ... 255
. . disposition of retained earnings ... 254
. . effect of judgment ... 248, 252
. . election of supervisory board members ... 251, 252
. . parties authorized to bring suit ... 245
. . subject matter in issue, value of ... 247
. . . transitional provisions ... 20 (Intro. Law)
. . transformation of company ... 375
. articles of incorporation, amendment of ... 179
. capital increase ... 182, 192, 202, 207
. capital reduction ... 222
. merger agreement, approval of ... 340
. nullity ... 241, 242
. . action for declaration of ... 249
. . disposition of retained earnings ... 253, 254
. . election of supervisory board members ... 250, 251
. partnership limited by shares ... 285
. preparation and implementation ... 83
. ratification of voidable resolutions ... 244
. separate vote ... 138

S

Secrecy, violation of ... 404
Shareholders
. auditor, objection to ... 163
. compensation for recurring performances in addition to contributions to capital ... 61
. contributions ... 55
. expulsion when in default ... 64, 11 (Intro. Law)
. insolvency ... 46
. limited ... 278
. obligations
. . contributions of assets ... 54
. . refund of prohibited payments ... 62
. . transfer of shares ... 55
. . waiver prohibited ... 66

*→References are to section (§) numbers of the German Stock Corporation Act
and the Law Introducing the Stock Corporation Act.*

Shareholders—continued
. obligations prior to effective date of
  Act ... 10 (Intro. Law)
. predecessor of expelled shareholder,
  liability for contributions called in ...
  65
. preferences in articles of incorporation
  ... 26
. protection of outside shareholders in
  enterprise agreements ... 304-307
. protective associations ... 128
. resolutions—see Resolutions of shareholders
. right to information ... 131
. . principal company of integrated com-
    panies ... 326
. rights ... 119
. . exercise of ... 118
. . protection in case of capital increase
    out of retained earnings ... 216
Shareholders' meeting ... 118-147
. agenda, publication of ... 124
. annual auditors, presence of ... 176
. articles of incorporation, resolution to
  amend ... 179
. attendance by managing and supervisory board members ... 118
. banks' duty to forward communications ... 128
. calling ... 121
. . minority request ... 122
. communications to shareholders and
  supervisory board members ... 125
. countermotions ... 126
. documents to be submitted ... 176
. establishment of annual financial statements ... 175
. expenses ... 122
. list of participants ... 129
. minutes, content of ... 130
. motions by shareholders ... 126
. nominations by shareholders ... 127
. . voting ... 137
. notice
. . period ... 123
. . publication ... 121
. partnership limited by shares ... 285
. place ... 121
. post-formation acquisitions ... 52
. protective association's duty to forward communications ... 128
. proxies ... 129
. proxy voting ... 134

Shareholders' meeting—continued
. release from responsibility of members
  of managing board and of supervisory
  board ... 120
. resolutions—see Resolutions of shareholders
. right of shareholders to information ...
  131, 13 (Intro. Law)
. . judicial decision ... 132
. right to attend or vote ... 123
. separate ... 138
. transitional provisions ... 13 (Intro.
  Law)
. voting requirements ... 133
. voting rights ... 134
. . exercise by banks, shareholders' pro-
    tective associations, and profes-
    sional agents ... 135
. . suspension ... 136

Shares
. acceptance as pledge ... 71
. acquisition
. . by shareholder for account of com-
    pany or through controlled or major-
    ity-owned enterprise...56
. . disclosure requirements ... 20, 21
. . of own shares by company ... 71
. . proof to enterprise in which interest
    has been acquired ... 22
. authorized capital increase
. . agreements on contributions of assets
    prior to registration of company
    ... 206
. . issuance of new shares ... 203, 204
. . . for assets ... 205
. bearer ... 10, 24
. cancellation for capital reduction ...
  237-239
. certificates
. . cancellation
. . . capital reduction ... 226
. . . change in legal circumstances ... 73
. . . lost or destroyed certificates ... 72
. . issuance ... 41, 191, 219
. . new certificate issued for damaged or
    defaced certificate ... 74
. . notice to surrender ... 73
. . signature ... 13
. . subscription to new shares ... 185
. classes ... 11

Shares—continued
. conditional capital increase
. . application to record issuance of new
    shares ... 201
. . declaration of exercise of preemptive
    rights ... 198
. . issuance of new shares ... 199
. . preemptive shares ... 197
. consideration for ... 9
. consolidation ... 4 (Intro. Law)
. controlled company ... 16
. conversion of bearer to registered
    shares ... 24
. dividend coupons, new, issuance of
    ... 75
. exchange when stock corporation trans-
    formed into limited liability com-
    pany ... 373
. forfeited ... 64
. fractional, resulting from capital
    increase ... 213
. held by another company ... 16
. interim certificates ... 8, 10, 41, 191, 219
. issuance
. . preemptive shares in conditional cap-
    ital increase ... 197
. . preferred shares with preference over
    or rights equal to non-voting pre-
    ferred shares ... 141
. liability of issuers ... 8
. minimum par value ... 8, 3 (Intro. Law)
. nominal value ... 6
. paid up in part, in case of capital
    increase ... 215
. period of ownership, computation of
    ... 70
. preference, cancellation or restriction
    ... 141
. preferred, non-voting ... 139
. . rights of holders ... 140
. registered ... 10, 24
. . entry in stock register ... 67
. . transfer ... 68
. . transitional provisions ... 9 (Intro.
    Law)
. rights held in common ... 69
. sale where unpaid ... 65
. signature on certificates ... 13
. subscription to new shares for increase
    of capital ... 185 - 187
. treasury, in case of capital
    increase ... 215

Shares—continued
. valuation for purposes of capital
    increase ... 220
. voting rights ... 12
. . multiple rights created prior to effec-
    tive date of Act ... 5 (Intro. Law)

Stock Corporation Act of 1937, repeal of
    ... 29 (Intro. Law)

Stock corporation defined ... 1

Supervisory board ... 95-116
. appointment of initial board ... 30
. . incorporation of existing enterprise
    ... 31
. changes, publication of ... 106
. committee meetings, attendance at
    ... 109
. composition ... 96
. . conflict with statutory provisions
    ... 97
. . jurisdiction of court ... 98, 99
. credit to members by company ... 115
. duties ... 111
. loans to members by company ... 115
. meetings
. . attendance at ... 109
. . calling of ... 110
. members
. . agreements to render services for
    company ... 114
. . appointment ... 101
. . . by court to fill quorum ... 104
. . . nullity ... 250
. . attendance at shareholders' meetings
    ... 118
. . dismissal ... 103
. . duty of care ... 116
. . false statements, penalty ... 399
. . liability ... 116
. . . control agreements ... 310
. . . damage to company caused by per-
    son influencing company ... 117
. . . formation of company ... 48
. . . post-formation acquisitions ... 53
. . misrepresentation, penalties ... 400
. . remuneration ... 113
. . term of office ... 102
. . violation of duties, penalties ... 402,
    404, 405
. membership ... 95, 96
. . incompatible with membership on
    managing board ... 105

→*References are to section (§) numbers of the German Stock Corporation Act and the Law Introducing the Stock Corporation Act.*

Supervisory board—continued
. membership—continued
. . limited liability companies and mining companies ... 27 (Intro. Law)
. . personal requirements ... 100
. organization ... 107
. partnership limited by shares ... 287
. reports submitted by managing board ... 90
. representation of company in dealings with managing board members ... 112
. resolutions ... 108
. rights ... 111
. transitional provisions ... 12 (Intro. Law)

T

Transfer of assets
. to mutual insurance company ... 360
. to public agencies ... 359
. transferee other than government or mutual insurance company ... 361
Transformations
. limited liability company into partnership limited by shares ... 389, 392
. . application to record ... 390
. . effect of registration ... 391
. limited liability company into stock corporation ... 376
. . application to record ... 379
. . dissenting quotaholders ... 383
. . examination of formation ... 378
. . liability of quotaholders ... 378
. . quotas, exchange of ... 382
. . registration, content of publication of ... 380
. . registration, effect of ... 381
. . supervisory board of stock corporation, composition of ... 377
. mining company into partnership limited by shares ... 393

Transformations—continued
. mining company into stock corporation ... 384
. . effect of registration ... 385
. partnership limited by shares into limited liability company ... 386, 388
. . effect of registration ... 387
. partnership limited by shares into stock corporation ... 366
. . application to record ... 367
. . effect of registration ... 368
. stock corporation into limited liability company ... 369
. . application to record ... 371
. . dissenting shareholders ... 375
. . effect of registration ... 372
. . exchange of shares ... 373
. . protection of creditors ... 374
. . supervisory board of limited liability company, composition of ... 370
. stock corporation into partnership limited by shares ... 362
. . application to record ... 364
. . effect of registration ... 365
. . supervisory board of partnership, composition of ... 363
. transitional provisions ... 24 (Intro. Law)
Transitional provisions ... 1-26 (Intro. Law)

V

Violations ... 399-408
. statute of limitations for prosecution ... 406
Voting rights of shares ... 12

W

Waiver or compromise of claims for damages ... 50, 53